The Slaughter of Farmed Animals

Practical Ways of Enhancing Animal Welfare

The Slaughter of Farmed Animals

Practical Ways of Enhancing Animal Welfare

Edited by

Temple Grandin

Department of Animal Science, Colorado State University, USA

and

Michael Cockram

Sir James Dunn Animal Welfare Centre, Atlantic Veterinary College, University of Prince Edward Island, Canada

CABI is a trading name of CAB International

CABI
Nosworthy Way
Wallingford
Oxfordshire OX10 8DE
UK

CABI
745 Atlantic Avenue
8th Floor
Boston, MA 02111
USA

Tel: +44 (0)1491 832111
Fax: +44 (0)1491 833508
E-mail: info@cabi.org
Website: www.cabi.org

Tel: +1 (617)682-9015
E-mail: cabi-nao@cabi.org

A catalogue record for this book is available from the British Library, London, UK.

Library of Congress Cataloging-in-Publication Data

Names: Grandin, Temple, editor.
Title: The slaughter of farmed animals : practical ways of enhancing animal welfare / edited by Temple Grandin and Michael Cockram.
Description: wallingford, Oxfordshire ; Boston : CABI, [2020] | Includes bibliographical references and index. | Summary: "From the ethics of slaughtering farmed livestock to the practical guidelines that must be put in place to maximise animal welfare, this book combines scientific evidence with down-to-earth practical advice for government and private industry managers, veterinarians and animal welfare practitioners"-- Provided by publisher.
Identifiers: LCCN 2019046143 (print) | LCCN 2019046144 (ebook) | ISBN 9781789240573 (paperback) | ISBN 9781789240580 (ebook) | ISBN 9781789240597 (epub)
Subjects: LCSH: Animal welfare--Moral and ethical aspects. | Meat animals--Moral and ethical aspects. | Animal industry--Moral and ethical aspects.
Classification: LCC HV4757 .S53 2020 (print) | LCC HV4757 (ebook) | DDC 179/.3--dc23
LC record available at https://lccn.loc.gov/2019046143
LC ebook record available at https://lccn.loc.gov/2019046144

References to Internet websites (URLs) were accurate at the time of writing.

ISBN-13: 9781789240573 (paperback)
9781789240580 (ePDF)
9781789240597 (ePub)

Commissioning Editor: Caroline Makepeace
Editorial Assistant: Lauren Davies
Production Editor: Shankari Wilford

Typeset by SPi, Pondicherry, India
Printed and bound in the UK by Severn, Gloucester

Contents

Contributors

Faith Baier, Department of Dairy Science, University of Wisconsin, Madison, USA. Email: fbaier@wisc.edu

Miki Ben-Dor, Department of Archaeology and Ancient Near Eastern Cultures, Tel Aviv University (TAU), Tel Aviv, Israel. Email: bendor.michael@gmail.com

Charlotte (Lotta) Berg, Department of Animal Environment and Health, Swedish University of Agricultural Sciences, Skara, Sweden. Email: Lotta.berg@slu.se

Michael Cockram, Sir James Dunn Animal Welfare Centre, Dept. of Health Management, Atlantic Veterinary College, University of Prince Edward Island, Charlottetown, PEI, Canada. Email: mcockram@upei.ca

Lily N. Edwards-Callaway, Department of Animal Science, Colorado State University, Fort Collins, Colorado, USA. Email: lily.edwards-callaway@colostate.edu

Temple Grandin, Department of Animal Science, Colorado State University, Fort Collins, Colorado, USA. Email: cheryl.miller@colostate.edu

Helen Kline, JBS Swift, Tolleson, Arizona, USA. Email: Helen.Kline@jbssa.com

Andy Lamey, Department of Philosophy, University of California, San Diego, California, USA. Email: alamey@ucsd.edu

Frédéric Leroy, Industrial Microbiology and Food Biotechnology, Faculty of Sciences and Bioengineering Sciences, Vrije Universiteit Brussel, Brussels, Belgium. Email: Frederic.leroy@vub.be

Frank Mitloehner, Department of Animal Science, University of California-Davis, Davis, California, USA. Email: fmmitloehner@ucdavis.edu

Mohan Raj, Formerly Reader in Animal Welfare, Department of Clinical Veterinary Science, University of Bristol, UK. Email: abmraj1957@gmail.com

Bernard Rollin, Department of Philosophy, Colorado State University, Fort Collins, Colorado, USA. Email: Bernard.rollin@colostate.edu

Peter Singer, University Center for Human Values, Princeton University. Email: singerp@gmail.com

Claudia Terlouw, Clermont Auvergne University, INRAE, VetAgro Sup, UMR Herbivores, F-63122 Saint-Genès-Champanelle, France. Email: claudia.terlouw@inrae.fr

Erika Voogd, Voogd Consulting, 28 West 225 Trieste Lane, West Chicago, Illinois, USA. Email: evoogd@voogdconsulting.com

Dennis Willson, Department of Animal Science, Colorado State University, Fort Collins, Colorado, USA. Email: dennis.willson@colostate.edu

Preface

This book provides both practical information that can be used in commercial abattoirs and in-depth reviews of scientific research on animal welfare. The two editors, Temple Grandin and Michael Cockram, provide different perspectives. Dr Grandin provides practical applied information that can be immediately put to use. Dr Cockram's chapters contain extensive literature reviews on transport, legislation, the condition of livestock and poultry that arrive at the abattoir, and on-farm welfare problems that can be assessed at the slaughter plant. Dr Grandin has chapters on stunning methods for livestock and poultry, determining unconsciousness, design of stun boxes and lairages, handling of animals, methods to prevent bruises, and the effects of pre-slaughter handling on meat quality. Other topics that are covered are assessment of animal welfare in slaughter plants and non-stunned religious slaughter. For a true international perspective, additional invited authors from Belgium, France, Sweden and the UK provide important research information on the welfare of livestock and poultry during stunning and slaughter. There is a comprehensive chapter on determining whether or not an animal is conscious. Five short chapters at the end of the book discuss the ethics of eating meat. It is important for the readers to understand differing viewpoints. This book will be especially useful for animal welfare officers in meat plants, veterinarians, meat scientists, regulatory officials, abattoir managers and students interested in animal welfare.

1 Introduction to Livestock and Poultry Welfare at Slaughter

TEMPLE GRANDIN*

Department of Animal Science, Colorado State University, USA

Our book on animal welfare at slaughter is aimed at abattoir managers, welfare officers, government regulators and supervisors of retail food supply chains. Retailers are increasingly enforcing private standards for their suppliers. Guidance from this book will assist quality assurance personnel, veterinarians and managers who are responsible for maintaining good animal welfare. It will also be a valuable text for students interested in either animal welfare or meat science. There is a major emphasis on cattle, pigs, sheep and broiler chickens. Information will also be included on other mammals and poultry.

This book is a combination of both practical 'how to' chapters by Temple Grandin and more in-depth scientific review chapters by Michael Cockram and invited authors. The first and second editors provide different perspectives. I have worked with the meat industry for over 40 years on equipment design, development of welfare auditing programmes and hands-on handling of livestock (Grandin, 2003, 2014, 2016). My chapters will cover methods to achieve the best possible welfare under commercial conditions. All stunning methods have welfare advantages and disadvantages. Scientific research on some methods, such as captive bolt and electrical stunning, has identified how these methods can be applied in practice to reduce the risk of welfare concerns. There are differences between the various types of controlled atmosphere (gaseous) stunning methods. The animal's reaction is highly variable depending on the type of gas, application method and species of animal (pigs versus poultry). The controversial subject of religious slaughter without stunning will also be covered (Chapter 11). Commercial application of methods of stunning

that some religious authorities will accept will also be discussed. In this introductory chapter, there is an overview of the topics that will be covered.

Michael Cockram has a veterinary and academic background in animal welfare. He has published research on the transport, lairage and handling of livestock and poultry, and other animal welfare issues. Much of this work has been undertaken within commercial slaughter plants. He has worked with several industry groups to apply the results of scientific research to commercial situations and has participated in the development of several animal welfare codes of practice. He presents the scientific evidence of welfare issues at slaughter in Chapter 2.

My Chapter 3 covers animal welfare tradeoffs when choosing between different technologies for commercial use. There are also chapters on the commercial application of stunning methods on cattle, pigs, sheep and poultry. Claudia Terlouw from the French National Institute for Agricultural Research covers the latest research studies for determining when an animal is unconscious (Chapter 14). Lotta Berg from the Swedish University of Animal Welfare Science covers the scientific research on poultry welfare during stunning (Chapter 7). Other issues covered by invited authors are prevention of bruising, by Lily Edwards-Callaway from Colorado State University (Chapter 5), and a series of shorter essays on the ethical arguments both for and against using animals for food (Chapter 18). Pre-slaughter handling of both livestock and poultry will be covered in detail. Practical guidance is provided on the design of restraint devices, lairages and races. There is a 'how to' chapter on behavioural principles of handling cattle, pigs and sheep (Chapter 6). Cockram has two additional

---

* Email: cheryl.miller@colostate.edu

1

chapters which cover problems that originate either on the farm or during transport and legislative issues (Chapters 4 and 17).

A Major Question About Welfare at Slaughter

A common question that people concerned about animal welfare often ask is: do animals know they are going to be slaughtered? When I first started my career in the early 1970s, I had to answer this question. To find out, I repeatedly travelled back and forth between a large beef slaughter plant and a local feedlot where people were vaccinating cattle. I was surprised to observe that the cattle behaved the same way in both the vaccinating race and the race that led to a captive bolt stunner. If they knew they were going to be slaughtered, their behaviour should have been much more agitated at the slaughterhouse. Research studies have shown that the levels of cortisol (stress hormone) have a similar range at both the ranch and the abattoir (Mitchell *et al.*, 1988; Grandin, 1997, 2014; Gruber *et al.*, 2010). In both places, the range of cortisol levels varied from very low to extremely high. The most important finding was that the range of cortisol values was similar in both places. Stress during handling can be lowered by training employees, better management supervision and simple modifications of equipment that are described in this book.

A common mistake made by people who want to improve animal welfare is to believe that buying the newest fancy equipment will fix all the animal welfare problems. I made this mistake early in my career when I thought that I could design a system that could replace management. Well-designed and engineered equipment is important, but it does not replace management and training of employees. Engineering and good equipment design can fix about half of the animal welfare problems, but the other half will require managers who care about animal welfare. One study showed that a major cause of poor stunning methods that failed to render cattle instantly unconscious was poor maintenance of the stunning equipment (Grandin, 2002). Poor maintenance is a management problem and not an equipment problem.

Simple Ways to Improve Existing Equipment

Maintaining an acceptable level of animal welfare is possible in abattoirs with basic modest equipment.

In many existing facilities, repairs and maintenance are often all that is required. There are many places where the best stunning equipment was purchased but the managers fail to maintain it. Ease of animal movement through a race can often be improved with easy fixes. Sometimes all that is required is to install a solid barrier to prevent approaching animals from seeing people or moving equipment ahead of them. Simple modifications, such as installing non-slip flooring in a stun box or changing lighting, will help keep pigs or cattle calmer. Illumination of a race entrance may make it possible to greatly reduce or eliminate electric goad (prod) use (Grandin, 2001). Pigs and cattle often refuse to enter dark places. Managers, veterinarians and plant employees will find lots of practical tips in this book.

Numerical Animal-based Measures of Welfare

I have worked hands-on in meat plants for over 40 years. During my career, I have been in over 300 beef, pork, lamb and poultry abattoirs in the USA, Canada, Mexico, South America, Europe, China, Australia and New Zealand. I have observed both the very best and the worst operations. I have designed stockyards (lairages), races and restrainer systems in abattoirs all around the world. At this late stage in my career, I am often asked what I am most proud of. During the 1970s, 1980s and early 1990s, I became increasingly frustrated that some of my clients did a poor job of operating facilities I had designed. What kept me motivated was that there were a few managers who did things right and supervised their employees.

In 1997, I developed a numerical scoring system, which used outcome indicators of poor animal welfare (Grandin, 1998). It became the basis of the US meat industry private standard. There are five simple outcome measures. To pass an audit, a plant had to achieve a good score on all five indicators. This system is discussed in detail in the book. The indicators are: (i) percentage of cattle, pigs or sheep effectively stunned with one application of the stunner; (ii) percentage rendered unconscious when hung on the bleed rail (must be 100%); (iii) percentage of cattle or pigs vocalizing (moo, bellow or squeal) during handling and restraint; (iv) percentage that fall down during handling; and (v) percentage moved with an electric prod. The advantage of numerical scoring is that it makes it easy to determine if handling and stunning practices are improving or becoming worse. There are also six acts of abuse which would be an immediate audit failure.

The next step in my career was to teach large retail meat buyers how to use the scoring system. In 1999 and 2000, after I started working with retail buyers, I observed more improvements in welfare than I had seen in my previous 25-year career. When the abattoirs were required to perform to an objective standard, they really improved (Grandin, 2005). It worked because it was objective and simple. Most of the abattoirs were able to pass the audits by improving employee training, better management supervision, increased stunner maintenance and simple modifications of facilities. This book can be used to teach people how to use behaviour principles to achieve low-stress livestock handling. People who work with animals need to be shown that handling will be more efficient if forceful methods are eliminated.

Did My Work Achieve Good Animal Welfare?

By using a combination of repairs, good management and simple modifications, I was able to make handling at a large slaughter plant less stressful than handling on many ranches. The average vocalization scores of cattle were lower at the abattoir (Grandin, 2001) than cattle handling on some ranches (Simon *et al.*, 2016). In cattle, vocalization during handling is related to physiological measures of stress (Dunn, 1990; Hemsworth *et al.*, 2011). For example, reducing the pressure applied by a head stanchion (head bail) reduced vocalization from 23% of the cattle down to 0%. Stress and pain have been greatly reduced compared with the bad old days of the 1970s, 1980s and 1990s. Many students and other people who are entering the industry today have never seen the awful conditions that existed during the first half of my career.

Welfare Issues that Originate at the Farm

I am becoming increasingly concerned about welfare issues that originate on the farm. Recently I was standing by the unloading ramp of a large plant that processed fed cattle. Many of the cattle were stiff and lame when they were unloaded off the truck. Fifteen years ago, problems with lame grain-fed beef were rare. The increased problems with lameness

in fed cattle are due to several factors that jointly increase stress on the animal's biology. They are heavier weights at a younger age, a genetic component, a lack of roughage in the diet and overuse of beta agonist growth promoters. At another abattoir, one of my colleagues has become increasingly disgusted at the condition of old dairy cows. They are allowed to deteriorate to a very poor condition before they are sold for slaughter. Most of these farm-related welfare problems come from a segment of poor producers. Over the years, many producers have greatly improved conditions on their farms. Slaughterhouses are the easiest part of the system to find remedies to improve animal welfare. The biggest challenge in animal welfare is to make sure that the animals on the farms had a life worth living.

The next step that can be taken to improve animal welfare is to measure welfare indicators of poor farm conditions at the abattoir. For livestock, some of the animal-based indicators that can be used are body condition score, lameness, swollen knee joints, hide cleanliness, bruises, death losses during transit, liver abscesses, lung lesions and infestations of lice. Poultry can also be assessed for conditions caused by poor housing. Some of the animal-based indicators for poultry are breast blisters, hock burn and foot pad lesions. The percentage of fractured wings can be used to audit poultry handling during catching.

In conclusion, I would like to add that pain, fear and discomfort can be reduced by following the best practices in our book.

References

Dunn, C.S. (1990) Stress reactions in cattle undergoing ritual slaughter using two methods of restraint. *Veterinary Record* 126, 522–525.

Grandin, T. (1997) Assessment of stress during handling and transport. *Journal of Animal Science* 75, 249–257.

Grandin, T. (1998) Objective scoring of animal handling and stunning practices in slaughter plants. *Journal of American Veterinary Association* 212, 36–39.

Grandin, T. (2001) Cattle vocalizations are associated with handling and equipment problems at beef slaughter plants. *Applied Animal Behavior Science* 71, 191–201.

Grandin, T. (2002) Return to sensibility problems after penetrating captive bolt stunning of cattle in commercial beef slaughter plants. *Journal American Veterinary Medical Association* 221, 1258–1261.

Grandin, T. (2003) Transferring results from behavioral research to industry to improve animal welfare on the farm ranch and the slaughter plant. *Applied Animal Behavior Science* 81, 215–228.

Grandin, T. (2005) Maintenance of good animal welfare standards in beef slaughter plants by use of auditing programs. *Journal American Veterinary Medical Association* 226, 370–373.

Grandin, T. (2014) Improving welfare and reducing stress on animals in slaughter plants. In: Grandin, T. (ed.) *Livestock Handling and Transport*. CAB International, Wallingford, UK, pp. 421–450.

Grandin, T. (2016) Preslaughter handling, welfare of animals and meat quality. In: Przybylski, W. and Hopkins, D.C. (eds) *Meat Quality Genetic and Environmental Factors*. CRC Press, Taylor Francis, New York, pp. 175–198.

Gruber, S.L., Tatum, J.D., Engle, T.E., Chapman, P.L., Belk, K.E. and Smith, G.C. (2010) Relationships of behavioral and physiological symptoms of preslaughter stress in beef longissimus muscle tenderness. *Journal of Animal Science* 88, 1148–1159.

Hemsworth, P.H., Rice, M., Karlen, M.C., Calleja, L., Barnett, J.L., Nash, J. and Coleman, G.J. (2011) Human animal interactions at abattoirs: relationships between handling and animal stress in sheep and cattle. *Applied Animal Behavior Science* 135, 24–33.

Mitchell, C., Hattingh, H.J. and Ganhao, M. (1988) Stress in cattle assessed after handling, after transport, and after slaughter. *Veterinary Record* 123, 201–205.

Simon, G.E., Hoar, B.R. and Tucker, C.B. (2016) Assessing cow-calf welfare. Part 2. Risk factors for beef cow health and behavior and stockperson handling. *Journal of Animal Science* 94, 3488–3500.

2 Welfare Issues at Slaughter

MICHAEL COCKRAM*

Sir James Dunn Animal Welfare Centre, Atlantic Veterinary College,
University of Prince Edward Island, Canada

Summary

This chapter discusses animal welfare in the context of slaughter and reviews the types of welfare issues that some animals can experience before and during slaughter. It shows how animal feelings such as pain, distress, fear, hunger, thirst, fatigue and discomfort can be affected by the procedures associated with slaughter and how responses to these states can be recognized. It concludes with a discussion on methods of assessing animal welfare at slaughter.

Learning Objectives

- Ethical approaches to welfare at slaughter.
- Criteria to assess slaughter methods.
- Potential causes of fear and stress.
- Understand possible causes of fear and stress.
- Learn physiological measures of stress.
- Animal welfare assessment methods.

Introduction

In introducing the broad concepts of animal welfare and humane slaughter, it is not the intention to imply that all of the potential welfare issues discussed will routinely occur during the slaughter of animals. The intention is to use the published literature to identify risks to animal welfare during slaughter, explain the nature of these potential welfare issues and show how to recognize them. Subsequent chapters will discuss how attention to detail, supervision and regulation (both self-regulation and external party regulation) can mitigate these risks to animal welfare.

Welfare issues can occur if animals arrive for slaughter already experiencing pain and discomfort,

if they experience problems during handling, lairage and restraint for stunning, and if stunning is ineffective. To avoid the risk of welfare issues during slaughter requires considerable attention to detail and conformity with best-practice guidelines. Close supervision is required to avoid a tendency to reduce the level of care provided in the misguided belief that optimal care is not required, due to the imminence of slaughter (Cortesi, 1994).

Grandin (2014) identified three categories of welfare issues that can arise during slaughter. One was when abuse, cruelty or neglect occurred due to the action of humans who were not adequately supervised. The second occurred where the operating procedures were appropriate, but there was a defect in the procedures undertaken that could be remedied by corrective action. The third category occurred where there were inherent welfare issues with the systems and procedures used for slaughter.

Humane Slaughter

Slaughter is the killing of animals for food, and humane slaughter is slaughter that shows sympathy with and consideration for the animals; it demonstrates compassion and is designed or calculated to inflict minimal pain (Oxford English Dictionary, 2018). It is, therefore, a combination of ethical treatment and a technical consideration of how to minimize any pain associated with slaughter. The term humane slaughter is used most often to refer to effective stunning, i.e. stunning that causes immediate loss of consciousness that persists until the animal is killed by exsanguination (bleeding or 'sticking') or by cardiac arrest. In developed countries, methods used for stunning and slaughtering

* Email: mcockram@upei.ca

animals have improved due to technical innovations and greater proficiency in their application. In developing countries, welfare standards at slaughter can be diverse, with a range of slaughter methods used that may be applied within domestic and communal settings rather than in specialized slaughter facilities (Lokuruka, 2016; Omotosho et al., 2016; Qekwana et al., 2017). Several examples of welfare issues at slaughter are provided from countries that have a different regulatory and commercial environment to those in, for example, North America, Europe and Australasia.

If animals are immediately killed or immediately stunned and rendered unconscious (i.e. a state of unawareness in which there is temporary or permanent disruption to brain function) and insensible (i.e. the animal is not able to experience pain and other mental states) until death occurs (Verhoeven et al., 2015), they will not experience pain or distress during the slaughtering procedure and the process is considered to be humane. Failure to respond to the application of a mildly painful stimulus that would be expected to be painful to a conscious animal is used as an indicator of loss of responsiveness after effective stunning (McKinstry and Anil, 2004; Hindle et al., 2010; Terlouw et al., 2016).

Ethical Approaches to Welfare at Slaughter

Slaughter is a topic where there are divergent ethical perspectives and some of these are absolute and prevent consensus. Sympathy with and compassion for animals has led some people to consider that the slaughter of animals or some types of animals is unethical. Although science is not able to answer ethical questions such as what is 'appropriate' (Rollin, 2015), animal welfare issues that form part of social debate can be investigated using scientific principles. This research attempts to understand how animals perceive their situation and whether practices can be modified to reduce the risk of suffering. If an animal is not subjected to pre-slaughter pain, fear or stress, is stunned instantaneously and does not recover consciousness before death, death itself is not a welfare issue (Broom, 1998). The aim of this chapter is not to challenge the consumption of meat or to persuade people away from meat eating, but to discuss the welfare issues that can arise during the slaughter of animals for food. The majority view is that it is ethically acceptable to slaughter animals, but most would impose the requirement to slaughter animals in the most humane manner consistent with the production of sufficient quantities of economical meat. Therefore, this chapter will not consider the death of an animal to be a welfare issue but only consider how it dies and the treatment of the animal during the pre-slaughter stages.

Ambivalence about livestock

Many people are ambivalent about the slaughter of animals for food and prefer not to consider or find it challenging to discuss the process of killing animals for their food (Abrams et al., 2015; Bray et al., 2016). This has led to the use of words that avoid reference to slaughter. Examples are the use of the word abattoir or processing plant rather than slaughterhouse or slaughter plant, and harvesting rather than slaughter, as ways of avoiding a direct description of slaughter or killing. The general public tends not to have a great deal of knowledge or experience of animal production and slaughter and therefore their views on many welfare issues may not be fully informed (Food Chain Evaluation Consortium, 2015; Cornish et al., 2016). Most consumers prefer to leave it to others such as regulators, the meat industry, food retailers and lobby groups to ensure that their meat is from animals slaughtered humanely. Therefore, political and commercial considerations have led to a range of animal welfare legislation, guidelines (Leary et al., 2016; OIE, 2016; European Commission, 2017; Grandin, 2017a), standards (Main et al., 2014; Lundmark et al., 2018) and audit procedures (Grandin, 2010) that place a responsibility on the slaughter plant for the welfare of the animals.

Meat Industry Practices and Animal Welfare

In developed countries, slaughterhouses are a centralized facility that can efficiently slaughter large numbers of animals in a regulated and industrialized environment and they avoid the use of numerous small dispersed locations within populated areas (Fitzgerald, 2010). However, one consequence is that this has separated contact between the public and the act of slaughter (Leroy and Praet, 2017). For economic reasons slaughterhouses have become large, specialized in specific types of animals and are fewer in number (MacDonald, 2003; Muth *et al.*, 2007). The risks to animal welfare are considered by some to be lower in small-scale slaughter facilities than in large ones (Hultgren *et al.*, 2016) and the levels of noise and stress experienced by the animals are thought to be greater in plants with a high throughput (Warriss *et al.*, 1994). In an attempt to avoid welfare risks (e.g. injury and stress) associated with the transportation of animals to slaughter in distant large plants, the use of mobile abattoirs that can move between farms has been investigated (Carlsson *et al.*, 2007). In one study, the signs of stress in sheep (serum cortisol concentration at exsanguination) were found to be lower after captive bolt stunning at a mobile on-farm abattoir than after transport, lairage, regrouping and handling followed by electrical stunning at a conventional abattoir (Eriksen *et al.*, 2013). However, mobile abattoirs have several economic and technical challenges compared with traditional slaughter plants (Hoeksma *et al.*, 2017) and represent a very small part of the industry.

Consider the entire food production chain

The slaughter of animals needs to be considered within the context of the entire food production chain: rearing on the farm, transport to slaughter, handling, lairage and slaughter, followed by processing, storage and delivery of the products to food manufacturers, distributors and retailers. Integrated companies that are involved in all or several stages in the food chain and some end users such as fast-food restaurants and large supermarkets that source their meat directly from specific slaughter plants aim to provide assurance on the quality and provenance of the meat and conformity with the standards of animal welfare that are required by the public and consumers (Harvey and Hubbard, 2013). Many companies that operate slaughter facilities in developed countries (but not necessarily those in some developing countries, e.g. see Frimpong *et al.*, 2014) give priority to animal welfare, but it is not the only consideration for the slaughter industry. The management of slaughter plants can be affected by a number of priorities and challenges that affect their viability (Charlebois and Summan, 2014). They need to manage their operations in a manner that is as economical as possible; delivers a product in sufficient quantity and quality to meet market demands; conforms to requirements for food safety, animal health, human health and safety; provides a service for the agricultural community; satisfies environmental concerns and is sustainable; and complies with industry or retail standards and legal regulations (Seng and Laporte, 2005).

Criteria to assess slaughter methods

There are several situations where animals might not be slaughtered using a method that poses the lowest risk to animal welfare. When developing guidelines on appropriate methods for humane slaughter, the American Veterinary Medical Association (Leary *et al.*, 2016) used some criteria that related to broader practical issues and not just those solely confined to animal welfare issues. They used the following criteria to assess methods used for slaughter:

- ability to induce loss of consciousness followed by death with a minimum of pain or distress;
- time required to induce loss of consciousness and the behaviour of the animal during that time, especially for religious slaughter;
- reliability and irreversibility of the methods resulting in death of the animal;
- safety of personnel;
- compatibility with intended animal use and purpose (i.e. meat consumption);
- potential psychological or emotional impacts on personnel;
- ability to maintain equipment in proper working order; and
- legal and religious requirements.

Market or societal demands

An example of the choice of a slaughter method that is not based on welfare criteria is where there is a market or societal demand for slaughter in conformity with religious practices, for example kosher or halal slaughter without adequate stunning. Another example is where electrical stunning is conducted with a low current to minimize the risk of product quality defects such as haemorrhages or bone fragments, but this can in some cases cause paralysis without insensibility to pain, whereas the use of a higher current would reduce the risk of an ineffective stun (Gregory and Wilkins, 1989; Raj, 1998). A similar situation applies to the use of head-back electrical stunning where there are welfare advantages compared with head-only stunning in that the animal is killed by cardiac arrest and the stun–stick interval is not critical (Raj, 1998).

However, this method might not be used due to the increased risk of bone fractures and meat quality defects (Gregory and Grandin, 1998). That said, there are often synergies between improved welfare and economic efficiency at slaughter (Støier *et al.*, 2016). It is easier and safer to handle animals that are calm compared with those that are stressed, fearful or in pain. Poor welfare conditions can often result in poor meat quality, such as pale soft exudative (PSE) and dark firm dry (DFD) meat, and damage (e.g. bruising) to meat, carcasses and hides/skins (Wigham *et al.*, 2018). As stress during pre-slaughter procedures (Hambrecht *et al.*, 2004) and the act of stunning can affect meat quality, considerable attention is given to the reduction of stress and this can influence the choice of handling and slaughter systems adopted.

Food Safety Risks and Animal Welfare

Food safety concerns can also influence the choice of stunning and killing method. Food safety risks preclude the use of chemicals that would remain in the body after death. Therefore, if the meat is used for human consumption, the chemicals that are available for euthanasia that cause sedation and suppression of heart and brain function cannot be used. There is a similar problem with the use of drugs to reduce pre-slaughter stress (Mota-Rojas *et al.*, 2011). Although pithing (the insertion and movement of a rod through the hole in the head made by the captive bolt) is an effective way of destroying brain and spinal cord tissue, thereby reducing muscle movements (clonic activity) and killing an animal after stunning, its use is now restricted to euthanasia rather than slaughter for human consumption (Appelt and Sperry, 2007). This is due to the risk of the spread of transmissible spongiform encephalopathies from cattle and sheep by the dissemination of central nervous system tissue (Anil *et al.*, 2002). Biosecurity and food safety requirements for ease of cleaning and disinfection require the extensive use of metal equipment and sometimes restricted use of bedding in the lairage (Small *et al.*, 2003). However, the use of metal fittings can be noisy and a source of fear to the animals (Waynert *et al.*, 1999). In some countries, in an attempt to reduce the surface contamination of animals with faeces and mud, and thereby reduce the risk of bacterial contamination of the meat, some sheep have been washed on arrival in the lairage using either a bath/dip or spray (Biss and Hathaway, 1996). However, this practice is stressful for sheep (Hargreaves and Hutson, 1990) and is not effective in reducing food safety risks. Emphasis is now given to ensuring that only clean animals arrive for slaughter.

Animal Welfare and Emotions/ Feelings in Animals

A central aspect of the study of animal welfare is attempting to understand the subjective mental feelings, experiences and emotions of animals (Duncan, 2005). Animals used for slaughter likely experience a range of feelings or subjective emotional experiences during pre-slaughter procedures and the act of slaughter (Terlouw *et al.*, 2008). Most regulations on slaughter require that animals are not subjected to avoidable pain, distress or suffering during slaughter and related operations. Increased knowledge and understanding of the underlying biology of domesticated animals together with advances in neuroscience, behaviour and psychology have formed the basis for scientific approaches to animal welfare issues (Broom, 2011). This scientific approach to animal welfare, i.e. one that follows a systematic methodology, based on evidence to pursue and apply knowledge and understand the natural and social world (Science Council, 2009), can provide valuable evidence to assist society and relevant stakeholders in making ethical decisions on animal welfare issues (Duncan, 2005).

Mental and affective states

Emotions and other feelings (such as hunger and thirst) that can be experienced as mental states are collectively described as affective states (Fraser, 2008) and are thought to have evolved in animals as a way of providing a more flexible way of meeting their basic needs than just relying on simple nervous reflexes (Duncan, 2005). Stimuli that affect an animal's allostasis (i.e. the balance in physiological systems that is adjusted according to the animal's situation) are thought to be responsible for creating an affective state. An affective state is characterized by its valence (i.e. whether it is a positive or negative feeling) and the degree of arousal or calming that is induced to enable the animal to respond to the information received concerning potential risks (Barrett *et al.*, 2007; Bliss-Moreau, 2017). Suffering occurs when an animal experiences one or more negative feelings such as pain, fear, hunger, thirst or discomfort for a prolonged period. The severity of any suffering is related to the duration and intensity of the negative state (Dawkins, 1990; Broom, 2011; Fraser, 2012).

Mental states in animals cannot be directly observed and measured (Fraser, 2009) and there is inconsistency both in psychological definitions and in concepts (de Vere and Kuczaj, 2016). Therefore, it is considered easier to attempt to assess welfare by making empirical measurements of health, biological function and the ability of animals to meet basic physiological needs. However, the ethical concerns about the welfare of animals, such as the risk of suffering during slaughter, relate to the capacity of domesticated animals to experience pain and other emotions and the circumstances that can induce these negative affective states. Therefore, the evidence for the main emotions and feelings that animals likely experience at a slaughter plant will be considered. The evidence to support the presence of emotions in animals is based on inductive reasoning, i.e. the balance of evidence, rather than on traditional empirical 'objective' science that can produce 'hard' evidence. The acknowledgement that animals that are killed for human consumption might or are likely to have the capacity to experience feelings such as pain, fear and stress can be challenging, especially for those involved in the meat industry. There can also be a tendency for those involved in food animal production to be more sceptical of the research that supports mental feelings in domestic animals than that of some other groups (Bastian *et al.*, 2012) who adopt a 'precautionary principle' approach in that they consider that it is preferable to assume that animals have the capacity to suffer. Although a scientific approach to animal welfare is an evidence-based approach rather than one that considers animal welfare issues solely from a moral or anthropomorphic perspective (the empathetic attribution of human characteristics including thoughts and emotions to domestic animals), it is nevertheless founded on a 'belief that animals have conscious feelings and are capable of experiencing pain and emotions' (Dawkins, 2017).

Similarities between animal and human neurology

The neurological basis of emotions, i.e. the type of activity in nerve cells in the brain of humans and other animals that produce emotions and other feelings, is not known (Dawkins, 2006). However, there are sufficient similarities between humans and domesticated animals in their brain structure and function, and in their behaviour and physiology, to suggest that animals likely experience affective states (Hemsworth *et al.*, 2015). When animals are in circumstances where humans would have an emotional experience, many of the responses made by domesticated animals are similar to those shown by humans when they report that they are experiencing a specific mental state. As affective states cannot be measured directly in animals, physiological and behavioural responses are measured that are thought to be related to these experiences (Hemsworth *et al.*, 2015). These responses can include neurophysiological and other physiological measurements, facial expressions and overt behaviours (Adolphs and Andler, 2018). In general, non-human mammals are motivated to seek similar emotional rewards and to avoid similar negative emotional events to those of humans. Human emotional feelings are dependent on similar subcortical brain systems that exist in both humans and many non-human animals (Panksepp, 2005). For example, in humans and other animals, the region of the brain known as the amygdala is considered to be involved in emotional experiences, such as fear, and in subsequent behavioural responses to fear, such as immobility (Cardinal *et al.*, 2002; Anderson and Adolphs, 2014). Electrical activation of these brain systems results in similar types of emotional expressions in humans and many non-human animals (Panksepp, 2005). The areas of the brain that are activated when humans experience a feeling such as thirst are also present in mammals and birds (Dawkins, 2006). There is pharmacological evidence that many drugs that control pain or fear/anxiety in humans appear to have similar effects in non-human animals (Hughes *et al.*, 1977). For example, lame broilers but not those with a normal gait have been shown to select food containing a non-steroidal anti-inflammatory drug over food without the drug and then show improved gait (Danbury *et al.*, 2000). Pigs given an anxiolytic will show reduced fear responses to novelty (Andersen *et al.*, 2000b; Dalmau *et al.*, 2009a).

Although domesticated animals likely have subjective feelings, they may not necessarily be similar to those experienced by humans (Dawkins, 2008). However, to act on suffering, it is not necessary to know exactly what an animal is feeling, only that there is evidence that the animal is likely experiencing a negative mental state, the severity of the suffering and its duration (Duncan, 2005). Examples of the factors that can cause negative affective states in animals at a slaughter plant are described below and signs that will assist in their recognition are discussed. It must be recognized that there are no consistent, discrete and specific markers of emotions, i.e. each emotion does not produce a distinct set of reproducible behavioural and physiological responses (Bliss-Moreau, 2017). Several emotions, e.g. pain and fear, can result in general arousal with increased activity, attention to surroundings and autonomic nervous system activity (fight or flight) or a passive response consisting of decreased activity and immobility. Events likely to induce different affective states can be associated with the same types of physiological responses. For example, increases in plasma cortisol concentrations and heart rate can be associated with negative emotions such as pain, fear and distress, as well as neutral events such as physical activity or positive ones such as feeding (Ralph and Tilbrook, 2016). Non-specific indicators of welfare can still be useful if they act as a warning of a potential issue that requires investigation and possibly corrective action.

Pain

Pain is 'an unpleasant sensory and emotional experience associated with actual or potential tissue damage' (International Association for the Study of Pain, 2017). Examples of potential causes of pain during pre-slaughter and slaughter procedures are shown in Table 2.1. Pain can potentially occur from injuries present on arrival, sustained in the lairage or during handling; from electricity and mechanical injury if stunning is not conducted appropriately; from starting to process an animal while it is still sensible to pain; and from undertaking exsanguination before stunning.

The consensus interpretation of the available evidence is that all mammals and birds are capable of experiencing pain (Sneddon et al., 2014). Bateson (1991) summarized the following similarities between humans and domesticated animals that suggest that domesticated animals can also experience pain. They both possess nervous system components that include receptors sensitive to noxious stimuli, brain structures equivalent to the human cerebral cortex, connections between these receptors and higher brain structures, and receptors for opioid substances in the brain. Analgesics modify responses to noxious stimuli and are selected by animals when they have damage likely to be associated with pain. In response to noxious stimuli, they attempt to avoid them or minimize the damage that they cause; these responses persist and animals learn how to associate neutral events with noxious stimuli. As there are differences in species-specific behaviour and neuroanatomy, this argument by analogy does not provide conclusive evidence. For example, it is also possible that some of the responses shown by animals are in response to nociception (i.e. a response to potentially damaging stimuli that does not require a subjective experience) rather than to pain (Sneddon, 2018). Body movements in response to nociception can be due to spinally-mediated reflex activity that does not require brain activity. The brain, and in particular the cerebral cortex and associated subcortical structures, must be functional for pain to be perceived. Therefore, if stunning is effective and the cerebral cortex is not functional because of physical disruption, hypoxia, an epileptic seizure or neuronal depression, pain cannot be experienced (Leary et al., 2016).

Absence of pain with effective stunning

Examples of research that supports the absence of pain with effective stunning are as follows.

- The disruption to brain activity that follows effective captive bolt stunning causes almost instantaneous loss of awareness to pain (Johnson et al., 2012).
- If an electric current is passed across the brain in a manner that induces epileptiform brain activity and causes loss of consciousness in less than 1 s, this is unlikely to be a painful experience (Berg and Raj, 2015). However, if an electric current is applied to the body before an animal loses consciousness, the animal can experience discomfort directly from the electricity, cardiac and skeletal muscle pain, and pain associated with heart failure (Gregory and Grandin, 1998).
- Leach et al. (1980) showed that sheep conditioned to expect electrical stunning by receiving prior exposure to a light source did not show an increase in heart rate when shown the light without electrical stunning. As no autonomic nervous system response was activated by the light, the absence of an increase in heart

Table 2.1. Examples of potential causes of pain in animals during pre-slaughter and slaughter procedures.

Examples of potential causes of pain	Reference
Injury, disease or neglected conditions present on arrival	
• pre-existing lesion, e.g. lameness that was present on the farm before loading	Flower and Weary (2009); Gentle (2011); Dalmau *et al.* (2016)
• severely debilitated or weak animals	
• lactating dairy cows that have not been dried up	
• injury sustained during handling or transport	Langkabel *et al.* (2015)
Injuries that occur during unloading, movement and handling	
• sharp protrusions causing skin lacerations or bruising, slippery floors resulting in slips and falls	Grandin (1997)
• physical force used by a handler on an animal either directly or with a tool	Hultgren *et al.* (2014)
• twisting an animal's tail	Pajor *et al.* (2000); Frimpong *et al.* (2014); Hultgren *et al.* (2014); Romero *et al.* (2017)
• lifting or dragging/pulling an animal by its head, horns, feet, tail or fleece	Jarvis *et al.* (1994); Frimpong *et al.* (2014)
Injuries in lairage	
• injuries caused by aggressive interactions between animals (especially in mixed social groups)	Warriss and Brown (1985); Warriss *et al.* (1998); Gispert *et al.* (2000); Faucitano (2001)
• animals slipping, falling and mounting during unloading or within the lairage	Kenny and Tarrant (1988); Miranda-de la Lama *et al.* (2012); Dalmau *et al.* (2016)
Use of electric goad/prod	
• especially on sensitive parts of the body[a]	Bourguet *et al.* (2011a); Hemsworth *et al.* (2011); Miranda-de la Lama *et al.* (2012); Hultgren *et al.* (2014); Romero *et al.* (2017)
Shackling before stunning	
• shackling of poultry before electrical stunning	Sparrey and Kettlewell (1994); Gentle and Tilston (2000)
Stunning	
• electrical shocks to poultry before stunning in water bath	Gregory and Grandin (1998); Raj (1998); Rao *et al.* (2013); Berg and Raj (2015)
• pigs or sheep in contact with another animal while it is electrically stunned or in contact with electricity from electrodes that are not placed appropriately on the head	Gregory and Wotton (1984); Grandin (2000)
• ineffective stunning not causing instantaneous unconsciousness or recovery of consciousness causing pain either directly from the stunning method or by susceptibility to painful stimuli from other slaughter procedures, e.g. exsanguination	Velarde *et al.* (2000); Hindle *et al.* (2010); Miranda-de la Lama *et al.* (2012); Zivotofsky and Strous (2012); Gallo and Huertas (2015)
• failure to apply sufficient current across the brain to cause insensibility before current is applied across the heart thereby inducing ventricular fibrillation in a conscious animal	Raj (1998)
• animals recovering from head-only electrical stunning due to a delay in exsanguination thereby becoming susceptible to painful stimuli	McKinstry and Anil (2004)
• animals that have not been effectively stunned and killed by exsanguination undergoing dressing (skin removal and cutting)	Ahsan *et al.* (2014)
• immersion of poultry and pigs in hot water when they enter a scalding tank conscious after ineffective electrical stunning and/or ineffective exsanguination	Griffiths (1985); EFSA (2013); Parotat *et al.* (2016)
Cutting neck tissues for exsanguination without prior stunning	
• pain from cutting tissues for exsanguination, especially when not undertaken with a sharp knife in one quick action	Barnett *et al.* (2007); Gibson *et al.* (2009a,b); Bourguet *et al.* (2011a); Johnson *et al.* (2012); Johnson *et al.* (2015)

[a]Use of electric goads/prods does not always cause a significant increase in plasma cortisol concentration or vocalizations (Probst *et al.*, 2014), but their use has been associated with vocalization and other physiological responses (Grandin, 2001; Warner *et al.*, 2007; Dupjan *et al.* 2008).

rate suggests that the sheep did not associate the light with a subsequent painful or fearful stimulus.

- Martin *et al.* (2016) investigated whether an analgesic reduced behavioural signs of pain/distress when broilers were exposed to low atmospheric pressure stunning. Although the results were not definitive, the behavioural responses suggested that the birds did not experience pain during the stunning procedure, for example from the expansion of trapped air in body cavities.

Pain assessment

Pain can be assessed by observing the behaviour and physiology of an animal. However, the behavioural signs that typically indicate pain and the associated changes in heart rate and respiratory rate are not specific to pain (National Research Council, 2009). Table 2.2 shows examples of common behavioural signs of pain, but there is considerable species variation, and individual variation within species, and many of the signs will depend on the type and severity of the pain.

Fear and Stress

Stress and distress

Before slaughter, animals are exposed to multiple potential stressors and each stage leading up to slaughter, including feed withdrawal, social mixing, handling, transport, lairage and slaughter, can be stressful (Table 2.3) (Terlouw *et al.*, 2008). The term stress describes the adaptive responses of an animal to environmental stimuli (stressors) that threaten its internal equilibrium (homeostasis/allostasis) (Ramos and Mormede, 1998; Mormède *et al.*, 2007). The term distress has many definitions, but in this context, it will be differentiated from stress by using it to describe an aversive, negative emotional state that occurs when adaptive responses fail to return the body to homeostasis (Sanford *et al.*, 1986; National Research Council, 2009).

If environmental stimuli are perceived and evaluated as a stressor, a range of neuroendocrine, metabolic and behavioural changes occur in an attempt to respond to the challenges presented (Veissier and Boissy, 2007). No single biological measurement adequately characterizes a stressful response and no single stress response is present in all stressful

Table 2.2. Examples of behavioral signs of pain (adapted from National Research Council, 2009).

Sign	Description
Guarding	The animal alters its posture to avoid moving or causing contact to a body part, or to avoid the handling of that body area.
Abnormal appearance	Different species show different changes in their external appearance, but obvious lack of grooming, changed posture and a changed profile of the body are all observable signs. In species capable of some degree of facial expression, the normal expression may be altered.
Altered behaviour[a,b]	Behaviour may be depressed; animals may remain immobile, or be reluctant to stand or move even when disturbed. They may also exhibit restlessness (e.g. lying down and getting up, shifting weight, circling or pacing) or disturbed sleeping patterns. Large animal species may grunt, grind their teeth, flag their tail, stomp or curl their lips (especially sheep and goats). Animals in pain may also show altered social interactions with others in their group.
Vocalization	An animal may vocalize when approached or handled, or when a specific body area is touched or palpated. It may also vocalize when moving to avoid being handled.
Mutilation	Animals may lick, bite, scratch, shake or rub a painful area.
Sweating	In species that sweat (horses), excessive sweating is often associated with some types of pain (e.g. colic).
Inappetence	Animals in pain frequently stop eating and drinking, or markedly reduce their intake, resulting in rapid weight loss.

[a]Animals in severe pain can have rapid and shallow respiration. On handling, they may react violently or adopt a rigid posture to immobilize the painful region. Localized pain may be associated with persistent licking or kicking at the offending area and, when the pain is severe, bellowing.
[b]Birds in pain show escape reactions, vocalization and excessive movement. Head movements increase in extent and frequency. There may also be an increase in heart and respiratory rates. Birds in chronic pain may exhibit a passive immobility characterized by a crouched posture with closed or partially closed eyes and head drawn toward the body. They may also become inappetent and inactive with a drooping appearance, holding their wings flat against the body and their neck retracted. When a bird is handled, its escape reaction may be replaced by immobility.

M. Cockram

Table 2.3. Examples of potential causes of fear and stress in animals during pre-slaughter and slaughter procedures.

Examples of potential causes of fear and stress	Reference
Handling and lairage	
• novel stimuli	Mormede and Dantzer (1978); Veissier and Le Neindre (1988); Keer-Keer *et al.* (1996); Grandin (2013)
• unpredictable stimuli such as noise from slamming gates or shouting by handler or exposure to loud noise	Waynert *et al.* (1999); Campo *et al.* (2005); Hambrecht *et al.* (2005); Terlouw and Rybarczyk (2008); Chloupek *et al.* (2009); Bourguet *et al.* (2010); Hultgren *et al.* (2014)
• proximity to humans	Hemsworth *et al.* (1994); Keer-Keer *et al.* (1996); Beausoleil *et al.* (2005); Petherick *et al.* (2009); Mazurek *et al.* (2011); Bassler *et al.* (2013)
• other animals (especially if in mixed social groups)	Arnone and Dantzer (1980); Terlouw and Rybarczyk (2008)
• lairage of suckled lambs	Linares *et al.* (2008)
• use of dogs for handling sheep	Beausoleil *et al.* (2005); Hemsworth *et al.* (2011); Zimerman *et al.* (2013)
• handling systems that separate/isolate animals from other members of the group before stunning	Terlouw *et al.* (2008); Bourguet *et al.* (2010)
• fast speed of movement of pigs from lairage to stunning area	Hemsworth *et al.* (2002)
• exposure to heat or cold stress during lairage	Hunter *et al.* (1998); Lowe *et al.* (2002); Debut *et al.* (2005); Knezacek *et al.* (2010); Scanes (2016)
Handling and restraint before stunning	
• handling of poultry by legs and inversion	Jones (1992); Kannan and Mench (1996)
• shackling of poultry before electrical stunning	Kannan *et al.* (1997); Debut *et al.* (2005); Bedanova *et al.* 2007;
• animals left in stunning pens or restraining facilities longer than necessary, e.g. when the line is stopped during breaks or equipment breakdown	Cockram and Corley (1991); Probst *et al.* (2014)
• escape from the restraining facilities during slaughtering operations	
• dragging, tying, shackling or hoisting livestock that are still conscious	Grandin (2003, 2014); Leary *et al.* (2016); Omotosho *et al.* (2016)
Stunning	
• breathlessness, asphyxia or choking and excitation responses of pigs to carbon dioxide stunning	Dodman (1977); Forslid and Augustinsson (1988); Raj (1998); Raj and Gregory (1996); Velarde *et al.* (2007); Llonch *et al.* (2012)
• consciousness or recovery from stunning due to inadequate stunning	
• incorrect positioning of stunning device	Anil and McKinstry (1998); Velarde *et al.* (2000); Njisane and Muchenje (2013); Romero *et al.* (2017)
• inadequate current/force	Anil and McKinstry (1998)
• more than one stun required	Miranda-de la Lama *et al.* (2012); Njisane and Muchenje (2013); Chulayo *et al.* (2016)
• recovery from stunning due to delay in exsanguination	Miranda-de la Lama *et al.* (2012); Bolaños-López *et al.* (2014); Romero *et al.* (2017)
• recovery from stunning due to ineffective exsanguination	Anil *et al.* (2000)
Exsanguination without prior stunning	
• inverted restraint before exsanguination without stunning	Westervelt *et al.* (1976); Dunn (1990); Bourguet *et al.* (2011a); Lambooij *et al.* (2012); Bozzo *et al.* (2018)
• blood entering trachea after exsanguination without stunning causing irritation and respiratory distress	Gregory *et al.* (2009)
• awareness before loss of consciousness after exsanguination without stunning	Daly *et al.* (1988); Anil *et al.* (1995a,b); Ceci *et al.* (2017); Cranley (2017)

situations (National Research Council, 2009). Stress responses can only provide evidence of arousal, as similar responses are also seen in response to a variety of negative affective states, including fear and pain (Ralph and Tilbrook, 2016), and are not even specific to negative/aversive situations (Rushen, 1986). The standard method of assessing stress responses is to measure increased activity of the hypothalamic–pituitary–adrenocortical axis (consisting of hypothalamus region of the brain, the anterior pituitary gland located below the brain and the cortex of the adrenal glands located near the kidneys) and the sympathoadrenomedullary system (consisting of the sympathetic nervous system that innervates the heart and other organs and the medulla of the adrenal glands). Increases in hormone concentrations, especially glucocorticoids produced by the adrenal cortex (cortisol in mammals and corticosterone in poultry) and catecholamines (epinephrine/adrenaline and norepinephrine/noradrenaline) produced by the adrenal medulla, heart rate and respiratory rate, and a redistribution of blood flow can occur in response to stressors to assist an animal to respond to challenges that might require exercise. These responses increase blood flow to the muscles and mobilize fat from adipose tissues and glycogen from the liver to increase blood glucose concentration to provide energy sources (Morméde et al., 2007). This is Cannon's 'fight or flight' syndrome (Cannon, 1939) that evolved to enable animals to respond to predators. Activation of the sympathoadrenomedullary system can occur within seconds, whereas the hypothalamic–pituitary–adrenocortical axis responses occur within minutes and can last several hours.

Physiological measures of stress

Animals can show physiological stress responses to a number of procedures undertaken during pre-slaughter and slaughter (Table 2.3). For example, during restraint before stunning/exsanguination, Westervelt et al. (1976) recorded a greater respiration rate in calves and a greater heart rate in sheep that were shackled and hoisted versus those restrained on a yoke with their feet elevated off the floor. Stress responses can consistent of overt and active behaviour, e.g. vocalization, and increased activity or passivity/withdrawal (immobility or freezing), e.g. tonic immobility and decreased maintenance behaviour (Ewbank, 1985). Some general signs of distress in livestock and poultry are thought to include tail flicking, head shaking, defecation, urination, shivering, eyelid flickering, head retraction and eye closure, gasping, yawning and vocalization (rate and change in character) (Gregory and Grandin, 1998; Briefer, 2012; Martin et al., 2016).

Compared with measurements made on the farm, several studies have shown successive increases in plasma cortisol concentration after handling, transport, lairage and slaughter (Fordham et al., 1989; Ceci et al., 2017), with the greatest signs of stress (e.g. greater urine concentrations of epinephrine and norepinephrine and greater plasma cortisol concentration) immediately after slaughter (Bourguet et al., 2010). Although each of the pre-slaughter stages can be stressful, whether a stress response occurs can depend on both animal factors and how the procedure is undertaken. For example, pigs that were routinely handled on-farm, transported a short distance, then kept in the lairage for 5 days before slaughter and handled carefully had a lower plasma cortisol concentration at slaughter than those that were mixed, transported for 2 h, kept in lairage for 0.5 h and then moved quickly before electrical stunning and exsanguination (Brown et al., 1998). Handling of pigs from the lairage to the stunning area without the use of electric goads is less stressful than when inappropriate handling consisting of the use of electric goads, shouting by handlers and increased movement of the pigs is used (Hambrecht et al., 2005).

Both genetics and previous experiences affect stress response

The physiological and behavioural responses of animals to the same stressor can vary between individuals and are influenced by the experience and genetics of the animal (Koolhaas and Van Reenen, 2016). For example, pigs heterozygous for the halothane gene had greater plasma cortisol concentrations after transport and after lairage than those that were homozygous negative for the halothane gene (Fàbrega et al., 2002). There can be differences between animals in how they perceive a stressor and differences in response styles to a stressor (Deiss et al., 2009). More excitable cattle have increased stress responses during handling compared with those with a calmer temperament (Curley et al., 2006; Cooke, 2014). Cattle reared extensively have less frequent interaction with humans and are more likely to show expressive behaviour during handling compared with cattle reared intensively (Fordyce *et al.*, 1985). The social grouping of cattle and the degree and type of handling that they experienced during rearing can affect the plasma cortisol concentration at the time of slaughter (Bourguet *et al.*, 2010). Repeated early gentle physical human contact with calves can reduce plasma cortisol concentration at slaughter (Probst *et al.*, 2012). In pigs that had been reared in a barren environment, de Jong *et al.* (2000) found an increased salivary cortisol concentration after pigs had been mixed, transported and lairaged compared with that measured on-farm before mixing. However, in pigs reared in an enriched environment (larger pens and straw) the salivary cortisol concentration was not significantly increased by these procedures.

Exercise and stress before slaughter can increase muscle activity, resulting in increased post-mortem muscle metabolism and in pigs and poultry in particular, a faster reduction in muscle pH and a slower fall in temperature that reduces meat quality (Terlouw *et al.*, 2012). The relationship between pre-slaughter stress and meat quality is complex. Whether pre-slaughter stress affects meat quality issues can depend on genetics and the carcass handling procedures (Gispert *et al.* 2000; Terlouw, 2005; Terlouw *et al.*, 2008). Warriss *et al.* (1998) did not find a clear relationship between pre-slaughter stress in pigs (as assessed by measurements of cortisol, lactate and creatine kinase at exsanguination) and measurements that characterized PSE meat. However, Choi *et al.* (2012) reported that high post-mortem muscle cortisol concentration in pigs was associated with increased muscle pH_{24}, reduced drip loss and increased tenderness. Increased pre-slaughter stress and/or activity can decrease muscle glycogen stores, resulting in a lower overall post-mortem muscle pH decline and an increased ultimate muscle pH that can affect meat quality (e.g. DFD meat). Foury *et al.* (2005) found positive correlations between post-mortem urinary catecholamines in pigs and muscle pH_{24}. Warriss *et al.* (1998) found signs of stress in pigs with DFD meat, but not all stressed pigs produced DFD meat, and Shaw *et al.* (1995) found greater concentrations of muscle cortisol in pigs with DFD meat than in those with normal meat. Although the presence of meat quality problems could indicate potential welfare issues, the absence of meat quality issues does not necessarily indicate that the animals had not been stressed during the pre-slaughter period.

Interpretation of physiological measures

The relevance of stress measurements in exsanguinated blood collected immediately after stunning as a way of assessing the effectiveness of different stunning methods requires careful interpretation. At slaughter, the sympathetic nervous system can be activated by an increase in intracranial pressure (Chiari *et al.*, 2000) at stunning and by a reduction in blood pressure at exsanguination (Gregory and Grandin, 1998). For example, the concentrations of catecholamines in blood samples collected at exsanguination increase after electrical and mechanical stunning (Shaw and Tume, 1992) and Althen *et al.* (1977) found an increased plasma concentration of epinephrine after pigs were electrically stunned or shot with a rifle, but not after shackling and exsanguination without stunning. Zulkifli *et al.* (2014) reported an increase in plasma norepinephrine concentration immediately after non-penetrating stunning and before exsanguination. However, they did not find a significant effect of penetrating or non-penetrating captive bolt stunning on plasma cortisol concentration immediately after stunning compared with immediately before stunning and there was no effect of stunning compared with exsanguination without stunning. If stunning causes immediate loss of consciousness it will not matter whether a particular stunning method causes sympathetic nervous system activation or not (Grandin, 2014). However, if a slaughter method does not cause immediate loss of consciousness and the animal experiences distress before it dies, an increase in stress may be detected. For example, Caballero *et al.* (1998) found greater signs of stress in cattle following cutting of the spinal cord (putilla) than in those stunned using a captive bolt. Ceci *et al.* (2017) reported greater plasma cortisol concentrations in blood collected during exsanguination in cattle that had not been stunned compared with those that had been stunned using a captive bolt. Chulayo *et al.* (2016) reported greater plasma cortisol concentration in blood collected during exsanguination in cattle that were given more than one captive bolt shot compared with those given one shot.

Fear

A major cause of stress at slaughter is fear of novel stimuli (Grandin, 2013) and fear from social disruption, especially isolation (Boissy, 1995; Forkman *et al.*, 2007). Animals are removed from their familiar environment on the farm, handled by humans, transported, mixed with unfamiliar animals in the lairage, exposed to novel sounds and odours and then moved to the point of slaughter. Fear is an emotional state induced by the perception of danger (Boissy, 1995). It is associated with escape or avoidance responses to a specific threat that is likely to cause harm (Dawkins, 2017). Anxiety is the emotional state experienced in anticipation of a threat to safety (Ledger and Mellor, 2018). Fear reactions can consist of autonomic nervous system responses such as increased heart rate, reflex withdrawal from the stimulus, and active and passive behavioural responses (Dawkins, 2017). Domesticated animals have maintained their fear responses that evolved as a way of avoiding potential predators (Rushen et al., 1999). Behavioural and physiological responses to fear prepare an animal to deal with danger and include defence (attack, threat), active avoidance (flight, hiding and escape) or passive avoidance (immobility) (Boissy and Erhard, 2014). Other behaviours such as feeding, exploration and social interactions can be inhibited. The characteristics of fearful stimuli are those that would have been associated with a predator, namely movement, suddenness, proximity and unpredictability (Désiré et al., 2004, 2006; Boissy and Erhard, 2014; Boissy and Lee, 2014). Humans can be perceived as potential predators and evoke fear responses due to their height and their quick or unpredictable movement (Rushen et al., 1999; Forkman et al., 2007). Fear of humans motivates animals to move away from handlers, and this response can be used to move the animals in the required direction. However, if excessive fear responses are caused, it can result in handling difficulties such as aggression, immobility or escape behaviour (Gregory and Grandin, 1998; Njisane and Muchenje, 2013). Animals that have been reared in an extensive system with minimal contact with humans are even more likely to experience fear during handling. Handling during rearing can reduce fear responses of livestock to humans, but this depends on the consistency, timing and type of interaction during rearing (Boissy and Bouissou, 1988; Hemsworth and Barnett, 1992). Geverink et al. (1998) found that pigs were easier to handle when they were moved out of a lairage pen if they had been subjected to regular handling on the farm.

Animals show individual differences in their fear responses and these can have a genetic basis (Boissy et al., 2005). Individual differences between sheep in the magnitude of their responses (vigilance and high-pitched bleating) to novelty and social isolation can affect their stress response to slaughter (as measured by the plasma cortisol concentration in exsanguinated blood) (Deiss et al., 2009). Pigs assessed as fearful (using a novel object test) can have a greater serum cortisol concentration at exsanguination following carbon dioxide stunning than those assessed as less fearful (Carreras et al., 2017).

Pigs can show behavioural and physiological responses to the sight and sound of other pigs in distress, but whether their responses indicate that they were distressed by the emotional state of the other pigs is not clear (Düpjan et al., 2011; Goumon and Špinka, 2016). Although subsequent discussion (Edgar et al., 2012) questioned whether the results obtained were sufficiently robust to permit practical application, Anil et al. (1996, 1997) concluded that the observation of the stunning and exsanguination of other animals was not stressful/fearful to sheep or pigs waiting for slaughter. There is evidence that animals can be affected by signals such as odours and alarm calls from other animals that have experienced or are experiencing fear (Reimert et al., 2017; Baciadonna et al., 2018). For example, some pigs avoided approaching a feeder sprayed with urine from stressed pigs but not one sprayed with urine from a non-stressed pig (Vieuille-Thomas and Signoret, 1992). In some studies, but not in others, compared with urine from non-stressed cattle, cattle can show increased latency to approach areas containing urine from stressed cattle (Boissy et al., 1998; Terlouw et al. 1998). Cattle can show increased sniffing and slower leg movements when approaching urine from stressed cattle or blood collected from a slaughter plant compared with their response to urine from non-stressed cattle or water (Terlouw et al., 1998).

Behavioural responses of fearful animals

Because of the complexity of the mechanisms underlying fear-related responses, it is not possible to attribute specific behavioural responses to fear (Forkman et al., 2007), but one response that has been used is tonic immobility, an anti-predator response seen in poultry and pigs after a handler turns the animal on its side. The animal remains immobile in an apparent attempt to distract the predator. The duration of tonic immobility is thought to be a measure of the fear experienced immediately preceding induction into tonic immobility (Jones, 1986; Erhard and Mendl, 1999; Andersen et al., 2000a) and has been used to assess fear responses of broilers following transportation to slaughter (Cashman *et al.*, 1989) and to shackling (Bedanova *et al.*, 2007). Fear responses thought to occur in slaughter plants are, for sheep and cattle, a head-down posture (when there is no obvious opportunity for escape from a fearful situation) (Hemsworth *et al.*, 2011), and for pigs and cattle, a reluctance to move (Hultgren *et al.*, 2014) or turning back from their direction of movement (Dalmau *et al.*, 2009b, 2010). Vocalization and changes in the characteristics of vocalization, e.g. loud, high-pitched vocalizations, can occur in pigs when they are aroused/excited (Reimert *et al.*, 2013; Leliveld *et al.*, 2017). Cattle and sheep vocalize when they are socially isolated (Manteuffel *et al.*, 2004; Deiss *et al.*, 2009), and cattle can vocalize when stressed by handling procedures at slaughter plants (Grandin, 1998a, 2001; Hemsworth *et al.*, 2011; Hultgren *et al.*, 2014). Other fear responses can include: piloerection; changes in facial expressions; head and ear position; defecation; urination; and the production of pheromones (Boissy, 1995; Reefmann *et al.*, 2009; Reimert *et al.* 2013).

Hunger and Thirst

Hunger

Hunger is part of an animal's normal daily rhythm associated with meal intake (Roche *et al.*, 2008; D'Eath *et al.*, 2009). There are anatomical and physiological differences in the digestive systems of ruminants, pigs, poultry and humans, but the mechanisms controlling hunger are thought to be similar (Baile and Della-Fera, 1981; Roche *et al.*, 2008). Hunger in animals is likely caused by a lack of gastrointestinal distention, by hormones that are influenced by circulating metabolites and metabolic signals from energy stores that reflect the energy status of the animal relative to metabolic demand, and by time of day. These signals are integrated by the hypothalamus, thalamus and other areas of the brain to produce the feeling of hunger (Tataranni *et al.*, 1999; Roche *et al.*, 2008). Hunger can be identified by an increased motivation to consume feed (Jackson *et al.*, 1999) and by increased activity to seek feed, e.g. foraging behaviour. Animals that have been fasted can show increased signs of arousal and anticipation before feed delivery (D'Eath *et al.*, 2009). However, Saucier *et al.* (2007) found no effects of fasting for up to 24 h on the lying behaviour, exploratory

behaviour or water intake of lairaged pigs. When offered feed, feeding rate is increased, and animals are likely to show increased competition to gain access to the feed (Beattie *et al.*, 2002).

It is normal practice to fast animals before slaughter; and if this period is prolonged, signs of hunger can become exaggerated and detrimental effects can occur. If fasting causes energy reserves to become exhausted (Warriss, 1982; Warriss *et al.*, 1988), this could increase the risk of fatigue and make animals more susceptible to cold environments. In some circumstances, especially if fasting is associated with social mixing, there can be an increased risk of fighting, resulting in skin injury in pigs (Brown *et al.*, 1999; Murray *et al.*, 2001) and bruising in cattle (Dodt *et al.*, 1979). There is some evidence that cattle fasted for 30 h are more susceptible to stressors such as novelty and show greater fear responses to sudden events and handling than those that have not been fasted (Bourguet *et al.*, 2011b; Terlouw *et al.*, 2012). Pigs fasted for 18 h before loading can vocalize more and be more difficult to orientate during loading than non-fasted pigs (Dalla Costa *et al.*, 2016).

Reasons for fasting before slaughter

There are several reasons why animals are fasted before slaughter and they include the following.

- For pigs and broilers, the risk of mortality during transport and lairage can be reduced (Averos *et al.*, 2008; Caffrey *et al.*, 2017).
- The stomach and intestines are not as distended (Bass and Duganzich, 1980; Warriss *et al.*, 2004; Faucitano *et al.*, 2006) and therefore there is less risk of inadvertent puncture/rupture during evisceration and a reduced risk of carcass contamination (Miller *et al.*, 1997; Morrow *et al.*, 2002).
- The amount of faeces produced during transport and lairage is decreased (Gregory *et al.*, 2000; Warriss *et al.*, 2004). This reduces the risk of faecal contamination of the animals and the amount of waste that requires disposal (Fisher *et al.*, 2012).
- There is insufficient time for feed consumed in the period before loading to be digested and converted into muscle and other tissues to justify an economic return from the cost of feeding (Carr *et al.*, 1971; Murray *et al.*, 2001; Kephart and Mills, 2005).
- It is thought that some aspects of meat quality might be improved (Sterten *et al.*, 2009; Faucitano

et al., 2010), e.g. in pigs, a reduction in drip loss (Salmi *et al.*, 2012). However, prolonged fasting can reduce carcass weight (Jones *et al.*, 1988) and reduce muscle glycogen, increasing the risk of DFD meat (Salmi *et al.*, 2012).

- For animals sold by weight, a period of fasting improves the prediction of the carcass weight (Hogan *et al.*, 2007).

The total duration of fasting is affected by the duration that feed is withdrawn on the farm before loading, the duration of transport (in many countries, animals are not normally offered feed during a journey to slaughter) and the duration of lairage without feeding. Even if animals are offered feed in the lairage, the latency to feed and the amount of feed consumed might be reduced by fear associated with: (i) the novelty of their environment, feed and feeding equipment; and (ii) unfamiliar animals in the same pen competing for limited access to feed (Boissy and Bouissou 1995; Dalmau *et al.*, 2009b). Although most animals readily consume feed when it is offered after a journey, a novel environment can decrease feed intake (Cockram *et al.*, 2000).

Thirst

Animals that do not have access to drinking water can become dehydrated during long journeys to slaughter and in hot environments (Arad *et al.*, 1985; Zhou *et al.*, 1999; Hoffman and Lühl, 2012). Thirst is a sensation that arises from dehydration and motivates animals to seek and drink water to maintain homeostasis (McKinley and Johnson, 2004). If thirst is severe and prolonged, it can be associated with significant dehydration and weakness. Thirst can be identified by increased water intake and reduced latency to drink after a period of water deprivation (Wythes *et al.*, 1980; Jensen *et al.*, 2016). It is initiated by an increase in the osmolality of body fluids, by a decrease in body fluid volume, and is affected by the presence of water in the oral cavity (de Araujo *et al.*, 2003). Dehydration can be assessed by measuring the total plasma protein concentration and plasma osmolality. As dehydration reduces carcass weight (Wythes *et al.*, 1980) and affects skin pliability, thereby making the skin more difficult to remove during carcass processing (Gregory and Grandin, 1998), it is avoided whenever possible. Withholding water during lairage to prevent a distended gastrointestinal tract is not required (Wythes *et al.*, 1985) and livestock (but not poultry) are normally provided with drinking water in the lairage. The susceptibility of different types of animals to dehydration varies. Suckling lambs that have recently been removed from their lactating mothers may not have learnt how to drink from a trough or drinker and are at risk of dehydration if they kept in a lairage too long (Jacob *et al.*, 2006; Velarde and Dalmau, 2012). Adult ruminants are more tolerant of short periods of water restriction and can utilize water from their rumen (Hecker *et al.*, 1964), but pigs are susceptible to water deprivation (Houpt and Yang, 1995).

Discomfort

Examples of potential causes of discomfort in animals during pre-slaughter and slaughter procedures are shown in Table 2.4. Discomfort as an affective state has not been studied extensively. It is likely to be associated with the physical environment and, depending on the cause, could be indicated by restlessness (increased activity such as walking and

Table 2.4. Examples of potential causes of discomfort in animals during pre-slaughter and slaughter procedures.

Examples of potential causes of discomfort	Reference
Inadequate protection from adverse weather conditions	Weeks (2008)
High temperature and/or humidity in lairage	Jacobs *et al.* (2017)
Exposure to cold conditions in lairage	Dalmau *et al.* (2016); Jacobs *et al.* (2017)
Inadequate ventilation in lairage, e.g. increased ammonia concentration	Weeks (2008)
Overcrowding resulting in insufficient floor space for rest or access to feed and water	Kim *et al.* (1994); Weeks (2008)
Hard or rough flooring in the lairage	Cockram (1990)
Physical pressure from restraint before stunning	Grandin (1998a, 2001); Bourguet *et al.* (2011a); Velarde *et al.* (2014)
Inhalation of water during electrical stunning of poultry	Gregory and Whittington (1992)
Electric prod use	Grandin (2001); Hemsworth *et al.* (2011)

M. Cockram

repeated standing up and lying down) (Guesgen and Bench, 2017), irritation or thermal discomfort caused by both heat and cold stress (Ledger and Mellor, 2018).

Fatigue

Although most animals do not show obvious signs of fatigue after long journeys, some animals that arrive at a slaughter plant after certain types of long journey and extended exercise associated with handling will be fatigued (Cockram *et al.*, 2012; Frese *et al.*, 2016). Signs of fatigue in pigs on arrival at a slaughter plant can include an inability to stand and walk, open-mouthed breathing, blotchy red skin and muscle tremors (Fitzgerald *et al.*, 2009). Signs of fatigue in cattle can include reluctance to move, stiff and shortened gait, failure to keep up with the rest of the group and muscle tremors (Thomson *et al.*, 2015; Frese *et al.*, 2016). Exercise during gathering and loading, the work required to maintain posture and balance during transport together with prolonged standing during a journey can cause muscle fatigue. After an extended period of exercise, physiological signs of fatigue can include: (i) a depletion of muscle glycogen and an accumulation of muscle metabolites, e.g. lactate, ammonia and electrolytes (Harman and Pethick, 1994); (ii) muscular damage, identified by leakage of intracellular enzymes, such as creatine kinase, across the cell wall and into the circulation; and (iii) raised body temperature (D'Allaire and DeRoth, 1986; Thomson *et al.*, 2015; Frese *et al.*, 2016). Signs of fatigue are likely to be more apparent in certain individuals and genetic strains, during periods of heat stress, and after transport at high stocking density (D'Allaire and DeRoth, 1986; Fitzgerald *et al.*, 2009; Frese *et al.*, 2016).

Animal Welfare Assessment

An animal welfare inspection or audit for certification or regulation can be undertaken by comparing what is observed at a slaughter plant with a list of minimal requirements (Botreau *et al.*, 2007a). The audit can be conducted using measurable outcomes that can be monitored and benchmarked to evaluate improvements with time (Grandin, 1998b, 2006). In some schemes, an overall evaluation can be made based on the number and severity of the non-conformances observed (Roberts *et al.*, 2012).

However, a comprehensive assessment of animal welfare is a complex task. Animal welfare is a multidimensional concept that cannot be measured directly but only inferred after making and interpreting multiple measurements of the various components thought to affect welfare (Blokhuis *et al.*, 2003). The UK's Farm Animal Welfare Council's 5 Freedoms (Farm Animal Welfare Council, 2009) provide a useful and reasonably comprehensive framework for consideration of the welfare of animals at slaughter plants:

1. Freedom from hunger and thirst.
2. Freedom from discomfort.
3. Freedom from pain, injury and disease.
4. Freedom to express normal behaviour.
5. Freedom from fear and distress.

The consideration of animal welfare in slaughter plants requires a slightly different approach to the assessment of welfare while animals are on the farm. For example, naturalness and positive welfare aspects are not as relevant, and the animals are normally only kept in the slaughter plant for less than a day or overnight. Slaughter can sometimes be arranged to replicate some aspects of natural predation, such as the killing of the animals *in situ* on the farm, while part of their social group. For example, it is less stressful for red deer to be shot while at pasture on-farm than it is for them to be transported to an abattoir for slaughter (Pollard *et al.*, 2002). However, even if the animals are slaughtered in the field, the use of some types of slaughter methods that do not cause instantaneous loss of consciousness is likely to cause greater suffering than methods used in the more controlled and regulated environment of a slaughterhouse (Reinert, 2012). Unless slaughter is undertaken as a form of euthanasia to relieve existing pain and suffering, it does not provide any positive welfare aspects that can be assessed.

Welfare assessment protocols

Welfare assessment protocols that have been or could be used to assess the welfare of cattle at slaughter were reviewed by Wigham *et al.* (2018). Welfare assessment systems are based on the identification of signs/indicators that are thought to reflect an animal's welfare status (animal-based or output measurements) and the risk factors (input measurements of the environment, management, genetics etc.) that could affect the output measurements

(Blokhuis et al., 2008). The risk factors that affect animal welfare at slaughter include the physical environment and the resources available to the animal such as space allowance, feed and water quantity and quality, bedding, etc., and management-based measures that can be assessed by documentation, e.g. staff training records and standard operating procedures. Depending on its characteristics (breed, sex, age, etc.) an animal will respond to these risk factors in varying ways, and their responses are assessed using animal-based measures. Input factors are easier to record than the responses of the animal and are more likely to be consistently recorded over time. Direct animal-based measures are made by observation, examination or inspection of the animals ante- or post-mortem (EFSA, 2012). Examples of animal-based measures are mortality, morbidity, lameness, injuries, body condition, signs of dehydration and the presence of overt behaviour indicative of pain or fear (Barnett and Hemsworth, 2009). Many animal-based measurements made under controlled experimental conditions are difficult to measure under commercial conditions and they often require information about the environment of the animals before they can be interpreted appropriately (Bracke, 2007).

Welfare Quality® system

Velarde and Dalmau (2012) and Dalmau et al. (2016) described how the European Welfare Quality® approach that was primarily developed for on-farm assessment could be used to assess the welfare of pigs and cattle at slaughter. The Welfare Quality® assessment scheme is based on 12 key criteria: (i) absence of prolonged hunger; (ii) absence of prolonged thirst; (iii) comfort around resting; (iv) thermal comfort; (v) ease of movement; (vi) absence of injuries; (vii) absence of disease; (viii) absence of pain induced by management procedures; (ix) expression of social behaviour; (x) expression of other behaviours; (xi) good human–animal relationship; and (xii) absence of general fear. In this scheme, data is collected on an animal unit and then converted into a score to evaluate the degree of compliance with these criteria. The scores obtained at this criterion level are then collated to assess unit compliance with four welfare principles (good feeding; good housing; good health; appropriate behaviour). Finally, these principle scores are used to make on an overall evaluation of the unit

as not classified, acceptable, enhanced or excellent (Botreau et al., 2009). To express the overall welfare status of a group of animals in a single integrated score or evaluation requires the interpretation and balancing of different types of data. Unfortunately, there is no standardized way of doing this and judgements on which criteria to use and how to weigh their relative importance involves a degree of subjectivity (Spoolder et al., 2003; Botreau et al., 2007a,b; de Graaf et al., 2018).

Welfare Quality® assessment protocols have been produced for cattle, pigs and broilers that incorporate some welfare assessments of finishing pigs, fattening cattle and broilers at the slaughter plant (Welfare Quality®, 2009a,b,c). All of these protocols assess the effectiveness of stunning. Observations are made during unloading, handling, lairage, slaughter and post-mortem (Dalmau et al., 2009b). The Welfare Quality® assessment protocols for pigs and cattle differ slightly, but in general, they score animals during unloading (by quantifying the frequency of slipping, falling, reluctance to move or turning back). In the lairage, they score the availability of food, the number of functional and clean drinking water sources, space allowance, the type of flooring, risk of injury and availability of bedding. Ante-mortem animal-based measurements used for cattle and pigs are scores for mortality, lameness and vocalizations and, for pigs only, signs of thermal discomfort (shivering, panting, huddling) and signs of respiratory disease. For cattle, the use of handling devices and direct physical contact by the handler together with struggling, kicking and jumping in the stunning box are assessed. Measurements on broilers include the duration of feed and water withdrawal, mortality, crate stocking density, panting and flapping on the shackle line and the recording of any pre-stun electric shocks. Some post-mortem measurements of pathology are also made. Brandt and Aaslyng (2015) used the Welfare Quality® protocol and additional measurements for the assessment of the welfare of pigs from the collection area on a farm during loading, transport, unloading, lairage, movement to stunning, stunning and exsanguination. Due to insufficient data to develop an expert consensus, a method for aggregation of the welfare scores at a slaughter plant was not developed during the original welfare quality project (Dalmau et al., 2016). However, Brandt et al. (2017) used the Welfare Quality® protocol, plus additional assessments (heart rate, duration of each stage, whether pigs were mixed, postures during lairage and how the pigs were handled), to make an overall assessment.

Use of animal-based measurements

Even if an animal-based measurement can be collected with relative ease, to be useful it should be valid, i.e. provide accurate information about a relevant welfare outcome. The specificity of an animal-based measure will depend on whether it responds to a single welfare factor or whether it relates or responds to several different factors. Some animal welfare outcomes that can be made at the time of slaughter or post-mortem represent the cumulative effect of various pre-slaughter factors on the animals, and their magnitude can be the consequence of the duration and intensity of a risk factor. Even though it is not always possible to attribute changes in these measurements to a particular factor or to relate them to a particular affective state, they can provide useful information on the influence of the overall pre-slaughter process on animal welfare. Examples of this type of measurement are: vocalizations (Grandin, 1998a); blood composition and temperature sampled during exsanguination, e.g. blood lactate concentration and creatine kinase activity; meat quality issues, e.g. bruising, skin damage, PSE meat, DFD meat; and mortality (Gispert et al., 2000; Brandt and Aaslyng, 2015). Although meat quality problems that are not caused by injury can be caused by factors associated with less than optimal welfare conditions, they are not reliable indicators of animal welfare. Rocha et al. (2016) recorded a range of pre-slaughter procedures in pigs and only found correlations between increased frequency of slipping at unloading and in the stunning chute area and increased drip loss and light reflectance, and between the use of electric prods in the stunning chute area and greater light reflectance of the longissimus lumborum muscle.

Defining the reasons why an animal welfare assessment is performed can assist in deciding whether it is necessary, appropriate and feasible to attempt to undertake all possible measurements and whether an overall welfare assessment, as used for an on-farm assessment, is a useful concept in the context of a slaughter plant. If the assessment is conducted to provide an assurance on the end product, or if the slaughter plant is part of an integrated company that has control of the production

and transport of the animals, then an overall assessment can be useful. Where responsibility for the various welfare issues is divided, the aggregation of different types of Welfare Quality® measurements into an overall score may not be as useful. Some of the welfare issues assessed in the Welfare Quality® protocols are primarily related to on-farm issues (such as genetic susceptibility to fear and stress, lameness, the presence of pathology and decisions on fitness for transport) and some of the issues are related to how the animals are transported. These aspects may not be directly under the control of the slaughter plant management.

Choosing welfare measurements

Only some of the list of potential measurements that could be made in an attempt to assess animal welfare at slaughter plants could be considered 'feasible' to record routinely in a commercial environment (Llonch et al., 2015; Losada-Espinosa et al., 2018). As discussed by EFSA (2012), the selection of which measurements are appropriate will depend on a number of factors, including the skills of the assessor, the conditions under which the information is collected, the time available and financial constraints. For example, in one study, the time taken to complete the Welfare Quality® assessment protocol in a pig slaughter plant was 5.5 h (range 4.3–7.3 h) (Dalmau et al., 2009b). The criteria for selection of a welfare indicator will also depend on issues such as the validity, sensitivity, specificity and robustness of the measurement (EFSA, 2012). The robustness of an animal-based measurement is influenced by how the measure is affected by changes in the environment, the person making the measurement and when it is taken. Repeatability and reliability of a measurement, i.e. the agreement between repeated measurements of the welfare outcome on the same sample by the same assessor (intra-observer) or a different assessor (inter-observer), affect the reproducibility of the assessment (EFSA, 2012). Inter-observer reliability is improved if there are not too many categories to observe and score (Grandin, 2017b). For example, Dalmau et al. (2010) assessed the repeatability of observations to assess lameness and the frequency of slipping and falling during unloading and movement of pigs to a lairage pen. They found it difficult to observe lameness until unloading was complete and the pigs were in the passageway. They also found it difficult to assess several variables simultaneously. The ability to observe and measure many animal-based measurements can be affected by: (i) fast processing speeds; (ii) the design and operation of facilities; (iii) the necessity to avoid interference with commercial operations and the movement of animals (Berg, 2012; Payne *et al.*, 2017; Wigham *et al.*, 2018); health and safety concerns in relation to (iv) the movement of animals and equipment; compliance with food safety regulations (e.g. movement between the lairage and the slaughter floor); difficulties in ensuring continuity of observations and (v) measurements on the same batch of animals during each stage of slaughter; and (vi) the necessity to be present at specific times outside of the normal working day. When measurements are made on a sample of animals, it is essential that the sample is unbiased and representative of all of the animals that pass through the slaughter plant. With automatic recording of measurements and development of techniques for precision livestock farming, an increased number of animal-based measurements, for example some of those discussed by Brandt and Aaslyng (2015), may become feasible (Støier *et al.*, 2016). Video recordings made for auditing and verification of slaughterhouse compliance with legislation and guidelines can be useful, especially if it becomes possible to have automated analysis of animal movements (Gronskyte *et al.*, 2016).

Conclusions

The animals slaughtered for food can experience a range of mental states, including pain, fear, distress, hunger, thirst, fatigue and discomfort. This chapter highlighted how pre-slaughter and slaughter procedures can affect the occurrence of these potential welfare issues. Subsequent chapters will describe approaches to avoid and mitigate suffering when animals are slaughtered. Animal welfare research continues to refine methods for identifying when animals are experiencing a negative welfare state, how to assess animal welfare at slaughter plants, how to provide optimal care for animals during pre-slaughter management and how to minimize the risks of pain and distress during stunning and slaughter.

References

Abrams, K.M., Zimbres, T. and Carr, C. (2015) Communicating sensitive scientific issues: The interplay between values, attitudes, and euphemisms in communicating livestock slaughter. *Science Communication* 37, 485–505. doi: 10.1177/1075547015588599

Adolphs, R. and Andler, D. (2018) Investigating emotions as functional states distinct from feelings. *Emotion Review* 10, 191–201. doi: 10.1177/1754073918765662

Ahsan, M., Hasan, B., Algotsson, M. and Sarenbo, S. (2014) Handling and welfare of bovine livestock at local abattoirs in Bangladesh. *Journal of Applied Animal Welfare Science* 17, 340–353.

Althen, T.G., Ono, K. and Topel, D.G. (1977) Effect of stress susceptibility or stunning method on catecholamine levels in swine. *Journal of Animal Science* 44, 985–989.

Andersen, I.L., Bøe, K.E., Færevik, G., Janczak, A.M. and Bakken, M. (2000a) Behavioural evaluation of methods for assessing fear responses in weaned pigs. *Applied Animal Behaviour Science* 69, 227–240. doi: 10.1016/S0168-1591(00)00133-7

Andersen, I.L., Færevik, G., Bøe, K.E., Janczak, A.M. and Bakken, M. (2000b) Effects of diazepam on the behaviour of weaned pigs in three putative models of anxiety. *Applied Animal Behaviour Science* 68, 121–130. doi: 10.1016/S0168-1591(00)00098-8

Anderson, D. and Adolphs, R. (2014) A framework for studying emotions across species. *Cell* 157, 187–200. doi: 10.1016/j.cell.2014.03.003

Anil, M.H. and McKinstry, J.L. (1998) Variations in electrical stunning tong placements and relative consequences in slaughter pigs. *Veterinary Journal* 155, 85–90. doi: 10.1016/S1090-0233(98)80042-7

Anil, M.H., McKinstry, J.L., Gregory, N.G., Wotton, S.B. and Symonds, H. (1995a) Welfare of calves: 2. Increase in vertebral artery blood flow following exsanguination by neck sticking and evaluation of chest sticking as an alternative slaughter method. *Meat Science* 41, 113–123. doi: 10.1016/0309-1740(94)00076-J

Anil, M.H., McKinstry, J.L., Wotton, S.B. and Gregory, N.G. (1995b) Welfare of calves: 1. Investigations into some aspects of calf slaughter. *Meat Science* 41, 101–112. doi: 10.1016/0309-1740(94)00075-I

Anil, M.H., Preston, J., McKinstry, J.L., Rodway, R.G. and Brown, S.N. (1996) An assessment of stress caused in sheep by watching slaughter of other sheep. *Animal Welfare* 5, 43–-441.

Anil, M.H., McKinstry, J.L., Field, M. and Rodway, R.G. (1997) Lack of evidence for stress being caused to pigs by witnessing the slaughter of conspecifics. *Animal Welfare* 6, 3–8.

Anil, M.H., Whittington, P.E. and McKinstry, J.L. (2000) The effect of the sticking method on the welfare of slaughter pigs. *Meat Science* 55, 315–319. doi: 10.1016/S0309-1740(99)00159-X

Anil, M.H., Love, S., Helps, C.R. and Harbour, D.A. (2002) Potential for carcass contamination with brain tissue following stunning and slaughter in cattle and sheep. *Food Control* 13, 431–436. doi: 10.1016/S0956-7135(01)00055-X

Appelt, M. and Sperry, J. (2007) Stunning and killing cattle humanely and reliably in emergency situations – a comparison between a stunning-only and a stunning and pithing protocol. *Canadian Veterinary Journal-Revue Veterinaire Canadienne* 48, 529–534.

Arad, Z., Arnason, S.S., Chadwick, A. and Skadhauge, E. (1985) Osmotic and hormonal responses to heat and dehydration in the fowl. *Journal of Comparative Physiology B* 155, 227–234. doi: 10.1007/BF00685217

Arnone, M. and Dantzer, R. (1980) Does frustration induce aggression in pigs? *Applied Animal Ethology* 6, 351–362. doi: 10.1016/0304-3762(80)90135-2

Averos, X., Knowles, T.G., Brown, S.N., Warriss, P.D. and Gosalvez, L.F. (2008) Factors affecting the mortality of pigs being transported to slaughter. *Veterinary Record* 163, 386–390.

Baciadonna, L., Duepjan, S., Briefer, E.F., Padilla de la, T. and Nawroth, C. (2018) Looking on the bright side of livestock emotions-the potential of their transmission to promote positive welfare. *Frontiers in Veterinary Science* 5, 218. doi: 10.3389/fvets.2018.00218

Baile, C.A. and Della-Fera, M.A. (1981) Nature of hunger and satiety control systems in ruminants. *Journal of Dairy Science* 64, 1140–1152.

Barnett, J.L. and Hemsworth, P.H. (2009) Welfare monitoring schemes: using research to safeguard welfare of animals on the farm. *Journal of Applied Animal Welfare Science* 12, 114–131. doi: 10.1080/108887 00902719856 ER

Barnett, J.L., Cronin, G.M. and Scott, P.C. (2007) Behavioural responses of poultry during kosher slaughter and their implications for the birds' welfare. *Veterinary Record* 160, 45–49.

Barrett, L.F., Mesquita, B., Ochsner, K.N. and Gross, J.J. (2007) The experience of emotion. *Annual Review of Psychology* 58, 373–403. doi: 10.1146/annurev. psych.58.110405.085709 ER

Bass, J.J. and Duganzich, D.M. (1980) A note on effects of starvation on the bovine alimentary tract and its contents. *Animal Production* 31, 111–113.

Bassler, A.W., Arnould, C., Butterworth, A., Colin, L., De Jong, I.C., Ferrante, V., Ferrari, P., Haslam, S., Wemelsfelder, F. and Blokhuis, H.J. (2013) Potential risk factors associated with contact dermatitis, lameness, negative emotional state, and fear of humans in broiler chicken flocks. *Poultry Science* 92, 2811–2826. doi: 10.3382/ps.2013-03208

Bastian, B., Loughnan, S., Haslam, N. and Radke, H.R.M. (2012) Don't mind meat? The denial of mind to animals used for human consumption. *Personality and Social Psychology Bulletin* 38, 247–256. doi: 10.1177/0146167211424291

Bateson, P. (1991) Assessment of pain in animals. *Animal Behaviour* 42, 827–839. doi: 10.1016/S0003-3472(05) 80127-7

Beattie, V.E., Burrows, M.S., Moss, B.W. and Weatherup, R.N. (2002) The effect of food deprivation prior to slaughter on performance, behaviour and meat quality. *Meat Science* 62, 413–418. doi: 10.1016/S0309-1740(02)00031-1

Beausoleil, N.J., Stafford, K.J. and Mellor, D.J. (2005) Sheep show more aversion to a dog than to a human in an arena test. *Applied Animal Behaviour Science* 91, 219–232. doi: 10.1016/j.applanim.2004.10.008

Bedanova, I., Voslarova, E., Chloupek, P., Pistekova, V., Suchy, P., Blahova, J., Dobsikova, R. and Vecerek, V. (2007) Stress in broilers resulting from shackling. *Poultry Science* 86, 1065–1069.

Berg, C. (2012) Monitoring animal welfare at slaughterhouses. In: Jakobsson, C. (ed.) *Sustainable Agriculture*. Baltic University Press, Uppsala University, Uppsala, Sweden, pp. 349–351.

Berg, C. and Raj, M. (2015) A review of different stunning methods for poultry-animal welfare aspects (stunning methods for poultry). *Animals* 5, 1207–1219. doi: 10.3390/ani5040407

Biss, M.E. and Hathaway, S.C. (1996) Effect of pre-slaughter washing of lambs on the microbiological and visible contamination of the carcasses. *Veterinary Record* 138, 82–86. doi: 10.1136/vr.138.4.82

Bliss-Moreau, E. (2017) Constructing nonhuman animal emotion. *Current Opinion in Psychology; Emotion* 17, 184–188. doi: 10.1016/j.copsyc.2017.07.011

Blokhuis, H.J., Jones, R.B., Geers, R., Miele, M. and Veissier, I. (2003) Measuring and monitoring animal welfare: transparency in the food product quality chain. *Animal Welfare* 12, 445–455.

Blokhuis, H.J., Keeling, L.J., Gavinelli, A. and Serratosa, J. (2008) Animal welfare's impact on the food chain. *Trends in Food Science and Technology* 19, S83. doi: 10.1016/j.tifs.2008.09.007

Boissy, A. (1995) Fear and fearfulness in animals. *Quarterly Review of Biology* 70, 165–191. doi: 10.1086/ 418981

Boissy, A. and Bouissou, M.-F. (1988) Effects of early handling on heifers' subsequent reactivity to humans and to unfamiliar situations. *Applied Animal Behaviour Science* 20, 259–273. doi: 10.1016/0168-1591(88) 90051-2

Boissy, A. and Bouissou, M.-F. (1995) Assessment of individual differences in behavioural reactions of heifers exposed to various fear-eliciting situations. *Applied Animal Behaviour Science* 46, 17–31. doi: 10.1016/0168-1591(95)00633-8

Boissy, A. and Erhard, H.W. (2014) How studying interactions between animal emotions, cognition, and personality can contribute to improve farm animal welfare. In: Grandin, T. and Deesing, M.J. (eds) *Genetics and the Behavior of Domestic Animals (Second Edition)*. Academic Press, San Diego, pp. 81–113.

Boissy, A. and Lee, C. (2014) How assessing relationships between emotions and cognition can improve farm animal welfare. *Revue scientifique et technique (International Office of Epizootics)* 33, 103–110.

Boissy, A., Terlouw, C. and Le Neindre, P. (1998) Presence of cues from stressed conspecifics increases reactivity to aversive events in cattle: evidence for the existence of alarm substances in urine. *Physiology and Behavior* 63, 489–495.

Boissy, A., Fisher, A.D., Bouix, J., Hinch, G.N. and Le Neindre, P. (2005) Genetics of fear in ruminant livestock. *Livestock Production Science* 93, 23–32.

Bolaños-López, D., Mota-Rojas, D., Guerrero-Legarreta, I., Flores-Peinado, S., Mora-Medina, P., Roldan-Santiago, P., Borderas-Tordesillas, F., García-Herrera, R., Trujillo-Ortega, M. and Ramírez-Necoechea, R. (2014) Recovery of consciousness in hogs stunned with CO_2: physiological responses. *Meat Science* 98, 193–197. doi: 10.1016/j.meatsci.2014.05.034

Botreau, R., Bonde, M., Butterworth, A., Perny, P., Bracke, M.B.M., Capdeville, J. and Veissier, I. (2007a) Aggregation of measures to produce an overall assessment of animal welfare. Part 1: A review of existing methods. *Animal* 1, 1179–1187. doi: 10.1017/S1751731107000535 ER

Botreau, R., Bracke, M.B.M., Perny, R., Butterworth, A., Capdeville, J., Van Reenen, C.G. and Veissier, I. (2007b) Aggregation of measures to produce an overall assessment of animal welfare. Part 2: Analysis of constraints. *Animal* 1, 1188–1197. doi: 10.1017/S1751731107000547 ER

Botreau, R., Veissier, I. and Perny, P. (2009) Overall assessment of animal welfare: strategy adopted in welfare quality (R). *Animal Welfare* 18, 363–370.

Bourguet, C., Deiss, V., Gobert, M., Durand, D., Boissy, A. and Terlouw, E.M.C. (2010) Characterising the emotional reactivity of cows to understand and predict their stress reactions to the slaughter procedure. *Applied Animal Behaviour Science* 125, 9–21.

Bourguet, C., Deiss, V., Tannugi, C.C. and Terlouw, E.M.C. (2011a) Behavioural and physiological reactions of cattle in a commercial abattoir: relationships with organisational aspects of the abattoir and animal characteristics. *Meat Science* 88, 158–168. doi: 10.1016/j.meatsci.2010.12.017

Bourguet, C., Deiss, V., Boissy, A., Andanson, S. and Terlouw, E.M.C. (2011b) Effects of feed deprivation on behavioral reactivity and physiological status in Holstein cattle. *Journal of Animal Science* 89, 3272–3285.

Bozzo, G., Barrasso, R., Marchetti, P., Roma, R., Samoilis, G., Tantillo, G. and Ceci, E. (2018) Analysis of stress indicators for evaluation of animal welfare and meat quality in traditional and Jewish slaughtering. *Animals* 8, 43.

Bracke, M.B.M. (2007) Animal-based parameters are no panacea for on-farm monitoring of animal welfare. *Animal Welfare* 16, 229–231.

Brandt, P. and Aaslyng, M.D. (2015) Welfare measurements of finishing pigs on the day of slaughter: a review. *Meat Science* 103, 13–23. doi: 10.1016/j.meatsci.2014.12.004

Brandt, P., Rousing, T., Herskin, M.S., Olsen, E.V. and Aaslyng, M.D. (2017) Development of an index for the assessment of welfare of finishing pigs from farm to slaughter based on expert opinion. *Livestock Science* 198, 65–71. doi: 10.1016/j.livsci.2017.02.008

Bray, H.J., Zambrano, S.C., Chur-Hansen, A. and Ankeny, R.A. (2016) Not appropriate dinner table conversation? Talking to children about meat production. *Appetite* 100, 1–9. doi: 10.1016/j.appet.2016.01.029

Briefer, E.F. (2012) Vocal expression of emotions in mammals: Mechanisms of production and evidence. *Journal of Zoology* 288, 1–20.

Broom, D.M. (1998) Welfare, stress, and the evolution of feelings. *Stress and Behavior* 27, 371–403.

Broom, D. (2011) A history of animal welfare science. *Acta Biotheoretica* 59, 121–137. doi: 10.1007/s10441-011-9123-3

Brown, S.N., Warriss, P.D., Nute, G.R., Edwards, J.E. and Knowles, T.G. (1998) Meat quality in pigs subjected to minimal preslaughter stress. *Meat Science* 49, 257–265.

Brown, S.N., Knowles, T.G., Edwards, J.E. and Warriss, P.D. (1999) Relationship between food deprivation before transport and aggression in pigs held in lairage before slaughter. *The Veterinary Record* 145, 630–634. doi: 10.1136/vr.145.22.630

Caballero, C.S., Sumano, L.H., Tapia, G. and Ocampo, C.L. (1998) Vanil-mandelic acid as indicator of acute stress in cows at slaughter. *Journal of Applied Animal Research* 14, 187–191.

Caffrey, N.P., Dohoo, I.R. and Cockram, M.S. (2017) Factors affecting mortality risk during transportation of broiler chickens for slaughter in Atlantic Canada. *Preventive Veterinary Medicine* 147, 199–208. doi: 10.1016/j.prevetmed.2017.09.011

Campo, J.L., Gil, M.G. and Dávila, S.G. (2005) Effects of specific noise and music stimuli on stress and fear levels of laying hens of several breeds. *Applied Animal Behaviour Science* 91, 75–84. doi: 10.1016/j.applanim.2004.08.028

Cannon, W.B. (1939) *Bodily Changes in Pain, Hunger, Fear and Rage: An Account of Recent Researches into the Function of Emotional Excitement.* Appleton-Centry Company, New York.

Cardinal, R.N., Parkinson, J.A., Hall, J. and Everitt, B.J. (2002) Emotion and motivation: the role of the amygdala, ventral striatum, and prefrontal cortex. *Neuroscience & Biobehavioral Reviews* 26, 321–352. doi: 10.1016/S0149-7634(02)00007-6

Carlsson, F., Frykblom, P. and Lagerkvist, C.J. (2007) Consumer willingness to pay for farm animal welfare: mobile abattoirs versus transportation to slaughter. *European Review of Agricultural Economics* 34, 321–344. doi: 10.1093/erae/jbm025

Carr, T.R., Allen, D.M. and Phar, P. (1971) Effect of preslaughter fasting on bovine carcass yield and quality. *Journal of Animal Science* 32, 870–873.

Carreras, R., Arroyo, L., Mainau, E., Valent, D., Bassols, A., Dalmau, A., Faucitano, L., Manteca, X. and Velarde, A. (2017) Can the way pigs are handled alter behavioural and physiological measures of affective state? *Behavioural Processes* 142, 91–98. doi: 10.1016/j.beproc.2017.06.005

Cashman, P.J., Nicol, C.J. and Jones, R.B. (1989) Effects of transportation on the tonic immobility fear reactions of broilers. *British Poultry Science* 30, 211–221. doi: 10.1080/000/1668908417141

Ceci, E., Marchetti, P., Samoilis, G., Sportelli, S., Roma, R., Barrasso, R., Tantillo, G. and Bozzo, G. (2017) Determination of plasmatic cortisol for evaluation of animal welfare during slaughter. *Italian Journal of Food Safety* 6, 134–137. doi: 10.4081/ijfs.2017.6912

Charlebois, S. and Summan, A. (2014) Abattoirs, meat processing and managerial challenges: a survey for lagging rural regions and food entrepreneurs in Ontario, Canada. *International Journal of Rural Management* 10, 1–20. doi: 10.1177/0973005214526504

Chiari, P., Hadour, G., Michel, P., Piriou, V., Rodriguez, C., Budat, C., Ovize, M., Jegaden, O., Lehot, J.J. and Ferrera, R. (2000) Biphasic response after brain death induction: prominent part of catecholamines release in this phenomenon. *The Journal of Heart and Lung Transplantation* 19, 675–682. doi: 10.1016/S1053-2498(00)00127-3

Chloupek, P., Voslářová, E., Chloupek, J., Bedáňová, I., Pištěková, V. and Vecerek, V. (2009) Stress in broiler chickens due to acute noise exposure. *Acta Veterinaria Brno* 78, 93–98. doi: 10.2754/avb200978010093

Choi, Y.M., Jung, K.C., Choe, J.H. and Kim, B.C. (2012) Effects of muscle cortisol concentration on muscle fiber characteristics, pork quality, and sensory quality of cooked pork. *Meat Science* 91, 490–498. doi: 10.1016/j.meatsci.2012.03.003

Chulayo, A.Y., Bradley, G. and Muchenje, V. (2016) Effects of transport distance, lairage time and stunning efficiency on cortisol, glucose, HSPA1A and how they relate with meat quality in cattle. *Meat Science* 117, 89–96. doi: 10.1016/j.meatsci.2016.03.001

Cockram, M.S. (1990) Some factors influencing behaviour of cattle in a slaughterhouse lairage. *Animal Production* 50, 475–481. doi: 10.1017/S0003356100004955

Cockram, M.S. and Corley, K.T.T. (1991) Effect of pre-slaughter handling on the behaviour and blood composition of beef-cattle. *British Veterinary Journal* 147, 444–454.

Cockram, M.S., Kent, J.E., Goddard, P.J., Waran, N.K., Jackson, R.E., McGilp, I.M., Southall, E.L., Amory, J.R., McConnell, T.I., O'Riordan, T. and Wilkins, B.S. (2000) Behavioural and physiological responses of sheep to 16 h transport and a novel environment post-transport. *Veterinary Journal* 159, 139–146. doi: 10.1053/tvjl.1999.0411

Cockram, M.S., Murphy, E., Ringrose, S., Wemelsfelder, F., Miedema, H.M. and Sandercock, D.A. (2012) Behavioural and physiological measures following treadmill exercise as potential indicators to evaluate fatigue in sheep. *Animal* 6, 1491–1502. doi: 10.1017/S1751731112000638

Cooke, R.F. (2014) Temperament and acclimation to human handling influence growth, health, and reproductive responses in *Bos taurus* and *Bos indicus* cattle. *Journal of Animal Science* 92, 5325–5333. doi: 10.2527/jas2014-8017

Cornish, A., Raubenheimer, D. and McGreevy, P. (2016) What we know about the public's level of concern for farm animal welfare in food production in developed countries. *Animals* 6. doi: 10.3390/ani6110074

Cortesi, M.L. (1994) Slaughterhouses and humane treatment. *Revue scientifique et technique (International Office of Epizootics)* 13, 171–193.

Cranley, J. (2017) Death and prolonged survival in nons-tunned poultry: a case study. *Journal of Veterinary Behavior: Clinical Applications and Research* 18, 92–95. doi: 10.1016/j.jveb.2016.09.005

Curley Jr, K.O., Paschal, J.C., Welsh Jr, T.H. and Randel, R.D. (2006) Technical note: Exit velocity as a measure of cattle temperament is repeatable and associated with serum concentration of cortisol in Brahman bulls. *Journal of Animal Science* 84, 3100–3103. doi: 10.2527/jas.2006-055

Dalla Costa, F.A., Devillers, N., Paranhos, D.C. and Faucitano, L. (2016) Effects of applying preslaughter feed withdrawal at the abattoir on behaviour, blood parameters and meat quality in pigs. *Meat Science* 119, 89–94. doi: 10.1016/j.meatsci.2016.03.033

D'Allaire, S. and DeRoth, L. (1986) Physiological responses to treadmill exercise and ambient temperature in normal and malignant hyperthermia susceptible pigs. *Canadian Journal of Veterinary Research – Revue Canadienne De Recherche Veterinaire* 50, 78–83.

Dalmau, A., Fabrega, E. and Velarde, A. (2009a) Fear assessment in pigs exposed to a novel object test. *Applied Animal Behaviour Science* 117, 173–180. doi: 10.1016/j.applanim.2008.12.014

Dalmau, A., Temple, D., Rodríguez, P., Llonch, P. and Velarde, A. (2009b) Application of the Welfare Quality® protocol at pig slaughterhouses. *Animal Welfare* 18, 497–505.

Dalmau, A., Geverink, N.A., Van Nuffel, A., Van Steenbergen, L., Van Reenen, K., Hautekiet, V., Vermeulen, K., Velarde, A. and Tuyttens, F.A.M. (2010) Repeatability of lameness, fear and slipping scores to assess animal welfare upon arrival in pig slaughterhouses. *Animal* 4, 804–809. doi: 10.1017/S1751731110000066

Dalmau, A., Nande, A., Vieira-Pinto, M., Zamprogna, S., Di Martino, G., Ribas, J.C.R., da Costa, M.P., Halinen-Elemo, K. and Velarde, A. (2016) Application of the Welfare Quality® protocol in pig slaughterhouses of five countries. *Livestock Science* 193, 78–87. doi: 10.1016/j.livsci.2016.10.001

Daly, C.C., Kallweit, E. and Ellendorf, F. (1988) Cortical function in cattle during slaughter – conventional captive bolt stunning followed by exsanguination compared with shechita slaughter. *Veterinary Record* 122, 325–329.

Danbury, T.C., Weeks, C.A., Chambers, J.P., Waterman-Pearson, A. and Kestin, S.C. (2000) Self-selection of the analgesic drug carprofen by lame broiler chickens. *Veterinary Record* 146, 307–311.

Dawkins, M.S. (1990) From an animal's point of view: Motivation, fitness, and animal-welfare. *Behavioral and Brain Sciences* 13, 1–9.

Dawkins, M.S. (2006) A user's guide to animal welfare science. *Trends in Ecology & Evolution* 21, 77–82. doi: 10.1016/j.tree.2005.10.017

Dawkins, M.S. (2008) The science of animal suffering. *Ethology* 114, 937–945. doi: 10.1111/j.1439-0310.2008.01557.x

Dawkins, M.S. (2017) Animal welfare with and without consciousness. *Journal of Zoology* 301, 1–10. doi: 10.1111/jzo.12434

de Araujo, I.E.T., Kringelbach, M.L., Rolls, E.T. and McGlone, F. (2003) Human cortical responses to water in the mouth, and the effects of thirst. *Journal of Neurophysiology* 90, 1865–1876. doi: 10.1152/jn.00297.2003

de Graaf, S., Ampe, B., Buijs, S., Andreasen, S.N., De Boyer, D.R. *et al.* (2018) Sensitivity of the integrated Welfare Quality® scores to changing values of individual dairy cattle welfare measures. *Animal Welfare* 27, 157–166. doi: 10.7120/09627286.27.2.157

de Jong, I.C., Prelle, I.T., van de Burgwal, J.A., Lambooij, E., Korte, S.M. *et al* (2000) Effects of rearing conditions on behavioural and physiological responses of pigs to preslaughter handling and mixing at transport. *Canadian Journal of Animal Science* 80, 451–458.

de Vere, A.J. and Kuczaj II, S.A. (2016) Where are we in the study of animal emotions? *Wiley Interdisciplinary Reviews: Cognitive Science* 7, 354–362. doi: 10.1002/wcs.1399

D'Eath, R.B., Tolkamp, B.J., Kyriazakis, I. and Lawrence, A.B. (2009) 'Freedom from hunger' and preventing obesity: the animal welfare implications of reducing food quantity or quality. *Animal Behaviour* 77, 275–288. doi: 10.1016/j.anbehav.2008.10.028

Debut, M., Berri, C., Arnould, C., Guemené, D., Santé-Lhoutellier, V. *et al.* (2005) Behavioural and physiological responses of three chicken breeds to pre-slaughter shackling and acute heat stress. *British Poultry Science* 46, 527–535. doi: 10.1080/00071660500303032

Deiss, V., Temple, D., Ligout, S., Racine, C., Bouix, J., Terlouw, C. and Boissy, A. (2009) Can emotional reactivity predict stress responses at slaughter in sheep? *Applied Animal Behaviour Science* 119, 193–202. doi: 10.1016/j.applanim.2009.03.018

Désiré, L., Veissier, I., Després, G. and Boissy, A. (2004) On the way to assess emotions in animals: do lambs (*Ovis aries*) evaluate an event through its suddenness, novelty, or unpredictability? *Journal of Comparative Psychology* 118, 363–374.

Désiré, L., Veissier, I., Després, G., Delval, E., Toporenko, G. and Boissy, A. (2006) Appraisal process in sheep (*Ovis aries*): interactive effect of suddenness and unfamiliarity on cardiac and behavioral responses. *Journal of Comparative Psychology* 120, 280–287.

Dodman, N.H. (1977) Observations on the use of the Wernberg dip-lift carbon dioxide apparatus for pre-slaughter anaesthesia of pigs. *British Veterinary Journal* 133, 71-80. doi: 10.1016/S0007-1935(17)34190-8

Dodt, R.M., Anderson, B. and Horder, J.C. (1979) Bruising in cattle fasted prior to transport for slaughter. *Australian Veterinary Journal* 55, 528–530. doi: 10.1111/j.1751-0813.1979.tb07018.x

Duncan, I.J.H. (2005) Science-based assessment of animal welfare: farm animals. *Revue Scientifique et Technique-Office International Des Epizooties* 24, 483–492.

Dunn, C.S. (1990) Stress reactions of cattle undergoing ritual slaughter using two methods of restraint. *Veterinary Record* 126, 522–525.

Düpjan, S., Schön, P-C., Puppe, B., Tuchscherer, A. and Manteuffel, G. (2008) Differential vocal responses to physical and mental stressors in domestic pigs (*Sus scrofa*). *Applied Animal Behaviour Science* 114, 105–115.

Düpjan, S., Tuchscherer, A., Langbein, J., Schön, P-C., Manteuffel, G. and Puppe, B. (2011) Behavioural and cardiac responses towards conspecific distress calls in domestic pigs (*Sus scrofa*). *Physiology & Behavior* 103, 445–452. doi: 10.1016/j.physbeh.2011.03.017

Edgar, J.L., Nicol, C.J., Clark, C.C.A. and Paul, E.S. (2012) Measuring empathic responses in animals. *Applied Animal Behaviour Science* 138, 182–193.

EFSA (2012) Statement on the use of animal-based measures to assess the welfare of animals. *EFSA Journal* 10, 2767. doi: 10.2903/j.efsa.2012.2767

EFSA (2013) Scientific opinion on monitoring procedures at slaughterhouses for poultry. *EFSA Journal* 11, 3521. doi: 10.2903/j.efsa.2013.3521

Erhard, H.W. and Mendl, M. (1999) Tonic immobility and emergence time in pigs – more evidence for behavioural strategies. *Applied Animal Behaviour Science* 61, 227–237. doi: 10.1016/S0168-1591(98)00196-8

Eriksen, M.S., Rødbotten, R., Grøndahl, A.M., Friestad, M., Andersen, I.L. and Mejdell, C.M. (2013) Mobile abattoir versus conventional slaughterhouse-impact on stress parameters and meat quality characteristics in Norwegian lambs. *Applied Animal Behaviour Science* 149, 21–29. doi: 10.1016/j.applanim.2013.09.007

European Commission (2017) *Preparation of Best Practices on the Protection of Animals at the Time of Killing*. European Commission, Brussels. doi: 10.2875/15243. Available at: https://publications.europa.eu/en/publication-detail/-/publication/ea4ef3e9-cda5-11e7-a5d5-01aa75ed71a1/language-en (accessed 15 April 2020).

M. Cockram

Ewbank, R. (1985) Behavioral responses to stress in farm animals. In: Moberg, G.P. (ed.) *Animal Stress*. Springer, New York, pp. 71–79. doi: 10.1007/978-1-4614-7544-6_3

Fàbrega, E., Manteca, X., Font, J., Gispert, M., Carrión, D., Velarde, A., Ruiz-de-la-Torre, J.L. and Diestre, A. (2002) Effects of halothane gene and pre-slaughter treatment on meat quality and welfare from two pig crosses. *Meat Science* 62, 463–472. doi: 10.1016/S0309-1740(02)00040-2

Farm Animal Welfare Council (2009) Five Freedoms. Available at: https://webarchive.nationalarchives.gov.uk/20110909181150/http://www.fawc.org.uk/freedoms.htm (accessed 15 April 2020).

Faucitano, L. (2001) Causes of skin damage to pig carcasses. *Canadian Journal of Animal Science* 81, 39–45.

Faucitano, L., Saucier, L., Correa, J.A., Méthot, S., Giguère, A. *et al.* (2006) Effect of feed texture, meal frequency and pre-slaughter fasting on carcass and meat quality, and urinary cortisol in pigs. *Meat Science* 74, 697–703. doi: 10.1016/j.meatsci.2006.05.023

Faucitano, L., Chevillon, P. and Ellis, M. (2010) Effects of feed withdrawal prior to slaughter and nutrition on stomach weight, and carcass and meat quality in pigs. *Livestock Science* 127, 110–114. doi: 10.1016/j.livsci.2009.10.002

Fisher, M.W., Gregory, N.G. and Muir, P.D. (2012) Current practices on sheep and beef farms in New Zealand for depriving sheep of feed prior to transport for slaughter. *New Zealand Veterinary Journal* 60, 171–175. doi: 10.1080/00480169.2011.645202

Fitzgerald, A.J. (2010) A social history of the slaughterhouse: from inception to contemporary implications. *Human Ecology Review* 17, 58–69.

Fitzgerald, R.F., Stalder, K.J., Matthews, J.O., Schultz Kaster, C.M. and Johnson, A.K. (2009) Factors associated with fatigued, injured, and dead pig frequency during transport and lairage at a commercial abattoir. *Journal of Animal Science* 87, 1156–1166. doi: 10.2527/jas.2008-1270

Flower, F.C. and Weary, D.M. (2009) Gait assessment in dairy cattle. *Animal* 3, 87–95. doi: 10.1017/S1751731108003194

Food Chain Evaluation Consortium (2015) Study on information to consumers on the stunning of animals. European Commission, Brussels. Available at: http://ec.europa.eu/food/animals/docs/aw_practice_slaughter_fci-stunning_exex-sum_en.pdf (accessed 15 April 2020).

Fordham, D.P., Lincoln, G.A., Ssewannyana, E. and Rodway, R.G. (1989) Plasma β-endorphin and cortisol concentrations in lambs after handling, transport and slaughter. *Animal Production* 49, 103–107. doi: 10.1017/S000335610000430X

Fordyce, G., Goddard, M.E., Tyler, R., Williams, G. and Toleman, M.A. (1985) Temperament and bruising of *Bos indicus* cross cattle. *Australian Journal of Experimental Agriculture* 25, 283–288.

Forkman, B., Boissy, A., Meunier-Salaün, M.-C., Canali, E. and Jones, R.B. (2007) A critical review of fear tests used on cattle, pigs, sheep, poultry and horses. *Physiology & Behavior* 92, 340–374. doi: 10.1016/j.physbeh.2007.03.016

Forslid, A. and Augustinsson, O. (1988) Acidosis, hypoxia and stress hormone release in response to one-minute inhalation of 80% CO_2 in swine. *Acta Physiologica Scandinavica* 132, 223–231.

Foury, A., Devillers, N., Sanchez, M.-P., Griffon, H., Le Roy, P. and Mormède, P. (2005) Stress hormones, carcass composition and meat quality in large White×Duroc pigs. *Meat Science* 69, 703–707. doi: 10.1016/j.meatsci.2004.11.002

Fraser, D. (2008) Toward a global perspective on farm animal welfare. *Applied Animal Behaviour Science* 113, 330–339. doi: 10.1016/j.applanim.2008.01.011 ER

Fraser, D. (2009) Animal behaviour, animal welfare and the scientific study of affect. *Applied Animal Behaviour Science* 118, 108–117. doi: 10.1016/j.applanim.2009.02.020

Fraser, D. (2012) A 'practical' ethic for animals. *Journal of Agricultural and Environmental Ethics* 25, 721–746. doi: 10.1007/s10806-011-9353-z

Frese, D.A., Reinhardt, C.D., Bartle, S.J., Rethorst, D.N., Hutcheson, J.P. *et al.* (2016) Cattle handling technique can induce fatigued cattle syndrome in cattle not fed a beta adrenergic agonist. *Journal of Animal Science* 94, 581–591. doi: 10.2527/jas2015-9824

Frimpong, S., Gebresenbet, G., Bobobee, E., Aklaku, E.D. and Hamdu, I. (2014) Effect of transportation and pre-slaughter handling on welfare and meat quality of cattle: case study of Kumasi abattoir, Ghana. *Veterinary Sciences* 1, 174–191. doi: 10.3390/vetsci1030174

Gallo, C.B. and Huertas, S.M. (2015) Main animal welfare problems in ruminant livestock during preslaughter operations: a South American view. *Animal* 10, 357–364. doi: 10.1017/S1751731115001597

Gentle, M.J. (2011) Pain issues in poultry. *Applied Animal Behaviour Science* 135, 252–258. doi: 10.1016/j.applanim.2011.10.023

Gentle, M.J. and Tilston, V.L. (2000) Nociceptors in the legs of poultry: Implications for potential pain in pre-slaughter shackling. *Animal Welfare* 9, 227–236.

Geverink, N.A., Kappers, A., Burgwal, V.D., Lambooij, E., Blokhuis, H.J. and Wiegant, V.M. (1998) Effects of regular moving and handling on the behavioral and physiological responses of pigs to preslaughter treatment and consequences for subsequent meat quality. *Journal of Animal Science* 76, 2080–2085. doi: 10.2527/1998.7682080x

Gibson, T.J., Johnson, C.B., Hulls, C.M., Mitchinson, S.L., Stafford, K.J. *et al.* (2009a) Electro-encephalographic responses of halothane-anaesthe-tised calves to slaughter by ventral-neck incision without prior stunning. *New Zealand Veterinary Journal* 57, 77–83. doi: 10.1080/00480169.2009.36882

Gibson, T.J., Johnson, C.B., Chambers, J.P., Stafford, K.J., Mellor, D.J. and Mellor, D.J. (2009b) Components of electroencephalographic responses to slaughter in halothane-anaesthetised calves: effects of cutting neck tissues compared with major blood vessels. *New Zealand Veterinary Journal* 57, 84–89. doi: 10.1080/00480169.2009.36883

Gispert, M., Faucitano, L., Oliver, M.A., Guàrdia, M.D., Coll, C. *et al.* (2000) A survey of pre-slaughter conditions, halothane gene frequency, and carcass and meat quality in five Spanish pig commercial abattoirs. *Meat Science* 55, 97–106. doi: 10.1016/S0309-1740(99)00130-8

Goumon, S. and Špinka, M. (2016) Emotional contagion of distress in young pigs is potentiated by previous exposure to the same stressor. *Animal Cognition* 19, 501–511.

Grandin, T. (1997) The design and construction of facilities for handling cattle. *Livestock Production Science* 49, 103–119.

Grandin, T. (1998a) The feasibility of using vocalization scoring as an indicator of poor welfare during cattle slaughter. *Applied Animal Behaviour Science* 56, 121–128.

Grandin, T. (1998b) Objective scoring of animal handling and stunning practices at slaughter plants. *Journal of the American Veterinary Medical Association* 212, 36–39.

Grandin, T. (2000) Effect of animal welfare audits of slaughter plants by a major fast food company on cattle handling and stunning practices. *Journal of the American Veterinary Medical Association* 216, 848–851.

Grandin, T. (2001) Cattle vocalizations are associated with handling and equipment problems at beef slaughter plants. *Applied Animal Behaviour Science*, 71, 191–201. doi: 10.1016/S0168-1591(00)00179-9

Grandin, T. (2006) Progress and challenges in animal handling and slaughter in the US. *Applied Animal Behaviour Science* 100, 129–139. doi: 10.1016/j.applanim.2006.04.016

Grandin, T. (2010) Auditing animal welfare at slaughter plants. *Meat Science* 86, 56–65. doi: 10.1016/j.meatsci.2010.04.022

Grandin, T. (2013) Making slaughterhouses more humane for cattle, pigs, and sheep. *Annual Review of Animal Biosciences* 1, 491–512. doi: 10.1146/annurev-animal-031412-103713

Grandin, T. (2014) Animal welfare and society concerns finding the missing link. *Meat Science* 98, 461–469. doi: 10.1016/j.meatsci.2014.05.011

Grandin, T. (2017a) *Recommended Animal Handling Guidelines & Audit Guide: A Systematic Approach to Animal Welfare*. North American Meat Institute, Washington, DC. Available at: http://animalhandling.org/sites/default/files/forms/animal-handling-guidelines-Nov32017.pdf (accessed 15 April 2020).

Grandin, T. (2017b) How to work with large meat buyers to improve animal welfare. In: Purslow, P.P. (ed.) *New Aspects of Meat Quality*. Woodhead Publishing, pp. 569–579.

Gregory, N.G. and Grandin, T. (1998) *Animal Welfare and Meat Science*. CAB International, New York.

Gregory, N.G. and Whittington, P.E. (1992) Inhalation of water during electrical stunning in chickens. *Research in Veterinary Science* 53, 360–362.

Gregory, N.G. and Wilkins, L.J. (1989) Effect of stunning current on carcass quality in chickens. *Veterinary Record* 124, 530–532.

Gregory, N.G. and Wotton, S.B. (1984) Sheep slaughtering procedures. 1. Survey of abattoir practice. *British Veterinary Journal* 140, 281–286.

Gregory, N.G., Jacobson, L.H., Nagle, T.A., Muirhead, R.W. and Leroux, G.J. (2000) Effect of preslaughter feeding system on weight loss, gut bacteria, and the physico-chemical properties of digesta in cattle. *New Zealand Journal of Agricultural Research* 43, 351–361.

Gregory, N.G., von Wenzlawowicz, M. and Holleben, K.v. (2009) Blood in the respiratory tract during slaughter with and without stunning in cattle. *Meat Science* 82, 13–16. doi: 10.1016/j.meatsci.2008.11.021

Griffiths, G.L. (1985) The occurrence of red-skin chicken carcasses. *British Veterinary Journal* 141, 312–314.

Gronskyte, R., Clemmensen, L.H., Hviid, M.S. and Kulahci, M. (2016) Monitoring pig movement at the slaughterhouse using optical flow and modified angular histograms. *Biosystems Engineering* 141, 19–30. doi: 10.1016/j.biosystemseng.2015.10.002

Guesgen, M.J. and Bench, C.J. (2017) What can kinematics tell us about the affective states of animals. *Animal Welfare* 26, 383–397.

Hambrecht, E., Eissen, J.J., Nooijen, R.I.J., Ducro, B.J., Smits, C.H.M. *et al.* (2004) Preslaughter stress and muscle energy largely determine pork quality at two commercial processing plants. *Journal of Animal Science* 82, 1401–1409.

Hambrecht, E., Eissen, J.J., Newman, D.J., Smits, C.H.M., Den Hartog, L.A. and Verstegen, M.W.A. (2005) Negative effects of stress immediately before slaughter on pork quality are aggravated by suboptimal transport and lairage conditions. *Journal of Animal Science* 83, 440–448.

Hargreaves, A.L. and Hutson, G.D. (1990) The stress response in sheep during routine handling procedures. *Applied Animal Behaviour Science* 26, 83–90.

Harman, N.G. and Pethick, D.W. (1994) The effects of sustained exercise on gluconeogenesis, glycogenolysis and glycogen synthesis in merino sheep. *Australian Journal of Agricultural Research* 45, 1189–1202.

Harvey, D. and Hubbard, C. (2013) The supply chain's role in improving animal welfare. *Animals* 3, 767–785.

Hecker, J.F., Budtz-Olsen, O. and Ostwald, M. (1964) The rumen as a water store in sheep. *Australian Journal of Agricultural Research* 15, 961–968. doi: 10.1071/AR9640961

Hemsworth, P.H. and Barnett, J.L. (1992) The effects of early contact with humans on the subsequent level of fear of humans in pigs. *Applied Animal Behaviour Science* 35, 83–90. doi: 10.1016/0168-1591(92)90018-7

Hemsworth, P.H., Coleman, G.J., Barnett, J.L. and Jones, R.B. (1994) Behavioural responses to humans and the productivity of commercial broiler chickens. *Applied Animal Behaviour Science* 41, 101–114. doi: 10.1016/0168-1591(94)90055-8

Hemsworth, P.H., Barnett, J.L., Hofmeyr, C., Coleman, G.J., Dowling, S. and Boyce, J. (2002) The effects of fear of humans and pre-slaughter handling on the meat quality of pigs. *Australian Journal of Agricultural Research* 53, 493–501. doi: 10.1071/AR01098

Hemsworth, P.H., Rice, M., Karlen, M.G., Calleja, L., Barnett, J.L. *et al.* (2011) Human–animal interactions at abattoirs: Relationships between handling and animal stress in sheep and cattle. *Applied Animal Behaviour Science* 135, 24–33. doi: 10.1016/j.applanim.2011.09.007

Hemsworth, P.H., Mellor, D.J., Cronin, G.M. and Tilbrook, A.J. (2015) Scientific assessment of animal welfare. *New Zealand Veterinary Journal* 63, 24–30. doi: 10.1080/00480169.2014.966167

Hindle, V.A., Lambooij, E., Reimert, H.G.M., Workel, L.D. and Gerritzen, M.A. (2010) Animal welfare concerns during the use of the water bath for stunning broilers, hens, and ducks. *Poultry Science* 89, 401–412. doi: 10.3382/ps.2009-00297

Hoeksma, D.L., Gerritzen, M.A., Lokhorst, A.M. and Poortvliet, P.M. (2017) An extended theory of planned behavior to predict consumers' willingness to buy mobile slaughter unit meat. *Meat Science* 128, 15–23. doi: 10.1016/j.meatsci.2017.01.011

Hoffman, L.C. and Lühl, J. (2012) Causes of cattle bruising during handling and transport in Namibia. *Meat Science* 92, 115–124. doi: 10.1016/j.meatsci.2012.04.021

Hogan, J.P., Petherick, J.C. and Phillips, C.J.C. (2007) The physiological and metabolic impacts on sheep and cattle of feed and water deprivation before and during transport. *Nutrition Research Reviews* 20, 17–28.

Houpt, T.R. and Yang, H.S. (1995) Water-deprivation, plasma osmolality, blood-volume, and thirst in young-pigs. *Physiology & Behavior* 57, 49–54.

Hughes, R.N., Syme, L.A. and Syme, G.J. (1977) Open-field behaviour in sheep following treatment with the neuroleptics azaperone and acetylpromazine. *Psychopharmacology* 52, 107–109. doi: 10.1007/BF00426609

Hultgren, J., Wiberg, S., Berg, C., Cvek, K. and Lunner Kolstrup, C. (2014) Cattle behaviours and stockperson actions related to impaired animal welfare at Swedish slaughter plants. *Applied Animal Behaviour Science* 152, 23–37. doi: 10.1016/j.applanim.2013.12.005

Hultgren, J., Algers, B., Atkinson, S., Ellingsen, K., Eriksson, S. *et al.* (2016) Risk assessment of sheep welfare at small-scale slaughter in nordic countries, comparing with large-scale slaughter. *Acta Veterinaria Scandinavica* 58. doi: 10.1186/s13028-016-0217-4

Hunter, R.R., Mitchell, M.A., Carlisle, A.J., Quinn, A.D., Kettlewell, P.J., Knowles, T.G. and Warriss, P.D. (1998) Physiological responses of broilers to pre-slaughter lairage: effects of the thermal micro-environment? *British Poultry Science* 39, S54.

International Association for the Study of Pain (2017) IASP Terminology. Pain Terms. Available at: https://www.iasp-pain.org/Education/Content.aspx?ItemNumber=1698#Pain (accessed 15 April 2020).

Jackson, R.E., Waran, N.K. and Cockram, M.S. (1999) Methods for measuring feeding motivation in sheep. *Animal Welfare* 8, 53–63.

Jacob, R.H., Pethick, D.W., Ponnampalam, E., Speijers, J. and Hopkins, D.L. (2006) The hydration status of lambs after lairage at two Australian abattoirs. *Australian Journal of Experimental Agriculture* 46, 909–912. doi: 10.1071/EA05327

Jacobs, L., Delezie, E., Duchateau, L., Goethals, K. and Tuyttens, F.A.M. (2017) Impact of the separate pre-slaughter stages on broiler chicken welfare. *Poultry Science* 96, 266–273. doi: 10.3382/ps/pew361

Jarvis, A.M. and Cockram, M.S. (1994) Effects of handling and transport on bruising of sheep sent directly from farms to slaughter. *The Veterinary Record* 135, 523–527. doi: 10.1136/vr.135.22.523

Jensen, M.B., Schild, S.-L.A., Theil, P.K., Andersen, H.M.-L. and Pedersen, L.J. (2016) The effect of varying duration of water restriction on drinking behaviour, welfare and production of lactating sows. *Animal* 10, 961–969. doi: 10.1017/S1751731115002736

Johnson, C.B., Gibson, T.J., Stafford, K.J. and Mellor, D.J. (2012) Pain perception at slaughter. *Animal Welfare* 21, 113–122. doi: 10.7120/096272812X13353700593888

Johnson, C.B., Mellor, D.J., Hemsworth, P.H. and Fisher, A.D. (2015) A scientific comment on the welfare of domesticated ruminants slaughtered without stunning. *New Zealand Veterinary Journal* 63, 58–65. doi: 10.1080/00480169.2014.964345

Jones, R.B. (1986) The tonic immobility reaction of the domestic fowl: a review. *World's Poultry Science Journal* 42, 82–96.

Jones, R.B. (1992) The nature of handling immediately prior to test affects tonic immobility fear reactions in laying hens and broilers. *Applied Animal Behaviour Science* 34, 247–254. doi: 10.1016/S0168-1591(05)80119-4

Jones, S.D.M., Schaefer, A.L., Tong, A.K.W. and Vincent, B.C. (1988) The effects of fasting and transportation on beef cattle. 2. Body component changes, carcass composition and meat quality. *Livestock Production Science* 20, 25–35. doi: 10.1016/0301-6226(88)90051-6

Kannan, G. and Mench, J.A. (1996) Influence of different handling methods and crating periods on plasma corticosterone concentrations in broilers. *British Poultry Science* 37, 21–31. doi: 10.1080/00071669608417833

Kannan, G., Heath, J.L., Wabeck, C.J. and Mench, J.A. (1997) Shackling of broilers: effects on stress responses and breast meat quality. *British Poultry Science* 38, 323–332. doi: 10.1080/00071669708417998

Keer-Keer, S., Hughes, B.O., Hocking, P.M. and Jones, R.B. (1996) Behavioural comparison of layer and broiler fowl: measuring fear responses. *Applied Animal Behaviour Science* 49, 321–333. doi: 10.1016/0168-1591(96)01055-6

Kenny, F.J. and Tarrant, P.V. (1988) The effect of oestrus behaviour on muscle glycogen concentration and dark-cutting in beef heifers. *Meat Science* 22, 21–31. doi: 10.1016/0309-1740(88)90024-1

Kephart, K.B. and Mills, E.W. (2005) Effect of withholding feed from swine before slaughter on carcass and viscera weights and meat quality. *Journal of Animal Science* 83, 715–721.

Kim, F.B., Jackson, R.E., Gordon, G.D.H. and Cockram, M.S. (1994) Resting behaviour of sheep in a slaughterhouse lairage. *Applied Animal Behaviour Science* 40, 45–54. doi: 10.1016/0168-1591(94)90086-8

Knezacek, T.D., Olkowski, A.A., Kettlewell, P.J., Mitchell, M.A. and Classen, H.L. (2010) Temperature gradients in trailers and changes in broiler rectal and core body temperature during winter transportation in Saskatchewan. *Canadian Journal of Animal Science* 90, 321–330. doi: 10.4141/CJAS09083

Koolhaas, J.M. and Van Reenen, C.G. (2016) Animal Behavior and Well-Being Symposium: Interaction between coping style/personality, stress, and welfare: relevance for domestic farm animals. *Journal of Animal Science* 94, 2284–2296.

Lambooij, E., van der Werf, J.T.N., Reimert, H.G.M. and Hindle, V.A. (2012) Restraining and neck cutting or stunning and neck cutting of veal calves. *Meat Science*, 91, 22–28. doi: 10.1016/j.meatsci.2011.11.041

Langkabel, N., Baumann, M.P.O., Feiler, A., Sanguankiat, A. and Fries, R. (2015) Influence of two catching methods on the occurrence of lesions in broilers. *Poultry Science* 94, 1735–1741. doi: 10.3382/ps/pev164

Leach, T.M., Warrington, R. and Wotton, S.B. (1980) Use of a conditioned stimulus to study whether the initiation of electrical pre-slaughter stunning is painful. *Meat Science* 4, 203–208.

Leary, S., Underwood, W., Anthony, R., Corey, D.G.T., Gwaltney-Brant, S., Meyer, R., Regenstein, J., Shearer, J. and Smith, S.A. (2016) *AVMA Guidelines for the Humane Slaughter of Animals: 2016 edition*. American Veterinary Medical Association, Schaumburg, Illinois. Available at: https://www.avma.org/KB/Resources/Reference/AnimalWelfare/Documents/Humane-Slaughter-Guidelines.pdf (accessed 15 April 2020).

Ledger, R.A. and Mellor, D.J. (2018) Forensic use of the five domains model for assessing suffering in cases of animal cruelty. *Animals* 8. doi: 10.3390/ani8070101

Leliveld, L.M.C., Düpjan, S., Tuchscherer, A. and Puppe, B. (2017) Vocal correlates of emotional reactivity within and across contexts in domestic pigs (*Sus scrofa*). *Physiology & Behavior* 181, 117–126. doi: 10.1016/j.physbeh.2017.09.010

Leroy, F. and Praet, I. (2017) Animal killing and postdomestic meat production. *Journal of Agricultural and Environmental Ethics* 30, 67–86. doi: 10.1007/s10806-017-9654-y

Linares, M.B., Bórnez, R. and Vergara, H. (2008) Cortisol and catecholamine levels in lambs: effects of slaughter weight and type of stunning. *Livestock Science* 115, 53–61. doi: 10.1016/j.livsci.2007.06.010

Llonch, P., Rodríguez, P., Gispert, M., Dalmau, A., Manteca, X. and Velarde, A. (2012) Stunning pigs with nitrogen and carbon dioxide mixtures: effects on animal welfare and meat quality. *Animal* 6, 668–675.

Llonch, P., King, E.M., Clarke, K.A., Downes, J.M. and Green, L.E. (2015) A systematic review of animal based indicators of sheep welfare on farm, at market and during transport, and qualitative appraisal of their validity and feasibility for use in UK abattoirs. *Veterinary Journal* 206, 289–297. doi: 10.1016/j.tvjl.2015.10.019

Lokuruka, M.N.I. (2016) A preliminary survey of animal handling and cultural slaughter practices among Kenyan communities: potential influence on meat quality. *African Journal of Food, Agriculture, Nutrition and Development* 16, 10666–10681. doi: 10.18697/ajfand.73.15255

Losada-Espinosa, N., Villarroel, M., María, G.A. and Miranda-de la Lama, G.C. (2018) Pre-slaughter cattle welfare indicators for use in commercial abattoirs with voluntary monitoring systems: a systematic review. *Meat Science* 138, 34–48. doi: 10.1016/j.meatsci.2017.12.004

Lowe, T.E., Gregory, N.G., Fisher, A.D. and Payne, S.R. (2002) The effects of temperature elevation and water deprivation on lamb physiology, welfare, and meat quality. *Australian Journal of Agricultural Research* 53, 707–714.

Lundmark, F., Berg, C. and Röcklinsberg, H. (2018) Private animal welfare standards – opportunities and risks. *Animals* 8. doi: 10.3390/ani8010004

MacDonald, J.M. (2003) Beef and pork packing industries. *Veterinary Clinics of North America: Food Animal Practice; Economics of the Red Meat and Dairy Industries* 19, 419–443. doi: 10.1016/S0749-0720(03)00022-7

M. Cockram

Main, D.C.J., Mullan, S., Atkinson, C., Cooper, M., Wrathall, J.H.M. and Blokhuis, H.J. (2014) Best practice framework for animal welfare certification schemes. *Trends in Food Science & Technology* 37, 127–136. doi: 10.1016/j.tifs.2014.03.009

Manteuffel, G., Puppe, B. and Schon, P.C. (2004) Vocalization of farm animals as a measure of welfare. *Applied Animal Behaviour Science* 88, 163–182. doi: 10.1016/j.applanim.2004.02.012 ER

Martin, J.E., Christensen, K., Vizzier-Thaxton, Y. and McKeegan, D.E.F. (2016) Effects of analgesic intervention on behavioural responses to low atmospheric pressure stunning. *Applied Animal Behaviour Science* 180, 157–165. doi: 10.1016/j.applanim.2016.05.007

Mazurek, M., McGee, M., Crowe, M.A., Prendiville, D.J., Boivin, X. and Earley, B. (2011) Consistency and stability of behavioural fear responses of heifers to different fear-eliciting situations involving humans. *Applied Animal Behaviour Science* 131, 21–28. doi: 10.1016/j.applanim.2011.01.004

McKinley, M.J. and Johnson, A.K. (2004) The physiological regulation of thirst and fluid intake. *News in Physiological Sciences* 19, 1–6.

McKinstry, J.L. and Anil, M.H. (2004) The effect of repeat application of electrical stunning on the welfare of pigs. *Meat Science* 67, 121–128. doi: 10.1016/j.meatsci.2003.10.002

Miller, M.F., Carr, M.A., Bawcom, D.B., Ramsey, C.B. and Thompson, L.D. (1997) Microbiology of pork carcasses from pigs with differing origins and feed withdrawal times. *Journal of Food Protection* 60, 242–245. doi: 10.4315/0362-028X-60.3.242

Miranda-de la Lama, G.C., Leyva, I.G., Barreras-Serrano, A., Perez-Linares, C., Sanchez-Lopez, E., Maria, G.A. and Figueroa-Saavedra, F. (2012) Assessment of cattle welfare at a commercial slaughter plant in the northwest of Mexico. *Tropical Animal Health and Production* 44, 497–504. doi: 10.1007/s11250-011-9925-y

Mormede, P. and Dantzer, R. (1978) Behavioural and pituitary-adrenal characteristics of pigs differing by their susceptibility to the malignant hyperthermia syndrome induced by halothane anesthesia. 2. pituitary-adrenal function. *Annales De Recherches Vétérinaires* 9, 569–576.

Mormède, P., Andanson, S., Aupérin, B., Beerda, B., Guémené, D. *et al.* (2007) Exploration of the hypothalamic-pituitary-adrenal function as a tool to evaluate animal welfare. *Physiology and Behavior* 92, 317–339.

Morrow, W.E.M., See, M.T., Eisemann, J.H., Davies, P.R. and Zering, K. (2002) Effect of withdrawing feed from swine on meat quality and prevalence of salmonella colonization at slaughter. *Journal of the American Veterinary Medical Association* 220, 497–502. doi: 10.2460/javma.2002.220.497

Mota-Rojas, D., Orozco-Gregorio, H., Gonzalez-Lozano, M., Roldan-Santiago, P., Martinez-Rodriguez, R. *et al.* (2011) Therapeutic approaches in animals to reduce the impact of stress during transport to the slaughterhouse: a review. *International Journal of Pharmacology* 7, 568–578. doi: 10.3923/ijp.2011.568.578

Murray, A., Robertson, W., Nattress, F. and Fortin, A. (2001) Effect of pre-slaughter overnight feed withdrawal on pig carcass and muscle quality. *Canadian Journal of Animal Science* 81, 89–97. doi: 10.4141/A99-129

Muth, M.K., Wohlgenant, M.K. and Karns, S.A. (2007) Did the pathogen reduction and hazard analysis and critical control points regulation cause slaughter plants to exit? *Review of Agricultural Economics* 29, 596–611. doi: 10.1111/j.1467-9353.2007.00374.x

National Research Council (2009) *Recognition and Alleviation of Pain in Laboratory Animals.* The National Academies Press, Washington, DC. doi: 10.17226/12526

Njisane, Y.Z. and Muchenje, V. (2013) Quantifying avoidance-related behaviour and bleeding times of sheep of different ages, sex and breeds slaughtered at a municipal and a commercial abattoirs. *South African Journal of Animal Science*, 43 (Suppl. 1), 38–42. doi: 10.4314/sajas.v43i5.7

OIE (2016) Terrestrial Animal Health Code. Slaughter of Animals. Office International des Epizooties. Available at: http://www.oie.int/index.php?id=169&L=0&htmfile=chapitre_aw_slaughter.htm (accessed 15 April 2020).

Omotosho, O.O., Emikpe, B.O., Lasisi, O.T. and Oladunjoye, O.V. (2016) Pig slaughtering in southwestern Nigeria: peculiarities, animal welfare concerns and public health implications. *African Journal of Infectious Diseases* 10, 146–155. doi: 10.21010/ajid.v10i2.11

Oxford English Dictionary (2018) 'Humane, Adj.' Available at: http://www.oed.com/view/Entry/89264?redirectedFrom=humane

Pajor, E.A., Rushen, J. and De Passillé, A.M.B. (2000) Aversion learning techniques to evaluate dairy cattle handling practices. *Applied Animal Behaviour Science* 69, 89–102. doi: 10.1016/S0168-1591(00)00119-2

Panksepp, J. (2005) Affective consciousness: core emotional feelings in animals and humans. *Consciousness and Cognition* 14, 30–80. doi: 10.1016/j.concog.2004.10.004 ER

Parotat, S., von Holleben, K., Arnold, S., Troeger, K. and Luecker, E. (2016) Hot-water spraying is a sensitive test for signs of life before dressing and scalding in pig abattoirs with carbon dioxide (CO_2) stunning. *Animal* 10, 326–332.

Payne, E., Starling, M. and McGreevy, P. (2017) Addressing the challenges of conducting observational studies in sheep abattoirs. *Animals* 7. doi: 10.3390/ani7110082

Petherick, J.C., Doogan, V.J., Holroyd, R.G., Olsson, P. and Venus, B.K. (2009) Quality of handling and holding yard environment, and beef cattle temperament: 1. relationships with flight speed and fear of humans. *Applied Animal Behaviour Science* 120, 18–27. doi: 10.1016/j.applanim.2009.05.008

Pollard, J.C., Littlejohn, R.P., Asher, G.W., Pearse, A.J.T., Stevenson-Barry, J. *et al.* (2002) A comparison of biochemical and meat quality variables in red deer (*Cervus elaphus*) following either slaughter at pasture or killing at a deer slaughter plant. *Meat Science* 60, 85–94. doi: 10.1016/S0309-1740(01)00110-3

Probst, J.K., Spengler Neff, A., Leiber, F., Kreuzer, M. and Hillmann, E. (2012) Gentle touching in early life reduces avoidance distance and slaughter stress in beef cattle. *Applied Animal Behaviour Science* 139, 42–49. doi: 10.1016/j.applanim.2012.03.002

Probst, J.K., Neff, A.S., Hillmann, E., Kreuzer, M., Koch-Mathis, M. and Leiber, F. (2014) Relationship between stress-related exsanguination blood variables, vocalisation, and stressors imposed on cattle between lairage and stunning box under conventional abattoir conditions. *Livestock Science* 164, 154–158. doi: 10.1016/j.livsci.2014.03.013

Qekwana, D.N., McCrindle, C.M.E., Oguttu, J.W., Grace, D. and Cenci-Goga, B. (2017) Assessment of welfare issues during traditional slaughter of goats in Pretoria, South Africa. *Journal of Applied Animal Welfare Science* 20, 34–41. doi: 10.1080/10888705.2016.1217486

Raj, M. (1998) Welfare during stunning and slaughter of poultry. *Poultry Science* 77, 1815–1819.

Raj, A.B.M. and Gregory, N.G. (1996) Welfare implications of the gas stunning of pigs 2. Stress of induction of anaesthesia. *Animal Welfare* 5, 71–78.

Ralph, C.R. and Tilbrook, A.J. (2016) Invited review: The usefulness of measuring glucocorticoids for assessing animal welfare. *Journal of Animal Science* 94, 457–470. doi: 10.2527/jas.2015-9645

Ramos, A. and Mormede, P. (1998) Stress and emotionality: a multidimensional and genetic approach. *Neuroscience and Biobehavioral Reviews* 22, 33–57.

Rao, M.A., Knowles, T.G. and Wotton, S.B. (2013) The effect of pre-stun shocks in electrical water-bath stunners on carcase and meat quality in broilers. *Animal Welfare* 22, 79–84. doi: 10.7120/09627286.22.1.079

Reefmann, N., Bütikofer Kaszàs, F., Wechsler, B. and Gygax, L. (2009) Ear and tail postures as indicators of emotional valence in sheep. *Applied Animal Behaviour Science* 118, 199–207.

Reimert, I., Bolhuis, J.E., Kemp, B. and Rodenburg, T.B. (2013) Indicators of positive and negative emotions and emotional contagion in pigs. *Physiology & Behavior* 109, 42–50. doi: 10.1016/j.physbeh.2012.11.002

Reimert, I., Fong, S., Rodenburg, T.B. and Bolhuis, J.E. (2017) Emotional states and emotional contagion in pigs after exposure to a positive and negative treatment. *Applied Animal Behaviour Science* 193, 37–42. doi: 10.1016/j.applanim.2017.03.009

Reinert, H. (2012) Knives for the slaughter – notes on the reform and governance of indigenous reindeer slaughter in Norway. *Acta Borealia* 29, 35–55. doi: 10.1080/08003831.2012.678719

Roberts, F., Lucas, A. and Johnson, S. (2012) The use of a single empirical outcome measure to assess welfare in slaughter plants: between- and within-sector comparisons of the supply base for a major retail multiple. *Animal Welfare* 21, 139–145. doi: 10.7120/0962 72812X13353700594003

Rocha, L.M., Velarde, A., Dalmau, A., Saucier, L. and Faucitano, L. (2016) Can the monitoring of animal welfare parameters predict pork meat quality variation through the supply chain (from farm to slaughter)? *Journal of Animal Science* 94, 359–376. doi: 10.2527/jas.2015-9176

Roche, J.R., Blache, D., Kay, J.K., Miller, D.R., Sheahan, A.J. and Miller, D.W. (2008) Neuroendocrine and physiological regulation of intake with particular reference to domesticated ruminant animals. *Nutrition Research Reviews* 21, 207–234. doi: 10.1017/S0954422408138744

Rollin, B.E. (2015) The inseparability of science and ethics in animal welfare. *Journal of Agricultural and Environmental Ethics* 28, 759–765. doi: 10.1007/s10806-015-9558-7

Romero, M.H., Uribe-Velásquez, L.F., Sánchez, J.A., Rayas-Amor, A. and Miranda-de la Lama, G.C. (2017) Conventional versus modern abattoirs in Colombia: impacts on welfare indicators and risk factors for high muscle pH in commercial Zebu young bulls. *Meat Science* 123, 173–181. doi: 10.1016/j.meatsci.2016.10.003

Rushen, J. (1986) Some problems with the physiological concept of 'stress'. *Australian Veterinary Journal* 63, 359–361.

Rushen, J., Taylor, A.A. and De Passillé, A.M. (1999) Domestic animals' fear of humans and its effect on their welfare. *Applied Animal Behaviour Science* 65, 285–303. doi: 10.1016/S0168-1591(99)00089-1

Salmi, B., Trefan, L., Bünger, L., Doeschl-Wilson, A., Bidanel, J.P. *et al.* (2012) Bayesian meta-analysis of the effect of fasting, transport and lairage times on four attributes of pork meat quality. *Meat Science* 90, 584–598. doi: 10.1016/j.meatsci.2011.09.021

Sanford, J., Ewbank, R., Molony, V., Tavernor, W.D. and Uvarov, O. (1986) Guidelines for the recognition and assessment of pain in animals. *Veterinary Record* 118, 334–338.

Saucier, L., Bernier, D., Bergeron, R., Giguère, A., Méthot, S. and Faucitano, L. (2007) Effect of feed texture, meal frequency and pre-slaughter fasting on behaviour, stomach content and carcass microbial quality in pigs. *Canadian Journal of Animal Science* 87, 479–487. doi: 10.4141/A06-072

Scanes, C.G. (2016) Biology of stress in poultry with emphasis on glucocorticoids and the heterophil to lymphocyte ratio. *Poultry Science* 95, 2208–2215. doi: 10.3382/ps/pew137

Science Council (2009) Our Definition of Science. Available at: https://sciencecouncil.org/about-science/our-definition-of-science/ (accessed 15 April 2020).

Seng, P.M. and Laporte, R. (2005) Animal welfare: the role and perspectives of the meat and livestock sector. *Revue Scientifique et Technique Office International Des Epizooties* 24, 613–623.

Shaw, F.D. and Tume, R.K. (1992) The assessment of pre-slaughter and slaughter treatments of livestock by measurement of plasma constituents – a review of recent work. *Meat Science* 32, 311–329. doi: 10.1016/0309-1740(92)90095-L

Shaw, F.D., Trout, G.R. and McPhee, C.P. (1995) Plasma and muscle cortisol measurements as indicators of meat quality and stress in pigs. *Meat Science* 39, 237–246. doi: 10.1016/0309-1740(94)P1824-F

Small, A., Reid, C.A. and Buncic, S. (2003) Conditions in lairages at abattoirs for ruminants in southwest England and in vitro survival of Escherichia coli O157, Salmonella Kedougou, and Campylobacter jejuni on lairage-related substrates. *Journal of Food Protection* 66, 1570–1575. doi: 10.4315/0362-028X-66.9.1570

Sneddon, L.U. (2018) Comparative physiology of nociception and pain. *Physiology* 33, 63–73. doi: 10.1152/physiol.00022.2017

Sneddon, L.U., Elwood, R.W., Adamo, S.A. and Leach, M.C. (2014) Defining and assessing animal pain. *Animal Behaviour* 97, 201–212. doi: 10.1016/j.anbehav.2014.09.007

Sparrey, J.M. and Kettlewell, P.J. (1994) Shackling of poultry – Is it a welfare problem? *World's Poultry Science Journal* 50, 167–176.

Spoolder, H., De Rosa, G., Horning, B., Waiblinger, S. and Wemelsfelder, F. (2003) Integrating parameters to assess on-farm welfare. *Animal Welfare* 12, 529–534.

Sterten, H., Frøystein, T., Oksbjerg, N., Rehnberg, A.C., Ekker, A.S. and Kjos, N.P. (2009) Effects of fasting prior to slaughter on technological and sensory properties of the loin muscle (M. longissimus dorsi) of pigs. *Meat Science* 83, 351–357. doi: 10.1016/j.meatsci.2009.06.002

Støier, S., Larsen, H.D., Aaslyng, M.D. and Lykke, L. (2016) Improved animal welfare, the right technology and increased business. *Meat Science* 120, 71–77. doi: 10.1016/j.meatsci.2016.04.010

Tataranni, P.A., Gautier, J., Chen, K., Uecker, A., Bandy, D. *et al.* (1999) Neuroanatomical correlates of hunger and satiation in humans using positron emission tomography. *Proceedings of the National Academy of Sciences of the United States of America* 96, 4569–4574. doi: 10.1073/pnas.96.8.4569

Terlouw, C. (2005) Stress reactions at slaughter and meat quality in pigs: genetic background and prior experience: a brief review of recent findings. *Livestock Production Science* 94, 125–135. doi: 10.1016/j.livprodsci.2004.11.032

Terlouw, E.M.C. and Rybarczyk, P. (2008) Explaining and predicting differences in meat quality through stress reactions at slaughter: the case of Large White and Duroc pigs. *Meat Science* 79, 795–805. doi: 10.1016/j.meatsci.2007.11.013

Terlouw, E.M.C., Boissy, A. and Blinet, P. (1998) Behavioural responses of cattle to the odours of blood and urine from conspecifics and to the odour of faeces from carnivores. *Applied Animal Behaviour Science* 57, 9–21. doi: 10.1016/S0168-1591(97)00122-6

Terlouw, E.M.C., Arnould, C., Auperin, B., Berri, C., Le Bihan-Duval, E. *et al.* (2008) Pre-slaughter conditions, animal stress and welfare: current status and possible future research. *Animal* 2, 1501–1517. doi: 10.1017/S1751731108002723

Terlouw, E.M.C., Bourguet, C. and Deiss, V. (2012) Stress at slaughter in cattle: role of reactivity profile and environmental factors. *Animal Welfare* 21, 43–49. doi: 10.7120/096272812X13353700593482

Terlouw, C., Bourguet, C. and Deiss, V. (2016) Consciousness, unconsciousness and death in the context of slaughter. Part II. Evaluation methods. *Meat Science* 118, 147–156. doi: 10.1016/j.meatsci.2016.03.010

Thomson, D.U., Loneragan, G.H., Henningson, J.N., Ensley, S. and Bawa, B. (2015) Description of a novel fatigue syndrome of finished feedlot cattle following transportation. *Journal of the American Veterinary Medical Association* 247, 66–72. doi: 10.2460/javma.247.1.66

Veissier, I. and Boissy, A. (2007) Stress and welfare: two complementary concepts that are intrinsically related to the animal's point of view. *Physiology and Behavior* 92, 429–433.

Veissier, I. and Le Neindre, P. (1988) Cortisol responses to physical and pharmacological stimuli in heifers. *Reproduction, Nutrition, Developpement* 28, 553–562.

Velarde, A. and Dalmau, A. (2012) Animal welfare assessment at slaughter in Europe: moving from inputs to outputs. *Meat Science* 92, 244–251. doi: 10.1016/j.meatsci.2012.04.009

Velarde, A., Gispert, M., Faucitano, L., Manteca, X. and Diestre, A. (2000) Survey of the effectiveness of stunning procedures used in Spanish pig abattoirs. *Veterinary Record* 146, 65–68.

Velarde, A., Cruz, J., Gispert, M., Carrión, D., Ruiz de, I.T. *et al.* (2007) Aversion to carbon dioxide stunning in pigs: effect of carbon dioxide concentration and halothane genotype. *Animal Welfare* 16, 513–522.

Velarde, A., Rodriguez, P., Dalmau, A., Fuentes, C., Llonch, P. *et al.* (2014) Religious slaughter: evaluation of current practices in selected countries. *Meat Science* 96, 278–287. doi: 10.1016/j.meatsci.2013.07.013

Verhoeven, M.T.W., Gerritzen, M.A., Kluivers-Poodt, M., Hellebrekers, L.J. and Kemp, B. (2015) Validation of behavioural indicators used to assess unconsciousness in sheep. *Research in Veterinary Science* 101, 144–153. doi: 10.1016/j.rvsc.2015.06.007

Vieuille-Thomas, C. and Signoret, J.P. (1992) Pheromonal transmission of an aversive experience in domestic pig. *Journal of Chemical Ecology* 18, 1551–1557. doi: 10.1007/BF00993228

Warner, R.D., Ferguson, D.M., Cottrell, J.J. and Knee, B.W. (2007) Acute stress induced by the preslaughter use of electric prodders causes tougher beef meat. *Australian Journal of Experimental Agriculture* 47, 782–788. doi: 10.1071/EA05155

Warriss, P.D. (1982) Loss of carcass weight, liver weight and liver-glycogen, and the effects on muscle glycogen and ultimate pH in pigs fasted pre- slaughter. *Journal of the Science of Food and Agriculture* 33, 840–846.

Warriss, P.D. and Brown, S.N. (1985) The physiological responses to fighting in pigs and the consequences for meat quality. *Journal of the Science of Food and Agriculture* 36, 87–92. doi: 10.1002/jsfa.2740360207

Warriss, P.D., Kestin, S.C., Brown, S.N. and Bevis, E.A. (1988) Depletion of glycogen reserves in fasting broiler chickens. *British Poultry Science* 29, 149–154.

Warriss, P.D., Brown, S.N., Adams, S.J.M. and Corlett, I.K. (1994) Relationships between subjective and objective assessments of stress at slaughter and meat quality in pigs. *Meat Science* 38, 329–340. doi: 10.1016/0309-1740(94)90121-X

Warriss, P.D., Brown, S.N., Barton Gade, P., Santos, C., Nanni Costa, L. *et al.* (1998) An analysis of data relating to pig carcass quality and indices of stress collected in the European Union. *Meat Science* 49, 137–144. doi: 10.1016/S0309-1740(97)00133-2

Warriss, P.D., Wilkins, L.J., Brown, S.N., Phillips, A.J. and Allen, V. (2004) Defaecation and weight of the gastrointestinal tract contents after feed and water withdrawal in broilers. *British Poultry Science* 45, 61–66. doi: 10.1080/0007166041668879

Waynert, D.F., Stookey, J.M., Schwartzkopf-Genswein, K., Watts, J.M. and Waltz, C.S. (1999) The response of beef cattle to noise during handling. *Applied Animal Behaviour Science* 62, 27–42. do: 10.1016/S0168-1591(98)00211-1

Weeks, C.A. (2008) A review of welfare in cattle, sheep and pig lairages, with emphasis on stocking rates, ventilation and noise. *Animal Welfare* 17, 275–284.

Welfare Quality® (2009a) Welfare Quality® assessment protocol for cattle. Welfare Quality® Consortium, Lelystad, Netherlands. Available at: http://www.welfarequality.net/media/1088/cattle_protocol_without_veal_calves.pdf (accessed 15 April 2020).

Welfare Quality® (2009b) Welfare Quality® assessment protocol for pigs (sows and piglets, growing and finishing pigs). Welfare Quality® Consortium, Lelystad, Netherlands. Available at: http://www.welfarequality.net/media/1018/pig_protocol.pdf (accessed 15 April 2020).

Welfare Quality® (2009c) Welfare Quality® assessment protocol for poultry (broilers, laying hens). Welfare Quality® Consortium, Lelystad, Netherlands. Available at: http://www.welfarequality.net/media/1019/poultry_protocol.pdf (accessed 15 April 2020).

Westervelt, R.G., Kirsman, D.M., Prince, R.P. and Giger, W. (1976) Physiological stress measurement during slaughter in calves and lambs. *Journal of Animal Science* 42, 831–837.

Wigham, E.E., Butterworth, A. and Wotton, S. (2018) Assessing cattle welfare at slaughter – why is it important and what challenges are faced? *Meat Science* 145, 171–177. doi: 10.1016/j.meatsci.2018.06.010

Wythes, J.R., Shorthose, W.R., Schmidt, P.J. and Davis, C.B. (1980) Effects of various rehydration procedures after a long journey on liveweight, carcasses and muscle properties of cattle. *Australian Journal of Agricultural Research* 4, 849–855.

Wythes, J.R., Johnston, G.N., Beaman, N. and O'Rourke, P.K. (1985) Pre slaughter handling of cattle: the availability of water during the lairage period. *Australian Veterinary Journal* 62, 163–165.

Zhou, W.T., Fujita, M. and Yamamoto, S. (1999) Thermoregulatory responses and blood viscosity in dehydrated heat-exposed broilers (*Gallus domesticus*). *Journal of Thermal Biology* 24, 185–192.

Zimerman, M., Domingo, E., Grigioni, G., Taddeo, H. and Willems, P. (2013) The effect of pre-slaughter stressors on physiological indicators and meat quality traits on Merino lambs. *Small Ruminant Research* 111, 6–9. doi: 10.1016/j.smallrumres.2012.12.018

Zivotofsky, A.Z. and Strous, R.D. (2012) A perspective on the electrical stunning of animals: are there lessons to be learned from human electro-convulsive therapy (ECT)? *Meat Science* 90, 956–961. doi: 10.1016/j.meatsci.2011.11.039

Zulkifli, I., Goh, Y.M., Norbaiyah, B., Sazili, A.Q., Lotfi, M. *et al.* (2014) Changes in blood parameters and electroencephalogram of cattle as affected by different stunning and slaughter methods in cattle. *Animal Production Science* 54, 187–193.

3 Tradeoffs Balancing Livestock and Poultry Welfare Concerns with the Commercial Reality of Slaughter

TEMPLE GRANDIN*

Department of Animal Science, Colorado State University, USA

Summary

When working with commercial companies, it is often more effective to actually achieve 70–80% of the desired welfare improvements than attempt to achieve 100% perfection and accomplish nothing. There are conditions that cause suffering that are always wrong and in these situations there is never a tradeoff. Some examples would be beating animals, restraint methods that cause injury, throwing or dragging animals or breaking tails. Government officials, managers of meat-buying supply chains and abattoir managers must always stop these abusive practices. However, there are often situations where there are legitimate welfare tradeoffs. Choice of stunning method is a major area of controversy. Electrical stunning induces instantaneous unconsciousness, but the handling methods to position the pigs or birds are more stressful than with gaseous stunning. When controlled atmosphere stunning is used, the pre-slaughter handling method causes much lower stress, but this must be balanced against the behavioural reaction to a slower induction of unconsciousness. During the induction phase, the animals may be exposed to aversive stimuli. This chapter will help readers make decisions about tradeoffs.

Learning Objectives

- Learn that when decisions are made about animal welfare, there are sometimes tradeoffs.
- List bad practices that are *never* acceptable and there are no tradeoffs.
- Discuss differences in animal behaviour that can have a detrimental effect on handling.
- Learn to balance handling stress versus stun method stress when evaluating electrical or controlled atmosphere stunning systems.
- Welfare assessment methods used in commercial programmes often have to be simpler than methods used in research.

Introduction

I have been designing equipment and working with abattoirs on improving animal welfare for over 40 years. My projects have ranged from huge US facilities to smaller operations in Europe, South America and Australia. To make real improvements in commercial abattoirs, I learned that it is often more effective to actually achieve 70–80% of what I want. If I had attempted to get to 100% improvements, I may have been less likely to have achieved anything.

There have been situations where equipment I had designed made big improvements in the welfare of livestock at abattoirs. In other situations, other people who subsequently visited the plant were still highly concerned about welfare. This was due to either employees not operating the equipment correctly or the wrong type of animal being handled in the equipment. In the late 1970s I was hired to design a system that would replace the worst shackling and hoisting system used on cattle for religious slaughter without stunning. This US abattoir was horrible. Almost every steer bellowed

---

* Email: cheryl.miller@colostate.edu

when it was jerked out of the box and hung up by one leg. This is still legal in the USA, because religious slaughter has legal exceptions to protect religious freedom (FSIS, 2017). The exemptions cover both slaughter without stunning and the restraint methods.

The plant's engineering department and I brainstormed to invent a better system to eliminate cruel shackling and hoisting of 150 cattle per hour (Grandin, 1980). We did this project before I had commercially developed the centre track (double rail) restrainer in the mid-1980s (Grandin, 1988a, 1993). Newer headholder and restrainer systems are much better than my early system (Grandin, 1993). When I look back on this older system, it was primitive compared with my more recent systems. The equipment was far from perfect, but it was a huge improvement compared with dragging live cattle around with chains. After the cattle were hung up, almost 100% of them were bellowing. Working on this early system also showed future clients that I was capable of designing even better systems.

Where Do You Draw the Line?

This is a chapter about tradeoffs. How do you draw the line to determine tradeoffs from an ethical perspective? For me to participate in changing a system that is really terrible, I draw the line at a 70–80% improvement. I would not have used my design expertise to design a slightly better shackle and hoist system. One reason I chose the 70–80% cutoff was that it was attainable in this particular slaughter plant. I remember big discussions with the plant engineer. He raised Angus cattle and he told me he would *never* bring his cattle to the old shackle and hoist system. After the new system was installed, he actually did bring his cattle to this abattoir. There was a joint decision between the engineer and me on what was acceptable. How was this decision made? Our goal was to eliminate the constant bellowing and struggling of tortured cattle. The new system achieved this. Compared with the old way, there was a huge improvement. To sell the expensive new system to plant management, we gave them an analysis on labour savings and safety for employees. To sell future systems, I documented the reduction in employee injuries.

It is Easier to Define Where There is Never a Tradeoff

In my work, I find it is often easier to clearly define what is not acceptable and where there are no tradeoffs (Grandin, 2014). The shackling and hoisting system described above should never be used. People who work in supply chain management buying meat often use terms such as critical non-compliances or non-negotiables for practices that are never allowed. There are certain bad practices that must be eliminated. There should never be tradeoffs with these practices; they should be banned. All the countries that participated in creating the World Organisation for Animal Health (OIE, 2018) welfare standards and the creators of many other government and private standards agreed that the following handling and transport practices are never acceptable.

- Beating, throwing or kicking animals (Defra, 2015, 2019; NAMI, 2019; OIE, 2018).
- Allowing livestock to die from either heat or cold stress during transport or handling. Some examples are parking a truck in the hot sun which causes death losses, or failure to cover a truck to prevent death from cold stress.
- Poking out eyes or cutting tendons to restrain animals (OIE, 2018).
- Restraining conscious mammals by hanging them upside down by the feet or legs (Defra, 2015; OIE, 2018).
- Moving animals by poking sensitive areas such as the rectum or genitals (NAMI, 2019; OIE, 2018).
- Deliberately slamming gates on animals or knocking animals down with gates (NAMI, 2019). Dragging pigs or other livestock with powered gates (FSIS, 2017).
- Multiple repeated shocks with an electric prod (goad).
- Transport of female animals that are likely to give birth during transport (Council of the EU, 2004; Defra, 2015; OIE, 2018).
- Breaking tails to move animals (Defra, 2015; OIE, 2018).
- Overloading vehicles to the point where it is impossible for a fallen animal to get back up, which results in it being trampled by other livestock.
- Immobilizing conscious animals with electricity (Grandin *et al.*, 1986; Pascoe, 1986; Defra, 2015; OIE, 2018). This must not be confused

with proper electrical stunning that causes instant insensibility.

- Deliberately driving animals over the top of other animals (NAMI, 2019; OIE, 2018).
- Dragging, dropping or throwing conscious animals during slaughter or transport (FSIS, 2017; OIE, 2018).
- Puntilla: severing the spinal cord to immobilize animals (Defra, 2015; HSA, 2016; OIE, 2018).

Determining Cut-off Points for Tradeoffs for Livestock Handling in Slaughter Plants

In other situations, the cut-off point for a tradeoff is less clear. There are three variables that have an effect on livestock welfare in races and alleys: (i) the skill level of the stock people handling the animals; (ii) the behavioural characteristics of the livestock; and (iii) the design of the facility. A system that could be operated with a high level of welfare in one situation may be highly detrimental to welfare in a different situation. Examples of conditions that would be detrimental to welfare would be excessive electric prod use, animals falling down or beating of animals for refusing to move. In this introductory chapter, examples will be provided to illustrate tradeoffs between the different components of a system.

People Want the New Piece of Equipment More Than Making the Effort Required for Good Management

During a long career, I have found that selling a fancy new piece of equipment is much easier than getting people to operate it correctly. If I have a choice between excellent management and older adequate equipment or a new state-of-the-art facility with poor management, I will always choose the older system that has a good management. Buying new equipment is easy because it is a one-time expense. Good management requires hard continuous work. Management is never done. It requires effort all day, every day. Attention to details and monitoring of procedures must be continued every day. It is not a one-time fix that some people think they can get with new equipment. I have a saying, 'People want the new thing more than they want the management.'

Tradeoff in Decisions on Race, Alley and Handling Facility Design

A facility design that may work well in one situation may be really poor in another. A simple handling system that may be used with a high level of welfare for tame cattle that are trained to lead could be very detrimental for the welfare of extensively raised wild cattle with large flight zones. There have been undercover videos of extensively raised cattle or sheep being handled in slaughter facilities that had been designed for tame animals. The slaughter plant had no chutes, single file races or restraining equipment to hold the wild livestock. The lack of the right equipment resulted in animals slipping on the floor, falling and serious abuse by the people. To correct these problems would have required construction of races, chutes and other systems shown in other chapters of this book. Abattoir designs for wild extensively raised cattle, bison and other livestock are shown in Grandin and Deesing (2008) and Grandin (2014). A basic principle is that extensively raised cattle and sheep that have not lived in close contact with people will require more expensive and elaborate facilities for handling, restraint and unloading transport vehicles. For tame livestock that are trained to lead, a race system may not be required.

Skill-dependent versus Less Skill-dependent Handling Facilities

When stock people are highly knowledgeable about the behavioural principles of livestock handing, simpler economical facilities may be very effective and provide good animal welfare. At an abattoir, it would be difficult to train people to the skill level that is described below. The author watched six wild Karakul sheep being herded by two very skilled stock people who moved them around the perimeter of a corral and expertly restrained them for injections behind a long gate. The sheep were moved calmly by two handlers, who worked the edge of the flight zone and stood at the correct positions. Their rudimentary corral system had no race and forcing pens. It would have been terrible if it had been used by less skilled people. In a place with high employee turnover or less skilled people, a system with races, alleys and a forcing pen would have been required. There has been increasing interest in learning low-stress cattle handling methods and an emphasis on using simpler facilities (Kidwell,

2011; Burt, 2008). People who successfully adopt this approach must develop their stock handling skills to a high level. This often requires several weeks of dedicated practice. To summarize, handling facilities can be either simple economical and highly handler-skill dependent, or more expensive and less dependent on the skill of the stock persons. The latter approach is recommended for abattoirs.

Condition of Livestock or Poultry Arriving at the Slaughter Plant – No Tradeoffs

To prevent suffering, producers and livestock dealers must deliver to the abattoirs an animal that can be easily handled (Grandin, 2017). Severely debilitated or sick livestock are impossible to handle while still maintaining good welfare. In Chapter 4, Michael Cockram discusses problems with old cull cows arriving at abattoirs in very bad condition. Another type of animal that is almost impossible to handle in a low-stress manner is the neonatal (bobby) dairy calf. When Holstein calves are a day old, they do not walk easily. Before dairy calves are shipped, they should have a dry navel cord and be able to walk easily without assistance from a person. The best way to improve neonatal calf welfare is to fatten them into larger steers or bulls that are easier to handle. Early in my career, I made the mistake of attempting to use engineering methods to handle neonatal calves that did not walk easily. Conveyors in the floor were not an effective solution. I tried this and they do not work. The solution is to bring animals to an abattoir that can walk easily. The problem must be fixed at the farm. Some of the worst animal welfare problems I observe in an abattoir are problems that must be fixed at the farm.

Livestock Behaviour Tradeoffs

Cattle and other livestock that have become accustomed to people walking through their pens will be much easier to handle in a low-stress manner at an abattoir. The livestock producer should do some work to improve the ease of handling of their animals when they arrive at a slaughter plant. A review of the literature clearly shows that acclimatizing livestock to handling will make them easier to handle at the abattoir (Abbott *et al.*, 1997; Geverink *et al.*, 1998; Krebs and McGlone, 2009). The question is: how much work should the farmer be required to do to get their animals acclimatized to

handling to prevent them from going berserk in the novel environment of a slaughter plant? Often simple procedures on the farm will improve the behaviour of cattle or pigs. These include walking through pens on foot to teach the pigs or cattle to move away quietly. It is my opinion that producers can easily do this. Animal-based outcome measures at the abattoir can be used to determine which producers have animals that are difficult to handle. Some of the measures that could be used to identify problems are: (i) baulking, refusing to move forward; (ii) turning back; (iii) falling; (iv) vocalization; and (v) electric goad use (Grandin, 1998a,b; Welfare Quality, 2009; Losada-Espinoza *et al.*, 2018). These assessments will be discussed further in Chapter 6.

Differences in Animals: Breed and Genetic Effects

The breed of cattle, sheep or pigs can have an effect on temperament and behaviour during handling (Baszczak *et al.*, 2006). This may make them more difficult to handle at the abattoir. Managers need to work with producers to help prevent handling problems at slaughter plants. More excitable animals exit more rapidly from squeeze chutes (crushes) and struggle more during restraint (Café *et al.*, 2011). Some animals are more excitable and have a higher startle response when they are suddenly introduced into a novel environment (Grandin, 1997). Animals with more excitable genetics may be calm and easy to handle when they are in a familiar environment on the home farm, but they may become highly agitated when brought to a slaughter plant or auction. Deiss *et al.* (2009), Bourquet *et al.* (2010) and Terlouw *et al.* (2012) conducted studies that showed that when temperament was tested on the farm, the novelty of the new environment at a slaughter plant caused more stress in animals that were more excitable than others. Agitation in animals during handing is caused by fear. The fear circuits in animals' brains have been mapped (Panksepp, 2010; Jones and Boissey, 2011; Morris *et al.*, 2011; LeDoux, 2012). Breed differences in behaviour during handling may be due to genetic differences in fearfulness.

Acclimatizing Livestock to Handling Procedures

Acclimatizing livestock to handling will require the producer to do some work to produce an animal that will have better welfare at the abattoir. Animal memories of previous experiences are very specific. If a horse becomes habituated to a blue and white umbrella, that learning will not transfer to an orange tarp (canvas) (Leiner and Fendt, 2011). Taming ewes to contact with people did not generalize to other procedures such as handling, shearing or movement through a race (Mateo *et al.*, 1991). If an experience that an animal will have in the future is similar to a previous experience, the animal may be able to generalize and be less stressed. Stress caused by moving through a loading ramp can be reduced by training pigs to go through alleys and ramps. Abbott *et al.* (1997), Geverink *et al.* (1998), Lewis *et al.* (2008) and Krebs and McGlone (2009) all did research that shows very clearly that pigs can be acclimatized to handling, which will make them easier to move in the future. Further studies with cattle showed that carefully acclimatizing cattle by moving them through yards and corrals reduced stress at the slaughter plant (Petherick *et al.*, 2009). The reactions of animals indicate that their memories are sensory based and stored as specific images or sounds (Grandin and Johnson, 2005). Cattle differentiate between a person on a horse and a person walking on the ground. Extensively reared cattle that have been handled exclusively on horseback may have only a 1 m flight zone, but when they first encounter a person walking on the ground at an abattoir, their flight zone may expand to 10 m. This can be dangerous for a handler in a small pen, because the animals may run wildly back and forth or attempt to leap the fence to get away from the person. The cattle perceive the person on foot as novel and frightening and the person on a horse as familiar and safe. Ideally cattle should be acclimatized to being moved on foot before they arrive at slaughter plants (Grandin and Deesing, 2008).

A similar problem can occur in pigs or cattle that are raised indoors. The animals differentiate between a person in the alley and a person walking through their pens. To produce calm animals that will be easy to load on to trucks and handle at an abattoir requires people walking through their pens during the entire fattening period. This will get the animals accustomed to moving quietly away when a person walks through them. Pigs that first experience a person in their pens on the day they are shipped are more likely to be difficult to handle. They may bunch together and squeal.

Acclimatization to a person walking through them is especially important with more excitable genetic lines. In the USA, the large integrated pork companies have a standard procedure that instructs people to walk through the finishing (fattening) pens every day.

Handling Bulls

Another factor that can affect animal handling is whether or not animals are socialized to other animals. Intact bulls that have been reared on small farms where they are always kept tied by a halter will often fight and mount each other when they are put in group pens. Fighting and mounting may be more severe compared with bulls reared in groups. Bulls reared together in a group pen or on pasture can be penned together with their herd mates at the slaughter plant. Fighting and mounting may be severe if bulls from different rearing pens are mixed. Bulls assessed as having low fear responses had more mounting than bulls with higher fearfulness (Mark Deesing, 2013, personal communication).

Livestock Breeding for Productivity Tradeoffs Affects Welfare

Producers have been breeding animals and using production methods to achieve greater amounts of meat or milk. Pushing the biological limits for more and more productivity can cause handling and welfare problems at the abattoir. At what point has pushing productivity gone too far? I suggest using outcome measurements at the abattoir such as lameness (mobility) scoring and panting scoring for heat stress (Welfare Quality, 2009; Grandin, 2017). Outcome measurements will be discussed in more detail in Chapter 12.

Genetic abnormalities can also contribute to handling and transport problems. Murray and Johnson (1998) reported that in pigs with the porcine stress syndrome (PSS) gene the death losses during transport were 9.2% in homozygotes, 0.27% in heterozygotes and 0.05% in PSS gene-free animals. Problems with the stress gene will vary in different countries. In the USA, a very low percentage of pigs carry the stress gene. Ninety-three per cent of pigs in midwestern US markets were homozygous negative (Ritter *et al.*, 2007). Indiscriminate selection for production traits such as rapid growth may result in a failure to select against structural leg defects. At a slaughter plant, the author made observations that showed that half of the market-weight pigs were lame (Grandin, 2014). The lameness was due to hereditary poor leg conformation. The pigs either had straight post-legged joints or their ankles were collapsed and they were walking on their dew claws. Ten years later, observations at the same abattoir indicated that the leg problems had been corrected by the elimination of one of their hybrid boar lines. The pigs I observed weighed between 270 and 290 lbs (123–132 kg) and all the pigs at this abattoir were ractopamine (beta agonist) free. They walked easily and were willing to trot during truck unloading. Selection for small feet in pigs to satisfy a specialized Asian market may also increase the percentage of lame pigs.

Tradeoff: Growth Promotors versus Welfare

Both research and my own observations show that high doses of beta agonists such as ractopamine and zilpaterol may also cause handling problems. Marchant-Forde et al. (2003) reported that pigs fed high doses of ractopamine were more difficult to handle. Ractopamine at high doses can also cause hoof lesions and fighting in pigs (Poletto et al., 2009, 2010). Further research has shown that problems with ractopamine in pigs are related to high dosage and physical exertion. When pigs are fed doses over 5 mg/kg per day, they may be more difficult to handle (Ritter et al., 2017). The percentage of non-ambulatory pigs may increase when pigs fed 20 mg/kg are handled in an aggressive manner (James et al., 2011; Peterson et al., 2015; Ritter et al., 2017). I have observed feedlot cattle that had been fed beta agonists that were both lame and heat stressed at the slaughter plant (Grandin, 2010, 2015). Cattle fed ractopamine for 28 days at a dose of 400 mg/day had a higher percentage of lame animals arriving at the abattoir (Hagenmaier et al., 2017a,b). This experiment was conducted during hot summer weather. The temperature was 31°C. Other research has also shown that cattle and sheep fed beta agonists had signs of heat stress and higher body temperatures (Marcia-Cruz et al., 2010; Vogel, 2011. In one very severe case, feedlot cattle fed high doses of zilpaterol had their outer hoof shells fall off (Thomson et al., 2016). I learned that the cattle originated from a feedlot that fed both high doses of zilpaterol and a diet high in potato starch. Heat stress signs and lameness were sometimes more likely when the outdoor temperature was over 32°C (90°F). Signs of severe heat stress in cattle include open-mouth breathing (Mader et al., 2005) followed by increased panting and, when the tongue becomes further extended, the internal body temperature of cattle rises (Gaughan and Mader, 2016). Loneragan et al. (2014) reported that feeding beta agonists increased death losses of cattle during the warmer summer months. I have observed that the detrimental effects were very uneven. A few animals in a group had severe heat stress and were reluctant to move. However, many of the other animals behaved normally. This may be due to uneven feed mixing, some cattle eating more and receiving a much higher dose or individual differences in ability to respond to heat. For example, cattle with black hides get hotter during hot weather compared with cattle with light-coloured hair.

Making Sensible Decisions on Beta Agonist Use

There is a tradeoff between welfare and sustainability. Beta agonists reduce the feed required to fatten an animal (Boles et al., 2012). Some importing countries have banned beta agonists. From a welfare standpoint, outcome measures of lameness and heat stress should be used to prevent producers from using doses that are too high. This is especially a problem when the weather is hot.

In beef, the use of either ractopamine or zilpaterol will make meat tougher (Lean et al., 2014). If the entire animal is going to be used for hamburgers or meatballs, this would not matter. In countries where beta agonists are permitted, people working in the lairage should be monitoring cattle for lameness or reluctance to move. A simple four-point scoring system can be used (Grandin, 2015; Edwards-Callaway et al., 2017): (1) =normal; (2) = lame, keeps with walking group; (3) = lame, does not keep up; and (4) = almost a downer.

Scientific studies, my own observations and reports from lairage managers all indicate that welfare problems in cattle are related to hot weather, high doses of beta agonists and physical exertion. In pigs, problems are related to high doses and physical exertion. Cattle on beta agonists should also be monitored for heat stress. Cattle at rest in a lairage should breathe with their mouths closed. If the mouth is open, they have severe heat stress (Gaughan and Mader, 2016).

Productivity Tradeoffs and Preventing Bad from Becoming Normal

The animal's biology has been pushed too far with either genetic selection or growth promotor substances if: (i) death losses increase; (ii) handling becomes more difficult; (iii) a higher percentage of animals are lame; or (iv) there is a greater percentage of animals showing signs of heat stress. Everybody needs to be careful to prevent bad conditions from slowly increasing and nobody noticing it. I call this 'bad becoming normal'. Surveys of dairy producers showed that they often underestimated the percentage of lame dairy cows by half. In the USA, beef cattle are being fed to heavier weights at younger ages. This may have increased the small percentage of beef cattle that die of heart failure before slaughter. At what point has pushing the animal's biology gone too far?

Electrical Stunning versus CO_2 Stunning Tradeoff for Pigs and Poultry

When animal welfare is being evaluated at a slaughter plant, both the stunning method and the handling methods associated with it should be evaluated as an entire system (Grandin, 2014). There are tradeoffs between the different parts of the system (Velarde and Raj, 2017). A good example is methods for stunning and handling pigs and chickens.

In both species, electrical stunning will produce instantaneous unconsciousness (Croft, 1952; Gregory and Wotton, 1990; Lines et al., 2011) but handling to position the animal is more stressful than for gaseous stunning. When chickens are electrically stunned, each bird is handled by a person and hung on a shackle. Hanging birds inverted on a shackle is highly stressful (Kannan et al., 1997; Bedanova et al., 2007). There is a new European system where the shackles are eliminated but each bird still has to be individually handled at the slaughter plant. From a handling standpoint, controlled atmosphere stunning is far superior. The birds enter the stunner in the transport containers and handling by people at the abattoir is eliminated. Since the gas used for stunning (CO_2) does not induce instantaneous insensibility, the question is: how much stress and discomfort does the animal have before it loses consciousness? Different researchers have reported different results. The stress of anaesthesia induction has to be balanced against the reduction in stress by eliminating

handling of individual birds at the slaughter plant. The author's opinion is that some discomfort during anaesthesia induction such as gasping and head shaking may be acceptable as a tradeoff against greatly lower handling stress. If the animals show escape movements and attempt to climb out of the container, the distress of induction is so severe that the system should not be used.

For poultry, five-stage CO_2 systems, where the level of CO_2 is slowly raised, are being used commercially (see Chapter 8). Gerritzen et al. (2013) concluded that the welfare of the chickens was overall improved compared with electrical waterbath stunning. To reduce the aversiveness of the CO_2 the container containing the chickens moves through five stages at 20%, 30%, 35%, 40% and 60% CO_2. There are commercial systems with more steps. Some commercial systems use 90% CO_2 at the final stage to ensure death of all the birds. I have observed anaesthesia induction in two of these systems and it is my opinion that they are a good tradeoff. The entire cycle to move the birds through the system is 6 min. Commercial systems must be closely monitored to prevent the time in the system from being speeded up. Speeding up movement through the machine could be very detrimental to animal welfare.

Gas mixtures that cause escape movements are not acceptable (see Chapter 9). In an abattoir, the reactions of poultry or pigs should be observed and monitored. Either a video camera or windows can be used. There are genetic differences in how pigs react to CO_2. Purebred Yorkshires (Large Whites) have a peaceful induction (Forslid, 1987) but some genetic lines violently attempt to escape when they first contact the gas (Grandin, 1988b). After the animal loses posture and the ability to stand, it has lost consciousness (Benson et al., 2012). Kicking and convulsions after loss of posture are not a welfare concern.

In pigs, group CO_2 systems can reduce handling stress because pigs do not have to line up in single file races. This makes it possible to totally eliminate electric prods. Electric prod use, jamming and other aversive events during the last 5 min before slaughter increase lactate levels and lead to poorer pork quality (Edwards et al., 2010a,b). Cattle are a species that will walk naturally in single file, but pigs may become more stressed when they have to line up. When single file races are used for pigs by highly skilled stock people, the use of electric prods can be reduced to 5–10% of the animals (Grandin,

2012). In this situation, welfare may be acceptable. The tradeoff is that electrical stunning causes no discomfort, but the handling system may be more stressful for the pigs compared with group handling with CO_2 stunning. Both the stunning method and the handling system should be evaluated together. The stress of handling has to be balanced against the aversiveness of the stunning method (Table 3.1).

High Amperage versus Low Amperage Electrical Stunning Systems for Poultry

From an animal welfare standpoint, an electrical stunning system that simultaneously induces unconsciousness and kills the animal by cardiac arrest is preferable to a system that induces a temporary period of unconsciousness. This is why the European Union and the OIE require 100 milliamperes per bird for broilers (EC Council Regulation 1099/2009; OIE, 2018; Defra, 2019; EFSA, 2019). Use of the EU standards will induce cardiac arrest (Gregory and Wotton, 1987; Berg and Raj, 2015; Bourassa et al., 2017).

In many countries, such as the USA and Brazil, lower amperages are used to prevent haemorrhages in the breast meat (Sirri et al., 2017). I have visited poultry slaughter plants in Brazil and the USA. At one abattoir, the stunner had settings labelled 'export' with high amperage settings and 'domestic' with lower settings. Electrical stunners that do not induce cardiac arrest are also used for halal (Muslim) slaughter (Sabow et al., 2017). Muslim religious authorities want the bird to die after the throat cut.

To prevent meat damage, low amperage systems that do not induce cardiac arrest are a commercial reality. I have worked with abattoirs that have these systems. To prevent birds from regaining consciousness, the automatic bleed machine was moved close to the stunner exit to shorten the stun-to-bleed time. This solved many problems with birds regaining consciousness. Research has also shown that using higher electrical frequencies and amperages can reduce meat damage (Girasole et al., 2015). However, birds stunned at 650 Hz showed more signs of ineffective stunning than those stunned at 300 Hz (Siqueira et al., 2017). When high frequencies are used, the period that the bird remains unconscious will be shorter (Siqueira et al., 2017).

Tradeoffs Between Environmental Sustainability and Animal Welfare Concerns

Long-distance shipping

There is great controversy today about shipping live cattle and other livestock to other countries for slaughter. This creates two problems: the stress of long-distance transport and the potential for poor slaughter facilities at the destination. In these situations, the trade is driven by customer preferences and economic factors. It may be possible to change customer preferences, but some of the economic factors will be difficult to overcome. A good example is the shipment of young Australian cattle to Indonesia for fattening and slaughter. Live cattle

Table 3.1. Animal welfare tradeoffs for electrical versus controlled atmosphere stunning of pigs and poultry.

Electrical	CO_2, LAPS[a] or other gas
Low purchase cost (both species)	High purchase cost (both species)
Unconsciousness is instantaneous (both species)	Unconsciousness is not instantaneous (both species)
Pre-slaughter handling is more stressful (both species)	Tradeoff in pigs and poultry is behaviour during anaesthesia induction must be balanced against the improved handling
Lower maintenance and operating cost (both species)	
Requires more supervision of employee behaviour (both species)	Pre-slaughter handling is less stressful (both species)
More blood spots in the meat of pigs	High maintenance and operating cost (both species)
High amperage electrical stunning causes more meat damage in broiler chickens	Requires less supervision of employee behaviour (both species)
	Requires careful monitoring of gas concentration or LAPS operation
	Meat damage varies with controlled atmosphere method (poultry)

[a]low atmospheric pressure stunning

T. Grandin

have the advantage of not requiring refrigeration in a country that has little infrastructure. Shipping refrigerated or frozen meat to countries such as Japan or Korea is economically viable because the customer is paying for a premium product. It is also easy to find a back haul, such as electronics, to fill the refrigerated shipping containers when they are returned. Customers buying premium meat products may also prefer to ship the meat by air.

The Indonesian situation has complex tradeoffs. Rural ranchers in Australia are engaging in sustainable production of cattle on pastures in the arid outback. Grazing animals are one of the best methods for raising food on their land. Shipping the cattle for final fattening in Indonesia increases the number of cattle that can be produced in a sustainable manner on the Australian outback. This land is too arid for growing crops. Grazing can be done with a favourable net carbon balance at moderate stocking rates (Bray *et al.*, 2014). Again, there is another tradeoff. If the system is pushed too hard by increasing stocking density on the pasture, the sustainability benefits may be lost. To make shipping refrigerated beef to Indonesia economically feasible would require finding a good back haul for the empty refrigerated containers. The most readily available back haul would be palm oil. This is really bad from an environmental standpoint. Rainforest is being destroyed for palm oil plantations. The best approach may be to ship the live cattle to Indonesia and have them sent to a modern slaughter house, run by Australian managers. This solution is not ideal for animal welfare, but it may be best from the standpoint of carbon footprint, sustainable agriculture and degradation of the environment. A reasonable level of animal welfare could be attained by enforcing rigorous standards for shipping and slaughter.

Tradeoffs on feed consumption

To improve animal welfare, some poultry growers are using slower-growing chickens. Use of the slower-growing strains will often cut death losses during rearing in half (Thornton, 2016). From a sustainability standpoint, the slowest-growing birds require much more feed. Up to 20% more feed may be required to produce the same amount of chicken meat (Thornton, 2016). This means that 20% more land would be required to grow the feed. A sensible compromise may be to use a slightly slower-growing bird and then breed to prevent problems such as

lameness. I have observed that the poultry industry is already doing this. Unfortunately, they are reluctant to publish their research on this topic.

Nutritional environmental tradeoffs: beta agonists

Recently there have been problems with broken legs and other bones during transport and handling at the slaughter plant. This is thought to be due to reducing minerals such as phosphorus in the ration to reduce phosphorus in the manure. Specimens sent to a diagnostic laboratory from pigs raised in the USA have shown that 19% of the animals had rickets, an old vitamin-deficiency disease (Canning *et al.*, 2017). This is due to reducing costs of the ration. Behavioural research indicates clearly that pigs should receive roughage for rooting and chewing (Van der Weerd *et al.*, 2008). Many producers are reluctant to feed roughage, because it increases the amount of manure. Again, there is a tradeoff of welfare versus sustainability issues related to manure.

Tradeoffs in Commercial versus Research Welfare Assessments

Animal welfare evaluation systems used in a commercial abattoir and in a research setting are different. To be effective, an assessment system for commercial use must be much simpler (Grandin, 2010). The reality is that auditors and managers have to be able to be trained in a day-and-a-half workshop. After the workshop, they have several shadow audits with an experienced auditor.

The trend in writing animal welfare guidelines is to use outcome measures that are animal-based instead of specifying exactly how a facility is designed (Wray *et al.*, 2003; Welfare Quality, 2009; Grandin, 2010; Velarde and Dalmau, 2012). Examples of outcome-based measurements are body condition score, lameness, bruises, panting score for heat stress, cleanliness of the animals, death loss, sickness, vocalization during handling, falling during handling and others. Grandin (2017) contained a review of welfare indicators that can be assessed at the abattoir. Producers, transporters and slaughter plant managers should track progress in reducing lameness and other problems by scoring these variables. On each numerically scored variable, cut-off points have to be determined for minimum acceptable levels. The cut-off points should be set where the best 25% of producers can attain them (Grandin, 2010). The other producers will need to be given time to bring their practices up to the standard. How did I decide where the cut-off point should be? This cut-off point worked well in previous work on assessing abattoirs on stunning and handling (Grandin, 2010). I have been on many welfare committees for many different species of animals. Unfortunately, I observed problems where the worst producers got on the committees so that they could set acceptable levels of lameness way too low. This enabled the worst farms to pass the audit.

Tradeoffs and Equipment Design

There have been many cases where expensive, difficult-to-maintain pieces of equipment have been installed in a developing country. The local people did not have the skills or resources to maintain it. Some examples of equipment that is only suitable for technologically advanced areas are controlled atmosphere stunning systems with complex conveyors or hydraulic lifting floors in livestock trucks. If the people cannot maintain the equipment, it is useless. In these situations, equipment with fewer difficult-to-maintain mechanical parts is more appropriate.

The corral, stockyard and race systems shown in this book and in Grandin and Deesing (2008) can all be built by local people with easily available materials such as steel or concrete. They also have the advantage of being low maintenance and they do not require automated or mechanized parts. In many developing countries, there is a lack of loading ramps for loading and unloading animals on to farm trucks. Loading ramps can be easily built from either metal or concrete. Moving parts are not required.

Economic Factors Can Either Improve Welfare or Make it Worse

When producers have to pay for bruises, they work to greatly reduce them (Grandin, 1981). However, if losses are passed on to the next segment of the marketing chain with no financial accountability, bruises and damage to livestock are usually greater (Grandin, 2015). Several studies have shown that cattle and sheep that pass through auctions have more bruises compared with livestock sold directly to a slaughter plant (Cockram and Lee, 1991; McNally and Warriss, 1996). The payment method for employees can also affect the quality of handling. Paying stock people based on the number of animals handled per hour may provide an incentive to handle animals roughly. Stock people should be paid based on the quality of handling by providing incentive pay for low levels of injuries or bruises.

How to Make Tradeoff Decisions

In my own work, to make decisions, I have used a combination of data collected during audits and my own observations from over 200 abattoirs in over 20 different countries. For example, how did I make the decision on the tradeoff between elimination of electric prods for pigs and elimination of shackling live birds and escape attempts from gas stunning systems? Escape movements are a well-defined behaviour that auditors and plant managers can easily observe. Everyone who cares about animal welfare can agree that escape attempts from the container are not acceptable. It is more difficult to make a definitive statement about which is worse: 15% of the pigs getting poked with an electrical prod, or four or five gasping movements before a pig falls over and loses posture in CO_2? This would require additional research. I also put management factors into my decisions. From my experience in slaughter plants, I have learned that supervising employees to keep electric prod use at low levels is more difficult than managing a group-handling CO_2 machine. To explain the tradeoff in simple terms: the CO_2 machine is expensive and more difficult to maintain, but day-to-day management of the people handling the pigs is easier. Electrical stunning systems are economical to buy and easy to maintain, but require much more supervision of the people handling and stunning the pigs.

Conclusions

Making ethical decisions on tradeoffs is sometimes difficult. There are tradeoffs between productivity and welfare and between sustainability and welfare. At what point has welfare been compromised? Welfare has been compromised if animals have higher death losses during transit, lameness or signs of heat stress. There are abusive practices that are always wrong and there is never a tradeoff. Numerical objective outcome measures should be used to evaluate welfare.

References

Abbot, T.A., Hunger, E.J., Guise, E.J. and Penny, R.A.C. (1997) The effect of experience of handling on pig's willingness to move. *Applied Animal Behaviour Science* 54, 371–375.

Baszczak, J.A., Grandin, T., Gruber, S.L., Engle, T.E. Platter, W.J., Laudert, S.B., Schroeder, A.L. and Tatum, J.D. (2006) Effects of ractopamine supplementation on behavior of British, Continental and Brahman crossbred steers during routine handling. *Journal of Animal Science* 84, 3410–3414.

Bedanova, I., Vaslarova, E., Chioupek, P., Pistekova, V., Suchy, P., Blahova, J., Dobsikova, R. and Vecerek, V. (2007) Stress in broilers resulting from shackling. *Poultry Science* 86, 1065–1069.

Benson, E.R., Alphin, R.L., Rankin, M.K., Caputo, M.P., Kinny, C.A. and Johnson, A.L. (2012) Evaluation of EEG based on determination of unconsciousness vs. loss of posture in broilers. *Research in Veterinary Science* 93, 960–964.

Berg, C. and Raj, M. (2015) A review of different stunning methods of poultry: animal welfare aspects. *Animals* 5, 1207–1219.

Boles, D.D., Shreck, A.L., Faulkner, D.B., Killefer, J. *et al.* (2012) Effect of ractopamine hydrochloride (Optaflexx) dose on live animal performance, carcass characteristics and tenderness in easily weaned steers. *Meat Science* 92, 458–463.

Bourasser, D.V., Bowker, B.C., Zhuang, H., Wilson, K.M., Harris, C.E. and Buhr, R.J. (2017) Impact of alternative electrical stunning parameters on the ability of broilers to recover conscious and meat quality. *Poultry Science* 96, 3495–3501.

Bourquet, C., Deiss, V., Brobert, M., Durand, D. Boissey, A., and Terlouw, W.M.C. (2010) Characterizing the emotional activity of cows to understand and predict stress reactions to the slaughter procedure. *Meat Science* 125, 9–21.

Bray, S., Duran-Brown, N. and O'Reagain, P. (2014) Northern Australian pasture and beef systems. Net carbon position. *Animal Production Science* 54, 1988–1994.

Burt, A. (2008) Bud Box, Not for amateurs. *BEEF*, October 1, 200, 52–53. Available at: http://beefmagazine.com/beef-quality/cattle-handling/1001-crowd-pen-stockmanship (accessed 15 October 2013).

Café, L.M., Robinson, D.L., Ferguson, D.M., McIntyre, B.L., Geesink, G.H. and Greenwood, P.L. (2011) Cattle temperament, persistence of assessments and associations with productivity efficiency, carcass and meat quality traits. *Journal of Animal Science* 89, 1452–1465.

Canning, P., Skoland, K., Ramirez, A. and Karriker, L. (2017) 4 top lameness diagnoses point to management strategies. *National Hog Farmer* August 2017, p. 30.

Cockram, M.S. and Lee, R.A. (1991) Some preslaughter factors affecting the occurrence of bruising in sheep. *British Veterinary Journal* 147, 120–125.

Council of the European Union (2004) European convention of the protection of animals during international transport, 2004/544EL.

Croft, P.S. (1952) Problems with electric stunning. *Veterinary Record* 64, 255–258.

Defra (2015) Guidance red meat slaughterhouses: restraining, stunning, and killing animals. Department of the Environment, Food and Rural Affairs. Available at: https://www.gov.uk/guidance/red-meat-slaughterhouses-restraining-stunning-killing-animals (accessed 15 April 2020).

Defra (2019) Guidance white meat slaughterhouses: unloading, handling, and holding, restraining, stunning, killing. Department of Environment, Food and Rural Affairs. Available at: https://www.gov.uk/guidance/white-meat-slaughterhouses-unloading-handling-and-holding-restraining-stunning-killing (accessed 15 April 2020).

Deiss, V., Temple, D., Ligout, S.L., Racine, C., Bouix, J., Terlouw, C., and Boisssey, A. (2009) Can emotional reactivity predict stress responses at slaughter in sheep? *Applied Animal Behaviour Science* 119, 193–202.

Edwards, L.N., Engle, T.E., Correa, J.A., Paradis, M.A., Grandin, T. and Anderson, D.B. (2010a) The relationship between exsanguination blood lactate concentration and carcass quality in slaughter pigs. *Meat Science* 85, 435–440.

Edwards, L.N., Grandin, T., Engle, T.E., Porter, S.P., Ritter M.J. *et al.* (2010b) Use of exsanguination blood lactate to assess the quality of pre-slaughter handling. *Meat Science* 86, 384–390.

Edwards-Callaway, L.N., Calvo-Lovenzo, M.S., Scanga, J.A. and Grandin, T. (2017) Mobility scoring of finished cattle. *Veterinary Clinics Food Animal Practice* 33, 235–250.

EFSA (2019) Slaughter of animals: poultry. *EFSA Journal* 17 (1). doi.org/10.2903/j.efsa.2019.5849

Forslid, A. (1987) Transient neocortical hippocampal and amygdaloid EEG silence induced by one minute infiltration of high concentration CO_2 in swine. *Acta Physiologica Scandinavica* 130, 1–10.

FSIS (2017) Humane Methods of Slaughter Act. Food Safety Inspection Service, US Department of Agriculture, Washington, DC. Available at: fsis.usda.gov (accessed 6 December 2017).

Gaughan, J.B. and Mader, T.L. (2016) Body temperature and respiratory dynamics in unshaded beef cattle. *International Journal of Biological Meteorology* 58, 1443–1450.

Gerritzen, M.A., Reimert, H.G.M., Hindle, V.A., Verhoeven, M.T.V. and Veerkamp, W.B. (2013) Multistage carbon dioxide gas stunning of broilers. *Poultry* 92, 41–50.

Geverink, N.A., Kappers, A., van de Bergwal, E., Lambooij, E., Blockhuis, E. *et al.* (1998) Effects of regular moving and handling on the behavioral and physiological responses of pigs to pre-slaughter treatment and consequences in meat quality. *Journal of Animal Sciences* 76, 2080–2085.

Girasole, M., Chirollo, C., Cenuso, M., Vollano, L., Chianese, A., and Cortesi, M.L. (2015) Optimization of stunning electrical parameters to improve animal welfare in a poultry slaughterhouse. *Italian Journal Food Safety*, 4576. doi: 10.4081/fs.2015).4576

Grandin, T. (1980) Problems with kosher slaughter. *International Journal for the Study of Animal Problems* 1(6),375–390.

Grandin, T. (1981) Bruises on southwestern feedlot cattle. *Journal Animal Science* 53 (Suppl. 1), 213 (abstract).

Grandin, T. (1988a) Double rail restrainer conveyor for livestock handling. *Journal of Agricultural Engineering Research* 41, 327–338.

Grandin, T. (1988b) Possible genetic effect on pig's reaction to CO_2 stunning. In: Chandler, C. and Thornton, T. (eds) *34th International Congress of Meat Science and Technology, 29 August–2 September 1988, Brisbane, Australia, Congress Proceedings*, Commonwealth Scientific and Industrial Research Organization, Canberra, Australia, pp. 96–97.

Grandin, T. (1993) Handling and welfare of livestock in slaughter plants. In: Grandin, T. (ed.) *Livestock Handling and Transport*. CAB International, Wallingford, UK, pp. 289–307.

Grandin, T. (1997) Assessment of stress during handling and transport. *Journal of Animal Science* 75, 249–257.

Grandin, T. (1998a) Objective scoring of animal handling and stunning practices in slaughter plants. *Journal of the American Veterinary Medical Association* 212, 36–39.

Grandin T. (1998b) The feasibility of using vocalization scoring as an indicator of poor welfare during slaughter. *Applied Animal Behaviour Science* 56, 121–128.

Grandin, T. (2010) Auditing animal welfare at slaughter plants. *Meat Science* 86, 56–65.

Grandin, T. (2012) Auditing animal welfare and making practical improvements in beef, pork, and sheep slaughter plants. *Animal Welfare* 21 (Suppl. 2), 29–34.

Grandin, T. (2014) A whole systems approach to assessing animal welfare during handling and restraint. In: Grandin, T. (ed.) *Livestock Handling and Transport*. CAB International, Wallingford, UK, pp. 1–13.

Grandin, T. (2015) *Improving Animal Welfare: A Practical Approach*. CAB International, Wallingford, UK.

Grandin, T. (2017) On-farm conditions that compromise animal welfare that can be monitored at the slaughter plant. *Meat Science* 132, 52–58.

Grandin, T. and Deesing, M. (2008) *Humane Livestock Handling*. Storey Publishing, North Adams, Massachusetts.

Grandin, T. and Johnson, C. (2005) *Animals in Translation: Using the Mysteries of Autism to Decode Animal Behavior*. Scribner, New York.

Grandin, T., Curtis, S.E., Widowski, T.M. and Thurmon, J.C. (1986) Electro-immobilization versus mechanical restraint in an avoid-avoid choice test for ewes. *Journal of Animal Science* 62, 1469–1480.

Gregory, N.G. and Wotton, S.B. (1987) Effect of electrical stunning on the electroencephalogram in chickens. *British Poultry Journal* 143, 175–183.

Gregory, N.G. and Wotton, S.B. (1990) Effect of stunning on spontaneous physical activity and evoked activity in the brain. *British Poultry Science* 31, 215–220.

Hagenmaier, J.A., Reinhardt, C.D., Ritter, M.J., Calvo-Lorenzo, M.S., Vogel, G.J. *et al.* (2017a) Effect of ractopamine hydrochloride on growth performance, carcass characteristics and physiological responses to different handling techniques. *Journal of Animal Science* 95, 1977–1992.

Hagenmaier, J.A., Reinhardt, C.D., Bartle, S.J., Henningson, J.N., Ritter, M.J. *et al.* (2017b) Effect of handling at the time of transport for slaughter on physiological response and carcass characteristics in beef cattle fed ractopamine hydrochloride. *Journal of Animal Science* 95, 1963–1976.

HSA (2016) Captive bolt stunning of livestock. Humane Slaughter Association, Wheathampstead, UK. Available at: www.hsa.org.uk (accessed 15 February 2020).

James, B.W., Tokoch, M.D., Goodband, R.D., Nelssen, J.L., Dritz, S.S. *et al.* (2011) Effects of dietary L-carnitine and ractopamine HCL on the metabolic response to handling in finishing pigs. *Journal of Animal Science* 91, 4426–4439.

Jones, B. and Boissy, A. (2011) Fear and other negative emotions. In: Appleby, M.C., Hughes, B.O., Mench, J.A. and Olsson, A. (eds) *Animal Welfare*, 2nd edn. CAB International, Wallingford, UK, pp. 78–97.

Kannen, G., Heath, J.L., Wabek, C.J. and Mench, J.A. (1997) Shackling broiler chickens affects stress responses and breast meat quality. *British Poultry Science* 38, 323–332.

Kidwell, B. (2011) Bud Box Bonanza. *Angus Journal*, February, pp. 163–164. Available at: http://www.angusjournal.com/articlepdf/bud%20box%2002-11%20aj.pdf (accessed 15 October 2013).

Krebs, N. and McGlone, J.J. (2009) Effects of exposing pigs to moving and odors in a simulated slaughter chute. *Applied Animal Behaviour Science* 116, 179–185.

Lean, I.J., Thompson, J.M. and Dunshea, F.R. (2014) A meta analysis of zilpaterol and ractopamine effects on feedlot performance, carcass traits, and shear strength of meat in cattle. *PLOS ONE* 9(12), e115904.

LeDoux, J. (2012) Rethinking the emotional brain. *Neuron* 73, 653–676.

Leiner, I. and Fendt, M. (2011) Behavioral fear and heart rate responses of horses after exposure to novel objects: effects of habituation. *Applied Animal Behaviour Science* 131, 104–109.

Lewis, C.R.G., Hulbert, L.E. and McGLone, J.J. (2008) Novelty causes elevated heart rate and immune changes in pigs exposed to handling, alleys, and ramps. *Livestock Science* 116, 338–341.

Lines, J.A., Raj, A.B.M., Wotton, S.B. and O'Callaghan, M. (2011) Head only electrical stunning of poultry using a water bath: a feasibility study. *British Poultry Science* 52, 432–438.

Loneragan, G.H., Thomsen, D.V. and Morgan, S. (2014) Increased mortality in groups of feedlot cattle administered B-adrenergic agonists ractopamine hydrochloride and zilpaterol hydrochloride. *PLOS ONE* 9(3), e91177. doi: 10.1371/journal.pone.0091177

Losada-Espinsoa, N., Villaroel, M., Maria, G.A. and Miranda de La Lama, G.C. (2018) Preslaughter cattle welfare indicators for use in commercial abattoirs with voluntary monitoring systems: a systematic review. *Meat Science* 138, 34–48.

Marcia-Cruz, I., Alvarez-Valenzuela, F.D., Torrentera-Olivera, G., Velazquez-Morales, J.V. and Correa-Calderon, A. (2010) Effect of zilpaterol hydrochloride on feedlot performance and carcass characteristics of ewe lambs during heat stress conditions. *Animal Production Science* 50, 983–989.

Mader, T.L., Davis, M.S. and Brown-Brandl, T. (2005) Environmental factors influencing heat stress in feedlot cattle. *Journal of Animal Science* 84, 712–719.

Marchant-Forde, J.N., Lay, D.C., Pajor, E.A., Richert, B.T. and Schinckel, A.P. (2003) The effects of ractopamine on the behavior and physiology of finishing pigs. *Journal of Animal Science* 81, 416–422.

Mateo, J.M., Estep, D.O., and McMann, J.S. (1991) Effects of differential handling on the behavior of domestic ewes. *Applied Animal Behaviour Science* 32, 45–54.

McNally, P.W. and Warriss, P.D. (1996) Recent bruising in cattle at abattoirs. *Veterinary Record* 138, 126–128.

Morris, C.L., Grandin, T. and Irlbeck, N.A. (2011) Companion Animal Symposium: Environmental enrichment for companion exotic and laboratory animals. *Journal of Animal Science* 89, 4227–4238.

Murray, A.C. and Johnson, C.P. (1998) Importance of halothane gene on muscle quality and preslaughter death in Western Canadian pigs. *Canadian Journal of Animal Science* 78, 543–548.

NAMI (2019) Recommended Animal Handling Guidelines and Audit Guide. North American Meat Institute, Washington, DC. Available at: www.animalhandling.org (accessed 15 April 2020)

OIE (2018) Slaughter of Animals. Chapter 7.5 in: *Terrestrial Animal Health Code*. World Organisation for Animal Health, Paris. Available at: oie.int/standard-setting/terrestrial-code/access-online (accessed 17 January 2020).

Panksepp, J. (2010) The basic emotional circuits of mammalian brains: do animals have affective lives? *Neuroscience and Behavioral Reviews* 35, 1791–1804.

Pascoe, P.J. (1986) Humaneness of an electroimmobilization unit for cattle. *American Journal of Veterinary Research* 47, 2252–2256.

Peterson, C.M., Pilcher, C.M., Rothe, H.M., Marchant-Forde, J.M., Ritter, M.J. *et al.* (2015) Effect of feeding ractopamine hydrochloride on growth performance and response to handling and transport in heavy-weight pigs. *Journal of Animal Science* 93, 1239–1249.

Petherick, J.C., Googan, V.J., Venus, B.K., Halroyd, R.C. and Olsson, P. (2009) Quality of handling and holding yard environment and beef cattle temperament, 2. Consequence for stress and productivity. *Applied Animal Behaviour Science* 120, 28–38.

Poletto, R., Rostagno, M.H., Richert, B.T. and Marchant-Forde, J.N. (2009) Effects of a 'step up' ractopamine feeding program, sex, and social rank on growth performance, beef lesions, and shedding in finishing pigs fed the beta ractopamine. *Journal of Animal Science* 87, 304–313.

Poletto, R., Cheng, H.W., Meisel, R.L., Garner, J.P., Richert, B.T. and Marchant-Forde, J.N. (2010) Aggressiveness and brain amine concentration in dominant and subordinate finishing pigs fed the B-adrenoreceptor agonist ractopamine. *Journal of Animal Science* 88, 3107–3120.

Ritter, M.J., Ellis, M., Hollis, G.R., McKeith, F.K. *et al.* (2007) Frequency of HAL-1843 mutation of the ryanodine receptor gene in dead and non-ambulatory non-injured pigs on arrival at the packing plant. *Journal of Animal Science* 86, 511–514.

Ritter, M.J., Johnson, A.K., Benjamin, M.E., Carr, S.N., Ellis, M. *et al.* (2017) Review: Effects of ractopamine hydrochloride (Paylean) on welfare indicators in market weight pigs. *Translational Animal Science* 1, 533–558.

Sabow, A.E., Nakyinsige, K., Adeyemi, K.D. and Sazili, A.Q. (2017) High frequency preslaughter electrical stunning in ruminants and poultry for halal meat production: a review. *Livestock Science* 202, 124–134.

Siqueira, T.S., Borger, T.D., Rocha, R.M.M., Figueira, P.T., Luciano, F.B. and Macedo, R.E.F. (2017) Effect of electrical stunning frequency and current wave form in poultry welfare and meat quality. *Poultry Science* 96, 2956–2964.

Sirri, F., Petracci, M., Zampiger, M., and Meluzzi, A. (2017) Effect of EU electrical stunning conditions on breast meat quality of chickens. *Poultry Science* 96, 3000–3004.

Terlouw, E.M.C., Bourquet, C. and Deiss, V. (2012) Stress at slaughter in cattle: role of reactivity profile and environmental factors. *Animal Welfare* 21 (Suppl. 2), 43–49.

Thomson, D.U., Loneragan, G.H., Henningson, J.N., Ensley, S. and Bhupinder-Bawa (2015) Description of a novel fatigue syndrome in finished feedlot cattle following transportation. *Journal of the American Veterinary Medical Association* 247, 66–72.

Thornton, G. (2016) The expanding market for slow growing broilers. Available at: www.wattagnet.com (accessed 2 June 2018).

Van der Weerd, R.A., Docking, C.M., Day, J.E.L., Brever, K. and Edwards, S.A. (2008) Effect of species relevant environmental enrichment on the behavior and productivity of finishing pigs. *Applied Animal Behaviour Science* 99, 230–242.

Velarde, A. and Dalmau, A. (2012) Animal welfare assessment at slaughter in Europe: moving from inputs to outputs. *Meat Science* 92, 244–251.

Velarde, A. and Raj, M. (2017) *Animal Welfare at Slaughter*. 5M Publishing, Sheffield, UK.

Vogel, K. (2011) Investigating the impact of husbandry and management practices on the interaction of animal wellbeing and product quality in beef, swine, and dairy systems. Dissertation, Colorado State University, Fort Collins, Colorado, USA.

Welfare Quality (2009) Protocols for Assessing Farm Animal Welfare. Available at: http://www.welfarequality.net/en-us/news/assessment-protocols/ (accessed 17 February 2020).

Wray, H.R., Main, D.C.J., Green, L.E. and Webster, A.J.E. (2003) Assessment of the welfare of dairy cattle using animal based measurements, direct observations, and investigation of farm records, *Veterinary Record* 153, 197–202.

4 Condition of Animals on Arrival at the Abattoir and Their Management During Lairage

MICHAEL COCKRAM*

Sir James Dunn Animal Welfare Centre, Atlantic Veterinary College, University of Prince Edward Island, Canada

Summary

Although most animals that arrive at an abattoir are in a reasonable state, i.e. they are fit, healthy and not suffering, some types of animals require immediate attention and additional care. They can arrive at an abattoir in poor condition for the following reasons.

- They were not fit for their journey to slaughter and should not have been loaded.
- They are compromised animals, in an impaired condition, at the end of their productive life and were culled and sent for slaughter because of their condition.
- They were injured during handling or during their journey or their health deteriorated during the journey.
- Their journey conditions or their management before and during transport were not satisfactory.

To reduce the numbers of animals that arrive at an abattoir in poor condition, guidance is discussed on how to:

- assess fitness for transport;
- undertake on-farm euthanasia for animals not fit for transport; and
- develop on-farm policies to avoid transporting animals in a deteriorated and compromised condition.

How lairage conditions and the management of animals in a lairage may or may not mitigate the condition of the animals on arrival and avoiding deterioration of their welfare during lairage will be discussed. Resting behaviour and the importance of physical and social environmental factors in meeting the behavioural and physiological requirements of the animals while in a lairage are emphasized.

Learning Objectives

- Categories of animals that have compromised welfare.
- Guidance on assessing fitness for transport.
- Guidance on developing on-farm policies to avoid transporting unfit animals.
- Understand animal welfare issues in the lairage at the abattoir.
- Learn about food safety and hygiene procedures in the lairage.

Arrival of Animals in the Lairage, Initial Welfare Assessment and Ante-mortem Inspection

It is a complex logistical task to coordinate the arrival of animal loads in relation to their time of slaughter so that vehicles are not kept waiting to unload, there is sufficient space available in the lairage to receive the animals and the animals are not kept too long in the lairage before slaughter. Ideally, loads should be provided with a specific arrival time; however, there can be delays because of loading difficulties, traffic and poor weather conditions etc. (Ljungberg *et al.*, 2007; Grandin, 2017).

---

* Email: mcockram@upei.ca

Whenever possible, the lairage staff and, if necessary, the veterinarian and animal welfare officer should be informed when and ideally before a load arrives that contains animals that require additional care and attention. Documentation on the fitness of the animals before loading or information from the driver of potential welfare issues that arose during loading or during the journey should be communicated to the slaughter plant. The driver's report and the initial assessment of the load by lairage staff represent a critical control point for animal welfare. For example, the load might need to be given priority for unloading and the animals slaughtered as soon as possible. One or more animals might not be suitable for unloading and could require either assistance to unload (Warren *et al.*, 2010), slaughter/euthanasia on the vehicle or separation after unloading into an isolation pen. Animals that are weak, fatigued, severely lame or neonatal ('bobby' veal calves) will require careful handling. Where the journey to slaughter was long, or the conditions were problematic, some animals can arrive in a state of hunger, thirst, fatigue, stress or be thermally compromised. The animals should be observed on arrival, during unloading and entry into the lairage for signs of heat stress, injury and painful conditions. Their management in the lairage should either reduce the duration that they continue to experience any aversive states by slaughtering them as soon as possible, mitigate the severity of any suffering or provide resources that rapidly resolve these difficulties. It is also important that steps are taken to communicate the nature of any serious welfare issues found on arrival at the slaughter plant with relevant parties, such as the transporter, the farm of origin of the animals and possibly any intermediary stages, such as an auction market. A discussion and guidance on how to reduce the risk of reoccurrence of these welfare issues should be initiated and, where necessary, practices amended.

Ante-mortem inspection

Before the animals are taken to slaughter an ante-mortem inspection is conducted to assess whether each animal is suitable for human consumption and can proceed for slaughter. If the inspection identifies an issue, the animal can be declared unsuitable for human consumption, and if necessary killed in the lairage, moved to an isolation pen in the lairage and possibly slaughtered separately from other animals, e.g. at the end of the day's

slaughter. A veterinarian or inspector would normally observe each animal (except poultry) at rest and while moving. The inspection is intended to identify animals showing clinical signs of disease, especially those conditions that may not be readily identifiable post-mortem, such as neurological signs. If necessary, this inspection is followed by a full clinical examination (Food Standards Agency, 2018). Another important function of ante-mortem inspection is to identify whether an animal is experiencing a welfare issue and to obtain information that might be required to take any necessary action, such as follow-up procedures with the farm of origin. This is an important opportunity for welfare surveillance as it could be the first occasion when an animal is exposed to inspection by someone other than the producer (Lahti and Soini, 2014). Examples of the types of welfare issues considered by the inspector during their inspection include poor body condition, difference in body size in relation to other animals in a group, and injuries and overgrown hoofs (Lahti and Soini, 2014). Ante-mortem inspection of poultry in containers is difficult, and it might only be possible to observe a sample of the birds for mortality, overcrowding and some obvious clinical signs, such as panting, prostration and nervous signs. Documentation on flock health can also be inspected (Allain *et al.*, 2018).

Animals That Arrive at an Abattoir in Poor Condition

Some animals arrive for slaughter in an unfit condition because they were not fit before the journey and should never have been loaded. In most countries, this would be a contravention of legal regulations and/or industry and international standards (OIE, 2011). In other cases, animals arrive unfit because their health deteriorated during the journey. Unless an unforeseen and unusual event occurred during the journey, the arrival of an animal in an unfit condition suggests that it was not fit for the intended or anticipated journey. However, some animals may have had pathology that was not readily apparent before loading (Harris *et al.*, 2018) and they may not have had any obvious clinical signs of disease or injury for a competent stockman or transporter to recognize. In some situations, an animal could become injured during handling, loading or during their journey. Some animals that are not in good health or optimal condition are transported to slaughter in a compromised

Table 4.1. Description of terms used to categorize the condition of animals on arrival at a lairage.

Category of animal	Description
Unfit for transport	Shows signs of infirmity, illness, injury or of a condition that indicates that it could not have been transported without suffering
Compromised	Shows signs of infirmity, illness, injury or of a condition that indicates that it had a reduced capacity to withstand transportation
Non-ambulatory	Unable to stand or move without assistance and unable to bear weight on two legs
Injured	Presence of skin injury, bleeding wound, bone fracture, joint dislocation or damaged prolapse, or other external lesion
Severely lame	Injured, crippled, or physically disabled with an abnormal gait and limp or walks with difficulty
Fatigued	Non-injured with a temporary reduction in the ability or motivation to walk and with increased motivation to rest
Dead-on-arrival	Animal found dead in the vehicle before unloading and entry into the lairage or was dead in a container on arrival or after lairage

or impaired condition because they are culled at the end of their productive life. In this situation, those involved would have considered that their condition was not so poor as to make them unfit for transport under the conditions provided for the journey. The economic value of compromised animals as a source of food for human consumption would have outweighed any potential welfare concerns regarding their transportation. Transportation can, in some circumstances, represent significant challenges even for fit and healthy animals. These challenges are greater for animals that are weak, diseased or injured. These types of animals were likely to have been experiencing welfare issues, such as pain and sickness, before loading and in this condition, they were less able to cope with the additional challenges associated with transport (Cockram, 2019). Animals that are not in good health are more likely to become fatigued, injured, non-ambulatory or die during transport.

Although in many or most loads the prevalence is zero, surveys of animals at slaughter plants show that some animals, especially cull animals, can arrive in poor condition (González et al., 2012). For example, Dahl-Pedersen et al. (2018b) assessed that 2% of the cull dairy cows that arrived at a Danish plant were severely lame. Many of the cull cows observed had become lame during the journey, or the severity of their lameness had increased during the journey. Unless there is strong regulatory enforcement or strict industry standards, some cull dairy and beef cows can arrive at slaughter plants in extremely poor condition. For example, they can be severely lame, extremely emaciated, have foot abnormalities, joint and jaw abscesses, swollen joints, mastitis, and rectal and vaginal prolapses

(Nicholson et al., 2013; Harris et al., 2017; Dahl-Pedersen et al., 2018c). In the USA, Vogel et al. (2011) assessed that 23% of cull dairy cows sent to slaughter via a market were sick. Cull sows can have foot lesions, abscesses and ulcers, signs of major pathology, such as pneumonia and peritonitis, and low body condition (Cleveland-Nielsen et al., 2004; Knauer et al., 2007). Although they occur less often, metritis, mastitis, chronic arthritis, fractures or osteomyelitis may also be present (Cleveland-Nielsen et al., 2004). In a survey of slaughter plants conducted in five countries, 0.2% of pigs were assessed as sick on arrival (Dalmau et al., 2016). When Jacobs et al. (2017c) undertook a rigorous assessment of the fitness of broilers before transport to slaughter, the main issues that they found were lameness, emaciation and clinical signs of illness or injury.

If neonatal bobby-veal male dairy calves are sent for slaughter, they can arrive in an extremely vulnerable, dehydrated and exhausted condition and some may require euthanasia (Stafford et al., 2001; Thomas and Jordaan, 2013). They are likely to experience difficulty walking and require very careful handling (Leary et al., 2016). Lactating dairy cows with obvious udder distension should be slaughtered as soon as possible or milked (OIE, 2016).

Euthanasia

Euthanasia is required if an animal:

- arrives at the slaughter plant and cannot be unloaded from a vehicle, e.g. it is non-ambulatory;
- cannot be moved to the slaughter area for stunning and exsanguination;

- cannot be moved to the slaughter area for exsanguination after stunning outside the stunning area without a risk of it regaining consciousness before it can be exsanguinated; or
- is suffering (see Chapter 2 for signs of pain) and immediate slaughter is not possible or appropriate.

The difference between euthanasia and slaughter in this context is that an animal that has passed ante-mortem inspection, been stunned and then killed by exsanguination or cardiac arrest can potentially enter the human food chain, whereas an animal that has been euthanized cannot, either because of the secondary method of killing, e.g. pithing following captive bolt stunning (see Chapter 2), or because it did not pass ante-mortem inspection. See later section for appropriate methods of euthanasia.

Dead-on-arrival and Mortality During Lairage

A small proportion of the animals transported to slaughter are dead-on-arrival (DOA) at the plant and others die during lairage (Knowles *et al.*, 1994; Fitzgerald *et al.*, 2009; Warren *et al.*, 2010). If DOAs are identified, it might indicate that the animals that survived the journey require extra care and attention (Ritter *et al.*, 2009). The frequency of DOAs is highest in poultry (Petracci *et al.*, 2006; Di Martino *et al.*, 2017; Cockram and Dulal, 2018). Broilers can die during handling and transport from heat or cold stress, trauma and disease (e.g. heart conditions, ascites and infectious disease) (Nijdam *et al.*, 2006; Kittelsen *et al.*, 2015). Mortality can occur in pigs (Ritter *et al.*, 2009) and the mortality risk is dependent on the genotype (Murray and Johnson, 1998; Grandin, 2001; Fabrega *et al.*, 2002) and the risk of heat stress (Averos *et al.*, 2008). In a survey of slaughter plants conducted in five countries, 0.09% of pigs were dead-on-arrival, and 0.008% were found dead in the lairage (Dalmau *et al.*, 2016). Especially for poultry, the recording and regular assessment of mortality rates is important: (i) to identify whether the mortality rate of a particular load is greater than normal and requires specific investigation; (ii) to examine flock/herd health, driver and transport records to identify risk factors that could be manipulated to reduce future deaths; and (iii) to provide benchmarking statistics to compare the plant with industry norms and to identify significant variations in performance between transporters, farms of origin, etc. In many countries, any livestock DOAs or a high percentage of poultry DOAs is likely to attract the attention of regulatory authorities, who will conduct their own investigation.

Non-ambulatory Animals

Although some animals can become non-ambulatory during transport (González *et al.*, 2012), many non-ambulatory animals that arrive at slaughter plants were either non-ambulatory or otherwise not fit for transport before loading (Stull *et al.*, 2007; Frimpong *et al.*, 2014). It is not possible to load non-ambulatory cattle without causing extensive pain and injury (Grandin, 2001). On-farm euthanasia should be considered for cows that have been non-ambulatory for more than 24 h (Green *et al.*, 2008). Most non-ambulatory cattle are dairy cows, but some beef cows can become non-ambulatory during transport (Stull *et al.*, 2007; Goldhawk *et al.*, 2015; Harris *et al.*, 2017). They are unable to stand and walk because they are injured (e.g. calving-related, slips and falls), weak (e.g. emaciated), or sick (e.g. metabolic and toxic conditions) (Stull *et al.*, 2007). Lameness, fractures, severe arthritis and various neurological conditions can increase the risk of pigs becoming non-ambulatory during a journey (Sutherland *et al.*, 2008). In one study, 0.24% of pigs that arrived at a slaughter plant were non-ambulatory and not injured; 0.08% were non-ambulatory and injured (Correa *et al.*, 2013). Non-injured, non-ambulatory pigs can have signs of metabolic acidosis and greater concentrations of serum cortisol and catecholamines than ambulatory pigs (Anderson *et al.*, 2002). This suggests that some pigs become non-ambulatory following the development of stress and fatigue during the journey to slaughter (Ritter *et al.*, 2009).

In many countries, non-ambulatory animals must not be dragged off the vehicle or lifted by the limbs, tail, neck or ears. Non-ambulatory cattle that arrive at a slaughter plant should be euthanized on the vehicle, i.e. stunned and then killed using a secondary method, such as pithing or exsanguination. In some countries, non-ambulatory pigs and sheep can be moved off the vehicle and into the slaughter plant on sleds, mats, specialized carts or mechanized equipment that supports the full length and weight of the animal. If a non-ambulatory animal impedes the unloading of ambulatory animals, it should be removed or euthanized before continuing with unloading (Leary *et al.*, 2016; Grandin, 2017).

Injured Animals

Some animals arrive with an injury that was caused during handling and transportation or was present before loading. These injuries can range from skin lacerations, bruising (Strappini *et al.*, 2009), trauma to the udder (Goldhawk *et al.*, 2015) and trauma to existing lesions, such as a hernia or damaged foot, to bone fractures and dislocations (Bueno *et al.*, 2013). Broilers and spent laying hens are susceptible to injury during handling and transport. Jacobs *et al.* (2017b) found that 1.9% of broilers examined in a lairage had wing fractures and 0.14% leg fractures. Cull sows can arrive with a range of injuries, such as skin and vulval wounds and shoulder ulcers (Fogsgaard *et al.*, 2018). Some cull animals are more susceptible to injury because they are weak and likely to acquire skin wounds and bruising during handling and transport (Strappini *et al.*, 2013; Goldhawk *et al.*, 2015; Dahl-Pedersen *et al.*, 2018b) or because their bones are fragile and are more likely to fracture (Newberry *et al.*, 1999; Grandin, 2001). If an animal is in pain, it should be killed as soon as possible (Chirico *et al.*, 2017). If an injured animal can be unloaded, it should either go immediately to slaughter or, if this is not possible, moved to a pen near the unloading area where it can be separated from other animals and provided with additional care. Extra care needs to be taken when moving injured animals, as movement of or pressure on a painful wound or area of inflammation causes additional pain.

Sick and Lame Animals

Some producers send animals to slaughter in a sick or diseased condition because they wish to obtain the maximum financial return from an animal that can no longer be treated economically or is unlikely to recover its productive performance. However, there is a financial risk that the animal may not survive transportation, or may be euthanized en route or on arrival at the slaughter plant; in some countries, the producer and transporter are at risk of regulatory enforcement penalties for transporting an animal that may not have been fit for transportation; and there is a high risk that part or the whole carcass will be condemned as unfit for human consumption (Jackowiak *et al.*, 2006;

White and Moore, 2009; Rezac *et al.*, 2014). There are extra costs to a slaughter plant in dealing with diseased animals. The line speed may have to be reduced to allow for careful inspection and extra trimming; and due to the risk of contamination, some animals may need to be slaughtered at the end of the normal period.

Severe lameness can be observed in some animals that arrive at a slaughter plant (Warren *et al.*, 2010). This is a serious welfare issue, as most lameness is caused by pain. Animals with painful foot lesions are more reluctant to bear weight on their feet than healthy animals, and pressure on a lesion causes additional pain (Dyer *et al.*, 2007; Flower *et al.*, 2008). Gait scoring systems are available to categorize the severity of alterations in gait (Angell *et al.*, 2015; Edwards-Callaway *et al.*, 2017; Fogsgaard *et al.*, 2018). However, in a Danish study, there was only moderate agreement between veterinarians and farmers and between veterinarians and livestock drivers on the assessment of lameness in cull dairy cows (Dahl-Pedersen *et al.*, 2018a). In a survey of slaughter plants conducted in five countries, 0.4% of the pigs were assessed as severely lame on arrival (Dalmau *et al.*, 2016). Harris *et al.* (2017) assessed cattle that arrived at slaughter plants in the USA and observed that 0.3% of cull dairy cows and 0.1% of cull beef cows were extremely reluctant to move even when encouraged, and 4.7% of cull dairy cows and 2.3% of cull beef cows were obviously lame. In a survey in Denmark of cull dairy cows selected by farmers for transport to slaughter, more than 1% were evaluated as not fit for transport because they were severely lame (i.e. obviously lame in one or more legs, and unable, unwilling, or very reluctant to bear weight on the affected leg) and 31% were classified as lame (Dahl-Pedersen *et al.*, 2018c).

Guidance on Assessing Fitness for Transport

The number of animals that arrive at slaughter plants in poor condition would be reduced if there was a more effective assessment of the fitness of animals before they are loaded on the journey to be sent to slaughter. In many countries, there are detailed legal regulations on the criteria for the fitness of animals for transport. In these countries, if an unfit animal arrives at a slaughter plant, there are procedures for the collection of evidence and the investigation of suspected breaches of welfare legislation with the possibility of penalties imposed on the producer and transporter (European Commission, 2016). The Office International des Epizooties chapter on the transport of animals by land (OIE, 2011) contains the following standards on the fitness of animals under section (c), which states that animals that are unfit to travel include, but may not be limited to:

i) those that are sick, injured, weak, disabled or fatigued;
ii) those that are unable to stand unaided and bear weight on each leg;
iii) those that are blind in both eyes;
iv) those that cannot be moved without causing them additional suffering;
v) newborn with an unhealed navel;
vi) pregnant animals which would be in the final 10% of their gestation period at the planned time of unloading;
vii) females travelling without young which have given birth within the previous 48 h;
viii) those whose body condition would result in poor welfare because of the expected climatic conditions.

Guidelines and decision trees that include examples of the types of clinical conditions that would make an animal unfit for transport are available. Some examples for cattle, pigs, sheep and poultry are Eurogroup for Animals *et al.* (2012, 2015), National Farm Animal Care Council (2013) and Poultry Industry Council (2017). However, different stakeholders have different views on the criteria that would make an animal unfit for transport (Grandin, 2016; Herskin *et al.*, 2017; Dahl-Pedersen *et al.*, 2018a). There is a potential conflict between the avoidance of the risk of suffering arising from a decision not to transport an animal that is not fit for transport and the financial loss associated with on-farm euthanasia compared with the potential return to a producer from transporting the animal for slaughter so that it can be sold for human consumption (Magalhães-Sant'Ana *et al.*, 2017). There are often very limited options for on-farm slaughter with the transport of the carcass to a slaughter plant, but where this option is available, it is likely to reduce some of the dilemmas associated with decisions on fitness for transport and economics (Magalhães-Sant'Ana *et al.*, 2017; Koralesky and Fraser, 2018). Greater dissemination of information on fitness for transport issues, guidance and training on the criteria for fitness for transport to producers, veterinarians and transporters, and enforcement of legal regulations or industry standards has been advocated (European Commission, 2016). A major difficulty with the enforcement of regulations on the fitness of animals is differentiating between conditions that were present and readily identifiable before loading and those that occurred during the journey. Ante-mortem and post-mortem inspection, together with an appreciation of the underlying pathological mechanisms and the age of lesions, can assist in resolving this issue (European Commission, 2016). A proportion of the animals sent for slaughter have pathological conditions that were only identified post-mortem, but were present before transportation and may not have been readily apparent before loading (Visser *et al.*, 1992; Cockram, 2019). Consideration of the pathophysiological implications of ill-health and injury on an animal's response to the potential physical and physiological challenges that can occur during transportation readily identifies the potential for suffering that can occur if compromised animals are transported (Cockram, 2019). It is therefore important that animals with identifiable conditions that make them unfit for transport are not sent for slaughter.

Guidance for On-farm Euthanasia of Animals Not Fit for Transport

For animals that are either experiencing suffering that cannot be mitigated, are not fit for transport, have no reasonable prospect of economic recovery or are not fit for human consumption, on-farm euthanasia is the preferred option (Fig. 4.1). Producers should be encouraged to develop a suitable on-farm euthanasia plan that is part of their health and welfare plan developed in consultation with the herd/flock veterinarian (Turner and Doonan, 2010). This should include clinical endpoints, decision trees, training of staff and appropriate methods of euthanasia. Developing clear agreed-upon criteria for euthanasia and effective training can assist those required to make difficult decisions on euthanasia and then undertake euthanasia (Turner and Doonan, 2010; McGee *et al.*, 2016). Shearer and Reynolds (2011) provide examples of conditions that often result in on-farm euthanasia. Examples of the reasons for euthanasia of dairy cows are mastitis/udder problems, lameness/locomotor disorders, calving problems, accidents and metabolic/digestive disorders (Thomsen

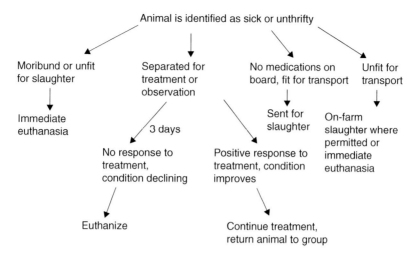

Fig. 4.1. Example of an algorithm used for developing an on-farm euthanasia protocol. (Source: Turner and Doonan, 2010, with permission.)

and Sørensen, 2009; McConnel *et al.*, 2010; Fusi *et al.*, 2017). Cull sows are euthanized because of traumatic injuries, fractures or paralysis; prolapse/dystocia; lameness; abscesses; and poor body condition (Engblom *et al.*, 2007, 2008; Jensen *et al.*, 2010).

In many countries, the percentage of animals euthanized on-farm has increased due to lowered thresholds for euthanasia to avoid animal suffering, to reduce treatment costs and to avoid penalties arising from the enforcement of animal welfare regulations (Thomsen and Sørensen, 2008). However, most producers will only undertake euthanasia in extreme circumstances. They are reluctant to undertake on-farm euthanasia because of the costs involved in undertaking euthanasia, the cost for disposal of the body and the loss of carcass value (Langford and Stott, 2012; Edwards-Callaway *et al.*, 2019). Another issue is the reluctance of a caretaker to kill an animal for which they have provided daily care (Rault *et al.*, 2017; Campler *et al.*, 2018). On some units, it may also be difficult to find a competent person and suitable equipment to undertake euthanasia (European Commission, 2016).

There are various options for on-farm euthanasia (Humane Slaughter Association, 2016) and guidelines are available (e.g. Leary *et al.*, 2016; National Pork Board, 2016; Poultry Industry Council, 2016; Shearer, 2018), but in some locations unacceptable methods that do not minimize suffering or cause instantaneous loss of consciousness and a reliable death are undertaken (Dalla

Costa *et al.*, 2019). Animals can be killed by a veterinarian using a lethal intravenous dose of an anaesthetic drug, but there are then restrictions on carcass disposal. A firearm that fires a free bullet or a shotgun that shoots multiple projectiles from close range into the brain of the animal can be an effective way of undertaking on-farm euthanasia. A rifle can be used to kill sheep, pigs and small cattle, but correct shot placement is important (Humane Slaughter Association, 2016). Captive bolt stunning, followed by bleeding or pithing, can be used where a free bullet is impractical for safety reasons. Although some animals will be killed by captive bolt stunning, if a secondary step is not used there is a risk that the animal will return to consciousness (Appelt and Sperry, 2007). Some types of captive bolt equipment have been designed specifically for euthanasia, but they do not always kill the animal after the first shot, and either a secondary step or multiple shots may be required (Derscheid *et al.*, 2016; Gilliam *et al.*, 2018). In one survey in the USA, 96% of the dairy cows that were euthanized were euthanized on-farm, 78% using a firearm, 7% with a captive bolt and 7% with a euthanasia solution (Aly *et al.*, 2014).

On-farm euthanasia of poultry can be required because of accidental injury or disease. Methods include the use of a percussive bolt, manual or mechanical cervical dislocation by stretching or crushing, and blunt trauma, followed by exsanguination (Bader *et al.*, 2014; Cors *et al.*, 2015).

Condition of Animals on Arrival and Management During Lairage

Where the condition of spent laying hens is poor (fragile bones, feather loss and poor body condition), there is no market for their carcasses and no plant within a reasonable distance that slaughters laying hens, on-farm euthanasia is undertaken. This avoids the welfare risks associated with pain from injury during handling and exposure to cold environments during transport (Newberry et al., 1999; Richards et al., 2012). The options for whole-flock euthanasia are the use of carbon dioxide in mobile containers or inside the barn, use of in-barn anoxic foam, handheld electrical stunners and maceration (McKeegan et al., 2013; Berg et al., 2014).

Guidance on Developing On-farm Policies to Avoid Transporting Animals in a Deteriorated and Compromised Condition

Improved on-farm procedures for decision making concerning if and when cull animals should be sent for slaughter would reduce the number of animals that arrive at abattoirs in poor condition (Grandin, 2001). Animals need to be culled before they become weak, debilitated and not fit for transport (Stojkov et al., 2018). For poultry, adopting a rigorous culling programme during rearing will reduce the risk of mortality during transport (Jacobs et al., 2017a). Culling procedures should form part of a written farm health and welfare plan developed in consultation with the unit's veterinarian that includes protocols for early identification of animals that need to be treated, culled and sent for slaughter or euthanized on-farm (Doonan et al., 2014). An effective health plan, regular health monitoring and veterinary advice on preventive measures, biosecurity and treatment protocols should improve the health and fitness of the animals and reduce the number of animals on a farm that need to be culled prematurely (LeBlanc et al., 2006; Scott et al., 2007). Regular on-farm health assessments using gait scoring (Schlageter-Tello et al., 2014) and body condition scoring (Roche et al., 2004; Bewley et al., 2008) are useful to identify animals suitable for culling before they become unfit for transport (Grandin, 2018). Thin animals are more likely to be injured or bruised during transport, have an increased risk of becoming non-ambulatory (Grandin, 2001) and can be more susceptible to cold conditions (Verbeek et al., 2012). Grandin (2001) suggested that improved genetic selection and breeding practices and the selection of transporters who provide

optimal standards for the transportation of animals would improve the condition of animals on arrival at slaughter plants. Ritter et al. (2006) showed that avoiding overcrowding during a journey reduced the risk of pigs becoming non-ambulatory. In broilers, the methods used for on-farm catching and handling (Cockram and Dulal, 2018) have a major influence on the prevalence of bone fractures, especially wing fractures (Kittelsen et al., 2015; Jacobs et al., 2017b).

Breeding animals are culled, i.e. removed from the herd or flock, for several reasons, including low production, poor breeding performance and health problems (Bascom and Young, 1998). There are many factors that affect culling decisions, including the age, stage of lactation, production, health status, behaviour, reproductive status and the producer's attitude to risk and uncertainty (Beaudeau et al., 2000). Economic factors such as the economic return from the output of the animal, e.g. milk or calf/piglet price, the price that can be obtained for cull animals at slaughter and the price and availability of replacement animals are major factors that can affect a culling decision (Bascom and Young, 1998; Beaudeau et al., 2000). If culling is 'voluntary,' i.e. planned, producers have the options of selling their animal immediately, waiting for increased prices or feeding the animal before auction. Depending on the type and condition of the animal, the options for cull animals that leave the farm can include sending the animal directly to slaughter for human consumption at either a large slaughter plant or a local abattoir, or to an auction market for sale for slaughter or further fattening.

The reason for culling can affect the fitness of the animals for transport. Animals that are culled 'involuntarily' because they are sick, lame, weak or injured are more likely to suffer during transport and can represent an economic loss to the producer (Chiumia et al., 2013). Health issues such as udder and mastitis problems, lameness, injury and disease are major causes for culling of dairy cows (Hadley et al., 2006). A proportion of dairy cows that arrive at slaughter plants are lame, in poor body condition and have mastitis (Nicholson et al., 2013). The timing of culling for dairy cows because of lameness can depend on the type of lesions (e.g. foot rot and sole ulcers), the stage of lactation and pregnancy status (Booth et al., 2004).

An important aspect of the culling decision is the marketing route chosen for the animals. Cull cows and sows may be sent for slaughter via auction markets, as this has the potential to maximize financial returns (Blair and Lowe, 2019; Edwards-Callaway et al., 2019). These animals may be collected from the farm by a dealer who then forms a batch of animals to send to a market or to a specialist slaughter plant that could be a considerable distance from the farm (Stojkov et al., 2018). Sending a compromised cull animal to an auction market can increase the journey duration and expose the animal to extra handling, novel environments, restricted availability of feed and water, and may provide reduced opportunities for rest and more opportunity for any existing health conditions to deteriorate.

In the absence of legal regulations and their effective enforcement, a producer might decide to risk transporting a compromised animal to attempt to obtain the maximum financial return and avoid the costs of undertaking on-farm euthanasia and subsequent carcass disposal. However, there are risks of mortality, animal suffering, failure to pass meat inspection and poor public perception of these practices (Edwards-Callaway et al., 2019). Even in situations where cull cows that are unfit for sale or further transport are prohibited from sale, a large proportion of cull cows sold at a market can be in poor body condition and lame. Although these conditions can reduce their value, the economic returns from selling these animals at a market can be high (Moorman et al., 2018).

Although not available in many locations, on-farm slaughter is an option that allows an animal to be slaughtered for human consumption without having to be transported alive to another location. This could be achieved using a mobile slaughter plant, or the animal could be slaughtered (using normal stunning and bleeding procedures) on the farm and then the carcass transported to a slaughter plant for post-mortem inspection (Koralesky and Fraser, 2018; Stojkov et al., 2018). In a study in Italy of on-farm mortality, 30% of the dairy cows that died on-farm were euthanized, and 25% were slaughtered on-farm and the carcasses sent to a slaughter plant (Fusi et al., 2017). On-farm slaughter is suitable for animals that pass ante-mortem inspection and are likely to pass post-mortem meat inspection, for example animals that have had an accident, are non-ambulatory or have locomotion problems due to trauma, arthritis or foot lesions (Hirvonen et al., 1997; Cullinane et al., 2010, 2012; Fusi et al., 2017; Koralesky and Fraser, 2018).

The ability of slaughter plants to exchange information within the meat production chain is influenced by the closeness of the relationship between a slaughter plant and individual producers or producer groups. This can be affected by the social, economic and regulatory environment (Deimel and Theuvsen, 2011), whether there are intermediary stages in the supply of animals to the plant, such as an auction market, and by the ownership of a slaughter plant and the production units that supply the animals for slaughter. If positive relationships can be established (Devitt et al., 2016) there are animal health and welfare and economic advantages to both parties in the communication of best-practice guidelines and feedback to producers on the ante-mortem and post-mortem condition of the animals received for slaughter (Willeberg et al., 1984; Harley et al., 2012). This can be achieved through direct contact and industry bodies. See Chapter 16 for further details on welfare issues that can be identified at slaughter.

Lairage

After arrival at a slaughter plant, animals that are not taken directly to slaughter are placed in a lairage (sometimes referred to as stockyards, holding pens, holding yards or holding barns). The original meaning of a lair or lairage is a place where animals can lie down and rest, but the lairage serves several potential functions. The main purpose is to act as a holding area to provide a reservoir of animals that are readily available to be taken for slaughter so that the speed of the slaughter line can be maintained without waiting for the arrival of animals. A lairage is preferable to leaving animals on a vehicle waiting to be unloaded just in time for slaughter. A lairage can provide more effective ventilation and facilities for resting, feeding and watering. It is often stated, that for welfare reasons, stressed and fatigued animals require lairage to rest and recover from handling and transportation. However, if animals are taken directly to slaughter shortly after unloading, they have little time to experience any further negative consequences arising from transportation, and it can be argued that this is preferable to keeping them in a lairage where they could continue to experience a negative affective state. This is especially the case where the lairage does not provide an optimal environment and causes further stress. The one welfare argument for providing animals with an opportunity to rest and recover from transportation is where animals have become so excited or agitated that they are difficult to handle and move to the point of slaughter and might also require additional restraint to ensure effective stunning (Chirico et al., 2017). Placing wet cattle and sheep in a lairage can provide an opportunity for them to dry off before slaughter and thereby reduce the risk of contamination of the meat during dressing procedures. Depending on the genotype and the pre-slaughter treatment, there is some evidence that a period of lairage can improve the meat quality of some pigs. A lairage also serves as a critical control point for food safety and animal welfare, as it provides an area for ante-mortem inspection of the animals (Jalakas et al., 2014). The condition of the animals and the facilities in the lairage should be checked regularly during the day by the lairage staff and at least daily by the slaughter plant management and a veterinarian. The principles affecting the design of lairage pens and handling in the lairage are covered in Chapters 6 and 12. Lairage pens should be of secure construction, without risk of injury to the animals, provide protection from predation and be arranged to permit inspection of animals at any time, with corridors between pens or overhead walkways, and facilities to remove sick or injured animals (Chirico et al., 2017).

There should be an emergency plan to deal with contingencies that could affect the welfare of the animals in the lairage and those that are en route to the lairage. Examples of potential events that require planning are an extended plant stoppage, disruption of services to the lairage (such as electricity and water), fire, extreme weather conditions and strict biosecurity procedures following a notifiable disease outbreak. The plan should be kept in a visible location and should be reviewed at least annually. For animals that are en route to the plant that cannot be returned to their farm of origin, there should be a designated place where animals can be unloaded and provided with adequate care (Leary et al., 2016; Grandin, 2017). If there is a risk of a delay in unloading animals after a vehicle has arrived at the lairage, the installation and use of a bank of fans with water misters just outside of the lairage can be effective in reducing the risk of heat stress while the vehicle is stationary (Pereira et al., 2018).

Duration in Lairage

There are several considerations that affect the duration that animals are held in the lairage (Warriss, 2003). Practical issues such as the timing of deliveries in relation to the timing and speed of slaughter can increase the duration that animals need to be held in the lairage. Limitation on the capacity of a lairage can reduce the duration that animals can be kept before slaughter. Some animals are slaughtered without spending any time in the lairage, but many animals spend several hours and some may be kept overnight (Small et al., 2007). There are animal welfare, meat quality and food safety issues that can influence this duration. Ideas on the optimal duration that animals need to be kept in a lairage have evolved. Practices vary between species and countries (e.g. see Gallo and Huertas, 2016), and can depend on factors such as the physical environmental conditions during transportation and lairage, duration of fasting and genotype.

A prolonged period in a lairage or holding barn is a major risk factor for broiler mortality (Nijdam et al., 2004; Knezacek et al., 2010; Chauvin et al., 2011; Caffrey et al., 2017). Providing appropriate ventilation and thermal conditions can, in some circumstances, be challenging. Some of the deaths during lairage can also be a delayed consequence of injury during catching and loading, others the result of problems experienced during the journey, e.g. hypothermia or hyperthermia (Caffrey et al., 2017), and some might occur due to a combination of factors, including the duration of fasting and chronic disease (Cockram and Dulal, 2018).

Animal Welfare

In most situations, from an animal welfare perspective that considers the affective state of animals, the duration that animals are present in a lairage should be kept to a minimum. There are several reasons for keeping this duration short. Some animals arrive in a lairage with a welfare issue such as a painful injury that arose during transport or was present on the farm. Early slaughter of these animals will reduce the duration of any suffering. For various reasons discussed in this chapter and Chapter 2, it is difficult to provide an optimal environment for animals in a lairage. Some environmental aspects can be harmful and the welfare of an animal can deteriorate with time in the lairage. Some animals in the lairage are kept in unstable social groups and interactions between animals such as fighting or mounting can cause stress and injury. The severity of these injuries can increase with duration in the lairage. With this reasoning, unless recovery is necessary to facilitate handling or stunning (Warriss, 2003), lairage is never beneficial for animal welfare.

Some confusion can nevertheless arise over whether lairage is beneficial for animal welfare, due to differences in how animal welfare is understood. The above reasoning and the discussion in Chapter 2 are based on the consideration that animal welfare is entirely dependent on what an animal feels. However, due to difficulties in assessing the affective state of an animal, some approaches to animal welfare assessment use disturbances to biological functioning or to the fitness of an animal as the criteria on which to assess animal welfare (Fraser et al., 1997; Fraser, 2003). If this approach to animal welfare is taken, it is possible to come to a different conclusion over optimal lairage durations. After transportation, it is not uncommon for several aspects of an animal's physiology to be affected, such as raised body temperature, increased plasma concentrations of cortisol, increased plasma creatine kinase activity, increased mobilization of metabolites associated with fasting and sometimes biochemical changes associated with dehydration. In favourable lairage conditions, these variables can return to normal with time in the lairage (Averos et al., 2007). The biological functioning approach would consider that the welfare of the animals would be improved if they were given the opportunity to recover from these physiological disturbances, e.g. provided with sufficient time for plasma cortisol concentrations to return to normal (Warriss et al., 1992; Perez et al., 2002; Liste et al., 2011). Using this approach, an optimal lairage duration would be based on how long these physiological variables take to return to 'normal' or baseline values. However, if the animals are stressed, do not rest, do not drink readily or do not have sufficient access to feed, their physiological variables may not stabilize in the lairage and their condition can deteriorate rather than improve.

Meat Quality

The evidence that animals require a short period in a lairage for improved meat quality is complex, variable between species and genotype within species, and dependent on other aspects of pre-slaughter management. However, there is convincing evidence that some aspects of meat quality can deteriorate with increased time in the lairage. With prolonged lairage, there can be reduced carcass weight and an increased risk that the animals will acquire a zoonotic infection (Warriss, 2003). Keeping some pigs for a short period in a lairage compared with immediate slaughtering upon arrival can in some circumstances be beneficial for meat quality. If the handling and transport of pigs have been stressful, resting them in a lairage can allow them to recover from some of this stress, and this can in some circumstances improve some aspects of meat quality (Warriss, 2003). Stress-susceptible pigs need more time to recover from transportation than stress-resistant pigs (De Smet et al., 1996). However, if halothane-negative pigs are transported for a relatively short duration, in conditions that do not cause heat stress, and are kept in small and stable social groups, slaughtering without a period of lairage may not necessarily result in poor meat quality (Aaslyng and Barton Gade, 2001).

Some pigs that are slaughtered on arrival can have a higher temperature and a faster post-mortem muscle pH decline than those kept in lairage for 1–2 h (Terlouw et al., 2008). A short period of lairage for 1–2 h before slaughter can in some circumstances improve meat colour and reduce the risk of pale, soft and exudative (PSE) meat (Dokmanović et al., 2014). However, long lairage periods allow more time for fighting between the pigs, the duration of fasting is longer, the amount of skin damage is increased, and muscle glycogen concentration is reduced, thereby increasing the risk of dark, firm and dry (DFD) meat (Guàrdia et al., 2009; Faucitano, 2010; Čobanović et al., 2016). After fasted pigs are placed in a lairage pen without access to feed, they can be active, investigating the pen, drinking water and mounting. This activity tends to decrease with time, but fighting can increase to maximum intensity after about 1 h. Fighting can be more intense and skin damage more severe with increased duration of fasting before loading (Brown et al., 1999b). Pigs that have been fighting are likely to be more stressed, have increased metabolic activity, higher body temperature and increased muscle lactate concentration and if slaughtered in this condition could have reduced meat quality (Faucitano, 2010). Other studies have shown that meat from pigs slaughtered immediately after transport had more desirable sensory properties (juiciness, tenderness, palatability) than those lairaged for 24 h (Śmiecińska et al., 2011). A meta-analysis of 13 studies on pigs with mixed social grouping, held in lairage for between 0.25 and 24 h, failed to identify a significant effect of lairage duration on muscle pH_{45}, muscle reflectance or drip loss. The only significant effect of lairage duration was a potentially negative effect on meat quality, namely an increase in pH_u in semimembranosus muscle (Salmi et al., 2012). However, fasting duration and transport duration also affected some aspects of meat quality; therefore, the effects of lairage duration on meat quality are also likely to be influenced by these factors.

In most cases, beef quality is not significantly improved by the time that cattle spend in lairage (Wythes et al., 1988; Ferguson et al., 2007). Del Campo et al. (2010) found a lower muscle pH_{24} after steers that had been transported for 4 h had been lairaged for 15 h compared with 3 h. However, prolonged lairage, e.g. 24 h, can increase live weight loss and increase the risk of DFD meat (Gallo et al., 2003). In young bulls, if lairage duration is kept to a minimum, meat quality is improved and the risks of DFD meat and bruising are reduced. Ideally, young bulls should be slaughtered as soon as possible after arrival. After long journeys lasting 1–2 days, the effect of lairaging young bulls with access to feed and water for longer than 2 days compared with 1–2 days on muscle pH_u is inconsistent and likely depends on the behavioural activity in the group (Liotta et al., 2007; Teke et al., 2014).

Availability of Water

There are no meat quality or food safety issues that preclude the provision of drinking water to animals in the lairage (Wythes et al., 1985). After animals have been transported on long journeys, most animals in a group may need to drink on arrival in the lairage (Wythes et al., 1980). For example, Jarvis et al. (1996) observed that 60% of cattle drank within the first 3 h of arrival in a lairage. Transportation can cause dehydration in livestock, but if offered ready access to water in the lairage the signs of dehydration are rapidly reduced (Gortel et al., 1992; Averos et al., 2007; Mota-Rojas et al., 2009). Pigs transported for 8–24 h regained 0.8% of their weight due to drinking during an 8 h lairage period (Becerril-Herrera et al., 2007). The volume of water drunk by pigs will depend on factors such as the temperature, the journey duration, duration of fasting and the type of feed previously offered (Saucier et al., 2007; Goumon et al., 2013).

Facilities for the provision of drinking water should be available in each lairage pen. Nipple drinkers, automatic troughs or buckets can be provided, but it is important to check that the animals can drink from the type of drinker provided and that it is placed at an appropriate height to allow the size of animal in the pen to drink. Water sources should be checked regularly to ensure that they are clean, in working order and used by the animals. It is good practice to provide more than one source of drinking water per pen and sufficient sources to allow easy access, e.g. one drinker per six cattle and one drinker per 12 pigs (Chirico et al., 2017). However, in practice, the number of animals per drinker frequently exceeds this ideal (Dalmau et al., 2009, 2016).

If animals are kept in a lairage for a prolonged period with access to water, not all animals will necessarily drink. After 15–28 h without water, Jongman et al. (2008) observed that only 80% of the sheep drank water during a 24 h lairage. Some animals may not drink enough to recover from dehydration associated with transportation, or they may not drink sufficient water to prevent progressive dehydration while kept in a lairage (Liu et al., 2012). If animals do not have access to water, they will become progressively dehydrated, especially in warm environments (Jacob et al., 2006; Pearce et al., 2008; Vanderhasselt et al., 2013). It is difficult to provide water to birds in containers and they should be slaughtered as soon as possible after arrival (Chirico et al., 2017).

Availability of Feed

As discussed in Chapter 2, it is normal practice to fast animals before slaughter. If the animals are only present in the lairage for a few hours, it has traditionally not been considered necessary to provide feed. However, on arrival in the lairage, some animals will already have experienced a period of fasting on the farm before loading, a second period without feed during transportation and will then experience a third period without feed in the lairage. Regulations and guidelines provide a limit on the duration without feed in the lairage, e.g. 12 h (OIE, 2016), but most guidelines do not take into consideration the length of fasting before arrival in the lairage. The guidelines also suggest that if animals are not slaughtered within 12 h, they should be provided with suitable feed on arrival and at subsequent intervals appropriate to the species.

M. Cockram

The lairage should provide facilities for feeding. Where feed troughs are provided, they should be sufficient in number and feeding space to allow adequate access for all animals to feed (OIE, 2016).

Hungry animals may be less likely to rest in a lairage. Pigs that have been fasted for a prolonged period can show increased activity and fighting that can adversely affect carcass and meat quality (Dalla Costa et al., 2018). Access to feed and water in the lairage for several hours allows the animals to regain some of the weight lost during transport, reduces the requirement to mobilize body energy reserves in response to an energy deficit and allows them to recover some of their energy reserves (Brown et al., 1999a; Cockram et al., 1999; Knowles et al., 1999). When offered feed in a lairage, most animals will eat it; for example, Jarvis et al. (1996) observed that 93% of cattle ate hay within the first 3 h in a lairage pen. After very long journeys, if feed and water are available for several days, most but not all sheep will eat, most sheep will recover from the effects of fasting, and muscle pH_u will improve (Shorthose, 1977). Pre-ruminant suckling lambs are more susceptible than ruminants to periods of food and water deprivation. As there is no improvement in meat quality with lairage, it is preferable to slaughter suckling lambs as soon as possible after arrival (Díaz et al., 2014).

Thermal Environment in the Lairage

Lairages can differ in the degree of protection provided to the animals from adverse weather conditions. Lairages can range from an environmentally controlled building, a naturally ventilated building, or a covered pen, to an uncovered pen or field (Small et al., 2007). In all situations, shelter must be provided to protect the animals from excessive wind and precipitation and to offer shade. The optimal temperature within a lairage is difficult to define, as several factors interact to influence the effective environmental temperature experienced by the animals. The thermal requirements of animals vary greatly, depending on factors such as body size, coat and tissue insulation, length of fasting, floor type and the availability of bedding, and there are differences between species in the mechanisms that they have for evaporative heat loss.

Young animals, pigs, poultry, shorn sheep, cull cattle and those in poor body condition, with a wet coat, exposed to draughts, fasted for prolonged periods and kept in pens without bedding, have

increased susceptibility to cold conditions and wind-chill (Grandin, 2017). In pigs, shivering and huddling are signs of cold stress that can sometimes be observed during lairage (Dalmau et al., 2009).

Heat stress in livestock

Livestock and poultry are susceptible to heat stress. Signs of heat stress in livestock are an increased respiration rate, decreased feed intake and increased drinking. This can be followed by panting, open-mouth breathing, salivation and, if severe, reduced coordination, trembling and recumbency (Huynh et al., 2005; Al-Dawood, 2017; Polsky and von Keyserlingk, 2017). The severity of heat stress can be identified using numerical scoring systems (e.g. Gaughan et al., 2008). Some animals can be hyperthermic on arrival, especially after long journeys in raised temperature and humidity (Miranda-de la Lama et al., 2018). On arrival in the lairage, some pigs can show panting, open-mouth breathing and hyperventilation, especially during warmer conditions, e.g. ≥ 17°C (Mota-Rojas et al., 2006; Kephart et al., 2010; Dalmau et al., 2016) and some cattle can be observed to be sweating on arrival (Warren et al., 2010).

Heat stress occurs when the metabolic heat produced by the animal is greater than its capacity to lose this heat to the surrounding environment. The exchange of heat between an animal and its environment is affected by the air temperature, humidity, air movement and radiant heat. Heat is lost to the environment through non-evaporative heat transfer to the air and surrounding surfaces by convection, conduction and thermal radiation exchange. The surface of an animal can gain heat from solar radiation; therefore, a roof or shade can provide protection from solar radiation. When an animal is lying down, heat exchange can occur through conduction to the floor. The type of floor surface and whether bedding is provided are especially important for the thermal conditions of pigs. In warm conditions, the pigs may lie down to increase body heat conduction to the floor, whereas in cooler conditions they stand and huddle (Fraqueza et al., 1998). Convective heat loss from air movement can remove surface heat, and this cooling is increased if the body surface is wet and water is evaporated from the surface. An air velocity of 0.2–0.5 m/s can remove the boundary layer of air insulation surrounding an animal (Berman, 2019) and faster speeds, e.g. 3 m/s, can disrupt air contained within the coat insulation and provide cooling (Collier and Gebremedhin, 2015).

Evaporative heat loss through the evaporation of water from the body surfaces, especially from the respiratory tract, is important as air temperature rises. This mode of heat transfer is influenced by the water vapour pressure difference between inhaled and exhaled air. The risk of heat stress increases when there is a combination of high temperatures and high humidity, and temperature–humidity index charts have been developed to indicate the risk of heat stress (Sullivan and Mader, 2018). If pigs are kept in hot and humid conditions in a lairage for several hours, meat quality can be affected (Santos et al., 1997) and the risk of mortality is increased (Vitali et al., 2014). This risk is reduced if the stocking density is kept low and water sprinklers are used for cooling (Vitali et al., 2014).

Water sprays and fans are used in hot conditions to assist cooling. If the humidity is not high, the evaporation of water from surfaces surrounding an animal can also cool the air. Recommendations for misting or wetting pigs are to avoid excess humidity by using a large droplet spray rather than a fine mist, allow pigs time to dry in an area with air movement before wetting them again, and avoid showering in cold conditions, as this can cause shivering and huddling (Weeding et al., 1993; Knowles et al., 1998; Dalmau et al., 2016; Grandin, 2017).

Heat and cold stress in poultry

Poultry are susceptible to both heat stress and cold stress during lairage. Prolonged exposure to thermal environmental extremes can result in mortality from either hyperthermia or hypothermia (Knezacek et al., 2010; Caffrey et al., 2017). A poultry lairage or holding barn should provide adequate shade and insulation from solar radiation (Ritz et al., 2005). Combinations of high temperature and high humidity pose a high risk of mortality (Tao and Xin, 2003a). The main way in which birds lose excessive heat is through the evaporation of water from the respiratory tract and through the skin (Genç and Portier, 2005). As the air temperature rises, the respiration rate increases and, eventually, panting occurs (Gleeson, 1985). High humidity impairs the ability of the birds to lose heat via respiratory evaporative cooling (Quinn et al., 1998; Genç and Portier, 2005). In hot and humid conditions, the survival time for broilers

before they collapse from heat exhaustion and die depends on the temperature rise within the container, the duration of exposure and the thermal regulatory ability of individual birds (Cockram and Dulal, 2018). The handling system and the lairage design can have a major influence on the thermal environment experienced by poultry. If the birds remain in crates on the trailer, the provision of sufficient ventilation to all of the birds in the load can be challenging (Cockram and Dulal, 2018). The temperature within the crates can rise above the external temperature and the body temperature of the birds can increase (Hunter et al., 1998; Warriss et al., 1999). Poultry kept in containers in a lairage are not provided with drinking water and will not have had access to water during catching, loading and the journey to slaughter. Birds that are exposed to high temperatures without access to water for prolonged periods are at an increased risk of dehydration and hyperthermia (Zhou et al., 1999). Bird behaviour should be monitored for signs of heat stress (panting and birds turning towards the side of modules to obtain fresh air) (Chirico et al., 2017). Jacobs et al. (2017a) reported a significant association between the percentage of birds panting during lairage and the risk of mortality. Air movement can reduce the risk of hyperthermia in broilers exposed to hot conditions (Hamrita and Conway, 2017). In hot conditions, an evaporative cooling system in addition to fan ventilation can reduce mortality in holding barns (Shackelford et al., 1984). In warm weather, water sprays can provide evaporative cooling and wetting of the birds (Tao and Xin, 2003b), but can increase the relative humidity.

A poultry lairage also has to protect the birds from wind, precipitation and extremely cold temperatures. The lower critical temperature for broilers at the time of slaughter is about 24°C (Meltzer, 1983) and at temperatures below this the birds must reduce their heat loss and/or increase heat production. When broilers are exposed to cold temperatures, they can respond by placing their head and feet under their body, huddling, ptiloerection, vasoconstriction, shivering and increasing their metabolic rate (Strawford et al., 2011). In a cold climate, the lairage needs temperature-controlled mechanical ventilation combined with heating. In some countries when poultry are transported during the winter months, the external temperature can be extremely low and during transport the birds (especially those near air inlets without external protection from cold air and water) are susceptible to hypothermia, frostbite and freezing (Hunter et al., 1999; Strawford et al., 2011). In cold conditions, broilers are at an increased risk of death the longer that they are kept in the lairage (Knezacek et al., 2010; Caffrey et al., 2017) and meat quality can be reduced (Bianchi et al., 2006; Dadgar et al., 2011, 2012).

Ventilation in the Lairage

Effective ventilation in the lairage is important to remove waste gases and avoid the build-up of metabolic heat and moisture and to replace these with fresh air distributed throughout the lairage. The ventilation system should be designed and when necessary adjusted to provide suitable temperatures for the types of animals in the lairage (Wathes et al., 1983). The ability of the ventilation system to remove waste products from the air and avoid poor air quality is dependent on the number of animals present in the air space and on their stocking density. In temperate climates, many livestock lairages are naturally ventilated and these are suitable for adult ruminants. The air movement is achieved by utilizing prevailing wind and thermal buoyancy. For natural ventilation to be effective the lairage has to be sited away from other buildings and obstructions that would block the prevailing wind. Thermal buoyancy will only work if the external temperature is lower than the internal temperature and there is a height difference between the outlets and the inlets. If a naturally ventilated building is too wide or understocked, air flow will not be sufficient in all parts of the building. A common design consists of inlets around the wall comprising space boarding and a raised roof ridge outlet. Ventilation can be adjusted by opening and closing doors and windows (Small et al., 2007; Mondaca, 2019).

In environments where the temperatures can be extreme, natural ventilation cannot be relied upon always to provide suitable conditions and adjustable mechanical ventilation is required. Temperature-controlled mechanical or fan ventilation with ducting is required for pig and poultry lairages to avoid the risk of heat and cold stress. This may need to be combined with air conditioning and heating systems. The ventilation system should function with minimum noise, avoid draughts and always provide sufficient air movement to extract stale air and replace it with fresh air. The ventilation rate can be increased by increasing the inlet area and the speed and number of fans in use. Extractor fans can be used to remove humidity and metabolic heat (Chirico et al., 2017). Mechanical ventilation systems require regular maintenance of equipment, and air quality should be monitored. When necessary, temperature, humidity and ammonia concentration should be measured, displayed and recorded. If there is a smell of ammonia, this indicates that there is insufficient minimum ventilation (Weeks, 2008). If mechanical ventilation is used, an alarm and emergency back-up facilities are required in case the system breaks down. The alarm system should be able to function even if there is a power failure and an emergency generator should be provided. There should be a contingency plan and an alternative (natural) means of providing ventilation must be available if the mechanical ventilation fails (Chirico et al., 2017).

Ventilation for poultry

In poultry lairages effective ventilation inside and between containers can reduce the mortality risk (Cockram et al., 2019). Ventilation can only be effectively achieved by unloading the containers from the vehicle and stacking them at appropriate locations in the lairage with a gap between them (Hunter et al., 1998). However, stacking containers concentrates metabolic heat and moisture production, reduces the surface area for cooling and reduces the airflow around each container. Ventilation within poultry containers is difficult, as there is little space above each layer of birds and, especially at high stocking density, side ventilation openings in the containers may be partially obstructed by the birds (Warriss et al., 2005). In both summer and winter, the temperature and humidity within a container are likely to rise during lairage and this can cause an increase in body temperature (Hunter et al., 1998; Quinn et al., 1998; Warriss et al., 1999). If the containers remain on the vehicle, banks of fans are required to provide side ventilation. In hot conditions, the load can also be placed under showers for several minutes after arrival (Freitas et al., 2016) and misting systems can be used to cool poultry (Quinn et al., 1998). However, if the humidity is high, the misting system will add humidity to the air and reduce the ability of the birds to lose heat by panting (Chirico et al., 2017).

Social Behaviour That Can Cause Stress or Injuries

The design and management of a lairage needs to consider the social behaviour of the animals. Different species should be penned separately. Ideally, animals should be kept in the same social groups that they were in when they were reared on the farm and then transported to slaughter. Mixing groups of either pigs or cattle together from different sources is likely to cause them to fight to establish a new social order. Animals likely to injure another animal should either be slaughtered as soon as possible or a fractious animal should be penned separately. Aggressive animals with horns or tusks capable of injuring other animals, breeding bulls and boars should be penned separately. Attention should also be given to ensuring that only animals of similar size are placed in the same pen. Sexual behaviour between entire boars or young bulls and between female cattle in oestrus can cause mounting, injury and poor meat quality (Kenny and Tarrant, 1988).

Either because insufficient numbers of pigs of the required weight range can be obtained from the same pen or because the size of the pens available during transport and lairage are often different from those used on farm, it can be difficult to avoid mixing different social groups of pigs (Guise and Penny, 1989; Grandin, 1990). If pigs are mixed, fighting can occur before loading, during transport and in lairage (Terlouw *et al.*, 2008; D'Eath *et al.*, 2010). If pigs are mixed, fighting during lairage can be reduced if the group size is kept low (Rabaste *et al.*, 2007), overcrowding is avoided, the period of fasting is not prolonged (Terlouw *et al.*, 2008), the pigs are kept in the dark and, if fed, sufficient feed is offered to reduce aggression at feeding (Barnett et al., 1994). Most of the fighting occurs within the first hour after arrival in the lairage (Moss, 1978). Temporarily dividing large lairage pens to keep pigs in small groups can reduce aggression (Faucitano, 2001). Some pigs are more aggressive than others, and unless these pigs are removed, they can cause increased fighting and skin damage (D'Eath *et al.*, 2010). Mixing pigs can decrease muscle pH_{45}, and increase skin damage, muscle pH_u and the risk of DFD pork (Guise and Penny, 1989; Karlsson and Lundstrom, 1992; D'Souza *et al.*, 1999). However, if pigs are not mixed, fighting is not common and most pigs lie down with in 1–2 h of arrival (Moss, 1978).

Social interactions, such as mounting and aggression, between young bulls are such a problem that keeping them in groups in a lairage should be avoided. If lairage is necessary, mixing should be avoided, the duration should be kept as short as possible, and mounting and aggressive behaviour reduced by keeping the animals in lowered light intensity or by providing an overhead barrier or electric grid (Kenny and Tarrant, 1987; Bartos *et al.*, 1988). If young bulls from different social groups are penned together, there is vigorous agonistic activity and mounting (Warriss *et al.*, 1984). This exercise increases muscle pH_{24} and causes DFD meat (Franc *et al.*, 1988; Bartos *et al.*, 1993). There is increased bruising, greater plasma creatine kinase activity and greater plasma cortisol concentration (Kenny and Tarrant, 1987).

Space Requirements in the Lairage

The design capacity of a lairage is affected by the number and type of animals required to be present at any one time, the number and size of pens required for holding animals while the slaughter line is operational, the space required to provide facilities for resting, drinking and feeding overnight, and the capacity of the ventilation system (Chirico *et al.*, 2017). If the stocking density exceeds the capacity of the ventilation system to remove metabolic heat, the animals could experience heat stress (Weeks, 2008). It is good practice to set and label each pen with maximum and minimum stocking rates and provide a temporary label indicating the date and time of arrival of the animals in the pen (Chirico *et al.*, 2017). The stocking density refers to the number or live weight of animals within a specified floor space, e.g. number of animals/m^2 or kg/m^2. Space allowance refers to the floor space provided per animal, e.g. m^2/animal. Space allowance ranges are specified depending on the weight and type of animal.

For livestock, the amount of space that an animal requires in a lairage depends to some extent on the length of time that it will remain there, as this affects what behaviour they need to perform (Petherick, 2007). For lairage lasting only a few minutes, an animal might require little more space that it occupies. For normal lairage lasting for more than a few minutes, each animal will require sufficient space to be able to rest, stand up, lie down, turn around, drink and thermoregulate. If held overnight they would normally require additional space to access feed. An estimation of the amount

Table 4.2. Minimal recommended space allowances for animals in lairages (adapted from Chirico *et al.*, 2017).

Type of animal	Weight (kg)	Presence of horns	Duration in lairage (h)	Space allowance (m²/animal)
Calves	200		< 3	0.7–0.8
			> 3	0.9–1
Cattle	550		< 3	1.4–1.5
			> 3	1.8–1.9
	700		< 3	1.6–1.7
			> 3	2.0–2.2
	< 150			≥ 1.5
	150–220			≥ 1.7
	> 220			≥ 1.8
		Without horns		≥ 2
		With horns		≥ 2.3
Piglets	25			0.14
Sows				> 1
Adult pigs other than sow or boar	115		< 12	≥ 0.5
			> 12	0.65
Lambs				≥ 0.25
Ewes	45–60			1.1–1.2
	60–90			1.2–1.4
Rams				1.5–2.0

of space that an animal will occupy can be approximated from its size and shape using the equation:

$$\text{surface area (m}^2) = k\,W^{2/3}$$

where W is the weight of the animal (kg), and k is a constant (Petherick, 2007). The estimate for this constant varies between 0.019 if sufficient space is required for just sternal recumbency or standing and 0.047 if sufficient space is allocated for lateral recumbency. The linear space (m) required for feeding and drinking from a trough can be estimated from length $= 0.064\,W^{0.33}$. However, this length will be affected by factors such as the competition for feed or water (Petherick, 2007). Table 4.2 gives minimal recommended space allowances.

Rest and Holding Time in the Lairage

Although it has been traditional practice to provide a period of rest before slaughter, lairages may not always provide an ideal environment for animals to rest. After arrival in a novel environment, animals can take several days before they adopt a normal sleeping pattern (Ruckebusch, 1975). Livestock can rest when lying down with their head raised, but for sleep they adopt a relaxed posture with reduced muscle tone and with their head resting (Merrick and Scharp, 1971). Their sleep is polyphasic in that they sleep in short periods rather than in one long period each 24 h (Ruckebusch, 1972; Ternman *et al.*, 2012). In a quiet environment, ruminants and pigs spend a large proportion of the day lying down (Ruckebusch, 1972). Before they sleep, they pass through a state of drowsiness that is characterized by a lack of behavioural activity and a low threshold of arousal (Ruckebusch, 1975; Campbell and Tobler, 1984). During this state, their rest can easily be disturbed by activity in the lairage (Tobler *et al.*, 1991). Most lying behaviour tends to occur during the evening and night when there is minimal human activity, with many animals standing up when human activity starts in the morning. To avoid disturbance of rest, it is preferable to avoid moving groups between pens (Jarvis *et al.*, 1996). The lighting in a lairage should be uniform and diffuse with sufficient intensity to enable inspection, but during the night the lighting should be dimmed to facilitate rest (Chirico *et al.*, 2017). Although they remain awake for long periods during the night, livestock sleep more during the night than during the day. When there is less activity during the day, they can also have some bouts of sleeping (Ruckebusch, 1975; Robert and Dallaire, 1986; Tobler *et al.*, 1991). Blue lighting is preferable for poultry (Adamczuk *et al.*, 2014). Poultry can rest while standing or sitting in a crouching posture with the neck withdrawn, tail lowered and sometimes with the wings drooping. Their posture is similar for sleeping, but their head is tucked into the feathers above the wingbase or behind the wing (Blokhuis, 1984).

How quickly animals start to lie down and for how long is likely to depend on factors such as the availability of feed, the novelty of the lairage environment, their degree of fatigue, disturbance from other animals, noise and human activity, the space provided, time spent drinking and the presence of bedding or the type of floor surface (Cockram, 1990, 1991; Kim et al., 1994; Jarvis and Cockram, 1995; Lebret et al., 2006; Barton Gade, 2008; Jongman et al., 2008; Torrey et al., 2013). Some animals lie down immediately after arrival in a lairage, but many take several hours to lie down, with the amount of lying increasing with increased duration in the lairage.

If the animals are kept in the lairage for longer than a few hours, a comfortable floor surface with low thermal conductivity should be provided to facilitate rest (Gordon and Cockram, 1995; Færevik et al., 2005). This can be achieved by providing bedding, such as straw or sometimes wood shavings (Small et al., 2007), or a soft surface such as rubber slats or mats. Where bedding is provided, it should be maintained in a condition that minimizes food safety risks from infection or surface contamination (Small et al., 2007). If animals are kept overnight, a solid, dry lying area should be provided.

Lairages can be noisier than many of the on-farm environments where the animals were reared (e.g. between 76 and 110 dB) (Talling et al., 1998; Weeks et al., 2009) and this can disturb the ability of animals to rest and can contribute to the stress experienced during lairage (Chloupek et al., 2009; Vermeulen et al., 2015). Livestock can respond to higher sound frequencies than humans (humans 20–20,000 Hz, cattle 25–35,000 Hz and pigs 42–40,500 Hz) (Weeks et al., 2009). The hearing range of broilers is 60–11,950 Hz (Hou et al., 1973).

There are several potential sources of noise in the lairage:

- vocalization of animals and people;
- slaughter and shackling equipment;
- movement of animals between and in and out of pens;
- opening and closing of metal gates;
- ventilation fans; and
- high-pressure water hoses (Talling et al., 1996, 1998; Weeks et al., 2009; Chirico et al., 2017).

Lairages tend to be quieter overnight when there is less activity than during the day (Weeks et al., 2009). Lairages should be designed and materials selected to minimize noise, such as the use of rubber baffles on doors and gates. However, due to the requirement to keep the lairage clean, surfaces in the lairage are hard and amplify sound. Separation of noisy activities, e.g. vehicle washing, away from the lairage is beneficial (Chirico et al., 2017).

Food Safety and Hygiene Procedures in the Lairage

The management of the lairage is influenced by food safety protocols to reduce the risk of contamination of the meat with bacteria such as *Escherichia coli* O157, salmonella and campylobacter. For example, there is a physical separation between the lairage and the 'clean' slaughter area of the plant to avoid direct movement of people, live animals and equipment between these areas. As livestock and poultry can be carriers of zoonotic bacteria, such as salmonella in their faeces, and these bacteria can be passed between groups in the lairage, cleaning and disinfection procedures are undertaken in the lairage to reduce surface contamination (Schmidt et al., 2004; Buncic and Sofos, 2012; Mannion et al., 2012; De Busser et al., 2013). This requirement means that surfaces should be easy to clean and made of hard materials, such as concrete and metal (Small et al., 2003). Roughened, grooved or smooth concrete, and concrete or metal slats are common types of floor surface used in lairages (Small et al., 2007). In pig lairages, salmonella contamination is lower where a slatted floor is used compared with a solid floor (Hurd et al., 2005). Cleaning and disinfection practices and the frequency of use of pressure washing or steam-cleaning vary between lairages (Small et al., 2007). To reduce bacterial contamination between groups, pens should be left to dry after cleaning and disinfection (Walia et al., 2017). Several lairage management practices are designed to reduce the risk of carcass contamination. Reducing the time spent in the lairage reduces the risk of the spread of infections between animals in the lairage. Whenever possible, animals are fasted in the lairage to limit defecation and coat contamination and the risk of spillage of gut contents during dressing procedures, but offering hay to cattle can reduce the risk of coat contamination with *Escherichia coli* O157 (Mather *et al.*, 2007, 2008). Hygiene practices that involve the removal of bedding between batches can restrict the use of bedding. However, the provision of bedding and providing time for wet and dirty coats to dry is sometimes used to improve the cleanliness of animals before slaughter. Alternatively, dirty animals might be slaughtered separately, the hair may be clipped, or the animals cleaned on arrival in a water bath or shower (Byrne *et al.*, 2007; McCleery *et al.*, 2008).

References

Aaslyng, M.D. and Barton Gade, P. (2001) Low stress pre-slaughter handling: effect of lairage time on the meat quality of pork. *Meat Science* 57, 87–92. doi: 10.1016/S0309-1740(00)00081-4

Adamczuk, G.O., Trentin, M.G., Lima, J.D., Motta, J. and Cantelli, R.P. (2014) Lighting in the shackling area: conciliating broiler welfare with labor comfort. *Brazilian Journal of Poultry Science* 16, 87–91.

Al-Dawood, A. (2017) Towards heat stress management in small ruminants – a review. *Annals of Animal Science* 17, 59–88.

Allain, V., Salines, M., Le Bouquin, S. and Magras, C. (2018) Designing an innovative warning system to support risk-based meat inspection in poultry slaughterhouses. *Food Control* 89, 177–186. doi: 10.1016/j.foodcont.2018.02.003

Aly, S.S., Rossow, H.A., Acetoze, G., Lehenbauer, T.W., Payne, M. *et al.* (2014) Survey of beef quality assurance on California dairies. *Journal of Dairy Science* 97, 1348–1357. doi: 10.3168/jds.2013-6856

Anderson, D., Ivers, D.J., Benjamin, M., Gonyou, H.W., Jones, D.J. *et al.* (2002) Physiological responses of market hogs to different handling practices. In: *Proceedings of the 33rd Annual Meeting of the American Association of Swine Veterinarians*. Kansas City, Missouri, pp. 399–401.

Angell, J.W., Cripps, P.J., Grove-White, D. and Duncan, J.S. (2015) A practical tool for locomotion scoring in sheep: Reliability when used by veterinary surgeons and sheep farmers. *Veterinary Record* 176, 521. doi: 10.1136/vr.102882

Appelt, M. and Sperry, J. (2007) Stunning and killing cattle humanely and reliably in emergency situations – a comparison between a stunning-only and a stunning and pithing protocol. *Canadian Veterinary Journal-Revue Veterinaire Canadienne* 48, 529–534.

Averos, X., Herranz, A., Sanchez, R., Commella, J.X. and Gosalvez, L.F. (2007) Serum stress parameters in pigs transported to slaughter under commercial conditions in different seasons. *Veterinarni Medicina* 52, 333–342.

Averos, X., Knowles, T.G., Brown, S.N., Warriss, P.D. and Gosalvez, L.F. (2008) Factors affecting the mortality of pigs being transported to slaughter. *Veterinary Record* 163, 386–390.

Bader, S., Meyer-Kühling, B., Günther, R., Breithaupt, A., Rautenschlein, S. and Gruber, A.D. (2014) Anatomical and histologic pathology induced by cervical dislocation following blunt head trauma for on-farm euthanasia of poultry. *Journal of Applied Poultry Research* 23, 546–556. doi: 10.3382/japr.2014-00977

Barnett, J.L., Cronin, G.M., McCallum, T.H. and Newman, E.A. (1994) Effects of food and time of day on aggression when grouping unfamiliar adult pigs. *Applied Animal Behaviour Science* 39, 339–347.

Barton Gade, P. (2008) Effect of rearing system and mixing at loading on transport and lairage behaviour and meat quality: Comparison of free range and conventionally raised pigs. *Animal* 2, 1238–1246. doi: 10.1017/S1751731108002565

Bartoš, L., Franc, Č., Albiston, G. and Beber, K. (1988) Prevention of dark-cutting (DFD) beef in penned bulls at the abattoir. *Meat Science* 22, 213–220. doi: 10.1016/0309-1740(88)90048-4

Bartoš, L., Franc, Č., Řehák, D. and Štípková (1993) A practical method to prevent dark-cutting (DFD) in beef. *Meat Science* 34, 275–282. doi: 10.1016/0309-1740(93)90077-U

Bascom, S.S. and Young, A.J. (1998) A summary of the reasons why farmers cull cows. *Journal of Dairy Science* 81, 2299–2305.

Beaudeau, F., Seegers, H., Ducrocq, V., Fourichon, C. and Bareille, N. (2000) Effect of health disorders on culling in dairy cows: a review and a critical discussion. *Annales De Zootechnie (Paris)* 49, 293–311.

Becerril-Herrera, M., Mota-Rojas, D., Guerrero-Legarreta, I., González-Lozano, M., Sánchez-Aparicio, P. *et al.* (2007) Effects of additional space during transport on pre-slaughter traits of pigs. *Journal of Biological Sciences* 7, 1112–1120. doi: 10.3923/jbs.2007.1112.1120

Berg, C., Yngvesson, J., Nimmermark, S., Sandström, V. and Algers, B. (2014) Killing of spent laying hens using CO_2 in poultry barns. *Animal Welfare* 23, 445–457. doi: 10.7120/09627286.23.4.445

Berman, A. (2019) An overview of heat stress relief with global warming in perspective. *International Journal of Biometeorology* 63, 493–498. doi: 10.1007/s00484-019-01680-7

Bewley, J.M., Peacock, A.M., Lewis, O., Boyce, R.E., Roberts, D.J. *et al.* (2008) Potential for estimation of body condition scores in dairy cattle from digital images. *Journal of Dairy Science* 91, 3439–3453.

Bianchi, M., Petracci, M. and Cavani, C. (2006) The influence of genotype, market live weight, transportation, and holding conditions prior to slaughter on broiler breast meat color. *Poultry Science* 85, 123–128.

Blair, B. and Lowe, J. (2019) Describing the cull sow market network in the US: A pilot project. *Preventive Veterinary Medicine* 162, 107–109. doi: 10.1016/j.prevetmed.2018.11.005

Blokhuis, H.J. (1984) Rest in poultry. *Applied Animal Behaviour Science* 12, 289–303. doi: 10.1016/0168-1591(84)90121-7

Booth, C.J., Warnick, L.D. Grohn, Y.T., Maizon, D.O., Guard, C.L. and Janssen, D. (2004) Effect of lameness on culling in dairy cows. *Journal of Dairy Science* 87, 4115–4122.

Brown, S.N., Knowles, T.G., Edwards, J.E. and Warriss, P.D. (1999a) Behavioural and physiological responses of pigs to being transported for up to 24 hours followed by six hours recovery in lairage. *Veterinary Record* 145, 421–429.

Brown, S.N., Knowles, T.G., Edwards, J.E. and Warriss, P.D. (1999b) Relationship between food deprivation before transport and aggression in pigs held in lairage before slaughter. *The Veterinary Record* 145, 630–634. doi: 10.1136/vr.145.22.630

Bueno, L.S., Caldara, F.R., Nääs, I.A., Salgado, D.D., García, R.G. and Almeida Paz, I.C.L. (2013) Swine carcass condemnation in commercial slaughterhouses. *Revista MVZ Córdoba* 18, 3836–3842.

Buncic, S. and Sofos, J. (2012) Interventions to control salmonella contamination during poultry, cattle and pig slaughter. *Food Research International; Salmonella in Foods: Evolution, Strategies and Challenges* 45, 641–655. doi: 10.1016/j.foodres.2011.10.018

Byrne, B., Dunne, G., Lyng, J. and Bolton, D.J. (2007) The development of a 'clean sheep policy' in compliance with the new Hygiene Regulation (EC) 853/2004 (Hygiene 2). *Food Microbiology* 24, 301–304. doi: 10.1016/j.fm.2006.04.009

Caffrey, N.P., Dohoo, I.R. and Cockram, M.S. (2017) Factors affecting mortality risk during transportation of broiler chickens for slaughter in Atlantic Canada. *Preventive Veterinary Medicine* 147, 199–208. 10.1016/j.prevetmed.2017.09.011

Campbell, S.S. and Tobler, I. (1984) Animal sleep – a review of sleep duration across phylogeny. *Neuroscience and Biobehavioral Reviews* 8, 269–300.

Campler, M.R., Pairis-Garcia, M.D., Rault, J.-L., Coleman, G. and Arruda, A.G. (2018) Caretaker attitudes toward swine euthanasia. *Translational Animal Science* 2, 254–262. doi: 10.1093/tas/txy015

Chauvin, C., Hillion, S., Balaine, L., Michel, V., Peraste, J. *et al.* (2011) Factors associated with mortality of broilers during transport to slaughterhouse. *Animal* 5, 287–293. doi: 10.1017/S1751731110001916

Chirico, S., Etienne, J., Jarvis, A., McEntaggart, K., Shah, P. *et al.* (2017) *Preparation of Best Practices on the Protection of Animals at the Time of Killing - Final Report.* European Commission, Brussels, Belgium. doi: 10.2875/15243

Chiumia, D., Chagunda, M.G.G., MacRae, A.I. and Roberts, D.J. (2013) Predisposing factors for involuntary culling in Holstein-Friesian dairy cows. *Journal of Dairy Research* 80, 45–50. doi: 10.1017/S002202991200060X

Chloupek, P., Voslářová, E., Chloupek, J., Bedáňová, I., Pištěková, V. and Večerek, V. (2009) Stress in broiler chickens due to acute noise exposure. *Acta Veterinaria Brno* 78, 93–98. doi: 10.2754/avb200978010093

Cleveland-Nielsen, A., Christensen, G. and Ersboll, A.K. (2004) Prevalences of welfare-related lesions at post-mortem meat-inspection in Danish sows. *Preventive Veterinary Medicine* 64, 123–131. doi: 10.1016/j.prevetmed.2004.05.003 ER

Čobanović, N., Karabasil, N., Stajković, S., Ilić, N., Suvajdžić, B. *et al.* (2016) The influence of pre-mortem conditions on pale, soft and exudative (PSE) and dark firm and dry (DFD) pork meat. *Acta Veterinaria* 66, 172–186. doi: 10.1515/acve-2016-0015

Cockram, M.S. (1990) Some factors influencing behaviour of cattle in a slaughterhouse lairage. *Animal Production* 50, 475–481.

Cockram, M.S. (1991) Resting behaviour of cattle in a slaughterhouse lairage. *British Veterinary Journal* 147, 109–119. doi: 10.1016/0007-1935(91)90100-2

Cockram, M.S. (2019) Fitness of animals for transport to slaughter. *The Canadian Veterinary Journal-Revue Veterinaire Canadienne* 60, 423–429.

Cockram, M.S. and Dulal, K.J. (2018) Injury and mortality in broilers during handling and transport to slaughter. *Canadian Journal of Animal Science* 98, 416–432. doi: 10.1139/cjas-2017-0076

Cockram, M.S., Kent, J.E., Waran, N.K., McGilp, I.M., Jackson, R.E. *et al.* (1999) Effects of a 15h journey followed by either 12h starvation or ad libitum hay on the behaviour and blood chemistry of sheep. *Animal Welfare* 8, 135–148.

Cockram, M.S., Dulal, K.J., Mohamed, R.A. and Revie, C.W. (2019) Risk factors for bruising and mortality of broilers during manual handling, module loading, transport, and lairage. *Canadian Journal of Animal Science* 99, 50–65. doi: 10.1139/cjas-2018-0032

Collier, R. and Gebremedhin, K.G. (2015) Thermal biology of domestic animals. *Annual Review of Animal Biosciences* 3, 10.1–10.20. doi: 10.1146/annurev-animal-022114-110659

Correa, J.A., Gonyou, H.W., Torrey, S., Widowski, T., Bergeron, R. *et al.* (2013) Welfare and carcass and meat quality of pigs being transported for two hours using two vehicle types during two seasons of the year. *Canadian Journal of Animal Science* 93, 43–55. doi: 10.4141/CJAS2012-088

Cors, J.-C., Gruber, A.D., Gunther, R., Meyer-Kuhling, B., Esser, K.-H. and Rautenschlein, S. (2015) Electro-encephalographic evaluation of the effectiveness of blunt trauma to induce loss of consciousness for on-farm killing of chickens and turkeys. *Poultry Science* 94, 147–155. doi: 10.3382/ps/peu038

Cullinane, M., O'Sullivan, E., Collins, G., Collins, D.M. and More, S.J. (2010) A review of bovine cases consigned under veterinary certification to emergency and casualty slaughter in Ireland during 2006 to 2008. *Irish Veterinary Journal* 63, 568–577.

Cullinane, M., O'Sullivan, E., Collins, G., Collins, D.M. and More, S.J. (2012) Veterinary certificates for emergency or casualty slaughter bovine animals in the Republic of Ireland: Are the welfare needs of certified animals adequately protected? *Animal Welfare* 21, 61–67. doi: 10.7120/096272812X13353700593563

Dadgar, S., Lee, E.S., Leer, T.L.V., Crowe, T.G., Classen, H.L. and Shand, P.J. (2011) Effect of acute cold exposure, age, sex, and lairage on broiler breast meat quality. *Poultry Science* 90, 444–457.

Dadgar, S., Crowe, T.G., Classen, H.L., Watts, J.M. and Shand, P.J. (2012) Broiler chicken thigh and breast muscle responses to cold stress during simulated transport before slaughter. *Poultry Science* 91, 1454–1464.

Dahl-Pedersen, K., Foldager, L., Herskin, M.S., Houe, H. and Thomsen, P.T. (2018a) Lameness scoring and assessment of fitness for transport in dairy cows: agreement among and between farmers, veterinarians and livestock drivers. *Research in Veterinary Science* 119, 162–166. doi: 10.1016/j.rvsc.2018.06.017

Dahl-Pedersen, K., Herskin, M.S., Houe, H. and Thomsen, P.T. (2018b) Risk factors for deterioration of the clinical condition of cull dairy cows during transport to slaughter. *Frontiers in Veterinary Science* 5. doi: 10.3389/fvets.2018.00297

Dahl-Pedersen, K., Herskin, M.S., Houe, H. and Thomsen, P.T. (2018c) A descriptive study of the clinical condition of cull dairy cows before transport to slaughter. *Livestock Science* 218, 108–113. doi: 10.1016/j.livsci.2018.11.001

Dalla Costa, F.A., Dalla Costa, O.A., Coldebella, A., de Lima, G.J.M.M. and Ferraudo, A.S. (2018) How do season, on-farm fasting interval and lairage period affect swine welfare, carcass and meat quality traits? *International Journal of Biometeorology* 1–9. doi: 10.1007/s00484-018-1527-1

Dalla Costa, F.A., Gibson, T.J., Oliveira, S.E.O., Gregory, N.G., Coldebella, A. *et al.* (2019) On-farm pig dispatch methods and stockpeople attitudes on their use. *Livestock Science* 221, 1–5. doi: 10.1016/j.livsci.2019.01.007

Dalmau, A., Temple, D., Rodríguez, P., Llonch, P. and Velarde, A. (2009) Application of the Welfare Quality® protocol at pig slaughterhouses. *Animal Welfare* 18, 497–505.

Dalmau, A., Nande, A., Vieira-Pinto, M., Zamprogna, S., Di Martino, G. *et al.* (2016) Application of the Welfare Quality® protocol in pig slaughterhouses of five countries. *Livestock Science* 193, 78–87. doi: 10.1016/j.livsci.2016.10.001

D'Eath, R.B., Turner, S.P., Kurt, E., Evans, G., Thölking, L. *et al.* (2010) Pigs' aggressive temperament affects pre-slaughter mixing aggression, stress and meat quality. *Animal* 4, 604–616. doi: 10.1017/S1751731109991406

De Busser, E.V., De Zutter, L., Dewulf, J., Houf, K. and Maes, D. (2013) Salmonella control in live pigs and at slaughter. *Veterinary Journal* 196, 20–27. doi: 10.1016/j.tvjl.2013.01.002

De Smet, S.M., Pauwels, H., De Bie, S., Demeyer, D.I., Callewier, J. and Eeckhout, W. (1996) Effect of halothane genotype, breed, feed withdrawal, and lairage on pork quality of Belgian slaughter pigs. *Journal of Animal Science* 74, 1854–1863. doi: 10.2527/1996.7481854x

Deimel, M. and Theuvsen, L. (2011) Networking in meat production systems: the influence of cooperative structures on farmers' participation. *International Journal on Food System Dynamics* 2, 23–35.

del Campo, M., Brito, G., Soares de Lima, J., Hernández, P. and Montossi, F. (2010) Finishing diet, temperament and lairage time effects on carcass and meat quality traits in steers. *Meat Science* 86, 908–914. doi: 10.1016/j.meatsci.2010.07.014

Derscheid, R.J., Dewell, R.D., Dewell, G.A., Kleinhenz, K.E., Shearer, L.C. *et al.* (2016) Validation of a portable pneumatic captive bolt device as a one-step method of euthanasia for use in depopulation of feedlot cattle. *Journal of the American Veterinary Medical Association* 248, 96–104.

Devitt, C., Boyle, L., Teixeira, D.L., O'Connell, N.E., Hawe, M. and Hanlon, A. (2016) Pig producer perspectives on the use of meat inspection as an animal health and welfare diagnostic tool in the Republic of Ireland and Northern Ireland. *Irish Veterinary Journal* 69, 2. doi: 10.1186/s13620-015-0057-y

Di Martino, G., Capello, K., Russo, E., Mazzucato, M., Mulatti, P. *et al.* (2017) Factors associated with pre-slaughter mortality in turkeys and end of lay hens. *Animal* 11, 2295–2300. doi: 10.1017/S1751731117000970

Díaz, M.T., Vieira, C., Pérez, C., Lauzurica, S., de Chávarri, E.G. *et al.* (2014) Effect of lairage time (0h, 3h, 6h or 12h) on glycogen content and meat quality parameters in suckling lambs. *Meat Science* 96, 653–660. doi: 10.1016/j.meatsci.2013.10.013

Dokmanović, M., Velarde, A., Tomović, V., Glamoclija, N., Marković, R. *et al.* (2014) The effects of lairage time and handling procedure prior to slaughter on stress and meat quality parameters in pigs. *Meat Science* 98, 220–226. doi: 10.1016/j.meatsci.2014.06.003

Doonan, G., Benard, G. and Cormier, N. (2014) Livestock and poultry fitness for transport – the veterinarian's role. *Canadian Veterinary Journal-Revue Veterinaire Canadienne* 55, 589–590.

D'Souza, D.N., Dunshea, F.R., Leury, B.J. and Warner, R.D. (1999) Effect of mixing boars during lairage and pre-slaughter handling on pork quality. *Australian Journal of Agricultural Research* 50, 109–113. doi: 10.1071/A98059

Dyer, R.M., Neerchal, N.K., Tasch, U., Wu, Y., Dyer, P. and Rajkondawar, P.G. (2007) Objective determination of claw pain and its relationship to limb locomotion score in dairy cattle. *Journal of Dairy Science* 90, 4592–4602. doi: 10.3168/jds.2007-0006 ER

Edwards-Callaway, L., Calvo-Lorenzo, M., Scanga, J.A. and Grandin, T. (2017) Mobility scoring of finished cattle. *Veterinary Clinics: Food Animal Practice* 33, 235–250. doi: 10.1016/j.cvfa.2017.02.006

Edwards-Callaway, L., Walker, J. and Tucker, C.B. (2019) Culling decisions and dairy cattle welfare during transport to slaughter in the United States. *Frontiers in Veterinary Science* 5. doi: 10.3389/fvets.2018.00343

Engblom, L., Lundeheim, N., Dalin, A.-M. and Andersson, K. (2007) Sow removal in Swedish commercial herds. *Livestock Science* 106, 76–86. doi: 10.1016/j.livsci.2006.07.002

Engblom, L., Eliasson-Selling, L., Lundeheim, N., Belák, K., Andersson, K. and Dalin, A.-M. (2008) Post mortem findings in sows and gilts euthanised or found dead in a large Swedish herd. *Acta Veterinaria Scandinavica* 50, 25. doi: 10.1186/1751-0147-50-25

Eurogroup for Animals, UECBV, Animals' Angels, ELT, FVE and IRU (2012) Practical Guidelines to Assess Fitness for Transport of Adult Bovines. Available at: https://www.agriculture.gov.ie/media/migration/animalhealthwelfare/transportofliveanimals/GuidelinesAssessFitnessTransportBovines050716.pdf (accessed 15 April 2020).

Eurogroup for Animals, UECBV, Animals' Angels, Cooperl Arc Atlantique, Copa-Cogeca *et al.* (2015) Practical Guidelines to Assess Fitness for Transport of Pigs. Available at: https://www.agriculture.gov.ie/media/migration/animalhealthwelfare/transportofliveanimals/GuidelinesAssessFitnessTranposrtPigs050716.pdf (accessed 15 April 2020).

European Commission (2016) Overview Report on Systems to Prevent the Transport of Unfit Animals in the European Union. Directorate for Health and Food Audits and Analysis (Directorate-General for Health and Food Safety). Available at: https://publications.europa.eu/en/publication-detail/-/publication/2bdfe42c-e33f-409e-8f02-4f0308205ede/language-en. doi: 10.2875/669512

Fabrega, E., Diestre, A., Carrion, D., Font, J. and Manteca, X. (2002) Effect of the halothane gene on pre-slaughter mortality in two Spanish commercial pig abattoirs. *Animal Welfare* 11, 449–452.

Færevik, G., Andersen, I.L. and Bøe, K.E. (2005) Preferences of sheep for different types of pen flooring. *Applied Animal Behaviour Science* 90, 265–276.

Faucitano, L. (2001) Causes of skin damage to pig carcasses. *Canadian Journal of Animal Science* 81, 39–45.

Faucitano, L. (2010) Invited review: Effects of lairage and slaughter conditions on animal welfare and pork quality. *Canadian Journal of Animal Science* 90, 461–469. doi: 10.4141/CJAS10020

Ferguson, D.M., Shaw, F.D. and Stark, J.L. (2007) Effect of reduced lairage duration on beef quality. *Australian Journal of Experimental Agriculture* 47, 770–773. doi: 10.1071/EA05212

Fitzgerald, R.F., Stalder, K.J., Matthews, J.O., Schultz Kaster, C.M. and Johnson, A.K. (2009) Factors associated with fatigued, injured, and dead pig frequency during transport and lairage at a commercial abattoir. *Journal of Animal Science* 87, 1156–1166. doi: 10.2527/jas.2008-1270

Flower, F.C., Sedlbauer, M., Carter, E., Von Keyserlingk, M.A.G., Sanderson, D.J. and Weary, D.M. (2008) Analgesics improve the gait of lame dairy cattle. *Journal of Dairy Science* 91, 3010–3014.

Fogsgaard, K.K., Herskin, M.S. and Thodberg, K. (2018) Transportation of cull sows-a descriptive study of the clinical condition of cull sows before transportation to slaughter. *Translational Animal Science* 2, 280–289. doi: 10.1093/tas/txy057

Food Standards Agency (2018) *Manual for Official Controls* (MOC), Volume 1, Chapter 2.2: Ante-mortem inspection. Available at: https://www.food.gov.uk/sites/default/files/media/document/chapter-2.2-ante-mortem-inspection_0.pdf (accessed 12 February 2020).

Franc, C., Bartos, L., Hanys, Z. and Tomes, Z. (1988) Pre-slaughter social activity of young bulls relating to the occurrence of dark-cutting beef. *Animal Production* 46, 153–161.

Fraqueza, M.J., Roseiro, L.C., Almeida, J., Matias, E., Santos, C. and Randall, J.M. (1998) Effects of lairage temperature and holding time on pig behaviour and on carcass and meat quality. *Applied Animal Behaviour Science* 60, 317–330. doi: 10.1016/S0168-1591(98)00156-7

Fraser, D. (2003) Assessing animal welfare at the farm and group level: the interplay of science and values. *Animal Welfare* 12, 433–443.

Fraser, D., Weary, D.M., Pajor, E.A. and Milligan, B.N. (1997) A scientific conception of animal welfare that reflects ethical concerns. *Animal Welfare* 6, 187–205.

Freitas, A.S., Carvalho, L.M., Soares, A.L., Neto, A.C.S., Madruga, M.S. *et al.* (2016) Simultaneous occurrence of broiler chicken hyper and hypothermia in-transit and lairage and dead on arrival (DOA) index under tropical climate. *International Journal of Poultry Science* 15, 459–466. doi: 10.3923/ijps.2016.459.466

Frimpong, S., Gebresenbet, G., Bobobee, E., Aklaku, E.D. and Hamdu, I. (2014) Effect of transportation and pre-slaughter handling on welfare and meat quality of cattle: case study of Kumasi abattoir, Ghana. *Veterinary Sciences* 1, 174–191. doi: 10.3390/vetsci1030174

Fusi, F., Angelucci, A., Lorenzi, V., Bolzoni, L. and Bertocchi, L. (2017) Assessing circumstances and causes of dairy cow death in Italian dairy farms through a veterinary practice survey (2013–2014).

M. Cockram

Preventive Veterinary Medicine 137, 105–108. doi: 10.1016/j.prevetmed.2017.01.004

Gallo, C.B. and Huertas, S.M. (2016) Main animal welfare problems in ruminant livestock during preslaughter operations: a South American view. *Animal* 10, 357–364.

Gallo, C., Lizondo, G. and Knowles, T.G. (2003) Effects of journey and lairage time on steers transported to slaughter in Chile. *Veterinary Record* 152, 361–364. doi: 10.1136/vr.152.12.361

Gaughan, J.B., Mader, T.L., Holt, S.M. and Lisle, A. (2008) A new heat load index for feedlot cattle. *Journal of Animal Science* 86, 226–234. doi: 10.2527/jas.2007-0305

Genç, L. and Portier, K.M. (2005) Sensible and latent heat productions from broilers in laboratory conditions. *Turkish Journal of Veterinary and Animal Sciences* 29, 635–643.

Gilliam, J.N., Woods, J., Hill, J., Shearer, J.K., Reynolds, J. and Taylor, J.D. (2018) Evaluation of the CASH dispatch kit combined with alternative shot placement landmarks as a single-step euthanasia method for cattle of various ages. *Animal Welfare* 27, 225–233. doi: 10.7120/09627286.27.3.225

Gleeson, M. (1985) Analysis of respiratory pattern during panting in fowl, *Gallus domesticus*. *Journal of Experimental Biology* 116, 487–491.

Goldhawk, C., Janzen, E., Gonzalez, L.A., Crowe, T., Kastelic, J. *et al.* (2015) Trailer temperature and humidity during winter transport of cattle in Canada and evaluation of indicators used to assess the welfare of cull beef cows before and after transport. *Journal of Animal Science* 93, 3639–3653. doi: 10.2527/jas.2014-8390

González, L.A., Schwartzkopf-Genswein, K., Bryan, M., Silasi, R. and Brown, F. (2012) Relationships between transport conditions and welfare outcomes during commercial long haul transport of cattle in North America. *Journal of Animal Science* 90, 3640–3651.

Gordon, G.D.H. and Cockram, M.S. (1995) A comparison of wooden slats and straw bedding on the behaviour of sheep. *Animal Welfare* 4, 131–134.

Gortel, K., Schaefer, A.L., Young, B.A. and Kawamoto, S.C. (1992) Effects of transport stress and electrolyte supplementation on body-fluids and weights of bulls. *Canadian Journal of Animal Science* 72, 547–553.

Goumon, S., Brown, J.A., Faucitano, L., Bergeron, R., Widowski, T.M. *et al.* (2013) Effects of transport duration on maintenance behavior, heart rate and gastrointestinal tract temperature of market-weight pigs in 2 seasons. *Journal of Animal Science* 91, 4925–4935. doi: 10.2527/jas.2012-6081

Grandin, T. (1990) Design of loading facilities and holding pens. *Applied Animal Behaviour Science* 28, 187–201. doi: 10.1016/0168-1591(90)90053-G

Grandin, T. (2001) Perspectives on transportation issues: the importance of having physically fit cattle and pigs. *Journal of Animal Science* 79, E201–E207.

Grandin, T. (2016) Transport fitness of cull sows and boars: a comparison of different guidelines on fitness for transport. *Animals* 6. doi: 10.3390/ani6120077

Grandin, T. (2017) *Recommended Animal Handling Guidelines and Audit Guide: A Systematic Approach to Animal Welfare*. North American Meat Institute, Washington, DC.

Grandin, T. (2018) Welfare problems in cattle, pigs, and sheep that persist even though scientific research clearly shows how to prevent them. *Animals* 8, 124. doi: 10.3390/ani8070124

Green, A.L., Lombard, J.E., Garber, L.P., Wagner, B.A. and Hill, G.W. (2008) Factors associated with occurrence and recovery of nonambulatory dairy cows in the United States. *Journal of Dairy Science* 91, 2275–2283. doi: 10.3168/jds.2007-0869

Guàrdia, M.D., Estany, J., Balasch, S., Oliver, M.A., Gispert, M. and Diestre, A. (2009) Risk assessment of skin damage due to pre-slaughter conditions and RYR1 gene in pigs. *Meat Science* 81, 745–751. doi: 10.1016/j.meatsci.2008.11.020

Guise, H.J. and Penny, R.H.C. (1989) Factors influencing the welfare and carcass and meat quality of pigs. 2. Mixing unfamiliar pigs. *Animal Production* 49, 517–521.

Hadley, G.L., Wolf, C.A. and Harsh, S.B. (2006) Dairy cattle culling patterns, explanations, and implications. *Journal of Dairy Science* 89, 2286–2296. doi: 10.3168/jds.S0022-0302(06)72300-1

Hamrita, T.K. and Conway, R.H. (2016) Effect of air velocity on deep body temperature and weight gain in the broiler chicken. *The Journal of Applied Poultry Research* 26, 111–121. doi: 10.3382/japr/pfw051

Hamrita, T.K. and Conway, R.H. (2017) Effect of air velocity on deep body temperature and weight gain in the broiler chicken. *The Journal of Applied Poultry Research* 26, 111–121. doi: 10.3382/japr/pfw051e

Harley, S., More, S., Boyle, L., O'Connell, N. and Hanlon, A. (2012) Good animal welfare makes economic sense: potential of pig abattoir meat inspection as a welfare surveillance tool. *Irish Veterinary Journal* 65. doi: 10.1186/2046-0481-65-11

Harris, M.K., Eastwood, L.C., Boykin, C.A., Arnold, A.N., Gehring, K.B. *et al.* (2017) National Beef Quality Audit–2016: Transportation, mobility, live cattle, and carcass assessments of targeted producer-related characteristics that affect value of market cows and bulls, their carcasses, and associated by-products. *Translational Animal Science* 1, 570–584. doi: 10.2527/tas2017.0063

Harris, M.K., Eastwood, L.C., Boykin, C.A., Arnold, A.N., Gehring, K.B. *et al.* (2018) National Beef Quality Audit–2016: Assessment of cattle hide characteristics, offal condemnations, and carcass traits to determine the quality status of the market cow and bull beef industry. *Translational Animal Science* 2, 37–49. doi: 10.1093/tas/txx002

Herskin, M.S., Hels, A., Anneberg, I. and Thomsen, P.T. (2017) Livestock drivers' knowledge about dairy cow fitness for transport – a Danish questionnaire survey. *Research in Veterinary Science* 113, 62–66. doi: 10.1016/j.rvsc.2017.09.008

Hirvonen, J., Hietakorpi, S. and Saloniemi, H. (1997) Acute phase response in emergency slaughtered dairy cows. *Meat Science* 46, 249–257.

Hou, S.M., Boone, M.A. and Long, J.T. (1973) An electro-physiological study on the hearing and vocalization in *Gallus domesticus. Poultry Science* 52, 159–164.

Humane Slaughter Association (2016) Emergency Slaughter. Available at: https://www.hsa.org.uk/downloads/publications/emergencyslaughterdownload-updated-2016-logo.pdf

Hunter, R.R., Mitchell, M.A., Carlisle, A.J., Quinn, A.D., Kettlewell, P.J. et al. (1998) Physiological responses of broilers to pre-slaughter lairage: effects of the thermal micro-environment? *British Poultry Science* 39, S53–S54. doi: 10.1080/00071669888377

Hunter, R.R., Mitchell, M.A. and Carlisle, A.J. (1999) Wetting of broilers during cold weather transport: a major source of physiological stress? *British Poultry Science* 40, S48–S49. doi: 10.1080/00071669986828

Hurd, H.S., Gailey, J.K., McKean, J.D. and Griffith, R.W. (2005) Variable abattoir conditions affect *Salmonella enterica* prevalence and meat quality in swine and pork. *Foodborne Pathogens and Disease* 2, 77–81. doi: 10.1089/fpd.2005.2.77

Huynh, T.T.T., Aarnink, A.J.A., Verstegen, M.W.A., Gerrits, W.J.J., Heetkamp, M.J.W. et al. (2005) Effects of increasing temperatures on physiological changes in pigs at different relative humidities. *Journal of Animal Science* 83, 1385–1396.

Jackowiak, J., Kiermeier, A., Kolega, V., Missen, G., Reiser, D. and Pointon, A.M. (2006) Assessment of producer conducted antemortem inspection of market pigs in Australia. *Australian Veterinary Journal* 84, 351–357.

Jacob, R.H., Pethick, D.W., Clark, P., D'Souza, D.N., Hopkins, D.L. and White, J. (2006) Quantifying the hydration status of lambs in relation to carcass characteristics. *Australian Journal of Experimental Agriculture* 46, 429–437. doi: 10.1071/EA04093

Jacobs, L., Delezie, E., Duchateau, L., Goethals, K. and Tuyttens, F.A.M. (2017a) Animal well-being and behavior. Broiler chickens dead on arrival: associated risk factors and welfare indicators. *Poultry Science* 96, 259–265. doi: 10.3382/ps/pew353

Jacobs, L., Delezie, E., Duchateau, L., Goethals, K. and Tuyttens, F.A.M. (2017b) Impact of the separate pre-slaughter stages on broiler chicken welfare. *Poultry Science*, 96, 266-273. 10.3382/ps/pew361

Jacobs, L., Delezie, E., Duchateau, L., Goethals, K., Vermeulen, D. et al. (2017c) Fit for transport? Broiler chicken fitness assessment for transportation to slaughter. *Animal Welfare* 26, 335–343. doi: 10.7120/09627286.26.3.335

Jalakas, S., Elias, T. and Roasto, M. (2014) From farm to slaughterhouse. In: Ninios, T., Lundén, J., Korkeala, H. and Fredriksson-Ahomaa, M. (eds) *Meat Inspection and Control in the Slaughterhouse.* John Wiley & Sons, Marblehead, Massachusetts, pp. 5–17.

Jarvis, A.M. and Cockram, M.S. (1995) Some factors affecting resting behaviour of sheep in slaughter-house lairages after transport from farms. *Animal Welfare* 4, 53–60.

Jarvis, A.M., Harrington, D.W.J. and Cockram, M.S. (1996) Effect of source and lairage on some behavioural and biochemical measurements of feed restriction and dehydration in cattle at a slaughterhouse. *Applied Animal Behaviour Science* 50, 83–94. doi: 10.1016/0168-1591(96)01070-2

Jensen, T.B., Bonde, M.K., Kongsted, A.G., Toft, N. and Sørensen, J.T. (2010) The interrelationships between clinical signs and their effect on involuntary culling among pregnant sows in group-housing systems. *Animal* 4, 1922–1928. doi: 10.1017/S1751731110001102

Jongman, E.C., Edge, M.K., Butler, K.L. and Cronin, G.M. (2008) Reduced space allowance for adult sheep in lairage for 24 hours limits lying behaviour but not drinking behaviour. *Australian Journal of Experimental Agriculture* 48, 1048–1051. doi: 10.1071/EA08039

Karlsson, A. and Lundström, K. (1992) Meat quality in pigs reared in groups kept as a unit during the fattening period and slaughter. *Animal Production* 54, 421–426. doi: 10.1017/S0003356100020882

Kenny, F.J. and Tarrant, P.V. (1987) The behaviour of young Friesian bulls during social re-grouping at an abattoir. Influence of an overhead electrified wire grid. *Applied Animal Behaviour Science* 18, 233–246. doi: 10.1016/0168-1591(87)90219-X

Kenny, F.J. and Tarrant, P.V. (1988) The effect of oestrus behaviour on muscle glycogen concentration and dark-cutting in beef heifers. *Meat Science* 22, 21–31. doi: 10.1016/0309-1740(88)90024-1

Kephart, K.B., Harper, M.T. and Raines, C.R. (2010) Observations of market pigs following transport to a packing plant. *Journal of Animal Science* 88, 2199–2203. doi: 10.2527/jas.2009-2440

Kim, F.B., Jackson, R.E., Gordon, G.D.H. and Cockram, M.S. (1994) Resting behaviour of sheep in a slaughterhouse lairage. *Applied Animal Behaviour Science* 40, 45–54. doi: 10.1016/0168-1591(94)90086-8

Kittelsen, K.E., Granquist, E.G., Vasdal, G., Tolo, E. and Moe, R.O. (2015) Effects of catching and transportation versus pre-slaughter handling at the abattoir on the prevalence of wing fractures in broilers. *Animal Welfare* 24, 387–389. doi: 10.7120/09627286.24.4.387

Knauer, M., Stalder, K.J., Karriker, L., Baas, T.J., Johnson, C. et al. (2007) A descriptive survey of lesions from cull sows harvested at two Midwestern US facilities. *Preventive Veterinary Medicine* 82, 198–212. doi: 10.1016/j.prevetmed.2007.05.017

Knezacek, T.D., Olkowski, A.A., Kettlewell, P.J., Mitchell, M.A. and Classen, H.L. (2010) Temperature gradients in trailers and changes in broiler rectal and core body temperature during winter transportation in Saskatchewan. *Canadian Journal of Animal Science* 90, 321–330.

Knowles, T.G., Maunder, D.I.I., Warriss, P.D. and Jones, T.W. (1994) Factors affecting the mortality of lambs in transit to or in lairage at a slaughterhouse, and reasons for carcase condemnations. *Veterinary Record* 135, 109–111. doi: 10.1136/vr.135.5.109

Knowles, T.G., Brown, S.N., Edwards, J.E. and Warriss, P.D. (1998) Ambient temperature below which pigs should not be continuously showered in lairage. *Veterinary Record* 143, 575–578. doi: 10.1136/vr.143.21.575

Knowles, T.G., Warriss, P.D., Brown, S.N. and Edwards, J.E. (1999) Effects on cattle of transportation by road for up to 31 hours. *Veterinary Record* 145, 575–582. doi: 10.1136/vr.145.20.575

Koralesky, K.E. and Fraser, D. (2018) Use of on-farm emergency slaughter for dairy cows in British Columbia. *Journal of Dairy Science* 101, 6413–6418. doi: 10.3168/jds.2017-14320

Lahti, P. and Soini, J. (2014) Ante-mortem inspection. In: Ninios, T., Lundén, J., Korkeala, H. and Fredriksson-Ahomaa, M. (eds) *Meat Inspection and Control in the Slaughterhouse*. John Wiley & Sons, Marblehead, Massachusetts, pp. 19–28.

Langford, F.M. and Stott, A.W. (2012) Culled early or culled late: economic decisions and risks to welfare in dairy cows. *Animal Welfare* 21, 41–55. doi: 10.7120/096272812X13345905673647

Leary, S., Underwood, W., Anthony, R., Corey, D.G., Gwaltney-Brant, S. *et al.* (2016) *AVMA Guidelines for the Humane Slaughter of Animals*, 2016 edn. Available at: https://www.avma.org/KB/Resources/Reference/AnimalWelfare/Documents/Humane-Slaughter-Guidelines.pdf

LeBlanc, S.J., Lissemore, K.D., Kelton, D.F., Duffield, T.F. and Leslie, K.E. (2006) Major advances in disease prevention in dairy cattle. *Journal of Dairy Science* 89, 1267–1279.

Lebret, B., Meunier-Salaün, M.C., Foury, A., Mormède, P., Dransfield, E. and Dourmad, J.Y. (2006) Influence of rearing conditions on performance, behavioral, and physiological responses of pigs to preslaughter handling, carcass traits, and meat quality. *Journal of Animal Science* 84, 2436–2447. doi: 10.2527/jas.2005-689

Liotta, L., Costa, L.N., Chiofalo, B., Ravarotto, L. and Chiofalo, V. (2007) Effect of lairage duration on some blood constituents and beef quality in bulls after long journey. *Italian Journal of Animal Science* 6, 375–384.

Liste, G., Miranda-De, L.L., Campo, M.M., Villarroel, M., Muela, E. and Mara, G.A. (2011) Effect of lairage on lamb welfare and meat quality. *Animal Production Science* 51, 952–958. doi: 10.1071/AN10274

Liu, H.W., Zhong, R.Z., Zhou, D.W., Sun, H.X. and Zhao, C.S. (2012) Effects of lairage time after road transport on some blood indicators of welfare and meat quality traits in sheep. *Journal of Animal Physiology and Animal Nutrition* 96, 1127–1135. doi: 10.1111/j.1439-0396.2011.01230.x

Ljungberg, D., Gebresenbet, G. and Aradom, S. (2007) Logistics chain of animal transport and abattoir operations. *Biosystems Engineering* 96, 267–277. doi: 10.1016/j.biosystemseng.2006.11.003

Magalhães-Sant'Ana, M., More, S.J., Morton, D.B. and Hanlon, A.J. (2017) Challenges facing the veterinary profession in Ireland: 1. clinical veterinary services. *Irish Veterinary Journal* 70. doi: 10.1186/s13620-017-0096-7

Mannion, C., Fanning, J., McLernon, J., Lendrum, L., Gutierrez, M. *et al.* (2012) The role of transport, lairage and slaughter processes in the dissemination of Salmonella spp. in pigs in Ireland. *Food Research International* 45, 871–879. doi: 10.1016/j.foodres.2011.02.001

Mather, A.E., Innocent, G.T., McEwen, S.A., Reilly, W.J., Taylor, D.J. *et al.* (2007) Risk factors for hide contamination of Scottish cattle at slaughter with *Escherichia coli* O157. *Preventive Veterinary Medicine* 80, 257–270. doi: 10.1016/j.prevetmed.2007.02.011

Mather, A.E., Reid, S.W.J., McEwen, S.A., Ternent, H.E., Reid-Smith, R. *et al.* (2008) Factors associated with cross-contamination of hides of Scottish cattle by *Escherichia coli* O157. *Applied and Environmental Microbiology* 74, 6313–6319. doi: 10.1128/AEM.00770-08

McCleery, D.R., Stirling, J.M.E., McIvor, K. and Patterson, M.F. (2008) Effect of ante- and postmortem hide clipping on the microbiological quality and safety and ultimate pH value of beef carcasses in an EC-approved abattoir. *Journal of Applied Microbiology* 104, 1471–1479. doi: 10.1111/j.1365-2672.2007.03670.x

McConnel, C.S., Garry, F.B., Hill, A.E., Lombard, J.E. and Gould, D.H. (2010) Conceptual modeling of postmortem evaluation findings to describe dairy cow deaths. *Journal of Dairy Science* 93, 373–386. doi: 10.3168/jds.2009-2296

McGee, M., Parsons, R., O'Connor, A., Johnson, A., Anthony, R. *et al.* (2016) A preliminary examination of swine caretakers' perspectives for euthanasia technology and training. *Journal of Animal Science* 94 (supplement 5), 32. doi: 10.2527/jam2016-0069

McKeegan, D.E.F., Reimert, H.G.M., Hindle, V.A., Boulcott, P., Sparrey, J.M. *et al.* (2013) Physiological and behavioral responses of poultry exposed to gas-filled high expansion foam. *Poultry Science* 92, 1145–1154. doi: 10.3382/ps.2012-02587

Meltzer, A. (1983) Thermoneutral zone and resting metabolic rate of broilers. *British Poultry Science* 24, 471–476. doi: 10.1080/00071668308416763

Merrick, A.W. and Scharp, D.W. (1971) Electroencephalography of resting behaviour in cattle, with observations on the question of sleep. *American Journal of Veterinary Research* 32, 1893–1897.

Miranda-de la Lama, G.L., Rodríguez-Palomares, M., Cruz-Monterrosa, R., Rayas-Amor, A., Pinheiro, R.S.B. *et al.* (2018) Long-distance transport of hair lambs: effect of location in pot-belly trailers on thermo-physiology, welfare and meat quality. *Tropical Animal Health and Production* 50, 327–336. doi: 10.1007/s11250-017-1435-0

Mondaca, M.R. (2019) Ventilation systems for adult dairy cattle. *Veterinary Clinics of North America: Food Animal Practice* 35, 139–156. doi: 10.1016/j.cvfa.2018.10.006

Moorman, A.K.G., Duffield, T.F., Godkin, M.A., Kelton, D.F., Rau, J. and Haley, D.B. (2018) Associations between the general condition of culled dairy cows and selling price at Ontario auction markets. *Journal of Dairy Science* 101, 10580–10588. doi: 10.3168/jds.2018-14519

Moss, B.W. (1978) Some observations on the activity and aggressive behaviour of pigs when penned prior to slaughter. *Applied Animal Ethology* 4, 323–339.

Mota-Rojas, D., Becerril, M., Lemus, C., Sánchez, P., González, M. *et al.* (2006) Effects of mid-summer transport duration on pre- and post-slaughter performance and pork quality in Mexico. *Meat Science* 73, 404–412. doi: 10.1016/j.meatsci.2005.11.012

Mota-Rojas, D., Becerril Herrera, M., Trujillo-Ortega, M., Alonso-Spilsbury, M., Flores-Peinado, S. and Guerrero-Legarreta, I. (2009) Effects of pre-slaughter transport, lairage and sex on pig chemical serologic profiles. *Journal of Animal and Veterinary Advances* 8, 246–250.

Murray, A.C. and Johnson, C.P. (1998) Impact of the halothane gene on muscle quality and pre-slaughter deaths in western Canadian pigs. *Canadian Journal of Animal Science* 78, 543–548. doi: 10.4141/A97-122

National Farm Animal Care Council (2013) Should this animal be loaded? Guidelines for transporting sheep. Code of Practice for the Care and Handling of Sheep. Available at: https://www.nfacc.ca/resources/codes-of-practice/sheep/appendix_h.pdf (accessed 15 April 2020).

National Pork Board (2016) On-farm Euthanasia of Swine Recommendations for the Producer. Available at: http://www.porkcdn.com/sites/porkorg/library/2016/11/2016-On-Farm-Euthanasia-of-Swine.pdf (accessed 15 April 2020).

Newberry, R.C., Webster, A.B., Lewis, N.J. and Van Arnam, C. (1999) Management of spent hens. *Journal of Applied Animal Welfare Science* 2, 13–29.

Nicholson, J.D.W., Nicholson, K.L., Frenzel, L.L., Maddock, R.J., Delmore Jr., R.J. *et al.* (2013) Survey of transportation procedures, management practices, and health assessment related to quality, quantity, and value for market beef and dairy cows and bulls. *Journal of Animal Science* 91, 5026–5036. doi: 10.2527/jas2013-6283

Nijdam, E., Arens, P., Lambooij, E., Decuypere, E. and Stegeman, J.A. (2004) Factors influencing bruises and mortality of broilers during catching, transport, and lairage. *Poultry Science* 83, 1610–1615. doi: 10.1093/ps/83.9.1610

Nijdam, E., Zailan, A.R.M., Van Eck, J.H.H., Decuypere, E. and Stegeman, J.A. (2006) Pathological features in dead on arrival broilers with special reference to heart disorders. *Poultry Science* 85, 1303–1308. doi: 10.1093/ps/85.7.1303

OIE (2011) Terrestrial Animal Health Code. Chapter 7.3. Transport of Animals by Land. Office International des Epizooties (World Organisation for Animal Health), Paris. Available at: http://www.oie.int/index.php?id=169&L=0&htmfile=chapitre_aw_land_transpt.htm (accessed 15 April 2020).

OIE (2016) Terrestrial Animal Health Code. Chapter 7.5. Slaughter of Animals. Office International des Epizooties (World Organisation for Animal Health), Paris. Available at: http://www.oie.int/index.php?id=169&L=0&htmfile=chapitre_aw_slaughter.htm (accessed 15 April 2020).

Pearce, K.L., Masters, D.G., Jacob, R.H., Hopkins, D.L. and Pethick, D.W. (2008) Effects of sodium chloride and betaine on hydration status of lambs at slaughter. *Australian Journal of Experimental Agriculture* 48, 1194–1200. doi: 10.1071/EA08034

Pereira, T.L., Titto, E.A.L., Conte, S., Devillers, N., Sommavilla, R. *et al.* (2018) Application of a ventilation fan-misting bank on pigs kept in a stationary trailer before unloading: effects on trailer microclimate, and pig behaviour and physiological response. *Livestock Science* 216, 67–74. doi: 10.1016/j.livsci.2018.07.013

Perez, M.P., Palacio, J., Santolaria, M.P., Acena, M.D., Chacon, G. *et al.* (2002) Influence of lairage time on some welfare and meat quality parameters in pigs. *Veterinary Research* 33, 239–250.

Petherick, J.C. (2007) Spatial requirements of animals: allometry and beyond. *Journal of Veterinary Behavior: Clinical Applications and Research* 2, 197–204.

Petracci, M., Bianchi, M., Cavani, C., Gaspari, P. and Lavazza, A. (2006) Preslaughter mortality in broiler chickens, turkeys, and spent hens under commercial slaughtering. *Poultry Science* 85, 1660–1664. doi: 10.1093/ps/85.9.1660

Polsky, L. and von Keyserlingk, M.A.G. (2017) Invited review: Effects of heat stress on dairy cattle welfare. *Journal of Dairy Science* 100, 8645–8657. doi: 10.3168/jds.2017-12651

Poultry Industry Council (2016) Practical Guidelines for On-Farm Euthanasia of Poultry. Available at: http://www.poultryindustrycouncil.ca/wp-content/uploads/2016/08/PIC-Practical-Guidelines-for-On-Farm-Euthanasia-of-Poultry.pdf (accessed 15 April 2020).

Poultry Industry Council (2017) Should This Bird Be Loaded? A Guide For Preparing, Loading, and Transporting Poultry. Available at: http://www.poultryindustrycouncil.ca/wp-content/uploads/2017/03/DT-Handbook-final.compressed.pdf

Quinn, A.D., Kettlewell, P.J., Mitchell, M.A. and Knowles, T. (1998) Air movement and the thermal microclimates observed in poultry lairages. *British Poultry Science* 39, 469–476. doi: 10.1080/00071669888610

Rabaste, C., Faucitano, L., Saucier, L., Mormède, P., Correa, J.A., Giguère, A. and Bergeron, R. (2007) The effects of handling and group size on welfare of pigs in lairage and their influence on stomach weight, carcass microbial contamination and meat quality. *Canadian Journal of Animal Science* 87, 3–12. doi: 10.4141/A06-041

Rault, J.-L., Holyoake, T. and Coleman, G. (2017) Stockperson attitudes toward pig euthanasia. *Journal of Animal Science* 95, 949–957. doi: 10.2527/jas2016.0922

Rezac, D.J., Thomson, D.U., Siemens, M.G., Prouty, F.L., Reinhardt, C.D. and Bartle, S.J. (2014) A survey of gross pathologic conditions in cull cows at slaughter in the Great Lakes region of the United States. *Journal of Dairy Science* 97, 4227–4235. doi: 10.3168/jds.2013-7636

Richards, G.J., Wilkins, L.J., Weeks, C.A., Knowles, T.G. and Brown, S.N. (2012) Evaluation of the microclimate in poultry transport module drawers during the marketing process of end-of-lay hens from farm to slaughter. *Veterinary Record* 171, 474. doi: 10.1136/vr.100844

Ritter, M.J., Ellis, M., Brinkmann, J., DeDecker, J.M., Keffaber, K.K. *et al.* (2006) Effect of floor space during transport of market-weight pigs on the incidence of transport losses at the packing plant and the relationships between transport conditions and losses. *Journal of Animal Science* 84, 2856–2864. doi: 10.2527/jas.2005-577

Ritter, M.J., Ellis, M., Berry, N.L., Curtis, S.E., Anil, L. *et al.* (2009) Transport losses in market weight pigs: I. A review of definitions, incidence, and economic impact. *Professional Animal Scientist* 25, 404–414.

Ritz, C.W., Webster, A.B. and Czarick III, M. (2005) Evaluation of hot weather thermal environment and incidence of mortality associated with broiler live haul. *Journal of Applied Poultry Research* 14, 594–602.

Robert, S. and Dallaire, A. (1986) Polygraphic analysis of the sleep-wake states and the REM sleep periodicity in domesticated pigs (*Sus scrofa*). *Physiology & Behavior* 37, 289–293.

Roche, J.R., Dillon, P.G., Stockdale, C.R., Baumgard, L.H. and VanBaale, M.J. (2004) Relationships among international body condition scoring systems. *Journal of Dairy Science* 87, 3076–3079.

Ruckebusch, Y. (1972) The relevance of drowsiness in the circadian cycle of farm animals. *Animal Behaviour* 20, 637–643. doi: 10.1016/S0003-3472(72)80136-2

Ruckebusch, Y. (1975) The hypnogram as an index of adaptation of farm animals to changes in their environment. *Applied Animal Ethology* 2, 3–18.

Salmi, B., Trefan, L., Bünger, L., Doeschl-Wilson, A., Bidanel, J.P. *et al.* (2012) Bayesian meta-analysis of the effect of fasting, transport and lairage times on four attributes of pork quality. *Meat Science* 90, 584–598. doi: 10.1016/j.meatsci.2011.09.021

Santos, C., Almeida, J.M., Matias, E.C., Fraqueza, M.J., Roseiro, C. and Sardina, L. (1997) Influence of lairage environmental conditions and resting time on meat quality in pigs. *Meat Science* 45, 253–262. doi: 10.1016/S0309-1740(96)00048-4

Saucier, L., Bernier, D., Bergeron, R., Giguère, A., Méthot, S. and Faucitano, L. (2007) Effect of feed texture, meal frequency and pre-slaughter fasting on behaviour, stomach content and carcass microbial quality in pigs. *Canadian Journal of Animal Science* 87, 479–487. doi: 10.4141/A06-072

Schlageter-Tello, A., Bokkers, E.A.M., Koerkamp, P.W.G.G., Van Hertem, T., Viazzi, S. *et al.* (2014) Manual and automatic locomotion scoring systems in dairy cows: A review. *Preventive Veterinary Medicine* 116, 12–25. doi: 10.1016/j.prevetmed.2014.06.006

Schmidt, P.L., O'Connor, A.M., McKean, J.D. and Hurd, H.S. (2004) The association between cleaning and disinfection of lairage pens and the prevalence of *Salmonella enterica* in swine at harvest. *Journal of Food Protection* 67, 1384–1388. doi: 10.4315/0362-028X-67.7.1384

Scott, P.R., Sargison, N.D. and Wilson, D.J. (2007) The potential for improving welfare standards and productivity in United Kingdom sheep flocks using veterinary flock health plans. *Veterinary Journal* 173, 522–531.

Shackelford, A.D., Whitehead, W.F., Dickens, J.A., Thomson, J.E. and Wilson, R.L. (1984) Evaporative cooling of broilers during pre slaughter holding. *Poultry Science* 63, 927–931.

Shearer, J.K. (2018) Euthanasia of cattle: practical considerations and application. *Animals* 8. doi: 10.3390/ani8040057

Shearer, J.K. and Reynolds J.P. (2011) Euthanasia techniques for dairy cattle. In: Risco, C.A. and Retamal, P.M. (eds) *Dairy Production Medicine*. John Wiley & Sons, Marblehead, Massachusetts, pp. 331–339.

Shorthose, W.R. (1977) The effects of resting sheep after a long journey on concentrations of plasma constituents, post-mortem changes in muscles, and meat properties. *Australian Journal of Agricultural Research* 28, 509–520.

Small, A., Reid, C.-A. and Buncic, S. (2003) Conditions in lairages at abattoirs for ruminants in southwest England and in vitro survival of *Escherichia coli* O157, *Salmonella* kedougou, and *Campylobacter jejuni* on lairage-related substrates. *Journal of Food Protection* 66, 1570–1575. doi: 10.4315/0362-028X-66.9.1570

Small, A., James, C., James, S., Davies, R., Howell, M. *et al.* (2007) Construction, management and cleanliness of red meat abattoir lairages in the UK. *Meat Science* 75, 523–532. doi: 10.1016/j.meatsci.2006.09.002

Śmiecińska, K., Denaburski, J. and Sobotka, W. (2011) Slaughter value, meat quality, creatine kinase activity and cortisol levels in the blood serum of growing-finishing pigs slaughtered immediately after transport and after a rest period. *Polish Journal of Veterinary Sciences* 14, 47–54. doi: 10.2478/v10181-011-0007-x

Stafford, K.J., Mellor, D.J., Todd, S.E., Gregory, N.G., Bruce, R.A. and Ward, R.N. (2001) The physical state and plasma biochemical profile of young calves on arrival at a slaughter plant. *New Zealand Veterinary Journal* 49, 142–149. doi: 10.1080/00480169.2001.36222

Stojkov, J., Bowers, G., Draper, M., Duffield, T., Duivenvoorden, P. *et al.* (2018) Hot topic: Management of cull dairy cows – consensus of an expert consultation in Canada. *Journal of Dairy Science* 101, 11170–11174. doi: 10.3168/jds.2018-14919

Strappini, A.C., Metz, J.H.M., Gallo, C.B. and Kemp, B. (2009) Origin and assessment of bruises in beef cattle at slaughter. *Animal* 3, 728–736. doi: 10.1017/S1751731109004091

Strappini, A.C., Metz, J.H.M., Gallo, C., Frankena, K., Vargas, R. *et al.* (2013) Bruises in culled cows: when, where and how are they inflicted? *Animal* 7, 485–491. doi: 10.1017/S1751731112001863

Strawford, M.L., Watts, J.M., Crowe, T.G., Classen, H.L. and Shand, P.J. (2011) The effect of simulated cold weather transport on core body temperature and behavior of broilers. *Poultry Science* 90, 2415–2424. doi: 10.3382/ps.2011-01427

Stull, C.L., Payne, M.A., Berry, S.L. and Reynolds, J.P. (2007) A review of the causes, prevention, and welfare of nonambulatory cattle. *Journal of the American Veterinary Medical Association* 231, 227–234.

Sullivan, K.F. and Mader, T.L. (2018) Managing heat stress episodes in confined cattle. *Veterinary Clinics: Food Animal Practice* 34, 325–339. doi: 10.1016/j.cvfa.2018.05.001

Sutherland, M.A., Erlandson, K., Connor, J.F., Salak-Johnson, J.L., Matzat, P. *et al.* (2008) Health of non-ambulatory, non-injured pigs at processing. *Livestock Science* 116, 237–245. doi: 10.1016/j.livsci.2007.10.009 ER

Talling, J.C., Waran, N.K., Wathes, C.M. and Lines, J.A. (1996) Behavioural and physiological responses of pigs to sound. *Applied Animal Behaviour Science* 48, 187–202.

Talling, J.C., Lines, J.A., Wathes, C.M. and Waran, N.K. (1998) The acoustic environment of the domestic pig. *Journal of Agricultural and Engineering Research* 71, 1–12.

Tao, X. and Xin, H. (2003a) Acute synergistic effects of air temperature, humidity, and velocity on homeostasis of market–size broilers. *Transactions of the American Society of Agricultural Engineers* 46, 491–497. doi: 10.13031/2013.12971

Tao, X. and Xin, H. (2003b) Surface wetting and its optimization to cool broiler chickens. *Transactions of the American Society of Agricultural Engineers* 46, 483–490.

Teke, B., Akdag, F., Ekiz, B. and Ugurlu, M. (2014) Effects of different lairage times after long distance transportation on carcass and meat quality characteristics of Hungarian Simmental bulls. *Meat Science* 96, 224–229. doi: 10.1016/j.meatsci.2013.07.009

Terlouw, E.M.C., Arnould, C., Auperin, B., Berri, C., Le Bihan-Duval, E. *et al.* (2008) Pre-slaughter conditions, animal stress and welfare: current status and possible future research. *Animal* 2, 1501–1517. doi: 10.1017/S1751731108002723

Ternman, E., Hanninen, L., Pastell, M., Agenas, S. and Nielsen, P.P. (2012) Sleep in dairy cows recorded with a non-invasive EEG technique. *Applied Animal Behaviour Science* 140, 25–32. doi: 10.1016/j.applanim.2012.05.005

Thomas, G.W. and Jordaan, P. (2013) Pre-slaughter mortality and post-slaughter wastage in bobby veal calves at a slaughter premises in New Zealand. *New Zealand Veterinary Journal* 61, 127–132. doi: 10.1080/00480169.2012.734374

Thomsen, P.T. and Sørensen, J.T. (2008) Euthanasia of Danish dairy cows evaluated in two questionnaire surveys. *Acta Veterinaria Scandinavica* 50. doi: 10.1186/1751-0147-50-33

Thomsen, P.T. and Sørensen, J.T. (2009) Factors affecting the risk of euthanasia for cows in Danish dairy herds. *Veterinary Record* 165, 43–45. doi: 10.1136/vetrec.165.2.43

Tobler, I., Jaggi, K., Arendt, J. and Ravault, J.-P. (1991) Long-term 24-hour rest activity pattern of sheep in stalls and in the field. *Experientia* 47, 744–749.

Torrey, S., Bergeron, R., Widowski, T., Lewis, N., Crowe, T. *et al.* (2013) Transportation of market-weight pigs: I. Effect of season, truck type, and location within truck on behavior with a two-hour transport. *Journal of Animal Science* 91, 2863–2871. doi: 10.2527/jas.2012-6005

Turner, P.V. and Doonan, G. (2010) Developing on-farm euthanasia plans. *Canadian Veterinary Journal* 51, 1031–1034.

Vanderhasselt, R.F., Buijs, S., Sprenger, M., Goethals, K., Willemsen, H. *et al.* (2013) Dehydration indicators for broiler chickens at slaughter. *Poultry Science* 92, 612–619. doi: 10.3382/ps.2012-02715

Verbeek, E., Oliver, M.H., Waas, J.R., McLeay, L.M., Blache, D. and Matthews, L.R. (2012) Reduced cortisol and metabolic responses of thin ewes to an acute cold challenge in mid-pregnancy: Implications for animal physiology and welfare. *PLoS ONE* 7. doi: 10.1371/journal.pone.0037315

Vermeulen, L., Van de Perre, V., Permentier, L., De Bie, S., Verbeke, G. and Geers, R. (2015) Pre-slaughter handling and pork quality. *Meat Science* 100, 118–123. doi: 10.1016/j.meatsci.2014.09.148

Visser, I.J.R., Odink, J., Smeets, J.F.M., Aarts, P.A.M.M., Elbers, A.R.W. *et al.* (1992) Relationship between pathological findings and values of haematological and blood-chemistry variables in apparently healthy finishing pigs at slaughter. *Journal of Veterinary Medicine, Series B* 39, 123–131. doi: 10.1111/j.1439-0450.1992.tb01147.x

Vitali, A., Lana, E., Amadori, M., Bernabucci, U., Nardone, A. and Lacetera, N. (2014) Analysis of factors associated with mortality of heavy slaughter pigs during transport and lairage. *Journal of Animal Science* 92, 5134–5141. doi: 10.2527/jas.2014-7670

Vogel, K.D., Claus, J.R., Grandin, T., Oetzel, G.R. and Schaefer, D.M. (2011) Effect of water and feed withdrawal and health status on blood and serum components, body weight loss, and meat and carcass characteristics of Holstein slaughter cows. *Journal of Animal Science* 89, 538–548. doi: 10.2527/jas.2009-2675

Walia, K., Lynch, H., Grant, J., Duffy, G., Leonard, F.C. *et al.* (2017) The efficacy of disinfectant misting in the lairage of a pig abattoir to reduce *Salmonella* and *Enterobacteriaceae* on pigs prior to slaughter. *Food Control* 75, 55–61. doi: 10.1016/j.foodcont.2016.12.028

Warren, L.A., Mandell, I.B. and Bateman, K.G. (2010) An audit of transport conditions and arrival status of slaughter cattle shipped by road at an Ontario processor. *Canadian Journal of Animal Science* 90, 159–167. doi: 10.4141/CJAS09068

Warriss, P.D. (2003) Optimal lairage times and conditions for slaughter pigs: a review. *Veterinary Record* 153, 170–176. doi: 10.1136/vr.153.6.170

Warriss, P.D., Kestin, S.C., Brown, S.N. and Wilkins, L.J. (1984) The time required for recovery from mixing stress in young bulls and the prevention of dark cutting beef. *Meat Science* 10, 53–68. doi: 10.1016/0309-1740(84)90031-7

Warriss, P.D., Brown, S.N., Edwards, J.E., Anil, M.H. and Fordham, D.P. (1992) Time in lairage needed by pigs to recover from the stress of transport. *The Veterinary Record* 131, 194–196. doi: 10.1136/vr.131.9.194

Warriss, P.D., Knowles, T.G., Brown, S.N., Edwards, J.E., Kettlewell, P.J. *et al.* (1999) Effects of lairage time on body temperature and glycogen reserves of broiler chickens held in transport modules. *The Veterinary Record* 145, 218–222.

Warriss, P.D., Pagazaurtundua, A. and Brown, S.N. (2005) Relationship between maximum daily temperature and mortality of broiler chickens during transport and lairage. *British Poultry Science* 46, 647–651. doi: 10.1080/00071660500393868

Wathes, C.M., Jones, C.D.R. and Webster, A.J.F. (1983) Ventilation, air hygiene and animal health. *Veterinary Record* 113, 554–559.

Weeding, C.M., Guise, H.J. and Penny, R.H.C. (1993) Factors influencing the welfare and carcass and meat quality of pigs: the use of water sprays in lairage. *Animal Production* 56, 393–397. doi: 10.1017/S0003356100006449

Weeks, C.A. (2008) A review of welfare in cattle, sheep and pig lairages, with emphasis on stocking rates, ventilation and noise. *Animal Welfare* 17, 275–284.

Weeks, C.A., Brown, S.N., Lane, S., Heasman, L., Benson, T. and Warriss, P.D. (2009) Noise levels in lairages for cattle, sheep and pigs in abattoirs in England and Wales. *Veterinary Record* 165, 308–314.

White, T.L. and Moore, D.A. (2009) Reasons for whole carcass condemnations of cattle in the United States and implications for producer education and veterinary intervention. *Journal of the American Veterinary Medical Association* 235, 937–941. doi: 10.2460/javma.235.8.937

Willeberg, P., Gerbola, M., Petersen, B.K. and Andersen, J.B. (1984) The Danish pig health scheme: nation-wide computer-based abattoir surveillance and follow-up at the herd level. *Preventive Veterinary Medicine* 3, 79–91. doi: 10.1016/0167-5877(84)90026-6

Wythes, J.R., Shorthose, W.R., Schmidt, P.J. and Davis, C.B. (1980) Effects of various rehydration procedures after a long journey on liveweight, carcasses and muscle properties of cattle. *Australian Journal of Agricultural Research* 4, 849–855.

Wythes, J.R., Johnston, G.N., Beaman, N. and O'Rourke, P.K. (1985) Pre slaughter handling of cattle: the availability of water during the lairage period. *Australian Veterinary Journal* 62, 163–165.

Wythes, J.R., Shorthose, W.R. and Powell, V.H. (1988) Cattle handling at abattoirs. 1. The effects of rest and resting conditions before slaughter and of electrical-stimulation of carcasses on carcass weight and muscle properties. *Australian Journal of Agricultural Research* 39, 87–95.

Zhou, W.T., Fujita, M. and Yamamoto, S. (1999) Thermoregulatory responses and blood viscosity in dehydrated heat-exposed broilers (*Gallus domesticus*). *Journal of Thermal Biology* 24, 185–192.

5

The Basics of Bruising in Cattle – What, When and How

LILY N. EDWARDS-CALLAWAY[1]* AND HELEN C. KLINE[2]

[1]*Department of Animal Science, Colorado State University, USA;* [2]*JBS Swift, Tolleson, Arizona, USA*

Summary

The welfare and economics of bruising have been a topic of discussion within the cattle industry over the past several years. Beginning in the early 1990s, the National Cattlemen's Beef Association implemented what is now called the National Beef Quality Audit to benchmark quality attributes of beef, bruising being one of the carcass defects measured. With these audits, the US cattle industry has been able to track the occurrence and subsequent economic impacts of bruising in the beef industry. During pre-slaughter transport and management, cattle are exposed to numerous events that can increase the risk of bruising such as multiple handling events, other animals, and various handling facilities and animal caretakers. Researchers and industry professionals can use the attributes of bruises, such as size, shape, pattern and color, to begin to understand where bruises are occurring within the supply chain. It is beneficial to couple post-mortem visual bruise assessment with ante-mortem assessment of handling in order to garner a more complete understanding of an animal's experience and subsequent bruise status. Incorporating visual bruise assessment into in-plant quality assurance programmes may be an effective way of raising awareness about bruising and its impacts on both quality and well-being. Even though this chapter is about cattle, most of the principles will also apply to sheep, bison, deer, goats or water buffalo.

Learning Objectives

- Bruising is a carcass defect caused by injury to the muscle that has economic and animal well-being implications.

- Bruises are not visible on the hides of live cattle. They must be assessed after hide removal during processing.
- Bruise characteristics such as location, size, colour and shape can provide clues as to how that bruise may have occurred.
- Coupling ante-mortem handling observations with post-mortem bruising assessment can be an effective method of understanding where bruises come from.
- Bruise monitoring programmes in the abattoir can help reduce bruise prevalence by increasing awareness.

Introduction

Bruising is something we all can relate to. We have grown up acquiring bruises on our legs from playing hard on the playground at school recesses, to being proud of a very large bruise we may have acquired participating in an exciting extreme sporting event, to lamenting over the bruises that happened after a mountain biking accident, or just being clumsy. Bruises are visible, everyone gets them, they are colourful (and the colour changes) and they come with a story. These everyday stories are often fond or embarrassing moments and we either remember exactly how the bruises were acquired or have no idea where they came from.

Unfortunately, there are also bruises that come from traumatic events, those associated with abuse, violence and crime. In these instances, it is often critical to understand what caused the bruise and when it occurred. The stories associated with these bruises are tragic and sometimes the victim cannot

---

* Email: Lily.Edwards-Callaway@colostate.edu

provide an explanation of events. Due to the high importance of understanding bruising in these contexts, there is a substantial body of research in the area of human forensics as it relates to bruising (Davis, 1998; DiMaio and DiMaio, 2001; Hughes *et al.*, 2004b). This information has been critical to human forensics but has also been beneficial in our understanding of bruising in livestock species. Forensic science has provided a platform of knowledge for many of the studies performed in animals to gain clarity on bruise characteristics, specifically bruise age.

Out of Sight, Out of Mind?

In humans, bruises are most likely visible at some point; if a bruise is deep it may take a few days to be visible on the skin surface and, depending on where the bruise is located, it may be covered by clothing. We notice other people's bruises, potentially enquire about them, and based on the visual clues often speculate about their origin. In many animals, bruises are not visible; thick hides and fur coats cover any bruises that an animal may have (pigs may be the exception when considering livestock). The fact that often we cannot see a bruise on an animal (livestock and pets included) sometimes diminishes the recognition that a particular, likely negative, event has resulted in a bruise and how painful that bruise could be. When bruises are out of sight, they are often out of mind and sometimes not even considered an 'injury'. This is not unique to livestock. A news article describing a 2007 Tour de France collision in which a rider collided with a dog on the racecourse (at race speed) comes to mind. After describing the significant crash in which the rider crashed into the dog's hind area at full speed, the reporter indicated that the dog 'was unhurt by the battering and clambered to its feet wagging its tail' but the rider had some 'cuts and bruises' (Robertson, 2007). It is likely that the crash would have caused some bruise formation on the dog, but the bruises were not visible and therefore were not considered.

The only way to see bruises in cattle is during post-mortem processing when the hides have been removed from the animal at the slaughter facility. Similar to criminal investigations, professionals in the livestock industry take the post-mortem bruising information and work backwards through the process to understand where the bruise came from and determine methods to prevent bruises in the future. Bruises are certainly visible on the processing floor at slaughter plants and the prevalence has spurred significant research and monitoring during pre-slaughter activities to understand where the bruises are coming from. Although general awareness has been raised about the welfare implications of bruising based on what is found post-mortem (Henderson, 2016; Grandin, 2018; Kline, 2018), at the moment when traumatic events that have the potential to cause bruising occur, there is still some lack of consideration for the impact on animal well-being. For example, when we watch cattle unload from a truck and see jamming at the exit to the trailer, we do not necessarily consider that a bruise may be a consequence. The damage/trauma is not immediately visible and therefore not fully considered.

The Welfare and Economics of Bruising in the Cattle Industry

There are numerous reasons that professionals within the cattle industry should be concerned about bruising, two of the primary reasons being the impacts that bruising has on animal well-being and the economic impact of carcass bruising. The welfare implications of bruising are multifaceted. The most obvious impact that bruises have on animal well-being is that they are painful. Consider a bruise you have had in the past. The event that caused the bruise likely caused pain (potentially not if it was a very small bruise) and, depending on the size and severity of the bruise, there was likely tenderness associated with the injury post development. Simply, bruises are painful. Additionally, consider the event that led to the formation of a bruise on the animal. An event that is forceful enough to cause a bruise is likely to be traumatic for the animal, due not only to the discomfort the bruise caused, and will cause, but also from the fear response that the event may have triggered. Although the majority of bruises seen in cattle are minimal, i.e. small (prevalence to be discussed in later sections), some animals do have severe bruises post-mortem. Observing these types of bruises post-mortem makes one question what happened to that animal that caused such significant trauma. With this questioning also comes a feeling of compassion when contemplating what that animal felt while the trauma-causing event was occurring.

It is necessary to note that not all handling events will cause bruising and not all events that cause bruising will cause severe bruises; likewise, not all handling events trigger fear and distress (most probably do not if low-stress handling is practised). It is important, though, to understand that these events can cause fear and distress, so that as we work with animals we should consider the implications of our behaviour, our approaches and our facilities. These trauma-causing events are not always caused by humans directly but since we are the stewards of livestock within our production systems, we do have a responsibility to try to prevent events like this from occurring, no matter the cause.

Bruised meat must not be used for human consumption

Additional consequences of bruising in livestock are the economic implications. Bruising is a carcass defect causing significant carcass damage. In slaughter facilities inspected by the US Department of Agriculture (USDA), bruises must be removed from the carcass during processing and this trimmed material is either rendered or discarded (CFR, 2019). In addition to the yield loss from trim, depending on the location and severity of the bruise, there is often an economic loss from devalued cuts, i.e. not an entire cut is lost but if a portion of a cut is removed the value will be reduced. Cattle industry stakeholders have estimated that bruising is currently costing the industry millions of dollars annually (Henderson, 2016; Lee et al., 2017). In the 1994 National Non-fed Beef Quality Audit (NBQA), the first of many audits to be conducted by the National Cattlemen's Beef Association (NCBA) benchmarking a multitude of quality defects in beef, bruising included, it was calculated that US$11.47 were lost per beef carcass due to bruising (National Cattlemen's Beef Association, 1994). Additionally, in the 1999 National Market Cow and Bull Beef Quality Audit, bruising was identified as the sixth leading cause of whole-carcass condemnation at the slaughter facility (Roeber et al., 2001). Although reductions in bruise prevalence have been made since the inception of these benchmarking audits (Eastwood et al., 2017; Harris et al., 2017), the 2016 NBQA estimated that bruises still account for US$3.41 per animal because of lost opportunity in carcass value within the beef industry (National Cattlemen's Beef Association, 2017).

Secondary to the carcass loss but also important are the reductions in slaughter plant efficiency associated with bruise removal. Depending on the prevalence and the severity of carcass bruising, sometimes processing speeds (chain speed) at the slaughter facilities are reduced to manage additional time needed to trim off bruises. Additional employees may be needed to assist with the amount of trimming required on groups of carcasses with a high rate of bruising. To the authors' knowledge, there is not a published value on this cost but, in conversations with industry partners, it is evident that any reduction in line speed (efficiency) at a processing facility has a financial implication and therefore is not preferred.

Prevalence: how big is the problem?

As indicated, the NBQAs have been documenting bruise prevalence via visual assessment in the US cattle industry at slaughter since the early 1990s. The most recent NBQA data collected in 2016 on market steers/heifers, cows and bulls reported a bruise prevalence of 38.8%, 64.1% and 42.9%, respectively (Eastwood et al., 2017; Harris et al., 2017). Although the percentage of minimal bruises observed has increased in market cows, the percentage of major, critical and extreme bruises has decreased over the past 20 years. Eastwood et al. (2017) compared the 2016 NBQA bruise prevalence with prior audit years, demonstrating an increase in the percentage of market cows with no carcass bruises present, potentially a testament to the attention and importance that has been given to bruising in market cows in recent years. Harris et al. (2017) reported approximately a 15% increase in fed cattle that were bruised in addition to an increased percentage of fed cattle with multiple bruises in the 2016 NBQA as compared with the 2011 NBQA. Perhaps as cattle increase in size, the industry will need to adjust facilities (as generally handling facilities have remained static) to accommodate this change, in order to reduce carcass bruising (Harris et al., 2017). Bruising will vary between facilities but the NBQAs provide a good reference point for comparison year over year. Wigham et al. (2018) provided a summary of bruise prevalence found in research studies globally, indicating a range of 37.5–97% bruising across studies.

'Iceberg Effect': bruises may not be visible on the carcass surface

In a recent bruising study assessing the actual trimmed bruise weight after visual bruise assessment in multiple slaughter facilities, it was found that a considerable number of carcasses scored as not having a bruise were in fact trimmed for bruising (Kline, 2018). Kline (2018) found that nearly 75% of carcasses did not have visible bruising. Of those, 41.7% had bruising trimmed off. The plant employees were able to identify clues on the carcass surface that there were deeper bruises not evaluated as a 'bruise' during visual assessment. The authors have named this observation the 'Iceberg Effect' since these deep-tissue bruises on cattle are not readily visible on the surface but penetrate deep into the muscle. This is a new finding that should be explored in future studies to understand identification of these bruises.

Bruising Basics

What is a bruise?

Bruising is most commonly caused by a blunt and/ or squeezing force trauma (Marshall, 1977; Nash and Sheridan, 2009; Venes, 2009). A bruise is the site of an injury/contusion and is technically defined as an 'extravasation of blood beneath an intact epidermis due to injury' (Capper, 2001). Three core criteria must be met for a bruise to occur: (i) the skin and tissues must be stretched and/or crushed with enough force to cause the small blood vessels to rupture but not break the surface of the skin (i.e. the trauma must be caused by a blunt force so that the skin is not punctured as to cause a laceration); (ii) there must be sufficient blood pressure within the blood vessels to move the blood from the damaged vessels to the surrounding areas; and (iii) the blood that leaves the blood vessels must be close to the surface of the skin to be visible with the naked eye for surface bruises (Langlois, 2007; Pilling et al., 2010). Considering the three criteria listed above, what does this mean in the context of bruises that are seen post-mortem at a slaughter plant in cattle? If a carcass bruise is identified, the event that caused that bruise must have been forceful enough to rupture blood vessels. Thinking about animals moving through a handling facility, not all bumps and jostles will result in a bruise, but ones with some force behind them will – this force could come from the behaviour of the animal itself, the behaviour of other animals in the contemporary group, and/or animal handlers. Additionally, deep tissue bruises will not be readily visible on the surface, due to the location of the trapped blood in the body tissues; this type of bruising may or may not be identified on the slaughter processing floor. The severity of a bruise is dependent on the amount and size of the blood vessels that are ruptured at the time of trauma (Marshall, 1977).

What do we know about how bruises are formed?

From personal experience, we have all seen bruises of many shapes and changing colours. The colour of a bruise reflects the physiological processes that have caused bruise formation and disappearance or 'healing'. As indicated, a bruise is formed from ruptured blood vessels underneath the skin. Blood contains haemoglobin, which is responsible for transporting oxygen from the lungs to the other tissues of the body (Langlois, 2007). The red discoloration in a contusion or bruise is the result of the haemoglobin that is present in the red blood cells that has been released from the damaged tissues due to the injury (Nash and Sheridan, 2009). The release of haemoglobin and/or red bloods cells initiates an inflammatory response within the body which includes vasodilation and this attracts macrophages to the traumatized area (Nash and Sheridan, 2009). The redness of the skin and freshly escaped blood then changes to a blue or purple colour due to the deoxygenated venous blood moving into the various body tissues (Pimstone et al., 1971; Nash and Sheridan, 2009). Macrophages then ingest the free red blood cells and degrade the attached haemoglobin on the red blood cells (Nash and Sheridan, 2009). Haemoglobin begins to break down by first converting to biliverdin, which contributes to the green colour seen in a healing contusion (Hughes et al., 2004a). Biliverdin then is converted to bilirubin, which accounts for the yellow colour seen in a healing bruise injury (Vanezis, 2001). Throughout this process some of the escaped iron can combine with ferritin, which creates haemosiderin, which can have a brown appearance in tissues (Hughes et al., 2004a,b). This process is illustrated in Fig. 5.1.

Bruise colour: what the black and blue is telling you

The colour of a bruise and how it relates to bruise age is the topic of great debate (Hamdy et al., 1957a; McCausland and Dougherty, 1978; Langlois

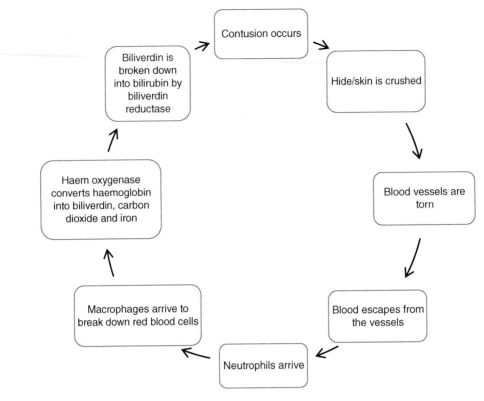

Fig. 5.1. Bruise pathophysiology cycle. (Information adapted from Vanezis, 2001; Hughes *et al.*, 2004a,b; Langlois, 2007; Nash and Sheridan, 2009.)

and Gresham, 1991; Langlois, 2007). When considering colour, the main objective or hope of understanding is to make some estimation of when the bruise occurred. As mentioned previously, in criminal investigations this is critical to understand. In the assessment of bruising post-mortem in livestock, professionals and researchers in the industry have been looking to bruise colour to provide some clues about when the bruise may have occurred. Bruise assessment is a mechanism to try to understand where bruises may be occurring and hopefully provide some ideas on how to mitigate risk factors associated with increased bruising. Unfortunately, the science of bruise colour is not exact, but it still is a useful tool to illuminate potential areas of opportunity. Despite some of the nuances of bruise colour, discussed below, bruise colour assessment post-mortem combined with visual observation of handling and management ante-mortem can provide valuable information to livestock producers and processors regarding critical control points within the pre-slaughter marking process.

There are many factors that affect the colour appearance of a bruise. Different species of animals can have varying bruise colour progressions and presentations (Hamdy *et al.*, 1957a; McCausland and Dougherty, 1978; Langlois and Gresham, 1991; Langlois, 2007). An older animal with less fat cover will bruise more easily than a younger animal with more fat cover. Statements that 'a blue bruise is recent' or 'a fresh bruise will be red' cannot be substantiated, because different tissues have various colour-retaining properties and there is inherent individual variation (Langlois, 2007). The perception of the colour of a bruise will change with the position of the trapped blood under the skin surface and the process of haemoglobin degradation (Langlois, 2007). Some authors have published guidelines for bruise colour appearance (Hamdy *et al.*, 1957a; Langlois and Gresham, 1991) but other experts claim that it is not possible to age a bruise solely based on colour (Langlois and Gresham, 1991).

L.N. Edwards-Callaway and H.C. Kline

Colour differences between fresh and old bruises

A general consensus seems to exist on the progression of the colour changes of a bruise but the exact time periods that match these colour changes are debated (Langlois and Gresham, 1991). Hamdy *et al.* (1957a) conducted a study in cattle that found that the red bruise colour could persist from 15 min to 2 days from the red blood cells and free haemoglobin in bovine tissue, green could be seen on days 3–4, and yellow and orange could be present on days 4–6 from the bilirubin in the tissues. The bruise colour cycle (Fig. 5.2) in livestock follows a predictable colour pattern, but the length of time of each colour stage can vary between livestock species. Studies were performed in cattle and rabbits and it was discovered that the order of the colour changes remained consistent between species, but that the age of the animals affected the rate at which the colour changes occurred (Hamdy *et al.*, 1957b, 1961b). McCausland and Dougherty (1978) conducted a study in calves that found the colour yellow appearing in the bruises within 48 h. There is much disagreement in the scientific community about only using colour to age a bruise (Langlois and Gresham, 1991), but a common theme shared in the literature is that yellow is a sign of 'older' bruising, 'old' being days. In practical application, the presence of yellow in a bruise at a slaughter facility likely indicates that the bruise did not occur during the marketing process (assuming this process occurred over no more than 2–3 days).

Impacting Factors

Factors that can affect the appearance of a bruise can include the environmental temperature, the laxity of the tissues, whether the tissue is near a bone surface, the age of the individual when the bruise occurs, pre-existing diseases, force and velocity level at impact, and pre-existing bruise trauma to the location (Hamdy *et al.*, 1961a,b; Langlois and Gresham, 1991; Randeberg *et al.*, 2007). The location of the injury can affect the amount of haemoglobin released from the vessels due to a bruise; for example, if the area is low in connective tissue and high in adipose tissue and vascularity, there can be a larger amount of blood released, changing what the bruise may look like (Johnson, 1990; Vanezis, 2001). The environmental temperature had an effect on the bruise healing rate of chicken broilers, because birds kept in colder temperatures healed at a slower rate and the bruises had overall more yellow colour present in the tissues (Hamdy *et al.*, 1961a).

Several studies conducted in humans and rabbits have indicated that age of the individual can also have an effect on the bruising process both in appearance and in healing time, which increases with age (Howes and Harvey, 1932; Hamdy *et al.*,

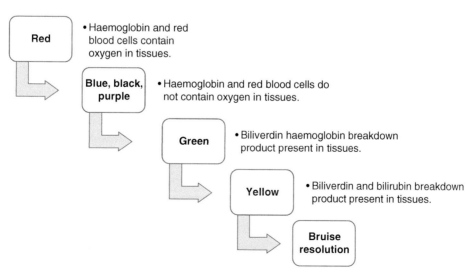

Fig. 5.2. Bruise colours and associated metabolite breakdown at various stages of bruise ageing. (Information adapted from Hamdy *et al.*, 1957a; McCausland and Dougherty, 1978; Langlois and Gresham, 1991; Langlois, 2007.)

1957b; Vanezis, 2001). Often elderly humans have thinning skin and the tissue around the blood vessels is weakened, thus impacting bruise occurrence and healing. The impact of age and body condition is a relevant point when thinking about cattle in particular, considering the range of ages seen between finished cattle and cull cows. Facilities that take a large range of cattle types and ages will potentially see a larger variation in the number of animals bruised.

The mass and the velocity of the object causing the bruise can affect the extent and severity of the bruise, but the sequence of visible and chemical changes of the bruise healing process remains constant (Hamdy et al., 1957b). A study with pigs was conducted to evaluate histological and gross changes in the bruised tissues at 2, 4, 6 and 8 h where the bruises had been caused by low, moderate or high force levels. All pigs were anaesthetized during this study and the appearance of the bruises was similar for all force levels until the 0.5 h mark. At this time point the visibility of the bruise depended on the amount of force used to inflict the bruise (Barington and Jensen, 2016).

How Do We Prevent Bruising?

Bruises can provide many clues regarding how an animal was managed, but it is up to the animal care professionals and scientists to use the clues provided from bruising and investigate how and when they may have occurred. Bruises occur when a traumatic event has occurred and injured bodily tissues. This can reveal facility design improvement opportunities, potential animal handling concerns or even animal-to-animal variation in bruising susceptibility.

What are the risk factors?

There has been a considerable amount of research exploring risk factors associated with increased chance of bruising in cattle during the pre-slaughter transport and management process. A review of this literature will not be included here but some factors will be mentioned in brief. In short, practices or events that increase an animal's chance of experiencing a 'traumatic event' (e.g. a bump, jam, fall) often are the factors that have been shown to be connected to increased bruising in cattle. Sometimes these factors are related to the environment and sometimes these factors are related to

individual animal characteristics. Rough handling (Huertas et al., 2010), mixing with horned animals (Shaw et al., 1976; Strappini et al., 2010; Mendonça et al., 2016), transport through auction markets (Grandin, 2000; Strappini et al., 2012) and inadequate facilities (Bethancourt-Garcia et al., 2019) are some pre-slaughter factors associated with increased risk of bruising.

Why, when and how did that bruise occur?

Understanding where bruises come from, and most importantly finding ways in which to prevent them, requires you to think like a detective: be observant, be creative, and be proactive examining key control points within your systems to make improvements. Determining the cause of a bruise is like a criminal investigation; you start at the 'scene of the crime', i.e. the bruised carcass, and have to work your way backwards through the system to determine what may have occurred during the process to cause the bruise. This is not always a straightforward process and it does not always deliver a definitive answer, but, if nothing else, it provides clues to follow as you continue to focus on reducing the prevalence of bruising within your systems.

Bruises can occur after stunning but not after bleeding

A study was conducted in cattle with applying force to bruise the cattle before and after exsanguination and it was determined that a bruise could form before and after stunning, but not after exsanguination when the blood pressure of the animal is close to zero (Hamdy et al., 1957b). Meischke and Horder (1976) stated that bruising is possible after an animal falls out of the 'knock box' after stunning but if the 'stun-to-stick' interval is decreased then this can decrease the amount of bruising. The depth of the injury can also affect the time it takes for the bruise to appear on the surface of the dermis; superficial bruises can appear almost immediately after the trauma occurs, while deep tissue bruising can take hours to appear or not appear at all on the surface, due to the body initiating the inflammatory response (Langlois and Gresham, 1991). Although there is potential for bruising to occur after an animal is rendered insensible at a slaughter facility, the extent of bruising at this time is likely low, due to the rate that exsanguination occurs and the handling process of the carcass during this period. However, artefacts arising from post-mortem changes and equipment damage can resemble a bruise (Vanezis, 2001).

Being a detective to find causes of bruises

What clues can we take from a bruise? By visually inspecting a carcass, you can gather many clues about what may have caused a bruise and when it may have occurred. Bruises provide clues with their shape, location, colour, size, severity, number of bruises, and similarity between individual animals (i.e. more than one animal from a group has the same bruise). There are many things a bruise can tell you if you take the time to look. Consider the bruised carcasses in Figs 5.3, 5.4 and 5.5. The actual causes of these bruises are unknown to the authors. Common causes of the bruises shown in the figures are listed in the captions.

Examine the bruising in Fig. 5.3. This is a bovine carcass with significant bruising down the dorsal midline, with a concentrated area at about the midpoint of the carcass that is somewhat circular in shape. There is significant bruising in the concentrated area, with an entire area of bruising along the spine, loin and ribs emanating from that midway point. This is a relatively large area of bruising. The colour, particularly of the focal point, is dark red and there is no evidence of yellowing, suggesting this bruise is not 'old' and likely occurred at some point during the marketing process (that time could vary, depending on where this animal came from). The pattern suggests that something made forceful contact with the animal's back although it is impossible to know exactly what occurred. Thinking about handling events that cattle experience, one could speculate that this bruise may have been caused by an overhead gate banging into the animal's back or potentially the animal bumped into part of a trailer or load-out during loading or unloading. During research projects, observations are made of handling events (Lee *et al.*, 2017), and/or video footage is taken (Kline, 2018) to help inform what could have occurred so that it can be prevented from occurring in the future.

Figure 5.4 shows an image of a smaller bruised area at the tailhead of a cow. This bruise is bright red with no yellow present, suggesting it is not an 'old' bruise. The shape is circular and it is located right above a bony protrusion, which potentially increased the likelihood of a bruise forming in this instance. Once again, similar to Fig. 5.3, this animal

Fig. 5.3. Bovine dorsal bruising along the back and shoulders of the carcass observed on the processing floor. When back bruises are observed, a possible cause is low compartment height in trucks. Strappini *et al.* (2013) found that many bruises were caused by the stunning box door hitting the back. (Photo courtesy of Helen Kline.)

likely bumped into some overhead edge of a facility or trailer that the animal moved through or past.

Lastly, in Fig. 5.5 the bruised area is similar in shape to Fig. 5.4. This bruise is a little bit of a deeper red/purple colour. It is on the hip region of the carcass, so once again matching the location with knowledge of the handling process before slaughter: one can imagine that this animal bumped into a gate or corner catching a bony part of its body on a protruding edge with some force, causing this bruise to form.

Fig. 5.4. Bovine tailhead (near the base of the tail) bruising on the carcass observed on the processing floor. (Photo courtesy of Helen Kline.)

Fig. 5.5. Bovine hip bruising on the carcass observed on the processing floor. Possible causes of hip (loin) bruises are: (i) two cattle jammed in a truck door; (ii) horns; (iii) animal caught between the end of gate and a fence; or (iv) hitting sharp edges in the handling facility. (Photo courtesy of Helen Kline.)

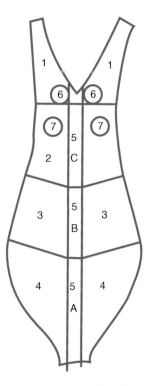

Fig. 5.6. Carcass diagram used for bruise scoring post-mortem and/or traumatic event scoring ante-mortem (adapted from Strappini *et al.*, 2012). Each region is identified by a unique number associated with that region.

Are bruises occurring inside or outside the slaughter plant?

These figures represent isolated examples of carcasses; we do not have information about bruising of other animals within the group or bruising of cattle in other groups. If any of these bruises (shape, location, colour) were repeatedly seen on carcasses from various groups of cattle, one can start to speculate that this may be occurring at the plant, i.e. if groups of cattle arriving from different origins have the same bruise markings, the plant is the location they have in common and were similarly exposed to. It is necessary to sample among multiple groups of cattle to gain

a clearer understanding of when and where bruises may be occurring.

Bruise Monitoring and Scoring

Packing companies can monitor bruising within their facilities. Employees can visually assess bruising and provide feedback to facility management. There are numerous ways to track bruising effectively, and any method can be adapted to a particular plant system. Some current methods used in research studies utilize some variation of a carcass chart (example in Fig. 5.6) on which bruise location and colour are marked by an observer. Figure 5.6 is a carcass scoring diagram adapted from Strappini *et al.* (2012); the dorsal section has been further divided into three subsections (5A–C) as opposed to one section in the original diagram. This diagram can be used to identify where on the carcass a bruise was observed. A similar diagram can be used when observing live animal handling.

L.N. Edwards-Callaway and H.C. Kline

Instead of scoring bruising, the observer will score where an animal 'bumped' into equipment or facilities, indicating the location of a potential bruise. Anecdotally, the authors used this diagram when scoring traumatic events in live cattle and inverted it to help mimic more realistically the orientation of cattle moving through the facility. This information can be paired with bruise scoring post-mortem to provide some integrated information about the animal's observed experience and the bruising pattern. Others studies have used similar diagrams (i.e. both sides of a carcass divided into regions) to track locations of bruises (Rezac, 2013; Lee *et al.*, 2017). These diagrams are useful for scoring location of bruising.

During the NBQAs, data is collected on the number, location and severity of bruises. The NBQA Bruise Key assesses severity of bruises visually by estimating the entire weight of the bruise on the carcass; the scale has 10 categories of severity, ranging in size from a quarter to an entire primal, but the severity is usually reported in larger categories of bruising: minimal = less than 0.45 kg trim loss; major = 0.46–4.54 kg trim loss; critical = 4.55–18.14 kg trim loss; extreme = loss of an entire primal (Eastwood *et al.*, 2017; Harris *et al.*, 2017). The authors recommend repeatability and reliability training for observers to ensure consistency in data collection.

Usually additional information, such as the origin of cattle (e.g. feedlot, farm, producer, sale barn), distance travelled, presence of horns and type of cattle (e.g. cow, bull, steer, heifer), should be collected as well in order to provide some information regarding the pre-slaughter management of the animals. As discussed above, some of the individual animal characteristics and management practices can increase the risk of bruising and therefore documenting these parameters may be helpful for in-plant bruising investigations. Performing targeted audits of different groups of animals at the processing facility is a way to measure and manage bruising. Incorporating a periodic bruise monitoring system into a quality assurance plan is a valuable way to benchmark bruising, target system changes and track improvement.

Evaluating pre-slaughter handling to find potential causes of bruising

In addition to scoring bruising on carcasses, it is often helpful to pair carcass bruising with an assessment of the handling prior to stunning, for example during loading, transport, unloading or movement within the slaughter facility. Bruising is sometimes challenging to monitor because obviously bruise prevalence cannot be assessed ante-mortem; thus, by the nature of bruising itself, it remains out of sight and out of mind until the opportunity for prevention has passed. Instead, the evaluation of handling, transport and movement ante-mortem to identify events that could potentially cause bruising needs to happen in tandem with the visual assessment post-mortem. These types of observations include watching animals unload at the facility and recording any bumps, jams or 'traumatic' impacts with the trailer, facility, handling aids or other animals. Additional observations could potentially occur at loading and during transport to the slaughter facility, depending on the resources and time available to do so. It is helpful to record where these 'traumatic' events occurred on a diagram to be used later in comparison with carcass bruising from those specific groups of animals. Although observing large groups of animals and assessing animals on a group ('lot') basis is helpful and provides valuable information, it is also helpful to focus on individual animals. By making observations on a specific animal and maintaining its identity as it moves through the slaughtering process, one is able more assuredly to make some inferences about the bruises found.

Weighing bruised trim meat

Additionally, it is possible to assess carcass loss (yield loss from bruised meat that has been trimmed and removed from the carcass) or damage by evaluating carcasses after trimming is complete. Collecting and weighing the bruise trim and the location in which this trim was located can provide valuable information on bruising. There are numerous ways to monitor bruising and they can be adapted to individual plants to help answer welfare and production questions.

Conclusion

Identifying the critical control points for bruising in the livestock supply chain is an ongoing process. By examining each step in the process, both the scientific community and abattoir management can evaluate the risk factors for bruising and develop methods to equip the livestock industry with relevant information that facility personnel can readily apply to current animal handling programmes. To decrease bruising requires an industry-wide effort to animal handling and well-being of cattle. Identifying the original cause of a bruise found on a carcass post-mortem is a complex and challenging task. The science of bruise assessment is not so precise that we can identify the hour, minute, location and day that a bruise occurred. What we can do is pair post-mortem bruise evaluation with ante-mortem handling and management evaluation to make some informed estimates of what could be targeted within the pre-slaughter system to improve our processes.

References

Barington, K. and Jensen, H.E. (2016) The impact of force on the timing of bruises evaluated in a porcine model. *Journal of Forensic and Legal Medicine* 40, 61–66.

Capper, C. (2001) The language of forensic medicine: the meaning of some terms employed. *Medicine, Science and the Law* 41(3), 256–259.

Bethancourt-Garcia, J.A., Vaz, R.Z., Vaz, F.N., Silva, W.B., Pascoal, L.L. *et al.* (2019). Pre-slaughter factors affecting the incidence of severe bruising in cattle carcasses. *Livestock Science* 222, 41–48.

CFR (2019) United States Code of Federal Regulations. 9 – Animals and Animal Products. Parts 311 (Disposal of diseased or otherwise adulterated carcasses and parts) and 381 (Poultry products inspection).

Davis, G.J. (1998) Patterns of Injury: blunt and sharp. *Clinics in Laboratory Medicine* 18(2) 339–350. doi: 10.1016/S0272-2712(18)30174-4

DiMaio, V.J. and DiMaio, D. (2001) *Forensic Pathology*. CRC Press, Boca Raton, Florida.

Eastwood, L., Boykin, C., Harris, M., Arnold, A., Hale, D. *et al.* (2017) National Beef Quality Audit - 2016: Transportation, mobility, and harvest-floor assessments of targeted characteristics that affect quality and value of cattle, carcasses, and by-products. *Translational Animal Science* 1(2), 229–238.

Grandin, T. (2000) *Livestock Handling and Transport*, 2nd edn. CAB International, New York.

Grandin, T. (2018) Welfare Problems in Cattle, Pigs, and Sheep that Persist Even Though Scientific Research Clearly Shows How to Prevent Them. *Animals* 8(7), 124. doi: 10.3390/ani8070124

Hamdy, M.K., Deatherage, F.E. and Shinowara, G.Y. (1957a) Bruised. I. Biochemical changes resulting from blunt injury. *Proceedings of the Society for Experimental Biology and Medicine* 95(2), 255–258.

Hamdy, M., Kunkle, L., Rheins, M. and Deatherage, F. (1957b) Bruised tissue III. Some factors affecting experimental bruises. *Journal of Animal Science* 16(2), 496–501.

Hamdy, M.K., May, K.N., Flanagan, W. and Powers, J.J. (1961a) Determination of the age of bruises in chicken broilers. *Poultry Science* 40(3), 787–789.

Hamdy, M.K., May, K.N. and Powers, J.J. (1961b) Some biochemical and physical changes occurring in experimentally-inflicted poultry bruises. *Proceedings of the Society for Experimental Biology and Medicine* 108(1), 185–188.

Harris, M., Eastwood, L., Boykin, C., Arnold, A., Gehring, K. *et al.* (2017) National Beef Quality Audit – 2016: Transportation, mobility, live cattle, and carcass assessments of targeted producer-related characteristics that affect value of market cows and bulls, their carcasses, and associated by-products. *Translational Animal Science* 1(4), 570–584.

Henderson, G. (2016) Beef's $35 million bruise. *Drovers Cattlenetwork*, September. Available at: http://digital edition.qwinc.com/publication/?i=338096&article_id= 2585141&view=articleBrowser#{%22issue_id%22: 338096,%22view%22:%22articleBrowser%22,%22 publication_id%22:%2240918%22,%22article_ id%22:%222585141%22} (accessed 15 July 2019).

Howes, E.L. and Harvey, S.C. (1932) The age factor in the velocity of the growth of fibroblasts in the healing wound. *Journal of Experimental Medicine* 55, 577–590.

Huertas, S.M., Gil, A.D., Piaggio, J.M. and Van Eerdenburg, F.J.C.M. (2010) Transportation of beef cattle to slaughterhouses and how this relates to animal welfare and carcase bruising in an extensive production system. *Animal Welfare* 19(3), 281–285.

Hughes, V., Ellis, P., Burt, T. and Langlois, N. (2004a) The practical application of reflectance spectrophotometry for the demonstration of haemoglobin and its degradation in bruises. *Journal of Clinical Pathology* 57(4), 355–359.

Hughes, V., Ellis, P. and Langlois, N. (2004b). The perception of yellow in bruises. *Journal of Clinical Forensic Medicine* 11(5), 257–259.

Johnson, C.F. (1990) Inflicted injury versus accidental injury. *Pediatric Clinics of North America* 37(4), 791–814.

Kline, H.C. (2018) Carcass bruising location and bruise trim loss in finished steers, cows, and bulls at five commerical slaughter facilities. Dissertation, Colorado State University, Fort Collins, Colorado.

Langlois, N.E. (2007) The science behind the quest to determine the age of bruises – a review of the English language literature. *Forensic Science, Medicine, and Pathology* 3(4), 241–251.

Langlois, N. and Gresham, G. (1991) The ageing of bruises: a review and study of the colour changes with time. *Forensic Science International* 50(2), 227–238.

Lee, T.L., Reinhardt, C.D., Bartle, S.J., Vahl, C.I., Siemens, M. and Thomson, D.U. (2017) Assessment of risk factors contributing to carcass bruising in fed cattle at commercial slaughter facilities. *Translational Animal Science* 1(4), 489–497.

L.N. Edwards-Callaway and H.C. Kline

Marshall, B. (1977) Bruising in cattle presented for slaughter. *New Zealand Veterinary Journal* 25(4), 83–86.

McCausland, I. and Dougherty, R. (1978) Histological ageing of bruises in lambs and calves. *Australian Veterinary Journal* 54(11), 525–527.

Meischke, H. and Horder, J. (1976) A knocking box effect on bruising in cattle [beef cattle, slaughtering]. *Food Technology in Australia* 28, 369–371.

Mendonça, F.S., Vaz, R.Z., Leal, W.S., Restle, J., Pascoal, L.L., Vaz, M.B. and Farias, G.D. (2016) Genetic group and horns presence in injuries and economic losses of bovine carcasses. *Semina: Ciências Agrárias* 37, 4265–4273. doi: 10.5433/1679-0359.2016v37n6p4265

Nash, K.R. and Sheridan, D.J. (2009) Can one accurately date a bruise? State of the science. *Journal of Forensic Nursing* 5(1), 31–37.

National Cattlemen's Beef Association (1994) *National Non-fed Beef Quality Audit. Executive Summary*. National Cattlemen's Beef Association, Englewood, Colorado.

National Cattlemen's Beef Association (2017) *National Beef Quality Audit – 2017: Market cows and bulls, Executive summary*. National Cattlemen's Beef Association, Englewood, Colorado.

Pilling, M., Vanezis, P., Perrett, D. and Johnston, A. (2010) Visual assessment of the timing of bruising by forensic experts. *Journal of Forensic and Legal Medicine* 17(3), 143–149.

Pimstone, N.R., Tenhunen, R., Seitz, P.T., Marver, H.S. and Schmid, R. (1971) The enzymatic degradation of hemoglobin to bile pigments by macrophages. *Journal of Experimental Medicine* 133(6), 1264–1281.

Randeberg, L.L., Winnem, A.M., Larsen, E.L., Haaverstad, R., Haugen, O.A. and Svaasand, L.O. (2007) In vivo hyperspectral imaging of traumatic skin injuries in a porcine model. *Proceedings of SPIE - The International Society for Optical Engineering* 6424. doi: 10.1117/12.699380

Rezac, D.J. (2013) Gross pathology monitoring of cattle at slaughter. Doctoral dissertation, Kansas State University.

Robertson, D. (2007) Canine spectator falls for Tour de France rider. *Daily Mail News*. Available at: https://www.dailymail.co.uk/news/article-469049/Canine-spectator-falls-Tour-France-rider.html (accessed 15 August 2019).

Roeber, D.L., Mies, P., Smith, C., Belk, K., Field, T. *et al.* (2001) National market cow and bull beef quality audit – 1999: a survey of producer-related defects in market cows and bulls. *Journal of Animal Science* 79(3), 658–665.

Shaw, F.D., Baxter, R.I. and Ramsay, W.R. (1976) The contribution of horned cattle to carcase bruising. *The Veterinary Record* 98(13), 255–257.

Strappini, A.C., Frankena, K., Metz, J.H.M., Gallo, B. and Kemp, B. (2010) Prevalence and risk factors for bruises in Chilean bovine carcasses. *Meat Science* 86, 859–864.

Strappini, A.C., Frankena, K., Metz, J.H.M., Gallo, C. and Kemp, B. (2012) Characteristics of bruises in carcasses of cows sourced from farms or from livestock markets. *Animal* 6(3), 502–509.

Strappini, A.C., Metz, J.H.M., Gallo, C., Frankena, K. *et al.* (2013) Bruises on culled cows when, where and how they are inflicted, *Animal* 7, 485–491.

Vanezis, P. (2001) Interpreting bruises at necropsy. *Journal of Clinical Pathology* 54(5), 348–355.

Venes, D. (2009) *Taber's Cyclopedic Medical Dictionary*. FA Davis, Philadelphia, Pennysylvania.

Wigham, E.E., Butterworth, A. and Wotton, S. (2018) Assessing cattle welfare at slaughter – Why is it important and what challenges are faced? *Meat Science* 145, 171–177.

6 Behavioural Principles of Stockmanship and Abattoir Facility Design

TEMPLE GRANDIN*

Department of Animal Science, Colorado State University, USA

Summary

Cattle, pigs, sheep and other livestock are very sensitive to visual stimuli and intermittent sounds. Removal of distractions from handling facilities will improve animal movement. Handlers also need to understand basic behavioural principles such as the flight zone and the point of balance. Low-stress handling of cattle and pigs requires moving small bunches. Good handling will require more walking to move small groups. Non-slip flooring is essential in stun boxes, races, unloading ramps and alleys. There are some species differences. Funnel-shaped crowd pens work well for cattle and sheep but poorly for pigs. To prevent pigs from jamming, there should be an abrupt entrance to a single file race. This chapter also contains a list for solving problems with handling and restraint equipment.

Learning Objectives

- Learn to find and remove visual and auditory distractions that cause animals to baulk, turn back, or refuse to move.
- Understand flight zone principles and point of balance when moving livestock.
- Learn how to design lairages, races, stun boxes and restrainers.
- Solve and fix handling problems that are detrimental to animal welfare.

Introduction

Good stockmanship when handling animals will improve both efficiency and animal welfare. When animals become difficult to move or handle, it is often due to the animal being fearful. Scientific research clearly shows that animals can experience fear (Davis, 1992; Panksepp, 2011). Stress hormone cortisol levels are similar during restraint, for veterinary procedures on the farm, and at the abattoir (Grandin, 1997a; Mitchell *et al.*, 1988). Novel experiences are often frightening to animals. In both cattle and sheep, the novelty of the abattoir environment may be a major cause of agitated fearful behaviour. Deiss *et al.* (2008) and Bourguet *et al.* (2010) showed that sheep and cattle that were more reactive to sudden novelty on the farm were also more reactive at slaughter. Therefore, the animals are more likely to be reacting to being in a novel place instead of being afraid of getting slaughtered (see Chapter 1). Calm animals are much easier to handle than frightened excited animals. People working with livestock need to understand that if an animal becomes highly agitated and fearful, 20–30 min is required for the heart rate to return to normal (Stermer *et al.*, 1981) and for stress hormones to decline (Lay *et al.*, 1992a,b). The best approach is to handle animals quietly so that they remain calm.

Signs of Agitated Fearful Livestock

People handling livestock need to be able to recognize when animals are becoming frightened. When an animal is becoming increasingly

* Email: cheryl.miller@colostate.edu

stressed, the following behavioural signs may be visible:

- the animal suddenly raises its heads in response to a stimulus;
- defecation with loose faeces;
- tail switching in cattle and horses (Grandin, 2017); and
- whites of the eyes show (Janczak *et al.*, 2008; Core *et al.*, 2009).

People moving and handling livestock need to understand how the animals perceive their surroundings. Cattle, sheep, pigs and other animals are extremely sensitive to things that move rapidly, shadows and reflections on shiny metal (Grandin, 1980a,b, 1996; Tanida *et al.*, 1996; Lanier *et al.*, 2000). These visual distractions can cause animals to baulk and refuse to move through a race or alley (Grandin, 1996). Removal of the distractions will usually improve animal movement. Later in this chapter, there will be further information on finding and removing distractions.

Vision and Hearing

Vision in cattle, pigs and sheep

Cattle, sheep and pigs have wide-angle vision and they can almost see all around themselves without turning their heads (Prince, 1970; Kilgour and Dalton, 1984; Hutson, 2014). Grazing animals, such as horses and sheep, have a horizontal band of sensitive retina (Shinozaki *et al.*, 2010). This enables them to easily scan their surroundings for danger during grazing. Grazing animals do have depth perception (Lemmon and Patterson, 1964), but it is likely that their depth perception is poor. Animals may stop and put their heads down when they see either a shadow on the floor, or a change in the surface such as moving from a concrete to a steel floor. They need to determine if the floor is safe to walk on. Farm animals are partially colour blind and they do not see red. Red may appear as grey or black. The retina of cattle, sheep and goats is most sensitive to yellowish-green (552–555 nm) and bluish-purple light (444–455 nm) (Jacobs *et al.*, 1998). This may explain why yellow safety vests may be a major distraction. The dichromatic vision of the horse is most sensitive at 428 nm and 539 nm (Carroll *et al.*, 2001). Dichromatic (two-colour) vision where the retina receptor for red is absent may also explain why livestock are so sensitive to sharp contrasts of light and dark.

Animal movement is highly influenced by vision

Compared with facilities on a farm, an abattoir usually has much more activity around the handling facilities. Solid sides are recommended on stun boxes and single file races to block the animal's view of nearby people, vehicles, conveyors and other equipment outside the race (Grandin, 1980a,b). Heather Ercolano (2018), an animal welfare specialist at a large slaughterhouse for cull dairy cows, experimented with both open and solid sides on the single file race (chute) that led to the stunner. The cows moved more easily when the solid sides were added. Muller *et al.* (2008) found that cattle remained quieter during restraint when they were not able to see a person standing beside them. In existing slaughter plants, experimentation should be done to determine if adding a solid side improves movement. Large pieces of cardboard work well for this purpose.

Cattle, pigs and sheep do not like to enter dark places. Adding a light to illuminate a dark stun box entrance can improve animal movement (Van Putten and Elshof, 1978; Grandin, 1982, 2001). A third principle on how vision has an effect on animal movement is that livestock may baulk and refuse to enter a stun box or race that appears to be a dead-end. Cattle will often enter a stun box more easily if they can see light through either the head-holder or a small window is installed in the front of the box. To prevent the incoming animals from seeing people or moving equipment, a solid shield should be located approximately 1 m in front of the box. In summary, there are three basic principles on how vision affects animal movement.

- Animals baulk and refuse to move forward when they see visual distractions ahead of them (Grandin, 1980a,b; Tanida *et al.*, 1996) (see Box 6.1).
- They are more willing to move from a darker area towards a more brightly illuminated area (Van Putten and Elshof, 1978; Grandin, 1982, 1996, 2001).
- They refuse to move towards a place that looks like a dead-end. This can be caused by layout mistakes in stun boxes, drive alleys and at the junction between a single file race (chute) and a crowd pen. An animal standing at the entrance of a single file race should be able to see two or three body lengths up the race. If the single file race is bent very abruptly at the junction, the animals may refuse to enter it.

Hearing in farm animals

Farm animals have sensitive hearing and are sensitive to high-pitched sounds. They can hear high-frequency sounds that people cannot hear. The human ear is most sensitive to sounds in the 1000–3000 Hz range. Cattle and horses are most sensitive to frequencies at 800 Hz and above (Heffner and Heffner, 1983). Sheep can hear up to 10,000 Hz (Wollack, 1963). High-pitched, intermittent sounds are also more likely to cause cattle or pigs to react (Talling *et al.*, 1998; Lanier *et al.*, 2000).

Designing equipment to reduce noise will help keep animals calmer. Air hissing should be muffled and metal clanging and banging should be silenced. Some equipment companies are building moving parts of equipment from heavy plastic panels to reduce noise (Fig. 6.1). Another advantage of plastic panels is that they are less reflective. A smartphone app can be used to monitor noise (Iulietto *et al.*, 2018) and assess the effectiveness of noise reduction methods.

Handlers should watch where animals point their ears. Cattle, sheep and many other animals will point their ears towards things that attract

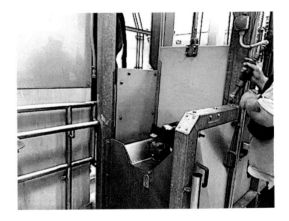

Fig. 6.1. The sliding panels that restrain the top of the bovine's neck and the box exit door are both constructed from thick plastic panels. This helps to reduce noise. (Photo courtesy of Temple Grandin.)

their attention. Yelling and screaming at livestock is highly stressful (Waynert *et al.*, 1999; Pajor *et al.*, 2003). Unlike equipment noise, yelling has intent; the animals know that the handler is yelling at them.

T. Grandin

Fig. 6.2. Cow's-eye view into a stun box with a head yoke. Note the reflections on the shiny metal. Moving a ceiling light may eliminate these reflections. Make sure that an approaching animal does not see people through the head yoke. This stun box has a good non-slip floor. (Photo courtesy of Temple Grandin.)

Flight Zone and Point of Balance

Flight zone principles for moving livestock

Handlers need to understand the behavioural principles of the flight zone and point of balance for moving cattle, pigs, sheep and other animals. To keep animals calm and move them easily, the handler should work on the edge of the flight zone (Grandin, 1980a,b, 2014; Grandin and Deesing, 2008) (Fig. 6.3). If cattle rear up or become agitated in a single file race, the handler should back up and retreat out of the animal's flight zone. Most animals will stop rearing and calm down when the handler backs out of their flight zone. The flight zone is the animal's personal space, and the size of the flight zone can vary from 0 m from a person to over 10 m.

Hedigar (1968) defined the process of taming an animal as removal of the flight zone to the point that the animal allows people to touch it. When a person penetrates the flight zone, the animals will turn and move away. The size of the flight zone will vary depending on how wild or tame the animals are. Completely tame animals that have been trained to lead have no flight zone. Usually, they should be led instead of being driven. If an animal

is trained to lead with a halter (head collar), it may be advisable to lead it into the stun box. Extensively raised animals that seldom see people will have a larger flight zone than animals that see people every day. When cattle are handled quietly, their flight zone will become smaller.

Understanding the flight zone

The size of the flight zone is determined by conditions on the farm where the animal was raised. There are three factors: (i) the amount of contact with people; (ii) the quality of the contact with people – calm and quiet versus shouting and hitting; and (iii) animal genetics. Animal temperament (flighty versus calm) is a heritable behaviour trait (genetic trait) (Hearnshaw and Morris, 1984; Voisinet et al., 1997a,b; Zambra et al., 2015; Littlejohn et al., 2016). Animals that see people every day on the farm when they are fed will usually have a smaller flight distance than animals on extensive pastures that see people only a few times a year. It is possible to have indoor intensively raised animals with large flight zones. This is caused by people never entering their pens during fattening. All species of livestock *must* become accustomed to people walking inside their pens before they come to an abattoir. Livestock that are properly acclimatized to people will quietly move away when a person walks through their pen. If pigs pile up and squeal during handling at the abattoir, this is usually an indicator that people never entered their pens on the farm.

Use the principle of pressure and release

To move extensively raised animals in a calm, controlled manner, the handler should work on the edge of the flight zone. The handler penetrates the flight zone to make the animals move and he backs up when he wants them to stop moving. The handler should avoid the blind spot behind the animal's rear. Animals may become agitated when a person is inside their personal space and the animals are unable to move away. This often occurs in either a race or small pen. If livestock turn and run back past the handler while being driven down a drive alley in the lairage, overly deep penetration of the flight zone is a likely cause. The handler should immediately back up and retreat from inside the flight zone when the animals give the slightest indication that they will turn back. Cattle and other

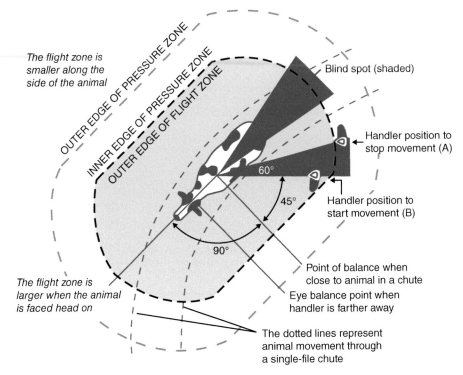

The flight zone is smaller along the side of the animal

OUTER EDGE OF PRESSURE ZONE

INNER EDGE OF PRESSURE ZONE

OUTER EDGE OF FLIGHT ZONE

Blind spot (shaded)

Handler position to stop movement (A)

60°

45°

Handler position to start movement (B)

90°

The flight zone is larger when the animal is faced head on

Point of balance when close to animal in a chute

Eye balance point when handler is farther away

The dotted lines represent animal movement through a single-file chute

Fig. 6.3. Flight zone and point of balance. To move a single animal forward, the handler must be behind the point of balance and stay out of the blind spot directly behind the animal. When the handler is close to the animal, the point of balance is at the shoulder. When the handler is farther away, the point of balance may move forward to just behind the eye. When the handler is on the outer edge of the pressure zone, the animal becomes aware of the handler's presence and turns around and looks. When the outermost edge of the flight zone is penetrated, the animal moves away. (Diagram courtesy of Temple Grandin, www.grandin.com)

livestock with very large flight zones may immediately turn back and run out of a lairage pen they have just entered. They are attempting to get away from the handler and they can be dangerous. Plant managers and livestock buyers need to work with producers to reduce problems with wild livestock with large flight zones.

Point of balance principles

The flight zone diagram (Fig. 6.3) shows the correct positions for the handler to move livestock through a single file race. The handler should stand behind the point of balance at the shoulder to make an animal go forward and in front of the point of balance at the shoulder to make an animal back up (Kilgour and Dalton, 1984; Smith, 1998; Grandin, 2014). The most common mistake that people make is to stand in front of the point of balance and poke the animal on the hindquarters to make

it move forward. This gives the animal conflicting signals and confuses it. The handler must be behind the shoulder when he wants to urge the animal forward. Another effective method to move animals forward in a single file race is to walk quickly by them in the opposite direction of desired movement (Fig. 6.4). The animal will move forward when the point of balance is quickly crossed.

Pressure zone or zone of awareness

When a person enters the edge of the flight zone, the animals will turn away from the person and move forward. When the person is just outside the flight zone, a group of cattle, pigs or sheep may turn and face the handler. This is called the pressure zone (Fig. 6.3). Other names for this zone are zone of awareness, or zone of influence. When a person is in this zone, they are outside the flight zone but the animals are watching and they know a person

T. Grandin

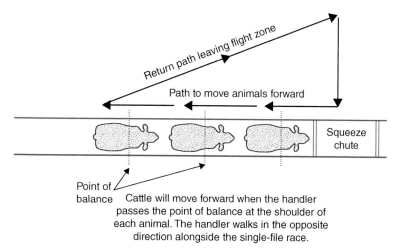

Return path leaving flight zone

Path to move animals forward

Squeeze
chute

Point of
balance   Cattle will move forward when the handler
passes the point of balance at the shoulder of
each animal. The handler walks in the opposite
direction alongside the single-file race.

Fig. 6.4. Handler movement pattern to induce cattle, pigs or sheep to move forward in a chute or race. (From Grandin, 1998, in Gregory, N.G. (ed.) *Animal Welfare and Meat Science*. CAB International, Wallingford, UK, p. 47.)

is there. On a pasture, cattle that are really far away will ignore you and continue to graze.

Use the bubble for moving groups out of pens

When cattle, sheep or pigs move past a handler standing at the gate, they will flow around the handler and keep the handler on the edge of their flight zone. It is like a 'force field' around the stock person. If the handler is positioned at the correct location at a gate, the animals will flow around the bubble formed around the person (Fig. 6.5). After movement is started, the handler should continue standing slightly outside the edge of the flight zone but inside the pressure zone. This method is very effective for moving animals out of large lairage pens. The flight zone diagram (Fig. 6.5) is mostly used in the single file race, because it prevents the animal from turning around, or for moving single animals, such as dairy cows or sows. When a group of animals is flowing out of a pen, the handlers must not attempt to keep moving back into the pen to stay behind the point of balance.

Timing bunches of cattle, pigs or goats to prevent turning around

Cattle, pigs and other livestock have a natural instinct to want to go back to where they came from. If they are allowed to stop too long in a drive alley or crowd pen, they will turn around to return to the lairage pens. When handlers learn to time

bunches, the animals can be kept moving and will not have the opportunity to turn around.

Moving small bunches and using following behaviour

Good stockmanship and low-stress handling at an abattoir will require more walking to bring small bunches of animals up to the crowd pen (forcing pen) that leads to the single file race (chute) (Fig. 6.6). Management in each facility should determine the number of animals that work well. A basic principle is that cattle, pigs and goats should be moved in small separate bunches. Sheep have the most intense following behaviour and larger bunches can be used. They can often be moved into the single file race in a continuous flow.

The crowd pen that leads to the single file race should be filled *half* full so that cattle and pigs will have room to turn. All livestock will follow the leader and handlers can take advantage of this natural behaviour to move animals easily. Cattle and pigs will enter a single file race more easily if it is allowed to become partially empty before attempting to fill it. A partially empty race takes advantage of following behaviour, because it provides enough space for four to ten animals to enter while following the leader. This will enable the group to pass through the crowd pen without stopping. Doing this will help prevent problems caused by animals stopping and having the opportunity to turn around.

Fig. 6.5. When the handler positions themselves in the correct position at a gate, pigs, cattle and sheep will flow around the bubble that is formed along the edge of the flight zone. (Photo courtesy of Temple Grandin.)

Fig. 6.6. Round crowd pen that has been filled half full. Note that the crowd gate is not pushed up tight against the animals. This design takes advantage of the natural behaviour of cattle and sheep to go back to where they came from. (From Grandin, T., 1998, in Gregory, N.G. (ed.) *Animal Welfare and Meat Science*. CAB International, Wallingford, UK.)

Trained leader animals

Trained goats or sheep will lead sheep through stockyards or lairages (Hutson, 2014). Lead animals also work really well for moving sheep on and off trucks. A specialist lead sheep or goat should be used for different handling procedures. Training the lead animals will be easier if one leader is trained to unload trucks, another is trained to load trucks and a third animal is trained to lead sheep out of pens and through the stockyards. In confined spaces such as trucks and small lairage pens at the slaughter plant, lead animals are recommended instead of

dogs. Dogs can be highly stressful for sheep (Hemsworth *et al.*, 2018). Lead sheep have been working very successfully for many years at the largest sheep slaughter plant in the USA.

Livestock become fearful when alone

A single cow in a pen that becomes agitated in an attempt to join its herdmates has caused many accidents that have severely injured people. Never get in a small, confined pen with a single, agitated bovine. Isolation away from herdmates is highly stressful for all livestock (Bates *et al.*, 2014). There are inherited genetic differences in an animal's response to isolation (Zambra *et al.*, 2015). It may jump a fence or run into people. If a lone animal becomes agitated, put some other animals with it.

Driving aids for moving livestock

Stock people should be trained to be quiet and avoid yelling. They need to learn how to move animals calmly and not be constantly poking them with a driving aid. A common mistake is to make lots of noise by banging driving aids on fences and other equipment. If the animals refuse to move, there may be distractions that need to be removed.

An electric goad should never be used as a person's primary driving tool. The World Organisation for Animal Health (OIE, 2016a,b) code recommends that only battery-operated goads should be used. Electric prod use will increase cortisol (stress hormone) levels in cattle and pigs (Hemsworth *et al.*, 2011) and fast movements by stock people and grabbing animals were detrimental for sheep

T. Grandin

(Hemsworth *et al.*, 2018). The OIE (2016a,b) code also states that electric goads should not be used on sheep, horses or very young animals such as piglets. The goad should only be picked up when other non-electrified methods fail to move an animal. Research has shown that the attitude of the handler towards the animal is better when shocks are not being used (Coleman *et al.*, 2003). Electric goads are also really detrimental to both meat quality and animal welfare (Benjamin *et al.*, 2001; Warner *et al.*, 2007; Ferguson and Warner, 2008; Edwards *et al.*, 2010a,b). Cattle that become behaviourally agitated have poor meat quality (Gruber *et al.*, 2010). However, a brief shock on the hindquarters is preferable to hard tail twisting or beating animals. Tail twisting is illegal in the UK. After the stubborn animal is moved with the electric goad, the goad should be put away. A plastic bag taped to the end of a stick or a flag is an excellent tool for moving cattle and directing their movement in crowd pens. For pigs, panels work really well in narrow alleys (McGlone *et al.*, 2004). Hard plastic panels are too heavy for people to carry all day. Plastic flags with a hand hold in the middle are effective for moving market-weight pigs out of lairage pens (Fig. 6.7). Some specialists in low-stress livestock handling prefer to use no driving aid. One reason for this recommendation is that it is difficult to stop people from constantly waving them. A skilled person can move the animals by making small movements of their bodies. Driving aids must never be applied to sensitive parts of the animal such as

the eyes, ears, nose, rectum, genitals or udder. The OIE code (OIE, 2016a,b) states:

> Painful procedures (including whipping, tail twisting, use of nose twitches, pressure on eyes, ears or external genitalia) or the use of goads or other aids which cause pain and suffering (including large sticks, sticks with sharp ends, lengths of metal piping, fencing wire or heavy leather belts) should be not be used.

Problems that originate at the farm

Problems that originate at the farm may make livestock difficult to handle at the slaughter plant. There are some cattle or pigs that may be difficult to move even when they are handled in well-designed facilities. This may be caused by lameness (difficulty walking) or being fed excessive amounts of beta agonist growth promoters (Peterson *et al.*, 2015). To solve these problems, conditions on the farm will need to be improved. Handlers should keep records to determine which producers send in animals that have handling problems. In one abattoir, problems with high numbers of downed non-ambulatory pigs were corrected by: (i) the producers reducing use of ractopamine beta agonists; (ii) genetic selection of breeding stock for good foot and leg conformation; and (iii) walking through the finishing (fattening) pens to get the pigs accustomed to people walking through them. Animals that are accustomed to being moved on the farm will be easier to handle (Abbot *et al.*, 1997; Geverink *et al.*, 1998; Lewis *et al.*, 2008; Krebs and McGlone, 2009). Brown *et al.* (2006) found that having people walk the finishing pens once or twice a week made pigs easier to drive at the slaughter plant. This teaches the pigs to move away quietly when people walk through them. High doses of beta agonists may have a detrimental effect on pig or cattle handling (Grandin, 2010; Peterson *et al.*, 2015; Ritter *et al.*, 2017).

Stockyards, Lairage and Races

Design of stockyard and lairages

A basic requirement is that cattle and sheep that are held overnight must have sufficient space to all lie down at the same time (see Chapter 11). The number of animals that can be carried in a truckload is usually used to determine the size of each lairage pen. Pens are usually designed to hold one or two truckloads.

Fig. 6.7. Flag with both a handle and a centre handhold for moving pigs. It is much lighter and easier to use than a panel. This photo also shows excellent non-slip flooring. (Photo courtesy of Temple Grandin.)

Resting time in lairage

Pigs require resting time in the lairage to preserve pork quality. At all times, pigs must always have sufficient space for all the animals to lie down at the same time (see Chapter 11). One hour is the minimum rest time and 2–4 h is recommended (Milligan *et al.*, 1998; Warriss, 2003). Pigs transported a short distance do not have sufficient time to calm down after being loaded and they need a longer resting time (Garcia-Celdran *et al.*, 2012). Lambs may benefit from overnight lairage or a 6–12-h holding time (Liste *et al.*, 2011; Liu *et al.*, 2012) (see Chapter 4).

One-way flow through the yards

Lairages and stockyards should be laid out to have one-way flow through the pens. The animals enter at one end of a pen and exit through the other end. Herringbone designs with the pens on a 60–70-degree angle work well (Fig. 6.8 and see Chapter 11). Do not put the pens on a 45-degree angle, because animals are more likely to become stuck in sharp corners. Pens can also be laid out in a straight configuration. Long narrow pens may help reduce fighting. Gates should be made to open on an angle. On a 2.5 m wide alley, use 3 m gates; and on a 3 m wide alley, use 3.5 m gates. The animals enter the pens through the outer alleys and move to the stunner through the central alley.

Use of non-slip flooring

A rough broom finish on concrete will quickly wear smooth. For pigs and sheep, printing the pattern of expanded metal mesh into the wet concrete is recommended. The grooved floor shown in Fig. 6.6 will also work well. Cattle and other large animals will need deeper grooves. A 20 cm × 20 cm diamond pattern that has grooves 2.5 cm deep is effective. Concrete slats can be used in the pens but the drive alleys should have solid concrete. More information on flooring can be found in the open-access sources of Grandin (2008) and www.grandin.com.

Handling intact bulls

Bulls fight more than steers. Mixing strange bulls can increase meat quality problems due to fighting and mounting. Bulls that have been reared on the farm in groups can be held in a regular group pen with their penmates. Do not mix bulls from other pens.

There are problems when bulls arrive as singles. If they are penned together, they will mount each other and fight. This is likely to cause poor-quality dark cutting meat or injuries. To prevent mounting and aggression, they can be unloaded into single file races. If this system is used, they should be delivered in a 'just in time' manner so that they spend less than an hour in single file races. This system should only be used when small numbers of one or two bulls are brought to an abattoir.

Design of single file race system

Single file races work well for cattle and sheep because they are animals that naturally walk in single file. Cattle will walk in single file when moving from pasture to pasture on the farm. Both of these species have a strong natural behaviour to follow the leader. In abattoirs, single file races are essential for low-stress handling of extensively raised cattle and sheep that have had little contact with people. In most countries, cattle and sheep are handled in systems with single file races and crowd pens to direct animals to the stun box. Since slaughter houses have many distractions, such as moving equipment and people, the use of solid sides on crowd pens, races and stun boxes is strongly recommended (Grandin, 1980a,b, 2014). This is especially important for animals with large flight zones. Blocking an animal's vision may result in calmer animals (Mitchell *et al.*, 2004; Muller *et al.*, 2008).

In small abattoirs in developing countries, a tame single bovine or water buffalo can be led to the slaughter area. Stunning can be performed while the animal is standing. In larger abattoirs, it is recommended to use a race and crowd pen system. All races should have solid outer fences to prevent the animals from seeing people, vehicles, moving equipment or other distractions outside the fence. Animal entry into the race can sometimes be facilitated if solid shields are installed to prevent approaching animals from seeing people standing by the race. A curved single file race is especially recommended for the moving of cattle and other large animals (Grandin, 1980a,b) (Fig. 6.9). A curved race works well for two reasons. It prevents incoming animals from seeing activity up ahead and it takes advantage of the natural behaviour to go back to where they came from. Pigs will move

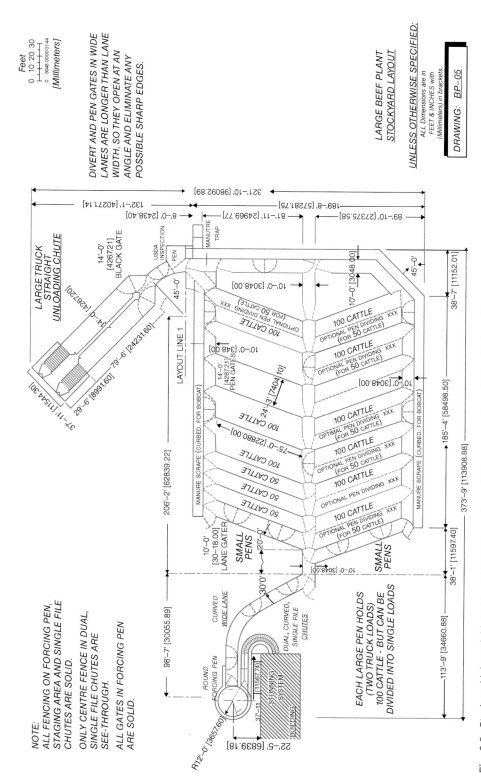

Fig. 6.8. Stockyard lairage laid out in a herringbone pattern. (Diagram courtesy of Temple Grandin.)

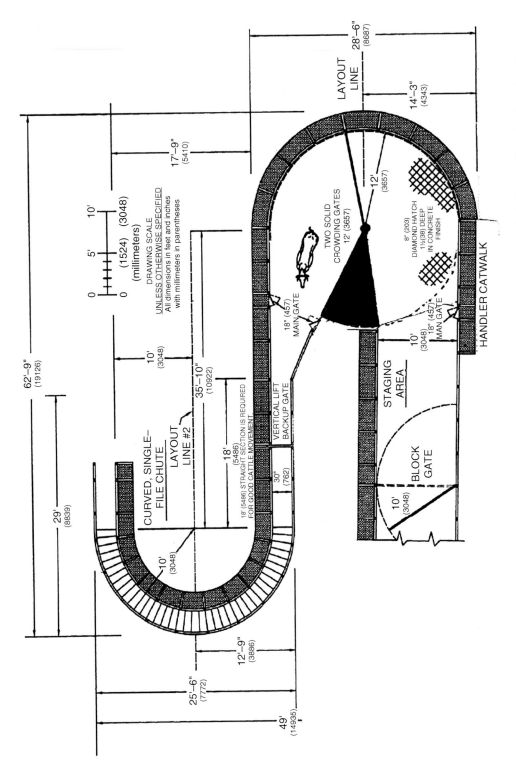

Fig. 6.9. Round crowd pen and curved race system for cattle. The round crowd pen has a 3.5 m (10 ft) radius. To facilitate cattle entry, there is a 5.4 m (18 ft) section of straight race before the curve. This enables the animal to see a place to go. One of the most common mistakes is bending the race too sharply where it joins the crowd pen. The stock person stands on the black shaded area to encourage the cattle to circle around him. This is called 'working the crowd gate pivot'. The crowd gate is latched as shown in Fig. 6.6. A small version of this design will also work with sheep. The round crowd pen radius can be shortened to 2.5 m (8 ft).

T. Grandin

easily in a straight race (Grandin, 1982). Figure 6.9 shows a round crowd pen and curved race that will work well for cattle and other large livestock. A stockperson stands in the black shaded area and uses a flag to encourage the animals to circle around. This takes advantage of the natural behaviour to go back to where they came from. The person stands at the pivot point of the crowd gate. This often works more efficiently than having the person move livestock when walking around the outer perimeter of the round crowd pen.

An inside radius of 5 m is ideal for cattle (additional recommendations are given in Grandin and Deesing, 2008). Walkways for the handler should run alongside the race, and the use of overhead walkways should be avoided. In slaughter plants with restricted space, a serpentine race system can be used (Grandin, 1984). A race system at an abattoir must be long enough to ensure a continuous flow of animals to the stunner, but not be so long that animals become stressed from waiting in line too long. A hold-down rack over the top of a single file race must not touch the backs of the animals, as they tend to panic if hold-down bars press on to their backs.

Crowd pen design leading to single file

A well-designed round crowd pen takes advantage of the animal's natural tendency to want to go back to where it came from. As animals move through the round pen, they will think they are going back to the lairage (Figs 6.6, 6.9). The recommended radius of the crowd pen is 3.5 m for cattle, 2.5 m for pigs or sheep. A funnel-shaped transition works well to direct cattle and sheep into a single file; one side of the funnel should be straight and the other should be on a 30-degree angle. Figure 6.9 shows the correct layout for cattle. Funnels work poorly

for pigs (Hoenderken, 1976). The entrance of the pig race should be abrupt (Fig. 6.10).

Unloading of trucks

Prompt unloading upon arrival at an abattoir is essential for good animal welfare. More than one unloading dock is strongly recommended. If animals have to be weighed or counted upon arrival, there should be an unloading pen for each unloading dock. These pens enable animals to be unloaded promptly prior to sorting, weighing or identification checking. After one or more procedures have been performed, the animals move to a holding pen in the lairage. Facilities used for unloading only should be 2.5–3.0 m wide to provide the animals with a clear exit into the alley (Grandin, 1980a).

A big problem in some developing countries is that there may be no unloading ramps. Animals are jumped out of vehicles and may break legs. Ramps can be easily built from either steel or concrete by local welders or masons. People skilled in welding and masonry are readily available in all developing countries. In most countries, two ramps will be needed: one for large trucks and one for smaller pickup ('ute') trucks. Stationary ramps are easier for local people to build than complicated devices such as hydraulic tailgate lifts or ramps that move up and down.

Ramps and slopes

Ideally, an abattoir should be built at truck deck level to eliminate ramps for both unloading and movement to the stunner. This is especially important for pigs. The maximum angle for non-adjustable livestock truck loading ramps should be 20–25 degrees. The ramp leading to the stunner should not exceed 10 degrees for pigs, 15 degrees for cattle

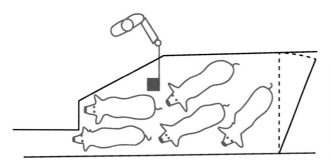

Fig. 6.10. The diagram shows a simple crowd pen design that has an offset step in the single-file race entrance which helps prevent jamming by allowing one pig to step aside. The handler is shown in the correct position to move pigs. The handler should work opposite to the straight edge. (From Grandin, 2015, p. 90.)

and 20 degrees for sheep. Ramp angles to the stunner should be more gradual than the maximum angles that will work for loading trucks. A loading ramp for pigs should not exceed 20 degrees (Warriss *et al.*, 1991). Pigs remain calmer on a ramp with a more gradual slope (Warriss *et al.*, 1991; Berry *et al.*, 2012). To reduce the possibility of falls, unloading ramps should have a flat deck at the top. This provides a level surface for animals to walk on when they first step off the truck. This same principle also applies to ramps to the stunner; a level portion facilitates animal entry into the restrainer or stunning box.

Grooved stair steps are recommended on concrete ramps (Grandin, 1980a, 2008) (Fig. 6.11). They are easier to walk on after the ramp becomes worn or dirty. The dimensions for cattle and other large animals are a 10 cm rise and a 30 cm or longer tread width. Steps 45 cm (18 in) long are recommended. For slaughter-weight pigs, cleats should be spaced 15 cm apart (Warriss *et al.*, 1991). For cattle, the spacing should be 20 cm of space between the cleats (Grandin, 2008). In pigs, there were very few differences in stress levels when they were loaded or unloaded with either a ramp or a hydraulic tailgate lift (Brown *et al.*, 2006). In developing countries, small livestock such as sheep may be handled manually during loading instead of using a ramp. Yardimci *et al.* (2012) reported that use of a ramp will reduce stress in sheep. Construction of a ramp is strongly recommended.

Handling systems for pigs

In Germany, Hartung *et al.* (1997) found that pigs were less stressed in a very short 3.5 m race than in a longer 11 m race. Figure 6.10 shows a crowd pen for pigs with an abrupt entrance. Funnel-shaped crowd pens work poorly with pigs. German plants run at slower speeds than plants in the USA and a race 3.5 m long may cause more stress in a plant running 800 pigs per hour, because the short race makes it more difficult to keep up with the line. In plants slaughtering 240 or fewer pigs an hour, stunning them with electric tongs in groups on the floor was less stressful than a double single-file race (Warriss *et al.*, 1994). In larger plants with a higher line speed, floor stunning with tongs tends to get rough and careless. In a small plant, pigs stunned in small groups on a floor had better meat quality (Stuier and Olsen, 1999).

In very small abattoirs where 20 or fewer market-weight pigs are processed per hour, some abattoirs use a captive bolt. The pigs are held in small groups of four to five animals in a small pen. The author observed that the other pigs had very little reaction when a pig was shot. Schaeperkoetter (2019) found that the last pig that was shot with a captive bolt was less stressed than the first pig in the group. The pen must have sufficient space so that the other pigs have sufficient space to move away. With a skillful stunning operator who seldom missed a shot, the other pigs did not squeal or become agitated. They

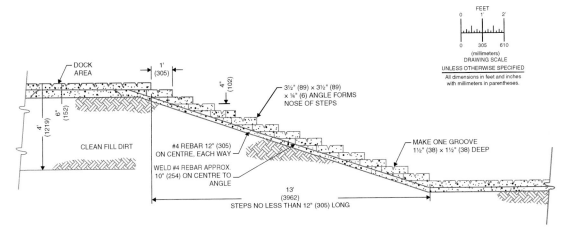

Fig. 6.11. For concrete ramps, stair steps are strongly recommended. One advantage of stair steps is that when they become worn, the animals can still walk easily on them. For unloading ramps, use 10 cm rise and 45 cm long tread length. The ramp has a level dock area so that animals exiting the truck will walk on a level floor. If cattle are wild, the level area should be 6 m (20 ft).

appeared to be unaware of what was happening. Anecdotal evidence suggests that the other animals should never observe the head being removed.

Group handling eliminates electric prods on pigs

Group handling systems for CO_2 stunning have significant advantages compared with handling pigs in single file races. Four to eight pigs at a time can be moved into the gondola and electric prods can be completely eliminated. Often the simpler systems with just a few powered pusher gates are better. Equipment companies like to sell many more powered pusher gates than are actually needed. The best systems have powered gates where a person can easily control forward movement. This prevents overcrowding of the pigs. Pigs must *never* be dragged or knocked over by powered gates. When vertical slide gates are used for pigs, injuries can be prevented by constructing the entire gate from a flexible piece of rubber conveyor or belting (Fig. 6.12). If the gate is closed on the pigs, the rubber flap will fold up.

Stun Boxes and Restrainers

Conventional stun boxes

A common mistake is to build stun boxes too wide. A stun box 76 cm wide will hold all cattle with the exception of some of the largest bulls. Stun boxes must have non-slip flooring to allow the animal to stand without slipping. A level or almost level floor is recommended. Stun boxes

with steeply sloped floors or stepped floors often cause animals to become agitated. Use of these floor designs should be avoided. In a conventional cattle stun box, stunning accuracy can be greatly improved by the use of a yoke to hold the animal's head. For cattle, yokes and mechanized head restraints are often used (Figs 6.1 and 6.2). Figure 6.13 shows an innovative stun box where a rear pusher gate has been eliminated. The headholder travels towards the animal instead of pushing the animal forward. Ewbank *et al.* (1992) found that cattle had higher stress levels when their heads were restrained. The system they observed was poorly designed and lacked a rear pusher gate. Forcing the animal's head into the restraint was difficult and took an average of 32 s. In well-designed systems, cattle will enter easily and the head is restrained within 5 s.

To minimize stress, the yoke must be designed so that the animal will enter it willingly (see Box 6.1). It must be stunned immediately after the head is caught. Munoz *et al.* (2012) and Paranhos de Costa *et al.* (2014) give additional information on correcting problems in stun boxes.

Restraint methods that cause suffering

The OIE (2019a,b) guidelines for animal welfare state that methods of restraint that cause avoidable suffering should not be used. Some of the worst methods that should never be used are:

- suspending or hoisting animals (other than poultry) by the feet or legs;

Fig. 6.12. Vertical slide gates constructed from flexible curtains made from conveyor belting will not injure the pigs if they are accidentally closed on them. (Photo courtesy of Temple Grandin.)

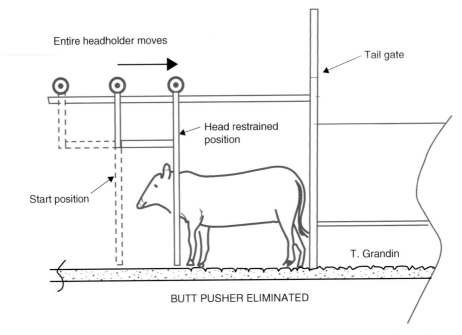

Fig. 6.13. This innovative stun box head yoke design eliminates the problems associated with pushing cattle forward with a rear pusher gate. The entire head yoke (headholder) assembly slowly moves backward towards the animal. Sudden jerky motion must be avoided. To block the animal's view of activity in front of the headholder, a solid shield should be installed in front of the headholder. (Diagram courtesy of Temple Grandin.)

- mechanical clamping of the legs of mammals;
- breaking legs or tails;
- cutting leg tendons;
- blinding by poking out eyes;
- severing the spinal cord with a puntilla (dagger) that paralyses the animals; and
- electrical immobilization with currents that are not sufficient to cause loss of sensibility (Lambooy, 1985; Grandin *et al.*, 1986; Pascoe, 1986; Rushen, 1986ab; Rushen *et al.*, 1986).

Conveyor restrainer systems

One advantage of conveyor systems is that animals follow their herdmates and will not have the stress of being alone (Bates *et al.*, 2014). One of the first modern systems was the 'V' conveyor restrainer for pigs (Regensburger, 1940). This consists of two obliquely angled conveyors that form a V. Pigs ride with their legs protruding through the space at the bottom of the V. The V restrainer is a comfortable system for pigs with round, plump bodies and for sheep (Grandin, 1980a). Pressure against the side of the pigs will cause it to relax (Fig. 6.14) (Grandin *et al.*, 1989). Both sides of the conveyor restrainer

Fig. 6.14. V conveyor restrainer for either pigs or sheep. The slats are constructed from insulating plastic for use with electrical stunning of either pigs or sheep. Both sides of the conveyor must run at the same speed to prevent animals from struggling. Photo courtesy of Temple Grandin.

must run at the same speed. Pigs may struggle or vocalize if one side runs faster than the other. However, the V restrainer is not suitable for restraining calves or extremely heavily muscled pigs with

T. Grandin

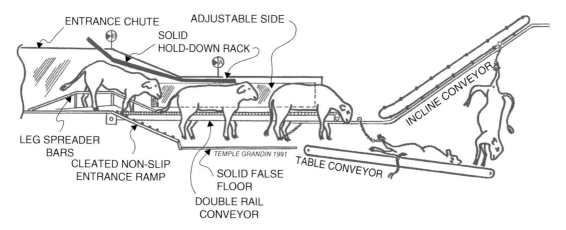

ENTRANCE CHUTE — ADJUSTABLE SIDE

SOLID
HOLD-DOWN RACK

INCLINE CONVEYOR

LEG SPREADER
BARS

CLEATED NON-SLIP
ENTRANCE RAMP

TEMPLE GRANDIN 1991

TABLE CONVEYOR

SOLID FALSE
FLOOR

DOUBLE RAIL
CONVEYOR

Fig. 6.15. Centre track double rail conveyor restrainer system for cattle. For cattle, it has many advantages compared with a V restrainer conveyor. (From Grandin, 1993, p. 303.)

large, overdeveloped hams (Lambooy, 1986). The V pinches the large hams and the slender forequarters are not supported. Some of the very lean, long pigs are also not supported properly by the V restrainer.

Researchers at the University of Connecticut, USA, developed a laboratory prototype for a double rail restrainer system to replace V conveyor restrainers (Westervelt *et al.*, 1976; Giger *et al.*, 1977). Calves and sheep are supported under the belly and the brisket by two moving rails. This research demonstrated that animals restrained in this manner were under minimal stress. Sheep and calves rode quietly on the restrainer and seldom struggled. The space between the rails provides a space for the animal's brisket and prevents uncomfortable pressure on the sternum. The prototype was a major step forward in humane restrainer design, but many components still had to be developed to create a system that would operate under commercial conditions.

In 1986, the first double rail restrainer was designed and installed in a large commercial calf and sheep slaughter plant by Grandin Livestock Handling Systems and Clayton H. Landis in Suderton, Pennsylvania, USA (Grandin, 1988). In the early 1990s, the Stork Company in the Netherlands developed a restrainer where pigs ride on a moving centre line conveyor.

In 1989, the first double rail restrainer was installed in large cattle slaughter plants by Grandin Livestock Handling Systems and Swilley Bond Equipment, Logan, Iowa, USA (Figs 6.14, 6.15) (Grandin, 1993). Half the cattle in North America are now handled in

Fig. 6.16. Large fed steer in the centre track double rail restrainer. The slats on the conveyor are shaped to fit the animal's brisket. Adjustable side panels move in and out to fit different sized cattle. (From Grandin, 1993, p. 303.)

this system, and it has been installed in over 30 plants. The double rail restrainer has many advantages compared with the V restrainer (Grandin, 1993) (Figs 6.15, 6.16). Stunning is easier and more accurate, because the operator can stand 28 cm closer to the animal. Cattle also enter more easily, because they can walk in with their legs in a natural position.

Proper design is essential for smooth, humane operation. Incoming cattle must not be able to see light coming up from under the restrainer. It must have a false floor below the restrained animal's feet, to provide incoming cattle with the appearance of a solid floor to walk on (Grandin, 1993). To keep cattle calm, they must be fully restrained and settled down on the conveyor before they emerge from under the hold-down rack. If the hold-down is too short, the cattle are more likely to become agitated. The principle is to block the animal's vision until it is fully restrained (Grandin, 2003).

Solving problems in stun boxes and conveyor restrainers

If animals struggle, vocalize or become agitated in the stun box, non-stun slaughter box or conveyor restrainer, their welfare is not acceptable. The most common causes of these problems are described in Box 6.2.

Box 6.2. Solving problems in stun boxes and conveyor restrainers

Use this outline to locate and remedy problems that cause livestock either to refuse to move forward or to become agitated.

- **Distractions that cause baulking** – This was discussed in the first part of this chapter.
- **Stun box floor is slick** – The animal becomes agitated because its feet do numerous rapid small sideways slips. Observe the animal's feet from the shackle side of the box. A steel floor made from diamond-embossed steel is often not adequate to prevent slipping. It should have either steel rods welded to it or a rubber mat. Never crisscross the rods on top of each other. The rods must lie flat on the floor of the box.
- **Stun box floor jiggles** – A metal floor that jiggles may scare animals. Animals may refuse to enter the stun box when they see the jiggling floor.
- **Baulking at visual cliff** – In both V restrainer conveyors and the double rail (centre track) conveyor restrainer, incoming cattle, pigs or sheep must not be able to see that the conveyor is raised up above the floor. It must have a false floor below the restrained animal's feet to provide the appearance of a solid floor to walk on. Block light that comes up from underneath the conveyors.
- **Excessive pressure applied by a headholder or other restraint device** (Grandin, 1998, 2001; Bourguet et al., 2011) – When there is excessive pressure, cattle or pigs will vocalize in direct response to being clamped in the device. The remedy is to reduce the pressure applied to the animal. Cattle vocalization is associated with higher cortisol levels (Dunn, 1990; Hemsworth et al., 2011).
- **Holding an animal in the fully restrained position too long** (Velarde and Raj, 2016) – This is especially a problem in non-stun slaughter boxes. This may cause cattle to vocalize. The animal should be stunned immediately after its head is restrained.
- **Sharp edges or pinching of the animal hide by the equipment** – A very small sharp edge or pinching of the skin will cause the animal to struggle or vocalize.
- **Excessive electric prod use** – This may cause animals to enter the box or conveyor in an agitated state and make stunning difficult. Train employees and remove distractions that cause baulking.
- **One side of a V conveyor restrainer runs faster than the other** – This will cause struggling due to pulling and stretching of the skin.
- **Animal thrown off balance causes struggling** – Restrainers that hold the animal's body with a squeeze side must not tilt it off balance. In systems where an upright animal is supported with its feet off the floor, it must be held in a balanced position. Examples of properly designed systems are in Regensburger (1940), Giger et al. (1977), Panepinto (1983) and Grandin (1988, 1992, 1993).
- **Animal's body not fully supported in rotating boxes** – Cattle will struggle if their bodies slip when the box rotates. The body must be held snugly.
- **Poorly designed controls on hydraulic or pneumatic equipment** – Pneumatic systems should be designed to enable the operator to have mid-stroke position control of the air cylinders that operate headholders and other restraint devices (Grandin, 1992). This will enable the operator to use lighter pressure for smaller animals. Controls should also be designed to limit the maximum pressure that can be applied. For example, a headholder requires a much lighter maximum pressure setting than a heavy door. Separate pressure relief valves on different parts of the system will prevent a careless operator from injuring an animal with either a headholder or rear pusher gate. Avoid air being powered down on vertical doors at the entrance and exit of a stun box. The control system should be designed so that the operator can immediately stop a gate from moving. This will help prevent bruising at the stun box door. On poorly designed systems, that door may continue to move downward when the operator pushes the control to raise it. There is more information and design of controls in Grandin (1992, 2016).

T. Grandin

Conclusions

Both good design of equipment and supervision of employees are required to have a high standard of animal welfare. Employees should be trained in the behavioural principles of livestock handling. Handling and welfare during handling and stunning can often be achieved after making simple improvements in facilities. Non-slip flooring in stun boxes and unloading areas is essential. Changing lighting or adding a light can be used to improve animal movement.

References

Abbott, T.A., Hunter, E.J., Guise, J.H. and Penny, R.H.C. (1997) The effect of experience of handling on pig's willingness to move. *Applied Animal Behaviour Science* 54, 371–375.

Bates, L.S.W., Ford, E.A., Brown, S.N., Richards, C.J., Hadley, P.J. *et al.* (2014) A comparison of handling methods relevant to religious slaughter of sheep. *Animal Welfare* 23, 251–258.

Benjamin, M.E., Gonyou, H.W., Ivers, D.L., Richardson, L.F., Jones, D.J. *et al.* (2001) Effect of handling method on the incidence of stress response in market swine in a model system. *Journal of Animal Science* 79 (Supplement 1), 279 (abstract).

Berry, N.L., Johnson, A.K., Hill, J., Longergan, S., Karriker, L.A. and Stalder, K.J. (2012) Loading gantry versus traditional chute for finisher pigs, effect on welfare at the time of loading and performance measures and transport losses at the harvest facility. *Journal of Animal Science* 90, 4028–4036.

Bourguet, C., Deiss, V., Gobert, M., Durand, D., Boissey, A. and Terlouw, E.M.C. (2010) Characterizing the emotional reactivity of cows to understand and predict their stress reactions to the slaughter procedure. *Applied Animal Behaviour Science* 125, 9–21.

Bourguet, C., Deiss, V., Tannugi, C.C. and Terlouw, E.M.C. (2011) Behavioural and physiological reactions of cattle in a commercial abattoir: relationships with organizational aspects of the abattoir and animal characteristics. *Meat Science* 88, 158–168.

Brown, N.S., Knowles, T.G., Wilkins, L.J., Chad, S.A. and Warriss, P.D. (2006) The response of pigs to being loaded or unloaded into commercial transporters using three systems. *The Veterinary Journal* 70, 91–100.

Carroll, J., Murphy, C.KJ., Neitz, M. and Van Hoeve, J.N. (2001) Photopigment basis for dichromatic vision in the horse. *Journal of Vision* 1, 80–87.

Coleman, G.J., McGregory, M., Hemsworth, P.H., Boyce, J. and Dowling, S. (2003) The relationship between beliefs, attitudes, and observed behaviors in abattoir personnel in the pig industry. *Applied Animal Behaviour Science* 82, 189–200.

Core, S., Miller, T., Widowski, T. and Mason, G. (2009) Eye white as a predictor of temperament in beef cattle. *Journal of Animal Science* 87, 2174–2178.

Davis, M. (1992) The role of the amygdala in fear and anxiety. *Annual Review of Neuroscience* 15, 353–375.

Deiss, V., Temple, D., Ligout, S., Racine, C., Boux, J. *et al.* (2008) Can emotional reactivity predict stress responses at slaughter in sheep? *Applied Animal Behaviour Science* 119, 193–202.

Dunn, C.S. (1990) Stress reactions of cattle undergoing ritual slaughter using two methods of restraint. *Veterinary Record* 126, 522–525.

Ercolano, H. (2018) Presentation at Animal Care Conference, North American Meat Institute, October 18–19, Kansas City.

Edwards, L.N., Engle, T.E., Correa, J.A., Paradis, M.A., Grandin, T. and Anderson, D.B. (2010a) The relationship between exsanguination blood lactate concentration and carcass quality in slaughter pigs. *Meat Science* 85, 435–440.

Edwards, L.N., Grandin, T., Engle, T.E., Porter, S.P., Ritter, M.J. *et al.* (2010b) Use of exsanguination blood lactate to assess the quality of pre-slaughter handling. *Meat Science* 86, 384–390.

Ewbank, R., Parker, M.J., and Mason, C.W. (1992) Reaction of cattle to head restraint at stunning: a practical dilemma. *Animal Welfare* 1, 55–63.

Ferguson, D.M. and Warner, R.D. (2008) Have we underestimated the impact of pre-slaughter stress on meat quality in ruminants? *Meat Science* 80, 12–19.

Garcia-Celdran, M., Ramis, G., Quereda, J.J. and Armero, E. (2012) Reduction in transport induced stress on finishing pigs by increasing lairage time at the slaughter house. *Journal of Swine Production* 20, 118–122.

Geverink, N.A., Kappers, A., van de Burgwal, E., Lambooij, E., Blokhuis, J.H. and Wiegant, V.M. (1998) Effects of regular moving and handling on the behavioral and physiological responses of pigs to pre-slaughter treatment and consequences for meat quality. *Journal of Animal Science* 76, 2080–2085.

Giger, W., Prince, R.P., Westervelt, R.G., and Kinsman, D.M. (1977) Equipment for low stress small animal slaughter. *Transactions of the ASAE* 20, 571–578.

Grandin, T. (1980a) Livestock behavior as related to handling facilities design. *International Journal for the Study of Animal Problems* 1, 33–52.

Grandin, T. (1980b) Observations of cattle behavior applied to the design of cattle handling facilities. *Applied Animal Ethology* 6, 9–31.

Grandin, T. (1981) Bruises on southwestern feedlot cattle. *Journal of Animal Science* 53 (Supplement 1), 213.

Grandin, T. (1982) Pig behaviour studies applied to slaughter-plant design. *Applied Animal Ethology* 9, 141–151.

Grandin, T. (1983) Welfare requirements of handling facilities. In: Baxter, S.H., Baxter, M.R. and

MacCormack, J.A.D. (eds) *Farm Animal Housing and Welfare*. Martinus Nihoff, Boston, Massachusetts, pp. 137–149.

Grandin, T. (1984) Race system for slaughter plants with 1.5 m radius curves. *Applied Animal Behaviour Science* 12, 295–299.

Grandin, T. (1988) Double rail restrainer for livestock handling. *Journal of Agricultural Engineering* 41, 327–338.

Grandin, T. (1992) Observation of cattle restraint devices for stunning and slaughtering. *Animal Welfare* 1, 85–91.

Grandin, T. (1993) Handling and Welfare of Livestock in Slaughter Plants, In: Grandin, T. (ed.) *Livestock Handling and Transport*. CAB International, Wallingford, UK, pp. 289–311.

Grandin, T. (1996) Factors that impede animal movement at slaughter plants. *Journal of the American Veterinary Medical Association* 209, 757–759.

Grandin, T. (1997a) Assessment of stress during handling and transport. *Journal of Animal Science* 75, 249–257.

Grandin, T. (1997b) The design and construction of handling facilities for cattle. *Livestock Production Science* 49, 103–119.

Grandin, T. (1998) The feasibility of using vocalization scoring as an indicator of poor welfare during slaughter. *Applied Animal Behaviour Science* 56, 121–128.

Grandin, T. (2001) Cattle vocalizations are associated with handling at equipment problems in beef slaughter plants. *Applied Animal Behaviour Science* 71, 191–201.

Grandin, T. (2003) Transferring results from behavioral research to industry to improve animal welfare on the farm, ranch and the slaughter plant. *Applied Animal Behaviour Science* 81, 215–228.

Grandin, T. (2008) Engineering and design of holding yards, loading ramps, and handling facilities for land and sea transport of livestock. *Veterinaria Italiana* 44(1).

Grandin, T. (2010) *Improving Animal Welfare: A Practical Approach*. CAB International, Wallingford, UK.

Grandin, T. (2014) Handling and welfare of livestock in slaughter plants. In: Grandin, T. (ed.) *Livestock Handling and Transport*. CAB International, Wallingford, UK, pp. 329–353.

Grandin, T. (2015) *Improving Animal Welfare: A Practical Approach*, 2nd edn. CAB International, Wallingford, UK.

Grandin, T. (2016) Practical methods to improve animal handling and restraint, In: Velarde, A. and Raj, M. (eds) *Animal Welfare at Slaughter*. 5M Publishing, Sheffield, UK, pp. 71–90.

Grandin, T. (2017) *Temple Grandin's Guide to Working with Farm Animals*. Storey Publishing, West Adams, Massachusetts.

Grandin, T. and Deesing, M. (2008) *Humane Livestock Handling*. Storey Publishing, North Adams, Massachusetts.

Grandin, T. and Deesing, M. (2013) Genetics and behaviour during restraint and handling. In: Grandin, T. and Deesing, M. (eds) *Genetics and the Behavior of Domestic Animals*, 2nd edn. Academic Press, Elsevier, San Diego, California, pp. 115–158.

Grandin, T., Curtis, S.E., Widowski, T. and Thurmon, J.C. (1986) Electro-immobilization versus mechanical restraint in an avoid-avoid choice test. *Journal of Animal Science* 62, 1469–1480.

Grandin, T., Dodman, N., and Shuster, L. (1989) Effect of naltrexone on relaxation induced by flank pressure in pigs. *Pharmacology and Biochemistry and Behavior* 33, 839–842.

Gregory, N.G. (ed.) (1998) *Animal Welfare and Meat Science*. CAB International, Wallingford, UK.

Gruber, S.L., Tatum, J.D., Engle, T.E., Chapman, P.L., Belk, K.E. and Smith, G.C. (2010) Relationships of behavioral and physiological symptoms of preslaughter stress on beef longissimus muscle tenderness. *Journal of Animal Science* 88, 1148–1159.

Hartung, V.J., Floss, M., Marahrens, M., Nowak, B. and Fedhsen, F. (1997) Stress response of slaughter pigs to electrical stunning in two different access systems. *Deutsch Tierztliche Wochenschrift* 104, 66–68.

Hearnshaw, H. and Morris, C.A. (1984) Genetic and environmental effect on temperament score in beef cattle. *Australian Journal of Agricultural Research* 35, 723.

Hedigar, H. (1968) *The Psychology and Behavior of Animals in Zoos and Circuses*. Dover Publications, New York.

Heffner, R.S. and Heffner, H.E. (1983) Hearing in large mammals: horse (*Equis caballus*) and cattle (*Bos taurus*). *Behavioral Neuroscience* 97(2), 299–309.

Hemsworth, P.H., Rice, M., Karlen, M.G., Calleja, L., Barnett, J.L., Nash, J. and Coleman, G.J. (2011) Human-animal interactions at abattoirs: relationships between handling and animal stress in sheep and cattle. *Applied Animal Behaviour Science* 135, 24–33.

Hemsworth, P.H., Rice, M., Borg, S., and Edwards, L.E. (2018) Relationships between handling, behaviour and stress of lambs at abattoirs. *Animal* 13(6), 1287–1296. doi: 10.1017/51751731/18002744

Hoenderken, R. (1976) Improved system for guiding pigs for slaughter to the restrainer. *Die Fleischwirtschaft* 56, 838–839.

Hutson, G.D. (2014) Behavioural principles of sheep handling. In: Grandin, T. (ed.) *Livestock Handling and Transport*. CAB International, Wallingford, UK, pp. 155–174.

Iulietto, M.F., Sechi, P., Gaudenzi, C.M., Grispoldi, L., Ceccarelli, M. *et al.* (2018) Noise assessment in slaughter houses by means of smartphone app. *Italian Journal of Food Safety* 7(2). doi:10.4081/ijfs.2018.7053

Jacobs, G.H., Deegan, J.F. and Neitz, J. (1998) Photo pigment basis for dichromatic colour vision in cows, goats, and sheep. *Visual Neuroscience* 15, 581–584.

Janczak, A.M., Salte, R. and Braastad, B.O. (2008) The use of diazepam as a pharmacological validation of eye white as an indicator of emotional state in dairy cows. *Applied Animal Behaviour Science* 96, 177–183.

Kilgour, R. and Dalton, C. (1984) *Livestock Behavior: A Practical Guide*. Westview Press, Boulder, Colorado.

Kilgour, R. and de Langen, H. (1970) Stress in sheep from management practices. *Proceedings, New Zealand Society of Animal Production* 30, 65–76.

Krebs, N. and McGlone, J.J. (2009) Effects of exposing pigs to moving and odors in a simulated slaughter chute. *Applied Animal Behaviour Science* 116, 179–185.

Lambooy, E. (1985) Electro-anesthesia or electro-immobilization of calves, sheep, and pigs by Feenix Stockstill. *Veterinary Quarterly* 7, 120–126.

Lambooy, E. (1986) Automatic electrical stunning of veal calves in a V-type restrainer. In: *Proceedings, 32nd European Meeting of Meat Research Workers*, August 24–29, 1986, Ghent, Belgium, pp. 77–80, Paper 2.2.

Lanier, J.L., Grandin, T., Green, R., Avery, D. and McGee, K. (2000) The relationship between reaction to sudden intermittent movements and sounds to temperament. *Journal of Animal Science* 78, 1467–1474.

Lay, D.C., Friend, T.H., Bowers, C.C., Grissom, K.K. and Jenkins, O.C. (1992a) A comparative physiological and behavioral study of freeze and hot iron branding using dairy cows. *Journal of Animal Science* 70, 1121–1125.

Lay, D.C., Friend, T.H., Randel, R.D., Bowers, C.C., Grissom, K.K. and Jenkins, O.C. (1992b) Behavioral and physiological effects of freeze branding and hot iron branding on crossbred cattle. *Journal of Animal Science* 70, 330–336.

Lemmon, W.B. and Patterson, G.H. (1964) Depth perception in sheep: effects of interrupting the mother-neonate bond. *Science* 145, 835–836.

Lewis, C.R.G., Hulbert, C.E. and McGlone, J.J. (2008) Novelty causes elevated heart rate and immune changes in pigs exposed to handling alleys and ramps. *Livestock Science* 116, 338–341.

Liste, G., Miranda-de la Lama, G.C., Campo, M.M., Villarroel, M., Muela, E. and Maria, G.A. (2011) Effect of lairage on lamb welfare and meat quality. *Animal Production Science* 51, 952–958.

Littlejohn, B.P., Riley, D.G., Welsh, T.H., Randal, R.D., Willard, S.T. and Vann, R.C. (2016) Heritability of temperament at weaning in a crossbred cattle population. *Journal of Animal Science* 94 (Suppl.) I. doi: 10.2527/55asas2015-001.

Liu, M.W., Zhong, R.Z., Zhou, D.W., Sun, H.X., and Zhao, C.S. (2012) Effects of lairage time after road transport on some blood indicators of welfare and meat quality traits in sheep. *Journal of Animal Physiology and Animal Nutrition* 96, 1127–1135.

McGlone, J.J., McPherson, R. and Anderson, D.L. (2004) Case study: moving devices for market-sized pigs: efficacy of electric prod, board, paddle or flag. *Professional Animal Scientist* 20, 518–523.

Miligan, S.D., Ramsey, C.B., Miller, M.F., Kaster, C.S. and Thompson, L.D. (1998) Resting of pigs and hot-fat trimming and accelerated chilling of carcasses to improve meat quality. *Journal of Animal Science* 76, 74–86.

Mitchell, G., Hattingh, J. and Ganhao, M. (1988) Stress in cattle assessed after handling after transport and after slaughter. *Veterinary Record* 123, 201–205.

Mitchell, K., Stookey, J.M., Laturnar, D.K., Watts, J.M., Haley, D.B. and Huyde, T. (2004) The effects of blindfolding on behaviour and heart rate in beef cattle during restraint. *Applied Animal Behaviour Science* 85, 233.

Muller, R., Schwartzkopf-Genswein, K.S., Shah, M.A. and von Keyserlinkg, M.A.G. (2008) Effect of neck injection and handler visibility on behavioral reactivity of beef steers. *Journal of Animal Science* 86, 1215–1222.

Munoz, D., Strappini, A. and Gallo, C. (2012) Indicadores de bienestar animal para detector problemas en al cajon de insensibilizacion de bovinos [Animal welfare indicators to detect problems in the cattle stunning box] *Archivos de Medicine Veterinaria* 44, 297–302.

OIE (2019a) Chapter 7.3. Transport of Animals by Land. *Terrestrial Animal Health Code*. World Organisation for Animal Health, Paris.

OIE (2019b) Chapter 7.5. Slaughter of Animals. *Terrestrial Animal Health Code*. World Organisation for Animal Health, Paris.

Pajor, E.A., Rushen, J. and dePaisille, A.M.B. (2003) Dairy cattle choice of handling treatments in a Y maze. *Applied Animal Behaviour Science* 80, 93–107.

Panepinto, L.M. (1983) A comfortable minimum stress method of restraint for Yucatan miniature swine. *Lab Animal Science* 33, 95–97.

Panksepp, J. (2011) The basic emotional circuits of mammalian brain. Do animals have affective lives? *Neuroscience and Biobehavioral Reviews* 35, 1791–1804.

Paranhos de Costa, M.J.R, Huertas, S.M., Strappini, A.C. and Gallo, C. (2014) Handling and transport of cattle and pigs in South America. In: Grandin, T. (ed.) *Livestock Handling and Transport*, 4th edn. CAB International, Wallingford, UK, pp. 39–64.

Pascoe, P.J. (1986) Humaneness of an electrical immobilization unit for cattle. *American Journal of Veterinary Research* 10, 2252–2256.

Peterson, C.M., Pilcher, C.M., Rothe, H.M., Marchant-Forde, J.N., Ritter, M.J. *et al.* (2015) Effect of feeding ractopamine hydrochloride on the growth performance and responses to handling and transport in heavy-weight pigs. *Journal of Animal Science* 93, 1239–1249.

Prince, J.H. (1970) The eye and vision. In: Swenson, M.J. (ed.) *Dukes Physiological of Domestic Animals*. Cornell University Press, New York, pp. 696–712.

Regensburger, R.W. (1940) Hog Stunning Pen. US Patent 2,185,949. US Patent and Trademark Office, Washington, DC.

Ritter, M., Johnson, A.K., Benjamin, M.E., Carr, S.N., Ellis, M. *et al.* (2017) Review: Effect of ractopamine hydrochloride (Paylean) on welfare indicators for market pigs. *Translational Animal Science* 1, 533–558.

Rushen, J. (1986a) Aversion of sheep to electro-immobilization and physical restraint. *Applied Animal Behaviour Science* 15, 315–324.

Rushen, J. (1986b) Aversion of sheep for handling treatments: paired-choice studies. *Applied Animal Behaviour Science* 16, 363–370.

Rushen, J. and Congdon, P. (1986) Sheep may be more averse to electro-immobilization than to shearing. *Australian Veterinary Journal* 63, 373–374.

Schaeperkoetter, M. (2019) Evaluating the impact of group stunning on the behavioral and physiological parameters of pigs and sheep in a small abattoir. Master's Thesis, Dept of Animal Science, Colorado State University, Fort Collins, Colorado.

Shinozaki, A., Hosaka, Y., Imagawa, T. and Vehara, M. (2010) Topography of ganglian cells and photo receptors in the sheep retina. *Journal of Comparative Neurology* 518, 2305–2315.

Smith, B. (1998) *Moving Em: a Guide to Low Stress Animal Handling*. Graziers Hui, Kamuela, Hawaii.

Stermer, R., Camp, T.H. and Stevens, D.C. (1981) *Feeder cattle stress during transportation*. American Society of Agricultural Engineers Paper No. 81–6001. American Society of Agricultural Engineers, St Joseph, Michigan.

Stuier, S. and Olsen, E.V. (1999) Dripless dependent on stress during lairage and stunning. Paper No. 4, p 29. In: *Proceedings of 45nd International Congress of Meat Science and Technology*, Yokohama, Japan, pp. 302–303.

Talling, J.C., Waran, N.K., Wathes, C.M. and Lines, J.A. (1998) Sound avoidance in domestic pigs depends on characteristics of the signal. *Applied Animal Behaviour Science* 58, 255–266.

Tanida, H., Miura, A., Tanaka, T. and Yoshimoto, T. (1996) Behavioral responses of piglets to darkness and shadows. *Applied Animal Behaviour Science* 49, 173–183.

van Putten, G. and Elshof, W.J. (1978) Observations of the effects of transport on the well-being and lean quality of slaughter pigs. *Animal Regulation Studies* 1, 247–271.

Velarde, A., Rodriguez, P., Dalmau, A., Fuentes, C., Llonch, P., von Hollenben, K.V. *et al.* (2014) Religious slaughter: evaluation of current practices in selected countries. *Meat Science* 96, 278–287.

Velarde, A. and Raj, M. (2016) *Animal Welfare at Slaughter*. 5M Publishing, Sheffield, UK.

Voisinet, B.D., Grandin, T., Tatum, J.D., O'Connor, S.F. and Struthers, J.J. (1997a) Feedlot cattle with calm temperaments have higher average daily gains than

cattle with excitable temperaments. *Journal of Animal Science* 75, 892–896.

Voisinet, B.D., Grandin, T., Tatum, J., O'Connor, S.F. and Struthers, J.J. (1997b) *Bos indicus*-cross feedlot cattle with excitable temperaments have tougher meat and a higher incidence of borderline dark cutters. *Meat Science* 46, 367–377.

Warner, R.D., Ferguson, D.M., Cottrell, J.J. and Knee, B.W. (2007) Acute stress induced by preslaughter use of electric prodders causes tougher meat. *Australian Journal of Experimental Agriculture* 47, 782–788.

Warriss, P.D. (2003) Optimal lairage times and conditions for slaughter pigs: a review. *Veterinary Record* 153, 170–176.

Warriss, P.D., Bevis, B.A., Edwards, J.E., Brown, S.N., and Knowles, T.G. (1991) Effect of angle on the ease with which pigs negotiate loading ramps. *Veterinary Record* 128, 419–421.

Warriss, P.D., Brown, S.N. and Adams, S.J.M. (1994) Relationship between subjective and objective assessment of stress at slaughter and meat quality in pigs. *Meat Science* 38, 329–340.

Waynert, D.E., Stookey, J.M., Schwartzkopf-Gerwein, J.M., Watts, C.S. and Waltz, C.S. (1999) Response of beef cattle to noise during handling. *Applied Animal Behaviour Science* 62, 27–42.

Westervelt, R.G., Kinsman, D., Prince, R.P. and Giger, W. (1976) Physiological stress measurement during slaughter of calves and lambs. *Journal of Animal Science* 42, 833–834.

Wollack, C.H. (1963) The auditory acuity of the sheep (*Ovis aries*). *Journal of Auditory Research* 3, 121–132.

Yardimci, M., Sahin, E.H., Cetingul, I.S., Bayram, I., Asian, R. and Sengor, E. (2012) Stress responses to comparative handling procedures in sheep. *Animal* 7, 143–150.

Zambra, N., Gimeno, D., Blache, D. and VanLier, E. (2015) Temperament and its heritability in Merino lamb. *Animals* 9(3), 373–379.

Useful Video References

Manitoba Pork (2014) Smart Pig Handling. Principles of Pig Handling, Part 2. Winnipeg, Manitoba, Canada. Available at: https://wwwyoutube.com/watch?v=aeCS71Zznys (accessed 15 April 2020)

Grandin, T. (2008) Handling Cattle Quietly in Pens. Grandin Livestock Handling Systems, Fort Collins, Colorado. Available at: https://wwwyoutube.com/watch?v=acDrG9b5uko (accessed 15 April 2020).

Grandin, T. (2008) Pig Behavior During Handling, by Temple Grandin. Available at https://www.youtube.com/watch?v=oA2x2_eAv4w (accessed 15 April 2020).

Grandin, T. (2014) Proper Use of Livestock Driving Tools, with Temple Grandin, Ph.D. Available at https://www.youtube.com/watch?v=d8mdhUqsi9s (accessed 15 April 2020).

7 Review of Scientific Research Studies on Poultry Stunning Methods

CHARLOTTE (LOTTA) BERG[1]* AND MOHAN RAJ[2]

[1]Department of Animal Environment and Health, Swedish University of Agricultural Sciences, Skara, Sweden; [2]Formerly Reader in Animal Welfare, Department of Clinical Veterinary Science, University of Bristol, UK

Summary

In this chapter, we will list the most commonly used methods for the stunning of poultry and the welfare aspects in relation to each method. The detailed physiological mechanisms for most of the stunning methods described can be found in, for example, the European Food Safety Authority (EFSA) report on the welfare aspects of the main stunning methods used by slaughterhouses for stunning commercial species of animals used for human food (EFSA, 2004). Based on the scientific evidence, the European Commission (EC) has legislated (EC Slaughter Regulation 1099/2009) certain minimum standards for stunning and killing of animals, including poultry. Similarly, Office International des Epizooties (OIE), the world organization for animal health and welfare, has produced guidelines for stunning and slaughter of animals.

In general, humane slaughter regulations and guidelines have the following requirements.

- No conscious animal shall be shackled or hoisted. However, poultry species are exempted for practical reasons.
- Animals, including poultry, must be rendered immediately unconscious prior to slaughter and they should remain so until death occurs through blood loss.
- Both carotid arteries supplying oxygenated blood to the brain must be severed.
- Animals, including poultry, must be dead before carcass dressing (including decapitation) or any other treatment (e.g. electrical stimulation or scalding) is carried out.

Learning objectives

- Understand how electrical stunning of poultry works.
- Understand the welfare issues associated with water-bath stunning.
- Understand the relevant electrical specifications and different types of electrical stunning.
- Be familiar with the use of captive bolt in poultry.
- Be familiar with the use of different types of gases for stunning poultry.
- Be familiar with the principles of low atmosphere pressure stunning of poultry.

Introduction

Legislation in many countries worldwide requires that poultry, just like mammals, should be stunned prior to exsanguination (Lambooij and Hindle, 2018). The reason behind this is that rendering the birds unconscious means that they will not experience pain, distress or unnecessary suffering during the neck cutting and bleeding phase of slaughter. Successful application of a stunning method should lead to immediate onset of unconsciousness that lasts until death occurs by bleed-out.

* Email: Lotta.berg@slu.se

The duration of unconsciousness induced by a stunning method must hence be longer than the sum of the time that elapses between the end of stun and neck cutting and the time to onset of death following neck cutting (Raj, 2010; Lines et al., 2011). Since the effect of a stunning method is momentary, the onus of preventing resumption of consciousness thereafter relies on the efficiency of the slaughter procedure, e.g. bleeding out by the prompt and accurate severance of carotid arteries supplying oxygenated blood to the brain. Some stunning procedures are therefore purposefully applied to induce humane death (e.g. killing with argon or nitrogen-induced anoxia, electrocution via head-to-body electrical stunning), rather than mere unconsciousness, and other methods lead to death due to structural damage to the brain (e.g. penetrating captive bolts) (Raj, 2010).

This chapter will also include some comments on the most commonly identified animal welfare problems in relation to each method and possible ways of minimizing these welfare risks. Furthermore, EFSA is currently updating its scientific review on slaughter of poultry, with a focus on animal welfare hazards, and a report has recently been published on the EFSA website (EFSA, 2019).

The methods dealt with in this chapter are electrical water-bath stunning, head-to-body dry electrical stunning, head-only electrical stunning, penetrating and non-penetrating captive bolt stunning, two- and multistage carbon dioxide stunning, exposure to inert gases with or without added carbon dioxide and low atmospheric pressure stunning. This covers the vast majority of the commercial broiler slaughter taking place globally. Broilers are by far the most common type of meat-producing poultry and in many cases the methods applied for broilers can be – and are – also used for stunning other types of poultry, such as end-of-lay hens, turkeys, ducks, geese and so on.

Electrical Water-bath Stunning

Mode of action

Electrical water-bath stunning is by far the most common stunning method used worldwide not only for broiler chickens but also for other types of poultry.

The brain mechanism behind electrical stunning is that application of a current of sufficient magnitude to the brain will induce a generalized epileptiform

activity and associated seizures; and this abnormal brain state is incompatible with the persistence of consciousness (Lambooy, 1981; Raj, 2006; Raj et al., 2006a,b; Lambooij and Hindle, 2018). Multiple-bird electrical water-bath stunning is the most common and cheapest method of rendering poultry unconscious prior to slaughter under commercial conditions, where high throughput rates are required (Raj, 2010). In this system, conscious birds are hung upside-down on a moving metal shackle line and passed through an electrified water-bath, such that the current flows through the whole body towards the shackle (the earth). This means that the entire bird is part of the electrical circuit (Raj, 2004).

Depending on the electrical parameter settings, water-bath stunning can be either reversible or irreversible. Exposure of poultry to low-frequency currents (e.g. less than 100 Hz) will lead to cardiac arrest via the induction of cardiac ventricular fibrillation, which would eliminate the risk of recovery of consciousness following stunning (Schütt-Abraham et al., 1983). Ventricular fibrillation can usually be achieved by delivering 120 mA per bird (for broilers) in a water-bath supplied with a 50 Hz sine wave alternating current (AC) (Berg and Raj, 2015). If higher frequencies are applied, it is usually not possible to achieve cardiac arrest in the birds, and hence the birds will recover consciousness if not immediately bled after stunning. The electrical requirements for poultry water-bath stunning have been reviewed by EFSA, with a focus on the time to induce consciousness and the duration of consciousness once achieved (EFSA, 2014b).

Animal welfare aspects of electrical stunning

From an animal welfare perspective, there are four main problems related to water-bath stunning of poultry:

- the inversion and shackling of conscious birds, which is an inevitable component of water-bath stunning;
- pre-stun shocks at the entrance to the stunners;
- the fact that several birds are stunned at the same time, and each receives a different amount of current inversely proportional to their electrical resistance; and
- the limited duration of unconsciousness induced.

Inversion and shackling are carried out as a restraining method to facilitate immersion of birds' heads in the water-bath (Fig. 7.1). Inversion in itself

Fig. 7.1. Inverted shackling of conscious birds is an unavoidable animal welfare problem related to poultry water-bath stunning. (Photo courtesy of C. Berg.)

is considered stressful (Kannan and Mench, 1996, 1997), and birds have pain receptors in their legs (Gentle and Tilston, 2000). Hence, birds will experience distress and pain when shackled. Bedanova *et al.* (2007) reported that the duration of shackling (i.e. birds hanging on shackles) was positively correlated with plasma corticosterone, glucose and lactate levels, tonic immobility duration and heterophil:lymphocyte ratio in broilers. Shackling has been considered as a major welfare issue associated with water-bath stunning of poultry (Sparrey *et al.*, 1992; Sparrey, 1994; Lambooij and Hindle, 2018). It has been reported that 90% of chickens start flapping their wings immediately after shackling and that this lasts on average for 14 s (Kannan and Mench, 1997). Wing flapping is triggered subsequently by several factors. In particular, in cases where shackle design is poor, breast support plates are absent or the birds are handled in a rough way during shacking, or jolts or vibration occur in the shackle line due to poor design, construction or maintenance, birds may start flapping their wings considerably between the point of shackling and reaching the water-bath (AVMA, 2016). Owing to the welfare concern, the duration between shackling and stunning is limited in the EC slaughter regulation to 1 min for broilers and 2 min for turkeys. By ensuring that staff are well trained (Berg, 2012) and are handling the birds carefully, and by using correctly designed

shackles of an appropriate size for the bird, by installing appropriate breast comfort plates and by applying a short interval from shackling to stunning (Lambooij and Hindle, 2018), these problems can be mitigated to some extent, but never completely. For heavy birds, such as turkeys, the shackling-related animal welfare problems are considered to be worse than in chickens. Dimming of lights or using blue light in the shackling area has been known to have a calming effect on birds and reduce wing flapping.

If birds are wing flapping as a result of pain or distress at shackling, because of long shackling lines (resulting in a long time interval from shackling to the water-bath entrance) or if the water-bath entrance is poorly constructed, birds may encounter electrical contact with the water-bath with the wings prior to the head. This will result in painful pre-stun electric shocks (Berg and Raj, 2015). Turkeys' wings hang lower than their heads and, owing to this, are predisposed to receiving pre-stun shocks at the entrance to the water-bath stunners.

Problems with variations in electrical resistance

In multiple-bird water-bath stunning systems, birds are constantly entering and leaving the water-bath with changing electrical resistance in the circuit. The electrical flow through each individual bird will be dependent on the resistance in the pathway for that particular bird. The effective electrical resistance can vary between birds, for example, between 1000 and 2600 ohms in broilers and between 1900 and 7000 ohms in layer hens (Schutt-Abraham *et al.*, 1987; Schutt-Abraham and Wormuth, 1991). Where water-bath stunners are supplied with constant voltage, birds with low electrical resistance will receive more current than necessary to achieve effective stunning, whereas those with high resistance will receive less current than necessary to achieve effective stunning. Birds in the former category will have good welfare outcome at stunning but could have poor carcass and meat quality, whereas the latter category will have poor welfare outcome and good meat quality. Most of the electrical resistance in the pathway is attributed to the poor contact between the legs and the metal shackle. The implication of this is that tighter shackle–leg fitting will reduce the electrical impedance, but this will have the negative effect of increased suffering due to pain. Nevertheless, routine cleaning of shackles using appropriate detergent to remove accumulation of fat and dirt and wetting the shackles prior to hanging live birds would help to improve electrical contact and minimize electrical resistance.

Although poultry flocks are often reasonably even in size and conformation, there is always some variation in size, weight, plumage condition, cleanliness or electrical contact between the legs and the metal shackle, and multiple-bird water-bath stunners supplied with a constant voltage will therefore not deliver effective stunning currents to all birds in the water-bath (Sparrey et al., 1992; Hindle et al, 2010) (Fig. 7.2). This is even more explicitly stated by EFSA, where a 2014 report stated that the electrical resistance varies widely between birds, making it impossible to deliver the same constant and predetermined current to each individual bird. Furthermore, EFSA stated that 'the complexity of such multiple-bird electrical water-bath stunning systems used in poultry slaughterhouses is not conducive to maintaining good animal welfare and, therefore, alternatives should be developed/implemented' (EFSA, 2014b).

Fig. 7.2. Due to variations in bird size, weight etc., multiple-bird water-bath stunners are unable to deliver the same predetermined current to each individual bird. (Photo courtesy of C. Berg.)

Reversible or irreversible stunning?

Although it is well known that a combination of high current (e.g. 120 mA) and low frequency (< 100 Hz) can be expected to result in cardiac arrest and death in the birds, and hence eliminate the risk of birds regaining consciousness before or during bleeding, many slaughterhouses do not use these electrical setting parameters. The reason for this is mainly related to product quality, as high-frequency stunning results in fewer problems with blood splash or fractures, which may lead to downgrading or rejection of the meat (Wilkins et al., 1998; Kranen et al., 2000) or to religious requirements (Sabow et al., 2017; Lambooij and Hindle, 2018). Hence, reversible stunning parameters are often used, which means that the stun-to-stick/cut interval must be kept to an absolute minimum. Globally, a large number of different settings are used commercially, not only with reference to current levels (amps) and frequencies (Hz), but also for waveforms (AC or DC) (Hindle et al., 2010; EFSA, 2013), sometimes without full understanding of how these parameters relate to each other and how the settings affect the stun quality of the birds. Indeed, electrical immobilization of conscious birds for the purpose of automatic neck cutting could not be excluded, in the worst-case scenario, especially when using low currents and high frequencies. Research has shown that sine or square wave alternating current is more effective than pulsed direct current, low frequencies (< 800 Hz) are more effective than high frequencies and that the minimum current necessary to achieve effective stunning increases as frequency of the current is increased (Raj, 2006). Girasole et al. (2016) evaluated electrical water-bath stunning of broilers with an average root mean square (RMS) current of 150, 200 and 250 mA and frequencies of 200, 400, 600, 800 and 1200 Hz. In this study, occurrence of corneal reflex, spontaneous eye blinking and a positive response to a painful stimulus were monitored and recorded immediately after the stunning and at 20 s post-stun during bleeding. The results clearly indicated that, at a current of 150 mA, the probability of a successful stun was over 90% at 200 Hz, approximately 40% at 400 Hz and below 5% for frequencies greater than 600 Hz. Therefore, the authors concluded that stunning at frequencies greater than 600 Hz cannot be recommended when RMS current of 150 mA is applied. The maximum probability of achieving a successful

C. Berg and M. Raj

stun required a current level of 200 mA at 400 Hz and a current level of 250 mA at 400 and 600 Hz, whereas the stunning treatments at 1200 Hz provided the lowest probability of a successful stun.

There are additional welfare concerns associated with water-bath stunning of ducks and geese. Firstly, heads of these poultry species are not always immersed in the water-bath; instead, the base of the neck or crop makes contact with the water (Humane Slaughter Association, 2015). This is because the birds bend their necks backwards, known as swan necking (Fig. 7.3).

The duration of reversible stunning is often limited, and hence prompt and accurate cutting of both carotids is essential to avoid the risk of birds regaining consciousness during bleeding or remaining alive whilst entering the scald tank.

A novel method of electrical water-bath stunning of individual birds has been developed for commercial use at broiler slaughter (Berg and Raj, 2015). In this system, birds are shackled as under the conventional water-bath stunning systems, but each bird is lowered into a separate water-bath and the body electrode is placed on the vent (Lambooij

et al., 2008, 2012). This means that each individual bird has its own water-bath, and hence the electrical parameters are not influenced by the impedance of other birds. Avoiding leg-to-shackle contact, which is the main source of electrical resistance in the circuit, is innovative and it may help to reduce the amount of voltage necessary to deliver the minimum current required to achieve effective stunning and killing.

Head-only Dry Electrical Stunning

Mode of action

There are commercial systems available for head-only electrical stunning of poultry using dry electrodes. One such system is built on the principle of restraining the bird in an inverted position in a cone and electrodes are automatically placed on each side of the head for stunning (Lambooij et al., 2014) (Fig. 7.4). In this way, a constant current can be applied to each bird (Berg and Raj, 2015). There are also commercial systems available with a less automated approach for small-scale slaughter of broilers, hens, turkeys or other types of poultry, where each bird is restrained manually and positioned horizontally in contact with the two metal electrodes on each side of the bird's head (Berg and Raj, 2015).

Research has shown that, when using sine wave alternating current to deliver a constant current, the effectiveness of head-only electrical stunning

Fig. 7.3. Ducks and geese tend to lift their heads by bending their necks backwards; hence there is a risk that the base of the neck or crop makes contact with the water first. (Photo courtesy of M. Raj.)

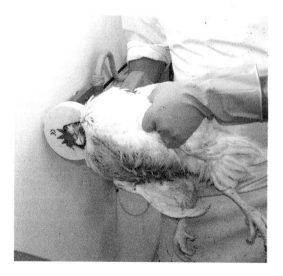

Fig. 7.4. Dry electrical stunning with manual restraint of the bird. (Photo courtesy of C. Berg.)

depends upon the frequency and amount of current delivered to individual birds (Raj and O'Callaghan, 2004). Based on the results, the authors concluded that minimum currents of 100, 150 and 200 mA should be delivered whilst using 50, 400 and 1500 Hz, respectively, to achieve adequate depth and duration of unconsciousness in broilers (Raj, 2004).

Animal welfare aspects of head-only stunning

From an animal welfare point of view, head-only electrical stunning system can deliver the required electrical current to an individual bird, if properly set up and managed. However, it only produces a reversible stun, often limited, and hence rapid cutting of both carotids is essential to avoid the risk of birds beginning to regain consciousness, i.e. the same issue as for reversible electrical water-bath stunning discussed above.

Penetrating and Non-penetrating Captive Bolt

Mode of action

A penetrating captive bolt can be used for stunning any species of poultry; however, it is used at commercial slaughterhouses as a back-up method. It is an option for small-scale slaughter or slaughter for private domestic consumption. Cartridge-powered, pneumatic (compressed air) and spring-operated captive bolts are available on the market (Raj and O'Callaghan, 2001; Gibson *et al.*, 2018) (Fig. 7.5). It has been suggested that the appropriate variables

Fig. 7.5. An example of a cartridge-powered captive bolt gun for any size and type of poultry. (Photo courtesy of C. Berg.)

for captive bolt stunning of broilers are a minimum of 6 mm bolt diameter driven at an air-line pressure of 827 kPa and a penetration depth of 10 mm (Raj and O'Callaghan, 2001).

To achieve effective stun, it is important that the bolt is correctly positioned (perpendicular to the skull), of sufficient width and penetration depth (if penetrating), and that the energy transmitted is sufficient (Raj and O'Callaghan, 2001; Martin *et al.*, 2019). Experience shows that spring-operated captive bolts do not necessarily meet these requirements and risk resulting in an insufficient stun. However, cartridge-powered, compressed air-powered and propane fuel cell-powered stun guns can consistently produce an effective stun, i.e. immediate insensibility, also in large birds such as turkeys (Erasmus *et al.*; 2010a,b; Gibson *et al.*, 2018; Woolcott *et al.*, 2018).

Animal welfare aspects of captive bolt stunning

In relation to animal welfare, the main risks related to the use of captive bolt guns are improper restraint of the bird, applying the bolt at an incorrect angle and using a bolt with too narrow diameter and/or too low velocity, all resulting in an insufficient stun. For example, Raj and O'Callaghan (2001) reported that when the captive bolt was shot at 110°, 120° or 130°, the majority of birds survived, continued breathing and showed no convulsions. Neck muscle tension and eye reflexes were also retained in these birds from the end of stunning. Post-mortem examination of the birds that survived after non-perpendicular shooting of the bolt revealed that the bolt either punctured a hole through the skin and skidded along the surface of the skull or only the rim of the bolt made contact with the skull, resulting in a compressed fracture. In the same study, examination of the skulls of broilers that were shot with a 3 mm bolt revealed that the bolt had penetrated the skull even though it failed to induce a stun. Evaluation of the spontaneous electroencephalogram (EEG) and visually evoked potentials (VEPs) indicated that these neurophysiological parameters also remained as that of pre-stun. This is because the crucial physical variable in determining the effectiveness of captive bolt stunning is the change of impulse per unit of time or, in other words, the product of mass and acceleration of the head upon the impact of the bolt. According to this, the maximum acceleration of the skull would be expected when the mass of impacting projectile is at least equivalent to that of the head and the velocity is high. By contrast, a projectile with a very small mass and a very high velocity will result in an ultra-short time span in which the skull as a whole will hardly move during transfer of energy. Instead, during impact there will be a high transfer of momentum and energy locally, resulting in perforation of the skull without acceleration of the head (Karger, 1995). In this situation, penetration of a narrow bolt into the brain tissue may not always produce immediate loss of consciousness.

Various types of novel mechanical devices

Erasmus *et al.* (2010a) evaluated the effectiveness of a commercially manufactured (Zephyr), pneumatically operated (air-line pressure of 758–827 kPa) non-penetrating captive bolt (25mm diameter, 17 mm protrusion beyond the barrel) for on-farm euthanasia of turkeys and compared it with blunt force trauma, manual cervical dislocation and mechanical cervical dislocation (crushing of the neck) using a burdizzo (a neck-crushing device originally intended for crushing spermatic cord). The results indicated that the Zephyr device and blunt trauma were effective in causing immediate unconsciousness. In contrast, neither method of cervical dislocation caused immediate unconsciousness. Several studies have shown that cervical dislocation induced by neck crushing or brain piercing does not lead to immediate unconsciousness (Erasmus *et al.*, 2010b; Martin *et al.*, 2016, 2017) and therefore is not considered to be humane.

Martin *et al.* (2019) examined three novel mechanical killing devices: Modified Armadillo (MARM, a brain-piercing device), Modified Rabbit Zinger (MZIN, a penetrating captive bolt device, 6 mm in diameter, 2.5–3.5 cm penetration depth), a novel mechanical cervical dislocation device (NMCD, a mechanical method that closely resembled the manual cervical dislocation technique) and traditional manual cervical dislocation (MCD). Post-mortem examination was carried out immediately after confirmation of death in all the chickens in order to establish treatment-specific post-mortem lesions. The percentage incidence of successfully causing death was MCD = 100.0%, NMCD = 96.0%, MZIN = 75.0% and MARM 48.7%. However, whether application of these methods produced immediate unconsciousness in all the birds is not reported.

Exposure to Gas Mixtures

Mode of action

Gas stunning systems are often referred to as controlled atmosphere stunning (CAS), if reversible, or controlled atmosphere killing (CAK), if irreversibly rendering the bird unconscious (Thaxton, 2018). In general, exposure to gas mixtures leads to a gradual loss of consciousness in the birds and is considered a suitable method not only for broilers, laying hens and turkeys, but also for ducks and geese.

There are a number of different systems commercially available using gas mixtures to stun poultry. The gas mixtures can be carbon dioxide (in two or several phases), carbon dioxide in combination with inert gases, or systems based primarily on inert gases (see below).

There are different designs of gas stunners. Some are horizontal and placed on the floor, where the birds are taken through the system (on a conveyor belt with or without the original transport containers) at two or more levels (Gerritzen *et al.*, 2013) (Fig. 7.6). Others are of a deep-pit design, i.e. constructed as a deep hole in the floor, where a paternoster system or a lift system brings the containers down into the higher concentration of carbon dioxide, and then up again (Fig. 7.7). The unconscious birds are then shackled prior to neck cutting. Depending on the concentration of carbon dioxide and the duration of the exposure to the higher concentrations of the gas, the duration of unconsciousness induced will vary (EFSA, 2013). If the concentration is high enough and the duration of exposure long enough,

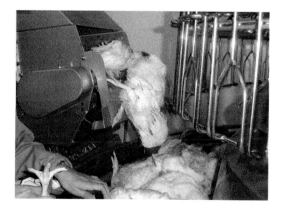

Fig. 7.6. A type of carbon dioxide stunning system where birds are first removed from the transport container, then taken on a conveyor belt through the two-stage carbon dioxide system, and finally shackled when unconscious. (Photo courtesy of C. Berg.)

Fig. 7.7. The shackling station at a multi-stage carbon dioxide system where the birds are stunned in their transport containers and shackled after becoming unconscious. (Photo courtesy of C. Berg.)

the stunning method will be irreversible, i.e. the birds will never resume breathing. Nevertheless, when birds are stunned using carbon dioxide or other gases in the context of slaughter, stunning should always be followed by bleeding. When birds are gas-stunned in groups, i.e. in their transport containers, the stunning duration has to be long enough to allow for shackling and bleeding of all the birds in that batch, before there is any risk of birds returning to consciousness.

Animal welfare aspects of gas stunning

The main advantage of gas stunning, from an animal welfare point of view, is that the birds do not have to be manually handled or shackled while conscious. Instead, the birds are stunned while sitting on a conveyor belt or still in their transport containers, eliminating the issue of removing the birds from the modules without causing injury. Shackling of freshly stunned birds can be performed in a well illuminated area; this and lack of wing flapping during shackling improves workers' health and safety.

Exposure to carbon dioxide

In the carbon dioxide stunners, the gas is administered in two or more phases (Meier *et al.*, 2015).

Birds are initially exposed to relatively low concentrations of CO_2 (less than 40%). Once the birds are unconscious, they are exposed to high concentrations of CO_2, typically 80–90% by volume in air (Berg and Raj, 2015). This process can, of course, be divided into more phases, where the CO_2 concentration is increased in smaller steps. The reason for gradually increasing the concentration of CO_2 instead of abruptly exposing the birds to high levels of the gas is that CO_2 is aversive, i.e. unpleasant to inhale. Both mammals and birds have chemoreceptors sensitive to CO_2 and therefore they will suffer pain and distress if exposed to high levels while still conscious (McKeegan *et al.*, 2006; Raj, 2006; Sandilands *et al.*, 2011; Berg *et al.*, 2014).

The main drawback from a bird welfare point of view is the aversiveness of CO_2 (Thaxton, 2018). Carbon dioxide is an acidic gas and is pungent to inhale (Raj and Tserveni-Gousi, 2000). Owing to this, chickens and turkeys, given a free choice, refuse to enter a feeding chamber containing high concentrations of CO_2 (Raj, 1996; McKeegan *et al.*, 2003; Sandilands et al., 2011). Carbon dioxide is also a potent respiratory stimulant and therefore inhalation of this gas at any concentration will lead to respiratory distress prior to the onset of

C. Berg and M. Raj

unconsciousness. By recording the firing rate of trigeminal nerve fibres and behavioural responses (avoidance tests) to inhalation of CO_2 in chickens, McKeegan et al. (2003) demonstrated that 11% by volume of CO_2 in air substantially increased the rate of firing and chickens certainly avoided an atmosphere containing 24% by volume of CO_2 in air. However, it can also be argued that the pain and distress associated with the induction of unconsciousness with a high concentration of CO_2 for a brief period, for example 30 s, can be less than the cumulative pain and suffering associated with the live bird handling and electrical water-bath stunning.

When CO_2 stunning is used, the gas concentration at relevant locations in the chamber should be monitored and maintained continuously, as should the exposure time. The gas may need humidification and under no circumstances must dry ice be used, as dry gas may cause severe irritation.

Exposure to inert gases, with or without added carbon dioxide

Inert gases, such as nitrogen or argon, can be used to stun poultry, sometimes in combination with CO_2. Exposure of birds to inert gases containing less than 2% by volume of oxygen leads to hypoxia, which renders them unconscious. Inert gases are not aversive to birds (or other animals), and the birds will hence not display head-shaking or gasping when coming in contact with the gas, which would make these gases more suitable for stunning purposes than CO_2 at high concentrations. For example, research has shown that chickens and turkeys do not show any aversion to the initial exposure to or inhalation of 90% argon in air with less than 2% residual oxygen (Raj, 1996; Sandilands et al., 2011). Webster and Fletcher (2001) showed that the behaviour of birds during exposure to argon was very similar to those exposed to atmospheric air, until the birds in argon lost consciousness.

However, hypoxia results in other types of negative effects, such as convulsions (wing flapping) after the loss of consciousness, which may be aesthetically unpleasant. In this regard, Ernsting (1965) reported that, under anoxic conditions, depression of activity in the mammalian brain extends progressively from the telencephalon to the diencephalon and then to the

mesencephalon. Anoxic convulsions result from the release of the caudal reticular formation from the suppression by higher centres, particularly the cerebral cortex and rostral reticular formation (Dell et al., 1961; Ernsting, 1965). The implication of this is that the onset of anoxic convulsions themselves can be used as an indicator of the loss of consciousness (Raj, 2004, 2010; Raj and Tserveni-Gousi, 2000).

Low Atmospheric Pressure Stunning (LAPS)

Mode of action

Low atmospheric pressure stunning (LAPS) is a reasonably new technology, which is currently commercially approved by USDA (Vizzier, 2015) and by the European Union for broiler chickens weighing up to 4 kg (European Commission, 2018) after evaluation by EFSA (EFSA, 2014a, 2017). However, it is not currently used commercially.

According to the manufacturers, LAPS involves exposure of birds in transport containers to hypoxia created by removal of air via gradual decompression in two phases. In the first phase, a relatively rapid reduction in pressure from standard sea level atmospheric pressure of 760–250 Torr is achieved in 50 s. In the second phase, the pressure is reduced to 160 Torr over a period of 210 s (McKeegan et al., 2013).

Animal welfare aspects of low atmospheric pressure stunning

The practical experiences from the LAPS system in relation to animal welfare are still limited, but the system shares the advantages of gas stunning systems by not having to shackle conscious birds. Time to reach the desired pressure should be monitored, as too rapid decompression is not acceptable on bird welfare grounds, and also temperature and humidity are of relevance (Holloway and Pritchard, 2017).

However, exposure of birds to LAPS results in other types of negative effects, such as convulsions (wing flapping) after the loss of consciousness, which may be aesthetically unpleasant. LAPS leads to irreversible stunning, i.e. when correctly carried out, birds will not regain consciousness.

References

American Veterinary Medical Association (AVMA) (2016) *Guidelines for the Humane Slaughter of Animals*, 2016 edn. American Veterinary Medical Association, Schaumburg, Illinois, p. 37.

Bedanova, I., Voslarova, E., Chloupek, P., Pistekova, V., Suchy, P. *et al.* (2007) Stress in broilers resulting from shackling. *Poultry Science* 86, 1065–1069. doi: 10.1093/ps/86.6.1065

Berg, C. (2012) Monitoring animal welfare at slaughterhouses. In: Jakobsson, C. (ed.) *Sustainable Agriculture*. Baltic University Programme, Uppsala, pp. 349–351.

Berg, C. and Raj, M. (2015) A review of different stunning methods for poultry – animal welfare aspects. *Animals* 5, 1207–1219. doi: 10.3390/ani5040407

Berg, C., Yngvesson, J., Nimmermark, S., Sandström, V. and Algers, B. (2014) Killing of spent laying hens using CO_2 in poultry barns. *Animal Welfare* 23, 445–457. doi: 10.7120/09627286.23.4.445

Dell, P., Hugelin, A. and Bonvallet, M. (1961) Effects of hypoxia on the reticular and cortical diffuse systems. In: Gustaut, H. and Meyer, J.S. (eds) *Cerebral Anoxia and the Electroencephalogram*. Charles C. Thomas, Springfield, Illinois, pp. 46–58.

EFSA (2004) Welfare aspects of the main systems of stunning and killing the main commercial species of animals. *EFSA Journal* 45, 1–29. doi: 10.2903/j.efsa.2004.45

EFSA (2013) Guidance on the assessment criteria for studies evaluating the effectiveness of stunning interventions regarding animal protection at the time of killing. *EFSA Journal* 11, 3486. doi: 10.2903/j.efsa.2013.3486

EFSA (2014a) Scientific opinion on the use of low atmosphere pressure system (LAPS) for stunning poultry. *EFSA Journal* 12, 3488. doi: 10.2903/j.efsa.2014.3488

EFSA (2014b) Scientific opinion on electrical requirements for poultry waterbath stunning equipment. *EFSA Journal* 12, 3745. doi: 10.2903/j.efsa.2014.3745

EFSA (2017) Low atmospheric pressure systems for stunning broiler chickens. *EFSA Journal* 15, 5056. doi: 10.2903/j.efsa.2017.5056

EFSA (2019) Slaughter of animals: poultry. *EFSA Journal* 17, 5849. doi: 10.2903/j.efsa.2019.5849

Erasmus, M.A., Lawlis, P., Duncan, I.J.H., and Widowski, T.M. (2010a) Using time to insensibility and estimated time of death to evaluate a nonpenetrating captive bolt, cervical dislocation, and blunt trauma for on-farm killing of turkeys. *Poultry Science* 89, 1345–1354. doi: 10.3382/ps.2009-00445

Erasmus, M.A., Turner, P.V., Nykamp, S.G. and Widowski, T.M. (2010b) Brain and skull lesions resulting from use of percussive bolt, cervical dislocation by stretching, cervical dislocation by crushing and blunt trauma in turkeys. *Veterinary Record* 167, 850–858. doi: 10.1136/vr.c5051 PMID: 21262650

Ernsting, J. (1965) The effect of anoxia on the central nervous system. In: Gillies, J.A. (ed.) *A Text Book of Aviation Physiology*. Pergamon Press, Oxford, pp. 271–289.

European Commission (2018) Commission implementing regulation (EU) 2018/723 of 16 May 2018 amending Annexes I and II to Council Regulation (EC) No. 1099/2009 on the protection of animals at the time of killing as regards the approval of low atmospheric pressure stunning. *Official Journal of the European Union* L122, 11–13. http://data.europa.eu/eli/reg_impl/2018/723/oj

Gentle, M.J. and Tilston, V.L. (2000) Nociceptors in the legs of poultry: Implications for potential pain in pre-slaughter shackling. *Animal Welfare* 9, 227–236.

Gerritzen, M.A., Reimert, H.G.M., Hindle, V.A., Verhoeven, M.T.W. and Veerkamp, W.B. (2013) Multistage carbon dioxide gas stunning of broilers. *Poultry Science* 92, 41–50. doi: 10.3382/ps.2012-02551

Gibson, T.J., Rebelo, C.B., Gowers, T.A. and Chancellor, N.M. (2018) Electroencephalographic assessment of concussive non-penetrating captive bolt stunning of turkeys. *British Poultry Science* 59, 13–20, doi: 10.1080/00071668.2017.1401215

Girasole, M., Marrone, R., Anastasio, A., Chianese, A., Mercogliano, R. and Cortesi, M.L. (2016) Effect of electrical water bath stunning on physical reflexes of broilers: evaluation of stunning efficacy under field conditions. *Poultry Science* 95, 1205–1210.

Hindle, V.A., Lambooij, E., Reimert, H.G.M., Workel, L.D. and Gerritzen, M.A. (2010) Animal welfare concerns during the use of the water bath for stunning broilers, hens, and ducks. *Poultry Science* 89, 401–412. doi: 10.3382/ps.2009-00297

Holloway, P.H. and Pritchard, D.G. (2017) Effects of ambient temperature and water vapor on chamber pressure and oxygen level during low atmospheric pressure stunning of poultry. *Poultry Science* 96, 2528–2539. doi: 10.3382/ps/pex066

Humane Slaughter Association (2015) Guidance Notes No. 7. *Electrical Waterbath Stunning of Poultry*. Humane Slaughter Association, Wheathampstead, UK.

Kannan, G. and Mench, J.A. (1996) Influence of different handling methods and crating periods on plasma corticosterone concentrations in broilers. *British Poultry Science* 37, 21–31. doi: 10.1080/00071669608417833

Kannan, G. and Mench, J.A. (1997) Prior handling does not significantly reduce the stress response to pre-slaughter handling in broiler chickens. *Applied Animal Behaviour Science* 51, 87–99. doi: 10.1016/S0168-1591(96)01076-3

Karger, B. (1995) Penetrating gun shots to the head and lack of immediate incapacitation I. Wound ballistics and mechanisms of incapacitation. *International Journal of Legal Medicine* 108, 53–61.

Kranen, R.W., Lambooij, E., Veerkamp, C.H., van Kuppevelt, T.H. and Veerkamp, J.H. (2000) Haemorrhages in muscles of broiler chickens. *World's Poultry Science Journal* 56, 93–126.

Lambooij, E. and Hindle, V. (2018) Electrical stunning of poultry. In: Mench, J.A. (ed.) *Food Science, Technology and Nutrition – Advances in Poultry Welfare*. Woodhead Publishing, Elsevier, Duxford, UK, pp. 77–98. doi: 10.1016/B978-0-08-100915-4.00004-X

Lambooij, E., Reimert, H., van de Vis, J.W. and Gerritzen, M.A. (2008) Head-to-cloaca electrical stunning of broilers. *Poultry Science* 87, 2160–2165. doi: 10.3382/ps.2007-00488

Lambooij, E., Reimert, H.G.M., Workel, L.D. and Hindle, V.A. (2012) Head-cloaca controlled current stunning: assessment of brain and heart activity and meat quality. *British Poultry Science* 53, 168–174. doi: 10.1080/00071668.2012.665434

Lambooij, E., Reimert, H.G.M., Verhoeven, M.T.W. and Hindle, V.A. (2014) Cone restraining and head-only electrical stunning in broilers: effects on physiological responses and meat quality. *Poultry Science* 93, 512–518. doi: 10.3382/ps.2013-03318

Lambooy, E. (1981) Some Neural and Physiological Aspects of Electrical and Mechanical Stunning in Ruminants. PhD Thesis, University of Utrecht, Utrecht, The Netherlands.

Lines, J.A., Raj, A.B.M., Wotton, S.B., O'Callaghan, M. and Knowles, T.G. (2011) Head-only electrical stunning of poultry using a waterbath: a feasibility study. *British Poultry Science* 52, 432–438. doi: 10.1080/00071668.2011.587180

Martin, J.E., McKeegan, D.E.F., Sparrey, J. and Sandilands, V. (2016) Comparison of novel mechanical cervical dislocation and a modified captive bolt for on-farm killing of poultry on behavioural reflex responses and anatomical pathology. *Animal Welfare* 252, 227–241.

Martin, J.E., McKeegan, D.E.F., Sparrey, J. and Sandilands, V. (2017) Evaluation of potential killing performance of novel percussive and cervical dislocation tools in chicken cadavers. *British Poultry Science* 58, 216– 223.

Martin, J.E., Sandilands, V., Sparrey, J., Baker, L., Dixon, L.M. and McKeegan, D.E.F. (2019) Welfare assessment of novel on-farm killing methods for poultry. *PLoS ONE* 14(2), e0212872. doi: 10.1371/journal.pone.0212872

McKeegan, D.E.F., Demmers, T.G.M., Wathers, C.M. and Jones, R.B. (2003). Chemosensitivity responses to gaseous pollutants and carbon dioxide: implications for poultry welfare. *Poultry Science* 82 (Suppl. 1), 16.

McKeegan, D.E.F., McIntyre, J., Demmers, T.G.M., Wathes, C.M. and Jones, R.B. (2006) Behavioural responses of broiler chickens during acute exposure to gaseous stimulation. *Applied Animal Behaviour Science* 99, 271–286. doi: 10.1016/j.applanim.2005.11.002

McKeegan, D.E.F., McIntyre, J.A., Demmers, T.G.M., Lowe, J.C., Wathes, C.M. et al. (2007) Physiological and behavioural responses of broilers to controlled atmosphere stunning: Implications for welfare. *Animal Welfare* 16, 409–426.

McKeegan, D.E.F., Sandercock, D.A. and Gerritzen, M.A. (2013) Physiological responses to low atmospheric pressure stunning and the implications for welfare. *Poultry Science* 92, 858–868. doi: 10.3382/ps.2012-02749

Meier, C., Veerkamp, W. and von Holleben, K. (2015) Evaluation of the Meyn Multistage CO2 stunning system for chicken with regard to animal welfare under practical conditions. In: *Proceedings of the 'Recent Advances II' – HSA International Symposium*, Zagreb, Croatia, 16–17 July 2015, p. 29.

Raj, A.B.M. (1996) Aversive reactions of turkeys to argon, carbon dioxide, and a mixture of carbon dioxide and argon. *Veterinary Record* 138, 592–593.

Raj, A.B.M. (2004) Stunning and slaughter of poultry. In: Mead, G.C. (ed.) *Poultry Meat Processing and Quality*. Woodhead Publishing, Cambridge, UK, pp. 65–89.

Raj, A.B.M. (2006) Recent developments in stunning and slaughter of poultry. *Word's Poultry Science Journal* 62, 467–484. doi: 10.1017/S0043933906001097

Raj, A.B.M. (2010) Slaughter and stunning. In: Duncan, J.H. and Hawkins, P. (eds) *The Welfare of Domestic Fowl and Other Captive Birds*. Springer Science + Business Media BV, London, pp. 259–277.

Raj, A.B.M. and O'Callaghan, M. (2001) Evaluation of a pneumatically operated captive bolt for stunning/killing broiler chickens. *British Poultry Science* 42, 295–299. doi: 10.1080/00071660120055232

Raj, A.B.M. and O'Callaghan, M. (2004) Effect of amount and frequency of head-only stunning currents on the electroencephalograms and somatosensory evoked potentials in broilers. *Animal Welfare* 13, 159–170.

Raj, A.B.M and Tserveni-Gousi (2000) Stunning methods for poultry. *World's Poultry Science Journal* 56, 291–304.

Raj, A.B.M., O'Callaghan, M. and Knowles, T.G. (2006a) The effect of amount and frequency of alternating current used in water bath stunning and neck cutting methods on spontaneous electroencephalograms in broilers. *Animal Welfare* 15, 7–18.

Raj, A.B.M., O'Callaghan, M. and Hughes, S.I. (2006b) The effect of amount and frequency of pulsed direct current used in water bath stunning and neck cutting methods on spontaneous electroencephalograms in broilers. *Animal Welfare* 15, 19–24.

Sabow, A.B., Nakyinsige, K., Adeyemi, K.D., Sazili, A.Q., Johnson, C.B. and Farouk, M.M. (2017) High frequency pre-slaughter electrical stunning in ruminants and poultry for halal meat production: a review. *Livestock Science* 202, 124–134. doi: 10.1016/j.livsci.2017.05.021

Sandilands, V., Raj, A.B.M., Baker, L. and Sparks, N.H.C. (2011) Aversion of chickens to various lethal gas mixtures. *Animal Welfare* 20, 253–262.

Schutt-Abraham, I. and Wormuth, H.J. (1991) Anforderungen an eine tierschutzgerechte elektrische betaubung von schlachtegeflugel. *Rundeschau für Fleischhygiene und Lebensmitteluberwachung* 43, 7–8.

Schütt-Abraham, I., Wormuth, H.-J., Fessel, J. and Knapp, J. (1983) Electrical stunning of poultry in view of animal welfare and meat production. In: Eikelenboom, G. (ed.) *Stunning of Animals for Slaughter*. Martinus Nijhoff, The Hague, Netherlands, p. 154.

Schutt-Abraham, I., Wormuth, H.J. and Fessel, J. (1987) Vergleichende untersuchungen zur tierschutzgerechten elektrobetaubung verschi edener schlachtgeflugelarten. *Berliner und Munchener Tierarztliche Worchenschrift* 100, 332–340.

Sparrey, J. (1994) Aspects in the design and operation of shackle lines for the slaughter of poultry. Unpublished MPhil. thesis, University of Newcastle upon Tyne, Newcastle upon Tyne, UK.

Sparrey, J.M. and Kettlewell, P.J. (1994) Shackling of poultry: is it a welfare problem. *World's Poultry Science Journal* 50, 167–176. doi: 10.1079/WPS19940014

Sparrey, J.M., Kettlewell, P.J. and Paice, M.E. (1992) A model of current pathways in electrical waterbath stunners used for poultry. *British Poultry Science* 33, 907–916. doi: 10.1080/00071669208417534

Thaxton, Y.V. (2018) Gas and low atmospheric pressure stunning. In: Mench, J.A. (ed.) *Food Science, Technology and Nutrition – Advances in Poultry Welfare*. Woodhead Publishing, Elsevier, Duxford, UK, pp. 99–110. doi: 10.1016/B978-0-08-100915-4.00005-1

Vizzier, T.Y. (2015) From idea to reality: the development of the low atmosphere stunning system. In: *Proceedings of the 'Recent Advances II'—HSA International Symposium*, Zagreb, Croatia, 16–17 July 2015, p. 36.

Webster, A.B. and Fletcher, D.L. (2001) Reactions of laying hens and broilers to different gases used for stunning poultry. *Poultry Science* 80, 1371–1377. doi:10.1093/ps/80.9.1371

Wilkins, L.J., Gregory, N.G., Wotton, S.B. and Parkman, I.D. (1998) Effectiveness of electrical stunning applied using a variety of waveform-frequency combinations and consequences for carcass quality in broilers. *British Poultry Science* 39, 511–518. doi: 10.1080/00071669888692

Woolcott, C.R., Torrey, S., Turner, P.V., Serpa, L., Schwean-Lardner, K. and Widowski, T.M. (2018) Evaluation of two models of non-penetrating captive bolt devices for on-farm euthanasia of turkeys. *Animals* 8, 42. doi:10.3390/ani8030042

8 Stunning Poultry with Controlled Atmosphere Systems

TEMPLE GRANDIN*

Department of Animal Science, Colorado State University, USA

Summary

A major advantage of controlled atmosphere stunning (CAS) or low atmospheric pressure stunning (LAPS) for poultry is that it eliminates handling of individual live birds at the slaughter plant. These systems are currently being used for both broiler chicken and turkeys. Research clearly shows that shackling of live birds is highly stressful (Kannan *et al.*, 1997; Bedanova *et al.*, 2007). When modern CAS systems are used, the birds are stunned in the same containers that were used to transport them to the abattoir. There are systems available that can handle birds in single drawers, small coops, decks or large modules that have multiple compartments. Chickens should not be exposed to greater than 40% CO_2 until they have loss of posture (LOP) and become unconscious. After the birds are rendered unconscious and killed, they are removed from the transport container. At this point, the dead birds are hung on the shackles by people, bled and processed in the conventional manner. The most common operational mistake is speeding up a system to increase poultry productivity. This may have serious detrimental effects on bird welfare. CAS and LAPS systems must be operated according to scientifically validated parameters. Specifications for gas concentrations, air withdrawal rates and exposure times must be strictly followed.

Learning Objectives

- Learn how controlled atmosphere stunning works.
- Learn differences between poultry handling systems.
- Monitoring bird behaviour for welfare during induction of unconsciousness.
- Understand common commercial systems.
- Solve common operational problems.

CAS and LAPS Solve a Big Management Problem

The implementation of controlled atmosphere stunning (CAS) and low air pressure atmospheric stunning (LAPS) is one of the few areas in animal handling where a piece of equipment can eliminate the need for management supervision of employee behaviour. All the problems of bad employee behaviour and the possibility of bird abuse during live shackling are eliminated. There are numerous animal activist videos online of people throwing, kicking, stomping on or hitting live broilers and turkeys. With CAS, the people are now removed from live bird handling. Mishandling of dead birds is not a welfare issue. The author has done welfare audits and auditor training at many poultry slaughter plants. In some facilities, poor supervision of employees handling of live birds was a major issue. From a welfare perspective, Table 8.1 compares electrical stunning with CAS or LAPS. It is essential that the transport containers are not overloaded. For all species of poultry, the birds must have sufficient space so that they can all lie down at the same time without being on top of each other. CAS systems are becoming increasingly popular. Raj (2017) reported that CAS is used on 60–65% of the broiler chickens in the UK and Germany. In Germany, 40% of the turkeys are stunned with CAS. The turkey industry in the USA is also increasing its use of CAS.

To maintain a high level of bird welfare, the CAS or LAPS process must be closely monitored. Supervision of

---

* Email: cheryl.miller@colostate.edu

Table 8.1. Welfare comparison of electrical versus controlled atmosphere stunning.

Stunning method	Advantages	Disadvantages
Electrical[a]	Instantaneous insensibility (Raj and O'Callaghan, 2004).	Birds are hung live inverted on the shackle line. This is stressful for the birds and increases plasma corticosterone (Kannan et al., 1997; Bedanova et al., 2007). Small birds mixed with large birds miss the water-bath and may not be stunned. Supervising and training employees is more difficult. Problems with people abusing birds are more likely because people handle each individual live bird. In poorly designed systems, the birds may get small pre-shocks before they enter the water bath.
Gas or low air pressure (LAPS)	Birds do not have to be removed from the transport containers for stunning. This greatly reduces handling stress. All birds in the container will be stunned. Less likely to have problems with employees abusing birds because they do not handle live birds.	Insensibility is not instantaneous. The distress and discomfort to the birds prior to the loss of insensibility will vary depending on the gas mixture or the speed of air removal. Requires very careful continuous monitoring of the gas mixtures. Wind around the plant building, changes in plant ventilation and opening and closing doors may change gas mixtures in some systems. These problems do not occur in LAP systems or closed gas systems. Much higher cost to install equipment compared with electrical stunning.

[a]Electrical stunning takes place in a water-bath

employee handling of live birds is eliminated, but it now has to be replaced by management attention to details of the stunning process. Specifications for timing, gas mixture and other parameters must be closely followed.

How CAS and LAPS Systems Handle Birds

Controlled atmosphere stunning uses automated systems to move transport containers into the CAS chamber. There are three basic types of transport container movement systems (Box 8.1). In all these systems, a forklift is used to put a large module containing the birds on an automated module handling system. In all the systems, dead chickens or turkeys are hung on shackles after they emerge from the stunner.

How CAS and LAPS Systems Work

There are three basic methods that are used to control gas mixtures. They are outlined in Box 8.2.

Is a Deep Pit Required?

The most modern poultry CAS machines do not require an expensive deep pit constructed from reinforced concrete. The largest pork CAS systems do require an

expensive pit. Some older poultry CAS systems have a deep pit. The newest systems can be easily mounted on a concrete slab at plant floor level. No digging or concrete forming is required. This also provides a safety advantage for people performing maintenance.

The Most Common Operational Problems with CAS or LAPS System

The number one problem which can cause poor bird welfare in any CAS or LAPS system is having an undersized machine. When the line speed exceeds the capacity of the machine, managers are tempted to speed up the process of induction of unconsciousness. This will result in poor welfare and bird suffering. When poultry CAS equipment is being purchased, it is strongly recommended to obtain a machine that has sufficient capacity for increased future production. This will enable a business to grow without compromising bird welfare. When CAS systems are speeded up and fail to follow scientifically validated exposure times, gas mixtures and gas concentrations, the birds will suffer.

Compared with electrical water-bath stunning, CAS systems require more maintenance and more highly trained technical people to maintain and calibrate them.

T. Grandin

Box 8.1. Transport container movement systems

- **Entire module systems** – An entire dump module or drawer module containing multiple bird compartments is placed on a conveyor table by the same forklift that was used to remove it from the truck. The birds are not touched by people until dead birds emerge from the stunning system. Entire module systems are often the best choice for large poultry plants that want to continue using their existing transport systems. This handling system is used with both CAS and LAPS.

- **Single drawer systems** – A module with multiple drawers containing birds is moved from the truck to an automated conveyor table by a forklift. Automatic equipment slides each individual drawer out of the module and moves it to a conveyor that goes into the CAS chamber. Single drawer systems require less floor space compared with entire module systems. This handling system is only used for CAS.

- **Live dump then move to CAS system** – This is an older style of CAS equipment that is being phased out when new abattoirs are built. In this system, live birds are dumped out and moved to a small conveyor that moves them through the CAS stunner. From a welfare standpoint, this system is inferior to the other systems because live birds are handled. It does eliminate live shackling. The main advantages of this system are that it often requires less floor space and that controlling the correct gas concentrations and mixtures is easier in a smaller chamber. It may be easier to install this system in an existing abattoir that is converting dump module electrical stunning to CAS. This would be especially true if floor space was limited or if there is not sufficient land for plant expansion. This handling system is only used for CAS.

- **Stacked deck modules** – This system has some definite advantages and may be a good choice for new poultry plants. It is not compatible with the systems described above. New modules and vehicles will be required. In both conventional drawer and dump module systems, there are three separate compartments on each deck. In a stacked deck system, there is one large compartment on each deck. During unloading at the plant, each deck is removed from the stack and moved through the CAS stunner like a giant drawer. There is no rack like a conventional drawer system, because the framework for the rack is built into each stackable deck. Automated equipment removes each deck from the bottom of the stack. The large decks move through the CAS stunner with multiple stations in the same manner that conventional drawers are moved (Fig. 8.1). Each deck stops in each CAS station. Out on the farm, a module is formed with four stacked decks. The four stacked decks are the same size as a conventional drawer module with multiple compartments. The bottom deck has holes for the forklift and the fourth deck on the top of the stack has a retractable plastic cover. To ready the stacked decks for poultry loading, the floor of each deck is slid open. The floor consists of several sliding panels that overlap each other when they are slid open. The bottom deck is loaded first. When it is full, the floor of the next deck is slid shut over it. This forms both a cover for the bottom deck and a floor for the next deck. This process is repeated for the other three decks. This system provides advantages from a welfare perspective because it is much easier to load birds into the large wide decks. The stacked decks are loaded into the transport vehicle with a conventional forklift. Since the four decks are stacked like shipping containers, the truck has a hydraulic roof which lowers and presses down on all the stacked decks (Fig. 8.2).

Monitoring Induction of Unconsciousness

Looking at meters is not a substitute for observing the birds during the induction of unconsciousness. The system must be equipped with either windows or video cameras. Captive bolt and electric stunning induce instantaneous unconsciousness. CAS or LAPS requires a period of time to make a bird unconscious. This is why observation of bird behaviour before loss of consciousness is extremely important. The birds must be visible from entry into the chamber until shortly after loss of posture (LOP). The birds are unconscious when they fall over and can no longer stand (Benson *et al.*, 2012a,b; AVMA, 2016; Mackie *et al.*, 2016). In turkeys, the birds are not able to stand in the transport containers. To substitute for LOP, watch for complete relaxation of their long necks. The turkeys will no longer be able to hold their heads up because they have lost the righting reflex. This is the same as LOP (Meyer, 2015).

Fig. 8.1. An assembled four-deck stacked module that has been placed in the curtain-sided transport trailer. (Photo courtesy of Temple Grandin.)

Fig. 8.2. Two decks from a stacked deck module system exiting the CAS stunning and moving towards the shackle system. (Photo courtesy of Temple Grandin.)

Behaviour Before LOP and Bird Welfare

To maintain acceptable welfare, bird behaviour must be observed before LOP. It is likely that the birds may experience some discomfort before they lose consciousness. Some stress during induction is probably less harmful to bird welfare compared with the obvious severe stress caused by live shackling (Grandin, 2015; Velarde and Raj, 2016). Shackling live chickens is highly stressful (Kannan *et al.*, 1997; Bedanova

et al., 2007). In a poorly managed CAS or LAPS stunner, there is a point where the induction process may become so poor that live shackling may be less stressful. It is the author's opinion that escape behaviour is *never* acceptable. If birds attempt to escape from the container, the gas parameters or air withdrawal specifications must be changed. If large numbers of birds vigorously flap before LOP, this is a definite indicator of severe distress. Other behaviours that may be observed are head shaking and mandibulation (beak opening and closing). The birds exhibiting these behaviours are probably experiencing some discomfort but it is likely that it is less severe compared with the stress of live shackling. Convulsions, flapping and other behaviours after LOP have no effect on bird welfare, but they may have a detrimental effect on meat quality. Many systems have windows that allow direct observation of the birds from the time they first enter the system until loss of posture and unconsciousness. Video cameras can also be used. All CAS and LAPS systems must have either video cameras or windows to view the birds.

CAS and LAPS Systems in Commercial Use

The guidelines from the OIE (2018) state that parameters for CAS stunning are still 'under study'.

- **Horizontal conveyor transport through a series of stations** – In this type of system, a single drawer deck or an entire module with multiple compartments is moved through five to six stations. At each station, the conveyor is stopped and flexible curtains are lowered. In a CO_2-only system, gas levels are slowly raised as an entire module or single drawers advance through a series of stations. CO_2 levels must remain under 40% until the birds lose consciousness. To ensure death, the final station contains 90% CO_2. Horizontal conveyor transport can also be used with other types of gases, such as oxygen and nitrous oxide.
- **Lowered into gas** – In this system either single drawers or modules containing chickens are lowered into a chamber that contains gradually increasing CO_2. This system is recommended for use with gases that are heavier than air, such as CO_2 or argon. Gravity holds the gas in the chamber. CO_2 levels start at 2–3% and are kept under 40% until the birds have lost posture and become unconscious. To reliably kill the birds, the module or drawer enters a second station containing higher levels of 90% CO_2. Exposure of chickens to greater than 40% CO_2 before loss of consciousness is stressful (Gerritzen et al., 2013).
- **Positive pressure systems** – Entire modules with multiple compartments or entire truck trailers are placed in a chamber and the gas is applied. Many different gases can be accurately applied in this type of system.
- **LAPS system** – Entire modules are moved into a chamber, where air is removed.

Since this book is about the practical application of CAS, this chapter will discuss the best practices for commercial use. The three major technologies that are currently in commercial use are outlined below. They are: (i) gradually increasing CO_2; (ii) biphasic CO_2 and oxygen; and (iii) LAPS (low atmospheric pressure). All good commercial systems are designed to kill the birds prior to discharge from the stunner.

Induction into Gradually Increasing Concentrations of CO_2

Gradual CO_2 induction is a common commercial system. Sudden introduction of chickens into high levels of CO_2 is very aversive to chickens. They will have violent reactions while they are still conscious. Research and the author's own observations indicate that a smooth gradual increase of CO_2 from 0% to 50–55% reduces the bird's reaction prior to LOP (Gerritzen et al., 2013). The mistake that is often made is raising the CO_2 concentration too quickly. Early patents for CO_2 stunning had a two-stage process. This is not recommended. Successful commercial equipment has five more steps to raise the concentration gradually over a period of several minutes (Bright Coop, 2019a,b; Meyn, 2019) (Fig. 8.1). Broiler chickens should show loss of posture (LOP) before the CO_2 levels reach 40%. It is important to keep the CO_2 levels at or below 40% until the chickens lose consciousness (Velarde and Raj, 2016). The final stage contains 90% CO_2 to kill the birds prior to shackling.

How gradual CO_2 systems work

Gradual CO_2 systems are commercially available in two types of systems. There are large systems where the birds are stunned in modules containing multiple compartments of broiler chickens (Fig. 8.3). The second type is a smaller system where individual drawers containing a group of chickens are removed from the module rack. Each individual drawer is conveyed through the CO_2.

Systems that can handle large modules containing multiple bird compartments use standard industrial freight handling equipment. These systems are similar to the roller platforms that cargo airlines use to move freight modules on to airplanes. The equipment moves the modules to the stunner entrance. As each module moves through the stunning tunnel, it is moved into stations with gradually increasing CO_2. To control CO_2 concentrations, doors or curtains slide down between the stations. After exposure, the doors slide up and the module advances to the next station, where it stops and another set of doors closes. All of the equipment is mounted on the floor. There is no pit.

In older types of gradual CO_2 systems, individual drawers containing chickens are lowered into a pit that contains gradually increasing levels of CO_2

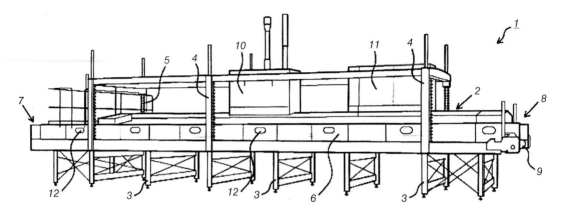

Fig. 8.3. Five-stage CO_2 stunning system for broiler chickens. Modules containing multiple chicken compartments move through a series of chambers with gradually increasing CO_2. (Photo courtesy of Patent Office.)

(Thuolen and Lyngholm, 2013). This type of system can only use gases that are heavier than air. In newer systems, the pit has been eliminated and the chamber is mounted on the floor. The drawers are lowered into increasing levels of CO_2 until 40%. After consciousness is lost, the drawers are transferred to another chamber with 90% CO_2 to ensure death.

Biphasic CO_2 and Oxygen System

Another gas system that is used commercially is the biphasic system. In this system, the chickens are initially exposed to an atmosphere of 40% CO_2, 30% oxygen and 30% nitrogen for 60 s (Abeyesinghe *et al.*, 2007; McKeegan *et al.*, 2007a,b; Coenen *et al.*, 2009). The second stage is the euthanasia phase, which has an atmosphere of 80% CO_2 and air. The biphasic system with added oxygen during the anaesthetic phase has advantages from both a welfare and a carcass quality standpoint (Abeyesinghe *et al.*, 2007; McKeegan *et al.*, 2007a,b; Coenen *et al.*, 2009). In the newest biphasic system, there are five stations with an exposure time of 60 s in each station (Figure 8.4). The first station has 27% CO_2 and 30% oxygen. As the broiler chickens progress through the system, the CO_2 levels are gradually raised. The fifth station has a CO_2 level of 70%. The author observed anaesthesia induction through observation windows and the birds' reactions were mild.

Fig. 8.4. Biphasic – Controlled atmosphere Biphasic stunning system. Marek Stork poultry – Processing patent 10085459b2. (Diagram courtesy of Humane-Aire, Bright Coop.)

The early biphasic systems had small tunnels, because it was easier to maintain the more complex gas mixture in a smaller space. In these early systems, the chickens were removed from the transport container before stunning. This method loses the welfare advantage of systems where the birds remain in the transport containers. They are hung on the shackling line after they are dead but they have to be handled by people or dumped out to put them on a small stunning conveyor. New biphasic systems are excellent from a welfare perspective because they are built with a larger tunnel that can accommodate an entire deck from a stacked deck module system. Maintaining the correct ratio of CO_2 to oxygen must be carefully monitored. McKeegan *et al.* (2007a,b) found that chickens from the CO_2 and oxygen system had fewer broken wings compared

T. Grandin

with a hypoxic system of argon and CO_2. From both a meat quality and welfare standpoint, the biphasic oxygen and CO_2 system was superior to 90% argon and air with less than 2% oxygen (Abeyesinghe et al., 2007).

Low Atmospheric Pressure Stunning (LAPS)

In this system, one to three large modules with multiple bird compartments are placed in a pressure vessel chamber. A vacuum pump is used to pull air out of the chamber. LAPS is now approved for use in the European Union for broiler chickens weighing up to 2.9 kg (EFSA, 2017). The conclusion was that LAPS provides a level of welfare at least equivalent to one currently approved method. LAPS, when done correctly, may be equivalent to stunning with inert gases (Martin et al., 2016a,b,c).

One advantage of this system is that it is mechanically simple and has fewer moving parts than staged CO_2 systems (Fig. 8.5a,b). Removal of the air is done in a two-stage process (Martin et al., 2016a). When LAPS is done correctly, there is no escape behaviour and LOP and unconsciousness occurred within an average of 81 s (Mackie et al., 2016). There are two phases in the LAPS cycle: an initial pressure reduction phase followed by a slower rate of decreasing pressure. The specifications for the LAPS in Martin (2016a,b,c) and Holloway and Pritchard (2017) must be followed exactly. Speeding up the process will be highly detrimental to broiler chicken welfare. Compared with gas stunning, more time is required for the chickens to lose consciousness. The process is also sensitive to environmental changes in barometric pressure and adjustments must be made (Holloway and Pritchard, 2017). The entire cycle is 270–280 s and it must never be speeded up. Monitoring of chicken welfare by observing behaviours before LOP is essential. Research has shown that the birds remain calmer if the chamber is kept dark (Martin et al., 2016b). This would make observation difficult, unless either an infrared camera or a small amount of blue light was used to provide illumination for conventional video.

From a safety standpoint, the metal pressure vessel has to be professionally engineered and built by a certified welder. Improper construction could result in collapse of the chamber. To achieve the air removal rate that has been specified in Mackie et al. (2016), a sliding gate valve controlled by a computer is used. One disadvantage of this system has been more broken wings and carcass damage compared with gas stunning systems. This caused one large chicken company to stop using it. Some of the problems at this company were caused by speeding up the air withdrawal time. To comply with EU requirements, LAPS must follow the specifications in Holloway and Pritchard (2017). When LAPS is used correctly, broiler chicken behaviour during induction is similar to inert gases (Mackie et al., 2016). LAPS may not work in turkeys. Informal experiments performed in the industry indicated that turkeys are much more resistant to hypoxia compared with chickens.

Hypoxic Systems Using Inert Gas

The use of an atmosphere that lacks oxygen is favoured by many welfare specialists, because it is

Fig. 8.5. LAPS low atmospheric stunning system for broiler chickens. (a) In a large slaughter plant, multiple modules containing numerous bird compartments can be placed in the chamber. A large abattoir may need two to four chambers. (b) A LAPS system designed for farm depopulation. (From http://www.lapsinfo.com/press-release)

not aversive to chickens (Berg and Raj, 2015). These systems use either nitrogen or argon, or these gases are mixed with CO_2. A major problem with these systems is strong convulsions after LOP when the chickens become unconscious. This causes high levels of meat damage (Abeyesinghe *et al.*, 2017). To reduce convulsions, the atmosphere must contain very low levels of oxygen. From an engineering standpoint, this is difficult to achieve in large commercial systems. Nitrogen is especially difficult to use, because it is a major component of air. Gravity will not hold it in a chamber. Attempting to mix nitrogen and CO_2 in equipment designed for CO_2 was a commercial failure due to high wing breakage. To effectively use inert gases in a commercial system would require use of a positive pressure chamber. The main problem with this type of system is that it requires huge quantities of gas. The chamber has to be completely refilled after each batch.

Back-up Systems

Both CAS and LAPS should have back-up systems so that the abattoir can operate if the stunner fails. The most common back-up is a separate electrical stunning line. In CAS or LAPS systems where more than one chamber supplies a single processing line, a back-up system is essential. This prevents the temptation to run the remaining operational chamber at an increased speed, which would be highly detrimental to bird welfare.

Other Types of Gases

It has been suggested to use carbon monoxide to euthanize poultry or other animals. This gas is too dangerous and can quickly kill people. From a safety standpoint, it should never be used in a commercial abattoir. A patent has been filed for a novel mixture of oxygen, CO_2 and nitrous oxide (Larsen *et al.*, 2016). This gas mixture will require further research before it is used commercially.

Whole Truck CAS Stunning System

Several turkey companies in the USA have systems where a truck loaded with turkey modules enters a building that looks like a truck wash (Lang *et al.*, 2008). Stainless steel panels automatically clamp on the sides of the trailer and pass gradually increasing levels of CO_2 into compartments that hold the turkeys. The trailer has to be modified with partitions to seal off each section. The author has observed this system and it does work. If it is cycled too rapidly and speeded up, the turkeys have a poor induction. The major problem with whole-trailer stunning is that it wastes vast quantities of CO_2 unless it is equipped with expensive devices to recapture the exhausted CO_2.

Removal of Birds Dead on Arrival (DOA)

From a food safety perspective, birds that arrive at the abattoir dead on arrival must not be processed for food. Practical experience has shown that birds that arrive dead can be easily identified and removed by shacklers. These birds are usually stiff or cold. Ouckama *et al.* (2018) reported that they could detect DOAs within 5 min post-mortem. They assessed hock stiffness, which is a sign that rigor mortis has started.

Choosing a System

To make a commercially viable system that protects bird welfare and has low levels of meat damage, gradually increasing levels of CO_2 or biphasic usually is the best option. All CAS and LAPS systems must be constantly monitored to maintain a smooth induction. Escape attempts should be abolished and wing flapping should occur in 5% or less of the birds. Outcome variables should be used to evaluate future innovations. See Chapters 11 and 13 for further information on assessing behaviour before loss of posture.

References

Abeyesinghe, S.M., McKeegan, D.E., McLeman, M.A., Low, J.C., Wathes, C.M. *et al.* (2007) Controlled atmosphere stunning of broiler chickens. 1 Effects on behaviour, physiology and meat quality in a pilot scale system at a processing plant. *British Poultry Science* 48, 406–423.

AVMA (2016) *Guidelines for the Humane Slaughter of Animals*, 2016 edn. American Veterinary Medical Association, Schaumberg, Illinois.

Benson, E.R., Alphin, R.L., Rankin, M.K., Caputo, M.P. and Johnson, A.L. (2012a) Electroencephalogram based methodology for determining unconsciousness during depopulation. *Avian Disease* 56 (4 Suppl.), 884–890.

Benson, E.R., Alphin, R.L., Rankin, M.K., Caputo, M.P., Kinny, C.A. and Johnson, A.L. (2012b) Evaluation of EEG based determination of unconsciousness vs.

loss of posture in chickens. *Research in Veterinary Science* 93, 960–964.

Bedanova, I., Vosarova, E., Chloupek, P., Pistekova, V., Suchy, P. *et al.* (2007) Stress in broilers resulting from shackling. *Poultry Science* 86, 1065–1069.

Berg, C. and Raj, M. (2015) A review of different stunning methods for poultry – animal welfare aspects. *Animals* 5, 1207–1219. doi: 10.3390/ani5040407

Bright Coop (2019a) A new day in processing. Bright Coop, Nacogdoches, Texas. Available at: www.brightcoop.com/humane-aire (accessed February 2019).

Bright Coop (2019b) Multilevel cage for transporting and stunning poultry, Patent 10165761B1.

Coenen, A.M., Lankhaar, J., Love, J.C. and McKeegan, D.E. (2009) Remote monitoring of electroencephalograms, electrocardiograms, and behavior during controlled atmosphere stunning of broilers: implications for welfare. *Poultry Science* 88, 10–19.

EFSA (2017) Low atmospheric pressure system for stunning broiler chickens. *EFSA Journal* 15(12), 1–125.

Gerritzen, M.A., Reimert, H.G., Hindle, V.A., Verhoeven, M.T., and Veerkamp, W.B. (2013) Multistage carbon dioxide gas stunning of broilers. *Poultry Science* 92, 41–50.

Grandin, T. (2015) *Improving Animal Welfare: A Practical Approach*. CABI International, Wallingford, UK.

Holloway, P.H. and Pritchard, D.G. (2017) Effects of ambient temperature and water vapor on chamber pressure and oxygen level during low atmospheric stunning of poultry. *Poultry Science* 96, 2528–2539.

Kannan, G., Heath, J.L., Wabeck, C.J. and Mench, J.A. (1997) Shackling broilers: effects on stress responses and breast meat quality. *British Poultry Science* 38, 323–332.

Lang, G.D., Nayini, N.R. and Rampersad, B.M. (2008) System and method for stunning poultry with gas, US Patent US8323080B2. US Patent Office, Washington, DC.

Larsen, H.D., Lykke, L.I., Aaslyng, M.D., Blaabjerg, L.O. and Brandt, P. (2016) Prestunning of animals with a combination of O_2, CO_2, and NO_2, US Patent US20180132495AI. US Patent Office, Washington, DC.

Mackie, N., Dorothy, E.F. and McKeegan, E.F. (2016) Behavioural responses of broiler chickens during low atmospheric pressure stunning. *Applied Animal Behaviour Science* 174, 90–98.

Martin, J.E., Christensen, K., Thaxton, V.T., Mitchell, M.A. and McKeegan, D.E.F. (2016a) Behavioural brain and cardiac responses to hypobaric hypoxia in broiler chickens. *Physiology and Behavior* 163, 25–36.

Martin, J.E., Christensen, K., Thaxton, Y.V. and McKeegan, D.E.F. (2016b) Effects of light on responses to low atmospheric pressure stunning in broilers. *British Poultry Science* 57, 585–600.

Martin, J.E., Christensen, K., Thaxton, Y.V. and McKeegan, D.E.F. (2016c) Effects of analgesic intervention on behavioural responses to low atmospheric pressure stunning. *Applied Animal Behaviour Science* 180, 157–165.

McKeegan, D.E.F., Abeyesinghe, S.M., McLamen, M.A., Lowe, J.C., Demmeus, T.G.M. *et al.* (2007a) Controlled atmosphere stunning of broiler chickens, II. Effect of behaviour, physiology and meat quality in a commercial processing plant. *British Poultry Science* 48, 430–442.

McKeegan, D.E.F., McIntyre, J.A., Demmers, T.G.M., Lowe, J.C., Wathes, C.M. *et al.* (2007b) Physiological and behavioral responses of broilers to controlled atmosphere stunning: implications for welfare. *Animal Welfare* 16, 409–426.

Meyer, R.E. (2015) Physiologic measures of animal stress during transitional states of consciousness. *Animals* 5(2), 702–716.

Meyn (2019) CO_2 stunning in transport container favorable for animal welfare. Meyn Food Processing Technology, Amsterdam. Available at: www.meyn.com/news/CO2-stunning-in-transport-container-favorable-for-animal-welfare (accessed February 2019).

OIE (2018) Chapter 7.5 – Slaughter of Animals. In: *Terrestrial Animal Health Code*. World Organisation for Animal Health, Paris.

Ouckama, R.M., Saigado-Bierman, F., Guerin, M.T. and Brash, M.L. (2018) Identifying dead on arrivals (DOA) at shackling in a slaughter line gas stunning system friend of lay hens: Part 1. Hock flexion resistance and wing position. *Journal of Applied Poultry Research* 27, 262–271.

Raj, M. (2017) Gas stunning of poultry. Gas mixture equipment: alternative adjustments and maintenance. Available at: www.embrapa.br (accessed February 2019).

Raj, A.B.M. and O'Callaghan, M. (2004) Effects of electrical water bath stunning current frequencies on the spontaneous electroencephalogram and somatosensory evoked potentials in hens. *British Poultry Science* 45, 230–236.

Thulin, P. and Lyngholm, M. (2013) Method and monitoring system for monitoring gas stunning of birds, Patent US9826745B2. US Patent Office, Washington, DC.

Velarde, A. and Raj, M. (2016) Gas stunning and killing methods. In: Velarde, A. and Raj, M. (eds) *Animal Welfare at Slaughter*. 5M Publishing, Sheffield, UK, pp. 133–151.

9 Stunning of Pigs and Sheep with Electricity and CO$_2$

T<small>EMPLE</small> G<small>RANDIN</small>*

Department of Animal Science, Colorado State University, USA

Summary

Properly applied electric stunning will instantaneously make an animal unconscious by inducing a grand mal epileptic seizure. The three types of electrical stunning are: (i) head-only reversible; (ii) head-to-back cardiac arrest; and (iii) sequential head-to-back or body cardiac arrest. The electrodes must be placed so that the electric current flows through the brain. Electrical stunning of dehydrated animals may be less effective. When CO$_2$ is used, induction of unconsciousness is not instantaneous. There are welfare concerns about the aversiveness of CO$_2$ inhalation. Some discomfort during induction may be a reasonable tradeoff because the group handling system eliminates electric prods. Behaviour before loss of posture (LOP) should be observed. If the animal attempts to escape, the stress during induction is excessive and not acceptable.

Learning Objectives

- How electrical stunning induces unconsciousness.
- Correct electrode positions for electrical stunning.
- What are the animal welfare concerns with CO$_2$ stunning.
- How to correct and fix operational problems with stunning in a commercial abattoir.

Introduction

For pigs, the commonly used methods in commercial abattoirs are either electrical or CO$_2$ stunning. For sheep or lambs, electrical stunning or captive bolt are common methods. In this chapter, the reader will learn the proper use of these methods. Effective stunning that reliably renders an animal unconscious requires the right equipment and also management who will pay close attention to both maintenance and details of the procedures.

Principles of Electrical Stunning for Pigs, Sheep or Goats

To induce instantaneous unconsciousness, a sufficient electric current must pass through the animal's brain to induce a grand mal epileptic seizure (Croft, 1952; Warrington, 1974; Lambooy and Spanjaard, 1982; Anil and McKinstry, 1998; AVMA, 2016; HSA, 2018). When head-only electrical stunning is done correctly, there will be a rigid tonic phase followed by a clonic kicking phase. During the tonic phase, the animal will be rigid. When the kicking phase stops, the animal will recover and becomes conscious. Electrical stunning methods are outlined in Box 9.1.

Tips on Electrical Stunner Positioning

An electrical stunning tong or other apparatus must never be applied to a sensitive part of the animal such as eyes, ears or rectum. Correct placement is essential to reliably make the animal instantly unconscious (Anil and MacKinstry, 1998). Acceptable positions for stunning are as follows.

- Simultaneous application to the forehead and back (cardiac arrest) of pigs and sheep (Gregory and Wotton, 1984; Wotton and Gregory, 1986). In a welfare audit, assess position of the head electrode. On sheep, the electrodes may also be placed on the top of the head and the chest (Mason *et al.*, 2018). This method will induce cardiac arrest. Due to their large size, do not use simultaneous head-to-body application for cattle.

* Email: cheryl.miller@colostate.edu

There are three basic methods for applying electrical stunning.

- **Reversible head-only** – Fig. 9.1 shows head-only electrical stunning. The tongs are used to pass an electric current through the brain. This is a fully reversible stun. To prevent recovery of consciousness, the animal must be bled within 10–15 s (Blackmore and Newhook, 1981; Lambooij, 1982; Grandin, 1986). This method will be discussed in detail in the chapter on religious slaughter (Chapter 11), because many religious authorities will accept a fully reversible stun where the animal can fully recover. Maintaining the full 1 amp is essential for effective head-only stunning of commercial pigs (Viegh et al., 2017).
- **Simultaneous head-to-body cardiac arrest** – Figs 9.2 and 9.3 show simultaneous head-to-back cardiac arrest stunning. When this method is used, the electric current is simultaneously passed through the animal's brain and heart. When correctly applied, it will simultaneously induce instantaneous unconsciousness and kill the animal by cardiac arrest. From an animal welfare standpoint, this is the preferred method (Gregory and Wotton, 1984; Wotton and Gregory, 1986). If bleeding is delayed, the animal will not recover. The head electrode must never be placed on the neck, because the current would fail to pass through the brain. Cardiac arrest would occur but the animal would still be conscious. In pigs, the head electrode can be placed in the hollow behind the ear (Fig. 9.2). In sheep, Velarde et al. (2000) found that the more forward position was more effective. Sheep have wool and it is an insulator. Stunning was more likely to be effective on sheep with short wool and when the application area was wetted. This is the reason why commercial head-to-back electrical stunners for sheep have a system for passing water through the electrodes to wet the skin surface.
- **Sequential head-to-body cardiac arrest stunning** – This method is especially useful in small abattoirs where the animals are electrically stunned with tongs while standing on the floor (Fig. 9.1). A head-to-back stunner (Figs 9.2 and 9.3) works poorly in this situation, because the animal will fall away from the head-to-back tong (wand). There is no restrainer conveyer or other restraint to hold the animal up. In the sequential method, the tong is first used to stun across the head to induce instantaneous unconsciousness. Immediately after removal from the head, the tong is re-applied right behind the elbow to induce cardiac arrest (Vogel et al., 2010) (Fig. 9.4). The electrodes must always be applied to the head first to induce unconsciousness. Before this method was developed, small abattoirs where pigs or sheep were head-only stunned on the floor often had problems with animals returning to consciousness. This occurred because recovery started before the sheep or pigs could be shackled, hoisted and bled. The sequential method is also used for cardiac arrest stunning of cattle (Wotton et al., 2000; Weaver and Wotton, 2008).

- Simultaneous application to the hollow behind the ear and body (cardiac arrest) of pigs. Assess position of head electrode only.
- Between the eye and ear on both sides of the head with a tong-type stunner for pigs and sheep (reversible head-only).
- Cattle nose-to-neck in a stanchion (reversible head-only for religious slaughter) (Wotton et al., 2000).
- Top of head and under the jaw with a tong-type stunning (reversible head-only).
- Two-stage cardiac arrest stun for cattle, nose-to-neck followed by neck-to-brisket electrode (Wotton et al., 2000; Weaver and Wotton, 2008).
- Two-stage cardiac arrest stun for pigs, sheep or goats. Application across the head followed by a second application to the chest (Vogel et al., 2010). The head stun must be applied first. This method is especially recommended for small abattoirs that stun groups of animals on the floor.

How Electricity Works

Electricity and water share some characteristics. Volts are analogous to water pressure and amperage is analogous to the amount (volume) of water. There has to be sufficient voltage to drive the required amperage through the animal's brain. Modern electrical stunning units will automatically deliver the required amperage. The voltage will automatically vary. On older stunning units, the voltage is set and the amperage will vary depending on the animal's

Fig. 9.1. Head-only electrical stunning with the tongs in the correct position to pass the current through the brain. This is essential to induce instant unconsciousness by causing a grand mal epileptic seizure. (From T. Grandin, 2010.)

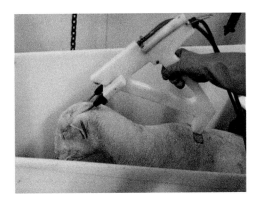

Fig. 9.2. Head-to-back cardiac arrest electrical stunning. It simultaneously induces unconsciousness and cardiac arrest. (From T. Grandin, 2010.)

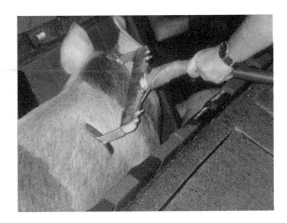

Fig. 9.3. Head-to-back cardiac arrest electrical stunner. The head electrode must never be placed on the neck. It must either be in the hollow behind the ears or on the forehead. Placing the body electrode on the side of the body helps reduce blood spotting in the meat. (From T. Grandin, 2010.)

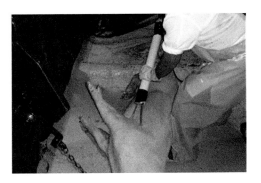

Fig. 9.4. Second step of a sequential cardiac arrest stunning procedure for pigs. The tong is first applied to the head to induce unconsciousness and then immediately applied to the chest to stop the heart. This chest position helps reduce meat damage. (Photo courtesy of Erika Voogd.)

resistance. Dehydrated animals or failure to wet the electrode application site can cause electrical stunning failures in all species of livestock (Grandin, 2001) and poultry. Dehydrated animals that have been off water for too long are poor conductors of electricity. If animals arrive at the slaughter plant in a severely dehydrated condition, a few hours in the lairage with drinking water may not be sufficient to recover. The author has observed that dehydration is a common cause of electrical stunning failures in cattle, sheep and pigs.

Minimum Amperage Requirements for Different Types of Livestock

Table 9.1 shows the minimum amperage requirements for different types of livestock. This table is

Table 9.1. Minimum current levels for head-only electrical stunning at 50–60 cycles (from AVMA, 2016; OIE, 2018).

Species	Current level
Cattle	1.5 amps
Calves (bovines of less than 6 months of age)	1.0 amps
Pigs	1.25 amps
Sheep and goats	1.0 amps
Lambs	0.7 amps[a]
Ostriches	0.4 amps

[a]Both EFSA (2015) and HSA (2016) require 1 amp for lamb

T. Grandin

in the latest version of the OIE 2018 slaughter guidelines.

The current levels should be maintained for 1 s after the initiation of the stun. To ensure reliable induction of unconsciousness, the tong should be applied for 2 or 3 s. When head-to-back stunning is used, a higher amperage may be required, because the current has to travel a greater distance through the body. When the original research was done to determine the 1.25 amp setting, lighter 100 kg (220 lb) pigs were used. In North America, larger 130 kg (275 lb) pigs are common. These larger animals will require higher amperage settings (NAMI, 2017).

Monitoring of Electrical Stunning

In many abattoirs, voltage and amperage meters are monitored to ensure that the stunner is delivering the required amperage (Velarde and Raj, 2016). Monitoring of meters is also done to comply with regulatory requirements. At regular intervals throughout the day, the readings are recorded. Computerized stunners are available that will automatically record the amperage and voltage of every stun.

Reading meters is not sufficient to ensure that all the animals are made instantly unconscious. Animal welfare officers, inspectors and auditors need to know how to determine if the stunner is causing a grand mal seizure. When head-only stunning is done for 2 or 3 s, it is easy to observe a distinct rigid (tonic) and kicking (clonic) phase. The presence of the tonic and clonic spasm is evaluated after the electrical stunner tong is removed from the head. When testing for tonic and clonic spasms, the tong should be held on for 1–3 s. Holding the tong on too long, for over 5 s, may depolarize the spine and mask the seizure.

Electrical stunner effectiveness may also be difficult to evaluate if a plant uses an immobilizing current to hold the carcass still after stunning. This is used in some beef abattoirs. To observe the clonic and tonic spasm, the immobilizer current must be turned off. If the stunner is not capable of inducing an epileptic seizure, it should not be used. The use of low currents or very high frequencies will result in paralysing a sensible animal. Electrical immobilization must never be used as a substitute for effective electrical stunning that induces a grand mal seizure (OIE, 2018). It is highly aversive

and detrimental to welfare (Lambooij and VanVorst, 1985; Grandin et al., 1986; Pascoe, 1986; Rushen, 1986).

If a head-only stunner is left on for 10–20 s, the seizure may be completely masked because the spinal column becomes depolarized. Head-to-back stunning and sequential electrical stunning can also mask the full tonic and clonic phases of the seizure. When it is applied for 2–3 s, there should still be slight signs of a tonic and a clonic phase. A sign that electrical stunning is not working is when the carcass is too still after a stun of 2–3 s.

Electrical Cycles (Frequency) on Stunning Effectiveness

Regular electric mains (house) current provided from a commercial power station operates at 50 cycles in Europe, Asia, Middle East, Russia and Africa. The electricity frequency is 60 cycles in Canada, USA, Mexico and Central America. South America is mostly 50 cycles with a few exceptions, such as Brazil, which is 60 cycles.

Low frequency 50- or 60-cycle electricity is more effective for stunning than higher frequencies. Figure 9.5 shows the difference between standard 50 or 60 Hz waveform and a 200 Hz waveform. The higher frequency has more cycles that the current makes per second.

Research clearly shows that 50 or 60 Hz provides superior stunning results compared with higher

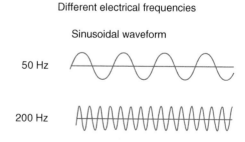

Different electrical frequencies

Sinusoidal waveform

50 Hz

200 Hz

Fig. 9.5. Tracing of electrical sinusoidal waveforms to show the difference between standard 50 Hz and 200 Hz electrical waveforms. Lower frequencies make electrical stunning more effective but they are more likely to cause meat damage in livestock and poultry. Research has been done to determine the best frequencies that reduce meat damage but still protect animal welfare with effective stunning.

frequencies. Low frequencies of 50–60 Hz have a greater ability to penetrate tissues. One of the reasons why people want to use higher frequencies is to reduce blood spotting and other damage to the meat. Higher frequencies can be used, but higher voltage will be required. For example, OIE (2018) guidelines for poultry require double the standard 100 mA recommendations for frequencies over 400 Hz. Another disadvantage of higher frequencies is that the time that the livestock or poultry remain unconscious is shorter.

Higher frequencies will reduce the length of time that pigs will remain insensible (Anil and McKinstry, 1992). Very high frequencies of 2000–3000 Hz fail to induce insensibility and should not be used (Croft, 1952; Warrington, 1974; Van der Wal, 1978). Frequencies of 1592 Hz sine wave or 1642 Hz square wave will induce insensibility in small pigs (Anil and McKinstry, 1992). Some effective commercial systems apply an 800 Hz current to the head, followed by a 50 Hz current applied to the body. This combination is effective (Lambooij et al., 1997; Berghaus and Troeger, 1998; Wenzlawowicz et al., 1999). High frequencies applied to induce cardiac arrest must never be used. Practical experience with a European tong-type stunner showed that 400 Hz applied to the chest failed to induce cardiac arrest in pigs.

Correcting Electrical Stunning Problems

Box 9.2 describes the reasons for problems that may be encountered during electrical stunning.

Carbon Dioxide (CO_2) Stunning of Pigs

CO_2 stunning of pigs is the major method that is used in large slaughter plants in both Europe and the USA. Electrical stunning induces instantaneous unconsciousness. When CO_2 stunning is used, the pigs have to breathe CO_2 gas for 20–30 s before they become unconscious. Smaller plants often use electrical stunning because the equipment is less expensive. One reason CO_2 has become the preferred method is that it reduces meat damage such as petechial haemorrhage and blood spots in the pork (Gregory, 2005). US abattoir managers have been motivated to switch to CO_2 to reduce broken backs in heavyweight 125 kg (275 kg) market pigs caused by electrical stunning. Broken backs are not a welfare concern, because the pig is unconscious, but they can cause serious meat damage. This is the commercial reality, even though there are animal welfare concerns about the aversiveness of CO_2 (Raj and Gregory, 1996; Becerill-Herrera et al., 2009; Dalmau et al., 2010).

One big advantage of the large CO_2 machines is that the pigs are handled in groups and the use of

---

Box 9.2. Electrical stunning problems

- **Pigs squeal or cattle bellow when the stunner is applied** – This occurs because the tong or other device was not pressed firmly against the animal before the current was turned on.
- **Poor electrical contact** – Wet either the animals or the electrodes. Never use sharp pin electrodes. Enlarging the surface area of electrode may improve electrical contact.
- **Sliding or bouncing the tong during application** – This can cause both meat quality problems and failure to induce instantaneous unconsciousness. If the wand bounces or slides, it causes the animal's muscles to contract more than once.
- **Dirty contacts, worn-out power receptacle or damaged wires** – May cause a drop in the current.
- **Meters are broken** – A faulty meter may give wrong readings. The electrical box must be kept dry. It must never be sprayed with water. Many

people get too reliant on the meters. Looking at the reaction of the animal is more important to make sure that a seizure is induced.
- **Dirty electrodes** – Electrodes must be kept clean to maximize current flow.
- **Electrode contact area too small** – In some systems, enlarging the contact area of the electrode may improve stunning.
- **DEHYDRATED ANIMALS** – This is in capital letters because electric stunning works poorly on dehydrated animals that have been off water for too long. If an electrical stunner suddenly starts failing, check where the animals came from. The author has observed problems with dehydrated animals in cattle, sows and lambs. This problem must be corrected by the producer or transporter. A drink of water in the lairage 2 h before stunning will usually not solve this problem.

T. Grandin

electric prods during handling can be completely eliminated. Cortisol levels were significantly lower in pigs handled in groups (Jongman *et al.*, 2017). Figure 9.6 shows a group of pigs ready to be moved into the chamber. Handling is greatly improved compared with moving several hundred pigs per hour through a single file race for electric stunning. When high numbers of pigs are moved through a single file race, electric prods will usually be needed to move about 15% of the pigs. Another advantage is that CO_2 stunning with long dwell times in the gas can almost eliminate problems with pigs regaining consciousness. In the USA, the Department of Agriculture's Food Safety and Inspection Service (FSIS) regulatory authority can shut an abattoir down if animals regain consciousness after stunning. This has motivated many abattoir companies to switch from electrical to CO_2 stunning. Pressure from animal activist groups has resulted in increased enforcement of US Humane Slaughter regulations. The author has observed that this has resulted in increased use of CO_2 because it makes it easier to comply with US regulations.

Welfare Controversy

The World Organisation for Animal Health (OIE) recommends that the CO_2 gas concentration must be 80% or 90%. Many commercial units in the USA are run at higher concentrations. The standard best practice is to quickly lower the pigs into 90% or greater levels of CO_2 (Becerril-Herrera *et al.*, 2009). One indicator of the continuing controversy about CO_2 stunning is that the OIE

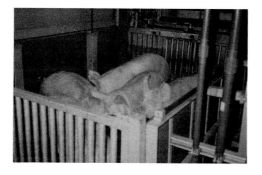

Fig. 9.6. A group of pigs getting ready to enter the CO_2 stunner. After the gate on the left side opens, the powered pusher gate on the right will move the pigs into the gondola. Group handling greatly reduces pre-stunning stress. (Photo courtesy of Temple Grandin.)

(2018) guidelines are still under study and the Humane Slaughter Association (HSA, 2018) has no guidance for CO_2 stunning of pigs. HSA has extensive guidance for electrical stunning, captive bolt stunning and gas (controlled atmosphere) stunning of poultry. Guidance from the European Food Safety Authority (EFSA) is also less detailed (EFSA, 2018) for controlled atmosphere stunning (CAS). EFSA has extensive guidance documents for other stunning methods. Both EFSA (2004, 2015) and the HSA are encouraging the development of new or modified gas stunning methods (EFSA, 2017, 2018).

One of the problems with alternatives to CO_2 has been pork quality (Llonch *et al.*, 2012a). CO_2 stunning had superior pork quality compared with head-to-brisket electrical stunning (Channon *et al.*, 2002). Another problem is that only gases that are heavier than air will work in the existing CO_2 machines. This limits the gases to CO_2 and argon. Other gases, such as nitrogen, will not stay in the chamber, because it is an open system dependent on gravity to confine the gas in a deep pit. The use of these gases may require the use of a different type of chamber. The use of other gases such as CO_2 and nitrogen, or CO_2 and argon, will reduce aversiveness (Raj and Gregory, 1996; Dalmau *et al.*, 2010; Llonch *et al.*, 2012b).

Assessing the Reaction of Pigs to CO_2 or Other Gases

Both captive bolt and electrical stunning induce instantaneous unconsciousness. When CO_2 or other controlled atmosphere methods are used, 20 or more seconds may be required before the pigs have loss of posture (LOP) (Velarde *et al.*, 2007). From an animal welfare standpoint, the most important part of the process is the induction phase before the pigs fall over and lose the ability to stand. The pigs will be unconscious either at the time of LOP or 2–10 s after LOP (Verhoeven *et al.*, 2016b). Verhoeven *et al.* (2016b) defined loss of posture as when the pig is in a recumbent position and it has totally lost control of posture. Convulsions, kicking and squealing that occur after LOP are less of a welfare concern.

Even though there is a possibility of some awareness after LOP, this measure is still useful for preventing the worst problems. Commercial abattoirs need assessment tools they can easily use. It is also possible that the pigs were in the transition zone between full consciousness and brain death in the Verhoeven *et al.* (2016a,b) study (see Chapter 14). Verhoeven *et al.* (2015) stated: 'The exact moment when unconsciousness sets in, based on EEG, is difficult to determine as change is often gradual.' Benson *et al.* (2012) determined that chickens became unconscious when they fell over and lost posture. Why have Verhoeven *et al.* (2016b) reported different results in pigs? This may be due to differences in the methods used to evaluate the EEG. Benson *et al.* (2012) used medical software that assessed the alpha–delta wave ratio and Verhoeven *et al.* (2016b) used a more subjective method of the visual appraisal of the EEG. When LOP occurs, it is the first step in becoming unconscious (Terlouw *et al.*, 2016a,b).

Another issue that has to be examined when assessing reactions to CO_2 or other controlled atmosphere stunning methods is the condition of the lungs. In commercial market-weight pigs, observations by people working in the industry indicate that 7–8% may have severe lung lesions. Lung lesions may increase the time required to lose consciousness. This is an area that will require more research.

Video Cameras Required to Evaluate Pig Reactions in Large CO_2 Machines

Assessment of the pigs' reactions in large commercial CO_2 machines will require the use of video cameras installed in the pit. In a typical large machine, the gondolas travel through the CO_2 on a continuous conveyor, similar to a skinny Ferris wheel. Viewing the pigs when they reach the bottom of the deep pit is extremely difficult, because the next gondola blocks the view. In small dip-lift machines that have a single gondola, which goes up and down like an elevator, it is easy to see the pigs through the entire process. Poultry systems are easier to evaluate through either windows or video cameras, because most systems are in cabinets that are mounted on top of the abattoir floor.

Researchers have found that there is an excitation phase that occurs before the loss of consciousness (Hoenderken, 1978, 1983; Rodrigues *et al.*, 2008). Loss of posture or escape movements could not be assessed by Rodrigues *et al.* (2008), because the pigs were held in a net sling. It is the author's opinion that some discomfort, such as head shaking or gasping, may be an acceptable tradeoff to achieve low-stress handling with no electric prods.

It is also the author's opinion that when escape attempts occur, the pig's welfare is not acceptable. An escape attempt is scored if a pig attempts escape from the gondola or other container. After the pigs were lowered into the gas, Verhoeven *et al.* (2016b) observed signs of pig aversion to CO_2 but 0% attempted to escape.

Genetic Differences in Pig Reaction to CO_2

A possible best way to improve animal welfare during induction of CO_2 anaesthesia is genetic selection. Dodman (1977) reported that the reaction of pigs to CO_2 was high variable. Forslid (1987) used EEG to determine that, in purebred Yorkshire (Large White) pigs, the excitation phase occurred after loss of consciousness. Unfortunately, he never tested any other breeds of pig.

Grandin (1988) observed pigs in small CO_2 machines where their reactions could be viewed. These observations were conducted before the large breeding companies had introduced large numbers of hybrid pigs. It would have been a genetically diverse population. The pigs were a mixture of breeds and colours. Some pigs struggled violently and others had a calm induction. The pigs were definitely having a reaction to the gas. The initial movement of the gondola had no effect on the pigs' behaviour. Grandin (1988) concluded that genetic factors may have had an effect on the pigs' reactions. Pigs that were white and had Yorkshire breed characteristics had a calmer induction than pigs that were black with a white belt, which is characteristic of the Hampshire breed. The next study, by Troeger and Wolsterdorf (1991), indicated that pigs with the halothane stress gene had a worse reaction during induction. Velarde *et al.* (2007) were the first researchers to test pigs with a known halothane genotype. They evaluated Duroc × Yorkshire pigs, which were homozygous halothane stress gene free, and Piétrain × Large White pigs that were carriers (heterozygotes). A concentration of 70–90% CO_2 was used, which is low compared with properly operated commercial units. For the carrier pigs, 67% attempted to escape from the gondola; for the pigs that were completely free of the stress gene, 46% of the animals attempted to escape (Velarde *et al.*, 2007). In Yorkshire × Landrace pigs, being shocked by an electric prod was more aversive than CO_2 (Jongman *et al.*, 2000).

T. Grandin

The author's own observations of pigs being introduced into CO_2 have ranged from a very peaceful induction in Danish homozygous halothane stress gene free pigs to the most vigorous escape attempts in other pig breeds. The pigs that had the worse reactions likely carried the stress gene and they were handled poorly with numerous electric prods. The Danish observations were made in a special research machine where a group of pigs entered the CO_2 very quietly. There was sufficient space in the gondola for the pigs to walk around. A few pigs sniffed the CO_2 and backed up. After LOP, the violent reaction occurred. The chamber had a concentration of 90% CO_2. Patricia Barton, a researcher at the Danish Meat Research Institute, always maintained that it is really important to have a calm pig entering the CO_2 gondola.

Observations in Large Butina Machine with Video

More recent observations of US commercial hybrid pigs by the author indicated that 20–30% had a calm induction before loss of posture. Eleven per cent had a definite escape reaction. The pigs were stunned with 90% CO_2 in a Butina machine with group handling. Determining the exact numbers of calm inductions was difficult, due to the gondola being loaded to the standard commercial capacity. All the pigs were quietly moved into the gondola and electric prods were not used on any of the pigs.

The pigs were all commercially available hybrids with unknown genetics. All the animals were white with grey areas on their hindquarters or shoulders. They had partially floppy ears that may indicate both Yorkshire and Landrace genetics. The grey areas may indicate Hampshire genetics. The coloration of the pigs indicates that it is likely they were free of Duroc or Piétrain genetics. They had no black spots or brown coloration.

Studies done in Australian abattoirs with CO_2 indicated that there was a large variation in escape/crawl reactions between different abattoirs and different farms (Jongman, 2017). Escape/crawl reactions varied from 6% to 46% of the pigs.

Evaluation of Future Controlled Atmosphere Stunning

EFSA (2018) adopted a document on guidelines for evaluating new systems. It has an excellent table (Table 9.2) for evaluating new systems. This table contains both behavioural and physiological measures. The table's behavioural measures should be used *before* loss of posture. Terlouw *et al.* (2016a,b) and Chapter 13 provide additional guidance.

When physiological measures are used, one must remember that increases in epinephrine that occur after the animal becomes unconscious have no effect on animal welfare. Captive bolt and electrical stunning both increase physiological measures of stress (Van der Wal, 1978). Since induction of unconsciousness is instantaneous, the increase in catecholamines would have no effect on the welfare of a properly stunned animal.

Operation Problems in the Slaughter Plant

Operation problems with CO_2 and other CAS methods that can compromise animal welfare are outlined in Box 9.3.

Management Decisions about Electrical or Controlled Atmosphere Stunning

CAS systems are expensive to buy and maintain but require less oversight by management during day-to-day operations compared with electrical stunning. When CAS is working properly, problems with pigs or poultry regaining consciousness can almost be eliminated. Electrical stunning is economical to buy and much cheaper to operate than CAS. To prevent pigs from regaining consciousness, electrical stunning requires a lot more attention to details of procedure such as electrode (tong) positioning and wetting the animals. Another disadvantage of electrical stunning is that it is more difficult to train people how to correctly evaluate unconsciousness. Stunning pigs in a large CO_2 machine with a long exposure time results in floppy pigs with all reflexes eliminated (Fig. 9.7). The floppy carcasses are both safer and easier to handle for the person who does the bleeding.

Conclusions

Both electrical stunning and CO_2 stunning require calm, low-stress handling. Agitated excited animals are more difficult to stun. There are tradeoffs. Electrical stunning, when properly applied, induces instantaneous unconsciousness, but low-stress

Table 9.2. EFSA (2018) overview of categories of animal-based measures associated with pain, distress and suffering during the induction of unconsciousness with CAS stunning. Assess behavioural measure *before* loss of posture (LOP). (Table adapted from EFSA, 2018, 'Guidance on the assessment criteria for application for new or modified stunning methods regarding animal protection at the time of killing'.)

Category of animal behaviour measures (ABMs)	ABMs	Examples	References
Behavioural measures	Vocalizations	Number and duration, intensity, spectral components	EFSA, 2005; Le Neindre et al., 2009; Atkinson et al., 2012; Landa, 2012; Llonch et al., 2012a, 2012b, 2013
	Postures and movements	Kicking, tail flicking, avoidance	Jongman et al., 2000; EFSA, 2005; McKeegan et al., 2006; Gerritzen et al., 2007; Velarde et al., 2007; Kirkden et al., 2008; Svendsen et al., 2008; Dalmau et al., 2010; Atkinson et al., 2012; Landa, 2012; Llonch et al., 2012a, 2012b, 2013; Verhoeven et al., 2015a,b
	General behaviour	Agitation, freezing, retreat attempts, escape attempts	EFSA, 2005; Velarde et al., 2007; Dalmau et al., 2010; Landa, 2012
Physiological measures	Hormone concentrations	HPA axis: corticosteroids, ACTH; sympathetic system; adrenaline, noradrenaline	Mellor et al., 2000; EFSA, 2005; LeNeindre et al., 2009; Coetzee et al., 2010; Landa, 2012
	Blood metabolites	Glucose, lactate, LDH	EFSA, 2005; Vogel et al., 2010; Landa, 2012; Mota-Rojas et al., 2012
	Autonomic responses	Heart rate and heart rate variability, blood pressure, respiratory rate, body temperature	Martoft et al., 2001; EFSA, 2005; Von Borell et al., 2007; Gerritzen et al., 2007; Rodriguez et al., 2008; Svendsen et al., 2008; Le Neindre et al., 2009; Dalmau et al., 2010; McKeegan et al., 2011; Atkinson et al., 2012; Landa, 2012; Llonch et al., 2012a, 2012b, 2013
Neurological measures	Brain activity	EEG, ECoG	Gibson et al., 2009a,b

Box 9.3. Operation problems with CAS methods that can compromise animal welfare

- **Undersized machine** – An overloaded, undersized machine is one of the worst problems with all types of gas stunning (Grandin, 2015). As a plant increases production, the machine may become overloaded. Plant managers who are purchasing a gas stunning machine should purchase a large enough machine to handle future increases in production. An overloaded machine has to be replaced. Specific signs of an overloaded machine are: (i) animals are not rendered insensible, because the exposure time has been decreased by speeding up the conveyor; and (ii) gondolas or containers are overloaded and pigs or birds do not have enough room to stand or lie down without being on top of each other. Pigs should never be forced to jump on top of other pigs when a gondola is being loaded.

- **Problems with maintaining the correct gas concentration** – Another problem that can occur is that gas is not evenly distributed in the chamber. This may be due to either a design fault in the chamber, or the ventilation system in the abattoir may be sucking the gas out of the chamber. Correcting this problem may require the expertise of an engineering professional skilled in ventilation systems. In open gas stunning systems that depend on gravity to hold either CO_2 or argon in the chamber, several problems may occur. Some of the problems are caused by wind blowing around the plant building, changes in the number of ventilation fans turned on in the abattoir, or opening and closing doors near the chamber. These factors can cause 'stack pressure' that may cause the gas to be sucked out (Grandin, 2015). Stack pressure is a common

Continued

T. Grandin

cause of a sudden appearance of conscious animals emerging from a chamber that has been operating effectively. This may occur when a certain specific sequence of either opening doors or turning on ventilator fans occurs. Doors that slam hard by themselves are moved by differences in air pressure between two rooms or between a room and the outdoors. Differences in air pressure in rooms near the gas stunning equipment may cause the stunner to fail. Stack pressure problems will have no effect on positive pressure (closed) systems where the gas is introduced into the chamber with a ventilation system. Low air pressure systems that are discussed in the poultry chapter (Chapter 8) are also not affected by air pressure differences within a building.

Fig. 9.7. Pigs discharged from a CO_2 machine are limp and floppy. The large CO_2 machines used in big commercial abattoirs have a dwell time that is sufficiently long to kill the pigs. This reduces many problems with pigs regaining consciousness. (Photo courtesy of Temple Grandin.)

handling of the animals before stunning is more difficult. When CO_2 or other CAS is used, low-stress handling before stunning is much easier and electric prods can be eliminated. All types of CO_2 or other controlled atmosphere stunning should be monitored with video cameras. Behaviour before loss of posture should be evaluated.

References

Anil, A.M. and McKinstry, J.L. (1992) The effectiveness of high frequency electrical stunning in pigs. *Meat Science* 31, 481–491.

Anil, M.H. and McKinstry, J.L. (1998) Variation in electrical stunning tong placements and relative consequences in slaughter pigs. *Veterinary Journal* 155, 85–90.

Atkinson, S., Velarde, A., Llonch, P. and Algers, B. (2012) Assessing pig welfare at stunning in Swedish commercial abattoirs using CO_2 group-stun methods. *Animal Welfare* 21, 487–495.

AVMA (2016) *Guidelines for the Humane Slaughter of Animals*, 2016 edn. American Veterinary Medical Association, Schaumberg, Illinois.

Becerril-Herrera, M., Alonso-Spilsbury, M., Lemus-Flores, C., Guerrero-Legarreta, I., Hernandez, A. et al. (2009) CO_2 stunning may compromise swine welfare compared to electrical stunning. *Meat Science* 81, 233–237.

Benson, E.R., Alphin, R.L., Rankin, M.K., Caputo, M.P., Kinnley, C.A. and Johnson, A.L. (2012) Evaluation of EEG based determination of unconsciousness vs. loss of posture in broilers. *Research in Veterinary Science* 93, 960–954.

Berghaus, A. and Troeger, K. (1998) Electrical stunning of pig's minimum current flow time required to induce epilepsy at various frequencies. *International Congress of Meat Science and Technology* 44, 1070–1073.

Blackmore, D.K. and Newhook, J.L. (1981) Insensibility during slaughter of pigs in comparison to other domestic stock. *New Zealand Veterinary Journal* 29, 2192.

Channon, H.A., Payne, A.M. and Warner, R.D. (2002) Comparison of CO_2 stunning with manual electrical stunning (50 Hz) of pigs on carcass and meat quality. *Meat Science* 60, 63–68.

Coetzee, J.F., Gehring, R., Tarus-Sang, J. and Anderson, D.E. (2010) Effect of sub-anesthetic xylazine and ketamine ('ketamine stun') administered to calves immediately prior to castration. *Veterinary Anesthesia and Analgesia* 37, 566–578.

Croft, P.S. (1952) Problems with electrical stunning. *Veterinary Record* 64, 255–258.

Dalmau, A., Rodriguez, P., Llonch, P. and Velarde, A. (2010) Stunning pigs with different gas mixtures: aversion in pigs. *Animal Welfare* 19, 325–333.

Dodman, N.H. (1977) Observations on the use of the Werberg dip–lift carbon dioxide apparatus for preslaughter anaesthesia of pigs. *British Veterinary Journal* 133, 71–80.

EFSA (European Food Safety Authority) (2004) Welfare aspects of the main systems of stunning and killing the main commercial species of animals. *EFSA Journal* 45, 1–29.

EFSA (European Food Safety Authority) (2005) Aspects of the biology and welfare of animals used for experimental and other scientific purposes. *EFSA Journal* 292, 1–46.

EFSA (European Food Safety Authority) (2015) Scientific opinion on the scientific assessment of studies on the electrical parameters of stunning small ruminants (ovine and caprine species). *EFSA Journal* 13(2), 4023.

EFSA AHAW Panel (EFSA Panel on Animal Health and Welfare) (2017) Scientific opinion on the low atmospheric pressure system for stunning broiler chickens. *EFSA Journal* 15(12), 5056.

EFSA (European Food Safety Authority) (2018) Guidance on the assessment criteria for applications for new or modified stunning methods regarding animal protection at the time of killing. Guidance of the Animal Health and Welfare (AHAW) Panel Document. *EFSA Journal* 16(7), 5343. doi: 10.2903/j.efsa.2018.5343

Forslid, A. (1987) Transient neocortisol, hippocampal and amygdaloid EEG silence induced by one minute inhalation of high concentration CO_2 in the swine. *Acta Physiologica Scandinavica* 130, 1–10.

Gerritzen, M., Lambooij, B., Reimert, H., Stegeman, A. and Spruijt, B. (2007) A note on behaviour of poultry exposed to increasing carbon dioxide concentrations. *Applied Animal Behaviour Science* 108, 179–185.

Gibson, T.J., Johnson, C.B., Murrell, J.C., Hulls, C.M., Mitchinson, S.L. *et al.* (2009a) Electroencephalographic responses of halothane-anaesthetized calves to slaughter by ventral-neck incision without prior stunning. *New Zealand Veterinary Journal* 57, 77–85.

Gibson, T.J., Johnson, C.B., Murrell, J.C., Chambers, J.P., Stafford, K.J. and Mellor, D.J. (2009b) Components of electroencephalographic responses to slaughter in halothane-anesthetized calves: effects of cutting neck tissues compared to major blood vessels. *New Zealand Veterinary Journal* 57, 84–89.

Grandin, T. (1986) Cardiac arrest stunning of livestock and poultry. In: Fox, M.W. (ed.) *Advances in Animal Welfare Science*. Martinus Nijhoff, Boston, Massachusetts, pp. 1–30.

Grandin, T. (1988) Possible genetic effect on pig's reaction to CO_2 stunning. *Proceedings of the 34th International Congress of Meat Science and Technology*, Brisbane, Australia. Commonwealth Scientific and Industrial Research Organization (CSIRO), Brisbane, Australia, pp. 96–97.

Grandin, T. (2001) Solving return to sensibility problems after electrical stunning in commercial pork slaughter plants. *Journal of the American Veterinary Medical Association* 219, 608–611.

Grandin, T. (2015) *Improving Animal Welfare: A Practical Approach*. CAB International, Wallingford, UK.

Grandin, T., Curtis, S.E., Widowski, T.M. and Thurmon, J.C. (1986) Electro-immobilization versus mechanical restraint in an avoid-avoid choice test for ewes. *Journal of Animal Science* 62, 1469–1480.

Gregory, N.G. (2005) Recent concerns about stunning and slaughter. *Meat Science* 70, 481–491.

Gregory, N.G. and Wotton, S.B. (1984) Sheep slaughtering procedures, II. Time to loss of brain responsiveness after exsanguination or cardiac arrest. *British Veterinary Journal* 140, 354–360.

Hoenderken, R. (1978) Electrical stunning of pigs for slaughter. Why? Hearing on preslaughter stunning. Kavlinge, Sweden, 19 May 1978.

Hoenderken, R. (1983) Electrical and carbon dioxide stunning of pigs for slaughter. In: Eikenboom, G. (ed.) *Stunning of Animals for Slaughter*. Martinus Nijhoff, Boston, Massachusetts, pp. 59–63.

HSA (2016) Electrical stunning of red meat animals. Humane Slaughter Association, Wheathampstead, UK. Available at: www.hsa.org.uk (accessed 12 January 2020).

HSA (2018) Captive bolt stunning of livestock. Humane Slaughter Association, Wheathampstead, UK. Available at: www.hsa.org.uk (accessed 12 January 2020).

Jongman, E.C., Barnett, J.L. and Hemsworth, P.H. (2000) The aversiveness of carbon dioxide stunning in pigs and a comparison of CO_2 rate vs. the V restrainer. *Applied Animal Behaviour Science* 67, 67–76.

Jongman, E., Woodhouse, R., Rice, M. and Rault, J.L. (2017) Behavioral responses to CO_2 stunning under commercial conditions. RSPCA Seminar, Canberra, Australia.

Kirkden, R.D., Niel, L., Lee, G., Makowski, I.J., Pfaffinger, M.J. and Weary, D.M. (2008) The validity of using an approach-avoidance test to measure the strength of aversion to carbon dioxide in rats. *Applied Animal Behaviour Science* 114, 216–234.

Lambooij, E. (1982) Electrical stunning of sheep. *Meat Science* 6, 123–135.

Lambooij, E. and Van Voorst, N. (1985) Electroanaesthesia of calves and sheep. In: Eikenboom, G. (ed.) *Stunning Animals for Slaughter*. Martinus Nijhoff, Boston, Masachusetts, pp. 117–122.

Lambooij, B., Merkus, G.S.M., Voorst, N.V., and Pieterse, C. (1997) Effect of low voltage with a high frequency electrical stunning on unconsciousness in slaughter pigs. *Fleischwirtschaft International* 2, 13–14.

Lambooy, E. and Spanjaard, W. (1982) Electrical stunning of veal calves. *Meat Science* 6, 15–25.

Landa, L. (2012) Pain in domestic animals and how to assess it: a review. *Veterinarni Medicina* 57, 185–192.

Le Neindre, P.G.R., Guemene, D., Guichet, J.L., Latouche, K., Leterrier, C. *et al.* (2009) Animal pain: identifying, understanding and minimizing pain in farm animals. Multidisciplinary scientific assessment. Summary of the expert report, INRA, Paris, 98 pp.

Llonch, P., Rodriguez, P., Gispert, M., Dalmau, A., Manteca, X. and Velarde, A. (2012a) Stunning pigs with nitrogen and carbon dioxide mixtures effects on animal welfare and meat quality. *Animal* 6, 668–675.

Llonch, P., Dalmau, A., Rodriguez, P., Manteca, X. and Velarde, A. (2012b) Aversion to nitrogen and carbon dioxide mixtures for stunning pigs. *Animal Welfare* 21, 33–39.

Llonch, P., Rodriguez, P., Jospin, M., Dalmau, A., Manteca, X, and Velarde, A. (2013) Assessment of unconsciousness in pigs during exposure to nitrogen and carbon dioxide mixtures. *Animal* 7, P492–498.

Martoft, L., Jensen, E.W., Rodriguez, B.E., Jurgensen, P.F., Forslid, A. and Pederson, H.D. (2001) Middle latency auditory evoked potentials during induction of thiopentone anesthesia in pigs. *Laboratory Animals* 35, 271–286.

Mason, A., Tolo, E., Hektoen, L., and Haga, H.A. (2018) The effect of electrical head to chest stunning on the EEG in sheep. *Animal Welfare* 27, 343–350.

McKeegan, D.E.F., McIntyre, J., Demmers, T.G.M., Wathes, C.M. and Jones, R.B. (2006) Behavioural responses of broiler chickens during acute exposure to gaseous simulation. *Applied Animal Behaviour Science* 99, 271–286.

McKeegan, D.E.F., Sparks, N.H.C., Sandilands, V., Demmers, T.G.M., Boulcott, P. and Wathes, C.M.C. (2011) Physiological responses of laying hens during whole house killing with carbon dioxide. *British Poultry Science* 52, 643–657.

Mellor, D.J., Cook, C.J. and Stafford, K.J. (2000) Quantifying some responses to pain as a stressor. In: Moberg, G.P. and Mench, J.A. (eds) *Biology of Animal Stress: Basic Principles and Implications for Welfare.* CAB International, Wallingford, pp. 171–198.

Mota-Rojas, D., Bolanos-Lopez, D., Concepcion-Mendez, M., Ramirez-Telles, J., Roldan-Santiago, P. *et al.* (2012) Stunning swine with CO2 gas: controversies related to animal welfare. *International Journal of Pharmacology* 8, 141–151.

NAMI (2019) Recommended Animal Handling Guidelines and Audit Guide. North American Meat Institute, Washington, DC.

OIE (2018) Slaughter of Animals. Ch. 7.5. In: *Terrestrial Animal Health Code.* World Organisation for Animal Health, Paris.

Pascoe, P.J. (1986) Humaneness of electro-immobilization unit for cattle. *American Journal of Veterinary Research* 10, 2252–2256.

Raj, A.B.M. and Gregory, N.G. (1996) Welfare implications of the gas stunning of pigs 2: Stress of induction of anesthesia. *Animal Welfare* 5, 71–78.

Rodriguez, P., Dalmau, A., Ruiz-de-la Torre, J.L., Manteca, X., Jensen, E.W. *et al.* (2008) Assessment of unconsciousness during carbon dioxide stunning in pigs. *Animal Welfare* 17, 341–349.

Rushen, J. (1986) Aversion of sheep to electro-immobilization and physical restraint. *Applied Animal Behaviour Science* 15, 315–324.

Svendsen, O., Jensen, S.K., Karlsen, L.V., Svalstoga, E. and Jensen, H.E. (2008) Observations on newborn calves rendered unconscious with a captive bolt gun. *Veterinary Record* 162, 90–92.

Terlouw, E.M.C., Bourquet, C. and Deiss, V. (2016a) Conscious, unconsciousness and death in the context of slaughter, Part 1. Neurological mechanisms underlying stunning and killing. *Meat Science* 118, 133–146.

Terlouw, E.M.C., Bourquet, C. and Deiss, V. (2016b) Conscious, unconsciousness and death in the context of slaughter, Part 2. Evaluation of methods. *Meat Science* 118, 147–156.

Troeger, K. and Woltersdorf, W. (1991) Gas anesthesia under laboratory conditions with fat pigs of known halothane reaction type: meat quality and animal protection. *Fleischwirtschaft* 4, 43–49.

Van der Wal, P.B. (1978) Chemical and physiological aspects of pig stunning in relation to meat quality, a review. *Meat Science* 2, 19–30.

Velarde, A. and Raj, M. (2016) *Animal Welfare at Slaughter.* 5M Publishing, Sheffield, UK.

Velarde, A., Ruiz de la Torre, J.L., Stub, C., Diestre, A., and Manteca, X. (2000) Factors affecting the effectiveness of head only electrical stunning in sheep. *Veterinary Record* 147, 40–43.

Velarde, A., Cruz, J., Gispert, M., Carrion, D., de la Torre, J.L.R. *et al.,* (2007) Aversion to carbon dioxide stunning in pigs: effect of carbon dioxide concentration and halothane genotype. *Animal Welfare* 16, 513–522.

Verhoeven, M.T.W., Gerritzen, A. and Hellebrekers, L.J. (2015a) Indicators used in livestock to assess unconsciousness after stunning: a review. *Animal* 9, 320–330.

Verhoeven, M.T.W., Gerritzen, M.A., Kiviers-Poodt, M., Hellebrekers, L.J. and Kemp, B. (2015b) Validation of behavioral indicators used to assess unconsciousness. *Research in Veterinary Science* 101, 144–153.

Verhoeven, M.T.W., Gerritzen, M.A., Hellebrekers, L.J. and Kemp, B. (2016a) Validation of indicators to assess unconsciousness in veal calves at slaughter. *Animal* 1(9), 1–9. doi: 10.1017/5173/16000422

Verhoeven, M.T.W., Gerritzen, M.A., Velarde, A., Hellebrekers, L. and Kemp, B. (2016b) Time of loss of consciousness and its relation to behavior in slaughter pigs during stunning with 80 to 95 carbon dioxide. *Frontiers in Veterinary Science* 3, 38.

Viegh, A., Abonyi-Toth, Z. and Rafal, P. (2017) Effectiveness of current intensity and duration on the effectiveness of head only electrical stunning in pigs under commercial conditions. *Acta Veterinaria Hungarica* 65, 13–28.

Vogel, K.D., Badtram, G., Claus, J.R., Grandin, T., Turpin, S. *et al.* (2010) Head only followed by cardiac arrest electrical stunning is an effective alternative to head only electrical stunning. *Journal of Animal Science* 89, 1412–1418.

Von Borell, E., Langbein, J., Despres, G., Hansen, S., Leterrier, C. *et al.* (2007) Heart rate variability as a measure of autonomic regulation of cardiac activity for assessing stress and welfare in farm animals: a review. *Physiology and Behavior* 92, 293–316.

Warrington, P.D. (1974) Electrical stunning: a review of literature. *Veterinary Bulletin* 44, 617–633.

Weaver, A.L. and Wotton, S.B. (2008) The Jarvis beef stunner: effects of a prototype chest electrode. *Meat Science* 81, 51–56.

Wenzlawowicz, M.V., Schutte, A., Hollenbon, K.V., Altrock, A.V., Bostelman, N. and Roeb, S. (1999) Field study on the welfare of meat quality aspects of Midas pig stunning device. *Fleischwirtschaft* 2, 8–13.

Wotton, S.B. and Gregory, N.G. (1986) Pig slaughtering procedures: time to loss of brain responsiveness after exsanguination or cardiac arrest. *Research in Veterinary Science* 40, 148–151.

Wotton, S.B., Anil, M.H., Whittington, P.E. and Parkman, I.D. (2000) Electrical stunning of cattle. *Veterinary Record* 147, 681–684.

T. Grandin

10 Basics of Captive Bolt Stunning of Cattle and Other Animals

FAITH BAIER[1]* AND DENNIS WILLSON[2]

[1]Department of Dairy Science, University of Wisconsin, Madison, USA;
[2]Department of Animal Science, Colorado State University, USA

Summary

Captive bolt guns and firearms are used to humanely induce unconsciousness in animals being slaughtered, euthanized or depopulated. A secondary method such as pithing, exsanguination or injectable agents should be used immediately after a captive bolt stun to ensure death occurs. Using a firearm does not require a secondary method to ensure death if the proper firearm and ammunition are chosen for the species being killed. The most important considerations in using captive bolt guns and firearms are regular cleanings, maintenance and safety. A captive bolt gun is safer than a firearm, because a firearm produces a free projectile. A review of the data shows that stunner placement at very small abattoirs accounts for the majority of humane handling enforcement actions in 2017 by the United States Department of Agriculture's Food Safety and Inspection Service (USDA FSIS). Low incidence of equipment failure indicates that abattoir managers have greatly improved gun maintenance.

Learning Objectives

- Learn about penetrating and non-penetrating captive bolt.
- The importance of good maintenance of stunners.
- Correct stunner placement for different types of animals.
- How to prevent stunning problems.
- Best practices for stunning.

Types of Captive Bolt Guns

Captive bolt guns are commonly used to stun animals, rendering them instantly insensible with no pain before exsanguination and dressing. A captive bolt gun applies physical trauma to the brain to produce an unconscious state in the animal. When a captive bolt gun is fired, a metal bolt or rod is propelled forward and out of the gun towards the animal's head. The bolt can be powered pneumatically or with a blank, powder-filled cartridge. There are two main types of captive bolt guns: large, pneumatically powered guns; and handheld guns powered by a cartridge. Captive bolt guns produce a penetrating or non-penetrating blow.

Penetrating captive bolt guns

Penetrating captive bolt guns have a bolt or rod that is propelled from the gun and enters the animal's head, specifically targeting the brain. The bolt then retracts into the shaft of the gun. Penetrating captive bolts cause irreversible physical damage to the animal's brain, making revival highly unlikely. Penetrating captive bolt guns are commonly used to stun cattle (AVMA, 2016). The humane slaughter of horses, swine and other food animals is discussed in the section, 'Recommendations of other species'.

Pneumatic captive bolt guns

Pneumatic captive bolt guns are powered by compressed air, which provides the energy to propel the bolt forward and out of the gun. Guns from different

---

* Email: fbaier@wisc.edu

manufacturers may have different air requirements for pressure and volume of air. Pneumatic captive bolt guns are commonly used at large cattle abattoirs. The gun is hung over the stun box as shown in Fig. 10.1. A pneumatic stunning system consists of three main parts: the gun; the spring-loaded cable balancer; and the air supply. It is critical to maintain all three parts for the pneumatic captive bolt gun to stun animals effectively. The balancer is mounted above the gun and compensates for the heaviness of the gun, providing the stun operator with a comfortable weight and ample range of gun movement. The air supply that powers the gun is a very important part and it must be regularly maintained. The main maintenance items are filling the lubricator, draining water from the tank and changing the air filter. For example, a Jarvis pneumatic stunner is operated with 190 pounds per square inch (psi) of air pressure (1310 kPa). The air pressure in an operating pneumatic gun should be tested for proper pressure regularly during a work shift. A Jarvis pneumatic gun set at 190 psi is sufficient to cause brainstem disruption, which ensures instantaneous insensibility and no chance of recovery (Oliveira *et al.*, 2017, 2018a). However, Kline *et al.* (2019) reported that cattle stunned with a Jarvis pneumatic captive bolt gun (200–210 psi) (1379–1448 kPa) were rendered unconscious instantly even when the brainstem remained intact. Furthermore, a similar study comparing bolt lengths in the Jarvis found that the longer bolt (17.8 cm versus 15.2 cm and 16.5 cm) caused increased visible brain damage (Wagner *et al.*, 2019). This study showed that there was no significant impact of the longer bolt length on specified risk material (SRM) dispersion from the brain. These two studies show that brainstem disruption is not necessary to induce instantaneous insensibility as long as the operator is using a high-powered pneumatic

penetrating captive bolt. A pneumatic stunner should have its own dedicated compressor. Running the stunner off the same system that runs other air tools in the abattoir may result in insufficient air pressure. This is especially a problem if many other tools are operated at the same time.

Hand-held

Hand-held captive bolt guns are powered by a blank cartridge. The gun is held in the operator's hand and is fired with a trigger. Hand-held captive bolt guns are commonly used in small abattoirs, or are a back-up gun in abattoirs using a pneumatic stunner. Hand-held captive bolt guns can be classified as either in-line, pistol-style, or long-handle. An in-line gun consists of two main interconnected pieces, which form a linear-shaped gun (Fig. 10.2). A pistol-style gun looks similar to a pistol firearm with a squeezable arched trigger and perpendicular handle (Fig. 10.3). A long-handle consists of a pistol-type captive bolt with an extended handle. This type of gun can either have a trigger or operate when bumped against the animal's forehead. The long-handle without a trigger is fired after the end of the barrel comes in contact with the animal. A small amount of force is required to fire this gun. The operator must always be careful not to tap the gun end on a surface that may cause it to fire unintentionally. A long-handle, hand-held captive bolt gun is used in situations where an animal may be out of reach. This type of device may also be used to humanely euthanize a non-ambulatory animal, or downer, in the abattoir lairage. Placement accuracy is critical for delivering an effective stun with a hand-held captive bolt gun, because it is less powerful than many pneumatic captive bolt guns.

Fig. 10.1. A pneumatic penetrating captive bolt gun. (Photo courtesy of Temple Grandin.)

Fig. 10.2. A hand-held in-line penetrating captive bolt gun. (Photo courtesy of Dennis William Willson.)

Non-penetrating captive bolt gun

Non-penetrating captive bolt guns have a mushroom-shaped bolt that does not fully penetrate the animal's head. It induces unconsciousness with a strong concussive force. Non-penetrating captive bolts are often used at abattoirs for halal slaughter of cattle. This type of gun may allow for the revival of an unconscious animal, especially if the animal is not bled immediately after stunning. As a general rule, the stun-to-stick interval should not exceed 60 s (AVMA, 2016). Depending on the type of gun, the non-penetrating force may or may not cause a skull fracture. Accurate placement of the stun is very important when using a non-penetrating captive bolt. There is a much smaller margin for error when using a non-penetrating captive bolt gun. The non-penetrating captive bolt must be placed perfectly perpendicular to the animal's forehead. A non-penetrating captive bolt is most effective when it makes a dent in the forehead of a bovine.

There is concern about the effectiveness of non-penetrating captive bolt guns for certain species. Recent studies in cattle report that a non-penetrating captive bolt gun is less effective at inducing instantaneous insensibility than a penetrating captive bolt gun. One study assessed zebu bulls' brains with portable electroencephalography (EEG) after the animals were stunned with a penetrating pneumatic captive bolt stunner or non-penetrating stunner

(Gibson *et al.*, 2019). The researchers found that only 82% of the bulls stunned with a non-penetrating captive bolt showed waveforms that indicated complete loss of consciousness, compared with 100% of bulls stunned with a penetrating captive bolt (Gibson *et al.*, 2019). Another study with zebu and crossbred (zebu and European breeds) bulls, steers and cows measured several variables related to stun effectiveness and signs of insensibility after being stunned with a non-penetrating or penetrating captive bolt. Oliveira *et al.* (2018b) reported that 99% of bulls stunned with a penetrating captive bolt immediately collapsed and only 12% required a second shot. In contrast, only 91% of bulls stunned with a non-penetrating captive bolt immediately collapsed and 29% required a second shot. Additional behaviours related to sensibility such as the righting reflex, eyeball rotation and response to nostril stimulations were observed more often after non-penetrating captive bolt stuns compared with penetrating captive bolt stuns (Oliveira *et al.*, 2018b).

Maintenance and Repair

The condition of a captive bolt gun reflects the level of care it has received. All captive bolt guns and stunning devices should be completely disassembled and cleaned every day. Supplies and procedures should be used according to the manufacturer's recommendations. Personnel should be familiar with each of the pieces and inner workings of the captive bolt gun (Fig. 10.4). Figure 10.5 shows an exploded parts diagram of an in-line penetrating captive bolt gun with labelled parts. Wire brushes are common tools used for cleaning (Fig. 10.6). Specific tools for cleaning may vary depending on the type of gun and

Fig. 10.3. A hand-held pistol-style penetrating captive bolt gun. (Courtesy of Jarvis Bunzl Processor Division.)

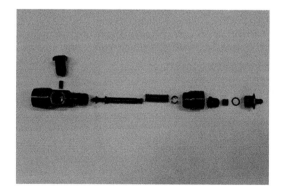

Fig. 10.4. Disassembled cartridge-fired in-line captive bolt gun. (Courtesy of Dennis William Willson.)

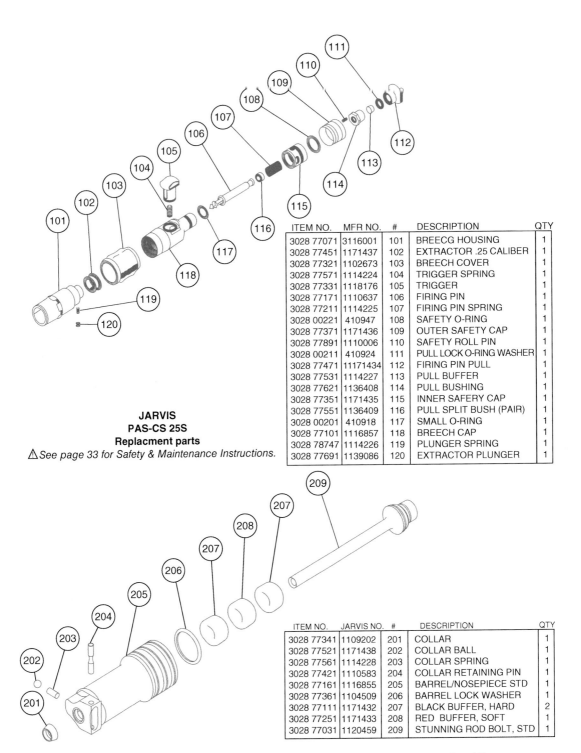

ITEM NO.	MFR NO.	#	DESCRIPTION	QTY
3028 77071	3116001	101	BREECG HOUSING	1
3028 77451	1171437	102	EXTRACTOR .25 CALIBER	1
3028 77321	1102673	103	BREECH COVER	1
3028 77571	1114224	104	TRIGGER SPRING	1
3028 77331	1118176	105	TRIGGER	1
3028 77171	1110637	106	FIRING PIN	1
3028 77211	1114225	107	FIRING PIN SPRING	1
3028 00221	410947	108	SAFETY O-RING	1
3028 77371	1171436	109	OUTER SAFETY CAP	1
3028 77891	1110006	110	SAFETY ROLL PIN	1
3028 00211	410924	111	PULL LOCK O-RING WASHER	1
3028 77471	11171434	112	FIRING PIN PULL	1
3028 77531	1114227	113	PULL BUFFER	1
3028 77621	1136408	114	PULL BUSHING	1
3028 77351	1171435	115	INNER SAFERY CAP	1
3028 77551	1136409	116	PULL SPLIT BUSH (PAIR)	1
3028 00201	410918	117	SMALL O-RING	1
3028 77101	1116857	118	BREECH CAP	1
3028 78747	1114226	119	PLUNGER SPRING	1
3028 77691	1139086	120	EXTRACTOR PLUNGER	1

JARVIS
PAS-CS 25S
Replacment parts
⚠ *See page 33 for Safety & Maintenance Instructions.*

ITEM NO.	JARVIS NO.	#	DESCRIPTION	QTY
3028 77341	1109202	201	COLLAR	1
3028 77521	1171438	202	COLLAR BALL	1
3028 77561	1114228	203	COLLAR SPRING	1
3028 77421	1110583	204	COLLAR RETAINING PIN	1
3028 77161	1116855	205	BARREL/NOSEPIECE STD	1
3028 77361	1104509	206	BARREL LOCK WASHER	1
3028 77111	1171432	207	BLACK BUFFER, HARD	2
3028 77251	1171433	208	RED BUFFER, SOFT	1
3028 77031	1120459	209	STUNNING ROD BOLT, STD	1

Fig. 10.5. Diagram of disassembled cartridge-fired in-line captive bolt gun. (Courtesy of Jarvis Bunzl Processor Division.)

F. Baier and D. Willson

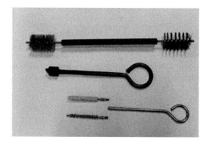

Fig. 10.6. An example of cleaning tools that can be used to regularly clean and maintain a captive bolt gun. (Courtesy of Dennis William Willson.)

Fig. 10.7. New, intact bumpers on a penetrating hand-held captive bolt gun. Be sure to check bumpers for wear regularly. The purpose of the bumpers is to automatically retract the bolt after each shot. If they become worn the rod may get stuck in the animal's head. (Courtesy of Dennis William Willson.)

Fig. 10.8. A Jarvis brand hand-held captive bolt gun testing station. (Courtesy of Dennis William Willson.)

manufacturer. In addition to cleaning, the bumpers should be checked for signs of wear (Fig. 10.7). Other parts that should be examined include the firing pin for signs of misalignment and any cracks or blemishes that may cause a malfunction. A review of cattle stunning with a penetrating captive bolt stressed the importance of regular cleaning and maintenance (Kamenik *et al.*, 2019). When there is a malfunction, the gun should immediately stop being used and thoroughly examined to find and fix the cause of the malfunction. The most common reasons for poor performance of a captive bolt gun are related to the lack of maintenance and cleaning of the device, as well as damp cartridges (Grandin, 2002). The second author has observed the bad practice of storing cartridges overnight on the damp windowsill of a kill floor. This resulted in frequent misfires.

Captive bolt guns should be tested frequently with a testing stand (Fig. 10.8). The test stand must be placed on a solid surface such as a concrete floor or sturdy steel work bench to obtain an accurate reading. Placing the test stand on a flimsy plastic cart resulted in inaccurate readings. Regular testing ensures that the gun is operating at the recommended settings. The bolt velocity should be 55 m/s for steers and cows and 70 m/s for bulls (Gregory, 2007; Gregory *et al.*, 2007). In addition, high-speed processing lines should rotate the use of multiple cartridge-fired captive bolts to prevent overheating, which can degrade the hitting power (Grandin, 2019).

Operator Training and Safety

Worker safety is of critical importance when working with captive bolt guns. All personnel should be thoroughly trained and familiar with the equipment before operating a captive bolt gun. Training should be administered to all employees who will be operating or near the stunning area. Often, training is administered on a regular basis to serve as safety updates and refreshers.

Gunshot

Accurate shot placement is of the utmost importance when stunning an animal (Schiffer *et al.*, 2017). In addition, it is important to use the right size, gun calibre and bullet, especially for very large animals (Shearer, 2018). The UK's Humane Slaughter Association (HSA) recommends ammunition that can generate a muzzle energy of at least 200 joules for killing large or mature animals (Humane Slaughter Association, 2019). When the same calibre of ammunition is used, a rifle is almost always superior to a pistol (AVMA, 2019). Bullets come in various qualities. All bullets are not the same, even though they may be the same calibre. Never use .22 shorts to stun an animal. Do not put the gun directly against the forehead of the animal. Hold the muzzle between 20 cm to half a metre away from the target when using a firearm, to minimize the risk of gun barrel explosion.

Additional information regarding stunning with firearms can be found in the American Veterinary Medical Association (AVMA) *Guidelines for the Euthanasia of Animals* (2020 Edition), the AVMA *Guidelines for Humane Slaughter* (2016 Edition) and the AVMA *Guidelines for the Depopulation of Animals* (2019 Edition).

Restraint

Restraint methods that cause suffering

The OIE guidelines (2019) for animal welfare state that methods of restraint that cause avoidable suffering should not be used. Methods of restraint that should never be used include:

- lifting or suspending a sensible animal by the feet or legs (except for poultry);
- mechanical clamping of a mammal's feet or legs;
- breaking bones;
- cutting tendons to immobilize;
- blinding; or
- severing the spinal cord to paralyse the animal.

Move animals quietly into restrainers

Animals should calmly enter a restrainer or stun box. If animals are baulking, observe why they are baulking, instead of using an electric prod. Poor lighting, shadows, slippery floors, contrast in flooring, air blowing in the face and visual distractions such as flapping objects or people can cause an animal to refuse to move (Grandin, 1996, 1998a). Simple fixes such as installing indirect lighting at the restrainer entrance, non-slip flooring and using cardboard to block the animals' vision reduces baulking and percentage of vocalizations due to electric prod use (Grandin, 2001). Equipment designers and animal handlers should be trained in using behavioural principles of low-stress livestock handling to control animals. The restraint device should be designed to provide optimal pressure on the sides of the animal, which keeps the animal calm and easy to handle. Other designs, including a knock box and headholder, can also be used with careful design considerations. (See Chapter 6 for more information about restraint.)

Stun Placement and Accuracy

One of the most important factors of humane slaughter is accurate stun placement. The correct placement of a stun varies, based on the species of animal. The exact placement may also vary slightly depending on the breed or head shape of a specific animal. In cattle, the preferred position for either captive bolt or gunshot is in the middle of the forehead (Fig. 10.9). The poll position should only be used if the forehead cannot be reached. When the poll position is used, the shot is located in the hollow behind the animal's poll.

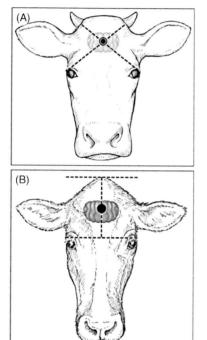

Fig. 10.9. Diagram of the anatomical shot placement for cattle. The shot should be placed at the intersection of two imaginary lines, each drawn from the outside corner of the eye to the centre of the base of the opposite ear (A). Alternatively, in long-faced cattle or young-stock (B), a point on the midline of the face that is halfway between the top of the poll and an imaginary line connecting the outside corners of the eyes can be used. (Adapted from the AVMA *Guidelines for the Humane Slaughter of Animals*, 2016 edition.)

Determining Insensibility

An animal should be rendered unconscious and insensible after one stun (EFSA, 2013a; CFR, 2018a). When captive bolt stunning is performed correctly, a single shot will cause immediate collapse with loss of posture, no rhythmic breathing, no righting reflex, no vocalizations, no corneal reflex and no menace reflex (AVMA, 2016, 2019). Gouveia *et al.* (2009) found that stunning efficiency with a captive bolt was greater in female animals compared with males (greater than 12 months of age), decreased with animal age in general and was better in dairy animals compared with beef animals. Signs of kicking should not be used to determine if an animal is conscious (Bartz *et al.*, 2015). An animal's spine will continue to fire signals to the walking circuit that will cause rhythmic movements related to walking even after the loss of consciousness. A properly stunned, unconscious animal may exhibit sideways head movements or post-stun leg paddling (Terlouw *et al.*, 2015). The observation of an animal that is kicking does not mean that an animal is conscious or returning to consciousness. (See Chapters 13 and 14 for more detailed information on determining insensibility.)

Recommendations for Other Species

The choice of captive bolt gun or firearm and placement depends on the species and field conditions. Delivering an effective stun safely with one shot should always be the number one priority. A penetrating captive bolt gun or gunshot to the middle of the forehead should always be used for cattle, especially mature bulls and aged animals, which have thickened frontal bones. Non-penetrating captive bolt guns have been found to be effective for euthanizing neonatal piglets, kid goats and lambs (Grist *et al.*, 2018a,b,c), as well as for young Holstein veal calves (Bartz *et al.*, 2015) and alpacas (Gibson *et al.*, 2015).

Sheep and goats

Sheep and goats can be stunned with either a captive bolt gun or firearm. There are three acceptable points of entry on sheep: the front of the head; the top of the head; and the back of the poll (Fig. 10.10). When delivering a forehead shot, position the gun so that entry is 2.0 cm above the eyes (Grandin, 2015). If using a gunshot, the ideal shooting

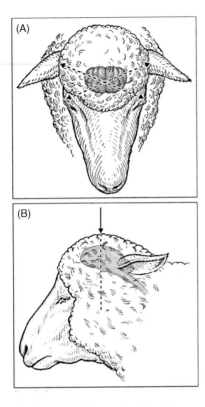

Fig. 10.10. Diagram of the anatomical shot placement for sheep. For polled sheep (A), the proper site is at or slightly behind the poll (B) or aiming toward the angle of the jaw or base of the tongue may be used. (Adapted from the AVMA *Guidelines for the Humane Slaughter of Animals*, 2016 Edition.)

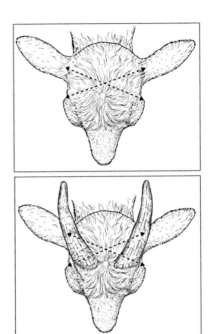

Fig. 10.11. Diagram of shot placement for goats. The optimal position is determined by using the intersection of two imaginary lines, each drawn from the outside corner of the eye to the centre of the base of the opposite ear with the projectile directed towards the back of the throat. (Adapted from the AVMA *Guidelines for the Humane Slaughter of Animals*, 2016 Edition.)

position for sheep is the top of the head at the midline of the skull, pointing straight down at the throat. In horned sheep, the most effective shot is behind the poll, which allows the projectile to avoid the extra bone mass created by the horns that cover the area in front of the brain (Grandin, 2015). Goats can be stunned just behind the poll with a captive bolt gun or firearm (Fig. 10.11). Plummer *et al.* (2018) verified that a penetrating captive bolt can be fired perpendicular to the skull at the poll position. In addition, Collins *et al.* (2017) examined the brains of goats stunned at the poll with a penetrating or non-penetrating captive bolt gun, using MRI and CT scans. The researchers reported severe skeletal and soft-tissue damage after impact with both types of captive bolt guns, suggesting that non-penetrating captive bolt stunning may be an acceptable method for goats.

Swine

Pigs are stunned in a similar fashion as cattle. Anderson *et al.* (2019) found that a frontal application of a penetrating captive bolt was the most effective position for stunning pigs (Fig. 10.12). The Zephyr-E, a non-penetrating captive bolt gun, has been very successful at rendering piglets (3–9 kg) insensible (Casey-Trotts *et al.*, 2014). Another study found that a non-penetrating captive bolt was effective for piglets (Grist *et al.*, 2018b). In small piglets, a standard non-penetrating captive bolt will crush the brain.

Horses

Horses that are slaughtered are commonly stunned with a captive bolt or a firearm. A frontal shot placement is recommended (Fig. 10.13). Gibson *et al.* (2015) reported that the use of a .22 calibre long rifle with hollow point ammunition was an effective method of stunning equines.

F. Baier and D. Willson

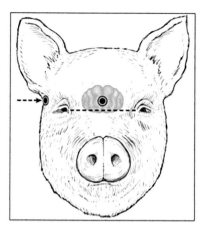

Fig. 10.12. Diagram of the two anatomical shot placements for pigs. The two positions include frontal and temporal. (Adapted from the AVMA *Guidelines for the Humane Slaughter of Animals*, 2016 Edition.)

Water buffalo

Water buffalo are often stunned with either a captive bolt or a firearm. Gregory *et al.* (2009) found that shooting water buffalo in the frontal position with a captive bolt gun was not always effective. They also stated that poll shooting can be effective but requires accurate placement to ensure that the animals are not shot through the spinal cord instead of the brain. A recent ballistics test showed that increased impact energy of a penetrating captive bolt or free projectiles from a firearm does not always correlate to higher perforation rate in the animal's skull, which led to a newly developed .357 Magnum stunning device specifically for water buffalo (Glardon *et al.*, 2018).

Cervids

A deer's brain is situated high in the skull. A captive bolt or gunshot should be placed 2.0 cm above the

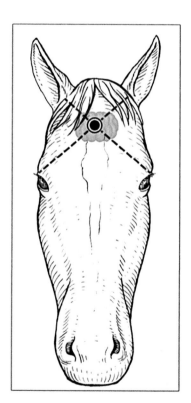

Fig. 10.13. Diagram of shot placement for horses. (Adapted from the AVMA *Guidelines for the Humane Slaughter of Animals*, 2016 Edition.)

intersection of an imaginary X drawn on the forehead, with each line starting at the inside corner of the eye and the base of the antler on the opposite side (Grandin, 2015). A gunshot to the back of the head or upper cervical region may also be sufficient to render deer and elk instantaneously insensible. Deer shot in the brain with a .223 calibre rifle from 10 m to 125 m died immediately from severe tissue damage to brain or spinal tissue (DeNicola *et al.*, 2019).

Poultry

The US Humane Slaughter Act of 1978 does not cover poultry; however, the Humane Slaughter of Livestock Regulations includes good commercial slaughter practices (CFR, 2018b). The regulations in Europe (EFSA, 2013b), Canada and Australia definitely include poultry in their Humane Slaughter regulations. A laboratory-made prototype of a pneumatic captive bolt gun operated most effectively with a minimum of 6 mm bolt diameter with an 872 kPa air-line pressure and a 10 mm penetration depth for effectively stunning broiler chickens (Raj and O'Callaghan, 2001). On turkeys, a non-penetrating captive bolt gun may be sufficient to induce immediate insensibility. A study by Gibson *et al.* (2018) used EEG to examine brain activity in turkeys stunned with one of three different concussive, non-penetrating captive bolt guns. The researchers found that all three types of non-penetrating captive bolt guns were effective at inducing unconsciousness if the shot was placed correctly and the power load performed as described in the manufacturer's specifications. Similarly, Woolcott *et al.* (2018) evaluated the effectiveness of two different non-penetrating captive bolt guns for stunning turkeys and found that both types of guns effectively caused immediate insensibility by traumatic brain injury.

Guinea pigs

Guinea pigs are often slaughtered for food in certain parts of the world. After a comparison of multiple stunning methods, captive bolt was deemed the most humane, effective and practical (Limon *et al.*, 2016). Cervical neck dislocation resulted in 97% of the guinea pigs showing behavioural or cranial/spinal responses indicative of possible suffering; therefore, this method should not be recommended (Limon *et al.*, 2016).

USDA Regulatory Actions Provide Insight into Stunning Problems

Livestock welfare problems at slaughter can be identified by looking at humane handling enforcement actions. The goal of determining welfare problems at slaughter is understanding the challenges so that practical solutions can be found. In 2017, 104 humane handling enforcement actions were issued to abattoirs by the FSIS. The USDA defines a very small abattoir as an establishment having up to nine employees or less than $2.5 million in annual sales. A small abattoir has 10–499 employees and a large abattoir has 500 or more employees (CFR, 1996). The FSIS takes official enforcement action against abattoirs found to be in violation of the Humane Slaughter Act of 1978 (USC, 2017), as regulated by the Humane Slaughter of Livestock Regulations (CFR, 2018a). A violation results in a notice of intended enforcement (NOIE) or a suspension by the FSIS. An NOIE is a warning that an infraction must be addressed. Failure to correct the noncompliance results in suspension. Inspection services cease during a suspension and the abattoir may be closed for hours or days. In 2017, 18% (19 of 104) of FSIS humane handling enforcement actions were NOIEs, 59% (61 of 104) were suspensions and 23% (24 of 104) were reinstatements of suspension. A reinstatement of suspension occurs when the establishment fails to take sufficient corrective action or commits another violation. The FSIS issues a deferral of the NOIE or abeyance of the suspension when evidence of appropriate corrective action and preventive steps has been established. The FSIS district office must approve a written response by the establishment before inspection services resume. A complete summary and discussion of the 2016 and 2017 humane handling enforcement actions can be found as a written article in the *National Provisioner* (Baier *et al.*, 2018).

Stunning violations summary

Stunning issues at very small abattoirs are the reason for the majority of FSIS humane handling enforcement actions (Table 10.1). In 2017, 88% (92 of 104) of enforcement actions were related to stunning, while the remaining 12% (12 of 104) were related to handling. Of the 92 enforcement actions related to stunning, 72% (66 of 92) were issued to very small abattoirs, 17% (16 of 92) to small abattoirs, and 11% (10 of 92) to large abattoirs.

Table 10.1. Summary table of 2017 USDA FSIS humane handling enforcement actions.

| | | Reason for enforcement action | | | | | | |
| Abattoir size | Handling | Stun placement | | | Restraint | Equipment failure | Knife (ritual) | N/A |
		CB	Gun	Electrical				
Very small	6	22	19	3	18	2	1	1
Small	3	6	3	1	0	3	1	2
Large	3	6	0	0	3	1	0	0

The designation of N/A was used when the main reason for the enforcement action was not stated. CB: captive bolt

Stunning was performed either electrically or mechanically by captive bolt or gunshot. Of the 92 enforcement actions related to stunning, 41% (38 of 92) involved captive bolt stunning and 30% (28 of 92) involved gunshot stunning. In addition, ten incidents involved captive bolt stunning followed by gunshot, and four incidents involved gunshot stunning followed by captive bolt. Two reports did not indicate whether the mechanical stunning violation involved captive bolt or gunshot. Finally, eight incidents involved electrical stunning and two incidents involved bovine halal knife slaughter.

Reasons for stunning problems

Stunning issues are due to poor placement, improper restraint and handling, or equipment failure. In 2017, 70% percent (64 of 92) of FSIS humane handling enforcement actions were due to poor placement of a captive bolt, gunshot, electrical stunner or problems with the cutting method for non-stunned religious slaughter, and 23% (21 of 92) were due to improper restraint (Fig. 10.14). Six reports stated equipment failure as the reason for the stunning issue, including four incidents of captive bolt failure, one occurrence of electrical failure and one gunshot failure.

Twenty years ago, Grandin (1998b) reported that maintenance was the number one reason for misfires and ineffective stuns in US abattoirs. A low incidence of equipment failure in 2017 indicates that the abattoirs are now doing a much better job at maintaining this equipment. This is due to both increased enforcement from the USDA and welfare auditing by meat-buying customers. This is why poor placement has become a main reason for ineffective stuns. In 2017, needing more than two stun attempts to render an animal insensible accounted for 61% (63 of 104) of FSIS humane handling enforcement actions, including 57% (36 of 63) bovine, 32% (20 of 63)

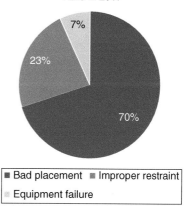

Reason for enforcement action by USDA-FSIS in 2017

- Bad placement
- Improper restraint
- Equipment failure

Fig. 10.14. A pie chart graphic summarizing the main reasons for the enforcement actions taken by the USDA FSIS in 2017. Action was taken in relation to three different events, including poor placement, improper restraint or equipment failure. Bad placement involves an inaccurate stun performed by the stunning operator, while equipment failure is related to the stunning device not working properly for a reason unrelated to the stun placement or accuracy. An improper restraint involves an animal that was not sufficiently held to ensure that a correct stun was performed.

porcine and 6% (4 of 63) ovine; 5% (3 of 63) did not list the species. In the UK, a gross examination of cattle heads shot multiple times showed that inaccurate placement was the determining factor in 83% (10 of 12) of cases where a second stun was delivered (Grist *et al.*, 2019). An ineffective stun occurs for several reasons (Box 10.3).

Auditing Stunning Practices

Abattoirs that have an effective, systematic approach to good captive bolt stunning practices will usually average about 96–98% of the animals being rendered insensible with a single shot (Grandin, 2005). Some plants will routinely shoot animals twice to ensure that they remain insensible, as a security knock. When the plant is being evaluated for stunning, the auditor or inspector should inspect the animal before the second shot is applied. The operator has to be able to demonstrate that they are capable of rendering 95% or more of the animals insensible with a single shot (Grandin, 2017). An experienced operator can easily achieve this (Atkinson *et al.*, 2013). The North American Meat Institute (NAMI) guideline allows 5% extra shots to enable the stunner operator to use an extra shot on a questionable animal (Grandin, 2017). Operators who attempt to never take an extra shot are more likely to have problems with return to sensibility (Grandin, 2019). Both the USDA and NAMI Guidelines have zero tolerance for starting invasive procedures such as skinning or leg removal on an animal showing signs of return to sensibility (CFR, 2018a; Grandin, 2017).

Stunner training resources

Training employees in basic principles of low-stress handling of livestock reduces baulking and facilitates animal movement, which increases efficiency. Dr Temple Grandin's website, Grandin.com, contains free resources for abattoir managers developing a livestock handling training programme for their employees. In addition, managers should make use of a free e-learning series posted at www.hsa.org.uk/publications/online-guides by the UK's Humane Slaughter Association about a variety of humane livestock slaughter topics. Certification courses in livestock welfare auditing, such as those offered by the Professional Animal Auditor Certification Organization (PAACO) in the USA, provide an opportunity for animal handlers to acquire professional-level expertise and credentials in evaluating livestock welfare at slaughter. Many countries have similar animal welfare training courses. Incentive programmes that reward employees who consistently demonstrate humane livestock handling skills should also be considered by abattoir managers.

Conclusion

Penetrating captive bolt is more effective than non-penetrating. Non-penetrating should not be used on bulls or mature pigs (AVMA, 2020). Captive bolt guns should be frequently cleaned and maintained to ensure that the devices perform properly. All employees should receive training regularly and always use caution when operating a captive bolt. Employee safety is the most important aspect when working with any type of gun. Accurate stun placement and adequate restraint are critical factors when efficiently and humanely stunning an animal with a captive bolt. Continuous improvement should be a consistent goal. Facilities and operators should stay informed and aware of new trainings or guidelines that may help improve any stunning-related practices or devices.

References

Anderson, K., Ries, E., Backes, J., Bishop, K., Boll, M. *et al.* (2019) Relationship of captive bolt stunning location with basic tissue measurements and exposed cross-sectional brain area in cadaver heads from market pigs. *Translational Animal Science* 3, txz097.

Atkinson, S., Velarde, A. and Algers, B. (2013) Assessment of stun quality at commercial slaughter in cattle shot with captive bolt. *Animal Welfare* 22, 473–481.

AVMA (2016) *Guidelines for the Humane Slaughter of Animals*. American Veterinary Medical Association, Schaumburg, Illinois.

AVMA (2019) *Guidelines for the Depopulation of Animals*. American Veterinary Medical Association, Schaumburg, Illinois.

AVMA (2020) *Guidelines for Euthanasia of Animals*. American Veterinary Medical Association, Schaumburg, Illinois.

Baier, F., Heimmermann, L., Odegard, S., Schiller, K. and Vogel K.D. (2018) A stunning issue: data pinpoints the need for a continued focus on stunning efficacy and management. *National Provisioner*. Available at: https://www.provisioneronline.com/articles/106362-data-pinpoints-need-for-a-continued-focus-on-stunning-efficacy-and-management (accessed June 2018).

Bartz, B., Collins, M., Stoddard, G., Appleton, A., Livingood, R. *et al.* (2015) Assessment of non-penetrating captive bolt stunning followed by electrical induction of cardiac arrest in veal calves. *Journal of Animal Science* 93, 4557–4563.

Bildstein, C. (2009) *Animal Care and Handling Conference*, 18–19 March, Kansas City, Missouri.

Casey-Trotts, T.M., Millman, S.T., Turner, P.V., Nykamp, S.G., Lawlis, P.C. and Widowski, T.M. (2014) Effectiveness of nonpenetrating captive bolt for euthanasia of 3 kg to 9 kg pigs. *Journal of Animal Science* 92, 5166–5174.

Collins, S.L., Caldwell, M., Hecht, S. and Whitlock, B.K. (2017) Comparison of penetrating and non-penetrating captive bolt methods in horned goats. *American Journal of Veterinary Research* 78, 151–157.

CFR (1996) *Pathogen reduction; hazard analysis and critical control point (HACCP) systems*. United States Code of Federal Regulations. 9 CFR Part 417, pp. 38819.

CFR (2018a) *Humane slaughter of livestock*. United States Code of Federal Regulations. 9 CFR Part 313, pp. 145–151.

CFR (2018b) *Poultry products and inspection services*. United States Code of Federal Regulations. 9 CFR Part 381.65.

DeNicola, A.J., Miller, D.S., DeNicola, V.L., Meyer, R.E. and Gambino, J.M. (2019) Assessment of humaneness using gunshot targeting the brain and cervical spine for cervid depopulation under field conditions. *PloS ONE* 14, e0213200.

EFSA (2013a) Scientific opinion on monitoring procedures at slaughterhouses for bovines. *EFSA Journal* 11(12), 3460.

EFSA (2013b) Scientific opinion on monitoring procedures at slaughterhouses for poultry. *EFSA Journal* 11(12), 3521.

Gibson, T.J., Bedford, E.M., Chancellor, N.M. and Limon, G. (2015) Pathophysiology of free-bullet slaughter of horses and ponies. *Meat Science* 108, 120–124.

Gibson, T.J., Whitehead, C., Taylor, R., Sykes, O., Chancellor, N.M. and Limon, G. (2015) Pathophysiology of penetrating captive bolt stunning in alpacas (*Vicugna pacos*). *Meat Science* 100, 227–231.

Gibson, T.J., Rebelo, C.B., Gowers, T.A., and Chancellor, N.M. (2018) Electroencephalographic assessment of concussive non-penetrative captive bolt stunning of turkeys. *British Poultry Science* 59, 13–20.

Gibson, T.J., Oliveira, S.E.O., Costa, F.A.D. and Gregory, N.G. (2019) Electro-encephalographic assessment of pneumatically powered penetrating and non-penetrating captive bolt stunning of bulls. *Meat Science* 151, 54–59.

Glardon, M., Schwenk, B.K., Riva, F., von Holzen, A., Ross, S.G. *et al.* (2018) Energy loss and impact of various stunning devices used for the slaughtering of water buffaloes. *Meat Science* 135, 159–165.

Gouveia, K.G., Ferreira, P.G., da Costa, J.C.R., Vaz-Pires, P. and da Costa, P.M. (2009) Assessment of the efficiency of captive-bolt stunning in cattle and feasibility of associated behavioural signs. *Animal Welfare* 18, 171–175.

Grandin, T. (1996) Factors that impede animal movement at slaughter plants. *Journal of the American Veterinary Medical Association* 209, 757–759.

Grandin, T. (1998a) Solving livestock handling problems in slaughter plants. In: Gregory, N.G. (ed.) *Animal Welfare and Meat Science*. CAB International, Wallingford, UK, pp. 42–63.

Grandin, T. (1998b) Objective scoring of animal handling and stunning practices in slaughter plants. *Journal of the American Veterinary Medical Association* 212, 36–93.

Grandin, T. (2001) Cattle vocalizations are associated with handling and equipment problems at beef slaughter plants. *Applied Animal Behaviour Science* 71, 191–201.

Grandin, T. (2002) Return to sensibility problems after penetrating captive bolt stunning of cattle in commercial beef slaughter plants. *Journal of the American Veterinary Medical Association* 221, 1258–1261.

Grandin, T. (2003) Transferring results of behavioural research to industry to improve animal welfare on the farm, ranch and the slaughter plant. *Applied Animal Behaviour Science* 81, 215–228.

Grandin, T. (2005) Maintenance of good animal welfare standards in beef slaughter plants by use of auditing programs. *Journal of the American Veterinary Medical Association* 226, 370–373.

Grandin, T. (2015) Recommended on-farm euthanasia practices. In: Grandin, T. (ed.) *Improving Animal Welfare: A Practical Approach.* CAB International, Wallingford, UK, p. 205.

Grandin, T. (2017) *Recommended animal handling guidelines and audit guide: a systematic approach to animal welfare.* North American Meat Institute (NAMI) Foundation, Washington, DC.

Grandin, T. (2019) Recommended captive bolt stunning techniques for cattle. Available at: https://grandin.com/humane/cap.bolt.tips.html (accessed 15 April 2020).

Gregory, N., Lee, C.J. and Widdicombe, J.P. (2007) Depth of concussion in cattle shot with penetrating captive bolt. *Meat Science* 77, 499–503.

Gregory, N. (2007) *Animal Welfare and Meat Production*, 2nd edn. CAB International, Wallingford, UK.

Gregory, N.G., Spence, J.Y., Mason, C.W., Tinarwo, A. and Heasman, L. (2009) Effectiveness of poll stunning water buffalo with captive bolt guns. *Meat Science* 81, 178–182.

Grist, A., Lines, J.A., Knowles, T.G., Mason, C.W. and Wotton, S.B. (2018a) Use of non-penetrating captive bolt on neonate goats. *Animals* 8, 58.

Grist, A., Lines, J.A., Knowles, T.G., Mason, C.W. and Wotton, S.B. (2018b) The use of a non-penetrating captive bolt for the euthanasia of neonate piglets. *Animals* 8, 48.

Grist, A., Lines, J.A., Knowles, T.G., Mason, C.W. and Wotton, S.B. (2018c) The use of a mechanical non-penetrating captive bolt for euthanasia of neonate lambs. *Animals* 8, 49.

Grist, A., Knowles, T.G. and Wotton, S. (2019) Macroscopic examination of multiple-shot cattle heads – an animal welfare due diligence tool for abattoirs using penetrating captive bolt devices? *Animals* 9, 328.

Humane Slaughter Association (2019) Humane killing of livestock using firearms. Available at: https://www.hsa.org.uk/ammunition/ammunition (accessed 5 August 2019).

Kamenik, J., Paral, V., Pyszko, M. and Voslarova, E. (2019) Cattle stunning with a penetrative captive bolt device: a review. *Animal Science Journal* 90, 307–316.

Kline, H.C., Wagner, D.R., Edwards-Callaway, L.N., Alexander, L.R. and Grandin, T. (2019) Effect of captive bolt lengths on brain trauma and post hind leg activity in finished cattle. *Bos taurus Meat Science* 155, 69–73.

Limon, G., Gonzales-Gustavson, E.A. and Gibson, T.J. (2016) Investigation into the humaneness of slaughter methods for guinea pigs (*Cavia procelus*) in the Andean region. *Journal of Applied Animal Welfare Science* 19, 1088–8705.

OIE (2019) *Terrestrial Animal Health Code: Guidelines for the Slaughter of Animals for Human Consumption*, 28th edn. World Organisation for Animal Health, Paris.

Oliveira, S.E.O., Gregory, N.G., Dalla Costa, F.A., Gibson, T.J. and Paranhos da Costa, M.J.R. (2017) Efficiency of low versus high airline pressure in stunning cattle with a pneumatically powered penetrating captive bolt gun. *Meat Science* 130, 64–68.

Oliveira, S.E.O., Gregory, N.G., Dalla Costa, O.A. and Paranhos da Costa, M.J.R. (2018a) Effectiveness of pneumatically powered penetrating and non-penetrating captive bolts in stunning cattle. *Meat Science* 140, 9–13.

Oliveira, S.E.O., Dalla Costa, F.A., Gibson, T.J., Dalla Costa, O.A. and Gregory, N. (2018b) Evaluation of brain damage resulting from penetrating and non-penetrating stunning in Nelore cattle using pneumatically powered captive bolt guns. *Meat Science* 145, 347–351.

Plummer, P.J., Shearer, J.K., Kleinhenz K.E. and Shearer, L.C. (2018) Determination of anatomic landmarks for optimal placement in captive-bolt euthanasia of goats. *American Journal of Veterinary Research* 79, 276–281.

Raj, A.B.M. and O'Callaghan, M. (2001) Evaluation of a pneumatically operated captive bolt for stunning/killing broiler chickens. *British Poultry Science* 42, 295–299.

Schiffer, K.J., Retz, S.K., Algers, B. and Hensel, O. (2017) Assessment of stun quality after gunshot used on cattle: a pilot study on effects of diverse ammunition on physical signs displayed after the shot, brain tissue damage and brain haemorrhages. *Animal Welfare* 26, 95–109.

Shearer, J. (2018) Euthanasia of cattle: practical considerations and application. *Animals* 8, 57.

Terlouw, E.M.C., Bourquet, C., Deiss, V. and Mallet, C. (2015) Origins of movements following stunning and bleeding in cattle. *Meat Science* 110, 136–144.

USC (2017) Humane Slaughter Act. USC Part 1901-1907, pp. 1001–1003.

Wagner, D.R., Kline, H.C., Martin, M.S., Alexander, L.R., Grandin, T. and Edwards-Callaway, L.N. (2019) The effects of bolt length on penetration hole characteristics, brain damage, and specified risk material dispersal in finished cattle stunned with a penetrating captive bolt stunner. *Meat Science* 155, 109–114.

Watts, J.M. and Stookey, J.M. (1999) Effects of restraint and branding on rates and acoustic parameters of vocalization in beef cattle. *Applied Animal Behaviour Science* 62, 125–135.

Woolcott, C., Torrey, S., Turner, P., Serpa, L., Schwean-Lardner, K. and Widowski, T. (2018) Evaluation of two models of non-penetrating captive bolt devices for on-farm euthanasia of turkeys. *Animals* 8, 42.

F. Baier and D. Willson

11 Religious Slaughter and How to Improve Welfare During Both Kosher and Halal Methods

TEMPLE GRANDIN[1]* AND ERIKA VOOGD[2]

[1]Department of Animal Science, Colorado State University, USA;
[2]Voogd Consulting, Chicago, Illinois, USA

Summary

There are three main issues when religious slaughter without stunning (kosher or halal) is discussed from the perspective of animal welfare. The first issue is the restraint method used to hold the animal in position and the second issue is the question of pain during the cut. The third issue is the time required to lose consciousness after the cut and possible distress during this period. Good cutting technique, well-designed restraint equipment and attention to details of the procedure will reduce animal welfare problems in both livestock and poultry. Many Muslim religious authorities will accept pre-slaughter stunning of livestock and poultry. Full reversible electrical stunning is preferred. The main religious concern is that the animal must be alive at the time of slaughter.

Learning Objectives

- Assessment of both restraint and cutting methods to improve animal welfare.
- Understand the design and operation of restraining devices.
- Methods to improve the cutting method to reduce the time the animal remains conscious.
- Learn about the different pre-slaughter stunning methods that may be permitted by religious authorities.

Introduction

Slaughter without prior stunning is a controversial subject from an animal welfare standpoint. Most

European Union (EU) countries, the OIE (World Organisation for Animal Health), and the USA, UK, Canada, Brazil, France and many other countries permit slaughter without stunning (Defra, 2015; Law Library of Congress, 2018). Allowing slaughter without stunning enables Jews and Muslims the freedom to practise this aspect of their religious beliefs. In Belgium, slaughter without stunning has been banned in some regions (Law Library of Congress, 2018). A discussion of all the religious freedom issues is beyond the scope of this chapter. When listing exceptions to a requirement that slaughter can only be conducted after stunning, legislation and guidelines often use the terms 'religious' or 'ritual' slaughter to refer to halal (Muslim) or kosher (Jewish) slaughter conducted without pre-slaughter stunning. Some halal slaughter is undertaken with either pre- or post-slaughter stunning. The purpose of this chapter is to provide practical guidance to people who are actually engaged in religious slaughter or otherwise involved, such as veterinarians, students, abattoir managers and inspectors. This guidance will help improve animal welfare during slaughter without prior stunning.

Some of the worst animal welfare issues that occur during religious slaughter are caused by sloppy procedures. It is the authors' opinion that religious slaughter can be done with an acceptable level of animal welfare, but it requires much greater attention to the details of procedure than conventional slaughter with stunning (Grandin, 1994; Grandin and Regenstein, 1994). Fortunately, many religious authorities will allow certain types of pre-slaughter

---

* Email: cheryl.miller@colostate.edu

stunning methods which will provide the highest level of welfare during halal slaughter. This chapter has four parts: (i) welfare during restraint for slaughter without stunning and assessment of restraint methods; (ii) welfare issues associated with the neck cut; (iii) methods to reduce the time the animal remains conscious; and (iv) use of permitted stunning methods. A major issue is that halal or kosher slaughter requires the animal to be alive at the time of the neck cut. There will be a discussion of how 'being alive' is defined.

Three Major Welfare Issues During Slaughter Without Stunning

Holding cattle, sheep or goats in position for slaughter without stunning requires restraining a fully conscious animal. There are three major welfare issues associated with either halal or kosher slaughter that is performed without pre-slaughter stunning. They are: (i) restraint and handling prior to the neck cut; (ii) possible pain during the neck cut; and (iii) possible distress during the time required for the animal to lose consciousness (Velarde and Dalmau, 2018). Some of the worst welfare problems observed by the first author are highly stressful methods of restraint. Some of the serious problems are excessive electric prod use and a high percentage of cattle bellowing. Vocalization of cattle during handling and restraint is associated with physiological measures such as cortisol (Dunn, 1990; Hemsworth et al., 2011). The OIE (2019), the State of Israel (IVSAH, 2017) the UK government's Department for Environment, Food & Rural Affairs (Defra, 2015), the EU and the DIALREL Report (2010) recommend avoiding highly stressful methods of restraint such as suspending livestock by the leg or legs, or dragging live animals. The OIE (2018) guidelines state:

> Methods of restraint causing avoidable suffering should not be used in conscious animals because they cause severe pain and stress: i) suspending or hoisting animals (other than poultry) by the feet or legs; ...

Although the OIE standards are guidelines, they provide a basis for the formulation of national legislation to comply with OIE standards. An Italian study showed that small ruminants in a mechanical rotating box struggled for a shorter period of time compared with animals that were suspended by a rear leg (Novelli et al., 2016). In the USA, there is a regulatory exemption which makes stressful restraint methods such as shackling and hoisting of conscious animals legal. The regulation, as cited by the Food Safety Inspection Service (FSIS) of the US Department of Agriculture (USDA), states: 'In order to protect freedom of religion, ritual slaughter and the handling and preparation of livestock for ritual slaughter are exempted from the terms of this chapter' (FSIS, 2011).

This USDA regulation is written into the laws of the USA. From a practical standpoint, the USA has no regulations for restraint of the animal during 'ritual slaughter'. A cutting method that is in accordance with the ritual requirements of a religious faith is deemed humane (USC, 1958). Private industry guidelines in the USA and Canada prohibit shackling and hoisting of conscious livestock (NAMI, 2019). In the USA, most kosher cattle plants have eliminated the shackling and hoisting of conscious cattle. Unfortunately, there are small abattoirs that perform either halal or kosher slaughter that still hoist up conscious sheep and goats by their rear legs. A major factor that has driven improvements is large meat-buying customers demanding improvements. Another driving factor has been reducing injuries to employees caused by struggling hanging livestock.

Restraint

Types of restraint that are acceptable

Livestock can be held in either an upright, inverted or lateral position. Keeping the animals as calm as possible is essential. The principles of good handling and stockmanship are covered in Chapter 6. When a calm animal is slaughtered without stunning, it may lose consciousness sooner (Grandin, 1994; Grandin and Regenstein, 1994). For small animals such as sheep and goats, the conscious animal can be held in an upright position by a person. Sheep can be easily straddled by a person and the head held up for the neck cut. They may become extremely stressed when they are separated from the flock. Sheep were less stressed when they were moved through a V restrainer in a continuous line than when there was a 20 s delay after the neck cut before the next sheep entered the V restrainer (Bates et al., 2014). In cattle, a well-designed upright restraint box was less stressful than a poorly designed rotating box (Dunn, 1990). Velarde and Dalmau (2018) stated that a conscious animal is more likely to be stressed if it is held on its side or if it is inverted on to its back in a rotary box than if it is restrained in an upright position. Figures 11.1, 11.2, 11.3 and 11.4 all show upright restraint devices for cattle and sheep. Figures 11.5 and 11.6 show rotating boxes for inverted restraint of cattle.

Assessing welfare problems with cattle restraint

Serious welfare problems and stress are occurring if a high percentage of cattle are vocalizing (mooing or bellowing) when they are held in a restraint device (Dunn, 1990; Grandin, 1998a,b; Munoz *et al.*, 2010). There is also a welfare issue that must be corrected if electric prod use while entering the restraint box is causing a high percentage of cattle to bellow. To assess vocalization, each animal is scored as either silent or vocalizing (Grandin, 1998a,b). When handling and restraint are done with good practices, the percentage of cattle vocalizing in a system with a head restraint should be 5% or less. Tables 11.1, 11.2 and 11.3 show scores for the percentage of cattle vocalizing in systems with good restraint practices and systems with poor restraint practices. A large review of

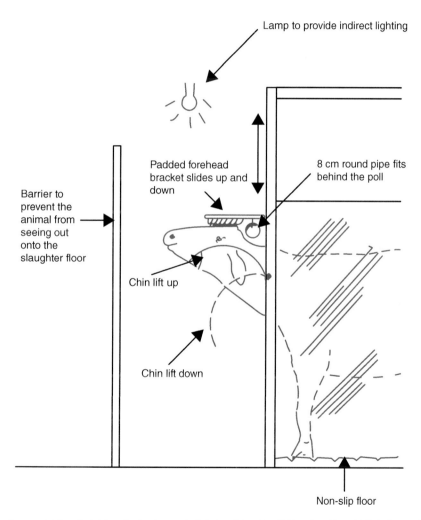

Fig. 11.1. Standing-upright restraint box for kosher or halal slaughter. A solid barrier 1.2 m (4 ft) in front of the headholder prevents incoming cattle from seeing people through the head opening. An overhead light illuminates the area because animals are attracted to a lighted opening. (Diagram courtesy of Temple Grandin.)

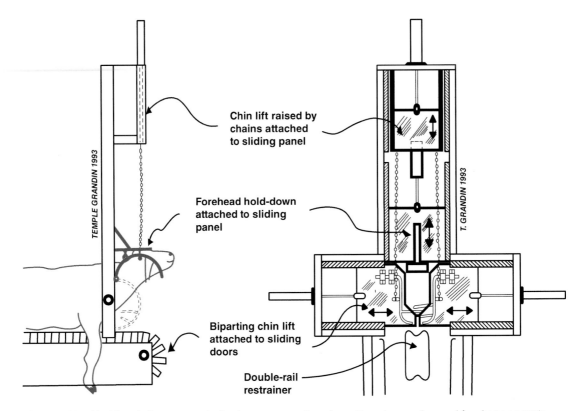

Chin lift raised by chains attached to sliding panel

Forehead hold-down attached to sliding panel

Biparting chin lift attached to sliding doors

Double-rail restrainer

TEMPLE GRANDIN 1993

T. GRANDIN 1993

Fig. 11.2. Head-holding device on a centre track conveyor system. A small version can be used for sheep or goats. The chin lift is attached to two biparting sliding doors. (From Grandin, 1993.)

Fig. 11.3. A calf is held in the head restrained position for religious slaughter. Note that the forehead is parallel to the floor and excessive bending of the neck is avoided. The round pipe behind the animal's poll prevents it from pulling its head out. (Photo courtesy of Temple Grandin.)

scientific articles reported that vocalization scoring was considered to be a valid way of assessing cattle welfare in commercial abattoirs (Losada-Espinoza *et al.*, 2018). Chapter 12 on auditing and assessing animal welfare has a more detailed

description of outcome-based numerical scoring for assessing animal welfare during slaughter.

The corrective actions that were implemented to improve the scores for electric prod use, slips/falls and cattle vocalizing shown in Table 11.3 were as follows.

- Discontinued use of high-pressure hose near the lead-up race, because it frightened the cattle.
- Raised open restraint box entrance door to reduce cattle baulking. Cattle may refuse to enter a box if back clearance is too low.
- Stopped banging the metal race with driving aids.
- Avoided jerky movement of the headholder and reduced pressure applied to the head.

Vocalization scoring does not work for sheep

Sheep will vocalize loudly when they are separated from the rest of the flock. This is due to

T. Grandin and E. Voogd

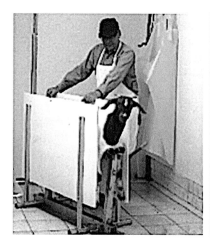

Fig. 11.4. Small restrainer for holding sheep or goats that is easy to build, based on a design by Westervelt *et al.*, 1976. (Photo courtesy of Spirit of Humane, Joe Regenstein.)

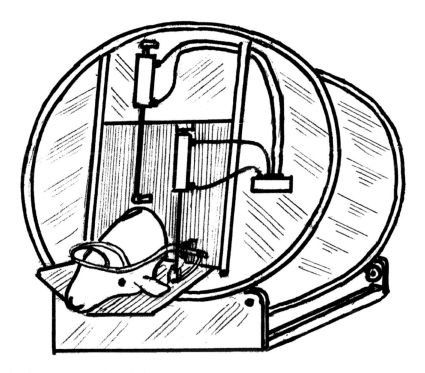

Fig. 11.5. Rotating box for restraint of cattle for kosher or halal slaughter. To prevent struggling, the box should have an adjustable side that will hold the animal snugly when it is rotated. This will prevent the animal from having the sensation of fear of falling. (Diagram courtesy of Temple Grandin.)

separation distress (Price and Thos, 1980). Separation distress (panic) is a separate emotional system from fear (Panksepp, 2011). When sheep are hurt or handled in a stressful manner, they almost never vocalize. The reason for this is that sheep are one of the most defenceless prey animals (Dwyer, 2004). A sheep that is hurt is more likely to get eaten by a predator if it vocalizes.

A sheep that is separated from the flock vocalizes, because being vocal may help it get back quickly to the safety of the flock.

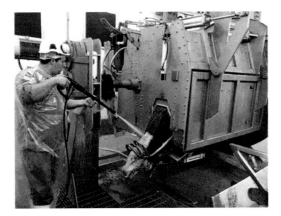

Fig. 11.6. Rotating box for cattle which holds two cattle. When one animal is in the inverted position, another animal is entering on the other side. The system rotates around a central pivot. Slaughter is conducted promptly after rotation. The vocalization score of approximately 20 Hereford cows was 0%. Washing the throat with the hose may increase stress and increases the length of time that the animal is restrained. (Photo courtesy of Temple Grandin.)

Table 11.1. Percentage of cattle vocalizing in a restraint box used for religious slaughter in abattoirs with good restraint practice.

	Percentage vocalizing	Type of box
Plant 1	2	Upright (Grandin, 2012)
Plant 2	1	Upright (Grandin, 2012)
Plant 3[a]	4.5	Rotating (Voogd, 2010–2014)

[a]Plant 3 score is an average taken from a series of audits. The range was 0% on the best days to 15% on the worst days (Erika Voogd, 2010–2014: data collected during commercial audits of abattoirs conducting religious slaughter)

Vocalization scoring in goats

Goats will vocalize loudly when they are isolated (Price and Thos, 1980) or mistreated. There is a need for research to determine vocalization thresholds for goats.

Monitoring of struggling during restraint

In all species of livestock and poultry, struggling during restraint is a sign of stress. Struggling must be evaluated before, during and after the neck cut. Small ruminants struggle for longer before the cut if they are suspended by one leg than when restrained in a rotating box (Novelli *et al.*, 2016). This is a welfare concern. After bleeding starts, struggling that is caused by convulsions is not a welfare concern, but continued struggling due to stress from the method of restraint, pain from the neck cut or from distress associated with continued consciousness is a concern. Velarde *et al.* (2014) assessed struggling in different types of restraint boxes and reported differences between restraint position in the percentages of cattle that were observed to be struggling after the neck cut. A major problem with this study was that struggling due to discomfort prior to the loss of consciousness and struggling due to post-cut convulsions induced by blood loss were not differentiated. If a conscious animal struggles excessively for a prolonged period of time after the neck cut (more than 15–30 s), it should be stunned. This will prevent needless suffering, even if the meat will be deemed non-kosher or non-halal.

Monitoring electric goad use and falling

Losada-Espinoza (2018) reported that scoring of falling during handling and interaction with people during handling are both scientifically valid measures for assessing cattle welfare at slaughter plants. Falling is most likely to be caused by slippery floors. One

Table 11.2. Percentage of cattle vocalizing in a restraint box used for religious slaughter in abattoirs with poor restraint practices.

	Percentage vocalizing	Type of box	Reason
Plant 1	23[a]	Upright	Excessive pressure on the neck (Grandin, 2001)
Plant 2	25	Rotating	Excessive pressure (Bourquet *et al.*, 2011)
Plant 3	47	Upright	Almost 100% electric prod use on the cattle (Hayes *et al.*, 2015)
Plant 4	32	Upright	Box was too short and applied excessive pressure to the rear of large cattle (Grandin, 1998a,b)

[a]When pressure was reduced on the neck, vocalization dropped to 0% (Grandin, 2001).

T. Grandin and E. Voogd

Table 11.3. Improvements in handling measurements after procedures were corrected.

	Cattle insensible on rail	Cattle electrically prodded	Cattle slipping	Cattle falling	Cattle vocalizing
NAMI (1) Pass percentage	100%	≤ 25.0%	≤ 3.0%	≤ 1.0%	≤ 5.0%
Before: N=29	100%	6.9%	3.4%	0%	10.3%
After: N=19	100%	0.0%	0.0%	0%	5.3%

of the problems is that flooring wears out slowly and people do not realize that the frequency of slipping and falling is increasing. This is why regular audit of slipping and falling is essential. Falling scoring is recommended by NAMI (2017), Welfare Quality (2009), OIE (2018) and Grandin (1998b). Boxes that are designed to make cattle fall should never be used. To facilitate shackling of fully conscious live animals, some boxes are mechanically designed to cause an animal to fall down. Use of this type of equipment would be an automatic failure of animal welfare audits. Boxes that are designed to restrain an animal by clamping its legs are also an automatic failed welfare audit.

Problems with restraint equipment

Problems with restraint equipment are outlined in Box 11.1. Common engineering problems with restraint boxes are outlined in Box 11.2.

Handling and restraint of poultry

Some plants that do either kosher or halal poultry without stunning hang the live birds on a conventional shackle line. This is allowed in all the countries and in the OIE (2018) guidelines. In small plants, each bird can be gently held by a person while the slaughterer makes the cut. After the cut, the bird is either hung on the slaughter line or placed inverted in a bleeding cone. Hanging live poultry on the shackle line is extremely stressful (Kannan et al., 1987; Bedanova et al., 2007). Restraining broiler chickens in cones is less stressful than shackling (Ismail et al., 2016). Both halal and kosher plants have developed systems where a series of cones are attached to a conveyor.

Welfare Issues During the Neck Cut

Extensive research has been done to determine the effects of slaughter without stunning on pain and stress during the neck cut. The three main issues associated with neck cutting in conscious cattle, sheep or goats for halal or kosher slaughter are as follows.

- Pain associated with the neck cut (Grandin, 1994; Gibson et al., 2009a,b,c; Gregory et al., 2012; Sabow et al., 2016).
- Aspiration of blood into the respiratory tract while the animal may still be conscious (Gregory et al., 2012).
- Time to lose consciousness after the cut. Loss of consciousness is not instantaneous after the cut (Grandin, 1980; Newhook and Blackmore, 1982; Blackmore, 1984; Gregory and Wotton, 1884a,b).

Painfulness of the cut

One of the biggest issues is defining what the animal is experiencing before it loses consciousness and the ability to feel pain. Grandin (1994), Levinger (1995) and Rosen (2004) maintained that when the super-sharp long kosher knife (Fig. 11.9) is used, there is little reaction to the neck cut. Waving a hand in front of a steer's face caused a bigger reaction than cutting with the special kosher knife (Grandin, 1994). These observations were made in a plant that had low-stress restraint. This made it possible to separate reactions to restraint from the reactions to the neck cut. Other researchers have provided evidence that the cut is painful. Gibson et al. (2009a,b) and Sabow et al. (2016) used EEG methods to determine if the cut was painful. Unfortunately, they did not use the special kosher knife. When halal slaughter is done without stunning, the only requirement is a sharp knife. For Jewish kosher slaughter, there are also length requirements (Levinger, 1995). The knife must be twice the width of the ventral aspect of the neck (Levinger, 1995). The blade must be smooth with no nick and a whetstone is required for sharpening.

In Gibson et al. (2009a,b), calves were slaughtered with a knife that had a 24.5 cm blade. The

---

Box 11.1. Fixing problems with restraint equipment for all species

- **Animals refuse to enter the restraint box** – The most common problem is that approaching animals can see people and activity through the headholder. A shield should be installed in front of the headholder to block the incoming animal's view (Fig. 11.1). Another problem is air blowing into the faces of approaching animals. For further information on refusal to enter, see Chapter 6.
- **Cattle vocalize in the box** – The first step is to determine which part of the restraining process is causing the vocalization. Observe carefully to determine which part of the box the vocalization is associated with. The main parts that can cause vocalization are:
  1. Tailgate slammed on the animal.

2. Rear pusher gate applies excessive pressure (Figs 11.7 and 11.8).
3. Headholder applies excessive pressure. Another cause of vocalization in cattle or struggling in all species is being clamped too long in the headholder. The neck cut should be performed immediately after the head is restrained.
4. Body shifts during rotation may cause all species to struggle. A rotating box must have an adjustable side so that the animal's body is supported when it is rotated. An adjustable side is required for the market in Israel (IVSAH, 2017). Rotation should not cause struggling in any species.
5. Sharp edges on equipment or the animal's skin is pinched.

Box 11.2. Common engineering problems with restraint boxes

- **Lack of cylinder mid-stroke position control of air cylinders on pneumatically (air-operated) systems** – In poorly designed systems, the amount of pressure applied to the animal is either none or applied at the maximum pressure setting. Well-designed pneumatic systems make it possible to have 'mid-stroke' position control of air cylinders. This enables the operator to stop movement of a headholder or pusher gate at an intermediate position (Grandin, 1992). This makes it possible for the operator to control the amount of pressure that is applied to the animal.
- **Lack of separate individually set pressure controls for different parts of the restraint box** – On both pneumatic and hydraulic systems, the headholder should be set at a much lighter pressure. Heavy vertical gates and the rotation

system on a rotating box require high settings. These high settings are usually too high for the parts that directly press against the animal. In cattle vocalization, scoring is useful to locate problems with excessive pressure. Different parts of the box will require separate pressure regulators on pneumatic systems and pressure relief valves on hydraulic systems.
- **Jerky motion** of different parts of the restraint box may cause all species to struggle. Flow controls and other devices should be used to provide smooth steady motion.
- **Lack of throttling ability** – This is especially important for the headholder. The best controls work like a car's accelerator. The operator can easily speed up or slow down movement.

---

blade was sharpened on a mechanical grinder. Regenstein (2017) stated that using a mechanical grinder may have made the blade rough. There is also a possibility that the blade was too short. The first author has observed neck cutting with knives that were too short. Cuts with these knives caused intensive struggling in both cattle and sheep. Sabow *et al.* (2016) had no knife description for their study on goats. Bozzo *et al.* (2018) measured stress hormones in Charolais cattle that were kosher slaughtered in a rotating box and compared them with cattle from the same farm that were

stunned with a captive bolt. Plasma cortisol, dopamine and norepinephrine concentrations at exsanguination were higher in the kosher group. Similar results were found by Petty *et al.*, (1994).

Aspiration of blood in respiratory tract

Researchers have found that while the cattle were still conscious, blood was aspirated into the trachea (windpipe) (Gregory *et al.*, 2009). It is likely that blood entering the respiratory tract would cause distress.

T. Grandin and E. Voogd

Fig. 11.7. Injury to the tail caused by excessive pressure from a poorly designed rump pusher gate. Photo shows hide on. (Photo courtesy of Erika Voogd.)

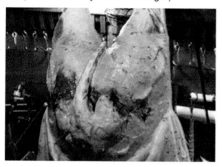

Fig. 11.8. Bruised rump caused by a gate either slamming on the rump or sharp edges on a rump pusher gate. Often the hide will appear normal but there are severe bruises. (Photo courtesy of Erika Voogd.)

Fig. 11.9. Special long knives used for kosher slaughter. The use of a knife that is too short will cause gouging of the wound. It is the opinion of both authors that these are the only type of knife that should be used on adult cattle. (Photo courtesy of Erika Voogd.)

Time to Loss of Consciousness After the Neck Cut

Effective captive bolt or electrical stunning causes all species to become unconscious instantly (Daly *et al.*, 1988). When good technique is used during kosher slaughter with the special knife, the length of time it takes for the bovine to collapse and lose consciousness can be greatly shortened. Table 11.5 shows the improvement in the time required to lose consciousness. In an upright position, the time is based on a loss of posture (LOP) or eye roll; and in the inverted position, until eye rollback. These are indicators that can be easily used in a slaughter plant to improve the procedure. Sometimes cattle or sheep can have prolonged onset of unconsciousness of over 60 s (Grandin, 1980; Blackmore, 1984; Gregory and Wotton, 1984a,b).

In the worst case, cattle remained conscious after being removed from the box and they walked around (Grandin, 1980). To achieve a shorter collapse time (LOP), the plant where these data were collected made the following changes in their procedure. The animal was held in an upright box in the restrained position with very light pressure applied to its body. The vocalization score averaged 4.5%. Within an average of 3.8 s after the head was restrained, the kosher cut was performed. This reduces stress, because cattle become stressed if they struggle and fight the headholder. After the cut, pressure from the rear pusher gate was immediately relieved. The headholder was loosened but it remained up to facilitate the flow of blood and observation of eye roll. It should be noted that this plant utilized a secondary cut of the carotid arteries, after shechita, to facilitate bleeding. If blood obstruction was

Table 11.4. Time to start of eye rollback in a rotating restraint box during kosher slaughter of 1810 cattle (data from: Erika Voogd (2010–2014); NAMI, 2019).

	Good technique	Poor technique baseline before good technique started
Average time	23 s	33 s
Standard Deviation	3.78 s	–
Maximum	38 s	120 s
Minimum	13 s	–
Per cent that collapsed within 30 s	94%	68%

Table 11.5. Improvement of halal cut efficiency after corrective actions, upright box.

	Cattle cut efficacy (collapse and eye roll within 30 s)	Cattle insensible when exiting box	Cattle insensible on rail
Grandin Pass Percent	≤ 95.0%	100%	100%
Before improvements: N=29	86.2%	100%	100%
After improvements: N=19	94.7%	100%	100%

observed, one or both arteries were severed again. The USA allows a secondary cut to facilitate bleeding (FSIS Directive 6900.2 Rev. 2); however, only one cut is permitted in Canada (Government of Canada, 2018; CFIA, 2019).

Gregory et al. (2010) had similar results. They assessed time to collapse in an upright restraint box. Immediately after the halal neck cut, pressure on the bovine's body was released. The average time to collapse was 20 s and 8% of the animals had collapse times of over 60 s. This may have prevented the problem reported by Verhoeven et al. (2016). They found that upright restraint increased the times required to lose consciousness. They performed upright restraint in a box designed for inversion. Loosening the headholder may have caused the head to slump down and occlude bleed out.

List of correction actions

- All the corrective actions listed Box 11.1 above.
- Replaced the knives and all knives were sharpened weekly by a service.
- A knife sharpener was installed for the slaughter person to use.
- To prevent needless suffering, all plants should implement a time limit (30–40 s) and a stun procedure for religiously slaughtered animals that fail to lose consciousness.

Methods to reduce the time to loss of consciousness

Gibson et al. (2015) and Gregory et al. (2012) reported that cutting the neck of a bovine close to C1 (cervical 1) position facilitated faster collapse. A high neck cut close to the jaw (cervical 1 position) averaged 13.5 s to collapse and a lower neck cut averaged 19 s. Similar results were reported by Gregory et al. (2012). It is also important to have a calm animal entering the restraint box. In cattle, there are sometimes problems with false aneurysms

that impede the flow of blood (Gregory et al., 2008). Seventy-one per cent of the cattle that failed to collapse within 75 s had a false aneurysm with swelling on the ends of carotid arteries (Gregory et al., 2010). The use of a sharp knife may reduce this problem.

The first author observed that, during kosher slaughter of large veal calves, a quick knife stroke induced a faster collapse than a slow knife stroke (Grandin, 1994).

Sheep lose consciousness more quickly than cattle

Many studies have shown that sheep will collapse and lose consciousness more quickly than cattle. Observations of behaviour, such as loss of posture, and EEG studies have confirmed this result (Newhook and Blackmore, 1982; Blackmore, 1984; Daly et al., 1988). On average, sheep will lose consciousness in 2–14 s (Newhook and Blackmore, 1982; Blackmore, 1984; Gregory and Wotton, 1984b) and cattle will lose it in 17–85 s (Blackmore et al., 1983; Blackmore, 1984; Gregory and Wotton, 1984a). All the sheep and cattle in these experiments were fully conscious when their necks were cut. There are differences between the blood vessel anatomy in the neck of cattle and sheep. Cattle have an additional blood supply to the brain from vertebral arteries in the back of the neck (Baldwin and Bell, 1963a,b; Blackman et al., 1986). When the neck cut is performed, the vessels in the back of the neck are not severed. In sheep, when a single horizontal cut is made across the neck, the entire blood supply to the brain is severed. DIAREL (2010) and Dalmau and Anil (2016) recommended that if an animal remains conscious for over 40 s, it should be immediately stunned with a captive bolt. In Canada, the CFIA Guidelines for ritual slaughter of food animals without pre-slaughter stunning have best-practice performance criteria for large bovines that state that if unconsciousness is not achieved within 30–40 s post-cut they should be stunned.

Ensuring loss of consciousness in poultry

Whether religiously slaughtered poultry are stunned or not stunned, the neck cut is important to ensure that the birds remain unconscious and bleed effectively. Most of the neck cuts are performed by trained slaughterers. The use of a sharp knife or chalef (for kosher operations) is critical to ensure that the cut is effective. Both carotid arteries should be cut, close to the head. If the cut is too shallow, bleeding may be slow or incomplete and birds may regain consciousness prior to scalding and/or feather removal. Poor bleeding can be visualized after scalding and feather removal by observing the presence of red pygostyles (red tail) and blood pooling in the neck. The preferred indicators for assessing unconsciousness are loss of eye reflexes in response to touch and loss of muscle tone (floppy head). Muscle tone should not be used alone (EFSA, 2013c).

Determining the onset of loss of consciousness and brain death in mammals

In Chapters 13 and 14 methods to determine the onset of unconsciousness and brain death are discussed in detail. Terlouw *et al.* (2016) made a differentiation between definitely conscious and brain dead. There is a transition zone between these two conditions. Verhoeven *et al.* (2016) found that EEG testing indicted that a veal calf held in the inverted position may still be conscious for a few seconds after loss of response to the menace/threat test (waving a hand in front of the eye) and a nose pinch. Righting reflex and time to collapse could not be evaluated, because the calf was inverted in a rotating box. Before invasive dressing procedures are performed, the animal must be brain dead. The corneal reflex and eyelash reflex and all other reflexes in the head must be absent. The Animal Health and Welfare (AHAW) Panel of the European Food Safety Authority (EFSA) recommended that, prior to invasive dressing procedures, livestock must have absence of rhythmic breathing, dilated pupils and complete loss of muscle tone (EFSA, 2013a,b). If a righting reflex occurs after hoisting, the animal is conscious (Grandin, 1998b). See Chapter 13 and Damau and Anil (2016).

When to remove an animal from the restraint box

Regulations will vary in different countries. From a welfare standpoint, the animal should remain in the restraint box until it is unconscious. It will be unconscious and probably in the transition zone to brain death after collapse (LOP), loss of righting, eye rollback and loss of menace/threat reflex. Before invasive dressing procedures are started, bleed-out must be completed and multiple indicators must show that the animal is brain dead. Some countries have regulations that, after the cut, an animal cannot be removed from the restraint box until 20 s have elapsed for sheep and 30 s for cattle. Trees (2018) recommended monitoring compliance with this interval with closed circuit TV.

Stunning Method and Religious Slaughter

Religious texts require that the animal must be alive when the neck is cut (Benzertiha *et al.*, 2017; Fuseini *et al.*, 2017). There is much discussion about how to define being alive. Some religious authorities want the animal to be conscious and others will accept rendering it unconscious before the cut. A fully reversible electrical stun does not kill the animal, but it renders it unconscious. Effective captive bolt stunning will cause instant loss of consciousness and destroy part of the brain, but the heart will remain beating for several minutes (Vimini *et al.*, 1983). If being alive is defined by a beating heart, this would make captive bolt stunning acceptable. A survey conducted in the UK found that 53% of Islamic scholars and > 95% of halal consumers considered reversible stunning to be halal compliant. Sabow *et al.* (2017, 2019) have an excellent review of halal-compliant electrical stunning methods.

Many Muslim religious authorities will allow pre-slaughter stunning of livestock and poultry (Nakyinsige *et al.*, 2013; Fuseini *et al.*, 2017; Lambooij and Hindle, 2017). The preferred method is electrical stunning that is fully reversible and the animal or bird could completely recover (if exsanguination was not performed). Sabow *et al.* (2017, 2019) had an excellent review of all the fully reversible electrical stunning methods for livestock and poultry. Muslims want death to be induced by the neck cut and not by the stunning method. Within the Muslim community, there has been much discussion (Fuseini *et al.*, 2016, 2017). When electrical stunning is used in halal cattle, sheep or poultry, it is designed to be fully reversible. It induces a period of unconsciousness that is sufficient to perform the neck cut. Head-only electrical stunning of sheep and calves will induce a period of unconsciousness for 18–42 s (Blackmore and Newhook, 1982). Velarde *et al.* (2000) found that sheep had a longer period of unconsciousness if the tongs were placed in a frontal position (between the eyes and ears on either side of the head) than in a caudal position (behind the ears on the occipital condyle on either side of the head). Research is also being conducted on novel reversible stunning with microwaves (Small *et al.*, 2019).

Reversible poultry stunning

Reversible electrical water-bath stunning methods for poultry are controversial because they often use lower amperages than in current European regulations. The first author has observed halal slaughter of chickens with fully reversible water-bath electrical stunning. To ensure that the birds did not recover, bleeding had to be done a few seconds after stunning. To prevent return to consciousness, signs of return to sensibility such as spontaneous natural blinking and loss of neck tension should be measured both before and after bleeding. EFSA (2014) reported that 104 mA, 126 volts at a frequency of 590 Hz was not effective in stunning poultry. Newer studies showed that a frequency of 750 Hz at 200 mA was effective for water-bath stunning of 88% of the broilers studied (Girasole *et al.*, 2015). Siquera *et al.* (2017) found that 650 Hz at 100 mA, AC was effective in 85% of the broilers studied. Allowing approximately 20% of the birds to be not effectively stunned would compromise the welfare of these birds. Girasole *et al.* (2015) conducted studies to determine the settings that would prevent return to sensibility in broiler chickens for 20 s. The electrical settings were 200 mA at 400 Hz and 250 mA at 400–600 Hz. The use of frequencies over 600 Hz is not recommended (Girasole *et al.*, 2015). Fuseini *et al.* (2018) discussed problems with conventional water-bath stunning from a halal perspective. They stated that a new head-only electrical stun system for broilers that uses tongs was effective in that eye reflexes were absent in 90% of the birds 90 s after stunning, but 95% recovered from the stun after 120 s (Fuseini *et al.*,

2018). One of their main concerns about electrical water-bath stunning was the bird dying before it was slaughtered.

Captive bolt and religious slaughter

Some Muslim religious authorities will accept pre-stunning with a captive bolt. It is allowed because the heart continues to beat for several minutes after both penetrating and non-penetrating captive bolt. If bleeding is delayed, the heart will beat for 8–10 min (Vimini *et al.*, 1983). A penetrating captive bolt is acceptable to some religious authorities but others will only accept a non-penetrating captive bolt. They would prefer that the skull not be fractured (Fuseini *et al.*, 2016). The author has observed that it is extremely difficult to avoid fracturing the skull and still render the animal unconscious. The basic concern is the fear of eating an animal that is dead before the neck cut (Fuseini *et al.*, 2016). The first author has also observed that a small dent is required to ensure instant unconsciousness. Oliveira *et al.* (2018) found that in large cattle a non-penetrating captive bolt was less effective for inducing loss of unconsciousness compared with a penetrating captive bolt. A study with bulls that recorded the EEG showed that a non-penetrating captive bolt was less effective than a penetrating captive bolt (Gibson *et al.*, 2019). In calves, a non-penetrating captive bolt was effective (Gibson *et al.*, 2009c; Bartz *et al.*, 2015). Muslim religious authorities are often more flexible about accepting stunning than Jewish rabbinical authorities. This may be partly due to Muslims having less reliance on centralized authorities. Decisions are more likely to be local. Orthodox glatt kosher slaughter never allows stunning. Less strict interpretation of Jewish law may accept an immediate post-cut stun. In the USA, it is common to have both types.

Labelling issues of non-stunned slaughtered meat

Another issue that abattoir managers must face is increasing requirements to label meat that originates from animals slaughtered without stunning. Alexander Trees, Editor of the *Veterinary Record*, stated that it should be labelled (Trees, 2018). Costain (2018) suggested a labelling system for identifying all types of both non-stunned and stunned slaughter. This would enable consumers to make choices about where their meat comes from.

These requirements will probably increase and this will require plant operation managers to keep stunned and non-stunned meat separated. The easiest way to accomplish this and to avoid mixing up carcasses is to have an entire day or days for non-stunned slaughter and other days for stunned.

Conclusions

Both authors, who have observed religious slaughter without stunning, consider that it can be done with an acceptable level of welfare, but careful attention to detail of the procedure is required. If procedures become sloppy, welfare will greatly deteriorate. Slaughter without stunning is more difficult to manage properly than conventional slaughter with stunning. Due to the attention to detail that is required for slaughter without stunning, serious welfare problems may be more likely to occur. Pre-slaughter stunning will improve welfare because it is easier to manage the process compared with slaughter without stunning.

References

Anil, M.H., McKinstry, J.L., Wotton, S.B., Gregory, N.G. (1995a) Welfare of calves – 1. Investigation into some aspects of calf slaughter. *Meat Science* 41, 101–112.

Anil, M.H., McKinstry, J.L., Gregory, N.G., Woman, S.B. and Symonds, H. (1995b) Welfare of calves – 3. Increase in vertebral artery blood flow following exsanguination by neck sticking and evaluation of chest sticking as alternative slaughter method. *Meat Science* 41, 113–123.

Baldwin, B.A. and Bell, F.R. (1963a) The effect of temporary reduction in cephalic blood flow on the EEG of sheep and calf. *Electroencephalography and Clinical Neurophysiology* 15, 465–473.

Baldwin, B.A., and Bell, F.R. (1963b) The anatomy of the cerebral circulation of the sheep and ox: the dynamic distribution of the blood supplied by the carotid and vertebral arteries to cranial regions. *Journal of Anatomy* 97, 203–215.

Bartz, B., Collins, M., Stoddard, G., Appleton, R., Livingood, R. *et al.* (2015) Assessment of non-penetrating captive bolt followed by electrical induction of cardiac arrest in veal calves. *Journal of Animal Science* 93, 4557–4563.

Bates, L.S.W., Ford, E.A., Brown, S.N., Richards, G., Hadley, P.J. and Knowles, T.G. (2014) A comparison of handling methods relevant to religious slaughter of sheep. *Animal Welfare* 23, 251–258.

Bedanova, I., Voslarova, E., Chloupek, P., Pistekova, V., Suchy, P. *et al.* (2007) Stress in broilers resulting from shackling. *Poultry Science* 86, 1065–1069.

Benzertiha, A., Kicrończyk, B., Rawski, M., Jozefiak, A., Mazurkiewicz, J. *et al.* (2018) Cultural and practical aspects of halal slaughtering in food production. *Medycyna Weterynaryjna* 74, 371–376. doi: 10.21521/mw.6023

Blackman, N.L., Cheetham, K., and Blackmore, D.K. (1986) Differences in blood supply to the cerebral cortex between sheep and calves during slaughter. *Research in Veterinary Science* 40, 252–254.

Blackmore, D.K. (1984) Differences in behavior between sheep and cattle during slaughter. *Research in Veterinary Science* 37, 223–236.

Blackmore, D.K. and Newhook, J.C. (1982) Electro-encephalographic studies of stunning and slaughter in sheep and calves – Part 3. The duration of insensibility induced by electrical stunning in sheep and calves. *Meat Science* 7, 19–28.

Blackmore, D.K., Newhook, J.C. and Grandin, T. (1983) Time of onset of insensibility in four- to six-week-old calves during slaughter. *Meat Science* 9, 145–149.

Bourquet, C., Deiss, V., Tannugi, C.C. and Terlouw, E.M.C. (2011) Behavioural and physiological reactions of cattle in a commercial abattoir: relationships with organization aspects of the abattoir and animal characteristics. *Meat Science* 88, 158–168.

Bozzo, G., Barrasso, R., Marchette, P., Roma, R., Samoilis, G. *et al.* (2018) Analysis of stress indicators for the evaluation of animal welfare and meat quality in traditional Jewish slaughtering. *Animals* 8(4). doi: 10.3390/ani8040043

Costain, F. (2018) Above all food labels require simplicity. *Veterinary Record* 182, 328.

CFIA (2019) *Guidelines for ritual slaughter of food animals without pre-slaughter stunning.* Canadian Food Inspection Agency, Government of Canada, Ottawa. Available at: www.inspection.gc.ca (accessed 10 March 2019).

Dalmau, A. and Anil, J. (2016) Slaughter without stunning, In: Velarde, A. and Raj, M. (eds) *Animal Welfare at Slaughter.* 5M Publishing, Sheffield, UK, pp. 177–198.

Daly, C.C., Kallweit, E. and Ellendorf, F. (1988) Cortical function in cattle during slaughter: conventional captive bolt stunning followed by exsanguination compared to shechita slaughter. *Veterinary Record* 122, 325–329.

Defra (2015) Guidance: Halal and kosher slaughter. Dept for Environment, Food & Rural Affairs, London. Available at: www.gov.uk/guidance/halal and kosher-slaughter#check-for-unconsciousness-and-signs-of-life (accessed 10 March 2019).

DIALREL (2010) Religious slaughter, improving knowledge and expertise through dialogue and debate on issues of welfare, legislation and socio-economic aspects. Available at: https://cordis.europa.eu/project/id/43075 (accessed 17 February 2020).

Dunn, C.S. (1990) Stress reactions of cattle undergoing ritual slaughter using two methods of restraint. *Veterinary Record* 126, 522–525.

Dwyer, C.W. (2004) How the risk of predation shaped the behavioral responses of sheep to fear and distress. *Animal Welfare* 13, 269–281.

EFSA (2013a) Scientific opinion on monitoring procedures at slaughterhouses for bovines. *EFSA Journal* 11(12), 3460. doi: 10.2903/j.efsa.2013.3460

EFSA (2013b) Scientific opinion on monitoring procedures at slaughterhouses for sheep and goats. *EFSA Journal* 11(12), 3522. doi: 10.2903/j.efsa.2013.3522

EFSA (2013c) Scientific opinion on monitoring procedures at slaughterhouses for poultry. *EFSA Journal* 11(12) 3521. doi: 10.2903/j.efsa 2013.3521

EFSA (2014) Scientific opinion on electrical requirements for poultry stunning water bath equipment. *EFSA Journal* 12(7), 3745.

FSIS (2011) 6900.2, Revision 2. Humane Handling and Slaughter of Livestock, Chapter III, Ritual Slaughter of Livestock, 1. General requirement (accessed 26 May 2019).

Fuseini, A., Knowles, T.G., Hadley, P.J. and Wotton, S.B. (2016) Halal stunning and slaughter: criteria of the assessment of dead animals. *Meat Science* 113, 132–137.

Fuseini, A., Wotton, S.B., Hadley, P.J. and Knowles, T.G. (2017) The perception and acceptability of preslaughter and post slaughter stunning on halal production. The views of UK Islamic scholars and halal consumers. *Meat Science* 123, 143–150.

Fuseini, A., Teye, M., Wotton, S.B., Lines, J.A. and Knowles, T.G. (2018) Electrical water bath stunning of Halal poultry meat production: animal welfare issues and compatibility with Halal rules. *CAB Reviews* 13, No. 016. doi: 10.1079/PAVSNNR2018/3016

Government of Canada (2018) Safe Food for Canadians Regulations SOR/2018-108. Available at: https://laws-lois.justice.gc.ca/eng/regulations/SOR-2018-108/FullText.html (accessed 10 March 2019).

Gibson, T.J., Johnson, C.B., Murrell, J.C., Hulls, C.M., Mitchinson, S.L. *et al.* (2009a) Electroencephalographic responses of halothane-anesthetized calves to slaughter by ventral-neck incision without stunning. *New Zealand Veterinary Journal* 57, 77–85.

Gibson, T.J., Johnson, C.B., Murrell, J.C., Chapters, J.P., Stafford, K.J. and Mellor, D.J. (2009b) Components of electroencephalographic responses to slaughter in halothane-anaesthetized calves. Effects of cutting neck tissues compared to major blood vessels. *New Zealand Veterinary Journal* 57, 84–89.

Gibson, T.J., Johnson, C.R., Murrell, J.C., Mitchinson, S.L., Stafford, K.J. and Mellor, D.J. (2009c) Amelioration of electroencephalographic responses to slaughter by nonpenetrative captive bolt stunning after ventral neck incision in halothane anesthetized calves. *New Zealand Veterinary Journal* 57, 96–101.

Gibson, T.J., Dadios, N., and Gregory, N.G. (2015) Effect of neck cut position on time to collapse in halal slaughtered cattle without stunning. *Meat Science* 110, 310–314.

Gibson, T.J., Oliveira S., Dalla-Costa, F.A. and Gregory, N.G. (2019) Electroencephalographic assessment of pneumatically powered captive bolt stunning of bulls. *Meat Science* 151, 54–59.

Girasole, M., Chiroilo, C., Ceruso, M., Voillano, L., Chianese, A. and Cortes, M.L. (2015) Optimization of electrical parameters to improve animal welfare in a poultry slaughterhouse. *Italian Journal of Food Safety* 4, 4576.

Grandin, T. (1980) Problems with kosher slaughter. *International Journal for the Study of Animal Problems* 16, 375–390.

Grandin, T. (1992) Observations of cattle restraint devices for stunning and slaughtering. *Animal Welfare* 1, 85–91.

Grandin, T. (1994) Euthanasia and slaughter of livestock, *Journal of the American Veterinary Medical Association* 204,1354–1360.

Grandin, T. (1998a) The feasibility of using vocalization scoring as an indicator of poor welfare during slaughter. *Applied Animal Behaviour Science* 56, 121–125.

Grandin, T. (1998b) Objective scoring of animal handling and stunning practices in slaughter plants. *Journal of the American Veterinary Medical Association* 212, 36–39.

Grandin, T. (2001) Cattle vocalizations associated with handling and equipment problems in slaughter plants. *Applied Animal Behaviour Science* 71, 191–201.

Grandin, T. (2012) Auditing animal welfare and making practical improvements in beef pork and sheep slaughter plants. *Animal Welfare* 21 (Suppl. 2), 29–34.

Grandin, T. and Regenstein, J.M. (1994) Religious slaughter and animal welfare: a discussion for meat scientists. *Meat Focus International* 3(1), 115–123.

Gregory, N.G. and Wotton, S.B. (1984a) Time to loss of brain responsiveness following exsanguination in calves. *Research in Veterinary Science* 37, 141–143.

Gregory, N.G. and Wotton, S.B. (1984b) Sheep slaughtering procedures: II. Time to loss of brain responsiveness after exsanguination or cardiac arrest. *British Veterinary Journal* 140, 354–360.

Gregory, N.G., von Wenzlawowicz, M., Alam, R.M., Anil, H.M., Yesildere, T. and Silva-Fletcher, A. (2008) False aneurysms in carotid arteries of cattle and water buffalo during shechita and halal slaughter. *Meat Science* 80, 2–11.

Gregory, N.G., von Wenzlawowicz, M. and von Hollenben, K.V. (2009) Blood in the respiratory tract during slaughter with and without stunning in cattle. *Meat Science* 82, 13–16.

Gregory, N.G., Fielding, H.R., von Wenzlawowicz, M. and von Hollenben, K.V. (2010) Time to collapse following slaughter without scanning of cattle. *Meat Science* 85, 66–69.

Gregory, N.G., Schuster, P., Mirabito, I., Kolesar, R. and McManus, T. (2012) Arrested blood flow during false aneurysm formation in the carotid arteries of cattle slaughtered with and without stunning. *Meat Science* 90, 368–372.

Hayes, N.S., Schwartz, C.A., Phelps, K.J., Borowicz, P., Maddock-Carlin, K.R. *et al.* (2015) The relationship between pre-harvest stress and carcass characteristics of beef heifers that qualified for kosher designation. *Meat Science* 100, 134–138.

Hemsworth, P.H., Rice, M., Karlen, M.G., Calleja, L., Barnett, J.L. *et al.* (2011) Human–animal interactions at abattoirs: relationship between handling and animal stress in sheep and cattle. *Applied Animal Behaviour Science* 135, 24–33.

Ismail, S.N., Sazili, A.Q., Idrus, Z., Meng, G.Y., Aghwan, Z.A. *et al.* (2016) Effect of shackling and cone restraining on meat quality of broiler chickens slaughtered at two categories of liveweight. *Journal of Biochemistry, Microbiology and Biotechnology* 4, 7.

IVSAH (2017) *IVSAH Guidelines for Humane Kosher Slaughter*. Ministry of Agriculture and Rural Development, Israel Veterinary Services and Animal Health. Available at: https://vmvt.lt/sites/default/files/humanisko_koserinio_skerdimo_gaires1.pdf (accessed 15 April 2020).

Kannan, G., Heath, J.L., Wabeck, C.J. and Mench, J.A. (1997) Shackling broilers: effects of stress responses on breast meat quality. *British Poultry Science* 38, 323-332.

Khalid, R., Knowles, T.G. and Wotton, S.B. (2015) A comparison of blood loss during halal slaughter of lambs following traditional religious slaughter without stunning, electrical head only stunning and post cut electric stunning. *Meat Science* 110, 15–23.

Lambooij, B. and Hindle, V. (2017) Electrical stunning of poultry. In: Mench, J. (ed.) *Advances in Poultry Welfare*. Woodhead Publishing, Cambridge, UK.

Law Library of Congress (2018) *Legal restrictions on religious slaughter in Europe*. Available at: www.loc.gov/law/help/religious-slaughter/europe.php (accessed 10 March 2019).

Levinger, I.M. (1995) *Shechita in the Light of the Year 2000*. Maskil L'David, Jerusalem, Israel.

Losada-Espinoza, N., Villarroel, M., Maria, G.S. and Miranda de la Lama, G.C. (2018) Pre-slaughter cattle welfare indicators for use in commercial abattoirs with voluntary monitoring systems: a systematic review. *Meat Science* 138, 34–48.

Munoz, D., Strappini, A., and Gallo, C. (2010) Animal welfare indicators to detect problems in cattle stunning box. *Archivos de Medicina Veterinaria* 44, 297–302.

Nakyinsige, K., Che Man, Y.B., Aghwan, Z.A., Zulkiffi, I., Gok, Y.M. *et al.* (2013) Stunning and animal welfare from an Islamic and scientific perspective. *Meat Science* 95, 352–361.

NAMI (2019) *Recommended Animal Handling Guidelines and Audit Guide*. North American Meat Institute, Washington, DC. Available at: www.animalhandling.org (accessed 15 February 2020).

Nangeroni, L.I. and Kennett, P.D. (1963) An electroencephalographic study of the effects of shechita slaughter on cortical function in ruminants. Report, Dept of Physiology, New York State Veterinary College, Cornell University.

Newhook, J.C. and Blackmore, D.K. (1982) Electroencephalographic studies of stunning and slaughter in sheep and calves: Part I – The onset of permanent insensibility in sheep during slaughter. *Meat Science* 6, 295–300.

Novelli, S., Sechi, P., Mattei, S., Julietto, M.F. and Cenci, G.B.T. (2016) Report on religious slaughter practices in Italy. *Veterinaria Italiana* 52. doi: 10.1.2834/Vwetti.189.920.1

OIE (2019) *Terrestrial Animal Health Code, Chapter 7.5 Slaughter of Animals*. World Organisation of Animal Health, Paris.

Oliveira, S.E., Gregory, N.G., Dalla Costa, F.A., Gibson, T.J., Dalla Costa, O.M. and Paranhos da Costa, M.J.R. (2018) Effectiveness of pneumatically powered penetrating and non-penetrating captive bolts in stunning cattle. *Meat Science* 140, 9–13.

Panksepp, J. (2011) The basic emotional circuits of mammalian brains: do animals have affective lives? *Neuroscience and Biobehavioral Reviews* 35, 1791–1804.

Petty, D.B., Hattingh, J., Ganhao, M.F. and Bezuidenhout, L. (1994) Factors which affect blood variables of slaughtered cattle. *Journal of the South African Veterinary Association* 65, 41–45.

Price, E.O. and Thos, J. (1980) Behavioral responses to short-term social isolation on sheep and goats. *Applied Animal Ethology* 6, 331–339.

Regenstein, R. (2017) Religious slaughter of animals: international efforts to meet this need responsibly. In: Barabosa-Cánovas, G., Pastore, G., Candoğan, K., Medina Meza, I.G., Caetano Da Silva Lannes, S. *et al.* (eds) *Global Food Security and Wellness*. Springer, pp. 339–355.

Rosen, S.D. (2004) Physiological insights into Shechita. *Veterinary Record* 154, 759–765.

Sabow, A.B., Colt, Y.M., Zulkifi, I., Sazili, A.Q., Kaka, V. *et al.* (2016) Blood parameters and electroencephalographic responses of goats to slaughter without stunning. *Meat Science* 121, 148–156.

Sabow, A.B., Nakyinsige, K., Adeyemi, K.D., Sazili, A.D., Johnson, C.B. *et al.* (2017) High frequency stunning of ruminants: a review. *Meat Science* 202, 124–134.

Sabow, A.B., Goh, Y.M., Zolkifli, I., Ab Kadir, M.A., Kaka, U. *et al.* (2019) Electroencephalographic and blood parameters change in anaesthetized goats subjected to slaughter without stunning and slaughter following different electrical stunning methods. *Animal Production Science* 59, 849–860.

Schulz, W., Schulze-Petxold, H., Hazam, A.S. and Grass, R. (1978) Experiments for the objectification of pain and consciousness during conventional (captive bolt

---

stunning) and religiously mandated ('ritual cutting') slaughter procedures for sheep and calves. *Deutsche Tierärztliche Wochenschrift* 85, 41–76.

Siquera, T.S., Borges, T.D., Rocha, R.M.M., Rigueira, P.T., Luciano, F.B. and Macado, R.E.F. (2017) Effect of electrical stunning frequency and current waveform on poultry welfare. *Poultry Science* 96, 2956–2964.

Small, A., Lea, J., Nicmeyer, D., Hughes, J., McLean, D. *et al.* (2019) Development of microwave stunning system for cattle 2. Preliminary observations on behavioral responses and EEG. *Research in Veterinary Science* 122, 72–80.

Terlouw, C., Bourquet, C. and Deiss, V. (2016) Consciousness, unconsciousness, and death in the context of slaughter, Part II. Evaluation of methods. *Meat Science* 118, 147–156.

Trees, A. (2018) Nonstun-slaughter: the elephant in the room. *Veterinary Record* 182, 177.

USC (1958) USC 1901-1907, Agriculture Chapter 48, Humane Methods of Livestock Slaughter.

Velarde, A. and Dalmau, A. (2018) Slaughter without stunning. In: Mench, J.A. (ed.) *Advances in Agricultural Animal Welfare. Science and Practice.* Food Science, Technology and Nutrition series. Woodhead Publishing, pp. 223–240.

Velarde, A., Ruiz-de-la-Torre, J.L, Stub, C., Diestra, A. and Manteca, X. (2000) Factors affecting head only electrical stunning in sheep. *Veterinary Record* 147, 40–43.

Velarde, A., Rodriguez, P., Dalmau, A., Fuentes, C., Llonch, P. *et al.* (2014) Religious slaughter: evaluation of current practices in selected countries. *Meat Science* 96, 278–287.

Verhouven, M.T., Gerritzen, M.A., Hellebrekers, L.J. and Kemp, B. (2016) Validation of indicators used to assess unconsciousness in veal calves at slaughter. *Animal* 10, 1457–1465.

Vimini, R.J., Field, A., Riley, M.L. and Varnell, T.R. (1983) Effect of delayed bleeding after captive bolt stunning and heart activity and blood removal in cattle. *Journal of Animal Science* 57, 628–631.

Welfare Quality® (2009) Welfare Quality® assessment protocol for cattle. Welfare Quality® Consortium, Lelystad, Netherlands. Available at: http://www.welfarequality.net/media/1088/cattle_protocol_without_veal_calves.pdf (accessed 10 March 2019).

Westervelt, R.G., Kinsman, D., Prince, R.P. and Giger, W. Jr (1976) Physiological stress measurements during slaughter of calves and lambs. *Journal of Animal Science* 42, 831–834.

Wotton, S.B.B., Zhang, X., McKinstry, J.J.L., Velarde, A. and Knowles, T.G. (2014) The effect of required current frequency combinations (EC1099-2009) on the incidence of cardiac arrest in broilers stunned and slaughtered for the halal market. *PeerJ PrePrints*, 2, e255v1.

Zulkiffi, I., Goh, Y.M., Narbyah, B., Sazili, A.Q., Lotfi, M. *et al.* (2013) Changes in blood parameters and electroencephalogram of cattle as affected by different stunning and slaughter methods. *Animal Production Science* 54, 187–193.

12 Auditing and Assessing the Welfare of Livestock and Poultry During Pre-slaughter Handling and Stunning

TEMPLE GRANDIN*

Department of Animal Science, Colorado State University, USA

Summary

Animal-based measures are an effective method for both auditing and monitoring handling and stunning of livestock and poultry in commercial abattoirs. The following variables should be measured. For livestock, the percentage of animals is assessed on five measures: (i) effective stunning with one application; (ii) insensible on the bleed rail; (iii) falling during handling; (iv) electric prod use; and (v) vocalization. For poultry, the percentage of birds is scored on six measures: (i) broken wings; (ii) broken legs; (iii) overloaded transport containers; (iv) broken transport containers; (v) effective stunning; and (vi) uncut red birds. Vocalization and electric prod use in cattle and pigs can be associated with higher physiological measures of stress. Legislative recommendations from the European Food Safety Authority (EFSA, 2013a–d) and OIE (2018) and legislative requirements from FSIS/USDA (2017) are outlined. Their similarities and differences are discussed. Written Standard Operating Procedures (SOPs) and corrective actions should comply with both legislative and customer requirements. SOPs should clearly state the specific operations in each abattoir and should not be copied from industry or government documents. Large abattoirs will need an animal welfare officer who has taken a training course that is approved in that country. Future welfare assessment methods such as gap analysis are explained.

Learning Objectives

- Learn how to use animal-based measures to assess stunning and handling.
- Explain the relationship between livestock vocalization and electric prod use with physiological measures of stress.
- Learn the similarities and differences between US, OIE and EU slaughter regulations.
- Explain how to write Standard Operating Procedures (SOPs).
- Introduce the duties of the animal welfare officer.

How to Maintain High Standards

Maintaining high standards of effective stunning and pre-slaughter handling requires constant supervision of all procedures. There is a difference between an effective welfare assessment system for practical everyday commercial use and more detailed assessments for scientific research. Effective systems for commercial use have to be simple and easy for people to learn, with a limited number of measurements (Grandin, 2010). They are designed to locate serious welfare issues that need immediate corrective action. Assessment tools designed for either research or more in-depth assessment of welfare can provide more detailed information (Wigham *et al.*, 2018).

The first section of this chapter will discuss the successful use of a simple numerical scoring system and the second half will discuss compliance with both FSIS/USDA and European Union (EU) regulations. The author has worked extensively with the creation and application of voluntary private industry standards that have been very effective for preventing serious welfare problems (Grandin 2000, 2001, 2010). In 1999, the use of an objective

---

* Email: cheryl.miller@colostate.edu

outcome-based numerical scoring system was first started in the USA. This occurred before the Humane Slaughter laws were strictly enforced by the Federal Government. Baseline data collected by Grandin (1998a) in federally inspected slaughter plants indicated that only 30% of the beef abattoirs could effectively stun 95% of the cattle with a single shot. The major cause of poor stunning was broken or poorly maintained captive bolts (Grandin, 1998a). At this time, the handling methods were very poor and some abattoirs used an electric prod on 100% of the animals (Grandin, 1998a). Today unpublished industry data indicate that 98–99% of the cattle are effectively stunned with a single shot.

In 1999, three major beef and pork buyers – McDonald's Corporation, Wendy's International and Burger King – started auditing their US federally inspected beef suppliers with simple objective numerical scoring. This resulted in huge improvements. The penalty for poor performance was removal from the approved supplier list. Out of 75 beef and pork plants on the McDonald's supplier list, only three had to purchase expensive equipment or build a new lairage or races to comply with the new standard (Grandin, 2005). To dramatically improve animal welfare, they performed a whole series of small changes that added up to great improvements. Box 12.1 gives a list of the most common modifications of handling procedures and equipment.

Simple Effective Assessment with Outcome-based Numerical Scoring

The scoring system was effective because it was simple to understand. It was like having easy-to-understand traffic laws for slaughter plants. Traffic laws are not vague. A stop sign means stop. Both speeding and alcohol levels in a driver's blood are numerically measured. If the police only enforced these three items, they would probably achieve significant public safety improvements.

Commercial meat buyers and regulatory officials need simple easy-to-use assessments, which enable auditors to be trained in a one- or two-day workshop. They also need clear guidance on critical non-compliances that must be corrected. Some examples would be acts of abuse such as dragging conscious non-ambulatory animals, beating livestock or deliberately slamming gates on them. These abuses would be grounds for either removal from an approved list or regulatory penalties. Guidance must be clear on what is acceptable and what is not acceptable. This avoids lawsuits when suppliers have to be removed from a buyer's approved supplier list.

Five Simple Numerically Scored Outcome-based Measurements for Assessing Livestock Stunning and Handling

An effective critical control point provides an assessment of multiple problems. It is based on directly

---

Box 12.1. Most common modifications of equipment and procedures to improve both animal welfare and numerical animal-based scores for livestock

- Stopped using electric goads (prods) as the primary driving tool. Handlers were not allowed to carry them constantly.
- Improved stunner maintenance – especially important for captive bolt.
- Non-slip flooring installed in stun boxes and unloading ramps.
- Reduced pushing pressure and installed manual controls on powered pusher gate systems used for moving pigs. This prevents the pigs from getting knocked over by the gates or being dragged.
- Training employees to move smaller groups of pigs and cattle from the lairage to the stunning area.
- Employees were taught behavioural principles of livestock handling, such as flight zone and point of balance (see Chapter 6).

- Changed lighting to remove reflections and added lamps to light up dark race entrances (see Chapter 6).
- Removed distractions that caused animals to baulk and refuse to move forward (see Chapter 6).
- Installed solid panels in strategic locations to prevent approaching animals from seeing people or moving conveyors up ahead of them.
- Reduced air hissing and metal clanging. A smartphone app can be used to monitor noise levels (Iulietto et al., 2018) and monitor progress on reducing noise.
- Stopped air blowing down a race towards approaching animals through the stun box door. Animals will often stop moving if air is blowing into their faces.

Auditing and Assessing the Welfare of Livestock and Poultry

observable events that can be numerically scored. Numerical scoring is used in many different guidelines (Grandin, 1998a; Welfare Quality, 2009; NAMI, 2019; Australian Meat Process Corp., 2018; OIE, 2018). It is not a paperwork audit. For example, poor stunning could be due to either poor maintenance or an untrained operator. Cattle or pig vocalization in the stunning area could be due to electric prods, excessive pressure from a restraint device, or a sharp edge (Grandin, 1998a, 2001; Bourquet et al., 2011). To pass the audit, the abattoir must have a passing score on all five variables.

1. Percentage of livestock rendered unconscious and insensible with a single application of the stunner (Grandin, 1998a, 2010; Welfare Quality, 2009). For captive bolt, it must be 96% to pass (NAMI, 2019). For electrically stunned animals, the tongs or other electrode application devices must be placed in the correct position on 99% of the livestock. The criterion is the same for both manual and automatic systems.

2. Percentage rendered unconscious before bleeding. Must be 100% to pass. The reason why the industry's voluntary standard allows a small percentage of second applications of the stunner is to help prevent hanging fully conscious animals on the rail. Stunner operators are encouraged to take an occasional second shot when necessary. When they try to be perfect, it increases the risk of hanging a conscious animal on the rail. If any sign of either consciousness or brainstem reflexes occurs during carcass processing (invasive dressing procedure) the audit is automatically failed.

3. Percentage of livestock moved with an electric prod (goad) (Grandin, 1998a, 2010; Simon et al., 2016; Woiwode et al., 2016). For an excellent score, an electric goad would be used on 5% or less of the cattle or pigs. In sheep and neonatal calves, electric prod use should be avoided (OIE, 2018). Use for both conventional and non-stunned religious slaughter.

4. Percentage of animals that fall during handling at any place in the abattoir from the unloading ramp to the stun box (Grandin, 1998a, 2010; Welfare Quality, 2009; Messori et al., 2016; Losada-Espinoza et al., 2017; OIE, 2018). Stun boxes that have floors which cause animals to fall would result in an automatic failed audit. Falls must be 1% or less of the animals. All falls caused by powered gates are counted. Use for both conventional and non-stun religious slaughter.

5. Percentage of cattle or pigs vocalizing in the stunning area (Grandin, 1998a, 2001; Welfare Quality, 2009; Losada-Espinoza et al., 2017) – bellowing or mooing in cattle, and pigs squealing. Each animal is scored as either silent or as a vocalizer. To make vocalization practical, it is much easier to score each animal as silent or vocalizing during stunning and handling. In cattle, all vocalizing animals in the stun box or non-stun religious slaughter box are counted. Cattle that vocalize in direct response to electric prods while entering the box are also counted. To pass, the percentage of cattle that vocalize must be 3% or less. If a headholder is used, then the acceptable percentage of vocalizing cattle is 5%. Use for both conventional and non-stun religious slaughter. Do not use vocalization scoring for sheep. For pigs, it is difficult to determine which pig in a group of pigs is squealing. If pigs are stunned on the floor with electric tongs, score each pig as silent or squealing when it is handled for stunning. If the pigs are held in a restrainer, score each pig as silent or squealing. For all species, never score vocalization in the lairage for the basic audit, because animals may vocalize for reasons unrelated to handling or restraint. The purpose of vocalization scoring is to identify severe problems with stressful handling or poor restraint. It can identify serious welfare issues with either restraint equipment or excessive electric goad use. For example, reducing pressure from a head restraint device reduced the percentage of cattle vocalizing from 23% to 0% (Grandin, 2001).

Clever Traffic Light Pig Squeal Meter

To help motivate a programme for continuous improvement in handling, some progressive managers have installed sound decibel meters in the room where the pig stunner is located. This will work with all types of stunners. The decibel meter is wired to a traffic light. The light is green when the squealing level is low and it turns red when the squeals increase. This is an excellent method for assessment within an abattoir. It will not work between plants, because each plant has a different number of pigs in the room. For all species, never score vocalization in the lairage. The purpose of vocalization scoring is to locate problems with either excessive electric goad use or problems with restraint equipment.

Most Common Modifications to Equipment and Procedures to Improve Animal Welfare and Numerical Scores for Poultry

- Improve maintenance of transport containers to prevent injuries to the birds.
- Use incentive pay for catchers to reduce broken wings and death losses.
- Limit catching shifts to 6 h. When workers get tired, bird injury increases.
- Eliminate people walking under the shackled birds or other disturbances at the entrance to the electric stunner.
- Sort out undersized birds that are too short to be properly stunned in an electric stunner.
- Install either a video camera or windows in controlled atmosphere stunners for constant monitoring of behaviour before loss of posture. Bird welfare has been seriously compromised if the birds attempt to escape from the container before loss of posture and losing consciousness (see Chapters 13, 14). If this occurs, the protocols for anaesthesia must be corrected.

Nine Simple Outcome Measures for Assessing Poultry Catching, Transport, Handling and Stunning

1. Percentage of birds with broken or dislocated wings. Score with the feathers on, to avoid confusion with defeathering machine damage. The percentage of birds with broken wings should be under 1% (Welfare Quality, 2009; Grandin, 2017; Jacobs et al., 2017).
2. Percentage of birds with a broken leg.
3. Percentage of overloaded transport containers. All birds should be able to lie down without being on top of each other. A container is defined as: (i) a single coop; (ii) a single drawer; or (iii) a single compartment in a dumping module. Limit 1% overstocked. Although overstocking is a major source of heat stress, understocking during cold weather can increase cold stress (Cockram et al., 2018). Each facility should determine clear cold-weather stocking densities.
4. Percentage of broken transport containers. A container is scored as broken if a plastic slat is missing or a piece of wire has broken loose. Limit 1% of the containers are broken.
5. Percentage of birds with body parts stuck in drawers or doors of transport containers (Vissar et al., 2014).

6. Percentage of birds that miss the electric stunner. Must be 99% or more correctly stunned.
7. Uncut red birds in electric stunning systems. Red birds occur when a bird fails to bleed out. After feather removal, it will be bright red because it did not bleed. A red bird that does not have its throat cut from either the cutting machine or the back-up bleeder person may have entered the scalder alive. A single uncut red bird is a failed audit.
8. Percentage of birds that are dead on arrival (Weeks et al., 2019).
9. Percentage of bruised birds. Count a bird as bruised if it has bruises larger than 19 mm (0.75 in) (Jacobs et al., 2017).

Acts of Abuse are Automatic Failed Audit

An audit is failed if any of the abuses listed in Chapter 2 are observed. Some examples are beating animals, dragging conscious non-ambulatory animals or poking sensitive areas such as the eyes, mouth or anus.

Effectiveness of Animal-based Measures

A review of the literature on pre-slaughter handling validated assessment of cattle welfare during handling by scoring: (i) interactions with handlers such as electric prod use; (ii) falling; and (iii) vocalization (Losada-Espinosa et al., 2017). These three measures can be easily conducted in a commercial slaughter plant. Previous research has clearly shown that procedures improve when stunning and handling are assessed with numerical scoring (Grandin, 2000, 2001, 2012). This is especially true when large meat-buying customers are insisting on high standards.

In poultry, scientific studies have validated scoring of bruises and broken wings (Kittelsen et al., 2015; Jacobs et al., 2017;). Extensive data has also been published on the incidence of bruises and dead on arrival (Langkebel et al., 2015; Caffrey et al., 2017; Jacobs et al., 2017). The other measures were developed by the author for use by large buyers of poultry (www.grandin.com). A recent problem in the poultry industry is that there are large amounts of commercial research on stunning and handling that are never published. The acceptable cut-off points for some of the variables were determined from unpublished information obtained during commercial audits.

A High Percentage of Animals Vocalizing and Electric Prod Use Is Related to Physiological Measures of Stress

In both cattle and pigs, vocalizations during handling and restraint are related to physiological measures of stress. In cattle, vocalization during restraint and handling is associated with higher cortisol levels (Dunn, 1990; Hemsworth *et al.*, 2011). In pigs, vocalization during handling was associated with poorer meat quality (Warriss *et al.*, 1994; Hambrecht *et al.*, 2004, 2005; Edwards *et al.*, 2010a,b).

Electric prod use is very detrimental to pigs (Benjamin *et al.*, 2001). When it occurs shortly before stunning, lactate levels increase and meat quality is lower (Faucitano, 1998, 2010; Hambrecht *et al.*, 2004, 2005; Correa *et al.*, 2010). In cattle, multiple shocks with an electric prod shortly before stunning resulted in tougher beef (Warner *et al.*, 2007). Gruber *et al.* (2010) reported that behavioural agitation in the stunning race resulted in higher lactate levels at bleeding. Dokmanovic and Baltic (2014) reported that pig squealing and electric prod use were associated with higher lactate levels in the blood. Vocalization scoring of pigs during pre-slaughter handling is a promising indicator (Brandt and Aaslyng, 2015).

Reducing Electric Prod Usage and Modifying Restraint Devices Reduces Vocalization

Grandin (1998b, 2001) reported that cattle vocalizations were directly associated with obvious aversive events such as electric prod use, excessive pressure from a restraint device or missed captive bolt stuns. In two abattoirs, when electric prod use was greatly reduced, the percentage of cattle that vocalized dropped from 32% to 12% in one plant and 12% to 3% in the second plant (Grandin, 1998b). In one survey, 86% of the cattle abattoirs had a vocalization score of 2% or less (Grandin, 2000). Simple improvements can greatly reduce the percentage of cattle that vocalize during handling and restraint. Reducing pressure applied by a headholder reduced the percentage of cattle vocalizing from 23% to 0% (Grandin, 2001). Bourquet *et al.* (2011) also reported that a high 25% vocalization score was due to excessive pressure from a restraint device. A plant that had almost 100% of the cattle moved with electric prods had 47% of cattle vocalizing (Hayes *et al.*, 2015). Simple changes to improve cattle movement, such as adding a light to a restrainer entrance, reduced vocalization due to electric prod use from 8% to 0% (Grandin, 2001).

In five abattoirs, modifications discussed previously were made to equipment. Before modification, 12.8% of the cattle vocalized; after modification, the percentage of cattle vocalizing dropped to 1% (Grandin, 2001).

How Stressful is Slaughter of Livestock?

An animal welfare officer at a slaughter plant may be asked, 'Do animals know they are going to be slaughtered?' The author has observed that animal behaviour during handling is similar in both the farm and in the slaughter plant. If animals knew they were going to be slaughtered, there should be greater agitation at the abattoir. Evaluation of physiological measures of stress indicated that levels of lactate, glucose or cortisol were similar to levels after on-farm cattle handling. Lactate and glucose respond very quickly to an aversive event such as an electric prod. Lactate and glucose measures could be used as an easy way to monitor handling quality of pigs at slaughter (Edwards *et al.*, 2010b). Meters for measuring lactate and glucose are easy to use and economical. Cortisol requires 15–20 min to reach peak levels (Lay *et al.*, 1992, 1998). Indicators such as adrenaline (epinephrine) and noradrenaline cannot be used, because stunning causes massive release (Warrington, 1974; Pearson *et al.*, 1977; Van der Wall, 1978). When electrical stunning or captive bolt stunning is done correctly, this massive release of stress hormones has no effect on welfare. The animal is rendered instantly unconscious and is not aware of the hormone release.

In some studies, cortisol levels are expressed in nanomoles per millilitre (nmol/ml) by multiplication of ng/ml by 0.36. Tame animals that are trained to lead often have baseline cortisol levels when they are handled for veterinary procedures. When brought to a slaughter plant, tame draught animals often show little or no behavioural signs of agitation.

Slaughter cortisol levels in cattle

When slaughtering is carried out carefully, cortisol levels in cattle can be substantially lower compared with on-farm handling of extensively raised cattle. Tume and Shaw (1992) reported that steers and heifers slaughtered in a small research abattoir had average cortisol levels of only 15 ng/ml and cattle slaughtered in a commercial slaughter plant had levels similar to those of on-farm handling of extensively raised cattle. Bison shot in the field had very low cortisol levels of 6.48 ng/ml and bison shot in a commercial plant had 36 ng/ml (Duane Lammers, 2012, personal communication).

For commercial slaughter of extensively raised cattle with captive bolt stunning, the following average cortisol values have been recorded: 45 ng/ml (Dunn, 1990), 25–42 ng/ml (Mitchell *et al.*, 1988), 44.28 ng/ml (Tume and Shaw, 1992), 24 ng/ml (Ewbank *et al.*, 1992), 66 ng/ml in two large export abattoirs (Hemsworth *et al.*, 2011). The high cortisol levels in Hemsworth *et al.* (2011) may have been due to extensively raised Brahman-cross cattle from the Australian outback. A French study with intensively raised young fed bulls had cortisol levels of 21 ng/ml at slaughter (Mounier et al., 2006). Bulls often have lower cortisol levels compared with steers. Gentle stroking of newborn calves for 10 min on five different days lowered cortisol levels at slaughter from 49 ng/ml to 29 ng/ml (Probst *et al.*, 2012). When things go wrong, the stress levels increase greatly. Cockram and Corley (1991) reported a median value of 63 ng/ml. One animal had a high of 162 ng/ml. This was probably due to constant slipping on the floor.

Cortisol levels similar to on-farm handling

Cortisol levels during handling at a slaughter plant are similar to on-farm handling and restraint for blood testing (Grandin, 1997, 2014). Baseline cortisol levels in cattle at rest can vary from a low of 2 ng/ml (Alam and Dobson, 1986) up to 9 ng/ml (Mitchell *et al.*, 1988). In another study, beef cattle on a research station that had become accustomed to being handled for different experiments had cortisol levels that ranged from 10 ng/ml in calm animals to 15 ng/ml in the more excitable individuals (King *et al.*, 2006). Restraining extensively raised semi-wild cattle for blood testing under farm conditions elicited cortisol readings of 25–33 ng/ml in steers (Zavy *et al.*, 1992), 63 ng/ml in steers and cows (Mitchell *et al.*, 1988), 27 ng/ml in steers, 63 ng/ml in steers and cows (Mitchell *et al.*, 1988), 27 ng/ml in steers, 24–46 ng/ml in weaner calves (Crookshank *et al.*, 1979) and 41 ng/ml in British/Continental beef breed (*B. taurus*) steers handled in the early morning (Vogel, 2011). Furthermore, cortisol has diurnal variations and may be higher earlier

in the day (Gygax *et al.*, 2006; Hemsworth *et al.*, 2011). In Braham and Brahman-cross cattle, cortisol values ranged from 30 to 35 ng/ml after 20 min restraint in a squeeze chute (Lay *et al.*, 1992, 1998); the levels were 12 ng/ml after 5 min and rose to 23 ng/ml after 10.5 min of restraint (Lay *et al.*, 1998).

Detrimental effects of poor handling of cattle

The slaughter plant observed by Cockram and Corley (1991) had a poorly designed forcing pen and slippery floors. About 38% of the cattle slipped after exiting the holding pens and 28% slipped just before entering the race. Cortisol levels also increased when delays increased waiting time in the single file race. This was the only study where vocalizations shortly before stunning were not correlated with cortisol levels. This can probably be partly explained by earlier stress caused by the slippery floors. Cortisol levels were lower and stress was reduced when cattle were transported and slaughtered with their penmates (Mounier *et al.*, 2006).

Ewbank *et al.* (1992) found a high correlation between cortisol levels and handling problems in the stun box. Use of a poorly designed head restraint device, which greatly increased behavioural agitation and the time required to restrain the animal, resulted in cortisol levels jumping from 24 to 51 ng/ml. In the worst animal, the level increased to 96 ng/ml. Cattle slaughtered in a badly designed restraining pen that turned them upside down had average values of 93 ng/ml (Dunn, 1990). Very few sexually mature bulls have been studied, though Cockram and Corley (1991) had a few in their study. Sexually mature bulls have much lower cortisol levels than steers, cows or heifers (Tennessen *et al.*, 1984).

Cortisol levels and stress in sheep and goats

Sheep research also shows that cortisol levels at an abattoir are similar to those in on-farm handling. Slaughter in a quiet research abattoir resulted in much lower average levels (40 ng/ml) compared with a large noisy commercial plant that had dogs (61 ng/ml) (Pearson *et al.*, 1977). In two large sheep export abattoirs in Australia, the mean cortisol level was 67 ng/ml (Hemsworth *et al.*, 2011). In a Brazilian abattoir, cortisol levels were 24 ng/ml after 3 h in large. Preventing sheep from seeing outside the truck during transport reduced cortisol at unloading from 35.49 ng/ml to 29 ng/ml (da Cunha

Leme *et al.*, 2012). Shearing and other on-farm handling procedures provoked similar or slightly greater stress levels of 73 ng/ml (Hargreaves and Hutson, 1990), 72 ng/ml (Kilgour and de Langen, 1970) and 60 ng/ml (Fulkerson and Jamieson, 1982). Restraint and isolation stress for 90–120 min increased cortisol levels to 80–100 ng/ml in sheep (Apple *et al.*, 1993; Rivalland *et al.*, 2007). Baseline levels were 22 ng/ml. Extremely high cortisol levels of 119 ng/ml were obtained in a slaughter plant where each sheep was individually picked up by a person to unload the trucks (Ekiz *et al.*, 2012). Five min of exposure to barking dogs increased cortisol levels in kids (Zimmerman *et al.*, 2012).

Do Blood Odours Upset Livestock?

Many people interested in the welfare of livestock are concerned about animals seeing or smelling blood. Cattle will baulk and sniff spots of blood on the floor (Grandin, 1980a,b), and washing the blood off facilitates movement. The baulking may be a reaction to novelty, as a piece of paper thrown in the race or stunning box elicits a similar response. Cattle will baulk and sometimes refuse to enter a stun box or restrainer if the ventilation system blows blood smells into their faces at the stun box entrance. They will enter more easily if an exhaust fan is used to create a localized zone of negative air pressure. This will suck smells away from cattle as they approach the stun box entrance. Application of mentholated ointment to a horse's nostrils may help to reduce stress at slaughter. Micera *et al.* (2012) reported that the ointment reduced adrenaline and noradrenaline levels.

Observations in Jewish religious (kosher) slaughter plants indicate that cattle will readily walk into a restraining box that is covered with blood. In kosher slaughter, the throat of a fully conscious animal is cut with a razor-sharp knife. Cattle will calmly place their heads into the head restraint device and some animals will lick blood or drink it. Pigs will eat or root in blood when they are slaughtered in groups (Schaeperkoetter *et al.*, 2019). Kosher slaughter can proceed very calmly with few signs of behavioural agitation if the restraining box is operated gently (Grandin, 1992, 1994). Research by Schaeperkoetter *et al.* (2019) indicated that watching other pigs being stunned and bled did not raise blood lactate levels.

However, if an animal becomes very agitated and frenzied during restraint, subsequent animals often become agitated and an entire slaughter day can turn into a continuous chain reaction of excited animals. The next day, after the equipment has been washed, the animals will be calm. The excited animals may be smelling an alarm pheromone from the blood of severely stressed cattle. Blood from relatively low-stressed cattle may have little effect, but blood from severely stressed animals that have shown signs of behavioural agitation for several minutes may elicit a fear response. Eible-Eibesefeldt (1970) observed that if a rat is killed instantly in a trap, the trap can be used again, but the trap will be ineffective if it injured the rat and failed to kill it instantly.

Research with pigs and cattle indicates that there are stress pheromones in saliva and urine. Vieuille-Thomas and Signoret (1992) and Boissy *et al.* (1998) reported that pigs and cattle tended to avoid places or objects sprayed with urine from a stressed animal. The stressor must be applied for 15–20 min to induce the effect. In the cattle experiment, the animals were given repeated shocks for 15 min (Grandin, 2014).

Complying with Government Legislation and Regulations

Abattoir managers need to comply with two sets of requirements. They are the specifications and private standards from customers and compliance with government regulations. In this section, the first part will cover US regulations (FSIS, no date, 2013, 2016, 2017) and the second part will cover recommendations for EU regulations (EFSA, 2013 a–d). Abattoirs that specialize in export often have to comply with both the US and EU requirements. One of the problems with regulations is that some of them are often vague. In FSIS regulations, the livestock have to be moved with 'minimum of excitement and discomfort' (Regulation 9CFR313). Determining excessive use of electric prods is based on the opinion of the inspector. In the EU, the term 'avoidable suffering' is used in many documents (Council of European Union, 1979). Vague wording results in variation in how the regulations are interpreted and enforced.

US Regulations

Increased enforcement of existing legislation

In the USA, recent lawsuits and other actions by animal activist groups have motivated the Food

Safety Inspection Service (FSIS) of the US Department of Agriculture (USDA) to strictly enforce Humane Slaughter Act regulations. The inspectors have the power to suspend federal meat inspection and shut an abattoir down until problems are corrected. The length of the shutdown ranges from a few hours to several days for serious violations. In the USA, the Humane Slaughter Act does not cover poultry. As discussed in Chapter 11, it also has an exemption for religious slaughter. Missed captive bolt or gunshots are the primary area of enforcement by FSIS. The US law basically states that stunning must be perfect. To avoid shutdowns, many US abattoirs that were previously using electrical stunning for pigs have switched to CO_2. The use of CO_2 machines with long dwell times in the gas almost eliminates pigs returning to consciousness after they exit the machine.

The FSIS inspectors are most likely to enforce the Humane Slaughter Act regulations that are clearly worded. The regulations that have vague wording are less likely to be enforced. The areas that are most critical for managers to supervise are as follows.

- Stunning efficacy. Since it is impossible to be perfect, there is some leeway if a plant has a robust systematic approach. There will be further explanations of this later in this chapter. The actual wording is 'all animals are rendered insensible to pain by a single blow or gunshot' (FSIS/USDA Humane Slaughter of Livestock Regulation 9 CFR 213).
- Provide water for all the livestock in the lairage. This is worded very clearly.
- Never drag non-ambulatory, conscious, downed animals. 'Stunned animals may be dragged.' Be really careful with power pusher gates to avoid dragging pigs. Dragging animals with gates can result in a violation.
- No pointed objects for driving livestock. The wording is those that 'in the opinion of the inspector would cause injury or unnecessary pain'. This wording has given the inspectors some flexibility.
- Never start invasive dressing procedures on animals showing any eye reflexes. Both FSIS and EU regulations require that animals are brain dead before carcass processing (invasive dressing procedure; also see Chapters 13 and 14).

Developing a robust systematic approach

People who manage both large and small US federally inspected meat plants need guidance that is simple and easy to understand. Some of the directives and documents from the FSIS are hard for managers and quality assurance employees to understand. A major issue was finding an easy-to-understand definition of a robust systematic approach for humane slaughter compliance.

I had the opportunity to talk to Patty Bennett, DVM, when she was the Humane Handling Enforcement Officer for FSIS. We were on a conference call during the 2017 North American Meat Institute's Animal Welfare Committee Meeting. I asked her to give me the definition of a robust systematic approach in plain, simple language that a plant manager could easily understand. After our discussion, the definition could be summarized to six major points. The first three points are clearly outlined in the document 'FSIS Compliance Guide for a Systematic Approach to the Human Handling of Livestock', which can be easily found on the internet. She outlined the first three points in plain easy-to-understand language:

1. **Written procedures are required** for a robust systematic approach. Written standard operating procedures (SOPs) must describe both the procedures in your plant and the corrective actions that will be taken if there is a failure of a procedure.

2. **Written records are required.** These records would contain the written procedures. They would also contain corrective actions and plant internal audits.

3. **FSIS review.** Records would be shared with the FSIS meat inspectors upon request.

The above three items are 'straight from the book' (FSIS, 2013). The next three items are paraphrased from notes from my conversation with Dr Bennett:

1. **The written program must match actual operations in the plant.** My interpretation of this is that the system is not robust if plant operations are different than the written document.

2. **Does it work?** There is need for constant monitoring to determine if the programme is working. Numerical scoring is a good method to determine if procedures are either improving or becoming worse. My interpretation is that both the internal monitoring methods and records of corrective actions for problems must be included in the written records. This would allow someone who is reviewing the records to determine if procedures are improving or becoming worse.

3. **Provide definite ways to fix problems.** This is especially relevant if there are re-occurring problems. Explains how problems were fixed.

Dr Bennett made it clear that a plant can have a robust systematic approach even if it is under an enforcement action.

FSIS/USDA HATS categories

The FSIS also has a system called HATS categories (FSIS, 2013). When an inspector sees a problem, they will write it up under a Humane Activity Tracing System (HATS) category. Below is a simplified list of HATS categories based on CFR 312.2 (FSIS, 2016).

1. Inclement weather – Includes both hot and cold weather. This section will include problems with slipping and falling on ice or frozen water troughs. During hot weather, lack of shade. Disabled livestock should be in a covered pen.
2. Truck unloading – This section includes slipping and falling, or forcing animals to move faster than a walking speed. Some inspectors will use numerical scoring to evaluate slipping, falling or excessive electric prod (goad) use.
3. Water/feed available – Water must always be available in lairage pens. Feed required after 24 h of holding in the lairage.
4. Ante-mortem inspection – Along with ante-mortem inspection for food safety, the inspectors will also observe handling. Major areas are excessive electric prod use and injuries due to handling practices.
5. Suspect and disabled animals – Never drag a conscious animal. Separate disabled animals from other animals.
6. Electric prod/alternative object use – No sharp objects. Does use of electric or other driving aids result in 'over excitement or injury'? Some inspectors will use numerical scoring of falls, vocalization and percentage electric prodded to determine if handling practices are acceptable.
7. Slips and falls – Can be due to either slick flooring or poor handling. Some inspectors will use numerical scoring on falling and electric prod use.
8. Stunning effectiveness (Regulation 9CFR 313.5, 313.15, 313.16 313.30) – A robust systematic approach may help avoid a plant shutdown if a stun is missed. Requires records of CO_2 concentrations.
9. No conscious animals hung on the bleed rail (Regulation 9 CFR 313.5, 313.15, 313.16, 313.30) – See Chapters 13 and 14 on determining insensibility.

European Council (EC) Regulations

There is an excellent discussion on European regulations by Pinellos (2016). Both the European Union and the OIE recognize the importance of promoting global animal welfare standards. Some of the wording that is used in the regulation is vague, such as preventing 'avoidable pain'. Below is a summary of the requirements for operators of slaughter plants. It has been summarized from Pinellos (2016).

1. Develop sampling practices to check efficacy of practices in your abattoir. Numerical scoring could be used for this.
2. Write SOPs for handling, restraining and stunning.
3. Maintain and keep clean all equipment used for handling, such as unloading ramps, waterers and pens. Keep maintenance records.
4. Always have a back-up stunner available.
5. Do not overstock lairage pens. Develop charts for number of animals that can be put in each pen. The author recommends that all the animals must be able to lie down without being on top of each other (Figs 12.1a, b and 12.2 could be used as part of an SOP on stocking density of the lairage).
6. Prompt unloading.
7. Good lairage conditions. Follow requirements for feeding and watering.
8. An Animal Welfare Officer is *required* for large abattoirs.
9. Monitor stunning. The author suggests that numerical scoring could be used for this purpose. Have documented maintenance procedures. The EU Regulation (Council Regulation (EC) No. 1099/2009) (European Council, 2009) requires SOPs that define parameters to indicate the effectiveness of stunning and the measures to be taken when checks indicate that an animal is not properly stunned. This wording would allow a few second applications to be legal.
10. Use equipment that complies with regulations.
11. Only accept the type of animals for which the slaughterhouse is officially approved.
12. Training of employees handling animals is essential. There should be documentation of the training materials that were used.
13. Manager must state maximum numbers, species and weight of animals that can be slaughtered per hour.

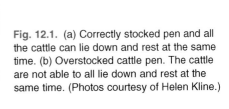

Fig. 12.1. (a) Correctly stocked pen and all the cattle can lie down and rest at the same time. (b) Overstocked cattle pen. The cattle are not able to all lie down and rest at the same time. (Photos courtesy of Helen Kline.)

Fig. 12.2. Lairage pen that is properly stocked with pigs. All the pigs have room to lie down without being on top of each other. A little extra space enables the pigs to get to the waterers. (Photo courtesy of Temple Grandin.)

Requirements for EU Animal Welfare Officers

The Animal Welfare Officer must directly report to the slaughter plant manager. To comply with EU regulations, a welfare officer is required for abattoirs that annually slaughter 1000 adult cattle or 5000 market-weight pigs. Poultry slaughter plants that process over 150,000 birds annually require a welfare officer. The duties of this person must be written as part of the abattoir's SOPs. There are two requirements for the animal welfare officer.

1. They must hold a certificate of competence for each of the operations for which they are responsible (European Commission, 2009. These are issued after completion of recognized training courses.

2. They must keep records of all actions for a year. The welfare officer should be involved in both implementation and development of SOPs and corrective actions.

The welfare officer has to have a programme for monitoring handling, stunning and condition of arriving animals. The author recommends numerical scoring of handling and stunning. See Chapter 4 on the condition of animals entering the abattoir. Some severely debilitated animals should never have been transported to the abattoir. They should have been euthanized on the farm. All employees who are handling, stunning or bleeding animals must have a training certificate. Use training courses that are approved in your country. There are often

Auditing and Assessing the Welfare of Livestock and Poultry

several different choices. There is an excellent webpage titled The Animal Welfare Officer in the European Union (European Union, 2012). Other sources of training materials are: NAMI (2019), Humane Slaughter Association (HSA, 2019), OIE slaughter guidelines (OIE, 2018) and www.Grandin.com.

Similarities Between OIE, EU and US Procedures for SOPs

Many of the requirements are similar for both the FSIS Robust Systematic Approvals and EU requirements for SOPs. Write SOPs in simple language describing what you do in your abattoir. Do not copy standards from other slaughter plants or quote verbatim from industry guidelines. Do not write a book. Box 12.2 gives an outline of a sample of SOPs.

Three Parts of an Effective Assessment System

A camera tripod has three legs. If one of the legs is missing, it will tip over. In a commercial assessment system, a third-party independent auditor will visit every facility. The second leg on the tripod is internal audits and assessments conducted by the animal welfare officer or other person designated by the plant management. The third leg is corporate buyer check audits. A management person from the buyer visits a sampling of abattoirs to ensure that the third-party auditors are doing their jobs.

In government regulatory systems, there are also three legs on the tripod. They are: (i) the government inspector assigned to the slaughter plant; (ii) the animal welfare officer at the plant; and (iii) the government inspector's supervisor. Both private standards and government systems have guidelines for the number of animals that should be sampled.

Remote Video Auditing

Video auditing using numerical scoring is being used in many abattoirs in the USA and closed-circuit TV is now required in the UK and Denmark. Auditors in a central control centre run by a private company randomly sample a group of animals in the stunning area, handling races, bleed rail and truck unloading area. If an auditor sees a non-compliance, the abattoir manager receives an email. Video auditing prevents the problem of people 'acting good' when they see a person with a clipboard.

Avoid Turning Compliance into a Paperwork Audit

Too many assessments have turned into paperwork audits, and observations of stunning and handling may be lacking. The paperwork may be in good order, but stunning and animal handling are terrible. Paperwork is important, but direct observation is most important. For EU, FSIS and private industry standards, records on training of people and maintenance of stunners and other equipment are important. Records also need to be kept of all non-compliances and corrective actions. Inspectors, animal welfare officers and auditors must get out in the lairage and stunning area and determine if the records accurately describe actual practices.

Training Materials

There are many sources of training materials for abattoir employees. In most countries, there are training materials that are readily available. Some good sources are NAMI (2019), Humane Slaughter Association in the UK, and OIE training materials. A particular buyer may have specific training materials and guidelines that should be used. The biggest problem the author has observed with training materials is failure to translate them into the languages used by the employees. Another approach is to use pictorial publications and videos where translation is not needed. A green check marker would show correct procedures and a red circle with a diagonal slash would show the wrong procedures.

Other Assessment Systems, ISO and Gap Analysis

There has been much discussion about assessing animal welfare with risk analysis, gap analysis or ISO. Some of this information has become really complicated. Below is a simplified explanation.

The International Organization for Standardization (ISO, 2016) has published an introductory document based on the World Organisation for Animal Health (OIE) published welfare standards for slaughter transport and production of beef cattle, dairy cattle and broiler chickens. This document is a guide for developing an animal welfare plan. The main guidance document is Chapter 7.1 Article 7.1.4 of the OIE Terrestrial Animal Health Code. This contains 11 General Principles of Animal Welfare. Fortunately, the document encourages the use of animal-based

Box 12.2. Outline of sample standard operating procedures (SOPs)

Write a few sentences for each item.

- Name of person who wrote the SOP
- Date written
- Name of supervisor

Description of Each Procedure – For example: (i) captive bolt stunning; (ii) unloading trucks; or (iii) handling non-ambulatory animals. Describe the procedures in your plant and write a separate SOP for each procedure.

    Monitoring the Procedure – Some examples would be maintenance records for stunners or numerical scoring of handling and stunning. The frequencies of the observations and monitoring should be stated.

    Corrective Actions – Describe procedures used to correct problems. Examples would be to re-train the employees or stop hiring a truck driver who dragged a downed animal. Acts of abuse should never be tolerated. It is recommended to state in very clear language the specific animal abuses that could result in termination of employment. These rules should be posted on signs in animal handling areas. If either a government meat inspector or a private industry auditor finds a deficiency, you have to respond and state what your corrective action will be. In both government and private programmes, follow-up inspections or auditor visits are usually required. This is to verify that improvements occurred after corrective actions were performed.

Examples of corrective actions performed daily in existing facilities:

- Establish procedures to prevent slipping and falling, such as washing the floor, or applying wood shavings.
- Rotate employees who perform the most physically strenuous jobs (state what the jobs are).

- Improve documentation of stunner maintenance to improve the percentage of animals effectively stunned with one application of the stunner (state changes to record keeping and stunner maintenance procedures).

Examples of corrective actions that are performed a single time:

- Purchase of new stunning equipment.
- Terminating the employment of an abusive truck driver.
- Installation of a non-slip flooring surface in a stun box, such as a ribbed rubber mat or welded steel rods.
- Construction of a solid barrier to prevent incoming livestock from seeing people and equipment movement through the headholder of the stun box (see Chapter 6).
- Changing lighting to improve animal movement (see Chapter 6).

Records – Written records of all corrective actions must be kept with the SOPs. Either paper or electronic records can be used.

    Clear descriptions of non-compliances – Both government inspectors and private industry auditors should write up non-compliances in clear language. If numerical scoring is used, both the target score and the score the plant actually received should be stated. The animal welfare officer or other designated person, such as a quality assurance supervisor, should respond with a corrective action plan. Below are examples of clearly written and vague/poorly written non-compliance and corrective actions. Clear wording also makes it easier to determine how serious a problem is. In the example below, the clearly written description shows that the problem was really serious. The vague description makes the problem less obvious.

	Clearly written	Vague, not clear
Noncompliance	A pig squealed when it entered the scalder and no attempt was made to either re-stun it or stop the line.	Poorly stunned pig entered the scalder
Corrective action	Station a person at the end of the bleed chain before the scalder to shoot with a captive bolt any pig that shows any signs of starting to regain consciousness. That person will be trained using [state materials used] training materials.	Better supervision of stunning and bleeding

measures where the threshold values are based on peer-reviewed scientific literature (Grandin, 1998a, 2001, 2010; Losada-Espinoza et al., 2004, 2017). For slaughter and handling, there is now extensive peer-reviewed literature that supports the thresholds for stunning, electric prod use, falling and vocalization that are found in the North American Meat Institute (NAMI) 2019 guidelines.

The booklet for ISO is *Animal Welfare Management: General Requirements and Guidance for Organizations in the Food Chain ISO/TS34700:2016*. It is an outline on how to set up your programme, but unfortunately it does not provide much practical guidance. It would be comparable to how each individual US slaughter plant had to develop its own individual Hazard Analysis and Critical Control Point plans to obey FSIS food safety regulations.

The section 'Developing an Animal Welfare Plan' discusses how to do a gap analysis of your plan. The directions are complicated and I will try to simplify them. A gap analysis is a method for looking at current performance and comparing it with a future performance goal. Your gap analysis should clearly identify your objectives for animal welfare (see chart in Box 12.3 for example).

On-farm Welfare Problems That Can Be Assessed at the Abattoir

Livestock

Another area where welfare could be improved is the condition of the livestock that enter the plant (Grandin, 2015, 2017; Dahl-Pedersen *et al.*, 2018; Edwards-Callaway *et al.*, 2018; Forsgaard *et al.*, 2018). Some of the threshold-based, animal-based outcome measures that can be used to assess on-farm conditions are:

- percentage of animals that arrive downed and non-ambulatory;
- percentage of livestock with poor body condition (Edwards-Callaway *et al.*, 2018; Munoz *et al.*, 2018);
- percentage of dirty animals (Munoz *et al.*, 2018);
- percentage of lame (difficulty walking) animals (Welfare Quality, 2009; Edwards-Callaway *et al.*, 2017, 2018; Dahl-Pedersen *et al.*, 2018; Munoz *et al.*, 2018);
- percentage with neglected health problems;
- percentage with severe liver abscesses (the most severe liver abscesses have adhesions to the carcass and large parts of the carcasses have to be trimmed due to contamination; Herrick *et al.*, 2018); and
- other diseases, such as mastitis or parasites (Dahl-Pedersen *et al.*, 2018).

You could use the NAMI lameness scoring system for assessing lameness (Edwards-Callaway *et al.*, 2017). An advantage of this four-point scoring tool is that it provides an assessment of lameness severity and it still provides high inter-observer reliability. The scores are: (1) = normal; (2) = lame, keeps up with walking group; (3) = lame, does not keep up and lags behind; and (4) = almost non-ambulatory and can barely walk. There are also readily available body condition scoring charts for assessing skinny cull cows and sows. Scoring tools for dirty animals and neglected conditions, such as hernias in pigs, are readily available.

Box 12.3. Example of how a plant's Animal Welfare Officers and Managers could create a gap analysis from their own records

Actual average scores in your abbatoir	
Stunning	96%
Electric prods	23%
Falling	1%
Vocalization	7%
Future goals – average scores	
Stunning	99%
Electric prods	15%
Falling	0.2%
Vocalization	3%

You would also explain the corrective actions you used to improve scores and reduce the gap between actual scores and the goals. A possible example for improving stunning would be including the balancer for a heavy pneumatic stunner as part of an enhanced maintenance programme. To reduce falling, you might replace the worn-out rubber mat in the stun box.

A large survey done in the USA showed that grain-fattened cattle had very low percentages of lame animals (Lee *et al.*, 2018). Observations by the author in 2018 also confirmed these results. Compiling averages across thousands of cattle may conceal very serious welfare conditions that a few poor producers are causing. Interviews with lairage workers clearly indicated that certain feedlots had greatly increased problems with lameness. On-farm issues that cause handling problems at the slaughter plant must be corrected at the farm. In a large pig slaughter plant, numbers of downed, non-ambulatory pigs were almost eliminated by changing on-farm practices. The following changes were made: (i) selection of breeding stock for good leg conformation; (ii) daily walking in the pens to get the pigs accustomed to people walking through them; and (iii) removal of beta agonists from the diet. When these observations were made, the temperature was over 38°C (100°F) with 41% humidity. During 1 h of observations, one pig arrived non-ambulatory on a truck and there were no downers in the stunning area. Approximately a thousand pigs were observed on this hot day. Before the on-farm production improvements were made, this same abattoir had five full-time people handling downers that were not able to walk.

In 2018, some of the most serious animal welfare issues that the author observed in US slaughter plants were issues that must be corrected at the farm. Producers who routinely deliver animals with serious welfare issues should be required to correct them. Dairy cows arriving in poor condition are still a major problem (Edwards-Callaway *et al.*, 2018).

Poultry

Many poultry welfare problems that occur on the farm can be easily assessed at the abattoir. There are problems related to housing and production:

- leg abnormalities, such as twisted or splayed;
- foot pad dermatitis;
- hock burn;
- skin lesions (breast blisters);
- plumage cleanliness; and
- cachexia (wasting syndrome), undersized.

Sources of information on these measures are Jacobs *et al.* (2016, 2017), Tuyttens (2017) and Tuyttens *et al.* (2018). Conditions caused by poor practices that occur during catching, transport or stunning have been covered in an earlier section of this chapter.

Conclusions

Maintaining a high standard of welfare of livestock and poultry during truck unloading, lairage, handling and stunning will require management to pay attention to many details of the procedure. Numerical scoring will help abattoir managers, regulatory officials and commercial auditors determine if practices are improving or deteriorating.

For the gap analysis, you could compare your baseline scores against goals for the future. Some of these goals could be based on published literature. There are many papers published in the peer-reviewed scientific literature. The ISO guidelines require periodic review of your animal welfare plan. During this review, you can determine if you are closing the gap between your current performance and your goals.

References

Alam, M.G. and Dobson, H. (1986) Effect of various veterinary procedures on plasma concentrations of cortisol, luteinizing hormone and prostaglandin F2 metabolite in the cow. *Veterinary Record* 118, 7–10.

Apple, J.K., Minton, J.E., Parson, K.M. and Unnuh, J.A. (1993) Influence of repeated restraint and isolation stress and electrolyte administration on pituitary-adrenal secretions, electrolytes, and other blood constituents in sheep. *Journal of Animal Science* 71, 71–77.

Australian Meat Processing Corporation (2018) Final Report. Development of reporting tools for the Australian Livestock Processing Industry Animal Welfare Certification System. Available at: ampc.com.air (accessed 6 January 2018).

Benjamin, M.E., Gonyou, H.W., Ivers, D.L, Richard, L.F., Jones, D.J. *et al.* (2001) Effect of handling method on the incidence of stress response in market swine in a model system. *Journal of Animal Science* 79 (Suppl. 1), 279 (abstract).

Boissy, A., Terlow, C. and Le Neindre, P. (1998) Presence of cues from stressed conspecifics increase reactivity to aversive events in cattle, evidence for the existence of alarm substances in urine. *Physiology and Behavior* 4, 489–495.

Bourquet, C., Deiss, V., Cohen-Tannugi, C. and Terlouw, E. (2011) Behavioral and physiological reactions of cattle in a commercial abattoir: relationships with organization aspects of the abattoir and animal characteristics. *Meat Science* 88, 158–168.

Brandt, P. and Aaslyng, M.D. (2015) Welfare measurements of finishing pigs on the day of slaughter: a review. *Meat Science* 103, 13–23.

Caffrey, N.P., Dohoo, I.R. and Cockram, M.S. (2017) Factors affecting mortality risk during transportation of broiler chickens in Atlantic Canada. *Preventive Veterinary Medicine* 147, 199–208.

Cockram, M.S. and Corley, K.T.T. (1991) Effect of preslaughter handling on the behaviour and blood composition of beef cattle. *British Veterinary Journal* 147, 444–454.

Cockram, M.S., Mohamed, R.A. and Revie, C.W. (2018) Risk factors for bruising and mortality of broilers during manual handling module loading, transport, and lairage. *Canadian Journal of Animal Science* 99(1), 50–65. doi: 10.1139/GJAS-2018-0032

Correa, J.A., Torrey, S., Devillers, N., Laforest, J.R., Gonyou, H.W. and Faucitano, L. (2010) Effects of different moving devices at loading on stress response and meat quality in pigs. *Journal of Animal Science* 88, 4086–4093.

Council of Europe (1979) European Convention for the Protection of Animals for Slaughter. European Treaty Series No. 102, Strasbourg 10.V.1979.

European Commission (2009) Council Regulation (EC) No. 1099/2009 of 24 September 2009 on the protection of animals at the time of killing. Available at: https://eur-lex. europa.eu/eli/reg/2009/1099/2018-05-18 (accessed 15 April 2020).

Crookshank, H.R., Elissalde, M.H., White, R.G., Clanton, D.C. and Smalley, H.E. (1979) Effect of transportation and handling of calves on blood serum composition. *Journal of Animal Science* 48, 430–435.

Dahl-Pedersen, K., Herskin, M.S., Houe, H. and Thornsen, P. (2018) A descriptive study of the clinical condition of cull dairy cows before transport to slaughter. *Livestock Science* 218, 108–113.

da Cunha Leme, T.M., Titto, E.A.L., Titto, C.G., Amadeu, C.C.B., Fantinato Neto, P., Vilela, R.A. and Pereira, A.M.F. (2012) Influence of transportation methods and pre-slaughter rest periods on cortisol level in lambs. *Small Ruminant Research* 107, 8–11.

Dokmanovic, M. and Baltic, M.S. (2014) The effect of lairage time and handling procedure prior to slaughter on stress and meat quality parameters in pigs. *Meat Science* 98, 220–226.

Dunn, C.S. (1990) Stress reactions of cattle undergoing ritual slaughter using two methods of restraint. *Veterinary Record* 126, 522–525.

Edwards, L.N., Engle, T.E., Correa, J.A., Paradis, M.A., Grandin, T. and Anderson, D.B. (2010a) The relationship between exsanguination blood lactate concentration and carcass quality in slaughter pigs. *Meat Science* 85, 43–440.

Edwards, L.N., Grandin, T., Engle, T.E., Porter, S.P., Ritter, M.J. *et al.* (2010b) Use of exsanguination blood lactate to assess the quality of pre-slaughter handling. *Meat Science* 86, 384–390.

Edwards-Callaway, L.N., Calvo-Lorenzo, M.S., Scanga, J.A. and Grandin, T. (2017) Mobility scoring of finished cattle. *Veterinary Clinics of North America: Food Animal Practice* 33, 235–250.

Edwards-Callaway, L.N., Walker, J. and Tucker, C. (2018) Perspective: culling decisions and dairy cattle welfare during transport and slaughter in the United States. *Frontiers in Veterinary Science* 5, 343. doi: 10.3389/ fvets.2018.00343

Eible-Eibesfeldt, I. (1970) *Ethology: The Biology of Behavior*. Holt Rinehart and Winston, New York.

Ekiz, B., Ekiz, E.E., Kocak, O., Yalcintah, H. and Yilmaz, A. (2012) Effect of pre-slaughter management regarding transportation and time in lairage on certain stress parameters, carcass, and meat quality in Kivircik lambs. *Meat Science* 90, 967–976.

EFSA (2013a) Scientific opinion on monitoring procedures at slaughterhouses for bovines. *EFSA Journal* 11(12) 3460.

EFSA (2013b) Scientific opinion on monitoring slaughterhouses for poultry. *EFSA Journal* 11(12), 3521.

EFSA (2013c) Scientific opinion on monitoring procedures at slaughterhouses for sheep and goats. *EFSA Journal* 11(12), 3522.

EFSA (2013d) Scientific opinion on monitoring procedures at slaughterhouses for pigs. *EFSA Journal* 11(12), 3523.

European Union (2012) *The Animal Welfare Officer in the European Union*. Directorate General Health and Consumers, European Commission, Brussels, Belgium.

Ewbank, R., Parker, M.J. and Mason, C.W. (1992) Reactions of cattle to head restraint at stunning: a practical dilemma. *Animal Welfare* 1, 55–63.

Faucitano, L. (1998) Preslaughter stressors effects on pork: a review. *Journal of Muscle Foods* 9, 293–303.

Faucitano, L. (2010) Invited review: Effects of lairage and slaughter conditions on animal welfare and pork quality. *Canadian Journal of Animal Science* 90, 461–469.

Fogsgaard, K.K., Herskin, M.S. and Thodberg, K. (2018) Transportation of cull sows, a descriptive study of the clinical condition of cull sows before transportation to slaughter. *Translational Animal Science* 2, 280–289.

Fulkerson, W.J. and Jamieson, P.A. (1982) Pattern of cortisol release in sheep following administration of synthetic ACTH and imposition of various stressor agents. *Australian Journal of Biological Sciences* 35, 215–222.

FSIS (2020) Humane Slaughter of Livestock Regulations 9 CFR 313. USDA Food Safety Inspection Service, Washington, DC.

FSIS (2013) *Approach to humane handling of livestock to achieve compliance with 9CFR Part 313*. USDA Food Safety Inspection Service, Washington, DC.

FSIS (2016) Humane Handling Verification for Livestock and Good Commercial Practices for Poultry. Humane Handling of Livestock and GCP in Poultry, 11/29/2016. USDA Food Safety Inspection Service, Washington, DC.

FSIS (2017) Humane Methods of Livestock Slaughter Act. USDA Food Safety and Inspection Service, Washington, DC.

Grandin, T. (1980a) Livestock behavior as related to handling facilities design. *International Journal of the Study of Animal Problems* 1, 33–52.

Grandin, T. (1980b) Bruises and carcass damage. *International Journal for the Study of Animal Problems* 1, 121–137.

Grandin, T. (1992) Observations of cattle restraint devices for stunning and slaughtering. *Animal Welfare* 1(2), 85–91.

Grandin, T. (1994) Euthanasia and slaughter of livestock. *Journal of the American Veterinary Medical Association* 204, 1354–1360.

Grandin, T. (1997) Assessment of stress during handling and transport. *Journal of Animal Science* 75, 249–257.

Grandin, T. (1998a) Objective scoring of animal handling and stunning practices in slaughter plants. *Journal American Veterinary Medical Association* 212, 36–39.

Grandin, T. (1998b) The feasibility of vocalization scoring as an indicator of poor welfare during slaughter. *Applied Animal Behaviour Science* 56, 121–128.

Grandin, T. (2000) Effect of animal welfare audits of slaughter plants by a major fast food company on cattle handling and stunning practices. *Journal American Veterinary Medical Association* 216, 848–851.

Grandin, T. (2001) Cattle vocalizations are associated with handling and equipment problems in slaughter plants. *Applied Animal Behaviour Science* 71, 191–201.

Grandin, T. (2005) Maintenance of good animal welfare standards in beef slaughter plants by use of auditing programs. *Journal American Veterinary Medical Association* 226, 370–373.

Grandin, T. (2010) Auditing animal welfare in slaughter plants. *Meat Science* 86, 56–65. doi: 10.1016/j.meatsci.2010.04.022

Grandin, T. (2012) Developing measures to audit animal welfare of cattle and pigs at slaughter. *Animal Welfare* 21, 351–356.

Grandin, T. (2014) *Livestock Handling and Transport*, 4th edn. CAB International, Wallingford, UK.

Grandin, T. (2015) *Improving Animal Welfare: A Practical Approach*. CAB International, Wallingford, UK.

Grandin, T. (2017) On-farm conditions that compromise animal welfare that can be monitored at the slaughter plant. *Meat Science* 132, 52–58.

Gruber, S.L., Tatum, T.D., Engle, T.E., Chapman, P.L., Belk, K.E. and Smith, G.C. (2010) Relationships of behavioral and physiological symptoms of preslaughter stress on beef longissimus muscle tenderness. *Journal of Animal Science* 88, 114–1159.

Gygax, L., Neuffer, J., Kaufmann, C., Hauser, R. and Wechsler, B. (2006) Milk cortisol concentration in automatic milking systems compared to auto tandem milking parlors. *Journal of Dairy Science* 89, 3447–3454.

Hambrecht, E., Eissen, J.J., Nooijent, R.I., Ducro, B.J., Smits, C.H.M. *et al.* (2004) Preslaughter stress and muscle energy determine pork quality at two commercial slaughter plants. *Journal of Animal Science* 82, 1401–1409.

Hambrecht, E., Eissen, J.J., Newman, D.J., Smits, C.H.M., Verstegen, M.W.A. and den Hartog, L.A. (2005) Preslaughter handling effects on pork quality and glycolytic potential in two muscles differing in fiber type composition. *Journal of Animal Science* 83, 900–907.

Hargreaves, A.L. and Hutson, G.D. (1990) The stress response of sheep during routine handling procedures. *Applied Animal Behaviour Science* 26, 83–90.

Hayes, N., Schwartz, C., Phelps, K., Borowicz, P., Maddock-Carlin, K. and Maddock, R. (2015) The relationship between pre-harvest stress and the carcass characteristics of beef heifers that qualified for kosher designation. *Meat Science* 100, 134–138.

Hemsworth, P., Rice, M., Karlen, M., Calleja, L., Barnett, J. *et al.* (2011) Human–animal interactions at abattoirs: relationships between handling and animal stress in sheep and cattle. *Applied Animal Behaviour Science* 125(1-2), 24–33.

Herrick, R., Rogers, C., Jones, T., McEvers, T., Brown, T. *et al.* (2018) Association of liver abscesses presence and severity of trim loss, harvest yield, carcass grading performance, lung lesions, and value of fed Holsteins. *Journal of Animal Sciences* (Suppl. 3), 269.

HSA (2019) Humane Slaughter Association, Wheathampstead, UK. Available at: www.hsa.org.uk (accessed 13 January 2019).

ISO (2016) ISO/T5334700: 2016, Animal welfare management – General requirements and guidance for organizations in the food supply chair. International Organization for Standardization, Geneva, Switzerland.

Iulietto, M.F., Sechi, P., Gaudenzi, C.M., Grispoldi, L., Ceccarelli, M. *et al.* (2018) Noise assessment in slaughter houses by means of smartphone app. *Italian Journal of Food Safety* 2(7), 7053.

Jacobs, L., Delezic, E., Duchateau, L., Goethals, K. and Tuyttens, F. (2016) Impact of separate preslaughter stages on broiler chicken welfare. *Poultry Science* 96, 266–273.

Jacobs, L., Delezic, E., Duchateau, L., Goethals, K. and Tuyttens, F.A.M. (2017) Broiler chickens dead on arrival: associated risk factors and welfare indicators. *Poultry Science* 96, 259–265.

Kilgour, R. and de Langen, H. (1970) Stress in sheep from management practices. *Proceedings of the New Zealand Society of Animal Production* 30, 65–67.

King, D.A., Schuehle-Pfeiffer, C.E., Randel, R., Welsh, T.H., Oliphant, R.A. *et al.* (2006) Influence of animal temperament and stress responsiveness on the carcass quality and beef tenderness of feedlot cattle. *Meat Science* 74, 546–556.

Kittelsen, K.E., Granquist, E.G., Vasdel, G., Tolo, E. and More, R.O. (2015) Effects of catching and transportation versus pre-slaughter handling at the abattoir on the prevalence of wing fractures in broilers. *Animal Welfare* 24, 387–389.

Langkebel, N., Baumann, M.P., Feller, A., Sanguanklat, A. and Fries, R. (2015) Influence of two catching methods on the occurrence of lesions in broilers. *Poultry Science* 94, 1735–1741.

Lay, D.C. Jr, Friend, T.H., Randel, R.D., Bowers, C.C., Grissom, K.K. and Jenkins, O.C. (1992) Behavioral and physiological effects of freeze and hot-iron branding on crossbred cattle. *Journal of Animal Science* 70, 330–336.

Lay, D.C. Jr, Friend, T.H., Randel, R.D., Bowers, C.L., Grissom, K.K. *et al.* (1998) Effects of restricted nursing on physiological and behavioural reactions of Brahman calves to subsequent restraint and nursing. *Applied Animal Behaviour Science* 56, 109–119.

Lee, T., Reinhardt, C.D., Bartle, S.J., Schwandt, E.F. *et al.* (2018) An epidemiological investigation to determine the prevalence and clinical manifestations of slow moving finished cattle presented at slaughter facilities. *Translational Animal Science* 2, 241–253.

Losada-Espinoza, N., Villarrael, M., Chacon, G. and Gebresenbet, G. (2004) Scoring system for evaluating the stress to cattle in commercial loading and unloading. *Veterinary Record* 154, 818–821.

Losada-Espinosa, N., Villarrael, M., Maria, G.A. and Miranda de la Lama, G.C. (2017) Preslaughter cattle welfare indicators for use in commercial abattoirs with voluntary monitoring systems: a systematic review. *Meat Science* 138, 34–38.

Messori, S., Visser, E.K., Buonanno, M., Ferrari, P., Barnard, S., Borciani, M. and Ferri, N. (2016) A tool for the evaluation of slaughter horse welfare during unloading. *Animal Welfare* 25(1), 101–113. doi: 10.7120/09627286.25.1.101

Micera, E., Moramarco, A.M. and Zarrilli, A. (2012) Reduction of the olfactory cognitive ability in horses during preslaughter: stress-related hormones evaluation. *Meat Science* 90, 272–275.

Mitchell, G., Hattingh, J. and Ganhao, M. (1988) Stress in cattle assessed after handling, after transport, and after slaughter. *Veterinary Record* 123, 201–205.

Mounier, L., Dubroeuck, H., Andanson, S. and Veissier, L. (2006) Variations in meat pH of beef bulls in relation to conditions of transfer to slaughter and previous history of the animals. *Journal of Animal Science* 84, 1567–1576.

Munoz, C., Campbell, A., Hemsworth, P.H., and Doyle, R. (2018) Animal based measures to assess the welfare of extensively managed ewes. *Animals* 8(1), 2. doi.org/10.3390/ani801002

NAMI (2019) *NAMI Recommended Animal Handling Guidelines and Audit Guide: A Systematic Approach to Animal Welfare*. North American Meat Institute, Washington, DC.

OIE (2018) Slaughter of animals. Chapter 7.5 in: *Terrestrial Animal Health Code*. World Organisation for Animal Health, Paris.

Pearson, A.J., Kilgour, R., de Langen, H. and Payne, E. (1977) Hormonal responses of lambs to trucking and handling. *Proceedings of the New Zealand Society of Animal Production* 37, 243–249.

Pinellos (2016) European Council Regulation (EC) 1099/2009 on the protection of animals at the time of killing, In: Velarde, A. and Raj, M. (eds) *Animal Welfare at Slaughter*. 5M Publishing, Sheffield, UK, pp. 219–232.

Probst, J.K., Spengler, N.A., Hillman, E., Kreuzer, M., Koch-Mathis, M. *et al.* (2015) Relationship between stress-related exsanguination blood variable, vocalization and stressors imposed on cattle between lairage and stunning box under conventional abattoir conditions. *Livestock Science* 164, 154–158.

Rivalland, E.T.A., Clarke, I.J., Turner, A.I., Pompolo, S. and Tilbrook, A.J. (2007) Isolation and restraint stress results in differential activation of corticotrophin-releasing hormone and arginine vasopressin neurons in sheep. *Neuroscience* 145, 1048–1058.

Schaeperkoetter, M.A., Grandin, T. and Edwards-Callaway, L.E. (2019) PSIII-16 Evaluating the impact of group stunning on physiological parameters of pigs in a small abattoir. *Journal of Animal Science* 97 (Suppl. 3), 185.

Simon, G.E., Hoar, B.R. and Tucker, C.B. (2016) Assessing cow–calf welfare. Part 2. Risk factors for beef cow health and behavior and stockperson handling. *Journal of Animal Science* 94, 3488–3500.

Tennessen, T., Price, M.A. and Berg, R.T. (1984) Comparative responses of bulls and steers to transportation. *Canadian Journal of Animal Science* 64, 333–338.

Tume, R.K. and Shaw, F.D. (1992) Beta-endorphin and cortisol concentrations in plasma of blood samples collected during exsanguination of cattle. *Meat Science* 31, 211–217.

Tuyttens, F. (2017) Broiler chicken welfare before slaughter. Monitoring protocol and integration tool now available. Research Institute for Agriculture, Fisheries and Food (ILVO), Belgium. Available at: https://www.ilvo.vlaanderen.be/language/en-US/EN/Press-and-Media/Newsletter/Survey/articleType/ArticleView/articleId/4648/Broiler-chicken-welfare-before-slaughter-Monitoring-protocol-and-online-integration-tool-now-available.aspx#.XpngUOQ1vnO (accessed 22 February 2020).

Tuyttens, F., Jacobs, L., Ampe, B., Goethals, K., Duchateau, L. and Delezic, E. (2018) Development of a user friendly protocol and web tool for monitoring and benchmarking broiler welfare during preslaughter. *15th European Poultry Conference*, Dubrovnik, Croatia.

Van der Wal, P.G. (1978) Chemical and physiological aspects of pig stunning in relation to meat quality: a review. *Meat Science* 2, 19–30.

Vieville-Thomas, C. and Signoret, J.P. (1992) Pheromonal transmission of aversive experiences in domestic pigs. *Journal of Chemical Ecology* 18, 1551–1557.

Warner, R.D., Ferguson, D.M., Cottrell, J.J. and Knee, B.W. (2007) Acute stress induced by preslaughter use of electric prodders causes tougher meat. *Australia Journal of Experimental Agriculture* 47, 782–788.

Warrington, R. (1974) Electrical stunning: a review of the literature. *The Veterinary Bulletin* 44, 617–635.

Warriss, P.D., Brown, S., Adams, S.J.M. and Corlett, I.K. (1994) Relationship between subjective and objective assessments of stress at slaughter and meat quality in pigs. *Meat Science* 38, 329–340.

Weeks, C.A., Tuyttens, F.A.M. and Grandin, T. (2019) Poultry handling and transport, In: Grandin, T. (ed.) *Livestock Handling and Transport*, 5th Edition, OAB International, Wallingford, Oxfordshire, UK, pp. 404–426.

Welfare Quality (2009) Assessment Protocols. Available at: www.welfarequality.net (accessed 25 June 2018).

Wigham, E.E., Butterworth, A. and Wotton, S. (2018) Assessing welfare at slaughter – why is it important and what challenges are faced? *Meat Science* 145, 171–177.

Woiwode, R., Patterson, J. and Grandin, T. (2016) Compliance of large feedyards in the northern high plains with Beef Quality Assurance Feedyard Assessment. *Professional Animal Scientist* 32, 750–757.

Zavy, M.T., Juniewicz, P.E., Phillips, W.A. and von Tungeln, D.L. (1992) Effect of initial restraint, weaning, and transport stress on baseline and ACTH stimulated cortisol responses on beef calves of different genotypes. *American Journal of Veterinary Research* 53, 551–557.

Zimmerman, M., Grigioni, G., Taddeo, H. and Domingo, E. (2012) Physiological stress responses and meat quality traits of kids subjected to different pre-slaughter stressors. *Small Ruminant Research* 100, 137–142.

13 Determining Unconsciousness and Insensibility in Commercial Abattoirs

TEMPLE GRANDIN*

Department of Animal Science, Colorado State University, USA

Summary

US and EU legislation require that an animal must be rendered insensible to pain before invasive dressing procedures start. If an animal shows any of the following clinical signs, it must be immediately re-stunned: (i) righting reflex or retains the ability to stand; (ii) species-specific vocalization; (iii) rhythmic breathing; (iv) menace/threat reflex or spontaneous (natural) blinking; (v) eyelash reflex; or (vi) corneal reflex (nictitating reflex in poultry). There is a transition zone between definitely conscious and definitely unconscious and brain dead. If an animal is re-stunned when it is in the transition zone, it is probably still insensible to pain. All of the above signs must be absent before invasive dressing procedures, such as skinning, scalding or dismemberment, are started.

Learning Objectives

- Determine if an animal is starting to return to sensibility.
- Determine when it is brain dead and invasive dressing procedures can be started.
- Provide easy-to-use guidance for people performing slaughter.

Introduction

An animal is unconscious if it is unable to respond to normal stimuli, including pain (von Hollenbon, 2010; AVMA, 2016). The definition used by the European Union's Food Safety Authority (EFSA) states (EFSA, 2013a–d):

> Unconsciousness is a state of unawareness (loss of consciousness) in which there is temporary

or permanent damage to brain function and the individual is unable to perceive external stimuli (which is referred to as insensibility) and control its voluntary mobility and, therefore, respond to normal stimuli including pain.

Council Regulation (EC) 1099/2009 defines sensibility as the ability of the animal to feel pain (EFSA, 2013a–d). The American Veterinary Medical Association defines unconsciousness as loss of awareness that occurs when the brain loses the ability to integrate information (AVMA, 2019).

In the USA, according to the Humane Methods of Slaughter Act, 'all animals must be rendered insensible to pain by a single blow or gunshot or an electrical, chemical, or other means that is rapid and effective'. In both Europe and the USA the regulations clearly state that after stunning the animal must not experience pain.

This has been interpreted by the Food Safety Inspection Service (FSIS) of the US Department of Agriculture (USDA) that every application of a stunner must be effective. This is extremely difficult for a commercial abattoir to achieve. Enforcement has been increased due to recent pressure from non-governmental animal activist groups. This wording originated in both the 1958 and 1978 Humane Slaughter Acts. The same statute is still being used today. The US laws do not cover poultry. In many other countries and in Europe, humane slaughter laws include poultry.

The European wording is less strict and requires appropriate measures to be taken immediately if an animal is not properly stunned. Council Regulation (EC) 1099/2009 also states that:

> Electrical stimulation shall only be performed once the unconsciousness of the animal has been verified.

---

* Email: cheryl.miller@colostate.edu

Further dressing or scalding shall only be performed once the absence of signs of life of the animal has been verified.

The EU regulations state that 'loss of consciousness and sensibility shall be maintained until the death of the animal'.

Dr E.M. Terlouw, author of Chapter 14 in this volume, published a paper which reviewed many research studies on assessing consciousness and unconsciousness (Terlouw *et al.*, 2016). Some of the studies were done with EEG to record electrical activity from the brain. When new stunning methods are evaluated, research methods in the laboratory should use the most sensitive methods for assessing unconsciousness. The studies should use methods such as electroencephalography (EEG) or electrocochleography (ECoG) (Gevelmeyer *et al.*, 2016). Terlouw *et al.* (2016) concluded that there should be a differentiation between when an animal is fully conscious and when it is unconscious and is brain dead.

How EEGs Work

There are various methods for evaluating EEG tracings. A normal EEG in a conscious animal will have low-amplitude high-speed alpha waves (8–23 Hz). When the animal becomes unconscious, the waves change to high-amplitude slow delta waves (0.5–4 Hz) (Fig. 13.1). Brain death occurs when the EEG flatlines. Methods for evaluating EEG are described in Benson *et al.* (2012), Gibson *et al.* (2019), March *et al.* (2005), Vlisides and Mashour (2017) and Hagihira (2017). Either visual appraisal or specialized computer programs are used to determine when the alpha waves transition to delta waves. For EEG to be useful, the animal has to stay still to prevent movement artifact. Gibson *et al.* (2019)

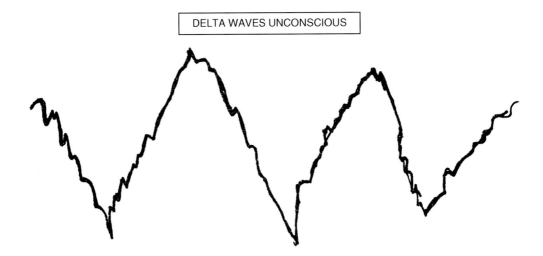

ALPHA WAVES AWAKE

DELTA WAVES UNCONSCIOUS

Fig. 13.1. Low-amplitude fast alpha waves in an awake conscious animal. High-amplitude slow delta waves under anaesthesia. These two waveforms are really distinct. The transition zone where the waves change from alpha to delta is not distinct.

T. Grandin

classified EEG tracings as: (i) movement artifact; (ii) normal; (iii) transitional between consciousness to unconsciousness; (iv) high-amplitude low-frequency (delta) (unconscious) and (v) isoelectric – flatline brain dead. The new research still shows an indistinct transition zone between consciousness and unconsciousness.

Transition Zone Between Consciousness and Unconsciousness

There is a transition zone between the state of being fully conscious and brain death (AVMA, 2016; Terlouw et al., 2016). VerHoeven et al. (2014) described the transition zone in a slightly different way: 'The exact moment when unconsciousness sets in based on EEG is difficult to determine as the change is often gradual.' A new document published by the AVMA (2019) stated that EEG data cannot provide a definite answer on the onset of unconsciousness. It occurs somewhere between behavioural unresponsiveness and flat (brain dead) EEG. Another way of explaining this is that it occurs at some point during the conversion of alpha waves to delta waves. When the animal is in the transition zone, it is probably insensible to pain. Regenstein (2017) used different words to describe the same concept. He stated there

should be a differentiation between 'loss of the ability to feel pain' and 'loss of all reflexes in the head'. USDA defines unconsciousness as 'not awake or aware, not able to respond to stimuli or the environment' (FSIS, 2018). People often ask if unconscious and insensible are the same. The FSIS PHV refresher training course on consciousness and stunning (FSIS, 2018) states that unconscious = insensible. They are the same.

The US law states that stunning should always render the animal insensible to pain with a single shot. It is nearly impossible for commercial abattoirs to eliminate 100% of every brainstem reflex with a single application of the stunner. From the Terlouw et al. (2016) paper the US industry learned that if a second stunner application was applied when an animal was in the transition zone, they would probably still be in compliance, because the animal would most likely still be insensible to pain. This would be true if the only signs that were present were the corneal reflex, eyelash reflex to touch or rhythmic breathing.

The North American Meat Institute (NAMI) in Washington, DC published a chart in its voluntary guidelines for assessing unconsciousness during (NAMI, 2019) adapted here in Table 13.1 and based on Terlouw et al. (2016) and other studies. For poultry, auditors from meat-buying customers often

Table 13.1. Assessing unconsciousness in livestock during slaughter (adapted from NAMI, 2017).

Possible state	Signs	Assessment	Action
Definitely unconscious and brain dead: ALL of the following signs are ABSENT	Menace reflex that occurs when a hand is waved in front of the eye without touch Eyelash reflex in response to touch Corneal reflex[a] Rhythmic breathing where the ribs move in and out at least twice	Unconscious	No action needed
Unconscious but beginning transition back to consciousness: ONE OR MORE of the following signs are PRESENT	Eyelash reflex in response to touch Rhythmic breathing where the ribs move in and out at least twice Corneal reflex[a]	Unconscious	Re-stun immediately
Definitely conscious: ANY of the following signs are PRESENT	No loss of posture (LOP) / animal standing Righting reflex on the rail[b] Spontaneous, unprovoked blinking Menace reflex that occurs when a hand is waved in front of the eye without touching Eye pursuit of a moving object	Conscious	Re-stun immediately

[a]For cattle, a finger may be used to test the corneal reflex. Because pigs and sheep have small eyes, a small blunt object like a pencil eraser or something similar may be used to touch the surface of the eyeball
[b]See Figs 13.2 and 13.3

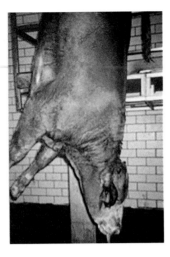

Fig. 13.2. A properly stunned bovine hanging on the rail has a straight back and a limp floppy head. Cattle and pigs will hang straight as shown in this photo. Some types of sheep will not hang straight due to strong suspensory ligament in the back of the head. In all species, the head and neck should be loose and floppy. (Photo courtesy of Temple Grandin.)

Fig. 13.3. Fully conscious bovine hung on the rail with an arched back righting reflex. Its back is arched and it is raising its head because it is fully conscious. The person doing the shackling failed to re-stun it before hoisting. This is a serious violation of animal welfare laws. It is important for people stunning and bleeding livestock to know what a righting reflex on the rail looks like. A single, properly applied stunning method will abolish the arched back righting reflex. This applies to all stunning methods. (Photo courtesy of Temple Grandin.)

audit suppliers and they will hold poultry companies to the same standards as plants slaughtering livestock. This is a situation where the use of private standards by commercial customers are improving welfare issues not covered by legislation.

Agreement Between USDA, EFSA, AVMA and NAMI on Consciousness Indicators for Livestock

There are some slight differences between researchers on the exact indicators that are in the transition zone between being conscious, and unconscious and brain dead. A commercial slaughter plant is not a research laboratory with an EEG. Therefore, indicators used under commercial conditions *must* be really conservative. The main area of possible disagreement is with spontaneous unprovoked (natural) blinking and the menace/threat reflex. The researchers' results are mixed. It is the author's opinion that to ensure that animals are unconscious under commercial conditions, these two indicators have been placed in the 'definitely conscious' category. When all types of stunning are done correctly, it is easy to completely abolish spontaneous blinking and the menace/threat reflex (Grandin, 2001, 2002). A single application of proper captive bolt or gunshot will eliminate the corneal reflex (Grandin, 2002; AVMA, 2016; Kamenik *et al.*, 2019). The corneal reflex and pupillary reflex to light may remain in a few properly stunned unconscious pigs that have been stunned with electricity (Vogel *et al.*, 2010). Corneal reflex, palpebral reflex and pupillary response to light may occur in unconscious animals after religious slaughter (Verhouven *et al.*, 2014).

The corneal reflex can occur in unconscious humans or animals (Vogel *et al.*, 2010). Vogel *et al.* (2010) reported that, with electrical stunning, it was not possible to eliminate all the brainstem reflexes in every single pig, prior to bleeding. Since the process of returning to consciousness is starting, the animal must be immediately re-stunned to prevent return to consciousness. Re-stunning with a captive bolt should be done immediately.

All reflexes in the eyes and head must be absent before carcass processing or invasive dressing procedures

To comply with EU (EFSA, 2004), OIE (2019), USDA (FSIS, 2017), AVMA (2016, 2019) and

NAMI (2017) regulations and guidelines, *all* reflexes in the head must be absent. To say it simply: *the head must be dead* before carcass processing begins. Invasive dressing procedures (carcass processing) include but are not limited to scalding, skinning, feather removal, limb removal, head removal and other procedures. This applies to all forms of slaughter, both stunning and religious slaughter without stunning. Bleeding the animal ensures brain death and it will eliminate eye and brainstem reflexes. For conventional slaughter with stunning, the EU requires re-stunning if the animal shows any of the signs listed below (EFSA, 2013a–d). The most common re-stunning method after all types of stunning is captive bolt. For both conventional and religious slaughter, without stunning, all of the reflexes below must be absent before invasive carcass processing.

- Menace/threat reflex – eye blinks when hand is waved in front of it. No touching. To learn what an eye blink looks like, observe live animals in the lairage (Fig. 13.4). During religious slaughter of cattle, this reflex may be difficult to interpret due to blood in the eye (see Chapter 14). This is especially a problem when the animal is inverted on to its back. Natural spontaneous blinking in poultry is an easy-to-use measure in a commercial slaughter plant. It is an indicator of sensibility in poultry (Girasole *et al.*, 2016).
- Corneal reflex to touch.
- Floppy-head – loss of neck tension in poultry hanging inverted on the shackle lines. Easy-to-use measure in a commercial poultry plant.
- Response to nose prick, or comb pinch in poultry.

- Rhythmic breathing – sides of the body move in and out. Do not confuse with gasping like a fish out of water.
- Failure to collapse and lose posture (ability to stand). Note that some papers use the term loss of balance instead of loss of posture (LOP). There are situations where the animal will fall and then get back up. This may be referred to as loss of balance. The animal is definitely unconscious when it permanently loses the ability to stand. This may also be called durable loss of posture, or loss of righting reflex (LORR) (AVMA, 2019).
- Palpebral (eyelash) reflex (nictitating membrane reflex in poultry).
- Species-specific vocalization absent.
- Nystagmus vibrating eye – not to be confused with true blinking (sign of a shallow stun with captive bolt) (Verhoeven *et al.*, 2014). Acceptable in electrically stunned animals.

Boxes 13.1, 13.2 and 13.3 contain signs that can be used easily in a commercial abattoir.

Ignore kicking: look at the head

In cattle, pigs, sheep and other mammals: *ignore kicking*. Kicking reflexes can occur in animals after the head is removed or the spinal cord has been severed (Terlouw *et al.*, 2015). The circuits that enable animals to walk are located in the middle of the spine (Grillner, 2011; Bouvier *et al.*, 2015; Martin *et al.*, 2018). Terlouw *et al.* (2015) discovered that kicking still occurs after the spinal cord is severed at the base of the skull. Foreleg movement

Fig. 13.4. People slaughtering animals must learn what spontaneous natural blinking and a response to the menace/threat reflex looks like. The best way to learn is to go into the lairage and look at live animals blinking. The menace reflex test is conducted by waving a hand in front of the eye without touching. It should not be confused with nystagmus (vibrating eye). (Photo courtesy of Temple Grandin.)

Box 13.1. Signs of insensibility (unconsciousness) in animals shot with properly applied captive bolt or gunshot that causes physical brain concussion (Grandin, 2015)

All four signs MUST BE ABSENT before invasive dressing procedures are started.

Rhythmic breathing

Occurs if ribs move in and out at least twice. Do not confuse with gasping (like a fish out of water), which may occur in properly stunned animals.

Natural blinking

Eye makes a fully open-and-close cycle like live animals in the lairage. Test by waving a hand in front of the eye (menace reflex). Do not touch the eyes. Nystagmus (vibrating eye) or weak corneal reflex may be present in unconscious animals. These reflexes must be absent before invasive dressing procedures are started.

Vocalization

Bellow, moo, squeal. It is permissible to have a small grunt due to chest compression when the animal falls.

Righting reflex (LOP or LORR)

When hung on the rail this can be observed as an arching of the back and sustained backward lifting of the head (Fig. 13.3). This should not be confused with a momentary flop of the head, which occurs when the back legs exhibit reflexive kicking. If the animal is on the floor, complete loss of posture (LOP) and loss of the ability to raise its head or stand.

Box 13.2. Signs of insensibility (unconsciousness) in animals stunned with electricity, CO_2 or other gases and LAPS, for methods that do not cause physical brain concussion (Grandin, 2015, updated)

All four signs MUST BE ABSENT before invasive dressing procedures are started.

Rhythmic breathing

Occurs if ribs move in and out at least twice. Do not confuse with gasping (like a fish out of water), which may occur in properly stunned animals.

Natural blinking

Eye makes a fully open-and-close cycle like live animals in the lairage. Test by waving a hand in front of the eye (menace reflex). Do not touch the eyes. Nystagmus (vibrating eye) or weak corneal reflex may be present in properly stunned animals. These reflexes must be absent before invasive dressing procedures are started.

Vocalization

Bellow, moo, squeal. It is permissible to have a small grunt due to chest compression when the animal falls.

Righting reflex (LOP or LORR)

When hung on the rail this can be observed as an arching of the back and sustained backward lifting of the head (Fig. 13.3). This should not be confused with a momentary flop of the head, which occurs when the back legs exhibit reflexive kicking. If the animal is on the floor, complete loss of posture (LOP) and loss of the ability to raise its head or stand.

Box 13.3. Signs of insensibility (unconsciousness) in properly stunned chickens (Grandin, 2015, updated)

- No nictitating membrane reflex – inner third eyelid closes in response to touching the edge of the outer eyelid.
- No spontaneous (natural) eye blinking that looks like eye blinks in live poultry in the lairage (easy to use in a commercial plant).
- Loss of muscle tone in jaw and neck (floppy) (easy to use in a commercial plant).
- No rhythmic breathing – some gasping like a fish out of water is permissible.
- No response to comb pinch.
- Electrical stunning: constant rapid tremors with wings held close to the body (HSA, 2016).

This is for electrical stunning only. When the chicken starts to recover, the wings will extend into extended flapping.

Recommendations based on EEG (brainwave) studies that were used to validate reflexes that could be observed at slaughter with signs of unconsciousness in chickens (Erasmus et al., 2010; Johnson, 2014; Sandercock et al., 2014; Poultry Industry Council, 2016; Martin et al., 2019). Girasole et al. (2016) is an excellent review of the relationship between electrical stunning methods and return to sensibility.

T. Grandin

may sometimes occur during knife insertion for bleeding. This is a reflex (Terlouw *et al.*, 2015).

Vogel *et al.* (2010) explained that the corneal reflex is the involuntary eyelid-closure response to protect the eyes from injury. There are two cranial nerves involved, one sensory and one motor, which converge in the brainstem. The corneal reflex occurs when a signal is sent from the brainstem to the eyelids to trigger closure. The corneal reflex only indicates brainstem activity, which is not indicative of consciousness by the stunned animal. Electrically (Vogel *et al.*, 2010) or gas-stunned animals with a weak corneal reflex triggered by the tip of a pen and no other signs of return to sensibility would be in a state similar to general anaesthesia. To prevent return to consciousness, they should be immediately re-stunned. If the animal has spontaneous, natural blinking that occurs when the eye is not touched, the animal is either definitely sensible (conscious) or close to regaining consciousness and must be re-stunned (Verhoeven *et al.*, 2014, 2015). People who are assessing insensibility should look at live animals in the lairage so that they will know what spontaneous blinking looks like (Fig. 13.4). For animals stunned with either gunshot or penetrating or non-penetrating captive bolt, the corneal reflex and all eye movements must be absent (Gregory, 2008; AVMA, 2016). The eyes should open into a wide, blank stare and not be rotated (Gregory, 2008). Do *not* use a finger or other thick blunt object to poke the eyes of animals with small eyes, such as pigs and sheep, when testing small animals for eye reflexes. This causes confusing signs that are difficult to interpret (Grandin, 2001). A finger may be used on animals with large eyes, such as cattle. Multiple indicators of return to consciousness must all be absent (Verhoeven *et al.*, 2015). Never rely on a single indicator.

The signs of insensibility in Boxes 13.1, 13.2 and 13.3 can be used when assessing stunning efficacy in cattle, pigs, sheep and other mammals (HSA, 2016a, 2016b, 2018). Additional information can be found in Gregory (2008) and Verhoeven *et al.* (2015).

Consciousness in the Fetus

There is concern that fetuses in livestock may suffer during slaughter. The EFSA Panel on Animal Health and Welfare (EFSA, 2017) reported that 3% of dairy cows, 1.5% of beef cows, 0.5% of sows, 0.8% of sheep and 0.2% of goats are in the final third of pregnancy when they arrive at the slaughterhouse. When fetal blood is collected, the recommended procedure is to leave the fetus inside the uterus until 15–20 min after the maternal neck cut (OIE, 2019). To reduce the possibility of the fetus becoming conscious, it should not be allowed to breathe air (Mellor and Gregory, 2003). A late-stage fetus that shows signs of life, or if there is any doubt about consciousness, requires stunning with a captive bolt (OIE, 2019). There is an extensive review of the literature in EFSA (2017).

Locations on the Processing Line to Evaluate Unconsciousness

The EU requires that the stunner operator, the shackler and the bleeder must have certificates to show that they have been trained to determine the signs that an animal is unconscious or starting to return to consciousness. For all stunning methods, the animal must be checked in three locations: (i) after release from the stun box, restrainer or CO_2 machine; (ii) at bleeding; and (iii) before invasive dressing procedures (carcass processing) starts. The checks should be done by two different people, a line slaughter employee and the animal welfare officer (EFSA, 2013). For religious slaughter without stunning, the animal should be checked before release from the restraint box and before invasive dressing procedures start.

Conclusions

When stunning is done correctly, all the indicators of return to consciousness will be absent. To maintain high standards, stunning equipment must be well maintained and applied by trained people. Poor maintenance of stunning equipment is a common cause of failure. The management of the abattoir must have a commitment to maintaining high standards.

References

AVMA (2016) *AVMA guidelines for the Humane Slaughter of Animals*, 2016 edn. American Veterinary Medical Association, Schaumburg, Illinois.

AVMA (2019) *AVMA Guidelines for the Depopulation of Animals*, 2019 edn. American Veterinary Medical Association, Schaumburg, Illinois.

Benson, E.R., Alphia, R.L., Ranin, M.K., Caputo, M.P. and Johnson, A.L. (2012) Electroencephalographic based methodology for determining unconscious during depopulation. *Avian Diseases* 56, 884–890.

Bouvier, J., Caggiano, V., Leiras, R., Caldera, V., Bellardita, C. *et al.* (2015) Descending command neurons in the brainstem half locomotion. *Cell* 163, 1191–1203.

Erasmus, M.A., Turner, P.V. and Widowski, T.M. (2010) Measures of insensibility used to determine effective stunning and killing of poultry. *Journal of Applied Poultry Research* 19, 288–298.

EFSA (2004) Welfare aspects of animal stunning and killing methods. Scientific report of the Scientific Panel for Animal Health and Welfare on a request from the Commission. Question. Adopted on 15 June 2004. European Food Safety Authority, Brussels.

EFSA (2013a) Scientific opinion on monitoring procedures at slaughterhouses for bovines. *EFSA Journal* 11(12) 3460.

EFSA (2013b) Scientific opinion on monitoring slaughterhouses for poultry. *EFSA Journal* 11(12), 3521.

EFSA (2013c) Scientific opinion on monitoring procedures at slaughterhouses for sheep and goats. *EFSA Journal* 11(12), 3522.

EFSA (2013d) Scientific opinion on monitoring procedures at slaughterhouses for pigs. *EFSA Journal* 11(12), 3523.

EFSA (2017) Animal welfare aspects in respect of the slaughter or killing of pregnant livestock (cattle, pigs, sheep, goats, horses). *EFSA Journal* 15(5), 4782. doi: 10.2903/j.efsa.2017.4782

FSIS (2017) *Humane Methods of Livestock Slaughter Act*. Food Safety and Inspection Service, US Department of Agriculture, Washington, DC.

FSIS (2018) PHV Refresher Training: Consciousness and Stunning. USDA Food Safety and Inspection Service. Available at: www.fsis.usda.gov (accessed 20 January 2020).

Gevelmeyer, A., Candian, D. and Berthe, F.G. (2016) Future trends to improve animal welfare at slaughter. In: Velarde, A., Raj, J. and Manteca, X. (eds) *Animal Welfare at Slaughter*. 5M Publishing, Sheffield, UK, pp. 233–250.

Gibson, T.J., Olivera, S.E.O, Dalla Costa, F.A. and Gregory, N.G. (2019) Electrocochleographic assessment of pneumatically powered captive bolt stunning of bulls. *Meat Science* 151, 54–59.

Girasole, M., Marrone, R., Anatasio, A., Chianese, A., Mercogliano, R. and Cortesi, L. (2016) Effect of electrical water bath stunning on physical reflexes of broilers: evaluation of stunning efficacy under field conditions. *Poultry Science* 95, 1205–1210.

Grandin, T. (2001) Solving return to sensibility problems after electrical stunning in commercial pork slaughter plants. *Journal of the American Veterinary Medical Association* 219, 608–611.

Grandin, T. (2002) Return to sensibility problems after penetrating captive bolt stunning of cattle in commercial beef slaughter plants. *Journal of the American Veterinary Medical Association* 221, 1258–1261.

Grandin, T. (2015) *Improving Animal Welfare: A Practical Approach*, 2nd edn. CAB International, Wallingford, UK.

Gregory, N.G. (2008) Animal welfare at markets and during transport and slaughter. *Meat Science* 80, 2–11.

Grillner, T. (2011) Human locomotor circuits conform. *Science* 334, 912–913.

Hagihira, S. (2017) Brain mechanisms during the course of anesthesia: what we know from EEG changes during induction and recovery. *Frontiers in Systems Neuroscience* 11, 39. doi: 10.3389/fnsys.2017.00039

HSA (2016a) Electrical stunning of red meat animals. Humane Slaughter Association, Wheathampstead, UK. Available at www.hsa.org.uk (accessed 19 February 2020).

HSA (2016b) Practical slaughter of poultry – a guide for small producers. Humane Slaughter Association, Wheathampstead, UK. Available at www.hsa.org.uk (accessed 19 February 2020).

HSA (2016c) Captive bolt stunning of livestock. Humane Slaughter Association, Wheathampstead, UK. Available at www.hsa.org.uk (accessed 30 December 2017).

Johnson, C.L. (2014) A review of bird welfare during controlled atmospheric and electrical water bottle stunning. *Journal American Veterinary Medical Association* 245, 60–68.

Kamenik, J., Paral, V., Pyszko, M. and Voslarova, E. (2019) Cattle stunning with captive bolt device: a review. *Animal Science Journal* 90(3), 307–316. doi: 10.1111/asj.13168

March, P.A. and Muir, W.W. (2005) Bispectral analysis of the electroencephalogram: a review of its development use in anesthesia. *Veterinary Anesthesia and Analgesia* 32, 241–255.

Martin, J.E., Sandilands, V., Sparrey, J., Baker, L., Dixon, L.M. and McKeegan, D.E.F. (2019) Welfare assessment of novel on-farm killing methods for poultry. *PLOS ONE* 14(2), e0212872. doi: 10.1371/journal.pone.0212871

Martin, M.S., Kline, H.C., Wagner, D.R., Alexander, L.R., Edwards-Calloway, L.N. and Grandin, T. (2018) Evaluation of different captive bolt lengths and breed influence upon post-stun hind limb and forelimb activity in fed cattle at a commercial slaughter facility. *Meat Science* 141, 159–164.

Mellor, D.J. and Gregory, N.G. (2003) Responsiveness, behavioral arousal, and awareness in fetal newborn lambs: experimental, practical, and therapeutic implications. *New Zealand Veterinary Journal* 51, 2–13.

NAMI (2019) NAMI Recommended Animal Handling Guidelines and Audit Guide: A Systematic Approach to Animal Welfare. North American Meat Institute, Washington, DC.

OIE (2019) Chapter 7.5 Slaughter of animals, In: *Terrestrial Animal Health Code*. World Organisation for Animal Health, Paris.

Pilge, S., Kreuzer, M., Karatchiviev, V., Kochs, E.F., Malcharck, M., and Schneider, G. (2015) Differences in state entropy and bispectral index during analysis of identical electroencephalogram signals. *European Journal of Anesthesiology* 32, 354–365.

Poultry Industry Council (2016) *Practical Guide for On-Farm Euthanasia of Poultry*, 2nd edn. Poultry Industry Council, Ontario, Canada.

Regenstein, J.M. (2017) Religious slaughter of animals: international efforts to meet this need responsibly. In: *Global Food Security and Wellness*. Springer, New York, pp. 339–355.

Sandercock, D.A., Auckburally, A., Flaherty, D., Sandilands, V. and McKeegan, D.E.F. (2014) Avian reflex and electroencephalographic responses in different states of consciousness. *Physiology and Behavior* 138, 252–259.

Terlouw, E.M., Bourquet, C., Deiss, V. and Mallet, C. (2015) Origin of movements following stunning and during bleeding in cattle. *Meat Science* 110, 135–144.

Terlouw, E.M.C., Bourguet, C. and Deiss, V. (2016) Consciousness, unconsciousness and death in the context of slaughter, Part 2. Evaluation of methods. *Meat Science* 118, 14–156.

Verhoeven, M.T.W., Gerritzen, M.A., Hellebrewders, L.J. and Kemp, B. (2014) Indicators used in livestock to assess unconsciousness after stunning: a review. *Animal* 9, 320–330.

Verhoeven, M.T.W., Gerritzen, M.A., Kiviers-Ooodt, M., Hellebrekers, L.J. and Kemp, B. (2015) Validation of behavioral indicators used to assess unconsciousness. *Research in Veterinary Science* 101, 1440153.

Vlisides, P.E. and Mashour, G.A. (2017) Clinical application of raw and processed EEG. In: Koht, A., Sloan, T.B. and Toleikis, J.R. (eds) *Monitoring the Nervous System for Anesthesiologists and Other Health Care Professionals* (2nd edn). Springer International, pp. 193 ff. doi.10.1007/978-3-319-46542-5_11

Vogel, K.D., Badtram, G., Claus, J.R., Grandin, T., Turpin, S. *et al.* (2010) Head only electric stunning is an effective alternative to head only electric stunning. *Journal of Animal Science* 89, 1412–1418.

von Holleben, M., von Wenzlawowicz, N., Gregory, H., Anil, A., Velarde, P. *et al.* (2010) Report on good and adverse practices – Animal welfare concerns in relation to slaughter practices from the viewpoint of veterinary sciences. Available at: http://www.dialrel.eu/images/veterinary-concerns.pdf (accessed 18 January 2020).

14 The Physiology of the Brain and Determining Insensibility and Unconsciousness

E.M. CLAUDIA TERLOUW*

Clermont Auvergne University, INRAE, VetAgro Sup, UMR Herbivores, France

Summary

In many countries, slaughter mostly involves two interventions: the animal is stunned to induce a loss of consciousness and then bled to induce death. In the context of religious slaughter (halal and shechita), animals may not be stunned before bleeding. In this case, the loss of blood first induces a loss of consciousness and then death. In certain cases of halal slaughter, the animal is stunned before or just after religious throat cutting to accelerate loss of consciousness.

Scientific studies show that mammals and birds are able to experience positive and negative emotions. The induction of unconsciousness before bleeding ensures that the animal does not experience pain, fear or other negative emotions during the slaughter process. The stunned, unconscious animal is insensitive to stimulations coming from its body or the environment: the brain is no longer capable of processing sensory information.

Animals showing any of the indicators of consciousness, of return to consciousness or risk of return to consciousness must be immediately re-stunned. The indicators of a conscious animal are: standing posture; head righting/righting reflex; species-specific vocalization; and response to menace/threat test. Indicators of risk of return to consciousness are: eye tracking; repeated spontaneous blinking; eyeball rotation or nystagmus; incomplete righting reflex; corneal reflex; or rhythmic breathing. Indicators of unconsciousness or death are: permanent loss of standing posture; absence of corneal reflex; absence of rhythmic breathing.

Learning Objectives

- Understand major parts of the brain associated with consciousness.
- Learn basic principles of stunning.
- Determine unconsciousness and death.
- Learn differences between animal species.
- Understand loss of consciousness during slaughter without stunning.

The Central Role of the Brain

Before describing how stunning or direct bleeding induces unconsciousness, the major parts of the brain and their relationship with normal, conscious functioning are presented.

Life consists of making of decisions, expressed in behaviour. An animal decides whether it should rest, care, eat, drink, look for a partner or for shelter, whether the ongoing behaviour should continue or be interrupted. The brain is the decision-making organ and it does so by combining all the information it has collected through different modalities. Various senses – hearing, seeing, smelling – allow the collection of information relating to the environment. Other sensors allow the collection of information on body condition. Oxygen and carbon dioxide sensors, baroreceptors and lung stretch receptors inform the brain in real time about the haemodynamic state of the body, allowing constant adjustments. Specialized sensory neurons give information on mechanical pressure and nociceptors on the presence of noxious stimuli on the body.

---

* Email: claudia.terlouw@inrae.fr

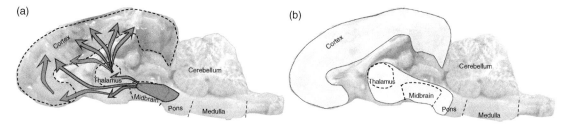

Fig. 14.1. Sagittal cut of a sheep brain (fresh). (a) The ascending reticular activating system (dark grey area and arrows) consists of three major pathways. One passes via the thalamus located just above the brainstem which in turn projects massively on the cortex (mammals) or pallium (birds) (Northcutt, 1984; Parvizi and Damasio, 2001). Another runs ventrally via the hypothalamus and basal forebrain, which in turn projects onto the cortex. The third pathway projects directly on the cortex (Parvizi and Damasio, 2003; Weiss *et al.*, 2007; Brown *et al.*, 2012). (b) Injury to the thalamus and hypothalamus, midbrain and/or rostral pons leads to impaired consciousness (Moruzzi and Magoun, 1949; Batini *et al.*, 1958; Gottesmann, 1988; Parvizi and Damasio, 2003). Impairment of large regions of the cortex, particularly the associative cortices, also causes unconsciousness (Laureys, 2005). Shaded areas indicate regions essential for consciousness. (Photo courtesy of V. Paulmier and C. Terlouw.)

Proprioceptors provide information about joint angles, muscle length and tension, which inform the brain on the posture and the spatial orientation of the body. Chemical sensors in the gut provide information about the digestive state. These sources of information, and others related to memory for example, are constantly compiled by the brain into an integrated coherent image in order to take appropriate decisions.

To carry out the integration of information properly, the brain has a highly organized architecture containing many specialized structures, but which at the same time are strongly interconnected to allow information aggregation. Mammals, humans included, have the same major brain structures. In its simplest form we can distinguish the forebrain, the midbrain and the hindbrain (Fig. 14.1; Box 14.1). The avian brain has many brain structures that are homologous to mammalian brain structures. For example, the avian pallium is homologous to the mammalian cortex.

appearance and is essential for conscious experiences. The visual, auditory, somatosensory, gustatory and olfactory cortices are the primary cortices, receiving, generally via the thalamus (Box 14.1), direct information from the senses. Their role is the first unscrambling of the signals. The primary motor cortex sends signals to the muscles, via the basal ganglia, allowing the animal to act on what it has perceived. Before the reaction, the integration of many types of information, on the environment, the body state, emotions and memory amongst others, takes place. This is the role of association cortices; they integrate and interpret information of primary areas, conceptualize information in a wider context and plan appropriate responses. The correct functioning of primary and associative cortices is necessary to know, understand and give a sense to what is perceived; to have a conscious perception of the environment and of the self (Crick and Koch, 2003; Laureys, 2005).

Brain Structures Involved in Consciousness

The cerebral cortex

Antonio Damasio defined consciousness as 'a state of mind in which there is knowledge of one's own existence and of the existence of surroundings' (Damasio, 2010). The cortex is the outer layer of the mammalian brain; it has a folded

The thalamus

The thalamus is placed centrally in the mammalian and avian brain. It is an essential relay station for visual, auditory, gustatory, somatosensory and motor information for the cortex (McCormick and Bal, 1994; McAlonan *et al.*, 2008; Huart *et al.*, 2009; Rees, 2009). The thalamus is involved in shifting attention from one stimulus to another one, which may seem more relevant or which attracts more, such as bright objects. Impairment of

Box 14.1. The major brain structures and their functions

The hindbrain is the lowest part of the brain (Fig. 14.1). It contains the cerebellum, of which the main function is to coordinate muscle movements, the medulla oblongata (or medulla), involved in the regulation of respiration and blood circulation, and the pons, involved in facial expression, sensation in the face, auditory processing, certain eye movements, respiration and sleep, among others.

The midbrain is situated just above the pons (Fig. 14.1). It is involved in eye movements, focusing of the eye lens, and auditory and visual processing. The midbrain, the pons and the medulla form together a structure called the brainstem. The brainstem and cerebellum play a major role in the maintenance of posture and balance.

The mammalian forebrain contains the cortex, involved in complex information processing such as remembering and planning, and the expression of purposeful behaviour, for example nest-building or searching for food or water (Fig. 14.1). In humans, the cortex is in charge of thinking, speaking and reasoning. It contains several subcortical structures, such as the hippocampus, involved in memory, the thalamus, which is an important relay station of most sensory and motor signals to the cerebral cortex, and the hypothalamus, which controls fluid and electrolyte balance, food ingestion, energy balance, reproduction, thermoregulation and immune and emotional responses. It further contains the basal ganglia, involved in motor functions.

The avian brain contains homologues of mammalian neocortical structures with similarities in connectivity and functional organization (Jarvis et al., 2005). The avian pallium receives information relative to the environment and the body state and projects to the brainstem and spinal cord, so that the organism can adapt, physiologically and behaviourally, to the incoming information. Like mammals, birds express complex cognitive behaviour. They can distinguish images that they can classify according to their content or group them according to abstract concepts, such as 'similar' or 'different'. Pigeons, for example, distinguish between photos containing humans and those that do not. Pigeons, hens and quail are also able to solve complex problems that require the application of a rule (Emery, 2006).

---

the thalamus and subthalamic regions abolishes consciousness (Moruzzi and Magoun, 1949; Gottesman, 1988) (Fig. 14.1).

The reticular formation and the ascending reticular activating system

The reticular formation plays an essential role in the level of arousal and consequently in consciousness (Fig. 14.1). It is located in the central and dorsal part of the brainstem, extending from the lower medulla to the upper midbrain, and consists of a network of interlacing neural fibres (Parvizi and Damasio, 2001). Projections arising from the reticular formation and surrounding structures activate the cortex, allowing it to function correctly and have conscious perception; it is called the ascending reticular activating system. Non-mammalian vertebrates, including birds, have similar structures (Ten Donkelaar and De Boer-Van Huizen, 1981; Northcutt, 1984). The function of the ascending reticular activating system is the maintenance of wakefulness and complex functions including motivation, attention, learning and memory (Zeman, 2001; Damasio, 2010; Brown et al., 2012). Impairment of

the ascending reticular activating system (rostral pons, midbrain and their projections) abolishes consciousness (Fig. 14.1).

Brain Structures Involved in Emotions and Pain

Scientific studies on animal behaviour and physiology as well as brain anatomy and function show that all mammals are able to experience positive and negative emotions (Paul et al., 2005; Boissy et al., 2007). Emotions are the driving force behind motivational states (Morgane et al., 2005). Emotions are processed by the limbic system, which consists of several cortical and subcortical structures essentially located in the forebrain (Morgane et al., 2005). The limbic system exists in humans and also in non-human mammals (LeDoux, 2000). The avian brain contains structures with similar functions as the mammalian limbic system and behavioural studies show that birds are capable of positive and negative emotions (Lowndes and Davies, 1996; Jarvis et al., 2005; Zimmerman et al., 2011). Pleasant experiences are associated with relatively greater activation in some of these limbic structures,

A stimulus is noxious when it can cause tissue damage. Nociceptors in the skin, joints, muscles and viscera are specialized nerves that transform noxious stimuli, whether chemical (often related to tissue lesions), mechanical or thermal, into a nervous message, which travels from its peripheral origin via the spinal cord to the brain, where the signal is interpreted. The sensory component (the type, location and intensity of the stimulus) of the pain experience is interpreted by the somatosensory cortices and the emotional (the unpleasantness of stimulus) by the limbic cortices (Bushnell *et al.*, 2013).

Local brain lesions may abolish one of the two components of pain. Ploner *et al.* (1999) described a patient with partial lesions of the somatosensory cortices. When thermal stimulation was applied on the body,

the patient had no information on the location, type and intensity of the stimulus. She did not even know there was a stimulus; she reported an 'unpleasant feeling' without being able to characterize its cause. She experienced the negative emotion, but did not understand the origin, lacking the nociceptive component.

The role of the limbic cortex in the emotional aspects of pain perception is illustrated by lesions in the limbic cortex of patients suffering severe incapacitating pain, interventions that were carried out in the past. When questioning the patients after the intervention, they reported that pain was still present, but no longer 'bothersome' (Foltz and White, 1962). Strictly speaking, we cannot speak of pain here because these patients perceive only the sensory and not the emotional component.

---

unpleasant experiences with activation in other limbic structures (Wager *et al.*, 2008). The term 'stress' refers to the presence of negative emotions, which occur when the animal feels threatened, whether the threat is real or imaginary. Stress is further associated with behavioural and physiological changes, which allow the animal to respond to the threat.

Pain is defined as 'an unpleasant sensory and emotional experience associated with actual or potential tissue damage, or described in terms of such damage' (International Association for the Study of Pain). Pain signals are difficult to ignore; as indicated by the definition, pain perception is associated with potential tissue lesion and danger and logically needs attending to (Eccleston and Crombez, 1999). By definition, pain refers to the situation where both the sensory and emotional components are perceived (Box 14.2). The bird pain system shows much similarity to that of mammals (Gentle, 1992).

The Basic Principles of Stunning

Stunning must induce a state of unconsciousness, which lasts until death is induced through exsanguination. The normal living brain is permanently active; it involves the permanent depolarization (losing electrical charge) and repolarization (regaining electrical charge) of its neurons. During unconsciousness, the electrical activity of the cortex is much reduced and may even be nearly absent (Newhook and Blackmore, 1982a,b; Raj *et al.*,

2006; Lambooij *et al.*, 2012). Depending on the method used, unconsciousness is induced by widespread dysfunction of the cerebral hemispheres, of which the cortex is part, or by impairment of the ascending reticular activating system, abolishing its stimulating effect on the cortex (Fig. 14.1). Particularly, damage to the thalamus and hypothalamus, or in the region of the midbrain and rostral pons, causes unconsciousness (Moruzzi and Magoun, 1949; Batini *et al.*, 1958; Parvizi and Damasio, 2003).

Mechanical stunning: the penetrating captive bolt

The penetrating captive bolt is a metal rod of generally 80–120 mm long and 12 mm thick and is used for any species, generally routinely for cattle and sheep and as a back-up stunning method for pigs (Kamenik *et al.*, 2019). It is contained in a stun gun placed against the forehead of the animal. The correct firing of the captive bolt causes unconsciousness due to one or several of the following effects: impact, mechanical destruction of parts of the brain, and widespread brain haemorrhage (Table 14.1).

The impact of the bolt on the skull sends a shockwave through the brain, repeatedly reflected and refracted by the skull and the boundaries between brain structures (Fig. 14.2). These reflections and refractions jumble the waves so that their crossings augment and cancel each other. Pressure gradients lead to tears and lesions in the brain tissue and disturbances

Table 14.1. Physiological events contributing to reversible or irreversible loss of consciousness, for the different stunning methods (not relevant for animals killed by the stunning method).

Stun technique	Event	Consequence	Reversibility of the effects in the short term
Captive bolt	Shock wave	Uncontrolled influx and efflux of ions: depolarisation of nerve cells	Reversible
		Slowing of energy production by the cells	Reversible
		Compression: decreased functioning of nerves and circuits	Reversible
	Bolt entering and exiting brain	Compression: decreased functioning of nerves and circuits	Potentially reversible
		Tears and rupture of brain tissue Shearing of vessels	Irreversible
	Brain haemorrhage	Insufficient blood circulation: lack of glucose and oxygen leading to lack of energy in the brain cells	Irreversible
		Compression: decreased functioning of nerves and circuits	Irreversible
Electrical	Current passing through the brain	Synchronised depolarisation of nerve cells, spreading to other brain regions	Reversible
	Current passing through the heart (head-body stunning only)	Heart fibrillation	Potentially reversible
	Current passing through the spinal cord (head-body only)	Weakness of skeletal muscle	Reversible
CO_2	Absorption and dissolution of CO_2 in the blood	Acidification of brain cells	Reversible

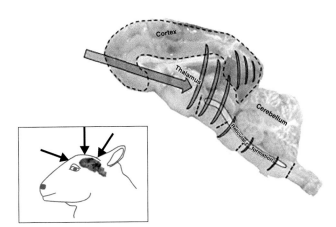

Fig. 14.2. Schematic illustration of the compression of brain tissue when the bolt enters the sheep brain frontally. Insert: possible positions of the stun gun on the sheep head (after Grandin, 2017). Notice that particularly with the frontal position the brainstem is easily missed if the gun is incorrectly oriented.

in the blood flow (Gibson *et al.*, 2015b; Martin, 2016; Terlouw *et al.*, 2016a). The impact causes a depolarization of the neurons of the cerebral hemispheres and potentially of the brainstem (Takahashi *et al.*, 1981; Katayama *et al.*, 1990; Martin, 2016). It disrupts normal cell function, particularly the production of energy and thereby slowing the potential repolarization of the neurons (Posner *et al.*, 2008). During subsequent deceleration, the cerebrum may swing on the brainstem, stretching and tearing it (Martin, 2016). The simple impact caused by the penetrating captive bolt is insufficient to obtain a long-lasting state of profound unconsciousness. The non-penetrating mushroom-shaped captive bolt induces

E.M.C. Terlouw

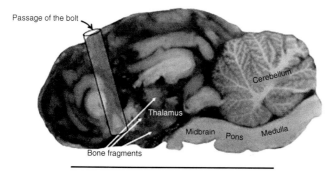

Fig. 14.3. Sagittal cut of a Charolais cow's brain (frozen after being removed from the skull) following effective captive bolt stunning, showing local destruction, bone fragments and widespread haemorrhage (dark aspects). The bolt did not reach the brainstem. (Photo courtesy of N. Bouko-Levy.)

unconsciousness through its impact via the skull on the brain, but its success rate is lower than that of the penetrating bolt (Gibson *et al.*, 2019).

The penetrating bolt causes further local fragmentation of the skull and pushes bone fragments, hair, skin and brain tissue through its trajectory (Terlouw *et al.*, 2016a). If the bolt reaches the thalamus and/or brainstem, it destroys part of the reticular formation and part of the ascending reticular activating pathways (Blackmore, 1979; Daly *et al.*, 1987; Daly and Whittington, 1989; Finnie, 2001) (Fig. 14.1), although the brainstem may be easily missed (Fig. 14.2) (Gilliam *et al.*, 2012; C. Bourguet, personal communication). The retraction of the bolt temporarily leaves a void in the tunnel created by its passage that sucks in the surrounding brain tissue, causing further tearing of axons and blood vessels (Terlouw *et al.*, 2016a).

Secondary damage, particularly widespread haemorrhage in many parts of the brain, is a major additional effect both for penetrating and non-penetrating stunning (Oliveira *et al.*, 2018; Kamenik *et al.*, 2019) (Fig. 14.3). Haemorrhage causes increased pressure on brain structures and further deprives them of blood supply; both severely hamper normal functioning of the neurons of the brain (Ommaya *et al.*, 1964; Terlouw *et al.*, 2016a). Cattle may be correctly stunned even if visual inspection of the brain indicates that the bolt has not caused direct damage to the brainstem. In these animals, generally widespread haemorrhage is observed in the cerebral ventricles and subdural area, surrounding the brain, while pinpoint haemorrhage may be observed in the white fibre tracts of the brainstem or other parts of the brain.

Mechanical stunning causes unconsciousness before the animal can perceive pain or fear-inducing stimuli. As an example, in a Holstein cow (Fig. 14.4),

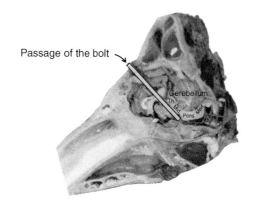

Fig. 14.4. Sagittal cut of a Holstein cow's head (frozen in the skull). The representation of the bolt is 9 cm long and demonstrates the distance to the brainstem. Th., thalamus, Mid., midbrain, Med., medulla. (Photo courtesy of C. Mallet.)

the distance between the skin of the forehead and the brainstem is approximately 7.5 cm and bolt velocities are between 27 and 61 m/s (Dörfler *et al.*, 2014; Gibson *et al.*, 2015b; Oliveira *et al.*, 2017). Hence, the brainstem is reached in 30 ms or less. The initial effect of the shock wave reaches deep brain structures within a few milliseconds (Chafi *et al.*, 2011; Zhu *et al.*, 2013; Martin, 2016). Thus, the delay to induce unconsciousness is much shorter than the 250 and 400 ms needed for conscious information processing (Box 14.3) and the animal has no conscious perception of the shot.

Stunning with an electrical current

Electrical stunning is used for sheep, poultry and pigs and in certain countries for calves or adult cattle. With this method, an electrical current of

Signals of the environment or arising from the body need time to travel towards the brain and to be consciously processed. The first, immediate pain stimulus travels towards the brain with a speed of 5–30 m/s while secondary, slow pain signals travel at speeds of below 2 m/s (Purves et al., 2004). Immediate pain needed 128 ms to travel from the hand receiving the painful stimulation to the somatosensory cortex (i.e. speed of about 8 m/s) and 271 ms to be processed, before the person could react (Ploner et al., 2006). Tactile stimuli travel faster, 30–70 m/s, and needed 36 ms to travel from the hand to the cortex (i.e. speed of about 30 m/s) but 333 ms to be processed (Ploner et al., 2006). Hence, following application, tactile and painful stimuli needed between 370 and 400 ms to be consciously processed, but this may be shorter if the distance between the stimulus site and the brain is shorter.

Visual, auditory and olfactory stimuli carry information on the environment that may indicate the presence of danger and therefore cause fear. Conscious perception of olfactory, visual or auditory information generally takes place 250–400 ms after the stimulus presentation (Comerchero and Polisch, 1999; Chennu and Bekinschtein, 2012). Thus different signals need variable times to reach the cortex, but the total time needed (travelling plus processing time) for conscious processing of sensory information is relatively standardized across modalities, ranging between 250 and 400 ms.

sufficient intensity crosses the brain, causing a generalized epileptiform seizure, followed by a brief period with greatly diminished brain activity, reflecting the massive and synchronized depolarization of the neurons (Blumenfeld, 2005) (Table 14.1). To induce unconsciousness, the seizure needs to be generalized, that is, to spread, and involve various brain structures such as the brainstem, thalamus and cortex (Lambooij and Spanjaard, 1982; Blumenfeld et al., 2003; Blumenfeld, 2005; Enev et al., 2007).

Other consequences include the release of neurotransmitters, particularly gamma-aminobutyric acid (GABA). Neurotransmitters are necessary for the transfer of information between neurons and the role of GABA is to slow brain activity; its release contributes to the state of unconsciousness (Cook et al., 1995; Treiman, 2001; Blumenfeld, 2005; Terlouw et al., 2016a). The blood circulation in the brain is modified and, in certain brain regions, blood flow may be insufficient to cover oxygen needs (Ingvar, 1986; Enev et al., 2007; Schridde et al., 2008; Posner et al., 2008).

There are two types of electrical stunning: head-only and head-body. In the first case, two electrodes are placed on either side of the head of the animal and the current crosses the brain. Following head-only stunning, after the seizure convulsions subside, the polarization of the neurons and metabolic brain state are restored, and the animal progressively regains consciousness (Posner et al., 2008; Vogel et al., 2011; Gibson et al., 2016). In the case of head-body electrical stunning, a current crosses the brain but also the heart. For sheep and pigs, two electrodes are placed on the head of the animal and a third on the chest, leg, sternum or back, depending on the species. Birds are hung by their legs on metal shackles suspended on a rail. The head is immersed in an electrified bath and the current flows between the head and legs. For adult cattle, electrical stunning also generally involves a head-body technique (Weaver and Wotton, 2009). Head-body stunning induces heart fibrillation that prevents proper blood flow. This causes further cerebral hypoxia that deepens and extends the duration of unconsciousness induced by the head electrodes (Pleiter, 2005; Vogel et al., 2011). While head-only electrical stunning is reversible, head-body stunning is generally irreversible, as the fibrillation often causes cardiac arrest (Lambooij and Spanjaard, 1982; Terlouw et al., 2016a).

During and immediately following correct application of the current, due to the massive discharges in the brain, the muscles are in a tonic contracted state for several seconds; the animal extends the forelegs and flexes the hind legs (Croft, 1952; Warrington, 1974; Blumenfeld et al., 2003). Subsequently, one or several clonic states follow, characterized by irregular jerking movements of the extremities and body (Croft, 1952; Warrington, 1974; Lambooij, 1982; Lambooij and Spanjaard, 1982; Velarde et al., 2002; Blumenfeld et al., 2009). Results on sheep suggested that, during the tonic phase and the first clonic phase, the animal was unconscious, representing a period of about 29 s (Croft, 1952; Velarde et al., 2002). In the case of head-body electrical stunning, depending on the species and site of the electrodes, part of the current aiming at inducing heart fibrillation may pass through the spinal cord. This has a paralysing effect and the tonic and clonic muscle contractions are less pronounced than following electrical head-only stunning (Wotton *et al.*, 1992). Therefore, the advantages of this method are not only a longer-lasting or irreversible unconscious state, but also a lesser degree of post-stun muscle contractions. The disadvantage is that the partially paralysing effect may mask possible signs of consciousness.

Hair, wool, feathers, bones, dirt, fat tissue and the outer layer of the skin have relatively high electrical resistance and may partly block the transfer of the current from the electrodes to the brain (Faes *et al.*, 1999; Velarde *et al.*, 2000; Grandin, 2019). The exact distribution of the electric field within the brain depends on the location of the electrodes and the characteristics of the animal (Terlouw *et al.*, 2016a). It is essential that sufficient electricity passes through the brain and that this occurs instantaneously (Lambooij, 1982; Lambooij and Spanjaard, 1982). As the resistance of the tissues diminishes once the current starts to flow (Kalinowsky, 1939; Wotton and O'Callaghan, 2002; Fish and Geddes, 2009), the initial voltage needed to reach the correct intensity instantaneously is higher than subsequently (Gregory, 2001). The administration of an electrical shock to the head, which does not induce immediate unconsciousness, is extremely painful (Impastato, 1954; Fish and Geddes, 2009). Once a current of sufficient intensity crosses the brain, the loss of consciousness occurs in 0.2 s (Kalinowsky, 1939; Liberson, 1948; Cook *et al.*, 1995); from that moment on, there is no longer a conscious perception of pain or fear signals. Taking into account the time that pain signals need to reach the cortex and the time needed for conscious processing, the maximal time allowance to reach the correct current intensity is relatively short (Fig. 14.5).

Stunning with a gas mixture

Gas stunning is used for pigs and poultry. Normal air contains 21% O_2, 0.03% CO_2 and the remainder is N_2. The principle of gas stunning is to immerse animals in a gas mixture most often containing high concentrations of CO_2, the remainder being air. Pigs are lowered in a gondola into a pit, while poultry are placed on a conveyor belt entering a tunnel, both filled with the CO_2 mixture.

Proper regulation of the concentration of blood gases, CO_2 and O_2, is vital. Oxygen is an essential need for energy metabolism of the body, while CO_2 is metabolic waste that must be eliminated. In the alveoli of the lungs, the molecules move from higher towards lower concentrations. When the CO_2 concentration is higher in the air inhaled than in the blood, CO_2 is absorbed into the bloodstream. The CO_2 dissolves in the blood, thereby acidifying it. This acidification is detected by sensors called chemoreceptors (Teppema and Dahan, 2010). The chemoreceptors are stimulated by low O_2 and/or high CO_2 in the blood and transmit their information to respiratory centres in the medulla of the brainstem, allowing the immediate faster and deeper breathing response (Timmers *et al.*, 2003; Forster and Smith, 2010; Chang *et al.*, 2015). However, when an animal is immersed in a mixture rich in CO_2, the elimination of CO_2 is not possible even if respiration is faster or deeper. The acidification of the blood results in the acidification of the brain cells, occasioning the depression of brain activity, causing the loss of consciousness. Respiration slows down and finally stops due to dysfunction of

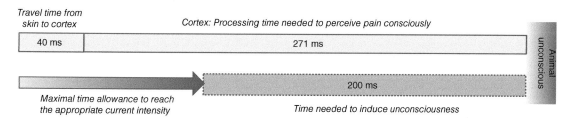

Fig. 14.5. Estimated time delays in the context of electrical stunning. The electricity causes a painful stimulus in the tissues beneath the electrodes, which the animal must not perceive consciously. The time needed for this stimulus to reach the cortex is unknown, but assuming a speed of 8 m/s (Box 14.3) and a travel distance of 30 cm in a pig, this could represent around 40 ms. Once a pain stimulus reaches the cortex, the processing time needed for conscious perception is on average 271 ms (Box 14.3). In this assumed case, the conscious pain perception starts after 311 ms. As 200 ms are needed to induce unconsciousness, maximal time allowance to reach sufficient current intensity would be 111 ms.

underlying nerve cells, resulting in death (Terlouw et al., 2016a). In parallel, the heart rate increases initially, but subsequently slows and stops if the situation continues (Terlouw et al., 2016a). The delay until loss of consciousness and induction of death are shorter with higher concentrations of CO_2 but this delay depends on the species (Conlee et al., 2005). In pigs and birds, loss of brain responsiveness occurred 21 s after the start of immersion in 80% and 86% of CO_2 in air, respectively (Raj and Gregory, 1994; Raj et al., 1997).

The disadvantage of gas stunning in terms of animal welfare is the relatively long delay until loss of consciousness, during which animals show reactions seemingly expressing aversion, such as avoidance behaviours and difficult breathing (Dodman, 1977; Forslid, 1987; Gerritzen et al., 2004). In pigs, the respiratory changes occur within seconds of immersion in CO_2 (Forslid, 1987; Velarde et al., 2007). Various studies have addressed the potential aversive nature of inhaling high CO_2 concentrations. Food-deprived pigs accepted to enter a box for a food reward when containing air, but not when it contained a mixture with 90% CO_2, indicating that high CO_2 concentrations are aversive, although another study found that in certain contexts aversion is limited (Raj and Gregory, 1995; Jongman et al., 2000). The aversive nature was confirmed in humans, in whom CO_2 inhalation causes pain and a sensation of discomfort; high CO_2 concentrations even induced apnoea (Anton et al., 1992; Brannan et al., 2001; Terlouw et al., 2016a).

During the immersion, animals often show convulsions (apparently involuntary muscle contractions). Some studies indicate that the muscle contractions take place only after the loss of consciousness, suggesting that these expressions are reflexes and not indicative of aversion (Forslid,

1987). Other studies showed the opposite (Velarde et al., 2007; Rodríguez et al., 2008). Overall, the occurrence of convulsions before, during or after the loss of consciousness seems to differ between studies, suggesting that their appearance may be context or animal dependent.

Some gas stunning systems are based on the use of inert gases, such as N_2 or argon (Raj et al., 1997; Dalmau et al., 2010; Llonch et al., 2012). The anaesthetic principle of these mixtures is the lack of O_2 (Box 14.4). Depending on the study context, compared with CO_2, behavioural responses to inert gases are less (Gerritzen et al., 2000; Sandilands et al., 2011) or on the contrary more pronounced, especially if induction time is taken into account (Lambooij et al., 1999; Gerritzen et al., 2004).

Bleeding with or without prior stunning

Bleeding can be performed on an intact animal (religious slaughter), a dead animal (some cases of gas or electrical stunning) or an unconscious animal. The initial physiological effects of massive haemorrhage of a living animal are essentially related to the lack of oxygenation of the brain. In the non-stunned animal, the lack of O_2 in the brain following bleeding leads to a slowing of brain activity, causing a progressive decrease in the level of consciousness until the animal is unconscious (Box 14.4). If O_2 and glucose continue to be lacking, the cerebral nervous tissue is irreversibly damaged and the animal dies. The different structures of the brain do not have the same vulnerability to blood loss: for example, the blood circulation in the brainstem and thalamus is better preserved than in other parts of the brain (Mueller et al., 1977). There is a reason for this: most vital functions are under the control of centres in the brainstem;

Box 14.4. The brain's needs

The brain has high glucose and oxygen needs but small storage capacities. In humans, the brain represents 2% of body weight, but uses 20% of total body O_2, 10–20% of the glucose and 15% of cardiac output (Zauner and Muizelaar, 1997). The amounts may be slightly lower in animals, but remain high. For example, the sheep brain uses 10% of body O_2 (Vernon, 2005).

When the brain lacks O_2, neurons can no longer produce energy and they progressively lose their

electrical charge. The lack of O_2 in the brain leads to further acidification of the cells, which also hampers normal functioning (Martoft et al., 2003; Nordström et al., 2012). Following the interruption of cerebral blood flow, brain activity stops after 12–72 s, depending on the experimental context and species, and energy reserves are exhausted after 1 min. Unconsciousness probably occurs before exhaustion of energy reserves (Terlouw et al., 2016a).

E.M.C.Terlouw

consequently, vital functions such as breathing and maintenance of homeostasis are preserved as long as possible despite blood loss.

The effects of bleeding on consciousness in non-stunned animals vary between species. Sheep lose consciousness on average after about 14 s (range 10–20 s) (Schulze *et al.*, 1978; Devine *et al.*, 1986; Verhoeven *et al.*, 2015a). In chickens and turkeys, bleeding without stunning caused loss of consciousness between 12–202 s and 18–51 s, respectively (Terlouw *et al.*, 2016b). In cattle, the results vary even more. In calves of different ages, loss of consciousness or death occurred between 5–336 s following bleeding (Terlouw *et al.*, 2016a). Part of this large variability in cattle is due to the formation of occlusions at the ends of severed carotids in part of the animals, slowing exsanguination. In these animals, the vertebral arteries continue to irrigate the brain and the animal remains conscious (Gregory *et al.*, 2006). In certain cases of halal slaughter, the animal is stunned before or just after religious throat cutting to accelerate loss of consciousness (Farouk, 2013; Nakyinsige *et al.*, 2013).

Determining Insensibility, Unconsciousness and Death

Following stunning, a number of indicators allow assessment of the state of consciousness or unconsciousness of the animal (Verhoeven *et al.*, 2015b; Terlouw *et al.*, 2016a,b). These observable signs are indirectly associated with brain functions involved in consciousness, particularly the brainstem and/or the cerebral cortex. To ensure unconsciousness, indicators of consciousness must be absent and indicators of unconsciousness must be present (Table 14.2). During unconsciousness, the cortical structures are no longer functional, including those involved in the perception of pain (Box 14.2). In other words, the unconscious animal does not perceive pain. The relevance of the main indicators of consciousness, unconsciousness and death and their limitations are discussed.

Indicators of Consciousness and Unconsciousness

Standing posture and righting

In the slaughter context, the permanent loss of the standing posture is an indicator of the loss of consciousness. Following a correct mechanical or electrical stun, the loss of the standing posture is immediate. During gas stunning and when bleeding animals without stunning, the loss of posture is progressive.

Postures and movements observed following penetrating captive bolt stunning depend on the extent and localization of the brain damage (Box 14.6). Experiments showed that small animals (cats, rats, rabbits) with damage involving only the thalamus but not the midbrain or pons are capable of standing and show spontaneous locomotion while keeping their balance in a near-normal manner (Magnus, 1925, 1926a,b; Siegel *et al.*, 1983; Musienko *et al.*, 2015). However, they lack spontaneous movement; an external stimulus is necessary to set them into motion (Takakusaki, 2017). No data are available for larger animals such as sheep or cattle with this type of brain damage; possibly, their weight makes effective standing more difficult, but it is probable that they show righting movements (Box 14.7). The degree of consciousness of animals with such damage depends on the presence of intact projections between the reticular formation and cortex (Fig. 14.1).

Damage reaching the midbrain or lower causes immediate loss of the standing posture. Immediately following effective penetrative captive bolt stunning, the animal lies down, often with extended limbs if it is on its side. This specific attitude is caused by dysfunction of motor pathways in the midbrain and pons (Bazett and Penfield, 1922; Pollock and Davis, 1930) (Fig. 14.6). The subsequent progressive relaxation of the muscles probably reflects the progression of impairments towards lower brainstem regions (medulla). The immediate collapse observed following electrical stunning is due to the seizure spreading through the subcortical structures and the brainstem (Terlouw *et al.*, 2016b). Gas stunning and bleeding without stunning induce gradually a loss of capacity to maintain the standing posture, probably due to a global progressive dysfunction of cortical and subcortical structures, including the brainstem: loss of posture is one of the first behavioural signs that overall brain activity has started to decrease (Mohan Raj and Gregory, 1990, 1994; Raj *et al.*, 1990; Gerritzen *et al.*, 2000; Gibson *et al.*, 2015a). At this stage, exposure to the gas needs to continue to make the slowing of brain activity more profound and widespread. During bleeding without stunning, some cattle regain the standing posture briefly, probably due to transient physiological adjustments partly restoring neurological function, before the final collapse (Gregory *et al.*, 2010; Bourguet *et al.*, 2011; Terlouw *et al.*, 2016a).

Table 14.2. Interpretation of indicators of consciousness and unconsciousness. Animals presenting one or more indicators of the first two categories (*Consciousness* and *Risk of consciousness or of return of consciousness*) must be immediately re-stunned.

Indicator	Anatomical interpretation	Comments	References
Consciousness			
Standing posture	Midbrain, pons, medulla functional	If the midbrain, pons, medulla are functional, while the thalamus and surrounding regions are extensively damaged, reflex standing is possible although the degree of consciousness of the animal may be altered (Fig. 14.1b). This situation is unlikely to occur in the slaughter context	Magnus, 1925, 1926; Pollock and Davis, 1927; Pollock and Davis, 1930; Halsey and Downie, 1966; Kao et al., 2006; Musienko et al., 2015
Coordinated head righting with or without body righting reflex	Midbrain, pons, medulla functional	A hoisted animal raising its head parallel to the floor with a stiff, hollow back presents a head righting reflex which is not acceptable following penetrating bolt stunning	Magnus, 1925, 1926; Pollock and Davis, 1927; Pollock and Davis, 1930; Siegel et al., 1986; Grandin, 2002
Species-specific vocalization	Midbrain functional		Behbehani, 1995; Jürgens, 2009
Response to the threat test	The cortex, retina, optical nerve and motor system in the brainstem are sufficiently functional to produce a positive response	Should not be confused with a corneal reflex caused by air movement Caution is advised in the interpretation as unconscious patients in a vegetative state were reported to present a blink response to the threat test	Limon et al., 2010; Verhoeven et al., 2015b, 2016; Terlouw et al., 2016b; Blumenfeld, 2009
Risk of consciousness or of return of consciousness			
Eye tracking	Relevant circuits in the midbrain and pons partly functional	Should not be confused with primitive orienting reflexes	Batini et al., 1958
Repeated spontaneous blinking	Relevant circuits in the midbrain, pons, medulla and upper cervical cord partly functional		Van de Werf and Smit, 2008; Blumenfeld, 2009; Kaminer et al., 2011; Terlouw et al., 2015
Eyeball rotation and/or nystagmus	Relevant circuits in the midbrain and pons partly impaired creating an imbalance in the vestibulo-ocular system	Damage to the cerebellum may also cause nystagmus	Abadi, 2002; Strupp et al., 2014
Incomplete head or body righting reflex	Relevant circuits in the midbrain, pons and/or medulla partly functional	Sheep may not hang completely straight. Certain reflex reactions to the manipulation of unconscious stunned or bled animals are normal	Magnus, 1925, 1926; Modianos and Pfaff, 1976; Musienko et al., 2015; Terlouw et al., 2015; Grandin, 2019
Presence of corneal reflex	Relevant circuit in the pons and medulla functional		Cruccu and Deuschl, 2000; Aramideh and Ongerboer de Visser, 2002 *Continued*

E.M.C.Terlouw

Table 14.2. Continued.

Indicator	Anatomical interpretation	Comments	References
Presence of rhythmic breathing	Relevant circuits in the pons and medulla functional		Ramirez et al., 1998; St John, 2009; Smith et al., 2013
Unconsciousness or death			
Instantaneous and permanent loss of standing posture without righting reflexes	Damage to the midbrain, pons and/or medulla	Specific, local lesions or impairments in the midbrain, pons and/or cerebellum may cause loss of standing posture with at least partial preservation of consciousness. Loss of standing posture is not a predictor of the *duration* of unconsciousness. Transection of medulla or upper spinal cord, by placing the stun gun (or puntilla) in the nape of the neck while orienting it towards the floor causes immediate collapse while the animal is *fully conscious*	Fulton et al., 1930; Pollock and Davis, 1930; Halsey and Downie, 1966; Tidswell, 1987; Limon et al., 2010; Musienko et al., 2015
Absence of corneal reflex	Damage to the pons and/or medulla	Electrical stunning: may be a false absence due to tonic or clonic muscle contractions. Direct bleeding: may be a false absence due to eye muscle contractions	Cruccu and Deuschl, 2000; Aramideh and Ongerboer de Visser, 2002; Terlouw et al., 2016b
Absence of rhythmic breathing	Damage to medulla	Captive bolt (frontal shot): impairment of medulla is indicative of profound damage and therefore longer-lasting unconsciousness. Electrical stunning: may be false absence due to muscle contractions interfering with respiratory muscles. Transection of medulla or upper spinal cord, by placing the stun gun (or puntilla) in the nape of the neck while orienting it downwards causes respiratory arrest while the animal is *fully conscious*	Limon et al., 2010; Smith et al., 2013

Box 14.5. Following stunning, the state of the animal often evolves

Following stunning, the brain is generally not in a static but rather in a progressively changing state. Following application of the captive bolt, brain functions may be progressively lost, due to spreading brain haemorrhage, or may recover, for example if the bolt has caused a shock wave but little irreversible brain damage. Following head-only electrical stunning, normal brain function progressively recovers. Heart fibrillation following head-body electrical stun often results in heart arrest and consequently death, but in some cases, the heart resumes normal functioning. Following immersion in CO_2, animals either die or progressively recover (Table 14.1). For these reasons, animals have to be monitored until the end of exsanguination.

Box 14.6. Brain control of posture and movement

Posture and movement involve several functions. Extensor and flexor muscles allow standing; they maintain an enduring and correctly balanced muscle tone, acting against the effect of gravity. Centres and pathways in the midbrain, pons and medulla control these functions. These structures assure further that the attitudes of different parts of the body change in a harmonized way; for example, if one part of the body changes, other parts assume a different attitude as well (Magnus, 1925, 1926a,b; Schepens and Drew, 2004; Takakusaki, 2017) (Box 14.7). These centres function automatically, that is, voluntary action is not needed.

Areas in the cortex are involved in initiating and controlling voluntary movement. These more complex activities combine many input sources, such as visual information on the environment, the positions of the joints and muscles, the body state and needs, and memory (Patla, 1997; Beloozerova and Sirota, 2003). Although the brainstem pathways can independently organize gross motor control, the motor cortex is essential for the voluntary and fine movements. The basal ganglia, situated between the cortex and the brainstem, are important intermediate stations, necessary for smooth changes between movements (Purves et al., 2004). The cerebellum plays a major role in the maintenance of posture and coordination of movements. Loss of the standing posture occurs with lesions at the level of the rostral midbrain.

Box 14.7. Relationships between posture, righting reflexes and balance

Righting functions assure that if, by its own active movements or by some outside force, the body of the animal is brought out of its normal posture, a series of reflexes are elicited so that it can reach or maintain its normal position.

Righting relative to gravity is controlled by labyrinthine information from the inner ear (in the temporal bone) and the vestibular nuclei (in the rostral medulla) and their interconnecting circuits. They allow putting the head correctly with respect to symmetry and gravity, even on an inclined surface.

Body and neck-righting reflexes consist of a relatively fixed chain of reflex movements: first, the head is brought into a normal position, subsequently the neck and the trunk. The automatic components of the righting reflex chain are generated in the brainstem; their voluntary control arises in the cortex (Magnus, 1925, 1926a,b; Pollock and Davis, 1930). Righting reflexes use labyrinthine information, but may exist without this. For example, moving the head of a labyrinthless animal (i.e. one from which the labyrinth, or inner ear, has been removed experimentally), even passively (by an experimenter), stimulates proprioceptors of the neck muscles which in turn act on the legs (e.g. turning the head to the side causes extension of the limbs on the side to which the head is turned). The centres for these righting reflexes lie in the medulla. Righting reflexes also use tactile stimuli: pressure on one side of the body (as when an animal is lying down) stimulates righting of the head. Pressure on two sides of the body does not. The centres for these righting reflexes lie in the midbrain (Magnus, 1926b).

Control of posture and righting are integrated functions. They have different inputs, but share the output pathways. Similarly, balance results from the combined corrective movements and depends on the capacities of the animal to maintain the standing posture and to correct its posture by righting. Balance is less good or absent if the circuits involved in standing and righting do not work correctly.

E.M.C.Terlouw

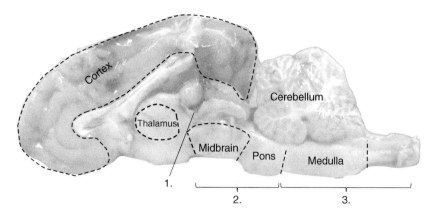

Fig. 14.6. Effects on standing and righting responses of different transections of the brainstem. These transections result from experimental surgical preparations and not from situations encountered in the slaughter context. 1. Animal capable of standing, locomotion when triggered, balance close to normal, righting reflex present. 2. No standing or locomotion, no righting; legs extended. 3. Animal flaccid but some reflex activity possible depending on context (Pollock and Davis, 1927; Ranson and Hinsey, 1929; Fulton *et al.*, 1930; Siegel *et al.*, 1986; Musienko *et al.*, 2015).

Permanent loss of the standing posture is closely associated with, but not identical to, loss of consciousness (Table 14.2): cell groups and pathways in the brainstem with a central role in maintenance of the standing posture and in righting reflexes are in close proximity to other brainstem cell groups and pathways, essential for the maintenance of consciousness. In the context of captive bolt stunning, loss of the standing posture indicates that the midbrain is injured; if this damage is widespread, the animal is unconscious. In the context of gas and electrical stunning, loss of the standing posture is a sign of widespread dysfunction of the brain, encompassing the midbrain.

Righting reflexes aim at bringing an animal into its normal posture (Box 14.7). Animals with lesions of the thalamus present righting reflexes (Magnus, 1925, 1926a,b; Pollock and Davis, 1930). Lesions of the midbrain or lower abolish coordinated righting reflexes (Magnus, 1925, 1926a,b) (Box 14.7). A complete oriented righting reflex following release from the stunning box involves the righting of the head, followed by righting of the trunk. The legs may be positioned and raise the trunk in a coordinated manner if the animal is physically capable (Magnus, 1926b). Coordinated, oriented righting reflexes must be absent following stunning because their presence indicates that the midbrain is not impaired; they are indicators of consciousness (Table 14.2).

After hoisting, an animal may present a head-righting reflex, raising its head parallel to the floor with a stiff, hollow back (Grandin, 2002) (Table 14.2). Following penetrating bolt stunning, such a head-righting reflex

on the slaughter line indicates that the brainstem was not sufficiently damaged and is not acceptable. Following religious slaughter without a stun, an animal that was bled correctly may present a stiff-hollow-back head-righting reflex on the slaughter line. In this case, the reflex is indicative of residual activity in the righting reflex circuit of an unconscious or dead animal (Terlouw *et al.*, 2015). However, in certain cases, the movement may be indicative of a risk of consciousness, particularly if the animal is not correctly bled. In this case, other signs of consciousness will be present (see Table 14.2 and below) and this situation is not acceptable.

The head, neck and trunk movements are inter-related (Boxes 14.6 and 14.7) and a passive change in the orientation of the head of animals with midbrain damage (e.g. an experimenter moves the head) may induce reflex leg movements (Bazett and Penfield, 1922; Pollock and Davis, 1930). The attitudes and movements of animals with midbrain damage depend further on whether they are lying down or suspended (Pollock and Davis, 1930). Following captive bolt stunning of cattle, hoisting or other forms of manipulation will change the position of the head with respect to the body (integrated in the medulla), and the animal loses its tactile information from the floor (integrated in the midbrain). This may explain certain reflex reactions of the legs or neck and head during manipulation or hoisting.

Leg movements may also result from residual nervous activity in pattern-generating centres in the brainstem and spinal cord, involved in the production of pattern movements, such as walking (Burke *et al.*, 2001;

Guertin, 2009; Frigon, 2012; Takakusaki, 2017). This explains some of the paddling movements that cattle present on the slaughter line following captive bolt stunning or following bleeding without stunning. The functioning of these generators is independent of consciousness; the simple presence of these movements does not indicate consciousness (Terlouw et al., 2015).

The loss of the standing posture or the presence of oriented righting reflexes may be difficult to evaluate when animals are physically restrained, for example fowl suspended on the rail, or animals maintained in restraining boxes or V-restrainers. Righting becomes very rudimentary (and more difficult to evaluate) if the animal cannot stand. Transection of the brainstem below the pons, or of the spinal cord without damaging the midbrain, which may occur if the stun gun is fired in the nape of the neck while oriented downwards, results in immediate collapse, while the animal is fully conscious as its upper brainstem remained intact (Figs 14.1b and 14.6; Table 14.2) (Fulton et al., 1930). Finally, immediate collapse is not a reliable predictor of the durability of the unconscious state, for which other signs are more appropriate (see Table 14.2 and below).

Eye movements and eye reflexes

Presence of spontaneous eye or eyelid movements or the absence of certain eye reflexes are often used to evaluate unconsciousness in the slaughter context. If the muscles of the eyes are passive, the eyeballs are centrally placed in the orbit (Box 14.8). Following an effective mechanical stun, the animal closes its eyes and immediately opens them. Following a gas stun, the eyes are generally open with eyelids and eyeballs immobile. After an effective electrical stun, the eyes are initially closed due to the tonic contraction of the muscles caused by the current, then reopened (Grandin, 2019).

The corneal reflex is tested by lightly touching the cornea: if the reflex is present, the eyelid closes. The reflex involves the transmission of sensory information to the pons eliciting a motor response via the reticular formation (Fig. 14.8) (Cruccu and Deuschl, 2000; Aramideh and Ongerboer de Visser, 2002). In the slaughter context, if the corneal reflex is absent, there is a large probability that the disruption is associated with a wider dysfunction, comprising part of the reticular formation and/or thalamus, and thus with a state of unconsciousness (Cruccu et al., 1997; Laureys, 2005). Hence, unconscious animals may show a corneal reflex, but an animal that does not is unconscious. In calves slaughtered without stunning, the corneal reflex was lost 1 min or more after the loss of consciousness (Lambooij et al., 2012; Verhoeven et al., 2016). For this reason, the absence of the corneal

---

Box 14.8. Brain control of eye movements

Eyes are highly specialized organs that collect important information. They function partly automatically controlled by several cell groups in the midbrain, pons and medulla (Fig. 14.7). Visual information is shared with other brain structures, such as the cortex, thalamus and basal ganglia.

In larger mammals, cell groups in the midbrain, the lower pons, the medulla and upper cervical cord control eyelid opening and closure (Schmidtke and Büttner-Evener, 1992; Bour et al., 2002; Van de Werf and Smit, 2008). Groups of nerve cells in the midbrain receive information from the optic nerve and control the muscles involved in pupillary constriction and lens accommodation to adjust for the amount of light that falls on the retina and to obtain a clear image (Figs 14.7 and 14.8).

In their neutral (relaxed) position, the eyeballs are centrally placed in the orbit. Eyes are capable of locking on to an object and maintaining a clear vision of it, even when the object is moving, a function called tracking. The eyes can also fixate on an object even when the head or the entire animal is moving. To take into account head and body position and movements, they exchange information with the circuits involved in locomotion and posture (Boxes 14.6 and 14.7). Six muscles are attached to the eyeballs to allow movement; several cell groups in the cerebellum, midbrain and the pons (Fig. 14.7) control them (Tehovnik et al., 2000; Enderle, 2006). Cell groups in midbrain and pons ensure that eyes are maintained in their position; otherwise, they would drift back into their neutral position.

Other cell groups in the midbrain and in the pons are involved in the coordination of eye movements. They receive information from cortical and subcortical areas. Figure 14.7 illustrates the complexity of this interconnected system. A local lesion in the midbrain or pons interrupting the network may create an imbalance, leading to unusual eye positions or movements such as eyeball rotation or nystagmus.

E.M.C. Terlouw

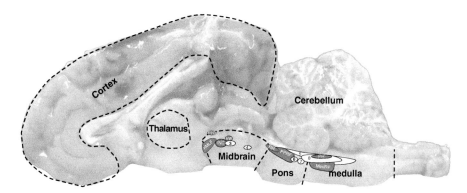

Fig. 14.7. Major cell groups involved in the control of eyelid and eyeball movements (Bhidayasiri *et al.*, 2000; Purves *et al.*, 2008). Cranial nuclei (light grey): oculomotor (3: horizontal and vertical eye movements, raising of the eyelid, eyeball retraction); trochlear (4: vertical eye movements), principal sensory trigeminal (5: sensory perception of the cornea and other areas of the face), abducens (6: horizontal eye movements, eyeball retraction), facial (7: eyelid closure, in larger animals also eyelid opening) and vestibular (8: smooth eye pursuit) nuclei. Other brainstem nuclei (dark grey): pretectal olivary and Edinger-Westphal nuclei (PTO and EW: pupillary constriction and lens accommodation), rostral Raphe group (RR: maintenance of eye position), the interstitual nucleus of cajal and prepositos hypoglossus (INC and PH: gaze holding), rostral interstitial nucleus of the medial longitudinal fasciculus and paramedian pontine reticular formation (riMLF and PPRF: control of saccades) and the medullary reticular formation (MedRF; organization of eye movements). For simplicity, connections between the cell groups are not depicted. Impairment of the nuclei or the connecting circuits leads to imbalance of the controlling system, which may be expressed in uncontrolled eye movements.

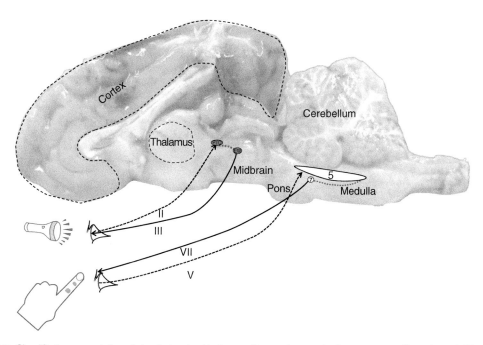

Fig. 14.8. Simplified representation of circuits involved in the pupillary and corneal reflex responses (Ongerboer de Visser and Moffie, 1979; Davidson *et al.*, 2000; Kozicz *et al.*, 2010). The pupillary reflex involves sensory information from the optic nerve (II) travelling via the pretectal olivary (PTO) nucleus, an interneuron, the Edinger-Westphal (EW) nucleus and the oculomotor nerve (III) to the sphincter muscle of the pupil, which contracts in response to increased light. The corneal reflex involves sensory information travelling via the trigeminal nerve (V), the trigeminal nucleus (5) and interneurons to the facial nucleus (7); the latter sending a signal via the facial nerve (VII) to the muscle of the eyelid allowing eyelid closure. Sensory and motor nerves are represented by dashed and continuous lines, respectively. Interneurons are represented by dotted lines.

Physiology of the Brain and Insensibility and Unconsciousness

reflex is a reliable indicator of unconsciousness at slaughter.

The palpebral reflex is tested by a light touch of the eyelid and the eyelash reflex by lightly brushing the eyelashes. The responses are also eyelid closure, and at least for the palpebral reflex the neural circuit is largely similar to that of the corneal reflex. During slaughter without stunning, the eyelash reflex is generally lost after the loss of corneal reflex, suggesting that it is more resistant to the effects of anoxia (Terlouw et al., 2016b). The exact procedure of these tests and their interpretation in terms of unconsciousness need further studies.

The nictitating membrane or third eyelid covers the eyeball in many birds, reptiles, amphibians and fish, and in some mammals such as rabbits, in response to touching the cornea. It is a passive reaction caused by the stimulation of the cornea and the active retraction of the eyeball by muscles and controlled by centres in the midbrain, pons and medulla (Berthier et al., 1983; Evinger et al., 1995). Following electrical stunning, the external eyelids close but the third eyelid remains open. In birds, the reflex can be tested even if external eyelids are closed as the movement of the membrane can be seen or felt underneath the eyelids (Erasmus et al., 2010).

The above reflexes cannot be tested correctly in the case of strong eye muscle contraction. After electrical stunning, the tonic state and the subsequent vigorous clonic movements may interfere with the eyelid response, or make it difficult to carry out the test or to interpret the results correctly (Grandin, 2019). Particularly in non-stunned cattle, eye muscles may present tonic contraction immediately after the start of the bleeding and the response may be absent while the animal is conscious. Finally, the corneal reflex test is difficult to interpret when the animal has blood in the eyes.

Persistent eyeball rotation is indicative of local impairments in the brainstem. For example, a lesion of specific nerves in the midbrain (oculomotor nerve) or lower pons (abducens nerve) causes the eye to turn inward or outward and downward, respectively. Eyeball rotation may be observed following captive bolt stunning; it may be full (iris hardly visible) or partial (half of the iris still visible) (Atkinson et al., 2013). It indicates a risk, as 50% of the cattle presenting full rotation also showed other signs of potential consciousness (Gouveia et al., 2009; Atkinson et al., 2013). The sign is particularly relevant for captive bolt stunning. During eyeball rotation, it may be impossible to touch the cornea to carry out the corneal reflex

and, in addition, the eye muscle contraction could interfere with the response (Terlouw et al., 2016b).

The pupillary reflex is the contraction of the pupil when suddenly exposed to light (Box 14.8; Fig. 14.8). The presence of fixed dilated pupils may be a useful indicator of a correct stun for all techniques and for bleeding of non-stunned animals (Table 14.2). It may be difficult to use immediately following electrical stun before bleeding, due to time constraints and muscle contractions. The pupillary reflex test necessitates further that the retina and optic nerve are functional (Box 14.8). The pupillary reflex is not valid if blood covers the cornea, or if blood loss reduces the functioning of the optic nerve (Lee et al., 2008).

Spontaneous blinking is initiated by reduced tear film thickness as well as a spontaneous blink generator and involves circuits in the brainstem and upper spinal cord (Box 14.8). Voluntary blinking involves, in addition, circuits in the cortex (Van de Werf and Smit, 2008; Kaminer et al., 2011; Xiao et al., 2015). The sign is relevant for all methods of stunning and for bleeding of non-stunned animals, but its absence does not necessarily indicate unconsciousness and its presence not necessarily consciousness (Table 14.2). Spontaneous blinking has been observed in vegetative patients and unconscious penetrative bolt-stunned bulls (Blumenfeld, 2009; Terlouw et al., 2015). Their presence in a stunned unconscious animal indicates that certain structures of the brainstem, possibly related to the blink generator, are still functional (Schmidtke and Büttner Ennever, 1992; Van de Werf and Smit, 2008).

Eye tracking involves different structures in the brainstem and in the cortex (Box 14.8). It does not occur in vegetative patients and the return of sustained and consistent eye tracking movements or fixation is one of the first signs of a return of consciousness in these patients (Blumenfeld, 2009). However, in the unconscious state primitive orienting reflexes may occur, consisting of eyes and head turning towards a visual or auditory stimulus, presumably mediated by intact brainstem circuits (Majerus et al., 2005; Blumenfeld, 2009). In the slaughter context, repeated eye tracking (Box 14.8) indicates consciousness or a risk of return of consciousness, but its absence does not necessarily indicate unconsciousness (Table 14.2). The sign is relevant for all methods of stunning and for bleeding of non-stunned animals.

Nystagmus is a vertical, horizontal or torsional rapid oscillation of the eyeball due to repeated contractions of muscles of the eye. Several neural circuits working in concert localized in the cerebellum, midbrain and pons, including the reticular formation, are involved in the coordination of eye movements (Box 14.8). Damage to one or more of these circuits may create an imbalance in their functioning and lead to nystagmus (Hüfner *et al.*, 2007). The direction of the nystagmus depends on the localization of the impairment of the circuits. In downbeat nystagmus the fast component of the oscillation is downward; it is generally caused by lesions in the cerebellum or lower pons (Hüfner *et al.*, 2007). In the context of slaughter, nystagmus is an indicator with low discriminatory power: when present, the brainstem is damaged but possibly not sufficiently to obtain a profound and long-lasting state of unconsciousness (Gregory *et al.*, 2007; Terlouw *et al.*, 2015). The sign is particularly relevant for captive bolt stunning (Table 14.2).

For the threat test, a finger or the hand is moved rapidly towards the eye of the animal and the presence of a withdrawal reaction (unrestrained animal) or a blinking response is checked. The test may be insufficiently sensitive, as a positive response could be obtained in unconscious humans (Blumenfeld, 2009). In sheep and cattle in the slaughter context, the presence of a reaction to the threat test was associated with other indicators of consciousness (Limon *et al.*, 2010; Verhoeven *et al.*, 2015b, 2016). The test is only valid if the eye is functional, if there is sufficient light and the corneal surface is not covered. The presence of a response to the threat test is indicative of a risk of consciousness or of a return to consciousness. The absence of a reaction does not prove that the animal is unconscious (Majerus *et al.*, 2005) (Table 14.2).

Rhythmic breathing

An unconscious animal breathes if only the midbrain is impaired, but the caudal pons and rostral medulla remained intact (Figs 14.1 and 14.8).

However, the absence of breathing is an indicator of unconsciousness; it indicates that the cell groups in the pons and medulla controlling respiration no longer function (Box 14.9; Fig. 14.8). Following captive bolt stunning, the absence of breathing indicates that there is damage to the deep structures of the brainstem and that there is a high probability that the unconsciousness will be durable. A successful electrical stun causes immediate respiratory arrest, because the seizure spreads to medulla, blocking normal function of the cell groups controlling respiration (Massey *et al.*, 2014; Box 14.9). However, following the electrical stun, breathing may change or stop for other reasons. Specifically, tonic and clonic muscle contractions following application of the current may hamper proper functioning of the respiratory muscles (James *et al.*, 1991). Following head-body stunning, the current flowing between the head and heart could also affect neurons in the spinal cord and/or respiratory muscles, which may cause respiratory arrest. Consequently, following an electrical stun, breathing is often difficult to evaluate and to interpret. However, the presence of breathing indicates consciousness (Table 14.2).

During bleeding without stunning or gas stunning, breathing ceases progressively. Bleeding of the non-stunned animal progressively causes a lack of O_2 of the nerve cells in the brainstem controlling breathing, which stop functioning (Terlouw *et al.*, 2016a). Due to the immersion in the gas mixture, these same nerve cells progressively lack O_2 and become acid, with the same consequence (Martoft *et al.*, 2003). The absence of breathing after gas stunning indicates that unconsciousness was achieved, but does not give information of the durability of the unconsciousness. If animals are

Box 14.9. Brain control of respiration

Several cell groups in the pons and medulla control respiration. Cell groups in the rostral medulla are responsible for inspiration and expiration, respectively. Other cell groups, located in the rostral and caudal pons and in the medulla, are in charge of the oscillation between inspiration and expiration (Feldman *et al.*, 2013; Smith *et al.*, 2013). A lesion at the level of rostral medulla causes irregular and abnormal breathing, over time often leading to respiratory failure (Ramirez *et al.*, 1998; McKay et al., 2005; Tan *et al.*, 2008) (Fig. 14.9). Lesions between the most caudal respiratory groups at the midlevel of the medulla, and the third cervical vertebra, lead to immediate respiratory arrest, without altering consciousness (Parvizi and Damasio, 2003; St John, 2009) (Fig. 14.9).

The integration of breathing with many other activities, such as movement, eating and drinking, and vocalization, sniffing and swallowing, takes place in the pons (Smith *et al.*, 2013). Voluntary breathing, controlled by regions in the cortex, may bypass or override the brainstem mechanisms controlling automatic breathing (McKay *et al.*, 2003).

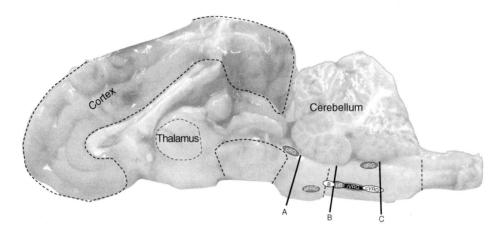

Fig. 14.9. Major cell groups involved in respiration (Smith *et al.*, 2013): pRG (pontine respiratory group: inspiratory–expiratory phase transition), pFRG (parafacial respiratory group: central chemosensory function), B (Bötzinger complex: expiration), pB (preBötzinger complex: pattern generator), rVRG (rostral ventral respiratory group: inspiration), cVRG (caudal ventral respiratory group: expiration), dRG (dorsal respiratory group: integration of sensory inputs related to breathing). Cell groups indicated in black, white and grey indicate inspiratory, expiratory and other (integrative) functions, respectively. Experimental transections at or rostral to level A do not influence breathing. Transections between A and B cause slow but regular breathing with a sustained hold of the breath at peak inspiration. The pB is both necessary and sufficient for spontaneous respiration. Therefore, transections between B and C cause irregular, abnormal breathing, and gasping, ultimately leading to respiratory arrest. Lesions between C and the third cervical vertebra cause immediate respiratory arrest (Box 14.9).

still alive following the release from the CO_2 mixture, they may resume respiration, which is indicative of a return of consciousness.

Thus, the absence of breathing is a reliable indicator of unconsciousness for mechanical (frontal shot) and gas stunning and the return of breathing for the return of consciousness in electrically stunned animals. However, transection of the medulla or spinal cord above the third cervical vertebra stops breathing, while the animal remains fully conscious (Table 14.2).

Vocalization

Vocalizations refer to species-specific sounds produced by the animal. A vocalization following the stun may be reflex vocalization, expressing pain or fear, and involves only the midbrain, or voluntary communication with conspecifics, involving the midbrain and the cortex (Warriss *et al.*, 1994; Grandin, 1998). In either case, species-specific vocalization is indicative of consciousness (Box 14.10; Table 14.2). In addition, if the vocalization expresses pain, the animal is sensitive, which also indicates consciousness. Guttural sounds should not be confused with vocalization; they may be secondary to breathing or gasping (see above).

Reaction to pain

The principle of nociceptive tests is to induce a noxious stimulus on the body or the head of the animal, for example a pinch (comb, ear tips or nasal septum), a skin prick with a hypodermic needle, or spraying with hot water (McKinstry and Anil, 2004; Limon *et al.*, 2010; Parotat *et al.*, 2015; Verhoeven *et al.*, 2015b).

Withdrawal of the stimulated body part is considered a positive reaction but the interpretation is difficult, because a nociceptive reflex response is difficult to distinguish from a conscious withdrawal response to perceived pain (Box 14.11). Properly stunned cattle may show a reflex response to exsanguination, involving a circuit through the spinal cord but not the brain; hence it is not a sign of consciousness. This type of reflex responses persisted 3 min after cessation of breathing (Terlouw *et al.*, 2015). Reflex withdrawal of the head exists also, possibly explaining the response to an ear pinch in pharmacologically anaesthetized sheep

Box 14.10. Brain control of vocalization

In general, animals produce two types of sound and a specific cell group in the caudal midbrain (periaqueductal grey) is essential for both. Elementary vocalizations associated with pain, fear or rage are mediated by a network inside this cell group, controlled by other brain areas to ensure that vocalizations are adapted to the context. For example, threatening calls are produced when in the presence of a subordinate, but not a dominant conspecific (Behbehani, 1995). More complex forms of communication arise in various regions in the cortex, which project to this midbrain cell group (Holstege, 1989; Behbehani, 1995; Jürgens, 2009). Vocalization is coordinated with respiratory activity (Zhang et al., 1995).

Box 14.11. Automatic nociceptive responses

The nociceptive reflex arc is a neural circuit that allows a rapid withdrawal of a limb when it is in contact with a noxious stimulus, even before the brain translates the signal into pain. This circuit involves a nociceptor carrying the message to the spinal cord, a short connecting neuron (interneuron) in the spinal cord and a motor nerve from the interneuron to the muscles in the limb. There is no intervention of the brain and the response is involuntary. In the conscious individual, the brain only subsequently interprets the stimulus in terms of pain.

A nociceptive reflex arc also allows the reflex withdrawal of the head in response to a noxious stimulus. The message is transmitted to cell groups in the pons (Manni et al., 1975; Abrahams et al., 1993; Serrao et al., 2003). The motor neurons responsible for the retraction of the head are located in the cervical vertebrae. This circuit appears to involve several neurons, but it does not involve the brain cortex and the response is therefore also involuntary.

showing an EEG indicative of unconsciousness (Verhoeven et al., 2015b) (Box 14.11).

Another difficulty is that the strength, location and/or type of the nociceptive stimulus seem to influence the likelihood of a response. After stunning and sticking, pigs presenting a corneal and pupillary reflex responded also to a hot-water spray as a nociceptive stimulus, but only one-third responded to a nasal septum pinch, another nociceptive stimulus (Parotat et al., 2015). Similarly, immediately following a neck cut of non-stunned sheep, the withdrawal response to an ear pinch was lost, while breathing and the corneal reflex were still present and the EEG indicated the presence of consciousness (Verhoeven et al., 2015b). These results suggest that, in the slaughter context, certain nociceptive stimuli may not be strong enough to evoke a reaction, or possibly that certain animals, although conscious, are physically unable to respond. Therefore, a pronounced reaction to a relatively moderate nociceptive stimulus, such as a pinch, may be indicative of consciousness. The presence of a reaction to a strong nociceptive stimulus may involve a reflex arc and is not necessarily indicative of con-

sciousness. The absence of a response is not a reliable indicator of unconsciousness. Reactions to nociceptive stimuli must be associated with other clinical signs to help interpret them.

Determining unconsciousness

Studies describing the neurological bases of the clinical signs discussed above generally do not describe the associated state of consciousness, though there are a few exceptions (Mettler, 1965; Halsey and Downie, 1966; Takakushi, 2017). Hence, knowledge of the exact relationships between clinical signs related to brainstem function and state of consciousness is still incomplete, mainly due to the complexity of the subject (Majerus et al., 2005).

In the context of slaughter, it is essential to use several indicators to verify unconsciousness (Table 14.2). The standing position, righting reflexes and vocalization indicate consciousness. Following captive bolt or gas stunning, the loss of the standing posture, the absence of eye movements and ocular reflexes and of rhythmic breathing indicate widespread dysfunction of the midbrain, pons and medulla and consequently unconsciousness. In the case of electrical stunning, the loss of the standing posture and the induction of a tonic state of at least 10 s indicate that sufficient electricity has crossed the brain and that the animal is unconscious, although consciousness may return if the animal is not bled rapidly (Croft, 1952; Warrington, 1974). A return of consciousness is accompanied by the return of the corneal reflex and of rhythmic breathing for all stunning techniques (Terlouw et al., 2016b).

Determining death

In the slaughter context, death is generally caused by a lack of O_2 supply to the brain, often associated with a lack of nutrient supply resulting from cardiac and/or respiratory arrest or exsanguination. It may also be caused by brain damage in the case of a mechanical stun, especially in small animals.

It is difficult to diagnose death formally in the slaughter context (Box 14.12). In practical terms, dressing or scalding is carried out after verification of the absence of certain signs of life; the animal is not breathing, shows no brainstem reflexes and, in addition, is bled properly. If these three points are confirmed, in the context of the abattoir and at this stage of slaughter, the loss of vital functions is irreversible because the animal is completely bled and can therefore be considered dead (Terlouw et al., 2016b).

Acknowledgements

I thank all the people, scientists and field workers, who asked me questions to which I had no immediate answer, and Temple Grandin for offering me the opportunity to deliver the results of my research and reflections on these questions.

References

Abadi, R.V. (2002) Mechanisms underlying nystagmus. *Journal of the Royal Society of Medicine* 95, 231–234.

Abrahams, V.C., Kori, A.A., Loeb, G.E., Richmond, F.J., Rose, P.K. and Keirstead, S.A. (1993) Facial input to neck motoneurons: trigemino-cervical reflexes in the conscious and anaesthetised cat. *Experimental Brain Research* 97, 23–30.

Anton, F., Euchner, I. and Handwerker, H.O. (1992) Psychophysical examination of pain induced by defined CO_2 pulses applied to the nasal mucosa. *Pain* 49, 53–60.

Aramideh, M. and Ongerboer de Visser, B.W. (2002) Brainstem reflexes: electrodiagnostic techniques, physiology, normative data, and clinical applications. *Muscle Nerve* 26, 14–30.

Atkinson, S., Velarde, A. and Algers, B. (2013) Assessment of stun quality at commercial slaughter in cattle shot with captive bolt. *Animal Welfare* 22, 473–481.

Batini, C., Moruzzi, G., Palestini, M., Rossi, G.F. and Zanchetti, A. (1958) Persistent patterns of wakefulness in the pretrigeminal midpontine preparation. *Science* 128, 30–32.

Bazett, H.C. and Penfield, W.G. (1922) A study of the Sherrington decerebrate animal in the chronic as well as the acute condition. *Brain* 45, 185–265.

Behbehani, M.M. (1995) Functional characteristics of the midbrain periaqueductal gray. *Progress in Neurobiology* 46, 575–605.

Beloozerova, I.N. and Sirota, M.G. (2003) Integration of motor and visual information in the parietal area 5 during locomotion. *Journal of Neurophysiology* 90, 961–971.

Berthier, N.E. and Moore, J.W. (1983) The nictitating membrane response: an electrophysiological study of the abducens nerve and nucleus and the accessory abducens nucleus in rabbit. *Brain Research* 258, 201–210.

Bhidayasiri, R., Plant, G.T. and Leigh, R.J. (2000) A hypothetical scheme for the brainstem control of vertical gaze. *Neurology* 54, 1985–1993.

Blackmore, D.K. (1979) Non-penetrative percussion stunning of sheep and calves. *Veterinary Record* 105, 372–375.

Blumenfeld, H. (2005) Cellular and network mechanisms of spike-wave seizures. *Epilepsia* 46, 21–33.

Blumenfeld, H. (2009) The neurological examination of consciousness. In: Laureys, S. and Tononi, G. (eds) *The Neurology of Consciousness*. Academic Press, San Diego, California, pp. 15–30.

Blumenfeld, H., Varghese, G.I., Purcaro, M.J., Motelow, J.E., Enev, M. *et al.* (2009) Cortical and subcortical networks in human secondarily generalized tonic-clonic seizures. *Brain* 132, 999–1012.

Blumenfeld, H., Westerveld, M., Ostroff, R.B., Vanderhill, S.D., Freeman, J. *et al.* (2003) Selective frontal, parietal, and temporal networks in generalized seizures. *NeuroImage* 19, 1556–1566.

Boissy, A., Manteuffel, G., Jensen, M.B., Moe, R.O., Spruijt, B. *et al.* (2007) Assessment of positive emotions in animals to improve their welfare. *Physiology & Behavior* 92, 375–397.

Bour, L., de Visser, B.O., Aramideh, M. and Speelman, J. (2002) Origin of eye and eyelid movements during blinking. *Movement Disorders* 17, S30–S32.

Bourguet, C., Deiss, V., Tannugi, C.C. and Terlouw, E.M. (2011) Behavioural and physiological reactions of cattle in a commercial abattoir: relationships with organisational aspects of the abattoir and animal characteristics. *Meat Science* 88, 158–168.

Brannan, S., Liotti, M., Egan, G., Shade, R., Madden, R. *et al.* (2001) Neuroimaging of cerebral activations and deactivations associated with hypercapnia and hunger for air. *Proceedings of the National Academy of Sciences* 98, 2029–2034.

Brown, R.E., Basheer, R., McKenna, J.T., Strecker, R.E. and McCarley, R.W. (2012) Control of sleep and wakefulness. *Physiological Reviews* 92, 1087–1187.

Burke, R.E., Degtvarenko, A.M. and Simon, E.S. (2001) Patterns of locomotor drive to motoneurons and last-order interneurons: clues to the structure of the CPG. *Journal of Neurophysiology* 86, 447–462.

Bushnell, M.C., Ceko, M. and Low, L.A. (2013) Cognitive and emotional control of pain and its disruption in chronic pain. *Nature Reviews Neuroscience* 14, 502–511.

Chafi, M.S., Ganpule, S., Gu, L. and Handra, N. (2011) Dynamic response of brain subjected to blast loadings: influence of frequency ranges. *International Journal of Applied Mechanics* 3, 803–823.

Chang, A.J., Ortega, F.E., Riegler, J., Madison, D.V. and Krasnow, M.A. (2015) Oxygen regulation of breathing through an olfactory receptor activated by lactate. *Nature* 527, 240–244.

Chennu, S. and Bekinschtein, T. (2012) Arousal modulates auditory attention and awareness: insights from sleep, sedation, and disorders of consciousness. *Frontiers in Psychology* 3, 65.

Comerchero, M.D. and Polich, J. (1999) P3a and P3b from typical auditory and visual stimuli. *Clinical Neurophysiology* 110, 24–30.

Conlee, K.M., Stephens, M.L., Rowan, A.N. and King, L.A. (2005) Carbon dioxide for euthanasia: concerns regarding pain and distress, with special reference to mice and rats. *Laboratory Animals* 39, 137–161.

Cook, C.J., Devine, C.E., Gilbert, K.V., Smith, D.D. and Maasland, S.A. (1995) The effect of electrical head-only stun duration on electroencephalographic-measured seizure and brain amino acid neurotransmitter release. *Meat Science* 40, 137–147.

Crick, F. and Koch, C. (2003) A framework for consciousness. *Nature Neuroscience* 6, 119–126.

Croft, P.G. (1952) Problems of electrical stunning. *Veterinary Record* 64, 255–258.

Cruccu, G. and Deuschl, G. (2000) The clinical use of brainstem reflexes and hand-muscle reflexes. *Clinical Neurophysiology* 111, 371–387.

Cruccu, G., Leardi, M.G., Ferracuti, S. and Manfredi, M. (1997) Corneal reflex responses to mechanical and electrical stimuli in coma and narcotic analgesia in humans. *Neuroscience Letters* 222, 33–36.

Dalmau, A., Rodriguez, P., Llonch, P. and Velarde, A. (2010) Stunning pigs with different gas mixtures: aversion in pigs. *Animal Welfare* 19, 325–333.

Daly, C.C. and Whittington, P.E. (1989) Investigation into the principal determinants of effective captive bolt stunning of sheep. *Research in Veterinary Science* 46, 406–408.

Daly C.C., Gregory, N.G. and Wotton, S.B. (1987) Captive bolt stunning of cattle: effects on brain function and role of bolt velocity. *British Veterinary Journal* 143, 574–580.

Damasio, A.R. (2010) *Self Comes to Mind: Constructing the Conscious Brain*. Pantheon Books, New York.

Davidson, C.M., Pappas, B.A., Stevens, W.D., Fortin, T. and Bennett, S.A. (2000) Chronic cerebral hypoperfusion: loss of pupillary reflex, visual impairment and retinal neurodegeneration. *Brain Research* 859, 96–103.

Devine, C.E., Tavener, A., Gilbert, K.V. and Day, A.M. (1986) Electroencephalographic studies of adult cattle associated with electrical stunning, throat cutting and carcass electro-immobilization. *New Zealand Veterinary Journal* 34, 210–213.

Dodman, N.H. (1977) Observations on the use of the Wernberg dip-lift carbon dioxide apparatus for pre-slaughter anaesthesia of pigs. *British Veterinary Journal* 133, 71–80.

Dörfler, K., Troeger, K., Lücker, E., Schönekeß, H. and Frank, M. (2014) Determination of impact parameters and efficiency of 6.8/15 caliber captive bolt guns. *International Journal of Legal Medicine* 128, 641–646.

Eccleston, C. and Crombez, G. (1999) Pain demands attention: a cognitive-affective model of the interruptive function of pain. *Psychological Bulletin* 125, 356–366.

Emery, N.J. (2006) Cognitive ornithology: the evolution of avian intelligence. *Philosophical Transactions of the Royal Society B* 361, 23–43.

Enderle, J.D. (2006) Eye movements. In: Akay, M. (ed.) *Wiley Encyclopedia of Biomedical Engineering.* Wiley, Hoboken, New Jersey, pp. 1597–1606.

Enev, M., McNally, K.A., Varghese, G., Zubal, I.G., Ootroff, R.D. and Blumenfeld, H. (2007) Imaging onset and propagation of ECT-induced seizures. *Epilepsia* 48, 238–244.

Erasmus, M.A., Turner, P.V. and Widowski, T.M. (2010) Measures of insensibility used to determine effective stunning and killing of poultry. *The Journal of Applied Poultry Research* 19, 288–298.

Evinger, C. (1995) A brain stem reflex in the blink of an eye. *Physiology* 10, 147–153.

Faes, T.J., van der Meij, H.A., de Munck, J.C. and Heethaar, R.M. (1999) The electric resistivity of human tissues (100 Hz–10 MHz): a meta-analysis of review studies. *Physiological Measurement* 20, R1–10.

Farouk, M.M. (2013) Advances in the industrial production of halal and kosher red meat. *Meat Science* 95, 805–820.

Feldman, J.L., Del Negro, C.A. and Gray, P.A. (2013) Understanding the rhythm of breathing: so near, yet so far. *Annual Review of Physiology* 75, 423–452.

Finnie, J. (2001) Animal models of traumatic brain injury: a review. *Australian Veterinary Journal* 79, 628–33.

Fish, R.M. and Geddes, L.A. (2009) Conduction of electrical current to and through the human body: a review. *Eplasty* 9, e44.

Foltz, E.F. and White, L.E. (1962). Pain 'relief' by frontal cingulumotomy. *Journal of Neurosurgery* 19, 89–100.

Forslid, A. (1987) Transient neocortical, hippocampal and amygdaloid EEG silence induced by one minute inhalation of high concentration CO_2 in swine. *Acta Physiologica Scandinavica* 130, 1–10.

Forster, H.V. and Smith, C.A. (2010) Contributions of central and peripheral chemoreceptors to the ventilatory response to $CO_2/H+$. *Journal of Applied Physiology* 108, 989–994.

Frigon, A. (2012) Central pattern generators of the mammalian spinal cord. *The Neuroscientist* 18, 56–69.

Fulton, J.F., Liddell, E.G.T. and Rioch, D.M. (1930) The influence of unilateral destruction of the vestibular nuclei upon posture and the knee-jerk. *Brain* 53, 327–343.

Gentle, M.J. (1992) Pain in birds. *Animal Welfare* 1, 235–247.

Gerritzen, M., Lambooij, B., Reimert, H., Stegeman, A. and Spruijt, B. (2004) On-farm euthanasia of broiler chickens: effects of different gas mixtures on behavior and brain activity. *Poultry Science* 83, 1294–1301.

Gerritzen, M.A., Lambooij, E., Hillebrand, S.J.W., Lankhaar, J.A.C. and Pieterse, C. (2000) Behavioral responses of broilers to different gaseous atmospheres. *Poultry Science* 79, 928–933.

Gibson, T.J., Dadios, N. and Gregory, N.G. (2015a) Effect of neck cut position on time to collapse in halal slaughtered cattle without stunning. *Meat Science* 110, 310–314.

Gibson, T.J., Whitehead, C., Taylor, R., Sykes, O., Chancellor, N.M. and Limon, G. (2015b) Pathophysiology of penetrating captive bolt stunning in alpacas (*Vicugna pacos*), *Meat Science* 100, 227–231.

Gibson, T.J., Taylor, A.H. and Gregory, N.G. (2016) Assessment of the effectiveness of head only and back-of-the-head electrical stunning of chickens. *British Poultry Science* 57, 295–305.

Gibson, T.J., Oliveira, S.E.O., Costa, F.A.D. and Gregory, N.G. (2019) Electroencephalographic assessment of pneumatically powered penetrating and non-penetrating captive-bolt stunning of bulls. *Meat Science* 151, 54–59.

Gilliam, J.N., Shearer, J.K., Woods, J., Hill, J., Reynolds, J. *et al.* (2012) Captive-bolt euthanasia of cattle: determination of optimal-shot placement and evaluation of the Cash Special Euthanizer KitReg for euthanasia of cattle. *Animal Welfare* 21, 99–102.

Gottesmann, C. (1988) What the cerveau isole preparation tells us nowadays about sleep-wake mechanisms? *Neuroscience and Biobehavioral Reviews* 12, 39–48.

Gouveia, K.G., Ferreira, P.G., da Costa, J.C.R., Vaz-Pires, P. and da Costa, P.M. (2009) Assessment of the efficiency of captive-bolt stunning in cattle and feasibility of associated behavioural signs. *Animal Welfare* 18, 171–175.

Grandin, T. (1998) The feasibility of using vocalization scoring as an indicator of poor welfare during cattle slaughter. *Applied Animal Behaviour Science* 56, 121–128.

Grandin, T. (2002) Return-to-sensibility problems after penetrating captive bolt stunning of cattle in commercial beef slaughter plants. *Journal of the American Veterinary Medicine Association* 221, 1258–1261.

Grandin, T. (2019) *Recommended Animal Handling Guidelines and Audit Guide: a Systematic Approach to Animal Welfare.* North American Meat Institute, Washington, DC.

Gregory, N.G. (2001) Profiles of currents during electrical stunning. *Australian Veterinary Journal* 79, 844–845.

Gregory, N.G., Fielding, H.R., von Wenzlawowicz, M. and von Holleben, K. (2010) Time to collapse following slaughter without stunning in cattle. *Meat Science* 85, 66–69.

Gregory, N.G., Lee, C.J. and Widdicombe, J.P. (2007) Depth of concussion in cattle shot by penetrating captive bolt. *Meat Science* 77, 499–503.

Gregory, N.G., Shaw, F.D., Whitford, J.C. and Patterson-Kane, J.C. (2006) Prevalence of ballooning of the severed carotid arteries at slaughter in cattle, calves and sheep. *Meat Science* 74, 655–657.

Guertin, P.A. (2009) The mammalian central pattern generator for locomotion. *Brain Research Reviews* 62, 45–56.

Halsey, J.H. and Downie, A.W. (1966) Decerebrate rigidity with preservation of consciousness. *Journal of Neurology, Neurosurgery, and Psychiatry* 29, 350–355.

Holstege, G. (1989) Anatomical study of the final common pathway for vocalization in the cat. *Journal of Comparative Neurology* 284, 242–252.

Huart, C., Collet, S. and Rombaux, P. (2009) Chemosensory pathways: from periphery to cortex. *B-ENT* 5 (Suppl. 13), 3–9.

Hüfner, K., Stephan, T., Kalla, R., Deutschländer, A., Wagner, J. *et al.* (2007) Structural and functional MRIs disclose cerebellar pathologies in idiopathic downbeat nystagmus. *Neurology* 69, 1128.

Impastato, D.J. (1954) The use of barbiturates in electroshock therapy. *Confinia Neurologica* 14, 269–275.

Ingvar, M. (1986) Cerebral blood flow and metabolic rate during seizures. Relationship to epileptic brain damage. *Annals of the New York Academy of Sciences* 462, 194–206.

James, M.R., Marshall, H. and Carew-McColl, M. (1991) Pulse oximetry during apparent tonic-clonic seizures. *The Lancet* 337, 394–395.

Jarvis, E.D., Gunturkun, O., Bruce, L., Csillag, A., Karten, H. *et al.* (2005) Avian brains and a new understanding of vertebrate brain evolution. *Nature Reviews Neuroscience* 6, 151–159.

Jongman, E.C., Barnett, J.L. and Hemsworth, P.H. (2000) The aversiveness of carbon dioxide stunning in pigs and a comparison of the CO_2 stunner crate vs. the V-restrainer. *Applied Animal Behaviour Science* 67, 67–76.

Jürgens, U. (2009) The neural control of vocalization in mammals: a review. *Journal of Voice* 23, 1–10.

Kalinowsky, L. (1939) Electric-convulsion therapy in schizophrenia. *The Lancet* 234, 1232–1233.

Kamenik, J., Paral, V., Pyszko, M. and Voslarova, E. (2019) Cattle stunning with a penetrative captive bolt device: A review. *Animal Science Journal* 90(3), 307–316.

Kaminer, J., Powers, A.S., Horn, K.G., Hui, C. and Evinger, C. (2011) Characterizing the spontaneous blink generator: an animal model. *Journal of Neuroscience* 31, 11256–11267.

Kao, C.D., Guo, W.Y., Chen, J.T., Wu, Z.A. and Liao, K.K. (2006) MR findings of decerebrate rigidity with preservation of consciousness. *American Journal of Neuroradiology* 27, 10174–1075.

Katayama, Y., Becker, D.P., Tamura, T. and Hovda, D.A. (1990) Massive increases in extracellular potassium and the indiscriminate release of glutamate following concussive brain injury. *Journal of Neurosurgery* 73, 889–900.

Kozicz, T., Bittencourt, J.C., May, P.J., Reiner, A., Gamlin, P.D. *et al.* (2011) The Edinger-Westphal nucleus: a historical, structural, and functional perspective on a dichotomous terminology. *Journal of Comparative Neurology* 519, 1413–1434.

Lambooij, E. (1982) Electrical stunning of sheep. *Meat Science* 6, 123–135.

Lambooij, E. and Spanjaard, W. (1982) Electrical stunning of veal calves. *Meat Science* 6, 15–25.

Lambooij, E., Gerritzen, M.A., Engel, B., Hillebrand, S.J.W., Lankhaar, J. and Pieterse, C. (1999) Behavioural responses during exposure of broiler chickens to different gas mixtures. *Applied Animal Behaviour Science* 62, 255–265.

Lambooij, E., van der Werf, J.T.N., Reimert, H.G.M. and Hindle, V.A. (2012) Restraining and neck cutting or stunning and neck cutting of veal calves. *Meat Science* 91, 22–28.

Laureys, S. (2005) Death, unconsciousness and the brain. *Nature Reviews Neuroscience* 6, 899–909.

LeDoux, J.E. (2000) Emotion circuits in the brain. *Annual Review of Neuroscience* 23, 155–184.

Lee, L.A., Deem, S., Glenny, R.W., Townsend, I., Moulding, J. *et al.* (2008) Effects of anemia and hypotension on porcine optic nerve blood flow and oxygen delivery. *Anesthesiology* 108, 864–872.

Liberson, W.T. (1948) Brief stimulus therapy. *American Journal of Psychiatry* 105, 28–39.

Limon, G., Guitian, J. and Gregory, N.G. (2010) An evaluation of the humaneness of puntilla in cattle. *Meat Science* 84, 352–355.

Llonch, P., Dalmau, A., Rodriguez, P., Manteca, X. and Velarde, A. (2012) Aversion to nitrogen and carbon dioxide mixtures for stunning pigs. *Animal Welfare* 21, 33–39.

Lowndes, M. and Davies, D.C. (1996) The effect of archistriatal lesions on 'open field' and fear/avoidance behaviour in the domestic chick. *Behavioural Brain Research* 72, 25–32.

Magnus, R. (1925) Croonian Lecture. Animal posture. *Proceedings of the Royal Society of London. Series B* 98, 339–353.

Magnus, R. (1926a) Some results of studies in the physiology of posture. Part I. *The Lancet* 211, 531–536.

Magnus, R. (1926b) Some results of studies in the physiology of posture. Part II. *The Lancet* 211, 585–588.

Majerus, S., Gill-Thwaites, H., Andrews, K. and Laureys, S. (2005) Behavioral evaluation of consciousness in severe brain damage. *Progress in Brain Research* 150, 397–413.

Manni, E., Palmieri, G., Marini, R. and Pettorossi, V.E. (1975) Trigeminal influences on extensor muscles of the neck. *Experimental Neurology* 47, 330–342.

Martin, G.T. (2016) Acute brain trauma. *Annals of the Royal College of Surgeons of England* 98, 6–10.

Martoft, L., Stodkilde-Jorgensen, H., Forslid, A., Pedersen, H.D. and Jorgensen, P.F. (2003) CO_2 induced acute respiratory acidosis and brain tissue intracellular pH: a 31P NMR study in swine. *Laboratory Animals* 37, 241–248.

Massey, C.A., Sowers, L.P., Dlouhy, B.J. and Richerson, G.B. (2014) Mechanisms of sudden unexpected death in epilepsy: the pathway to prevention. *Nature Reviews Neurology* 10, 271–282.

McAlonan, K., Cavanaugh, J. and Wurtz, R.H. (2008) Guarding the gateway to cortex with attention in visual thalamus. *Nature* 456, 391–394.

McCormick, D.A. and Bal, T. (1994) Sensory gating mechanisms of the thalamus. *Current Opinion in Neurobiology* 4, 550–556.

McKay, L.C., Evans, K.C., Frackowiak, R.S. and Corfield, D.R. (2003) Neural correlates of voluntary breathing in humans. *Journal of Applied Physiology (Bethesda, MD: 1985)* 95, 1170–1178.

McKay, L.C., Janczewski, W.A. and Feldman, J.L. (2005) Sleep-disordered breathing after targeted ablation of preBotzinger complex neurons. *Nature Neuroscience* 8, 1142–1144.

McKinstry, J.L. and Anil, M.H. (2004) The effect of repeat application of electrical stunning on the welfare of pigs. *Meat Science* 67, 121–128.

Mettler, F.A. (1965) Mesencephalic hemisection in the primate. *American Journal of Physiology* 209, 312–318.

Modianos, D.T. and Pfaff, D.W. (1976) Brain stem and cerebellar lesions in female rats. I. Tests of posture and movement. *Brain Research* 106, 31–46.

Mohan Raj, A.B. and Gregory, N.G. (1990) Effect of rate of induction of carbon dioxide anaesthesia on the time of onset of unconsciousness and convulsions. *Research in Veterinary Science* 49, 360–363.

Morgane, P.J., Galler, J.R. and Mokler, D.J. (2005) A review of systems and networks of the limbic forebrain/limbic midbrain. *Progress in Neurobiology* 75, 143–60.

Moruzzi, G. and Magoun, H.W. (1949) Brain stem reticular formation and activation of the EEG. *Electroencephalography and Clinical Neurophysiology* 1, 455–473.

Mueller, S.M., Heistad, D.D. and Marcus, M.L. (1977) Total and regional cerebral blood flow during hypotension, hypertension and hypocapnia. Effect of sympathetic denervation in dogs. *Circulation Research* 41, 350–356.

Musienko, P., Gorskii, O., Kilimnik, V., Kozlovskaya, I., Courtine, G. *et al.* (2015) Regulation of posture and locomotion in decerebrate and spinal animals. *Neuroscience and Behavioral Physiology* 45, 229–237.

Nakyinsige, K., Man, Y.B.C., Aghwan, Z.A., Zulkifli, I., Goh, Y.M. *et al.* (2013) Stunning and animal welfare from Islamic and scientific perspectives. *Meat Science* 95, 352–361.

Newhook, J.C. and Blackmore, D.K. (1982a) Electroencephalographic studies of stunning and slaughter of sheep and calves. Part 2: The onset of permanent insensibility in calves during slaughter. *Meat Science* 6, 295–300.

Newhook, J.C. and Blackmore, D.K. (1982b) Electroencephalographic studies of stunning and slaughter of sheep and calves. Part 1: The onset of permanent insensibility in sheep during slaughter. *Meat Science* 6, 221–233.

Nordstrom, T., Jansson, L.C., Louhivuori, L.M. and Akerman, K.E. (2012) Effects of acute hypoxia/acidosis on intracellular pH in differentiating neural progenitor cells, *Brain Research* 1461, 10–23.

Northcutt, R.G. (1984) Evolution of the vertebrate central nervous system: patterns and processes. *American Zoologist* 24, 701–716.

Oliveira, S.E.O., Gregory, N.G., Dalla Costa, F.A., Gibson, T.J. and da Costa, M.J.R.P. (2017) Efficiency of low versus high airline pressure in stunning cattle with a pneumatically powered penetrating captive bolt gun. *Meat Science* 130, 64–68.

Oliveira, S.E.O., Dalla Costa, F.A., Gibson, T.J., Dalla Costa, O.A., Coldebella, A. and Gregory, N.G. (2018) Evaluation of brain damage resulting from penetrating and non-penetrating stunning in Nelore cattle using pneumatically powered captive bolt guns. *Meat Science* 145, 347–351.

Ommaya, A.K., Rockoff, S.D., Baldwin, M. and Friauf, W.S. (1964) Experimental concussion. *Journal of Neurosurgery* 21, 249–265.

Ongerboer de Visser, B.W. and Moffie, D. (1979) Effects of brain-stem and thalamic lesions on the corneal reflex: an electrophysiological and anatomical study. *Brain* 102, 595–608.

Parotat, S., von Holleben, K., Arnold, S., Troeger, K. and Luecker, E. (2015) Hot-water spraying is a sensitive test for signs of life before dressing and scalding in pig abattoirs with carbon dioxide (CO_2) stunning. *Animal* 1–7.

Parvizi, J. and Damasio, A.R. (2003) Neuroanatomical correlates of brainstem coma. *Brain* 126, 1524–1536.

Patla, A.E. (1997) Understanding the roles of vision in the control of human locomotion. *Gait & Posture* 5, 54–69.

Paul, E.S., Harding, E.J. and Mendl, M. (2005) Measuring emotional processes in animals: the utility of a cognitive approach. *Neuroscience and Biobehavioral Reviews* 29, 469–491.

Pleiter, H. (2005) Electrical stunning before ritual slaughter of cattle and sheep in New Zealand. *Animal Welfare at Ritual Slaughter*, pp. 72–76.

Ploner, M., Freund, H.J. and Schnitzler, A. (1999) Pain affect without pain sensation in a patient with a postcentral lesion. *Pain* 81, 211–214.

Ploner, M., Gross, J., Timmermann, L. and Schnitzler, A. (2006) Pain processing is faster than tactile processing in the human brain. *Journal of Neuroscience* 26, 10879–10882.

Pollock, L.J. and Davis, L. (1927) Studies in decerebration: IV. Integrated reflexes of the brain stem. *Archives of Neurology & Psychiatry* 17, 18–27.

Pollock, L.J. and Davis, L. (1930) The reflex activities of a decerebrate animal. *Journal of Comparative Neurology* 50, 377–411.

Posner, J.B., Saper, C.B., Schiff, N. and Plum, F. (2008) *Plum and Posner's Diagnosis of Stupor and Coma.* Oxford University Press, Oxford.

Purves, D., and Augustine, G., Fitzpatrick, D. *et al.* (eds) (2004) *Neuroscience*, 3rd edn. Sinauer Associates, Sunderland, Massachusetts.

E.M.C.Terlouw

Raj, A.B.M., Johnson, S.P., Wotton, S.B. and McKinstry, J.L. (1997) Welfare implications of gas stunning pigs: 3. The time to loss of somatosensory evoked potentials and spontaneous electrocorticogram of pigs during exposure to gases. *The Veterinary Journal* 153, 329–340.

Raj, A.B.M. and Gregory, N.G. (1995) Welfare implications of the gas stunning of pigs. 1. Determination of aversion to the initial inhalation of carbon dioxide or argon. *Animal Welfare* 4, 273–280.

Raj, A.B.M., O'Callaghan, M. and Hughes, S.I. (2006) The effects of amount and frequency of pulsed direct current used in water bath stunning and of slaughter methods on spontaneous electroencephalograms in broilers. *Animal Welfare* 15, 19–24.

Raj, M. and Gregory, N.G. (1994) An evaluation of humane gas stunning methods for turkeys. *The Veterinary Record* 135, 222–223.

Raj Mohan, A.B., Gregory, N.G. and Wotton, S.B. (1990) Effect of carbon dioxide stunning on somatosensory evoked potentials in hens. *Research in Veterinary Science* 49, 355–359.

Ramirez, J.M., Schwarzacher, S.W., Pierrefiche, O., Oliveira, B.M. and Richter, D.W. (1998) Selective lesioning of the cat pre-Bötzinger complex in vivo eliminates breathing but not gasping. *The Journal of Physiology* 507(3), 895–907.

Ranson, S.W. and Hinsey, J.C. (1929) Extensor tonus after transection of the brain stem at varying levels. *The Journal of Nervous and Mental Disease* 70, 584–597.

Rees, G. (2009) Visual attention: the thalamus at the centre? *Current Biology* 19, R213–R214.

Rodríguez, P., Dalmau, A., Ruiz-de-la-Torre, J.L., Manteca, X., Jensen, E.W. *et al.* (2008) Assessment of unconsciousness during carbon dioxide stunning in pigs. *Animal Welfare* 17, 341–349.

Sandilands, V., Raj, A.B.M., Baker, L. and Sparks, N.H.C. (2011) Aversion of chickens to various lethal gas mixtures. *Animal Welfare* 20, 253–262.

Schepens, B. and Drew, T. (2004) Independent and convergent signals from the pontomedullary reticular formation contribute to the control of posture and movement during reaching in the cat. *Journal of Neurophysiology* 92, 2217–2238.

Schmidtke, K. and Buttner-Ennever, J.A. (1992) Nervous control of eyelid function. A review of clinical, experimental and pathological data. *Brain: a Journal of Neurology* 115(1), 227–247.

Schridde, U., Khubchandani, M., Motelow, J.E., Sanganahalli, B.G., Hyder, F. and Blumenfeld, H. (2008) Negative BOLD with large increases in neuronal activity. *Cerebral Cortex* 18, 1814–1827.

Schulze, W., Schultze-Petzold, H., Hazem, A.S. and Gross, R. (1978) Experiments for the objectification of pain and consciousness during conventional (captive bolt stunning) and religiously mandated ('ritual cutting') slaughter procedures for sheep and calves. *Deutsche Tieraerztliche Wochenschrift (German Veterinary Weekly)* 85, 62–66.

Serrao, M., Rossi, P., Parisi, L., Perrotta, A., Bartolo, M. *et al.* (2003) Trigemino-cervical-spinal reflexes in humans. *Clinical Neurophysiology* 114, 1697–1703.

Siegel, J.M., Nienhuis, R. and Tomaszewski, K.S. (1983) Rostral brainstem contributes to medullary inhibition of muscle tone. *Brain Research* 268, 344–348.

Siegel, J.M., Tomaszewski, K.S. and Nienhuis, R. (1986) Behavioral states in the chronic medullary and midpontine cat. *Electroencephalography in Clinical Neurophysiology* 63, 274–288.

Smith, J.C., Abdala, A.P., Borgmann, A., Rybak, I.A. and Paton, J.F. (2013) Brainstem respiratory networks: building blocks and microcircuits. *Trends in Neurosciences* 36, 152–162.

St John, W.M. (2009) Noeud vital for breathing in the brainstem: gasping – yes, eupnoea – doubtful. *Philosophical Transactions of the Royal Society of London. Series B* 364, 2625–2633.

Stiegler, P., Sereinigg, M., Puntschart, A., Seifert-Held, T., Zmugg, G. *et al.* (2012) A 10 min 'no-touch' time – Is it enough in DCD? A DCD Animal Study. *Transplant International* 25, 481–492.

Strupp, M., Kremmyda, O., Adamczyk, C., Bottcher, N., Muth., C. *et al.* (2014) Central ocular motor disorders, including gaze palsy and nystagmus. *Journal of Neurology* 261 (Suppl. 2), S542–S558.

Takahashi, H., Manaka, S. and Sano, K. (1981) Changes in extracellular potassium concentration in cortex and brain stem during the acute phase of experimental closed head injury. *Journal of Neurosurgery* 55, 708–717.

Takakusaki, K. (2017) Functional neuroanatomy for posture and gait control. *Journal of Movement Disorders* 10, 1–17.

Tan, W.B., Janczewski, W.A., Yang, P., Shao, X.M., Callaway, E.M. and Feldman, J.L. (2008) Silencing preBotzinger Complex somatostatin-expressing neurons induces persistent apnea in awake rat. *Nature Neuroscience* 11, 538–540.

Tehovnik, E.J., Sommer, M.A., Chou, I.H., Slocum, W.M. and Schiller, P.H. (2000) Eye fields in the frontal lobes of primates. *Brain Research Reviews* 32, 413–448.

Ten Donkelaar, H.J. and De Boer-Van Huizen, R. (1981) Ascending projections of the brain stem reticular formation in a nonmammalian vertebrate (the lizard *Varanus exanthematicus*), with notes on the afferent connections of the forebrain. *The Journal of Comparative Neurology* 200, 501–528.

Teppema, L.J. and Dahan, A. (2010) The ventilatory response to hypoxia in mammals: mechanisms, measurement, and analysis. *Physiological Reviews* 90, 675–754.

Terlouw, C., Bourguet, C. and Deiss, V. (2016a) Consciousness, unconsciousness and death in the context of slaughter. Part I. Neurobiological mechanisms underlying stunning and killing. *Meat Science* 118, 133–146.

Terlouw, C., Bourguet, C. and Deiss, V. (2016b) Consciousness, unconsciousness and death in the context of slaughter. Part II. Evaluation methods. *Meat Science* 118, 147–156.

Terlouw, E.M.C., Bourguet, C., Deiss, V. and Mallet, C. (2015) Origins of movements following stunning and during bleeding in cattle. *Meat Science* 110, 135–144.

Tidswell, S.J., Blackmore, D.K. and Newhook, J.C. (1987) Slaughter methods: electroencephalographs (EEG) studies on spinal cord section, decapitation and gross trauma of the brain in lambs. *New Zealand Veterinary Journal* 35, 46–49.

Timmers, H.J.L.M., Wieling, W., Karemaker, J.M. and Lenders, J.W.M. (2003) Denervation of carotid baro- and chemoreceptors in humans. *The Journal of Physiology* 553, 3–11.

Treiman, D.M. (2001) GABAergic mechanisms in epilepsy. *Epilepsia* 42 (Suppl. 3), 8–12.

Van der Werf, F. and Smit, A.E. (2008) The world according to blink: blinking and aging. In: Cavallotti, C.A.P. and Cerulli, L. (eds) *Age-related Changes of the Human Eye*. Humana Press, Totowa, New Jersey, pp. 319–341.

Velarde, A., Cruz, J., Gispert, M., Carrin, D., Ruize-de-la-Torre, J.L., Diestre, A. and Manteca, X. (2007) Aversion to carbon dioxide stunning in pigs: effect of carbon dioxide concentration and halothane genotype. *Animal Welfare* 16, 513–522.

Velarde, A., Ruiz-de-la-Torre, J.L., Rosello, C., Fabtega, E., Diestre, A. and Manteca, X. (2002) Assessment of return to consciousness after electrical stunning in lambs. *Animal Welfare* 11, 333–341.

Velarde, A., Ruiz-de-la-Torre, J.L., Stub, C., Diestre, A. and Manteca, X. (2000) Factors affecting the effectiveness of head-only electrical stunning in sheep. *Veterinary Record* 147, 40–43.

Verhoeven, M.T.W., Gerritzen, M.A., Kluivers-Poodt, M., Hellebrekers, L.J. and Kemp, B. (2015a) Validation of behavioural indicators used to assess unconsciousness in sheep. *Research in Veterinary Science* 101, 144–153.

Verhoeven, M.T., Gerritzen, M.A., Hellebrekers, L.J. and Kemp, B. (2015b) Indicators used in livestock to assess unconsciousness after stunning: a review. *Animal* 9, 320–330.

Verhoeven, M.T.W., Gerritzen, M.A., Hellebrekers, L.J. and Kemp, B. (2016) Validation of indicators used to assess unconsciousness in veal calves at slaughter. *Animal* 10, 1457–1465.

Vernon, R.G. (2005) Metabolic regulation. In: Dijkstra, J., Forbes, J.M. and France, J. (eds) *Quantitative Aspects of Ruminant Digestion and Metabolism*, 2nd edn. CABI, Wallingford, UK.

Vogel, K.D., Badtram, G., Claus, J.R., Grandin, T., Turpin, S. *et al.* (2011) Head only followed by cardiac arrest electrical stunning is an effective alternative to head-only electrical stunning in pigs. *Journal of Animal Science* 89, 1412–1418.

Wager, T.D., Davidson, M.L., Hughes, B.L., Lindquist, M.A. and Ochsner, K.N. (2008) Prefrontal-subcortical pathways mediating successful emotion regulation. *Neuron* 59, 1037–1050.

Warrington, P.D. (1974) Electrical stunning: a review of literature. *The Veterinary Bulletin* 44, 617–633.

Warriss, P.D., Brown, S.N., Adams, S.J.M. and Corlett, I.K. (1994) Relationships between subjective and objective assessments of stress at slaughter and meat quality in pigs. *Meat Science* 38, 329–340.

Weaver, A.L. and Wotton, S.B. (2009) The Jarvis Beef Stunner: Effects of a prototype chest electrode. *Meat Science* 81, 51–56.

Weiss, N., Galanaud, D., Carpentier, A., Naccache, L. and Puybasset, L. (2007) Clinical review: Prognostic value of magnetic resonance imaging in acute brain injury and coma. *Critical Care* 11, 230.

Wotton, S.B. and O'Callaghan, M. (2002) Electrical stunning of pigs: the effect of applied voltage on impedance to current flow and the operation of a fail-safe device. *Meat Science* 60, 203–208.

Wotton, S.B., Anil, M.H., Whittington, P.E. and McKinstry, J.L. (1992) Pig slaughtering procedures: head-to-back stunning. *Meat Science* 32, 245–255.

Xiao, F.L., Gao, P.Y., Sui, B.B., Wan, H., Lin, Y. *et al.* (2015) Time-course of changes in activation among facial nerve injury: a functional imaging study. *Medicine (Baltimore)* 94, e1582.

Zauner, A. and Muizelaar, J.P. (1997) *Head injury*. Chapman and Hall, London, pp. 217–227.

Zeman, A. (2001) Consciousness. *Brain: a Journal of Neurology* 124, 1263–1289.

Zhang, S.P., Bandler, R. and Davis, P.J. (1995) Brain stem integration of vocalization: role of the nucleus retroambigualis. *Journal of Neurophysiology* 74, 2500–2512.

Zhu, F., Skelton, P., Chou, C.C., Mao, H., Yang, K.H. and King, A.I. (2013). Biomechanical responses of a pig head under blast loading: a computational simulation. *International Journal for Numerical Methods in Biomedical Engineering* 29, 392–407.

Zimmerman, P.H., Buijs, S.A.F., Bolhuis, J.E. and Keeling, L.J. (2011) Behaviour of domestic fowl in anticipation of positive and negative stimuli. *Animal Behaviour* 81, 569–577.

15 The Importance of Good Pre-slaughter Handling to Improve Meat Quality in Cattle, Pigs, Sheep and Poultry

TEMPLE GRANDIN*

Department of Animal Science, Colorado State University, USA

Summary

Careful low-stress handling at the slaughter plant can help maintain meat quality. Poor handling practices shortly before stunning can increase problems with tough meat in cattle and pale soft exudative (watery) (PSE) meat in pigs. There is a basic principle of the effects of the stress of handling and transport on meat quality. Short-term stresses such as electric prod use in the stunning race cause lower pH in the meat and increase lactate and glucose levels (Edwards *et al.*, 2010). Longer-term stresses such as long transport times raise pH and increase dark cutting. To explain it simply, short-term stresses a few minutes before stunning tend to make meat tougher and light in colour. Longer-term stresses darken meat colour and reduce shelf life. Both PSE and dark cutting or dark firm dry (DFD) meat are severe quality defects.

There are exceptions to the short-term versus long-term stress rule, but in general, this principle is true. To explain it in an easy to understand manner, dark cutters occur when the muscle glycogen is depleted and lactic acid can no longer be produced. This causes the muscle pH to rise. A good analogy is a car running out of fuel. When the glycogen runs out, the pH will rise and meat color will darken. There are many factors that can contribute to the 'fuel' running out. Dark cutting may be caused by a combination of long transit times, fluctuating hot and cold temperatures, nutrition, hormone implant programs, animal genetics, bulls fighting

and mounting in the lairage, and other factors (Ponnampalam *et al.*, 2017). In both livestock and poultry, careful handling will reduce the percentage of bruised animals.

Learning Objectives

- Understand factors that can cause meat quality problems during handling and transport.
- Learn the importance of low-stress handling to maintain meat quality.
- How on-farm conditions have an effect on meat quality.
- Bruises can be reduced in all species with careful handling.

The Importance of Maintaining High Meat Quality

Both PSE and DFD meat are severe quality problems (Przbylski and Hopkins, 2016). Figure 15.1 shows both normal and dark cutting beef. PSE pork has poor water binding and it has greater cooking losses (Fig. 15.2). Dark cutting beef and lamb is darker and has a shorter shelf life in the grocery store (Adzitey and Nurul, 2011). Consumers generally prefer high-quality pork, beef and lamb (Viljoen *et al.*, 2002). Handling practices at the abattoir can have a significant effect on meat quality (Grandin, 2015; Faucitano, 2018).

---

* Email: cheryl.miller@colostate.edu

Detrimental Effects of Short-term Stress

Jamming in the race and electric prod use within 5 min prior to stunning increased blood lactate levels in pigs and had a detrimental effect on pork quality (Edwards *et al.*, 2010; Vermeulen *et al.* 2015a,b; Oliveira *et al.*, 2018. Faucitano (2018) reported that improving handling reduces PSE and skin damage. Hambrecht *et al.* (2005a,b) found that some of the most detrimental effects of poor handling occurred close to the time of stunning. Lactate levels can be easily measured at bleeding as an indicator of the quality of handling (Edwards *et al.*, 2010; Rocha *et al.*, 2016). Squealing shortly before stunning is associated with both physiological measures of stress and poor pork quality (Warriss *et al.*, 1994) (see Chapter 12).

When pigs are handled carefully, lactate levels will be in the single-digit range of 4–6 mM (Benjamin *et al.*, 2001; Edwards *et al.*, 2010). Other studies have shown that lactate levels can range from 4.4 mM to 31 mM depending in the quality of handling (Warriss *et al.*, 1994; Hambrecht *et al.*, 2004,

2005a,b). Lactate can be easily measured with a handheld meter (Burfeind and Heuwieser, 2012). Rapid chilling will reduce PSE, but it will not prevent poor-quality pork caused by high pre-slaughter stress (Hambrechet *et al.*, 2004).

Similar results have been found in cattle. Repeated shocking of cattle with an electric prod shortly before stunning resulted in tougher meat (Warner *et al.*, 2007). Cattle with high lactate levels at bleeding had tougher meat (Gruber *et al.*, 2010). Meat tenderness was measured with the Warner Bratzler shear test.

For assessment of stress shortly before slaughter, there are two easy-to-use temperature measurements. Pigs at risk for poor-quality PSE meat had higher body temperatures (Vermeulen *et al.*, 2015a,b). Body temperatures can be measured in live pigs shortly before stunning with infrared thermography (Rocha *et al.*, 2016). Continuous scoring of handling practices should be used to maintain low-stress handling. Either the animal welfare officer or the quality assurance manager should monitor handling practices. Scoring of handling is covered in Chapter 12. Low levels of electric prod use, animals falling down, jamming or vocalizing in the stunning area will help preserve meat quality.

To preserve meat quality, it is essential that the producer deliver to the slaughter plant animals that are easy to handle. Weak or lame animals that are less willing to move may be more likely to be handled roughly with excessive electric prod use. Highly excitable animals or aggressive animals are also difficult to handle. Many welfare issues that occur at abattoirs are due to conditions outside the plant.

Good Lairage Practices

Low-stress handling is difficult if the livestock refuse to move easily. Pigs should be rested in the

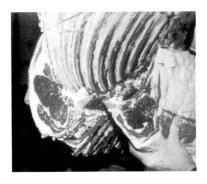

Fig. 15.1. Dark cutting (DFD) beef is shown on the right hand side and normal red beef is shown on the left. Dark cutting beef is a severe quality defect.

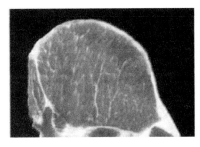 

Fig. 15.2. The picture on the right shows pale soft exudative (PSE) pork and the picture on the left shows normal pork. Pale soft pork has poor water-binding capacity and has a low pH. (Photo from www.fao.org.)

T. Grandin

lairage pens (stockyard) for 1–3 h before stunning. This will make them easier to handle. Research clearly shows that resting reduces PSE (Milligan et al., 1998; Perez et al., 2002; Warriss, 2003). The time of resting is calculated as the total time the pigs are in the lairage holding pen. They should have a minimum of 1 h of undisturbed rest. Overnight resting provides no advantages. In some cases, too many hours spent in the lairage may result in stiff difficult-to-move animals. Stress was reduced if pigs were held in a lairage for under 4 h. Perez et al. (2002) concluded that both a failure to rest pigs in the lairage or an excessively long period in the yards without food is detrimental to pork quality. Cattle should have a short period to settle down after truck uploading. In some countries, long lairage periods are required. Unfortunately, there may be some situations where this could cause dark cutters.

Handling Bulls

Ideally, bulls should be kept in farm penmate groups throughout transport and during lairage at the plant. Mixing bulls from different pens will cause fighting and mounting, because the animals have to establish a new dominance order. Agonistic (fighting) behaviour between bulls that are mixed increases dark cutting (Price and Tennessen, 1981). Bulls have a tendency to have more dark cutters than steers. Mounting behaviour, and the increased physical exertion associated with it, increases the incidence of dark cutting (Tarrant, 1989). Many abattoirs that slaughter bulls construct a roof with steel bars over each pen in the lairage. This prevents bulls from mounting if they have to be mixed with strange bulls. Devices that prevent mixed bulls from mounting will reduce dark cutters (Bartos et al., 1988).

Handling Practices on the Farm Will Affect Handling Ease at the Abattoir

An animal's experience with handling on the farm will have an effect on its behaviour at the slaughter plant. Pigs will differentiate between a person walking in the alley and a person walking through their pens. Pigs that have never experienced people walking through their pens on the farm may be more difficult to handle at the plant (Grandin, 2014, 2015). They may be more likely to pile up and squeal when people attempt to move them. Producers should walk through the fattening (finishing)

pens every day to train pigs to move quietly away from people walking through them. Research clearly shows that previous experiences with handling at the farm will make pigs easier to handle in the future (Abbot et al. 1997; Geverink et al., 1998; Krebs and McGlone, 2009). Pigs that move easily will be less likely to be subjected to poor handling practices such as excessive electric prod use, pile-ups, jamming in races and squealing.

In cattle, on-farm handling practices can also have an effect on behaviour at the plant. Cattle that have never been moved by a person on foot can be difficult and dangerous to handle by a person walking on the ground (Grandin, 2015). This is more likely to be a problem with extensively raised cattle that are handled by cowboys on horseback. A person on a horse and a person on the ground look totally different. When cattle have become accustomed to the person on the horse, it is perceived as safe and familiar. The sudden appearance of a person on the ground is perceived as novel and frightening. This can greatly increase the animal's flight zone (see Chapter 6). This may also contribute to meat quality problems.

Pork Quality and Stunning Method

One reason why some pork abattoirs have switched from electrical stunning to CO_2 is to improve pork quality. The biggest problems associated with electrical stunning are bone fractures and ecchymosis (blood spots in the pork) (Channon et al., 2003a,b; Marcon et al., 2019). Fractured vertebrae can damage the loins. From a welfare perspective, fractures are a non-issue because the pig is rendered instantly unconscious. There is also some evidence that electrical stunning may increase PSE and cooking losses. This is especially a problem if long application times of 19 s are used (Channon et al., 2003a,b). Short electrical stunning times of 4 s or less reduced problems with PSE.

During years of consulting, the author has learned how to greatly reduce problems with ecchymosis and bone fractures associated with electrical stunning. The following are recommendations to preserve pork quality.

- Do not energize the tongs until they are pressed firmly against the animal.
- Do not double stun.
- Do not slide the tongs during the stun. This is likely to cause the muscles to contract more than

once. This may increase the occurrence of fractures or ecchymosis.

- Keep the wiring connections and switches dry. All electrical equipment must be protected from water when the plant is cleaned. Store the tongs in a dry location. If possible, mount the stunner power unit in a separate utility room. Water in the wiring may increase electrical fluctuations and increase ecchymosis. Electrical current fluctuations may cause the muscles to contract more than once.
- Periodic replacement of tong wiring switches and connectors may reduce ecchymosis. Carbon deposits on electrical switch contacts may cause current fluctuations.
- Animals must be wetted, but electrical components such as switches must be kept dry.
- Frequently clean the electrodes that contact the animal.

Practical experience in many pork abattoirs by the author indicates that the meat quality difference between CO_2 and electrical stunning are greatly reduced by careful management of electrical stunning. Economics may not justify the use of CO_2 when it is compared with well-managed electrical stunning. Electrical stunning requires continuous attention to the details of the procedure. Some good reviews are in Grandin (1986) (see also Chapter 14).

Genetic Effects on Meat Quality

Pigs and cattle with a more excitable temperament may have poorer meat quality. In cattle, the animals with a more excitable temperament may have more dark cutters and meat quality problems (Voisinet et al., 1997; King et al., 2006; Café et al., 2010; Hall et al., 2011; Ponnanpalom et al., 2017; Della Rosa et al., 2018). High death losses and increased PSE can occur in pigs that are homozygous for the porcine stress syndrome (PSS) halothane gene (Murray and Johnson, 1998). Fortunately, in many modern pig populations, this gene has been greatly reduced through selective breeding (Ritter et al., 2009). There are still some populations of pigs with the halothane gene. It can be very detrimental to pork quality because the pigs may have more PSE. Pigs with the stress gene may quiver all over, lie down and become non-ambulatory. Sometimes their skin will have a red splotching area. To cool the pig, wet the floor around it. Spraying cold water directly on the pig may kill it.

Porcine Stress Gene Genetics

There are some older pig populations that may have been deliberately bred to have the halothane gene (named because of the adverse effects noticed under halothane anaesthesia), because it is associated with lean low-fat pork. The halothane gene is a classical Mendelian trait. For a pig to exhibit the PSS condition with high death losses, it has to inherit the halothane gene from both the sire and the dam. This creates a homozygous positive animal. The carrier (heterozygote) pig is created by inheritance of only one PSS gene from either one of the parents. The heterozygote animal will be less likely to have increased death losses. Its tendency to have PSE meat may be greater than pigs completely free of the halothane gene (Band et al., 2005). A pig completely free of the halothane gene is homozygous negative. If a sire and dam that are carriers (heterozygotes) are mated, some but not all of the piglets will be homozygous positive for PSS.

Leg Conformation Problems and Lameness (Difficulty Walking)

Indiscriminate breeding for meat traits may be associated with poor leg conformation (Grandin, 2015). Pigs and cattle with poor leg conformation may have difficulty walking and be lame. Lame animals are more difficult to handle, which may lead to more electric prod use and rough handling. Producers should be encouraged to select both cattle and pigs with correct feet and legs (Le et al., 2015a,b) (Fig. 15.3).

Lameness can be caused by other factors, such as poorly designed dairy freestalls (cubicles) and poorly bedded housing (Fulwider et al., 2007; Grandin, 2015) (see Chapter 16 for lameness scoring methods). Another factor is housing cattle for long periods on bare concrete (Wagner et al., 2016). Producers who deliver high percentages of lame animals to the abattoir should work to reduce lameness. There are many different causes of lameness and most of them originate at the farm. The first step in reducing lameness is to measure it and work with producers (Cook et al., 2015; Grandin, 2017). The author has observed that cattle with swollen knee joints are more likely to lie in an abnormal position. Normal cattle will tuck both front legs under their bodies when they are lying down in sternal recumbency (lying on their brisket). If one of the front legs is sore, the animal will

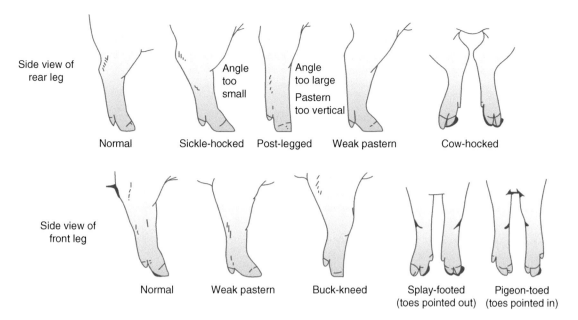

Fig. 15.3. Leg conformation chart. Diagrams of common poor conformation of the feet and legs of cattle, pigs and other livestock. Poor leg and hoof structure is a major cause of lameness (difficulty in walking). Breeders should select animals with the normal correct hoof and lower leg angle. An animal's hoof should point straight forward. The two diagrams on the bottom show poor conformation with toes pointed either in or out.

lie down and extend the leg straight out. The other front leg will be tucked under the body. Figure 15.4 shows a scoring chart for eroded knee joints in fattened feedlot cattle.

Factors that may be contributing to joint damage and lameness in livestock include:

1. Heavier weights at a younger age.
2. Leg conformation problems associated with indiscriminate genetic selection for carcass traits. In the late 1980s and early 1990s the pork industry had serious problems with lame pigs due to poor leg and ankle conformation. The author has observed that problems with downed non-ambulatory pigs were greatly reduced when pork producers stopped using a boar genetic line with poor legs. To prevent lameness, the Angus Association in the USA now has guidelines for leg conformation. Vollmar (2016) reported that cattle originating from ranches in northern USA were more likely to have the crooked-class hoof defects compared with cattle from Texas. This is possibly due to the more intensive breeding programmes at the larger northern ranches.
3. Feeding diets with excessive levels of concentrates such as grain. The animals may be being pushed too hard with high concentrate ratios.

4. Feeding young cattle for long periods on concrete slats. Wagner (2016) found that cattle housed on bare concrete slats had increased swollen knee joints compared with slats covered with rubber. The author observed that young 180 kg (400 lb) cattle housed for 100 days or less on bare concrete slats had knee joints with normal appearance, but similar cattle housed for longer periods on concrete slabs had leg problems. These cattle were fed a high grain diet. It appears that the length of time housed on the concrete slats is a factor. More mature heavy (539 kg) cattle placed on concrete slats were free of adverse effects (Earley *et al.*, 2017). This may be due to the cattle being more mature and fed more roughage. Elmore *et al.* (2015) also reported that rubber mats reduced joint swelling. Reducing the number of days that cattle are housed on slats will reduce joint swelling and leg abnormalities.

Cardiac Weakness, Liver Abscesses, Lung Lesions and Other On-farm Factors That May Affect Meat Quality

During my observations at slaughter plants, there are more and more welfare and meat quality prob-

Fed Cattle Knee Joint Score

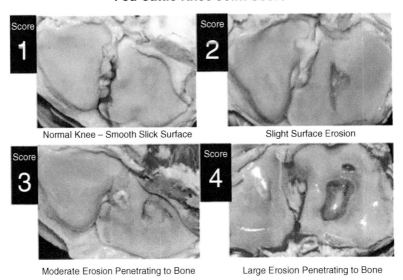

Score 1 — Normal Knee – Smooth Slick Surface

Score 2 — Slight Surface Erosion

Score 3 — Moderate Erosion Penetrating to Bone

Score 4 — Large Erosion Penetrating to Bone

Fig. 15.4. Cattle knee joint scoring chart developed by Dr Scott Crain. A score of 1 is normal and a score of 4 is severe.

lems that will have to be corrected at the farm. These issues may cause death losses, more difficult handling or lower meat quality. To solve these problems will require changes in either production or breeding practices. A complete review of all the causes is beyond the scope of this book. However, it is important to be aware that many meat quality and livestock handling issues must be addressed at the farm. These issues may require changes in genetic selection, feeding or housing.

Poultry breeders have known for years that fast-growing broilers would often die from 'flip over' disease. Birds bred for meat have a higher suscepti-bility to cardiac arrhythmia problems (Gesek *et al.*, 2016). The livestock industry needs to avoid repeating some of these same mistakes. Research clearly shows that some heavy chickens have a severe meat quality problem called woody breast or white striping (Permentier *et al.*, 2015; Kuttapan *et al.*, 2016, 2017; Tijare *et al.*, 2016). Muscle can grow so rapidly that the circulatory system cannot keep up. In extreme cases, an area of necrosis will form in the middle of a poultry muscle (Velleman, 2015). In pigs, animals with reduced cardiac func-tions were more likely to die during transport (Zurbrigg *et al.*, 2017, 2019).

In beef cattle, some animals living at very high altitudes have cardiac problems. Some are more resistant to the hypoxic effects of high altitudes than others. This condition is heritable (Will *et al.*, 1975; Newman *et al.*, 2015). Beef cattle bred to have superior carcass traits may have more difficulty living at high altitudes. Unfortunately, US ranchers are starting to observe cardiac problems in cattle that were originally only seen at high altitudes. Heart issues are occurring at much lower elevations (Neary *et al.*, 2015). It is possible that indiscriminate breeding selection for larger cattle and improved carcass traits has contributed to this problem. Genomic analysis found a possible weak association between growth and pulmonary arterial pressure (PAP) test of high-altitude sickness (Cockrum *et al.*, 2019). Heavy Angus steers with increased levels of adiposity (fat) were at increased risk of heart failure during finishing (fattening) (Neary *et al.*, 2015). Researchers at Kansas State University have described a new condition in beef cattle called fatigued cattle syndrome (Thomson *et al.*, 2015). It is most likely to occur in very large grain-fed cattle when they are subjected to physical exertion. Cattle that become non-ambulatory have high lactic acid levels (Thomson *et al.*, 2015). This is similar to fatigued pigs. This is extremely detrimental to both meat quality and animal welfare.

T. Grandin

Liver Abscesses and Lung Lesions

Amachawadi and Nagaraja (2015) reported that 10–20% of fed beef cattle had liver abscesses. The problem was worse in grain-fed Holstein cattle (Amachawadi and Nagaraja, 2015). Holsteins with edible livers had higher carcass weights (Herrick et al., 2018). McCoy et al. (2017) found that fed steers with severe liver abscesses had tougher meat and a reduction in carcass weights (Brown and Lawrence, 2010). Researchers in New Zealand found similar problems with an increased incidence of liver abscesses in pastured bulls. Meat inspection reports from 137,675 bulls indicated that dairy breed bulls had 10.3% abscessed livers and the beef breeds had only 4.7% (Trotter, 2016). Both studies illustrate that there is a genetic effect on the likelihood that an animal will get liver abscesses.

There may be a great variation in the percentage of cattle having liver abscesses. Groups of cattle may have a range of 0% to 70% (Reinhardt and Hubbert, 2015). This illustrates that feeding practices and other on-farm factors are associated with increased liver abscesses. Mild to moderate liver abscesses had a minimal effect on cattle performance (Davis et al., 2007). Baier (2019) found that liver abscesses had no significant effect on measures of stress. Most liver abscess scoring systems do not differentiate between severe liver abscesses that adhere to the body wall and ones that do not. Research is needed to determine the effects of abscesses that cause adhesions. Trim loss from adhesions can destroy large amounts of meat.

Some groups of pigs will have a high percentage of lung lesions. Scollo et al. (2017) found that there was a strong relationship between certain farms and lung lesions observed at slaughter. Observations in the USA indicate that 10–15% may have lung lesions that adhere to the body wall. Lung lesions can greatly increase pork quality problems and downgraded carcasses (Permentier et al., 2015; Karabasil et al., 2017).

Effects of Growth Promoters and Hormones on Meat Quality, Handling and Death Losses

An animal's biology can be overloaded either by overzealous genetic selection for production traits or by administering too many growth or milk production promoters. Unless it is used very carefully, the hormone rBST, which is used for increasing milk production, has caused problems in dairy cows. The cow may have increased difficulty maintaining her body condition and suffer more illness from mastitis (Kronfeld, 1994, 2000; Collier et al., 2001). Problems with rBST may be closely related, with higher doses causing more problems. Cows given a high dose of 30.9 mg tended to have more days open and re-breeding required more artificial insemination (AI) services (Endman et al., 1990).

Beta agonists (zilpaterol and ractopamine) increase muscle mass (Scamlin et al., 2009). These products are not hormones or antibiotics. They may also make meat tougher (Shook et al., 2009; Merez-Murillo et al., 2016). The author and other people who work in slaughter plants have observed that cattle fed high doses of beta agonists are sometimes lame and stiff when they arrive (Grandin, 2015). This problem is more likely to occur during hot weather. Hagenmaier et al. (2017) also reported increased lameness in feedlot cattle during unloading at the abattoir during hot weather. Physical exertion and muscle fatigue during handling and transport may make it worse. Frese et al. (2016) reported that running 563 kg heavy fed steers for 1540 m raised physiological indicators of stress compared with walking them. Observations in the field indicate that problems are more likely to occur during hot weather over 32°C (90°F) on the day of slaughter (Grandin, 2015). Higher doses tend to worsen the detrimental effects. When pigs were fed a high dose of ractopamine, they were more difficult to handle (Marchant-Forde et al., 2003; Ritter et al., 2017). Aggression between pigs also increased in pigs fed high doses (> 10 mg) of ractopamine (Poletto et al., 2008). During hot weather, death losses in cattle may be increased (Montgomery et al., 2008; Longeragan et al., 2014). Zilpaterol may also increase cardiac problems in cattle (Neary et al., 2018). Pigs fed 20 mg ractopamine/kg were more likely to become stressed if they were handled roughly (James et al., 2013). An increase in downed non-ambulatory pigs was related to the dose. A dose of 5 mg/kg had no effect and a dose of 7.5 mg/kg, fed for 28 days, increased downed fatigued pigs (Peterson et al., 2015). Another study showed that ractopamine fed at a dose of 10 mg for 28 days increased epinephrine levels and had only minor effects on handling (Puls et al., 2014). One study showed that heat stress may be increased in sheep fed beta agonists (Marcias-Cruz et al., 2010). Another study done with zilpaterol showed minor heat stress effects

(Boyd *et al.*, 2015); 78% of the cattle had red hides and the temperature during the beta agonist feeding period was high, but it dropped below 32°C (90°F) on the day of slaughter. In the USA, zilpaterol has a 3-day withdrawal period prior to slaughter. The cattle in this study had an extra (fourth) day of withdrawal prior to slaughter. There is a possibility that this may have reduced the detrimental effects during handling and transport.

There is also evidence that high doses of ractopamine may be associated with hoof cracking in pigs (Poletto *et al.*, 2009). Feeding zilpaterol increased abnormal lateral lying posture in 31% of the cattle (Tucker *et al.*, 2015). Cattle fed a combination of a high-starch diet of potato waste and high doses of zilpaterol had sloughing off of the outer hoof shell during hot weather (Huffstutter and Polansek, 2013). Most problems were associated with either a combination of high doses or hot temperatures greater than 32°C (90°F), either shortly before or on the day of slaughter. In cattle and pigs, problems with both animal welfare and handling associated with beta agonists were associated with higher doses and longer periods of time on the additive. Baszczak *et al.* (2006) found that feeding ractopamine to cattle at a dose of 200 mg/day for 28 days had little effect. A review of the literature in pigs also indicated that higher doses cause more problems (Ritter *et al.*, 2017). To prevent problems with beta agonists, high doses must be avoided. Reports from veterinarians in the field indicate that feedlots can make their records appear to have low doses. This form of cheating is done by inputting into the computer that the animal will eat a smaller amount of feed than it actually does.

Synthetic male hormone ear implants containing trenbolone acetate can increase dark cutters if given at excessive doses (Scanga *et al.*, 1998). The author has observed that high doses can also cause fed feedlot heifers to have a masculine appearance.

Methods to Reduce Bruises in Livestock

The first step is to determine if bruises are happening within the abattoir or outside it. Bruises that originate from a problem inside the plant will usually occur on livestock from many different sources and they will be fresh. Exact ageing of bruises is difficult but fresh bruises on the day of slaughter will be bright red. Bruises that are 48 h old may be yellow or yellow/red (Hamdy *et al.*, 1957; McCausland and Dougherty, 1978; Strappini *et al.*,

2009). Old injuries that are several weeks or months old may have yellow discoloration (Grandin, 2015). In broiler chickens, bruises can be distinguished between recent and old. Chicken bruises that are over 24 h old will be greenish (Northcutt and Rowland, 2000). Fresh poultry bruises will be red.

Good record keeping is essential to document origin of bruises

To determine the origin of bruises (Boxes 15.1, 15.2), careful records should be kept of the location of bruises and the origin of the livestock. To reduce bruises in the abattoir, the first step is to find and prevent the bruises that are occurring inside the plant. The next step is to find bruises that are associated with certain truckers or farms. Research clearly shows that certain truckers or farms are associated with higher levels of either bruises or death losses (Gonzales *et al.*, 2012).

One of the most effective ways to reduce bruises and other losses is to hold transporters and producers economically accountable (Grandin, 1981, 2015). When people have to pay for bruises, they will work to reduce them.

Solving Bruise and Injury Problems in Poultry

Bruised legs

The author has observed that rough shackling is a major cause of bruised drumsticks. The people doing the shackling squeeze the legs too hard when they put the birds on the shackles. An understaffed shackle line where people have to hurry is one cause of bruised legs (Grandin, 2015).

Bruised chicken breasts

There are two major causes of bruised chicken breasts. One cause is jamming birds too quickly through the small opening in the top of the coop. The other results from machine catching systems when birds are jammed against the coop door by a conveyor that is out of alignment.

Smashed heads

This injury is most likely to occur when drawer systems are used for transporting chickens,

Box 15.1. Common causes of fresh bruises in the abattoir and during transport

- **Stun box door** – The door strikes the back of the animal due to either poorly designed controls or operation carelessness. One study showed that the door often hit cattle (Munoz et al., 2012). Bruising can still occur after stunning and prior to bleeding (Meischke and Horder, 1976).
- **Rough livestock handling** – Poor handling methods can cause animals to fall down, jump on each other or get trampled. Cattle handled roughly had more bruises (Grandin, 1981; Weeks et al., 2002; Mendonca et al., 2016).
- **Sharp edges on equipment** – Edges with a small diameter are more likely to causes bruises (Fig. 15.5). Bruises caused by an equipment problem inside the abattoir will often be at the same location on animals from many different sources.
- **Overloaded trucks** – Transporters should follow truck loading guidelines. Overloaded trucks may have more bruised cattle and dead pigs (Ritter et al., 2006, 2009; Schwartzkopf-Genswein and Grandin, 2014). Sheep are less likely to slip or fall during transport if they have adequate space (Jones et al., 2010). If an animal goes down and it is stepped on by other animals, it may have severe bruising over large areas of the carcass.
- **Poor driving** – Sudden stops and starts may throw animals off-balance and increase bruising. Good driving practices will reduce bruises (Tarrant et al., 1992; Schwartzkopf-Genswein and Grandin, 2014).
- **Truck compartments too low** – If tall cattle are getting more back bruises, the height of the truck compartments may be too low (Fig. 15.6). One study showed that tall Holstein steers had more bruises than shorter beef breed cattle (Lee et al., 2017). This is likely due to taller animals hitting the underside of the decks.
- **Grabbing sheep by the wool** – Lifting sheep by the wool will cause severe bruises. Managers must train employees never to grab sheep by the wool.
- **Sticks with nails in them** – Poking animals with sticks with nails on the end will damage the hides and causes bruises. Pointed objects for driving animals should be prohibited.
- **Slippery floors** – Slick floors in trucks, races, lairage pens and other areas can cause animals to fall.
- **Worn-out metal** – Animals rubbing against metal equipment can wear holes through pipes and sheet metal. These worn areas may have extremely sharp edges that can tear hides and cause bruises.

Box 15.2. Common causes of older bruises

Older bruises will no longer be red. They will be darker and have areas with yellowish mucus. The author has observed that yellowish mucus can still be present several months after an injury.

- **Auctions and livestock markets** – Livestock that pass through markets will usually have more bruises than animals sold to the abattoir directly from the farm of origin (Cockram and Lee, 1991; Hoffman et al., 1998; Weeks et al., 2002).
- **Fighting and mounting** – Mixing strange animals at markets can increase bruises.
- **Number of times handled and transported** – Livestock that are handled multiple times or loaded and unloaded many times often have more bruises.
- **Hail damage** – Cattle hit by hail will often have multiple small bruises.
- **Swinging gates into animals** – Animals can become bruised if gates are swung at them in an attempt to stop animal movement down an alley. The worst bruises occur if the animal gets stuck between the end of a gate and a fence.
- **Tieback gates** – Gates in markets and lairages should be equipped with tiebacks to prevent them from accidentally swinging out into groups of approaching livestock.

---

where the birds are put in trays that are slid into rack-like dresser drawers. Drawer systems that have been redesigned so that there is a gap between the stop of the drawer and the rack frame seldom have this problem. This gap prevents the head of a chicken from being smashed when the drawer full of chickens is slid back into the rack.

Importance of Good Pre-slaughter Handling

Fig. 15.5. Edges with a small diameter such as steel angle irons are more likely to cause bruises than larger rounded surfaces. Steel T shapes and angles are not recommended for lairage construction.

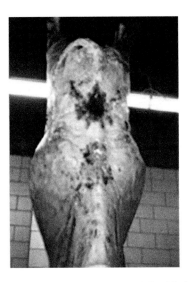

Fig. 15.6. Back bruise on a tall animal that hit the underside of a low truck compartment. Cattle can be severely bruised and the hide may have no visible damage. (Photo courtesy of Helen Kline, Colorado State University.)

Broken wings

The number one cause of this problem is rough handling during catching. Chickens should *never* be picked up by a single wing. Measuring the percentage of broken wings is a sensitive indicator of how people are handling the birds. Broken wings can also occur in systems where birds have to be removed from the coop through a small door. When individual coops are used, the best ones have a small door for loading the birds and the entire top opens to remove the birds for shackling at the plant. Figure 15.7 shows both broken and bruised wings on broiler chickens.

There is a big difference in the percentage of chickens with broken wings between the best and worst plants. Some ethicists are hesitant to state an acceptable level of broken wings, because that translates into thousands of birds with broken wings. The author has observed that when numerical standards were introduced for measuring broken wings, they were greatly reduced. In the USA before measurement started, 5–6% of the birds had broken wings. With the present data, the maximum acceptable level would be 1% and plants with 3% are clearly not acceptable.

Broken legs

In spent hens, weak bones are a major contributor to fractures (Webster, 2004). Old hens have high percentages of keel bone fractures due to osteoporosis (Sherwin *et al.*, 2010; Wilkins *et al.*, 2011). In broiler chickens, rough handling is a major cause. There is much controversy among welfare specialists on the correct way to pick up chickens during catching. Some specialists state that they should never be picked up by a single leg. In some countries, this is the normal catching method. The author has observed one-legged catching where the number of birds injured was very low. The coops were brought into the barn close to the catcher. The catcher never walked more than 3 m to load the chickens into the coops (Grandin, 2015).

Recommendations on Poultry Catching Methods

It is the author's opinion that instead of arguing over whether poultry are hand caught or machine-caught, caught by one leg or two legs, or lifted by the entire body, the best approach is to measure injuries and deaths.

These percentages will measure the outcome of poor handling. Broken wings should be counted when the feathers are on, to prevent counting breakage from the feather-removal picking machine. The broken wing score should include both breaks and discolorations.

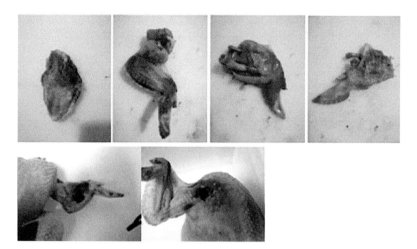

Fig. 15.7. Wing damage on broiler chickens. The top row shows broken wings after the feathers have been removed. When assessing broken wings at the abattoir, scoring the birds with the feathers on avoids confusion between damage from feather removal equipment and damage from handling. When chickens are hung on the line, a broken wing hangs straight down. The bottom two photos show bruised wings that are not broken.

Trouble-shooting Problems

Sometimes a problem, such as high percentages of downed non-ambulatory pigs, is caused by a combination of factors. At one large slaughter plant, correcting three different contributing factors almost eliminated non-ambulatory pigs. The three factors that brought about improvements were: (i) instructing producers to walk through the finishing fattening pens to get the pigs accustomed to quietly moving away when people walked through them (Grandin, 2015); (ii) reducing or eliminating ractopamine use; and (iii) stopping using genetic lines with either the PSS halothane gene or poor leg conformation.

Conclusions

Conditions in the slaughter plant and conditions outside the slaughter plant can both contribute to meat quality issues. The first step is to determine if the problem is occurring in the abattoir or outside it. The next step is to correct in-plant problems such as poor handling, lack of lairage rest time for pigs or mounting behaviour in bulls. Problems that are usually caused by on-farm factors are (i) animals that are difficult to handle; (ii) lameness; (iii) high death losses; (iv) bruises; or (v) tough meat caused by feed additives. These issues must be corrected at the farm. Use measurements with numerical scoring to determine the origin of the problem.

References

Abbot, T.A., Hunter, E.J., Guise, J.H. and Penny, R.H.C. (1997) The effect of experience of handling on a pig's willingness to move. *Applied Animal Behaviour Science* 54, 371–375.

Adzitey, F. and Nurul, H. (2011) Pale soft exudative (PSE) and dark firm dry (DFD) meats causes and measures to reduce these incidences – a mini review. *International Food Research Journal* 18(1).

Amachawadi, R.G. and Nagaraja, T.G. (2015) Liver abscesses in cattle: a review of incidence in Holsteins and of bacteriology and vaccine approaches to control in feedlot cattle. *Journal of Animal Science* 94, 1620–1632.

Baier, S.F. (2019) Evaluation of different hair characteristics and the impact of liver abscess presence on stress-related physical and physiological parameters associated with well-being in beef feedlot steers. Master's Thesis, Colorado State University, Fort Collins, Colorado.

Band, G.O., Guimarães, S.E.F., Lopes, P.S., Schierholt, A.S., Silva, K.M. et al. (2005) Relationship between the porcine stress syndrome gene and pork quality trials of F2 pigs resulting from divergent crosses. *Genetics and Molecular Biology* 28, 88–91.

Bartos, L., Franc, C., Albiston, G. and Beber, K. (1988) Prevention of dark cutting (DFD) beef in penned bulls at the abattoir. *Meat Science* 22, 213–220.

Baszczack, J.A., Grandin, T., Gruber, S.L., Engle, T.E., Platter, W.J. et al. (2006) Effects of ractopamine supplementation on the behavior of British, Continental and Brahman crossbred steers during routine handling. *Journal of Animal Science* 84, 3411–3414.

Benjamin, M.E., Gonyou, H.W., Ivers, D.L., Richard, L.F., Jones, D.J. *et al.* (2001) Effect of handling method on the incidence of stress response in market swine in a model system. *Journal of Animal Science* 79 (Suppl. 1), 379 (Abstract).

Boyd, B.M., Shackelford, S.D., Hales, K.E., Brown-Brandi, T.M. *et al.* (2015) Effect of shade and feeding zilpaterol hydrochloride to finishing steers on performance, carcass quality, heat stress, mobility and body temperature. *Journal of Animal Science* 93, 5801–5811.

Brown, T.R. and Lawrence, T.E. (2010) Association of liver abnormalities with carcass grading, performance and value. *Journal of Animal Science* 88, 4037–4043.

Burfeind, O. and Heuwieser, W. (2012) Validation of handheld meters to measure blood L-lactate concentration in dairy cows and calves. *Journal of Dairy Science* 95, 6449–6456.

Café, L.M., Robinson, D.L., Ferguson, D.M., McIntyre, B.L., Geesink, G.H., and Greenwood, P.L. (2010) Cattle temperament: persistence of assessments and associations with productivity, efficiency, carcass, and meat quality traits. *Journal of Animal Science* 89, 1452–1465.

Channon, H.A., Payne, A.M. and Warner, R.D. (2003a) Halothane genotype, pre-slaughter handling and stunning method all influence pork quality. *Meat Science* 56, 291–299.

Channon, H.A., Payne, A.M. and Warner, R.D. (2003b) Effect of stun duration and current level applied during head to back and head only electrical stunning of pigs on pork quality compared to pigs stunned with CO_2. *Meat Science* 65, 1325–1332.

Cockram, M.S. and Lee, R.A. (1991) Some preslaughter factors affecting the occurrence of bruising in sheep. *British Veterinary Journal* 147, 120–125.

Cockrum, R.R., Speidal, S.E., Crawford, N.F., Zeng, X, Blackburn, H.D. *et al.* (2019) Genotypes identified by genome wide association analysis influence yearling pulmonary arterial pressure and growth traits in Angus heifers from a high altitude beef production system. *Livestock Science* 224, 75–86.

Collier, R.J., Byatt, J.C., Denham, S.C., Eppard, P.J., Fabellar, A.C. *et al.* (2001) Effects of sustained release bovine somatropin (sometribove) on animal health in commercial dairy herds. *Journal of Dairy Science* 84, 1098–1108.

Cook, N.B., Hess, J.P., Foy, M.R., Bennett, T.B. and Brotzman, R.L. (2015) Management characteristics, lameness, and body injuries of dairy cattle housed in high performance dairy herds in Wisconsin. *Journal of Dairy Science* 99, 1–3.

Davis, M.S., Koers, W.C., Vander Pol, K.J. and Turgeon, O.A. (2007) Liver abscess score and carcass characteristics of feedlot cattle. *Journal of Animal Science* 85, 126–137.

Della Rosa, M.M., Pavan, E., Marasca, S., Spetter, M. and Ramiro, F. (2018) Performance, carcass and meat traits of grazing cattle with different exit velocity. *Animal Production Science* 59(9), 1752–1761. doi.org/10.1071/AN18064

D'Souza, D.N., Dunshea, F.R., Leaury, B.J. and Warner, R. (1999) Effect of mixing boars during lairage and preslaughter handling on meat quality. *Australian Journal of Agricultural Research* 50, 109–113.

Earley, B., McNamara, J.D., Jerrams, S.J. and O'Riordan, E.G.O. (2017) Effect of concrete slats, three mat types and out wintering pads on performance and welfare of finishing beef steers. *Acta Veterinaria Scandinavica* 59, 34.

Edwards, L.N., Grandin, T., Engle, T.E., Porter, S.P., Ritter, M.J. *et al.* (2010) Using exsanguination blood lactate to assess the quality of pre-slaughter pig handling. *Meat Science* 86, 384–390.

Elmore, M.R., Elischer, M.F., Claeys, M.C. and Pajor, E.A. (2015) The effects of different flooring types on the behavior, health and welfare of finishing beef steers. *Journal of Animal Science* 93, 1258–1266.

Endman, R.A., Sharma, B.K., Shaver, R.D. and Cleale, R.M. (1990) Dose response of recombinant bovine somatatropin from weeks 15 to 14 postpartum in lactating dairy cows. *Journal of Dairy Science* 83, 2907–2915.

Faucitano, L. (2018) Preslaughter handling practices and their effects on animal welfare and pork quality. *Journal of Animal Science* 96, 728–738.

Frese, D.A., Reinhardt, C.D., Bartle, S.J., Rethorst, D.N., Hutcheson, J.P. *et al.* (2016) Cattle handling technique can induce fatigued cattle syndrome in cattle not fed a beta-agonist. *Journal of Animal Science* 94, 581-591.

Fulwider, W.K., Grandin, T., Garrick, D.J., Engle, T.E., Lamm, W.D. *et al.* (2007) Influence of freestall base on tarsal joint lesions and hygiene in dairy cows. *Journal of Dairy Science* 90, 3559–3566.

Gesek, M., Otrocka-Domagat, E., Sokoi, R., Pazdzion-Czapula, B.D. and Lambert, A.M. (2016) Histopathological studies of the heart in three lines of broiler chickens. *British Poultry Science* 57, 219–226.

Geverink, N.A., Kappers, A., van de Bungwal, E., Lambooij, E., Blokhuis, J.H. and Wiegant, V.M. (1998) Effects of regular moving and handling on the behavioral and physiological responses of pigs to pre-slaughter treatment and consequences for meat quality. *Journal of Animal Science* 76, 2080–2085.

Gonzales, L.A., Schartzkopf-Genswein, K.B., Bryan, M., Silasi, R. and Brown, F. (2012) Benchmarking study of industry practices during commercial long haul transport of cattle in Alberta. *Journal of Animal Science* 90, 3618–3629.

Grandin, T. (1981) Bruises on southwestern feedlot cattle. *Journal of Animal Science* 53 (Suppl. 1), 213 (abstract).

Grandin, T. (1986) Cardiac arrest stunning of livestock and poultry. In: Fox, M.W. (ed.) *Advances in Animal Welfare Science*. Martinus Nijhoff, Boston, Massachusetts, pp. 1–30.

Grandin, T. (2014) *Livestock Handling and Transport*, 4th edn. CAB International, Wallingford, UK.

Grandin, T. (2015) *Improving Animal Welfare: A Practical Approach*. CABI International, Wallingford, UK.

Grandin, T. (2017) On-farm conditions that compromise animal welfare that can be monitored at the slaughter plant. *Meat Science* 132, 52–58.

Gruber, S.L., Tatum, J.D., Engle, T.E., Chapman, P.L., Belk, K.E. *et al.* (2010) Relationships of behavioral and physiological symptoms of preslaughter stress on beef longissimus muscle tenderness. *Journal of Animal Science* 88, 1148–1159.

Hagenmaier, J.A., Reinhardt, C.D., Ritter, M.J., Calvo-Lorenzo, M.S. *et al.* (2017) Effects of ractopamine hydrochloride on growth performance, carcass characteristics and physiological response to different handling techniques. *Journal of Animal Science* 35, 1977–1998.

Hall, N.L., Buchanan, D.S., Anderson, V.L., Ilse, B.R., Carlin, K.R. and Berg, E.P. (2011) Working chute behavior of feedlot cattle can be an indicator of cattle temperament and beef carcass composition and quality. *Meat Science* 89, 52–57.

Hambrecht, E., Eissenn, J.J., Deklein, W.J.H., Ducro, B.J., Smits, C.H.M. *et al.* (2004) Rapid chilling cannot prevent inferior pork quality caused by high preslaughter stress. *Journal of Animal Science* 82, 551–556.

Hambrecht, E., Eissen, J.J., Newman, D.J., Smits, C.H.M., den Hartog, L.A. *et al.* (2005a) Negative effects of stress immediately before slaughter on pork quality are aggravated by suboptimal transport and lairage conditions. *Journal of Animal Science* 83, 440–448.

Hambrecht, E., Eissen, J.J., Newman, D.J., Verstegen, M.W. and Hartog, L.A. (2005b) Preslaughter handling affects pork quality and glycolytic potential of two muscles differing in fiber type composition. *Journal of Animal Science* 83, 900–907.

Hamdy, M.K., Kunkle, L.E. and Deatherage, F.E. (1957) Bruised tissue. II. Determining of the age of a bruise. *Journal of Animal Science* 16, 490–495.

Herrick, R., Rogers, C., Jones, T., McEvers, T., Brown, T. *et al.* (2018) Association of liver abscesses presents and severity with trim loss, harvest yield, carcass grading performance, lung lesions and value of fed Holsteins. *Journal of Animal Science* 96 (Suppl. 3), 269 (abstract).

Hoffman, D.E., Spire, M.F., Schwenke, J.R. and Unruh, J.A. (1998) Effect of source of cattle and distance transported to a commercial slaughter facility on carcass bruises in mature beef cows. *Journal of the American Veterinary Medical Association* 212, 668–672.

Huffstutter, P.J. and Polansek, T. (2013) Special Report: Lost hooves, dead cattle before Merck halted Zilmax sales. Available at: www.reuters.com/article/2013/12/31/us-zilmax-merck-cattle-special-report-idUSBRE9BT0NV20131231 (accessed 19 January 2020).

James, B.W., Tokach, M.D., Goodband, R.D., Nelssen, J.H., Dritz, S.S. *et al.* (2013) Effect of dietary L-carnitine and ractopamine HCL on the metabolic response to handling in finishing pigs. *Journal of Animal Sciences* 91, 4426–4429.

Jones, T.A., Waitt, C. and Dawkins, M.S. (2010) Sheep lose balance, slip and fall less when loosely packed in transit where they stand close to but not touching their neighbors. *Applied Animal Behaviour Science* 123, 16–23.

Karabasil, N., Cobanovic, N., Vucicevic, I., Stajkovic, S., Becskei, Z. *et al.* (2017) Association of severity of lung lesions with carcass and meat quality in slaughter pigs. *Acta Veterinaria Hungarica* 65. doi: 10.1556/004_2017.034

King, D.A., Schuelhle-Pfeiffer, C.E., Randel, R.D., Welsh, T.H. Jr, Oliphint, R.A. *et al.* (2006) Influence of animal temperament and stress responsiveness on the carcass quality and beef tenderness of feedlot cattle. *Meat Science* 74, 546–556.

Krebs, N. and McGlone, J.J. (2009) Effects of exposing pigs to moving and odors in a simulated slaughter chute. *Applied Animal Behaviour Science* 116, 179–185.

Kronfield, D.S. (1994) Health management of dairy herds treated with bovine somatotropin. *Journal of American Veterinary Medical Association* 204, 116–130.

Kronfield, D.S. (2000) Recombinant somatotropin and animal welfare. *Journal of the American Veterinary Medical Association* 216, 1719–1722.

Kuttappan, V.A., Hargis, B.W. and Owens, C.W. (2016) White striping and woody breast myopathies in the modern poultry industry: a review. *Poultry Science* 95, 2724–2733.

Kuttappan, V.A., Owens, C.M., Coon, C., Hargis, B.W. and Vazquez-Anan, M. (2017) Incidence of broiler breast myopathies at two different ages and its impact on selected raw material quality parameters. *Poultry Science* 96, 3005–3009.

Le, T.H., Madsen, P., Lundeheim, N., Nilsson, K. and Norberg, E. (2015a) Genetic association between leg conformation in young pigs and sow longevity. *Journal of Animal Breeding and Genetics* 133(4), 283–290.

Le, T.H., Nisson, K., Norberg, E. and Lundeheim, N. (2015b) Genetic association between leg conformation in young pigs and sow longevity. *Livestock Science* 176, 9–17.

Lee, T.L., Reinhardt, C.D., Cartle, S.J., Vahl, C.I., Siemens, M. and Thomson, D.U. (2017) Assessment of risk factors contributing to carcass bruising in fed cattle at commercial slaughter facilities. *Translational Animal Science* 1, 489–497.

Longeragen, G.H., Thomson, D.U. and Scott, H.M. (2014) Increased mortality in groups and cattle administered the β-adrenergic agonists ractopamine hydrochloride and zilpaterol hydrochloride. *PLOS ONE* 9(3), e91177. doi: 10.1371/journal.pone.0091177

Marchant-Forde, J.N., Lay, D.C., Pajor, E.A., Richert, B.T. and Schinckel, A.P. (2003) The effects of ractopamine on the behavior and physiology of finishing pigs. *Journal of Animal Science* 81, 416–422.

Marcias-Cruz, U., Alvarez-Valenzuela, F.D., Torrentera, N., Velaquez-Morales, J.V., Correa-Calderon, A. *et al.* (2010) Effect of zilpaterol hydrochloride on feedlot and carcass characteristics of ewe lambs under heat stress condition. *Animal Production Science* 50, 983–989.

Marcon, A.V., Caldara, F.R., Oliviera, G.F. de, Gonçalves, L.M.P., Garcia, R.G. *et al.* (2019) Pork quality after electrical or carbon dioxide stunning at slaughter. *Meat Science* 156, 93–97.

McCausland, I.P. and Dougherty, R. (1978) Histological aging of bruises in lambs and calves. *Australian Veterinary Journal* 54(11), 525–527.

McCoy, E.J., O'Quinn, T.G., Schwandt, E.F., Reinhardt, C.D. and Thompson, D.U. (2017) Effects of liver abscesses severity and quality grade and meat tenderness and sensory attributes in commercially finished beef cattle fed with and without tylosin phosphate. *Translational Animal Science* 1, 304–310.

Meischke, H.R.C. and Horder, J.C. (1976) Knocking box effect on bruising in cattle. *Food Technology, Australia* 28, 369–371.

Mendonca, F.R., Vaz, F., Cardoso, J., Restle, F., Vaz, L. *et al.* (2016) Pre-slaughtering factors related to bruises on cattle carcasses. *Animal Production Science* 58, 385–392.

Merez-Murillo, F.J., Avendano-Reyes, L., Perez-Linares, C., Figueroa-Saavedra, F., Torres-Rodriguez, V. *et al.* (2016) Feedlot performance, carcass characteristics and meat quality in zebu heifers supplemented with two b-adrenergic agonists. *Animal Production Science* 57, 2125–2132.

Milligan, S.D., Ramsey, C.B., Miller, M.F., Kaster, C.S. and Thompoon, L.D. (1990) Resting of pigs and hot fat trimming and accelerated chilling of carcasses to improve meat quality. *Journal of Animal Science* 76, 74–86.

Montgomery, J.L., Krehiet, C.R., Cranston, J.J., Yates, D.A., Hutcheson, J.P. *et al.* (2008) Effects of dietary zilpaterol hydrochloride on feedlot performance and carcass characteristics of beef steers fed without nonensin and tylosin. *Journal of Animal Science* 87, 1013–1023.

Munoz, D., Strappini, A. and Gallo, C. (2012) Indicadores de bienestar animal para detector problemas en al cajon de insensibilizacion de bovinos [Animal welfare indicators to detect problems in the cattle stunning box]. *Archivos de Medicina Veterinaria* 44, 297–302.

Murray, A.C. and Johnson, C.P. (1998) Importance of the halothane gene on muscle quality and pre-slaughter death in Western Canada pigs. *Canadian Journal of Animal Science* 78, 543–548.

Neary, J.M., Garry, F.B., Holt, T.N., Thomas, M.G. and Enns, R.M. (2015) Mean pulmonary arterial pressures on Angus steers increase from cow-calf to feedlot finishing phases. *Journal of Animal Science* 93, 3854–3861.

Neary, J.M., Gary, F.B., Gould, D.H., Holt, T.N. and Brown, R.D. (2018) The beta agonist zilpaterol hydrochloride may predispose feedlot cattle to cardiac remodeling and dysfunction. *F1000 Research* 7, 399.

Newman, J.H., Holt, T.N., Cogan, J.D., Womack, B., Phillips, J.A. *et al.* (2015) Increased prevalence of EPASI variant in cattle with high altitude pulmonary hypertension. *Nature Communications* 6, article 6863.

Northcutt, J.K. and Rowland, G.N. (2000) Relationship of broiler bruise age to appearance and tissue histological characteristics. *Journal of Applied Poultry Science Research* 9, 13–20.

Oliveira, E.A. de, Dall'Olio, S., Tassone, F., Arduini, A. and Costa, L.N. (2018) The effect of stress prior to stunning on proglycogen, macroglycogen, lactate, and meat quality traits in different pig breeds. *Italian Journal of Animal Science* 17, 879–883.

Perez, M.P., Palacio, J., Santolaria, M.P., del Acena, N.C., Chacon, G., Verde, M.T. *et al.* (2002) Influence of lairage time on some welfare and meat quality parameters in pigs. *Veterinary Research* 33, 239–250.

Permentier, L., Meenhout, D., Delay, W., Broekmann, K., Vermeulen, L. *et al.* (2015) Lung lesions increase risk of reduced meat quality in slaughter pigs. *Meat Science* 108, 106–108.

Peterson, C.M., Pilcher, C.M., Rothe, H.M., Marchant-Forde, J.N., Ritter, M.J. *et al.* (2015) Effect of feeding ractopamine hydrochloride on the growth performance and responses to handling and transport in heavy-weight pigs. *Journal of Animal Science* 93, 1239–1249.

Poletto, R., Garner, J., Cheng, H.W. and Marchant-Forde, J. (2008) The effects of ractopamine gender and social rank on aggression and peripheral monamine levels in finishing pigs. *Journal of Animal Science* 86 (E.Suppl.2), Abstract 352.

Poletto, R., Rostagno, M.H., Richert, B.T. and Marchant-Forde, J.N. (2009) Effects of a 'step up' ractopamine feeding program, sex, and social rank on growth performance hoof lesions, and Enterobacteriaceae shedding in finishing pigs. *Journal of Animal Science* 87, 304–313.

Ponnampalam, E.N., Hopkins, D.L., Bruce, H., Li, D., Baldi, G, and Bekhit, A.E. (2017) Causes and contributing factors to dark cutting meat: current trends and future directions: a review. *Comprehensive Reviews in Food Science and Food Safety* 16(3), 400–430. doi.org/10.1111/1541-4337.12258

Price, M.A. and Tennessen, T. (1981) Preslaughter management and dark cutting in the carcasses of young bulls. *Canadian Journal of Animal Science* 61, 205–208.

Przbylski, W. and Hopkins, D. (2016) *Meat Quality Genetic and Environmental Factors*. CRC Press, Boca Raton, Florida.

Puls, G.L., Trout, W.E., Ritter, M.J., McKeith, F.K., Carr, S.N. and Ellis, W. (2014) Impact of ractopamine hydrochloride on growth performance, carcass and pork quality characteristics, and responses to handling and transport in finishing pigs. *Journal of Animal Science* 93, 1229–1238.

Reinhardt, C.D. and Hubbert, M.E. (2015) Control of liver abscesses in feedlot cattle: a review. *Professional Animal Scientist* 31, 101–108.

Ritter, M.J., Ellis, M., Brinkmann, J., DeDecker, J.M., Keffaber, K.K. *et al.* (2006) Effect of floor space during transport of market-weight pigs on the incidence of transport losses at the packing plant and the relationships between transport conditions and losses. *Journal of Animal Science* 84, 2856–2864.

Ritter, M.J., Ellis, M., Berry, N.L. and Curtis, S.E. (2009) Review: Transport losses in market weight pigs, 1. A review of definitions incidence and economic impact. *Professional Animal Scientist* 25, 404–414.

Ritter, M.J., Johnson, A.K., Benjamin, M.E., Carr, S.N., Ellis, M. *et al.* (2017) Review: Effects of ractopamine hydrochloride (Paylean) on welfare indicators for market weight pigs. *Translational Animal Science* 1, 533–558.

Rocha, L.M., Velarde, A., Dalmau, A., Saucier, L. and Faucitano, L. (2016) Can monitoring of animal welfare parameters predict pork meat variation through the supply chain (from farm to slaughter). *Journal of Animal Science* 94, 359–376.

Scamlin, S.M., Platter, W.J., Gomez, R.A., McKeith, F.K. and Killefer, J. (2009) Comparative effects of ractopomine hydrochloride and zilpaterol hydrochloride on growth performance, carcass traits, and longissimus tenderness of finishing steers. *Journal of Animal Science* 88, 1823–1829.

Scanga, J.A., Belk, K.E., Tatum, J.D., Grandin, T. and Smith, G.C. (1998) Factors contributing to dark cutting beef. *Journal of Animal Science* 76, 2040–2047.

Schartzkopf-Genswein, K. and Grandin, T. (2019) Cattle transport by road in America. In: Grandin, T. (ed.) *Livestock Handling and Transport*, 5th edn. CAB International, Wallingford, UK, pp. 153–170.

Scollo, A., Gottardo, F., Contiera, B., Mazzoni, C., Leneveu, P. and Edwards, S. (2017) Benchmarking pluck lesions at slaughter as a health monitoring tool for pigs slaughtered at 170 kg (heavy pigs). *Preventive Veterinary Medicine* 144, 20–28.

Sherwin, C.M., Richards, G.J. and Nicol, C.J. (2010) Comparison of welfare of layer hens in four housing systems in the UK. *British Poultry Science* 51, 488–499.

Shook, J.N., VanOverbeke, D.L., Kinman, L.A., Krebbiel, C.R., Holland, B.P. *et al.* (2009) Effects of zilpaterol hydrochloride and withdrawal time on beef carcass cutability composition and tenderness. *Journal of Animal Science* 87, 3677–3685.

Strappini, A.C., Metz, J.H.M., Gallo, C.B., and Kemp, B. (2009) Origin and assessment of bruises in beef cattle at slaughter. *Animal* 3, 728–736.

Tarrant, P.V. (1989) Animal behaviour and the environment in the dark cutting condition in beef: a review. *Irish Journal of Food Science and Technology* 3(1), 1–21.

Tarrant, P.V., Kenny, F.J., Harrington, D. and Murphy, M. (1992) Long distance transportation of steers to slaughter effect of stocking density on physiology behavior and carcass quality. *Livestock Production Science* 3, 223–238.

Thomson, D.L., Longeragan, G.H., Hennington, J.N., Ensley, S. and Bawa, B. (2015) Description of novel fatigue syndrome of finished feedlot cattle following transportation. *Journal of the American Veterinary Medical Association* 247, 66–72.

Tijare, V.V., Yang, F.L., Huttappan, V.A., Alvarado, C.Z., Coon, C.N. and Owens, C.M. (2016) Meat quality of broiler breast fillets and white striping and woody breast muscle myopathies. *Poultry Science* 95, 2167–2173.

Trotter, C. (2016) Liver abscesses in pasture based beef bulls in the South Island of New Zealand: the incidence and effect on carcass weight. *Animal Production, Australian Society of Animal Production, Proceedings*, 109, Abstract NZSp-9.

Tucker, C.B., Calvo-Lorenza, M.S. and Mitloehner, F.M. (2015) Effects of growth promoting technology on feedlot cattle behavior 21 days before slaughter. *Applied Animal Behaviour Science* 162, 1–8.

Velleman, S.G. (2015) Relationship of skeletal muscle development and growth to breast muscle: a review. *Avian Diseases* 59, 525–531.

Vermeulen, L., Van de Perre, V., Permentier, L., DeBic, S., Verbeka, G., and Geers, R. (2015a) Preslaughter handling and pork quality. *Meat Science* 100, 118–123.

Vermeulen, L., Van de Perre, V., Permentier, L., DeBic, S. and Geers, R. (2015b) Preslaughter rectal temperature as an indicator of pork meat quality. *Meat Science* 105, 53–56.

Viljoen, H.F., de Kock, H.L. and Webb, E.C. (2002) Consumer acceptability of dark firm and dry (DFD) and normal pH beef steaks. *Meat Science* 61, 181–185.

Voisinet, B.D., Grandin, T., Tatum, J.D., O'Connor, S.F. and Struthers, J.J. (1997) Feedlot cattle with calm temperaments have higher average daily gains than cattle with excitable temperaments. *Journal of Animal Science* 75, 892–896.

Vollmar, K. (2016) Survey of prevalence of conformational leg defects in feedlot receiving cattle in the United States. Master's Thesis, Colorado State University, Fort Collins, Colorado.

Wagner, D. (2016) Behavioral analysis and performance responses of feedlot steers on concrete slats versus rubber slats. (Abstract) *ASAS/ADSA Joint Annual Meeting* July 22, 2016, Salt Lake City, Utah.

Warner, R.D., Ferguson, D.W., Cottrell, J.J. and Knee, B.W. (2007) Acute stress induced by the preslaughter use of electric prodders causes tougher beef meat. *Australian Journal of Experimental Agriculture* 47, 782–788.

Warriss, P.D. (2003) Optimal lairage times and conditions for slaughter pigs: a review. *Veterinary Record* 153, 170–176.

Warriss, P.D., Brown, S., Adams, S.J.M. and Corlett, I.K. (1994) Relationships between subjective and objective assessments of stress at slaughter and meat quality in pigs. *Meat Science* 38, 239–340.

Webster, A.B. (2004) Welfare implications of avian osteoporosis. *Poultry Science* 83, 184–192.

Weeks, C.A., McNally, P.W. and Warriss, P.D. (2002) Influence of the design of facilities at auction markets and animal handling procedures on bruising in cattle. *Veterinary Record* 150, 743–748.

Wilkins, L.J., McKinstry, J.L., Avery, N.C., Knowles, T.G., Brown, S.N. *et al.* (2011) Influence of housing system and design on bone strength and keel bone fractures in laying hens. *Veterinary Record* 169, 414.

Will, D.H., Hicks, J.L., Card, C.S., and Alexander, A.F. (1975) Inherited susceptibility of cattle to high altitude pulmonary hypertension. *Journal of Applied Physiology* 38, 491–494.

Zurbrigg, K., Van Dreumal, T., Rothchild, M., Alves, D., Friendship, R. and O'Sullivan, T. (2017) Pig level risk factors for in transit losses in swine: a review. *Canadian Journal of Animal Science* 97, 339–346.

Zurbrigg, K., Van Dreumel, T., Rothschild, M.F., Alves, D., Friendship, R.M. and O'Sullivan, T.L. (2019) Rapid Communication: A comparison of cardiac lesions and heart weights from market pigs that did and did not die during transport to one Ontario abattoir. *Translational Animal Science* 3, 149–154.

T. Grandin

16 The Use of Abattoir Data to Provide Information on the Welfare of Livestock and Poultry on the Farm and During Transport

TEMPLE GRANDIN[1]* AND MICHAEL COCKRAM[2]†

[1]Department of Animal Science, Colorado State University, USA; [2]Sir James Dunn Animal Welfare Centre, Atlantic Veterinary College, University of Prince Edward Island, Canada

Summary

A range of conditions that may compromise animal welfare can be assessed at the abattoir. Injuries associated with handling and transport and pathology associated with conditions that were present on the farm can be identified (Grandin, 2017). Some examples are fitness for transport, lameness, bruises, wounds, skin lesions on poultry and death losses. It can be more efficient to undertake some types of welfare assessments on animals after they have been transported to slaughter at a limited number of locations than to attempt to visit the large number of farms that supply each abattoir. Studies have shown that many welfare problems can be assessed at the slaughter plant (EFSA Panels, 2011; Harley *et al.*, 2012a,b; Llonch *et al.*, 2015; Souza *et al.*, 2018). It is also easier to identify some conditions postmortem than in live animals. The collection of slaughter plant data is an integral part of many welfare assessment schemes, such as Welfare Quality (2009) and commercial (private) programs that are outlined in Grandin (2012, 2015), Lundmark *et al.* (2018) and Vogeler *et al.* (2019). Data is collected from routine ante-mortem and post-mortem inspections of carcasses and viscera (internal organs) for gross pathological changes. Although this data collection is undertaken for food safety reasons, it provides relevant animal welfare information. However, there are some issues with the quality and nature of these data that need to be considered when they are used for welfare assessment. The provision of feedback to producers on welfare issues identified at slaughter remains an underutilized tool for reducing on-farm health and welfare issues. Fully integrated systems, especially in the poultry and pig industries, for additional data collection by specific assessors and provision of producer feedback have been developed. Providing feedback to producers is more difficult in segmented marketing chains where an animal passes through auctions or dealers.

Learning Objectives

- Learn the on-farm animal welfare problems that can be easily identified at the abattoir.
- Understand the limitations of these assessments.
- Provide information for implementing these assessments.
- Introduce the scientific studies on assessment methods.

Introduction

The first section of this chapter will cover how to get started in assessing animal welfare issues at the

---

* Email: cheryl.miller@colostate.edu
† Email: mcockram@upei.ca

abattoir that occur during transport or on the farm. The second section will cover an in-depth review of the literature on welfare assessments at the abattoir. In the next section, the most important indicators for a practical commercial programme are outlined. There will also be a discussion on the limitations of in-abattoir welfare audits. For example, they cannot be used to determine the influence of some aspects of the type of housing that the animals were raised in or to determine if analgesics or anaesthetics were used during painful surgical procedures.

Tables 16.1, 16.2 and 16.3 contain an overview of conditions that can be easily assessed at the abattoir.

Different Types of Measurement Systems and Choosing the Most Suitable Scoring Tools

There are many different published scoring systems available for scoring condition of animals on the farm. Some of the measures that have good inter-observer reliability are lameness (difficulty walking), sores and lesions, feather/coat condition, animal or bird cleanliness and neglected injuries (Gibbons *et al.*, 2012; Llonch *et al.*, 2015) (Tables 16.1 and 16.2). Scoring tools are also used for assessing internal indicators of poor health such as liver abscesses, lung lesions and stomach ulcers (Hardstaff *et al.*, 2012; Leruste *et al.*, 2012) (Table 16.3).

A scoring tool has good inter-observer reliability if several different people use the tool and the results agree most of the time. Agreement can never be perfect but it should be the same 70–90% of the time. Some of the best scoring tools have photographs to show normal and varying degrees of a problem ranging from normal to severe (Fig. 16.1). To help improve inter-observer reliability, auditors, government inspectors and abattoir quality assurance people should be trained to always keep the scorecard with them. The scorecard can either be a plastic laminated card or kept on a smart phone. When assessors are well trained, they can achieve substantial agreement (Leruste *et al.*, 2012).

Use of Critical Control Points (CCPs)

As used by Grandin (2019), a critical control point is a factor in an audit or assessment that is extremely important. If a factor that is a CCP is failed, there would be a severe welfare problem.

Some welfare issues that can be detected at the abattoir are more serious than others. It is the first author's opinion that lameness is an example of a CCP. Lame animals are in pain (Flower *et al.*, 2008). An example of a less serious welfare indicator may be a few small scratches on a pig. The principle of CCPs comes from food safety. In Hazard Analysis Critical Control Points (HACCPs), the CCP is a point, step or procedure in a process where hazards can be controlled or reduced to an acceptable level (critical limit) (Hulebak and Schlosser, 2002). A basic HACCP programme measures the really important welfare indicators. In the next section of this chapter, the CCPs for each species will be covered.

Some of the most important variables that should be assessed at the abattoir are as follows:

- dead animals, all species;
- non-ambulatory downers;
- lameness in livestock;
- broken wings (poultry);
- bruises and fractures;
- skin lesions, both livestock and poultry;
- dirty livestock or poultry;
- poor body condition;
- obvious neglected health problems;
- liver abscesses in cattle;
- lung lesions in livestock;
- hernias in pigs; and
- udder problems in dairy animals.

Commercial versus research assessment tools

There is a difference between a scoring system that is used in a research study and a system used under commercial conditions. Commercial systems often have to be simpler. A more complex system can provide more graduations of severity, but it will be harder to train people to use it accurately under commercial conditions. A good commercial system will usually have fewer categories than the most sensitive research tools.

There is much discussion in the scientific literature and in the industry on the number of categories a scoring tool should have. An assessment tool assessing animal welfare during stunning and handling with simple yes/no scoring is described in Chapter 11 (Grandin, 1998, 2000, 2005, 2010). Each animal is either stunned correctly or is not stunned correctly with single application of the

Table 16.1. Overview of conditions associated with either poor fitness for transport or poor handling and transport practices.

Welfare problem	Comments	References
Dead on arrival	The prevalence and where possible the reasons should be recorded	Murray and Johnson (1998); Averos *et al.* (2008); Caffrey *et al.* (2017); Di Martino *et al.* (2017); Cockram and Dulal (2018)
Dead in lairage	The prevalence and where possible the reasons should be recorded	Knowles *et al.* (1994); Fitzgerald *et al.* (2009); Knezacek *et al.* (2010)
Moribund (near death)	The prevalence and where possible the reasons should be recorded	Stafford *et al.* (2001)
Recumbent/ non-ambulatory (not able to walk)	Where possible determine whether the condition was associated with injury or fatigue. The cause should be recorded	Ritter *et al.* (2009); Thomson *et al.* (2015)
Heat stress	Identified using clinical signs (open-mouth breathing). Cattle with open mouth breathing at rest have severe heat stress	Mader *et al.* (2005); Gaughan *et al.* (2008); Kephart *et al.* (2010); Jacobs *et al.* (2017a)
Cold stress	Identified using clinical signs (shivering)	Hunter *et al.* (1999); Ontario Court of Justice (2014); Caffrey *et al.* (2017)
Frozen/frostbite	Identified by skin lesions and sometimes by the presence of ice	Schoning and Hamlet (1989a,b); Wellehan (2003); Goumon *et al.* (2013)
Dehydration	Identified by drinking behaviour and clinical signs	Jarvis *et al.* (1996)
Surface wounds	In pigs, skin lesions due to fighting can be identified and scored. Damage from driving instruments may also be apparent, e.g. reddened areas on the skin or petechiae in the anus of pigs and cattle	White (1999); Aaslyng *et al.* (2013); Blagojevic *et al.* (2015); Carroll *et al.* (2016, 2018)
Fractures and dislocations	Severe lameness often with limb dragged in a flexed position and non-weight bearing	Tiong and Bin (1989); Rakestraw (1996); Dalla Costa *et al.* (2019)
Bruises	Traumatic injury to the muscle that must be trimmed out. Caused by rough handling, bumping into sharp edges on handling facilities or overloading of trucks	Tarrant *et al.* (1992); Costa *et al.* (2006); Strappini *et al.*, (2009, 2012, 2013); Grandin (2015, 2017); Bethancourt-Garcia *et al.* (2019). For additional references, see Chapter 15
Poor body condition (skinny or emaciated)	Prominent bone structure with little evidence of fat deposits or muscling. Some thin animals may be weak and not fit for transport	Edmonson *et al.* (1989); Grandin (2015); Munoz *et al.* (2018)

stunner. An animal either falls down during handling or does not fall down. It is either poked with an electric goad (prod) or not poked with it.

Yes/no scoring works poorly for some welfare problems such as foot pad lesions in poultry or lameness. When yes/no or presence/absence scoring is used, each bird or animal is scored as either normal or has a foot pad lesion. It provides no indication of the severity of a problem. For example, a chicken with a small foot pad lesion that may be a minor welfare issue is combined in the same category with a bird that has a severe lesion that would cause pain. There is evidence that yes/no scoring may have better inter-observer reliability and training of

auditors is easier. To use this approach, a normal foot and a very slight foot pad lesion may have to be placed in an acceptable category and a more severe one is placed in the fail category. When the yes/no approach is used, each animal receives either an acceptable or not acceptable designation.

The next question is: how many categories should a scoring system have when a degree of severity is included? If there are too many categories, training of auditors becomes more difficult. The first author's experience and studies have shown that three should be the minimum number of categories and five should be the maximum. A three-point system would have

Table 16.2. Conditions associated with on-farm management that can cause pain or discomfort.

Welfare problem	Comments	References
Lameness	Identified using locomotion scoring and swollen joints	Mouttotou et al. (1997); Winter (2008); Jensen et al. (2012); Shearer et al. (2013); Angell et al., (2015); Llonch et al. (2015); Edwards-Callaway et al. (2017); Deeming et al. (2018); Munoz et al. (2018)
Hernia	Scored by size, severity of skin lesions and proximity to the ground	Straw et al. (2009); Welfare Quality (2009b); Schild et al. (2015)
Rectal prolapse	Straining, protrusion and swelling of the rectum	Blagojevic et al. (2015)
Vaginal prolapse	Straining, protrusion and swelling of the vagina	Hardstaff et al. (2012)
Surface wounds in pigs	Areas with loss of body coat, skin redness and swellings can occur following trauma, infection and external parasites. In pigs, bite wounds can occur on the flank, neck, head, ears, vulva and tail	White (1999); Faucitano et al. (2001); Hardstaff et al. (2012)
Damaged or diseased eye	Trauma, cancer or infection of the eye can occur. High ammonia levels on the farm can cause eye damage	Hamir and Parry (1980); Miles et al. (2006)
Swollen leg joints (hock lesions)	Cattle housed indoors on a hard surface	Fulwider et al. (2007); Barrientos et al. (2013); Kester et al. (2014); Phythian et al. (2019)
Breast blisters (poultry)	Poor litter	Haslam et al. (2007); Allain et al. (2009)
Hock burn (poultry)	Poor litter	Allain et al. (2009)
Foot pad lesions (poultry)	Poor litter	Ekstrand et al. (1997); Michel et al. (2012); Heitmann et al. (2018)
Respiratory signs	Cough, nasal discharge, dyspnoea	Leruste et al. (2012); Llonch et al. (2015)
Diarrhoea	Faecal staining of the perineum	Hardstaff et al. (2012)
Nervous signs	Ataxia, circling, convulsions, paralysis etc.	Konold et al. (2006)
Dirty livestock or poultry[a]		Welfare Quality (2009c); McKeith et al. (2012); Grandin (2015, 2017); Saraiva et al. (2016); Lundmark et al. (2018); Munoz et al. (2018)

[a]Cleanliness is used in a number of animal welfare assessment schemes. Its relevance depends to some extent on the approach adopted for welfare assessment (Lassen et al., 2006), but extremely dirty cattle may have discomfort because their hides are sometimes damaged.

Table 16.3. Examples of conditions associated with on-farm management that are assessed during inspection of the internal organs.

Welfare problem	Comments	References
Lung lesions (pneumonia)	The worst ones have adhesions to the chest wall	Hardstaff et al. (2012); Leruste et al. (2012); Rezac et al. (2014)
Liver abscesses	The worst ones have adhesions to the abdominal wall	Nagaraja and Lechtenberg (2007); Amachawadi and Nagaraja (2015)
Cardiac (heart) abnormalities	Brisket disease in cattle. Cardiac pathology associated with death losses	Neary et al. (2015); Newman et al. (2015); Zurbrigg et al. (2019)
Parasites	Liver flukes	Innocent et al. (2017)
Peritonitis	Can result in adhesions to the abdominal wall	
Stomach ulcers		Brščić et al. (2011b); Swaby and Gregory (2012)

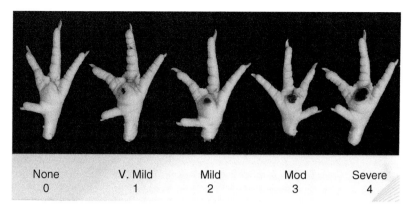

Fig. 16.1. Foot pad lesion scoring for broiler chickens, with four levels of severity. The bird that has a severe score 4 lesion would have much poorer welfare than a bird with a score 1 very mild lesion. If yes/no or absence/presence scoring is used, scores 0, 1 and 2 may be scored as acceptable and scores 3 and 4 as not acceptable. A score 4 must never be merged with a score 1 bird. (Photo from Temple Grandin, 2015.)

normal, mild and severe. A five-point system would have more gradations of severity.

Differences in numbering of scoring system

There are differences between published scoring systems on how the different categories are numbered. Grandin (2015) used 1 = normal, 2 = mild, and 3 = severe. It is becoming a more common practice to label the categories 0 = normal, 1 = mild, and 2 = severe (Welfare Quality, 2009a,b,c). When comparing data between different scientific studies or different abattoirs, make sure that everybody is using both the same scoring tool and the same numbering method. For commercial use and for scientific studies, both the scoring tool and its numbering system must be stated. For example, a four-point cattle lameness scoring was used with a 1, 2, 3, 4 numbering (Edwards-Callaway et al., 2017). The welfare quality scoring tool for Welfare Quality (2009a) was used with a three-point numbering system. Another example is the three-point Bristol poultry gait scoring (Knowles et al., 2008).

Do not use aggregate (integrated) scoring

When aggregate scoring is used, the scores for many welfare indicators such as lameness, injuries, foot pad lesions and other factors are combined into a single welfare score. This often works poorly because sometimes a severe problem where an audit should have been failed can be masked. One study of on-farm dairy audits had a farm with 47%

lame cows that was still able to pass a welfare audit (DeVries et al., 2013, 2015). Good scores on other welfare measures masked the poor lameness scores. A dairy with almost half their cows being lame should fail a welfare audit. DeGraaf et al. (2017) found that the Welfare Quality integrated scoring system put too much emphasis on water troughs and not enough emphasis on lameness and mortality. Further concerns about problems with aggregate scoring are in Sandøe et al. (2017).

Comparisons between different farms

For many of the welfare indicators, there are big differences between the best farms and worst farms (Grandin, 2015). This is true for lameness in dairy cows (Cook et al., 2016), death losses, downed non-ambulatory animals and swollen hocks in dairy cows (Fulwider et al., 2007). Producers can be motivated to improve if reports are published so that they can determine how they rank compared with other producers (Chapinal et al., 2014). Incentive pay can also be used to help reduce problems caused by either rough handling or poor management of housing.

Poultry Indicators of Poor On-farm Conditions

Compared with other species, poultry have welfare issues that are easy to measure. If a house has poor litter quality, there will be an increase in foot pad lesions, hock burn and breast blisters in broiler chickens (Mayne, 2005; deJong *et al.*, 2014; Saraiva *et al.*, 2016). Some of the scoring tools that are available are breast blisters (Allain *et al.*, 2009), foot pad lesions (Ekstrand *et al.*, 1997; Dawkins *et al.*, 2004) and hock burn (Allain *et al.*, 2009; Saraiva *et al.*, 2016). There are many factors both on the farm and during handling and transport that will increase the percentage of dead-on-arrival poultry. Some of the factors are dirty birds, injuries and thermal stress (Jacobs *et al.*, 2017a). For abattoirs that process spent laying hens, there are easy-to-use scoring tools that are available online at Featherwel (2016) and Laywel (2006). These sites have pictorial scoring tools for feather condition and problems with feet and legs. These scoring tools can be used to determine if layers on the farm have either been pecked by other hens or have poor feather condition caused by a variety of housing problems on the farm (Morrissey *et al.*, 2016).

Wet litter will increase foot pad lesions in broilers (de Jong *et al.*, 2014). Allain *et al.* (2009) did extensive work on assessing hock burn and foot pad lesions. Foot pad lesions are a serious welfare issue, because they cause pain in turkeys (Wyneken *et al.*, 2015). The first author has observed that there are different types of lesions. Baby chicks will sometimes get damaged. When the bird gets older, this damage is no longer irritated and it has grown into whitish, rough tissue. The worst damage is caused by wet mucky litter. On a three-point scoring system, the worst footpads are ulcerated (Michel *et al.*, 2012). One study showed that new litter is not always better than old litter (Jacob *et al.*, 2016). This is why it is important to perform measurements. The first author has observed that maintaining sufficient ventilation rates is essential to keep litter dry. In cold climates, producers are reluctant to increase ventilation rates, because it increases costs to heat the barn. The percentage of soiled dirty birds should also be measured. The type of food fed to the birds may have an effect on bird cleanliness. Birds fed wheat and kept in a poorly ventilated barn during cold weather may have black tarry muck on them. Another factor that needs to be examined is genetic factors that may increase susceptibility to hock burn (Kjaer *et al.*, 2016). Slow-growing birds were less susceptible (Kjaer *et al.*, 2016). Dirty chickens can be easily assessed with a three-point system (Saraiva *et al.*, 2016): 0 = clean,

1 = soiling on breast, 2 = very dirty (dirt caked on feathers). Welfare Quality (2009a) also has a three-point system.

Cattle Indicators of Poor On-farm Conditions

When cattle are unloaded at the abattoir, it is easy to assess lameness, body condition, swollen leg joints and hock lesions. Cattle are one of the most extensively studied species. An increased prevalence of lameness, swollen leg joints or hock lesions is often associated with housing problems on the farm. There are some cattle that are definitely not fit for transport to an abattoir. These animals should have been euthanized on the farm. Animals that are not able to walk, are blind in both eyes, or females in the last 10% of gestation which are likely to give birth during transport should not be transported. Unfortunately, there are some dairy cows arriving at the abattoir in poor condition (Edwards-Callaway *et al.*, 2018). The Organisation for Animal Health (OIE, 2019), the EU and many producers have guidelines on fitness for transport. A recent study showed that there is often disagreement between producers and veterinarians on whether or not a cow was fit for transport (Dahl-Pederson *et al.*, 2018). Every producer, abattoir manager and truck driver should ask: how would this animal look if it was photographed on a phone and the video went viral on the internet? Phones are everywhere. If it would look bad on a phone and you would not want to show the pictures to your city friends, then do not ship it.

Lameness in cattle

Lameness is a serious welfare issue that causes pain (Flower *et al.*, 2008). The first author prefers the four-point lameness scoring system (Edwards-Callaway *et al.*, 2017). It is easy to use when trucks are being unloaded. It is the author's opinion that the three-point welfare quality lameness scoring loses too much information. In a three-point system, there is no differentiation between mild and severe lameness. The scores are 0 = normal, 1 = lame, 2 = downed non-ambulatory. A five-point system is too difficult for use under commercial conditions. For cattle, a three-point lameness score loses all measurements of severity. March *et al.* (2007) reported that it is easier to teach people to score lame and normal cows. When a five-point lameness scoring tool was used, Schlageter-Tielo *et al.* (2014) found problems with inter-observer reliability. Agreement between observers was worse in differentiating mild lameness from moderate lameness. Below is a simple four-point lameness (difficulty in walking) scoring for cattle, pigs and other mammals when they are being unloaded from a truck (Grandin, 2015). It has been validated by Edwards-Callaway *et al.* (2017).

1. Walks normally with smooth, even steps.
2. Walks with a limp or has a stiff gait, with head down or bobbing head. The animal keeps up when a group of animals are walking (classify as mild lameness).
3. Walks with difficulty but still fully mobile. It cannot keep up and is left behind when a group of animals is walking (classify as severe lameness).
4. Can barely stand and walk, and may become non-ambulatory. Same as a score 5 on the Zinpro dairy cow scales (classify as severe lameness and not fit for transport).

It is easy for observers to differentiate between an animal that keeps up with the walking group or falls behind. This is the main factor that differentiates a score 2 from a score 3. Note that some guidelines will label normal walking as 0 and will number the degrees of lameness with 1,2,3. A detailed photographic guide to identify hoof lesions that cause lameness can be found on the Zinpro website (Zinpro, no date).

Lameness is often associated with housing problems, hoof diseases or swollen hocks (Fulwider *et al.*, 2007; Von Keyserlingk *et al.*, 2012; Higginson-Cutler *et al.*, 2013; Kester *et al.*, 2014). There is a big difference between the worst and the best dairy farms. In one study, the best dairy farm had 2.8% lame cows and the worst one had 36% (Cook *et al.*, 2016). One way to motivate producers to reduce lame cows is to publish reports on how a producer ranks compared with other producers (Chapinal *et al.*, 2014).

Dirty cattle

For scoring dirty cattle coming out of feedlots, McKeith *et al.* (2012) used a three-point system. A simple four-point scoring system used in Grandin (2015) is shown below. For most types of housing systems, this simple scoring system is effective. For cattle housed on dirt lots, the soiled area can range from slight discoloration of the hair to large chunks of manure and dirt. Welfare concerns would be greater if large areas of the animal's body are covered with thick chunks of soil.

1 = Completely clean
2 = Legs are soiled, belly is clean
3 = Legs and belly soiled
4 = Legs, belly and sides of body soiled

If the '0 = normal' scoring system is used, the scores would be 0,1,2,3.

Cattle body condition score

The main causes of poor (skinny) body condition are either disease or poor nutrition. In extensively raised cattle, the body condition of cows may become thin during the dry season, but when the rains return the animals will fatten and regain condition. In an extensively raised animal there are many questions about what is an acceptable level of body condition. Figure 16.2 shows cows in the Australian outback during the dry season. The first author observed these cows and they were healthy and alert. For intensively raised dairy cows, many scoring tools are available (Wildman *et al.*, 1982; Ferguson *et al.*, 1994; Elanco, 2009). The author recommends using scoring tools that are recommended by the cattle producers in your country. Five-point scales are often used. There needs to be a pictorial score card to show a skinny body condition that is never acceptable. When body score data are being compared, it is essential to determine which scoring tools are being used. A search online revealed a wide variety of pictorial body condition scoring tools.

Udder problems

One of the most common problems is that the farmer fails to dry up a cow before shipping her to the abattoir. This will result in a distended udder that drips milk. This is a common welfare issue that must be corrected at the farm.

Neglected health problems in cattle

A large survey in the USA with both dairy and beef cattle indicated that timely marketing was a major problem (Roeber *et al.*, 2001). Producers should market cull cows to a slaughter plant before they deteriorate and become too debilitated for transport. Some common neglected health problems in cattle are necrotic cancer eye, where the eyeball has

Fig. 16.2. These thin cattle on the arid Australian outback are in good health and alert. When the rains come, they will fatten back up. Body condition scoring charts may have to be adapted to local conditions. If they become thinner than this photo, their welfare would probably be compromised. (Photo courtesy of Temple Grandin.)

ruptured, and necrotic infected prolapses. If the eye is not intact, the cow should not be transported (Canadian Food Inspection Agency, 2013).

Coat condition in cattle and bald spots

Bald spots on cattle are often caused by lice. When cattle normally shed their long winter hair, the new coat underneath is glossy. When they get lice, bald skin will be visible. Large bald spots on cattle are never acceptable. Bald spots are never caused by normal shedding of winter hair.

Abnormal behaviour in cattle

Tongue rolling is an abnormal behaviour that can be easily observed in a slaughter facility. The cow will raise its head and rapidly waggle its tongue. It is common in Jersey dairy cattle and it is associated with both genetic and environmental factors. It is an abnormal behaviour. Jerseys may be less likely to do it if they have access to pasture.

Internal organ inspection in cattle

Liver abscesses are discussed in Chapter 15. The worst livers have abscesses that adhere to the abdominal wall. The Elanco Scoring System (Elanco, 2019) does not differentiate between a severe abscess that adheres to the abdominal wall and one that does not. The Elanco system scores liver abscesses as normal, mild and severe with a three-point system. It is the first author's opinion that a fourth score should be added for adhering to the abdominal wall. Other internal problems that can be easily assessed are parasites, pneumonia and other disease conditions (Table 16.3). For a more detailed discussion, see the literature review in the second part of this chapter.

Injection site damage in cattle and pigs

Studies clearly show that injections of either vaccines or medicines deep into the muscle will damage the meat of cattle and pigs (Geaze et al., 1996; Cresswell et al., 2017; Ko et al., 2018; Pfeiffer *et al.*, 2019). In beef, George *et al.* (1995) found that a deep muscle injection can cause an area of toughness 7–8 cm away from the lesion. This is the reason why cattle producers in many countries have stopped giving injections in the rump. They have switched to the neck position and use the subcutaneous route. In South America, injections in the rump are still common. Some medications and vaccines are more irritating than others. Injection site damage can range from old healed fibrous areas in the beef (Fig. 16.3) to more recent lesions with pus. A recent study showed that injection site damage is still a problem in cow carcasses (Pfeiffer *et al.*, 2019). There are good photos of fresh injection site damage in Ko *et al.* (2018).

Pig Indicators of Poor On-farm Conditions

The same four-point lameness systems (Grandin, 2015; Edwards-Callaway, 2017) can be easily used for lameness evaluation in pigs. During truck unloading, the pigs that lag behind when the group is moving are easy to see. Pigs have shorter legs and it may be more difficult to see the lame stiff-legged animals that can still keep up with the walking group. Pfeifer *et al.* (2019) found that interobserver reliability for lameness was poor. For pigs, it may be best to use the Welfare Quality three-point scoring system (Welfare Quality, 2009b).

Breeding for good feet and legs can help prevent lameness (Le *et al.*, 2015).

It is possible that some problems with interobserver reliability are due to the Welfare Quality pig-scoring system combining normal and mild lameness and then having two categories of severe lameness (Welfare Quality, 2009b). It may be easier for assessors to understand the following scale:

0 = Normal
1 = Fully mobile but lags behind a group of walking pigs during truck unloading
2 = Can barely walk and is almost a downer, non-ambulatory

From the first author's own experience, observing stiff lame cattle is much easier. In pigs, it is easy to differentiate between 0 = normal, 1 =lame and does not keep up with the group, and 2 = downer, non-ambulatory.

Dirty pigs

Pigs will roll in the mud to keep cool. This natural behaviour must not be confused with soil from dirty, poorly-maintained housing. For high-welfare sow herds, groups on straw bedding are often used. To keep the animals clean, sufficient bedding must be continually added to provide a dry, clean surface for the pigs to lie on. The biggest problem the first author has observed with these systems is failure to use sufficient bedding to keep the pigs clean.

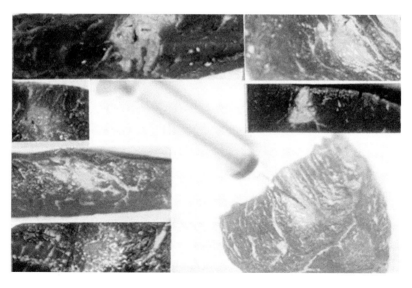

Fig. 16.3. Old healed injection site lesions in meat. Every injection with a needle damages the meat. More recent injection site damage may have pus or oozing fluid. (Photo courtesy of Temple Grandin.)

Body condition score in pigs

In intensively raised herds, pigs should be kept in good body condition. An easy way to determine if a sow is too skinny is to look for a series of vertebrae bumps down her back. A sow that is in good body condition will have a smooth back.

Skin lesions in pigs

Increasing the body condition of sows will help prevent skin lesions on the shoulder. Shoulder lesions often occur in sows housed in stalls. The presence of shoulder lesions cannot be used to identify producers who have sow gestation stalls where the sow is not able to turn around. The first author has observed shoulder lesions on sows housed in a straw-bedded pen. Lundeheim *et al.* (2014) found that thin back fat was associated with more lesions.

Hernias

Another problem that is relatively common in pigs is umbilical hernias. These can range from the size of a golf ball to a large distension dragging on the floor (Welfare Quality, 2009b). Pigs must be marketed before a hernia interferes with walking or gets injured by dragging on the floor. There is a genetic component to hernias (Grindflek *et al.*, 2018; Li *et al.*, 2019).

Tail biting and fighting in pigs and signs of abnormal behaviour

Pigs from certain farms or specific genetic lines may show more tail-bitten pigs compared with those from other farms. There are genetic differences in the tendency of pigs to tail bite, fight or chew on things (D'Eath *et al.*, 2009; Zunderland *et al.*, 2011; Chu *et al.*, 2017). Some pigs are naturally more aggressive (Chu *et al.*, 2017). Brunberg *et al.* (2013a,b) have done some interesting research on tail biting. Some pigs are the perpetrators of tail biting; others are more likely to tolerate having their tails bitten. Breeding programmes that select for rapid growth and lean backfat may have more problems. Within a group of pigs on a farm, there may be three types of pigs: (i) pigs that bite other pigs' tails; (ii) pigs that tolerate other pigs biting their tails; and (iii) neutral pigs who both avoid getting bitten or actively biting other pig's tails.

Scoring tools are available for assessing tail biting and scratches on pigs due to fighting. At an abattoir, it is possible to determine if scratches on pigs occurred during transport and lairage or if they occurred earlier in the pig's life. Carroll *et al.* (2018) found that many skin and tail lesions that occurred 10 weeks earlier could be observed at slaughter. A Swedish study indicated that providing straw helped to reduce tail biting. Tail docking is banned in Sweden, where at slaughter 1.6% of the pigs had bitten tails (Wallgren *et al.*, 2016).

Internal organ inspection in pigs

Two farm-related health problems that can be easily tabulated are lungs that adhere to the chest wall and gastric ulcers (Swaby and Gregory, 2012). Both of these are conditions that would definitely compromise welfare. Harley *et al.* (2012a,b) and Knage-Rasmussen *et al.* (2015) used meat inspection reports as an animal welfare surveillance tool. They examined the prevalence of tail biting and carcass condemnations at slaughter (see the literature review in the second half of this chapter for more information).

Problems with Livestock on High-dose Beta Agonists

Lameness, non-ambulatory animals and handling problems may be associated with high doses of the beta-agonists ractopamine and zilpateral. See Chapter 15 for a full discussion of this problem.

Sheep and Goats Indicators of Poor On-farm Conditions

Munoz *et al.* (2018) is an open access paper and has a table for scoring body condition, rumen fill, fleece cleanliness, fleece condition, skin lesions, tail length, dag (dirty breech) area, foot wall integrity, hoof wall integrity, hoof overgrowth and lameness.

Lameness

One advantage that assessors have when they score lameness in sheep, goats and cattle is that all three of these species will head bob while walking when they are lame. Munoz *et al.* (2018) used a four-point lameness scale for extensively raised ewes. They had good inter-observer agreement.

Foddai *et al.* (2012) contained information on scoring systems for foot rot in sheep.

Munoz *et al.* (2018) had a four-point scale:

0 = Normal
1 = Shorter stride, head bobbing
2 = Not weight-bearing on the affected limb
3 = Reluctant to move or stand

The Munoz *et al.* (2018) scoring tool is designed for on-farm use where evaluating animals walking as a group would not be possible. At an abattoir, livestock are unloaded from a truck and the four-point system (Edwards-Callaway *et al.*, 2017) would be easy to use for sheep or goats. Deeming *et al.* (2018) used both four-point and five-point systems for evaluating lameness in dairy goats. To use a five-point system accurately requires more training.

Dirty sheep and goats and hair coat condition

Munoz *et al.* (2018) found that the scoring system they used for fleece cleanliness and fleece condition had perfect agreement between four observers. Scores for dags (dirty breech area) had only moderate agreement. Hair coat condition is a valid indicator of dairy goat welfare (Battini *et al.*, 2015).

Munoz *et al.* (2018) used a four-point scale for fleece cleanliness and a three-point scale for fleece condition (see also Estevez *et al.*, 2017; Munoz *et al.*, 2019).

0 = Clean and dry
1 = Dry, slight mud/dirt
2 = Wet, some areas contaminated with dung
3 = Filthy, very wet and coated in mud or dung

Body condition score

Since sheep have wool, it is often difficult to assess body condition in live sheep with thick wool. Munoz *et al.* (2018) found that inter-observer agreement was poor. For accurate assessment of body condition in sheep at an abattoir, it is recommended that it should be done in the carcass after the pelt (skin) is removed.

Lesions and joint problems in sheep

Phythian *et al.* (2019) found that inter-observer agreement was high for assessing joint swelling.

Abnormal behaviour in sheep

Sheep living in confined systems will sometimes bite and pull the wool off each other. Feeding programmes or close confinement can have an effect on wool pulling (Huang and Takeda, 2016, 2018). Wool pulling is abnormal behaviour that is detrimental to animal welfare. There are often individual differences in the tendency to wool bite.

Prohibited Surgical Procedures

It is easy to determine if an animal has had certain surgical procedures that may be prohibited, either in some countries or under a specific marketing programme.

- Tail docking of dairy cows. Research shows that docking provides no health or cleanliness advantage for dairy cows (Frantz *et al.*, 2019). Trimming the end of the switch is easy to do and should be used instead of tail docking.
- Mulesing in sheep (removal of strips of wool-bearing skin from around breech to prevent flystrike).
- Chopping long horns off large cattle.
- Tail docking in pigs.

Animal Welfare Issues that Must be Assessed with On-farm Visits

Provision of pain relief for surgeries done on the farm

Provision of analgesics and anaesthetics for surgeries such as castration or dehorning provides a reduction of stress and pain in cattle, sheep, pigs and goats (Stafford and Mellor, 2015).

Type of animal housing on the farm

Welfare criteria that specify a certain type of housing cannot be verified at the abattoir. Specific welfare requirements such as group sow housing or pasture access cannot be assessed at slaughter.

Euthanasia methods used on the farm

The public is increasingly concerned about the methods that are used to euthanize animals on the farm. There are many videos online that show euthanasia methods that are abusive and not acceptable. Evaluations at slaughter will not address this problem.

Environmental enrichment

There is increasing concern that livestock and poultry do not receive sufficient environmental enrichment to fulfil behaviour needs. Some examples of methods to accommodate behaviour needs are nest boxes for hens, straw for pigs to root in or perches for poultry. The use of environmental enrichment on the farm cannot be assessed at the abattoir.

Abusive rough handling

Sometimes it is possible to observe injuries from abusive on-farm handling at the abattoir. This is especially true if the poor handling occurred recently (see Chapters 5 and 15). Other abuses such as rough abusive on-farm handling of young animals are impossible to evaluate on an older animal.

Detailed Review of the Literature on the Use of Abattoir Data for Animal Welfare Assessment

Ante-mortem and post-mortem inspection of livestock and poultry at a slaughterhouse provides a major collection point where animals from different farms could be assessed. There are many welfare issues that occur during rearing on the farm that can be identified at slaughter. Welfare issues associated with transport and slaughter can also be assessed at the abattoir (EFSA Panels, 2011) (Table 16.1). Assessments at slaughter will be especially useful in regions where on-farm welfare assessments are not performed. The existing regulatory frameworks and infrastructure for food safety inspection can be used to assess on-farm welfare (Stärk et al., 2014).

Limitations of on-farm assessments

Many animals can be difficult to handle, examine and sample on-farm. It can be difficult to examine some animals fully and effectively on-farm and to score the severity of lesions, such as bite wounds in pigs. For example, on-farm pigs may be kept in highly stocked pens with poor lighting, and they could be resting and dirty, making inspection difficult (Dalmau et al., 2014). If inspection or sampling at the slaughterhouse is effective, it can represent a more economical and safer procedure than undertaking on-farm examination or sampling (Schärrer et al., 2015). If a blood sample or other tissue is required at the time of slaughter or post-mortem, there is no negative impact on animal welfare compared with sampling a live animal (Birkegård et al., 2017). As there are strict biosecurity

measures, especially at pig and poultry farms, it is difficult to sample a large number of farms in a short period. Convenience sampling at an abattoir is inexpensive compared with undertaking numerous farm visits (Birkegård et al., 2017).

There are some welfare conditions that can be more readily identified at the slaughter plant than during an on-farm inspection. Many types of injuries, such as bruising, skin wounds, footpad dermatitis and hock burns, are more apparent and more accurately recorded during post-mortem examination when the animals are on the slaughter line and after various degrees of processing, such as defeathering, scalding or skin removal, than during an on-farm inspection of live animals. Scalding in hot water cleans poultry carcasses and feet, making it easier to identify contact dermatitis after slaughter than in live birds. Scalding and hair removal from pig carcasses improves the visibility of tail lesions, severe skin lesions from fighting and lesions from trauma inflicted by handling instruments (Barington and Jensen, 2013; Carroll et al., 2016). Bruising cannot be observed in cattle and sheep until the skin has been removed.

Limitations of slaughter welfare assessment

The main problem with the use of slaughter data is that it is only suitable for the identification of health and welfare issues that cause lesions that are detectable at slaughter. The recording of lesions at the time of slaughter will not detect lesions that were present earlier in the life of the animal and have subsequently resolved (Sanchez-Vazquez et al., 2011). It will not record pathology that was present in animals that died on-farm, were euthanized or were not fit for transport (Petersen et al., 2008). The type and prevalence of health and welfare conditions identified at an abattoir are affected by whether the condition was readily recognizable on-farm, whether it was subsequently treated and whether preventive measures were instigated. Conditions that cause severe clinical signs were likely to be detected on-farm. Animals with mild or non-detectable clinical signs are more likely to be sent to slaughter than those with more severe external signs (Hardstaff et al., 2012).

Several of the Welfare Quality schemes (finishing pigs, broilers and fattening cattle) for welfare assessment incorporate post-mortem abattoir recordings from batches of animals that were observed on-farm and scored using a range of animal-based welfare indicators (Welfare Quality, 2009a,b,c). This requires good communication and planning with the slaughter plant to ensure that the animals assessed on-farm can also be assessed at slaughter. The slaughter plant assessments are confined to a limited number of specific lesions, mostly conducted on a sample of the animals from each batch. Most lesions are scored by reference to a description and image. 'Warning' and 'alarm' thresholds are set for the prevalence of each lesion. Some measurements use the meat inspection data collected by meat inspectors, whereas others require assessors to be present to collect additional data. De Jong et al. (2016) discussed some practical issues with the use of the broiler welfare assessment protocol. An additional 1–2 h per flock at a slaughter plant is needed as well as a welfare assessment during a farm visit. In Dutch slaughterhouses, the speed of the slaughter line only allowed a scoring system that identified either 'no' or 'mild' hock burn and the prevalence of condemnations for different lesions was not recorded by meat inspectors; only the total percentage of rejected carcasses was recorded (De Jong et al., 2016).

Different approaches to assessing animal welfare at the abattoir

When considering data collection on animal welfare at abattoirs, there are differences in approach as to which of the conditions recorded at slaughterhouses are identified as relevant to animal welfare. Sometimes only conditions that instigate enforcement action on regulations to protect the welfare of animals are considered to be a welfare issue. Another approach is to identify a condition as relevant to animal welfare if it occurred on-farm or during transport following a management problem or some other form of human culpability (Blagojevic et al., 2015). Many conditions are listed under the heading of animal health rather than animal welfare because they either pose a public health risk or are associated with an economic loss if control and treatment measures are not undertaken to reduce their prevalence and severity.

The approach taken in this chapter is that all conditions that are likely to have been associated with an aversive emotional state in the animal, such as pain or discomfort, are considered relevant to animal welfare. As a consequence, many of the conditions that are normally listed as animal health

conditions are considered to be relevant to animal welfare. This approach was also taken by EFSA Panels (2011) and Nielsen et al. (2017) when they discussed the use of meat inspection data for animal welfare assessment. Injuries and diseases identified either ante-mortem or post-mortem were likely to have been associated with experiences of pain, suffering and discomfort when the animals were on-farm and during transport to slaughter. Many diseases that cause gross pathology in animals are also likely to have caused the animals to feel ill and experience clinical signs associated with unpleasant sensations, such as inappetence, thirst, fever and nausea. Many of the diseases that cause identifiable lesions at the abattoir would have had poor welfare consequences for the animals when they were alive by causing them weakness, reduced ability to undertake important physiological functions, and to obtain feed, water and rest (Cockram and Hughes, 2018).

Determining the prevalence of animal welfare issues in a country, province or state

Within a country, there is a limited number of abattoirs through which almost all livestock and meat birds pass. This structure should provide an ideal opportunity for surveillance of animal welfare issues. Systematically collected data are essential for the accurate description of animal welfare issues that can then be used to contribute to the planning, implementation and evaluation of risk-mitigation actions by government or industry. Estimates of the prevalence of conditions relevant to animal welfare can be monitored over time and significant changes can be detected (Correia-Gomes et al., 2016). To produce valid estimates, surveillance to measure the level of a welfare problem at an abattoir has to avoid bias and therefore needs to be based on either a census or a representative sample of the relevant population (EFSA Panels, 2011). Abattoir characteristics, such as the number of days or weeks on which animals are slaughtered, and the number of animals processed, may affect condemnation rates at different plants (Alton et al., 2010). As animal welfare is a sensitive topic, many producers consider that information for their farm is confidential and access to their data should not be provided to external parties (Shadbolt et al., 1987). However, there are ways of maintaining the anonymity of individual producers when regional or national statistics are compiled.

Use of abattoir data for enforcement of legal regulations on animal welfare

In some countries, if the prevalence of a specific welfare issue in a batch of animals exceeds an established 'target' value, or if the severity of a welfare issue in an individual animal requires action, a regulatory response may be instigated. In some countries, enforcement inspectors are required to identify welfare issues in live or dead animals that appear to have originated on-farm or during transport, gather evidence and report the details to the regulatory authority (EFSA Panels, 2011). In the EU, a directive (European Council, 2007) that regulates the on-farm stocking density of broilers requires slaughter plant monitoring of the prevalence of specific welfare outcomes to ensure that they do not exceed specified thresholds; or, if they do, the producer has to reduce the on-farm stocking density to a prescribed level. If a producer rears broilers at a floor stocking density greater than 33 kg/m^2 they must provide documentation on the daily mortality rate and the cumulative daily mortality rate and this is assessed alongside the percentage of broilers that are dead on arrival. The prevalence of post-mortem lesions (e.g. ascites/oedema, cellulitis and dermatitis, emaciation, joint lesions, septicaemia/respiratory lesions and foot pad dermatitis) that are indicators of contact dermatitis, parasitism and systemic illness cannot exceed specified thresholds (Butterworth *et al.*, 2016). Where levels exceed a threshold (trigger level), the owner/keeper of the birds and the government welfare regulatory authority are notified.

Use of Data Collected Primarily for Food Safety Reasons for Animal Welfare Assessment

Almost all food-producing animals (except those that die, or are killed, on-farm) are slaughtered for human consumption and subjected to ante- and post-mortem inspection at abattoirs. Although this information is collected primarily for food safety reasons, it is a valuable source of surveillance data for animal health and welfare at farm, regional and national levels. If this information is provided to the producer, it can be used to inform their herd/flock health planning. The relative merits of the use of meat inspection data to provide information on animal welfare have been discussed by several authors (Cleveland-Nielsen *et al.*, 2004; Harley *et al.*,

2012a; Stärk *et al.*, 2014; Huneau-Salaün *et al.*, 2015; Devitt *et al.*, 2016b; Correia-Gomes *et al.*, 2017; Grandin, 2017; van Staaveren *et al.*, 2017).

The aim of meat inspection is to protect public health by reducing the risk of hazardous material entering the food chain. An integrated 'farm-to-fork' approach is used to identify infectious risks to human health that may not be associated with gross pathology that is readily identifiable during post-mortem inspection. This can require the supplier of the animals to provide the abattoir with food-chain documentation on the management of their animals while they were on the farm (Butler *et al.*, 2003). Ante-mortem inspection, i.e. of live animals, is conducted to identify any clinical signs of disease in the animals that might affect human health and to identify diseases of economic significance to animal health. Ante-mortem inspection is increasingly used to identify any signs that animal welfare has been compromised during the handling and transport of the animals to the abattoir or during rearing on the farm of origin. The post-mortem visual inspection of the carcass and the viscera is designed to detect and withdraw from the food chain (i.e. condemn as unfit for human consumption) any carcasses and viscera that show grossly identifiable abnormalities that may affect their safety or wholesomeness. Condemnation statistics for carcasses, parts of carcasses and viscera will list the prevalence of conditions assessed as unfit for human consumption (Government of Canada, Agriculture and Agri-Food Canada, 2018a,b).

Food chain records as a source of information

Food chain information is information shared between farms and slaughterhouses, primarily to reduce the risk of food safety issues, but it also has relevance for meat quality, animal health and animal welfare. A producer (especially of pigs and poultry) is increasingly required to provide information on production performance and mortality during rearing to enable a veterinary inspector at the slaughter plant to evaluate the food safety risk associated with a batch of animals. However, there is a tendency for some producers to provide insufficient and inaccurate food chain information (Felin *et al.*, 2016; Allain *et al.*, 2018). Mortality rates during rearing provide useful information, but ideally, for welfare assessment, the records need to differentiate between animals that die and those that are killed due to euthanasia. For all-in/all-out systems, the batch is identifiable and a batch mortality rate can be calculated. For continuous systems, where only some animals are selected for slaughter, the group is not as clearly defined and the mortality rate over a specific period is provided (Food Control Consultants, 2015).

Ante-mortem meat inspection of live animals as a source of information

The ante-mortem inspection of live animals in the lairage is intended to detect animals with clinical signs of disease that might pose an increased food safety risk because they could have a condition that might not readily be identifiable during post-mortem examination or might require more detailed attention during post-mortem examination. It can also be used to identify diseases that pose major risks to animal health. Depending on the type of condition identified, the ante-mortem inspection might be used to adjust the timing of slaughter to earlier than scheduled (if, for example, a condition is associated with discomfort or suffering) or, if there is a risk of contamination, to later than scheduled. Watson *et al.* (2011) provided examples of common conditions recorded ante-mortem in calves, sheep and pigs in Great Britain.

The ante-mortem inspection is also used to identify any signs that indicate that animal welfare has been compromised during handling and transport or that the animals are affected by conditions associated with poor on-farm management (Tables 16.1 and 16.2). However, the ante-mortem inspection might only have fair to moderate sensitivity for the detection of health and welfare conditions that produce obvious clinical signs (EFSA Panels, 2011). The sensitivity of ante-mortem inspection is affected by factors such as: the duration of the examination of each animal; whether the animals are observed during movement or by pen-side inspection; the intensity of the lighting; any overcrowding in the lairage pens; the skill and experience of the examiner; and whether specific case definitions for animal welfare conditions are provided (Petersen *et al.*, 2004; Schemann *et al.*, 2010; EFSA Panels, 2011).

If signs that animal welfare has been compromised are detected by abattoir staff during unloading or lairage and reported to an inspector, or are identified by an inspector conducting ante-mortem inspection, there can be an expectation or requirement that an inspector will take specific actions directed at the transporter and/or the consignor of the animal(s) to reduce the risk of reoccurrence. Therefore, an inspector might be inclined only to record severe animal welfare conditions that require specific intervention. There is a risk that some less severe welfare conditions seen during ante-mortem inspection will not be recorded and this can reduce the value of ante-mortem inspection results as a means of identifying the prevalence of some animal welfare conditions (Food Control Consultants, 2015).

Limitation of data from meat inspection records

Meat inspection data is attractive as a data source as it saves time and resources on the collection of data and provides information from a wide geographical area (Houe *et al.*, 2011). However, there are several concerns about the accuracy and usefulness of meat inspection data for animal welfare assessment (Huneau-Salaün *et al.*, 2015; Mathur *et al.*, 2018). Information collected for primary databases that are used for research or advisory services is normally recorded using precise case definitions with instructions to assessors on how to identify and record the severity of each of the disease conditions. When secondary databases, such as meat inspection data, are used for a purpose that is different to that for which it was designed, there can be technical and practical limitations on their use (Houe *et al.*, 2011). There can be significant differences between the meat inspection condemnation rates for various conditions at different slaughterhouses due to inconsistencies between the visual criteria used by different inspectors to evaluate the reasons for condemnation (Lupo *et al.*, 2008; Schleicher *et al.*, 2013). Meat inspection results may be recorded with varying levels of detail. For example, lungs may be recorded as 'abnormal' or as showing signs of gross pathology associated with a specific case definition (e.g. enzootic pneumonia-like lesions) and sometimes with a measure of severity. Case definitions of post-mortem conditions that provide standard definitions for disease/condition categories in the form of text and photographs/diagrams can improve the consistency of recording (Food Control Consultants, 2015; Horst *et al.*, 2019). Compared with detailed systematic laboratory evaluation by trained pathologists, routine meat inspection does not always provide the correct identification of some lesions (Bisaillon *et al.*, 1988; Nielsen *et al.*, 2015). There may be differences in the thresholds used to identify whether a lesion is recorded. Bonde *et al.* (2010) found that, compared with trained pathologists, meat inspectors tended to have a low sensitivity in that they may not have recorded less severe conditions, but they had very high specificity in that they required the presence of typical signs before they identified and recorded a condition.

The reliability of the recording of conditions can be affected by the number of conditions that meat inspectors have to record, their training and opportunities for continuing professional development (CPD) and the extent of the monitoring of inspection results between inspection teams, abattoirs or regions. The lighting, the speed of the slaughter line and the number of inspectors can also affect the reliability of data recording (Watson *et al.*, 2011; Food Control Consultants, 2015; Horst *et al.* 2019). Touch-screen terminals close to the inspection points that automatically identify the animal being inspected, or the batch to which it belongs, can be used to record meat inspection data. However, manual collection methods that utilize paper, boards, or mechanical counters are also used. These manual systems often require transcription, manual data processing or digital entry on to computer software when the inspector has completed their inspection period on the slaughter line (Food Control Consultants, 2015).

Problems with comparing meat inspection data between countries

When comparing the prevalence of conditions recorded using meat inspection data over time or between countries, there can be differences in the way in which conditions have been identified and recorded (Watson *et al.*, 2011). There is also a risk of double recording of the same post-mortem finding, e.g. pleurisy, in a single animal at both the carcass and offal inspection points, or an abscess could be recorded in more than one location (Watson *et al.*, 2011; Food Control Consultants, 2015). If multiple conditions are observed, only the dominant condition may be recorded. When a whole carcass is rejected, the viscera and offal may also be rejected without inspection. Superficial bruising may be trimmed and not recorded in condemnation data (Watson *et al.*, 2011).

Conditions Associated with Injury that Compromise Animal Welfare

Skin conditions in poultry

Although not part of normal meat inspection conducted for food safety reasons in poultry, foot pad dermatitis, hock burn and breast blisters are increasingly monitored on the slaughter line as part of quality assurance and animal welfare surveillance. These conditions are a form of contact dermatitis that occurs on-farm when the litter quality is poor. The prevalence and severity of footpad dermatitis, hock burn and breast blisters are affected by the litter quality, stocking density and other aspects of management during rearing. If the litter condition deteriorates, ammonia from the accumulation of urea in the litter causes a chemical burn on the skin and poor air quality (Haslam *et al.*, 2007). The severity of foot pad dermatitis can be scored on the slaughter line by the size and pathological characteristics of the lesions (Michel *et al.*, 2012; Heitmann *et al.*, 2018). Cellulitis occurs in poultry as a diffuse inflammation of the subcutaneous tissue. It can be associated with skin scratches from other birds at feeders that can introduce bacterial infection (Norton *et al.*, 1999; St-Hilaire and Sears, 2003). The prevalence of skin scratches in broilers is affected by the stocking density during rearing (Allain *et al.*, 2009). Spent laying hens can experience feather loss during the laying period. They can be scored for plumage condition (on the neck, breast, cloaca/vent, back, wings and tail), skin damage from feather pecking to the rear body and comb, and for aggressive pecking to the head (Tauson *et al.*, 2005).

Skin conditions in livestock

Photographic scales can be used to record the location and severity of skin lesions in pigs due to fighting (Faucitano, 2001). When the skin damage is caused by fighting during transport and lairage, more damage tends to occur on the head and shoulder areas than on the middle or rear of the pig. The lesions are typically comma shape, 5–10 cm long and numerous (Faucitano, 2001). Fresh wounds indicate that the damage likely occurred during transport and lairage. Healed (non-red) skin lesions, scars, notches and necrosis indicate older wounds that likely occurred on the farm (Dalmau *et al.*, 2014; Bottacini *et al.*, 2018; Carroll *et al.*, 2018). In pigs, tail bite lesions can be recorded as injuries to the tail and by a short or missing tail. Skin damage on the middle, back and hind regions of pigs can occur due to inappropriate use of driving instruments, mounting by other pigs, or contact with overhead rails during handling (Geverink et al. 1996; Faucitano, 2001). The skin over joints such as the shoulder and over hernias can be examined for abscesses, abrasions and ulcers (Knauer et al., 2007). Most ulceration lesions are due to external trauma or fistulation to the skin surface from an underlying condition. If granulation tissue is not present, the ulceration is likely to be recent (Barington et al., 2016b). Occasionally skin erythema due to urine scald can occur in pigs due to inadequate bedding in transit or on-farm (White, 1999). Parasitic skin infection, e.g. flystrike in sheep and mange in pigs, may be observed (Davies et al., 1996; White, 1999; Wall and Lovatt, 2015). In cattle, hide damage can occur from the use of sticks containing nails during handling (Grandin, 2017).

Bruising on poultry and livestock

Bruising can be observed after defeathering of poultry, after skin removal in ruminants and on the skin surface of live pigs, but it is clearer after carcass processing (Barington and Jensen, 2013). Bruising can be present in subcutaneous fat and muscle. There are several methods for scoring the severity of bruising, but most involve recording the number, size, shape, colour, depth and location of the bruising (Strappini et al., 2012). Differences in the way in which bruising is identified and recorded can have large effects on the reported prevalence (Knowles and Broom, 1990). The manner in which broilers are handled during loading can affect the degree of bruising observed on the slaughter line (Cockram and Dulal, 2018). Handling, conditions during transport (e.g. high stocking density) and mounting interactions during lairage can affect the occurrence of bruising in livestock (Kenny and Tarrant, 1987; Eldridge and Winfield, 1988; Tarrant et al., 1992; Jarvis et al., 1995; Costa et al., 2006; Romero et al., 2013; Goldhawk et al., 2015; Dalla Costa et al., 2019). The severity of haemorrhage and the amount of necrotic muscle tissue in a bruise are dependent on the force of impact (Barington and Jensen, 2016a). The pattern and shape of bruising can often resemble the object used to inflict the trauma (Barington and Jensen, 2016b). Excessive use of driving instruments during handling can cause bruising (Geverink et al., 1996). For example, in pigs and cattle, bruising in a tramline pattern consisting of two longitudinal, parallel lines of haemorrhage separated by apparently normal skin is indicative of trauma from the excessive use of a stick or bar. Bruising in pigs in the shape of the handle of a plastic pig paddle and the pattern of a metal chain has been recorded (McNally and Warriss, 1996; Barington et al., 2016a). Skin-penetrating lesions due to excessive use of tattoo hammers can also occur in pigs (Nielsen et al., 2014).

In cattle and pigs, a large proportion of the bruising seen on the slaughter line has been estimated to occur at the abattoir (McCausland and Millar, 1982; Strappini et al., 2013; Barington et al., 2018). The colour of a bruise is initially red, and then it changes through various shades of purple, green and yellow due to the breakdown of haemoglobin into bilirubin and biliverdin. It is difficult to accurately estimate the age of a bruise just from its colour (Barington and Jensen, 2015), but laboratory analysis can provide a reasonable estimate of the age of the bruising (Barington et al., 2018). Some bruising seen on the slaughter line can be caused during stunning and post-mortem by machinery or the handling of the carcass (Hamdy et al., 1961; Kranen et al., 2000; Strappini et al., 2009; Kittelsen et al., 2015b).

Fractures

Fractures can occur in the wings and legs of broilers and laying hens during handling before loading, but also during shackling and electrical stunning at the abattoir (Gregory and Wilkins, 1990; Gregory et al., 1990; Raj et al., 1990; Newberry et al., 1999; Kittelsen et al., 2015b; Jacobs et al., 2017b). Fractures can also occur at other sites, especially in birds that are dead on arrival (Kittelsen et al., 2015a). In laying hens, wing and keel bone fractures can occur on-farm associated with cage and non-cage housing systems, respectively (Gregory et al., 1990; Wilkins et al., 2011). Leg fractures can occur in pigs during handling and transport (Tiong and Bin, 1989; Dalla Costa et al., 2019). A recent fracture is likely to be recognized post-mortem by fresh haemorrhage at the fracture site (Hardstaff et al., 2012). In cattle, a healed, broken tail due to poor handling can be apparent as a permanent bend or kink in the tail (Grandin, 2017).

Conditions Associated with On-farm Management

Emaciation and poor body condition

Emaciation can occur for several reasons, including overproduction, disease (e.g. parasites and wasting diseases), dental problems and undernutrition. Body condition score can be evaluated while the carcass is on the slaughter line (Knauer *et al.*, 2007). During processing, emaciated carcasses can be recognized as those with little subcutaneous and intracavity fat. Any carcass fat that is present tends to be oedematous and jelly-like in appearance (Hardstaff *et al.*, 2012). In poultry, a carcass condemned due to emaciation/cachexia has little muscle, almost no fat and a prominent keel bone. Emaciation in poultry is caused by poor management and chronic health conditions (Nery *et al.*, 2017).

Dehydration

Dehydration can occur due to water restriction during transport and lairage (Jones *et al.*, 1990; Brown *et al.*, 1999; Jacob *et al.*, 2006) and occasionally due to an inability to obtain sufficient water on-farm due to management problems, disease or heat. Dehydration can cause a loss in carcass weight, a drier appearance to the meat, a reduction in the contents of the gastrointestinal tract and greater difficulty in separating the skin (hide) from the subcutaneous tissues (Jones *et al.*, 1990).

Conditions associated with lameness

Arthritis (inflammation of a joint) is a common cause of lameness in pigs, cattle and poultry that is recognized post-mortem by swelling and excessive fluid in the joint (Cross and Edwards, 1981; Dupuy *et al.*, 2013). Arthritis can be caused by infection and degeneration of the joint due to a range of factors, including repeated trauma and structural abnormalities associated with genetics and rapid growth (Bradshaw *et al.*, 2002). In pigs, the prevalence of arthritis is affected by housing and on-farm management (Heinonen *et al.*, 2007). Scoring of lameness of poultry at an abattoir is extremely difficult. However, it is easier to measure abnormalities such as twisted legs. Knowles *et al.* (2008) has a good review of leg disorders in broiler chickens.

Tenosynovitis with or without tendon rupture can occur in broilers as a result of infection and trauma and cause lameness (Johnson, 1972; Duff

and Randall, 1986). Bursitis lesions are inflamed and enlarged bursae (fluid-filled sacs located where muscles and tendons move over bones). In pigs and cattle, they are caused by trauma and, in particular, pressure on hard surfaces during lying (Gillman *et al.*, 2008; Brščić *et al.*, 2011a). Bursitis can affect locomotion in finishing pigs (Kilbride *et al.*, 2009).

In cattle and pigs, lesions in the feet are a major cause of lameness. Although not normally part of routine meat inspection (the feet from pigs and poultry might be kept for human consumption), valuable information could be gained by an examination of the feet. Feet from cattle, sheep and pigs could be examined for the presence of claw and hoof wall cracks, heal lesions, abscesses, interdigital inflammation and abnormal overgrowth conditions (upward or inward curvature of the toes or excessive hoof growth) (Murray *et al.*, 1994; Knauer *et al.*, 2007; Foddai *et al.*, 2012; Nalon *et al.*, 2013). The condition of the feet in cattle and pigs can be affected by many on-farm factors: environmental, genetic, nutritional or infectious (Mouttotou *et al.*, 1999; Pluym *et al.*, 2013). For ruminants, the lower part of the limbs (at the carpal and hock joints) and feet are normally removed and discarded early in the carcass dressing procedures, before the carcass is skinned (but they are sometimes left attached to the hide). Although the feet from a batch of animals could be examined after the carcasses have been processed and moved along the slaughter line, to avoid the risk of contamination this is likely to require a separate area and different personnel to conduct the assessment (Llonch *et al.*, 2015). Spent laying hens can be assessed for the severity of foot damage (inflamed bumble foot lesions) (Tauson *et al.*, 2005). Poor management of freestalls (cubicles) in dairy farms or stalls that are too small can cause swollen hocks in dairy cows (Fulwider *et al.*, 2007). Dairy cows with swollen hocks are more likely to be lame. There is a big difference between the best and the worst dairy farms in the percentage of lame cows (Espejo *et al.*, 2006; Grandin, 2015).

Conditions Associated with On-farm Management or Infection That Can Cause Aversive Pathophysiological Effects

Cardiovascular conditions

Ascites in broilers is an accumulation of fluid in the lungs and abdomen that can result in respiratory distress. It is caused by an imbalance between oxygen supply and the oxygen required for rapid growth. The heart has to work harder than normal to maintain effective blood flow throughout the body and this can result in chronic congestive heart failure, increased systemic pressure and excess fluid. It is a multifactorial problem influenced by environmental, nutritional and genetic factors (Wideman, 2001; Julian, 2005; Hassanzadeh et al., 2014). Pericarditis and endocarditis can occur in cattle due to traumatic reticulopericarditis and bacterial infection, respectively. These conditions can cause pain and discomfort; and if severe heart disease develops, this can be associated with respiratory difficulties and ascites (Buczinski et al., 2010). In pigs, pericarditis can be caused by several types of bacterial and mycoplasma infection. Adhesions between the heart and the pericardium might cause discomfort (Buttenschøn et al., 1997).

In cattle, problems with brisket disease (congestive heart disease) have become more common (Neary et al., 2015). Heavy Angus steers are more susceptible (Neary et al., 2015). In the USA, heavy fed cattle may lie down and refuse to move. Thomson et al. (2015) called this fatigued cattle syndrome. In both pigs and cattle, there are some animals that do not tolerate physical exertion and there are various causes of this problem. The fatigued cattle problem is caused by a variety of factors such as genetic selection for carcass traits. Excessive concentrates in the diet or indiscriminate use of growth-promoting agents may also be contributing factors (Grandin and Whiting, 2018).

Respiratory conditions

Pneumonia (inflammation of the lung) can be recognized by palpation and identification of dark purple areas of consolidation that can be scored by the percentage of the lung area affected (Ostanello et al., 2007). Animals with pneumonia will likely have experienced fever, inappetence (Escobar et al., 2007), increased respiratory frequency and decreased tidal volume. The severity of these physiological effects is related to the degree of pathological changes in the lungs, such as the constriction of airways, accumulation of mucus within the lumen of airways, oedema and thickening of the mucous membranes (Reinhold et al., 2002). In animals with pneumonia, reduced physiological function can result in hypoxia from impaired oxygen supply (Linden et al., 1995). If an animal is showing signs of laboured breathing over a prolonged period, this will result in an excessive respiratory effort, discomfort, distress and fatigue (Beausoleil and Mellor, 2015). Pneumonias in calves and pigs are multifactorial diseases involving several potential pathogens. The prevalence of pneumonia is influenced by environmental factors (e.g. housing and ventilation), factors affecting susceptibility to the pathogens, and management factors, such as mixing, stocking density, vaccination and biosecurity procedures (Stärk, 2000; Lorenz et al., 2011). Air sacculitis in broilers is caused by bacterial infections and its occurrence is affected by several management factors (Gross, 1961; d'Arc Moretti et al., 2010).

Pleurisy is an inflammation of the pleura (serous membranes that line the inside of the chest and enclose the lungs) that can be associated with pain and discomfort while breathing or coughing, due to the sliding of the inflamed visceral and parietal pleura against each other and from the development of adhesions. Pleurisy can develop after bacterial and mycoplasma infection and following pneumonia (Meyns et al., 2011). Several management factors, such as biosecurity procedures, stocking density and mixing, are associated with the prevalence of pleurisy (Jäger et al., 2012).

Hepatic and renal conditions

In cattle, sheep and pigs, parasites in the liver can cause hepatitis and cirrhosis that, if severe, can lead to weight loss and anaemia (Sanchez-Vazquez and Lewis, 2013). Jaundice can occur from excessive destruction of red blood cells or an accumulation of bilirubin associated with liver disease or a bile duct blockage (Pearson, 1981). On-farm parasite control measures can be based on the prevalence of liver conditions recorded in condemnation data (Innocent et al., 2017; Mendes et al., 2017). Liver condemnation due to hepatic lipidosis (fatty liver) can occur in cull dairy cows (Rezac et al., 2014). Kidney conditions such as nephritis can be observed and scored by the extent of the macroscopic changes that can occur following various types of infections (Martinez et al., 2006) (see Chapter 15).

Infection

Septicaemia is caused by the spread of pathogenic bacteria, and toxaemia is caused by the spread of bacterial toxins in the blood. In animals condemned with these conditions, a wide range of pathological changes will have occurred while the animal was alive, including effects on the blood supply to the muscles (cyanosis and hyperaemia) and widespread inflammation of the viscera (Fisher *et al.*, 1998). Animals with gross pathology identified post-mortem as septicaemia would have experienced systemic illness, muscle weakness (Ochala *et al.*, 2011) and difficulty maintaining normal physiological function (Wester *et al.*, 2011; Olsen *et al.*, 2016). An abscess is a collection of pus contained within a fibrous capsule and is formed by bacteria. Abscesses can occur throughout the body, including the liver and lungs, and cause weight loss (Brown and Lawrence, 2010). Some abscesses arise from bacterial contamination following an injection (George *et al.*, 1995). Liver abscesses can occur in cattle following rumen acidosis and ruminitis caused by a high-grain and low-roughage diet (Nagaraja and Chengappa, 1998; Nagaraja and Lechtenberg, 2007). In pigs, abscesses can be found throughout the body as a result of tail biting and other types of trauma (Huey, 1996; Heinonen *et al.*, 2010; Ellerbroek *et al.*, 2011). Peritonitis is an inflammation of the peritoneal cavity and its serosal surface (peritoneum). It can be caused by systemic infection, trauma, or gastrointestinal ulceration, blockage or ischaemia (restriction of blood supply). In animals that are condemned due to peritonitis, there was likely to have been an initial systemic response and abdominal pain, followed by adhesion formation (Fecteau, 2005). Animals condemned due to mastitis will likely have experienced pain and discomfort and possibly sickness (Leslie and Petersson-Wolfe, 2012).

Dark-coloured meat

Although sometimes recorded as part of meat quality control and, if the meat is very dark, as part of meat inspection, the significance of dark firm dry meat (DFD) as an indicator of animal welfare is problematic. EFSA Panels (2011) suggested that the presence of DFD meat indicates 'that the transport or lairage conditions did not comply with legislation or with codes of practice'. Although many of the risk factors for DFD in cattle, pigs and poultry are associated with less than optimal welfare conditions, the relationships between factors such as stress, exercise, cold exposure and the occurrence of DFD in susceptible animals are not fully understood (Mach *et al.*, 2008; Dadgar *et al.*, 2012). Therefore, the occurrence of DFD should be used to indicate that management practices should be revised, but not as a trigger for regulatory action on animal welfare (see Chapter 15 for additional information).

Conditions Recorded in Condemnation Data That Have No Direct Relevance to Animal Welfare

There are several reasons for the condemnation of a carcass or viscera that do not have direct relevance to animal welfare. These include contamination (e.g. by faeces or gut contents), post-slaughter damage from machinery, poor plucking, overscalding, pigmentation or abnormal colour, and abnormal smell. Condemnations due to poor bleeding can arise for several reasons not associated with inadequate exsanguination that might have delayed loss of consciousness or death. Therefore, quantifying the total number of condemnations might not provide sensitive or accurate information on animal welfare.

Feedback of Information to Producers to Improve On-farm Animal Welfare

As discussed above, there are on-farm risk factors for many of the conditions recorded during meat inspection (Bisaillon *et al.*, 2001; Lupo *et al.*, 2010). If abattoirs provide data on disease prevalence to producers and their veterinarians, this can be used to inform herd/flock health planning and enable them to make changes to their production systems to improve animal health and welfare, and potentially provide economic benefits (Dalmau *et al.*, 2014; Food Control Consultants, 2015). For example, the presence of some types of gross pathology such as lung lesions in cattle and pigs has been shown to reduce growth during rearing (Pagot *et al.*, 2007; Caucci *et al.*, 2018). There are also advantages to abattoirs if producers can reduce the prevalence of pathology in animals sent for slaughter. Abscesses and adhesions impede evisceration and this, together with the need for more detailed inspection and subsequent condemnation, can slow the slaughter line (Nagaraja and Chengappa, 1998).

Feedback to producers on condemnation data to identify subclinical disease present on a unit is potentially valuable. Some conditions that are not readily identifiable in live animals on the farm can be more readily detected during post-mortem inspection at the slaughterhouse (Green *et al.*,

Abattoir Data on the Welfare of Livestock and Poultry

1997; Food Control Consultants, 2015). Some examples are liver abscesses in cattle (Nagaraja and Chengappa, 1998) and poor rumen development and abomasal lesions in veal calves (Brščić *et al.*, 2011b). Some parasitic skin conditions can be more readily and objectively assessed during an inspection at slaughter than on-farm (Cargill *et al.*, 1997). Although bovine respiratory disease is commonly diagnosed on-farm using clinical signs of illness, monitoring of lung lesions at slaughter can be a more accurate way of identifying the prevalence of this condition (White and Renter, 2009).

For the provision of feedback to producers and their veterinarians, the number of conditions per animal or body part in the batch of animals should be calculated. When data is compiled and presented to producers and other stakeholders, the provision of categories by species, age and class of animal (for example, by differentiating between animals slaughtered in prime condition, young and cull animals) provides the most useful information (Food Control Consultants, 2015). Many producers do not effectively utilize the information provided by abattoirs (Shadbolt *et al.*, 1987; Meat and Livestock Commercial Services, 2013). Some producers express dissatisfaction with the accuracy and consistency of meat inspection results (Food Control Consultants, 2015; Devitt *et al.*, 2016a). Traditionally, when any information was supplied by an abattoir to a producer, it consisted of information on the weight, grades/classification, prices and deductions for condemnations (Pointon *et al.*, 2008). The producer would likely view the condemnation data with scepticism, as it would describe what financial deductions the abattoir had made for the product that was condemned or otherwise rejected, and would not necessarily consider the information to be accurate if there had been few signs of ill-health in the animals sent to slaughter. If an all-in–all-out system is used, all of the animals in a slaughtered batch will no longer be present on the farm and condemnation data might be considered to have less relevance than that for units where some animals reared in similar groups, or from the same group, are still present. However, for batch-reared groups, there can be common management issues that could affect subsequent groups of animals and condemnation data can be valuable (Heinonen *et al.*, 2001). There can also be a concern that data generated to assist producers might be used by regulatory authorities to enforce animal welfare standards (Devitt *et al.*, 2016a).

Benchmarking of information and providing data summaries to producers

Industry bodies have an opportunity to provide data summaries, analysis and benchmarking of meat inspection data to their members. In several countries, there are examples of national and industry systems that provide frequent feedback of benchmarked results from targeted abattoir inspections to participating producers and their herd veterinarians (Neumann *et al.*, 2014; Eze *et al.*, 2015). Holt *et al.* (2011) and Sanchez-Vazquez *et al.* (2011) described industry-financed initiatives that provided producers within the scheme with a report on every batch of pigs that they sent on specific days to an abattoir within the scheme. The report provided the farm-level frequency of gross pathological lesions observed in their pigs at slaughter. A more detailed inspection of a limited number of specific conditions than that undertaken for routine meat inspection was conducted by trained inspectors provided by the scheme. The inspection involved palpation and manipulation of the organs in addition to visual inspection (but no incision), and a measure of the severity of the lesion by reference to specific descriptions of the conditions to be recorded. Information on lesions was recorded directly on to hand-held touchscreen computers at the time of the assessment on the slaughter line. After each assessment day, the electronically recorded information was transferred electronically to a central database. The scheme provided training for assessors, quality control on the information recorded, data processing, analysis and electronic communication of reports, and knowledge transfer activities. This type of scheme has the potential to provide relevant information on the prevalence of certain diseases on particular farms and to identify management practices, e.g. vaccinations, parasite control and biosecurity practices, that minimize the risk of disease. The reports not only increase the awareness of producers and their veterinarians of individual problems present on their farms, but also provide a comparison between different units within their businesses and a comparison of their units with the industry as a whole. This benchmarking provides peer/industry pressure to control diseases and other welfare issues that cause identifiable lesions in their animals.

Traceability and the meat production chain

The ability to follow animals either individually or as a batch through the meat production chain is an essential component of any system to utilize slaughter plant data to provide information on welfare issues during transport and on the farm. Food safety issues and commercial pressure on product quality have led to an increase in the use of systems for the traceability of live animals and the exchange of food chain information (Schwägele, 2005).

Traceability systems can be introduced by industry-wide private sector initiatives, individual supply chain initiatives and public sector regulation. A lack of adequate and standardized data collection and an effective means of data exchange can often mean that internal traceability (within a company) is easier than chain traceability (between companies in the supply chain) (Bosona and Gebresenbet, 2013). In the EU, abattoirs must have a traceability system that can identify the supplier of each animal that it receives (Schwägele, 2005). Cattle and sheep have to be individually identified and groups of pigs identified by their farm of origin. The electronic identification of animals makes it easier to follow animals through the supply chain. However, a frequent logistical issue is maintaining the identification of either individual animals or the batch during slaughter processes when the physical identification of an animal is removed when the head, hide, viscera and feet are separated from the carcass (Crandall et al., 2013). Batches are usually identified on the slaughter line by local systems for marking the first and last animals in a batch.

Common interests between each of the partners in a supply chain can improve information exchange and result in benefits in product quality, food safety and animal health and welfare (Deimel and Theuvsen, 2011). Participation of producers and processors in cooperatives or specialized networks can be beneficial to the competitiveness of individual farms and companies. Producer cooperation with an abattoir can depend on many factors, such as the degree of mutual interdependence, the availability of other suppliers and processors, the price received by a producer from the abattoir, and whether there is personal contact between the producer and the abattoir (Schulze et al., 2006).

Structure of the food chain and traceability

The degree of vertical integration in the supply chain can vary greatly between different sectors. In the pig and poultry sectors, there tends to be a high amount of vertical integration. Large vertically integrated pig and poultry companies often control each stage in the production of pigs and poultry for slaughter. In most countries, nearly all of the pigs and poultry reared for slaughter are transported directly from a farm to the abattoir and are delivered in clearly defined batches (often separated into different rearing barns from the same unit). If cull poultry (breeding birds and laying hens) are sent to slaughter, they are similarly sent directly to a processor in defined batches. However, there is often a lack of vertical integration in some other sectors, such as the beef and sheep industries, where animals can pass through several different companies between birth and slaughter. Groups of cattle or sheep that arrive at a slaughterhouse may consist of: (i) animals that were born and reared on the farm where the animals were loaded; (ii) animals that were born on a number of different farms and finished on the farm where the animals were loaded; or (iii) mixed animals from a range of units that have come from a market or have spent only a short period on the farm where the animals were loaded. Cull dairy cows, cull breeding sows and boars may be sent to slaughter via dealers and collection centres and often arrive at abattoirs as mixed groups (Food Control Consultants, 2015). Mixed groups make it more difficult to provide traceability of animal welfare issues. If animals have moved and changed ownership in the immediate pre-slaughter period (e.g. finishers or dealers), the decision about which holding or farm of origin should be contacted in relation to welfare issues identified at slaughter is problematic. For animals that have undergone a finishing period, the most relevant party will depend on the duration of the finishing period and the nature and epidemiology of the problem(s) identified (Food Control Consultants, 2015).

References

Aaslyng, M.D., Brandt, P., Blaabjerg, L. and Støier, S. (2013) Assessment and incidence of skin damage in slaughter pigs. In: *Proceedings of the 59th International Congress of Meat Science and Technology.* Izmir, Turkey. Available at: https://www.dti.dk/international/icomst-2013/assessment-and-incidence-of-skin-damage-in-slaughter-pigs/33756,2

Allain, V., Mirabito, L., Arnould, C., Colas, M., Le Bouquin, S. *et al.* (2009) Skin lesions in broiler chickens measured at the slaughterhouse: relationships between lesions and between their prevalence and rearing factors. *British Poultry Science* 50, 407–417. doi: 10.1080/00071660903110901

Allain, V., Salines, M., Le Bouquin, S. and Magras, C. (2018) Designing an innovative warning system to support risk-based meat inspection in poultry slaughterhouses. *Food Control* 89, 177–186. doi: 10.1016/j.foodcont.2018.02.003

Alton, G.D., Pearl, D.L., Bateman, K.G., McNab, W.B. and Berke, O. (2010) Factors associated with whole carcass condemnation rates in provincially-inspected abattoirs in Ontario 2001-2007: implications for food animal syndromic surveillance. *BMC Veterinary Research* 6. doi: 10.1186/1746-6148-6-42

Amachawadi, R.G., and Nagaraja, T.G. (2015) Liver abscesses in cattle: a review of incidence in Holsteins of bacteriology and vaccine approaches to control in feedlot cattle. *Journal of Animal Science* 94, 1620–1632.

Angell, J.W., Cripps, P.J., Gove-White, D.H. and Duncan, J.S. (2015) A practical tool for locomotion scoring of sheep: reliability when used by veterinary surgeons and sheep farmers. *Veterinary Record* 176, 521.

Averos, X., Knowles, T.G., Brown, S.N., Warriss, P.D. and Gosalvez, L.F. (2008) Factors affecting the mortality of pigs being transported to slaughter. *Veterinary Record* 163, 386–390.

Barington, K. and Jensen, H.E. (2013) Forensic cases of bruises in pigs. *Veterinary Record* 173, 526. doi: 10.1136/vr.101854

Barington, K. and Jensen, H.E. (2015) Experimental animal models of bruises in forensic medicine – a review. *Scandinavian Journal of Laboratory Animal Science* 41, 1–8.

Barington, K. and Jensen, H.E. (2016a) The impact of force on the timing of bruises evaluated in a porcine model. *Journal of Forensic and Legal Medicine* 40, 61–66. doi: 10.1016/j.jflm.2016.03.005

Barington, K. and Jensen, H.E. (2016b) A novel, comprehensive, and reproducible porcine model for determining the timing of bruises in forensic pathology. *Forensic Science, Medicine, and Pathology* 12, 58–67. doi: 10.1007/s12024-016-9744-6

Barington, K., Agger, J.F.G., Nielsen, S.S., Dich-Jørgensen, K. and Jensen, H.E. (2016a) Gross and histopathological evaluation of human inflicted bruises in Danish slaughter pigs. *BMC Veterinary Research* 12. doi: 10.1186/s12917-016-0869-3

Barington, K., Dich-Jorgensen, K. and Jensen, H.E. (2016b) A retrospective study of forensic cases of skin ulcerations in Danish pigs from 2000 to 2014. *Acta Veterinaria Scandinavica* 58, 48. doi: 10.1186/s13028-016-0229-0

Barington, K., Skovgaard, K., Henriksen, N.L., Johansen, A.S.B. and Jensen, H.E. (2018) The intensity of the inflammatory response in experimental porcine bruises depends on time, anatomical location and sampling site. *Journal of Forensic and Legal Medicine* 58, 130–139. doi: 10.1016/j.jflm.2018.06.005

Barrientos, A.K., Chapinal, N., Weary, D.M, Gallo, E., and von Keyserlingk, M.A.G. (2013) Herd level risk factors for hock injuries in freestalled-housed dairy cows in the northeastern United States and Canada. *Journal of Dairy Science* 96, 3758–3765.

Battini, M., Peric, T., Ajuda, I., Viera, A., Grosso, L., Barbiera, S. *et al.* (2015) Hair coat condition: a valid and reliable indicator for on-farm welfare assessment of adult dairy goats. *Small Ruminant Research* 123, 197–203.

Beausoleil, N.J. and Mellor, D.J. (2015) Introducing breathlessness as a significant animal welfare issue. *New Zealand Veterinary Journal* 63, 44–51. doi: 10.1080/00480169.2014.940410

Bethancourt-Garcia, J.A., Vaz, R.Z., Vaz, F.N., Silva, W.B., Pascoal, L.L. *et al.* (2019) Preslaughter factors affecting the incidence of severe bruising in cattle carcasses. *Livestock Science* 222, 41–48.

Birkegård, A.C., Halasa, T. and Toft, N. (2017) Sampling pig farms at the abattoir in a cross-sectional study – evaluation of a sampling method. *Preventive Veterinary Medicine* 145, 83–90. doi: 10.1016/j.prevetmed.2017.07.002

Bisaillon, J., Meek, A.H. and Feltmate, T.E. (1988) An assessment of condemnations of broiler chicken carcasses. *Canadian Journal of Veterinary Research* 52, 269–276.

Bisaillon, J., Feltmate, T.E., Sheffield, S., Julian, R., Todd, E. *et al.* (2001) Classification of grossly detectable abnormalities and conditions seen at postmortem in Canadian poultry abattoirs according to a hazard identification decision tree. *Journal of Food Protection* 64, 1973–1980. doi: 10.4315/0362-028X-64.12.1973

Blagojevic, B., Dadios, N., Reinmann, K., Guitian, J. and Stärk, K.D.C. (2015) Green offal inspection of cattle, small ruminants and pigs in the United Kingdom: impact assessment of changes in the inspection protocol on likelihood of detection of selected hazards. *Research in Veterinary Science* 100, 31–38. doi: 10.1016/j.rvsc.2015.03.032

Bonde, M., Toft, N., Thomsen, P.T. and Sørensen, J.T. (2010) Evaluation of sensitivity and specificity of routine meat inspection of Danish slaughter pigs using latent class analysis. *Preventive Veterinary Medicine* 94, 165–169. doi: 10.1016/j.prevetmed.2010.01.009

Bosona, T. and Gebresenbet, G. (2013) Food traceability as an integral part of logistics management in food and agricultural supply chain. *Food Control* 33, 32–48. doi: 10.1016/j.foodcont.2013.02.004

Bottacini, M., Scollo, A., Edwards, S.A., Contiero, B., Veloci, M., Pace, V. and Gottardo, F. (2018) Skin lesion monitoring at slaughter on heavy pigs (170 kg): Welfare indicators and ham defects. *Plos ONE* 13, e0207115.

Bradshaw, R.H., Kirkden, R.D. and Broom, D.M. (2002) A review of the aetiology and pathology of leg weakness in broilers in relation to welfare. *Avian and Poultry Biology Reviews* 13, 45–103.

Brown, T.R. and Lawrence T.E. (2010) Association of liver abnormalities with carcass grading performance and value. *Journal of Animal Science* 88, 4037–4043. doi: 10.2527/jas.2010-3219

Brown, S.N., Knowles, T.G., Edwards, J.E. and Warriss, P.D. (1999) Behavioural and physiological responses of pigs to being transported for up to 24 hours followed by six hours recovery in lairage. *Veterinary Record* 145, 421–429.

Bršćić, M., Gottardo, F., Leruste, H., Lensink, J., van Reenen, K.C.G and Cozzi, G. (2011a) Prevalence of locomotory system disorders in veal calves and risk factors for occurrence of bursitis. *Agriculturae Conspectus Scientificus* 76, 291–295.

Bršćić, M., Heutinck, L.F.M., Wolthuis-Fillerup, M., Stockhofe, N., Engel, B. *et al.* (2011b) Prevalence of gastrointestinal disorders recorded at postmortem inspection in white veal calves and associated risk factors. *Journal of Dairy Science* 94, 853–863.

Brunberg, E., Jansen, P., Isaksson, A., and Keeling, L.J. (2013a) Brain gene expression differences are associated with abnormal tail biting behavior in pigs. *Genes, Brain and Behavior* 12, 275–281. doi: 10.1111/gbb.12002

Brunberg, E., Jensen, P., Isaksson, A. and Keeling, J.J. (2013b) Behavioral and brain gene expression profiling in pigs during tail biting outbreaks *PLoS ONE* 8(6), e66513. doi: 10.1371/journal.pone.0066513

Buczinski, S., Rezakhani, A. and Boerboom, D. (2010) Heart disease in cattle: Diagnosis, therapeutic approaches and prognosis. *The Veterinary Journal* 184, 258–263. doi: 10.1016/j.tvjl.2009.05.005

Butler, R.J., Murray, J.G. and Tidswell, S. (2003) Quality assurance and meat inspection in Australia. *OIE Revue Scientifique et Technique* 22, 697–712. doi: 10.20506/rst.22.2.1430

Buttenschøn, J., Friis, N.F., Aalbaek, B., Jensen, T.K., Iburg, T. and Mousing, J. (1997) Microbiology and pathology of fibrinous pericarditis in Danish slaughter pigs. *Journal of Veterinary Medicine Series A* 44, 271–280.

Butterworth, A., de Jong, I.C., Keppler, C., Knierim, U., Stadig, L. and Lambton, S. (2016) What is being measured, and by whom? Facilitation of communication on technical measures amongst competent authorities in the implementation of the European Union broiler directive (2007/43/EC). *Animal* 10, 302–308. doi: 10.1017/S1751731115001615

Caffrey, N.P., Dohoo, I.R. and Cockram, M.S. (2017) Factors affecting mortality risk during transportation of broiler chickens for slaughter in Atlantic Canada. *Preventive Veterinary Medicine* 147, 199–208. doi: 10.1016/j.prevetmed.2017.09.011

Canadian Food Inspection Agency (2013) Transportation of Animals Program, Compromised Animals Policy, Ottawa, Canada. Available at: https://www.inspection.gc.ca/animals/terrestrial-animals/humane-transport/compromised-animals-policy/eng/1360016317589/1360016435110 (accessed June 17, 2018).

Cargill, C.F., Pointon, A.M., Davies, P.R. and Garcia, R. (1997) Using slaughter inspections to evaluate Sarcoptic mange infestation of finishing swine. *Veterinary Parasitology* 70, 191–200. doi: 10.1016/S0304-4017(96)01137-5

Carroll, G.A., Boyle, L.A., Teixeira, D.L., Van Staaveren, N., Hanlon, A. and O'Connell, N.E. (2016) Effects of scalding and dehairing of pig carcasses at abattoirs on the visibility of welfare-related lesions. *Animal* 10, 460–467. doi: 10.1017/S1751731115002037

Carroll, G.A., Boyle, L.A., Hanlon, A., Collins, L., Griffin, K. *et al.* (2018) What can carcass-based assessments tell us about the lifetime welfare status of pigs? *Livestock Science* 214, 98–105. doi: 10.1016/j.livsci.2018.04.020

Caucci, C., Di Martino, G., Schiavon, E., Garbo, A., Soranzo, E. *et al.* (2018) Impact of bovine respiratory disease on lung lesions, slaughter performance and antimicrobial usage in French beef cattle finished in north-eastern Italy. *Italian Journal of Animal Science* 17(4), 1065–1069. doi: 10.1080/1828051X.2018.1426395

Chapinal, N., Weary, D.M., Collings, L. and von Keyserlingk, M.A.G. (2014) Lameness and hock injuries improve on-farms participating in an assessment program. *Veterinary Journal* 202, 646–648.

Chu, Q., Linag, T., Fu, L., Li, H. and Zhou, B. (2017) Behavioral and genetic differences between American and European pigs. *Journal of Genetics* 90, 707–715.

Cleveland-Nielsen, A., Christensen, G. and Ersboll, A.K. (2004) Prevalences of welfare-related lesions at postmortem meat-inspection in Danish sows. *Preventive Veterinary Medicine* 64, 123–131. doi: 10.1016/j.prevetmed.2004.05.003 ER

Cockram, M.S. and Dulal, K.J. (2018) Injury and mortality in broilers during handling and transport to slaughter. *Canadian Journal of Animal Science* 98, 416–432. doi: 10.1139/cjas-2017-0076

Cockram, M.S. and Hughes B. O. (2018) Health and disease. In: Appleby, M.C., Olsson, I.A.S. and Galindo, F. (eds) *Animal Welfare*. CABI, Wallingford, UK, pp. 141–159.

Cook, N.B., Hess, J.P., Foy, M.R., Bennett, T.B. and Bratzman, R.L. (2016) Management characteristics, lameness, and body injuries of dairy cattle housed in high performance dairy herds in Wisconsin. *Journal of Dairy Science* 99, 5879–5891.

Correia-Gomes, C., Smith, R.P., Eze, J.I., Henry, M.K., Gunn, G.J. *et al.* (2016) Pig abattoir inspection data: can it be used for surveillance purposes? *PLoS ONE* 11, e0161990.

Correia-Gomes, C., Eze, J.I., Borobia-Belsué, J., Tucker, A.W., Sparrow, D. *et al.* (2017) Voluntary monitoring systems for pig health and welfare in the UK: Comparative analysis of prevalence and temporal patterns of selected non-respiratory post mortem conditions. *Preventive Veterinary Medicine* 146, 1–9. doi: 10.1016/j.prevetmed.2017.07.007

Costa, L.N., Fiego, D.P.L., Tassone, F. and Russo, V. (2006) The relationship between carcass bruising in bulls and behaviour observed during pre-slaughter phases. *Veterinary Research Communications* 30 (Suppl. 1), 379–381.

Crandall, P.G., O'Bryan, C.A., Babu, D., Jarvis, N., Davis, M.L. *et al.* (2013) Whole-chain traceability, is it possible to trace your hamburger to a particular steer, a US perspective. *Meat Science* 95, 137–144. doi: 10.1016/j.meatsci.2013.04.022

Cresswell, E., Butterworth, A. and Wapenaar, W. (2017) Injection site lesion prevalence and potential risk in UK beef cattle. *Veterinary Record* 180 (70). doi: 10.1136/vr.103778

Cross, G.M. and Edwards, M.J. (1981) The detection of arthritis in pigs in an abattoir and its public health significance. *Australian Veterinary Journal* 57, 153–158. doi: 10.1111/j.1751-0813.1981.tb00500

d'Arc Moretti, L., Dias, R.A., Telles, E.O. and Balian, S.d.C. (2010) Time series evaluation of traumatic lesions and airsacculitis at one poultry abattoir in the state of São Paulo, Brazil (1996–2005). *Preventive Veterinary Medicine* 94, 231–239. doi: 10.1016/j.prevetmed.2010.02.013

Dadgar, S., Lee, E.S., Crowe, T.G., Classen, H.L. and Shand, P.J. (2012) Characteristics of cold-induced dark, firm, dry broiler chicken breast meat. *British Poultry Science* 53, 351–359. doi: 10.1080/00071668.2012.695335

Dahl-Pedersen, K., Foldager, L., Herslin, M.S., Houe, H. and Thomson, P.T. (2018) Lameness scoring and assessment of fitness for transport in dairy cows Agreement among and between farmers, veterinarians and livestock drivers. *Research in Veterinary Science* 119, 162–166.

Dalla Costa, O.A., Dalla Costa, F.A., Feddern, V., Lopes, L.d.S., Coldebella, A. *et al.* (2019) Risk factors associated with pig pre-slaughtering losses. *Meat Science* 155, 61–68. doi: 10.1016/j.meatsci.2019.04.020

Dalmau, A., Fabrega, E., Manteca, X. and Velarde, A. (2014) Health and welfare management of pigs based on slaughter line records. *Journal of Dairy, Veterinary & Animal Research* 1, 73–78. doi: 10.15406/jdvar.2014.01.00016

Davies, P.R., Bahnson, P.B., Grass, J.J., Marsh, W.E., Garcia, R. *et al.* (1996) Evaluation of the monitoring of papular dermatitis lesions in slaughtered swine to assess Sarcoptic mite infestation. *Veterinary Parasitology* 62, 143–153. doi: 10.1016/0304-4017(95)00853-5

Dawkins, M.S., Donelly, C.A. and Jones, T.A. (2004) Chicken welfare is influenced more by housing conditions than by stocking density. *Nature* 427, 342–344.

D'Eath, R.B., Ruehe, R., Turner, S.P., Ison, S.H., Farish, M. *et al.* (2009) Genetics of animal temperament: aggressive behavior at mixing is genetically associated with handling in pigs, *Animal* 3, 1544–1554.

Deeming, L.E., Beausoleil, N.J., Stafford, K.J., Webster, J.R. and Zobel, G. (2018) Technical note: The development of a reliable 5-point gait scoring system for dairy goats. *Journal of Dairy Science* 101, 4491–4497.

De Graaf, S., Ampe, B., Winckler, C., Radeski, M., Mounier, L. *et al.* (2017) Trained-user opinion about Welfare Quality measures and integrated scoring of dairy cattle welfare. *Journal of Dairy Science* 100, 6376–6388.

de Jong, I.C., Gunnink, K.H. and van Harn, J. (2014) Wet litter not only induces footpad dermatitis but also reduces overall welfare, technical performance, and carcass yield in broiler chickens. *Journal of Applied Poultry Research* 23, 51–58.

de Jong, I.C., Hindle, V.A., Butterworth, A., Engel, B., Ferrari, P. *et al.* (2016) Simplifying the Welfare Quality® assessment protocol for broiler chicken welfare. *Animal* 10, 117–127. doi: 10.1017/S1751731115001706

Deimel, M. and Theuvsen, L. (2011) Networking in meat production systems: the influence of cooperative structures on farmers' participation. *International Journal on Food System Dynamics* 2, 23–35.

Devitt, C., Boyle, L., Teixeira, D.L., O'Connell, N.E., Hawe, M. and Hanlon, A. (2016a) Pig producer perspectives on the use of meat inspection as an animal health and welfare diagnostic tool in the Republic of Ireland and Northern Ireland. *Irish Veterinary Journal* 69, 2. doi: 10.1186/s13620-015-0057-y

Devitt, C., Boyle, L., Teixeira, D.L., O'Connell, N.E., Hawe, M. and Hanlon, A. (2016b) Stakeholder perspectives on the use of pig meat inspection as a health and welfare diagnostic tool in the Republic of Ireland and Northern Ireland; a SWOT analysis. *Irish Veterinary Journal* 69, 17. doi: 10.1186/s13620-016-0076-3

de Vries, M., Bokkers, E.A.M., van Schaik, G., Botreau, R. *et al.* (2013) Evaluating the results of the Welfare Quality multi-criteria evaluation model for classification of dairy cattle welfare at the herd level. *Journal of Dairy Science* 96, 6254–6273.

de Vries, M., Bokkers, E.A.M., van Reenen, C.G., Engel, B., van Schaik, G. *et al.* (2015) Housing and management factors associated with indicators of dairy cow welfare. *Preventive Veterinary Medicine* 118, 80–92.

Di Martino, G., Capello, K., Russo, E., Mazzucato, M., Mulatti, P. *et al.* (2017) Factors associated with pre-slaughter mortality in turkeys and end of lay hens.

Animal 11, 2295–2300. doi: 10.1017/S1751731117 000970

Duff, S.R.I. and Randall, C.J. (1986) Tendon lesions in broiler fowls. *Research in Veterinary Science* 40, 333–338. doi: 10.1016/S0034-5288(18)30545-9

Dupuy, C., Morignat, E., Maugey, X., Vinard, J.-L., Hendrikx, P. *et al.* (2013) Defining syndromes using cattle meat inspection data for syndromic surveillance purposes: a statistical approach with the 2005-2010 data from ten French slaughterhouses. *BMC Veterinary Research* 9. doi: 10.1186/1746-6148-9-88

Edmonson, A.J., Lean, I.J., Weaver, L.D., Farver, T. and Webster, G. (1989) A body condition scoring chart for Holstein dairy cows. *Journal of Dairy Science* 72, 68–78. doi: 10.3168/jds.S0022-0302(89)79081-0

Edwards-Callaway, L.N., Calvo Lorenzo, M.S., Scanga, J.A. and Grandin, T. (2017) Mobility scoring in finished cattle. *Veterinary Clinics, Food Animal Practice* 33, 235–250.

Edwards-Callaway, L.N., Walker, J. and Tucker, C.B. (2018) Culling decisions and dairy cattle welfare during transport to slaughter in the United States. *Frontiers in Veterinary Science* 18. doi: 10.3389/fuets.2018.00343

EFSA Panels (2011) Scientific opinion on the public health hazards to be covered by inspection of meat (swine). *EFSA Journal*, 9, 2351.

Ekstrand, C., Algers, B. and Swedberg, J. (1997) Rearing conditions and footpad dermatitis in Swedish broiler chickens. *Preventive Veterinary Medicine* 31, 167–174.

Elanco (2009) *The 5-point body condition scoring system*. Elanco Animal Health, Greenfield, Indiana.

Elanco (2019) Liver Check Service. Available at: www.elanco.us/liver-check-service (accessed 1 August 2019).

Eldridge, G.A. and Winfield, C.G. (1988) The behaviour and bruising of cattle during transport at different space allowances. *Australian Journal of Experimental Agriculture* 28, 695–698.

Ellerbroek, L., Mateus, A., Stärk, K., Alonso, S. and Lindberg, A. (2011) Contribution of meat inspection to animal health surveillance in swine. *EFSA Supporting Publications* 8, 191E. doi: 10.2903/sp.efsa.2011.EN-191

Escobar, J., Van Alstine, W.G., Baker, D.H. and Johnson, R.W. (2007) Behaviour of pigs with viral and bacterial pneumonia. *Applied Animal Behaviour Science* 105, 42–50. doi: 10.1016/j.applanim.2006.06.005

Espejo, L.A., Endres, M.I., and Saifer, J.A. (2006) Prevalence of lameness in high-producing Holstein cows housed in freestall barns in Minnesota. *Journal of Dairy Science* 89, 3052–3058.

Estevez, M., Battini, E., Canali, R., Ruiz, G. *et al.* (2017) 013 AWIN mobile apps: animal welfare assessment at your fingertips. *Journal of Animal Science* 95, 6–7.

European Council (2007) Council Directive 2007/43/EC of 28 June 2007 laying down minimum rules for the protection of chickens kept for meat production. *Official Journal* L 182 12.7.2007, 19–28.

Eze, J.I., Correia-Gomes, C., Borobia-Belsué, J., Tucker, A.W., Sparrow, D. *et al.* (2015) Comparison of respiratory disease prevalence among voluntary monitoring systems for pig health and welfare in the UK. *PLoS ONE* 10, e0128137.

Faucitano, L. (2001) Causes of skin damage to pig carcasses. *Canadian Journal of Animal Science* 81, 39–45.

Featherwel (2016) Why feather score? University of Bristol, UK. Available at: https://www.featherwel.org/injuriouspecking/howtofeatherscore.html (accessed 21 February 2020).

Fecteau, G. (2005) Management of peritonitis in cattle. *Veterinary Clinics: Food Animal Practice* 21, 155–171. doi: 10.1016/j.cvfa.2004.12.007

Felin, E., Jukola, E., Raulo, S., Heinonen, J. and Fredriksson-Ahomaa, M. (2016) Current food chain information provides insufficient information for modern meat inspection of pigs. *Preventive Veterinary Medicine*, 127, 113–120. doi: 10.1016/j.prevetmed.2016.03.007

Ferguson, J.O., Galligan, D.T. and Thomsen, N. (1994) Principle descriptors of body condition score in Holstein cows. *Journal of Dairy Science* 77, 2695–2703.

Fisher, M.E., Trampel, D.W. and Griffith, R.W. (1998) Postmortem detection of acute septicemia in broilers. *Avian Diseases*, 42, 452–461. doi: 10.2307/1592671

Fitzgerald, R.F., Stalder, K.J., Matthews, J.O., Schultz Kaster, C.M. and Johnson, A.K. (2009) Factors associated with fatigued, injured, and dead pig frequency during transport and lairage at a commercial abattoir. *Journal of Animal Science*, 87, 1156–1166. doi: 10.2527/jas.2008-1270

Flower, F.C., Sedlbauer, M., Carter, E., von Keyslerlingk, M.A.G., Sanderson, D.J. and Weary, D.M. (2008) Analgesics improve the gait of lame dairy cattle. *Journal of Dairy Science* 91, 3010–3014.

Foddai, A., Green, L.E., Mason, S.A. and Kaler, J. (2012) Evaluating observer agreement of scoring systems for foot integrity and footrot lesions in sheep. *BMC Veterinary Research* 8, article 65. doi: 10.1186/1746-6148-8-65

Food Control Consultants (2015) Project FS 517005. Improved Food Chain Information (FCI) and Collection and Communication of Inspection Results (CCIR). A Project Implemented by Food Control Consultants Ltd (FCC) for the Food Standards Agency. Available at: https://www.food.gov.uk/sites/default/files/media/document/fs517005finalreport.pdf (accessed April 2013).

Frantz, L.M., Morabito, E.A., Dolecheck, K.A. and Bewley, J.M. (2019) Short communication: A comparison of cow cleanliness, fly population and fly avoidance behaviors among docked switch trimmed and switch intact dairy cows in 3 commercial dairy herds. *Journal of Dairy Science* 102, 1584–1588.

Fulwider, W., Grandin, T., Garrick, D.J., Engle, T.E., and Rollin, B.E. (2007) Influence of freestall base on tarsal joint lesions and hygiene in dairy cows. *Journal of Dairy Science* 90, 3559–3568.

Gaughan, J.B., Mader, T.L., Holl, S.M. and Lisle, A. (2008) A new heat load index for feedlot cattle. *Journal of Animal Science* 86, 226–234.

Geaze, M.H., Cowman, G.L., Tatum, J.D. and Smith, G.C. (1996) Incidence and sensory evaluation of injection site lesions in beef top sirloin butts. *Journal of Animal Science* 74, 2095–2103.

George, M.H., Heinrich, P.E., Dexter, D.R., Morgan, J.B., Odde, K.G. *et al.* (1995) Injection-site lesions in carcasses of cattle receiving injections at branding and at weaning. *Journal of Animal Science* 73, 3235–3240. doi: 10.2527/1995.73113235x

Geverink, N.A., Engel, B., Lambooij, E. and Wiegant, V.M. (1996) Observations on behaviour and skin damage of slaughter pigs and treatment during lairage. *Applied Animal Behaviour Science* 50, 1–13. doi: 10.1016/0168-1591(96)01069-6

Gibbons, J., Vasseur, E., Rushen, J. and de Pasille, A.M. (2012) A training program to ensure high repeatability of injury scoring of dairy cows. *Animal Welfare* 21, 379–388.

Gillman, C.E., KilBride, A.L., Ossent, P. and Green, L.E. (2008) A cross-sectional study of the prevalence and associated risk factors for bursitis in weaner, grower and finisher pigs from 93 commercial farms in England. *Preventive Veterinary Medicine* 83, 308–322.

Goldhawk, C., Janzen, E., Gonzalez, L.A., Crowe, T., Kastelic, J. *et al.* (2015) Trailer temperature and humidity during winter transport of cattle in Canada and evaluation of indicators used to assess the welfare of cull beef cows before and after transport. *Journal of Animal Science* 93, 3639–3653. doi: 10.2527/jas.2014-8390

Goumon, S., Brown, J.A., Faucitano, L., Bergeron, R., Widowski, T.M. *et al.* (2013) Effects of transport duration on maintenance behavior, heart rate and gastrointestinal tract temperature of market-weight pigs in 2 seasons. *Journal of Animal Science* 91, 4925–4935. doi: 10.2527/jas.2012-6081

Government of Canada. Agriculture and Agri-Food Canada (2018a) Condemnation Reports. Department of Agriculture and Agri-Food (Agriculture and Agri-Food Canada). Available at: http://www.agr.gc.ca/eng/industry-markets-and-trade/canadian-agri-food-sector-intelligence/poultry-and-eggs/poultry-and-egg-market-information/condemnations/?id=1384971854399 (accessed 15 April 2020).

Government of Canada. Agriculture and Agri-Food Canada (2018b) Red Meat Condemnation Reports. Available at:http://www.agr.gc.ca/eng/industry-markets-and-trade/canadian-agri-food-sector-intelligence/red-meat-and-livestock/red-meat-and-livestock-market-information/condemnations/

Grandin, T. (1998) Objective scoring of animal handling and stunning practices at slaughter plants. *Journal of the American Veterinary Medical Association* 212, 36–39.

Grandin, T. (2000) Effect of animal welfare audits of slaughter plants by a major fast food company on cattle handling and stunning practices. *Journal of the American Veterinary Medical Association* 216, 848–851.

Grandin, T. (2005) Maintenance of good animal welfare standards in beef slaughter plants by using auditing programs. *Journal of the American Veterinary Medical Association* 226, 370–373.

Grandin, T. (2010) Auditing animal welfare at slaughter plants. *Meat Science* 86, 56–65.

Grandin, T. (2012) Developing measures to audit welfare of cattle and pigs at slaughter. *Animal Welfare* 21, 351–356.

Grandin, T. (2015) *Improving Animal Welfare: A Practical Approach*, 2nd edn. CABI International, Wallingford, UK.

Grandin, T. (2017) On-farm conditions that compromise animal welfare that can be monitored at the slaughter plant. *Meat Science* 132, 52–58. doi: 10.1016/j.meatsci.2017.05.004

Grandin, T. (2019) Animal Welfare Audits for Cattle, Pigs, and Chickens that use the HACCP Principles of Critical Control Points with Animal Based Outcome Measures. Available at: https://www.grandin.com/welfare.audit.using.haccp.html (accessed 15 April 2020).

Grandin, T. and Whiting, M. (2018) *Are we Pushing Animals to Their Biological Limits?* CAB International, Wallingford, UK.

Green, L.E., Berriatua, E. and Morgan, K.L. (1997) The relationship between abnormalities detected in live lambs on farms and those detected at post mortem meat inspection. *Epidemiology and Infection* 118, 267–273. doi: 10.1017/S0950268897007401

Gregory, N.G. and Wilkins, L.J. (1990) Broken bones in chickens: effect of stunning and processing in broilers. *British Poultry Science* 31, 53–58. doi: 10.1080/00071669008417230

Gregory, N.G., Wilkins, L.J., Eleperuma, S.D., Ballantyne, A.J. and Overfield, N.D. (1990) Broken bones in domestic fowls: effect of husbandry system and stunning method in end-of-lay hens. *British Poultry Science* 31, 59–69. doi: 10.1080/00071669008417231

Grindflek, E., Hansen, M.H.S., Lien, S. and van Son, M. (2018) Genome wide association study reveals a QTL and strong candidate genes for umbilical herniasinpigs.*BMLGenomics*19,412.doi:10.1186/s12864-018-4812-9

Gross, W.B. (1961) The development of 'air sac disease'. *Avian Diseases* 5, 431–439. doi: 10.2307/1587774

Hamdy, M.K., May, K.N. and Powers, J.J. (1961) Some physical and physiological factors affecting poultry bruises. *Poultry Science* 40, 790–795. doi: 10.3382/ps.0400790

Hamir, A.N. and Parry, O.B. (1980) An abattoir study of bovine neoplasms with particular reference to ocular squamous cell carcinoma in Canada. *Veterinary Record* 106, 551. doi: 10.1136/vr.106.26.551

Hardstaff, J., Nigsch, A., Dadios, N., Stärk, K., Alonso, S. and Lindberg, A. (2012) Contribution of meat inspection to animal health surveillance in sheep and goats. *EFSA Supporting Publications* 9, 320E. doi: 10.2903/sp.efsa.2012.EN-320

Harley, S., More, S., Boyle, L., O'Connell, N. and Hanlon, A. (2012a) Good animal welfare makes economic sense: potential of pig abattoir meat inspection as a welfare surveillance tool. *Irish Veterinary Journal* 65, 11. doi: 10.1186/2046-0481-65-11

Harley, S., Moore, S.J., O'Connell, N.E., Hanlon, A., Teixiera, D. and Bogle, L. (2012b) Evaluating the prevalence of tail biting and carcass condemnations in slaughter pigs in the Republic and Northern Ireland and potential abattoir meat inspection as a welfare surveillance tool. *Veterinary Record* 171, 621. doi: 10.1136/vr.100986

Haslam, S.M., Knowles, T.G., Brown, S.N., Wilkins, L.J., Kestin, S.C. *et al.* (2007) Factors affecting the prevalence of foot pad dermatitis, hock burn and breast burn in broiler chicken. *British Poultry Science* 48, 264–275. doi: 10.1080/00071660701371341

Hassanzadeh, M., Buyse, J., Toloei, T. and Decuypere, E. (2014) Ascites syndrome in broiler chickens: a review on the aspect of endogenous and exogenous factors interactions. *Journal of Poultry Science* 51, 229–241.

Heinonen, M., Hakala, S., Hämeenoja, P., Murro, A., Kokkonen, T. *et al.* (2007) Case-control study of factors associated with arthritis detected at slaughter in pigs from 49 farms. *Veterinary Record* 160, 573. doi: 10.1136/vr.160.17.573

Heinonen, M., Gröhn, Y.T., Saloniemi, H., Eskola, E. and Tuovinen, V.K. (2001) The effects of health classification and housing and management of feeder pigs on performance and meat inspection findings of all-in–all-out swine-finishing herds. *Preventive Veterinary Medicine* 49, 41–54. doi: 10.1016/S0167-5877(01)00175-1

Heinonen, M., Orro, T., Kokkonen, T., Munsterhjelm, C., Peltoniemi, O. and Valros, A. (2010) Tail biting induces a strong acute phase response and tail-end inflammation in finishing pigs. *The Veterinary Journal* 184, 303–307. doi: 10.1016/j.tvjl.2009.02.021

Heitmann, S., Stracke, J., Petersen, H., Spindler, B. and Kemper, N. (2018) First approach validating a scoring system for foot-pad dermatitis in broiler chickens developed for application in practice. *Preventive Veterinary Medicine* 154, 63–70. doi: 10.1016/j.prevetmed.2018.03.013

Higginson-Cutler, J.H., Cramer, G., Walter, J.J., Millman, S.T. and Kelton, D.F. (2013) Randomized clinical trial of tetracycline hydrochloride bandage and paste treatments for resolution of lesions and pain associated with digital dermatitis in cattle. *Journal of Dairy Science* 90, 7550–7557.

Holt, H.R., Alarcon, P., Velasova, M., Pfeiffer, D.U. and Wieland, B. (2011) BPEX pig health scheme: a useful monitoring system for respiratory disease control in pig farms? *BMC Veterinary Research* 7. doi: 10.1186/1746-6148-7-82

Horst, A., Gertz, M. and Krieter, J. (2019) Challenges and opportunities of using meat inspection data to improve pig health traits by breeding: a review. *Livestock Science* 221, 155–162. doi: 10.1016/j.livsci.2019.02.001

Houe, H., Gardner, I.A. and Nielsen, L.R. (2011) Use of information on disease diagnoses from databases for animal health economic, welfare and food safety purposes: strengths and limitations of recordings. *Acta Veterinaria Scandinavica* 53, S7. doi: 10.1186/1751-0147-53-S1-S7

Huang, C.-Y. and Takeda, K. (2016) Influence of feed type and its effect on repressing wool-biting behavior in housed sheep. *Animal Science Journal* 88, 546–552. doi: 10.1111/asj.12664

Huang, C.-Y. and Takeda, K.-I. (2018) Effect of the proportion of roughage fed as rolled and baled hay on repressing wool-biting behavior in sheep. *Animal Science Journal* 89, 227–231. doi: 10.1111/asj.12895

Huey, R.J. (1996) Incidence, location and interrelationships between the sites of abscesses recorded in pigs at a bacon factory in Northern Ireland. *Veterinary Record* 138, 511–514. doi: 10.1136/vr.138.21.511

Hulebak, K.L. and Schlosser, W. (2002) Hazard analysis and critical control point (HACCP) history and conceptual overview. *Risk Analysis* 22, 547–552. doi: 10.1111/0272-4332.00038

Huneau-Salaün, A., Stärk, K.D.C., Mateus, A., Lupo, C., Lindberg, A. and Le Bouquin-Leneveu, S. (2015) Contribution of meat inspection to the surveillance of poultry health and welfare in the European Union. *Epidemiology and Infection* 143, 2459–2472. doi: 10.1017/S0950268814003379

Hunter, R.R., Mitchell, M.A. and Carlisle, A.J. (1999) Wetting of broilers during cold weather transport: a major source of physiological stress? *British Poultry Science* 40, S49.

Innocent, G.T., Gilbert, L., Jones, E.O., McLeod, J.E., Gunn, G. *et al.* (2017) Combining slaughterhouse surveillance data with cattle tracing scheme and environmental data to quantify environmental risk factors for liver fluke in cattle. *Frontiers in Veterinary Science* 4, 65.

Jacob, F.G., Baracho, M.S., Naas, I.A., Salgado, D.A., and Souza, R. (2016) Incidence of pododermatitis in broiler reared under two types of environment. *Revista Brasileira de Ciencia, Avicola* 18, 247–253. doi: 10.1590/1806-9061-2015-0047

Jacob, R.H., Pethick, D.W., Clark, P., D'Souza, D.N., Hopkins, D.L. and White, J. (2006) Quantifying the hydration status of lambs in relation to carcass characteristics. *Australian Journal of Experimental Agriculture* 46, 429–437. doi: 10.1071/EA04093

Jacobs, L., Delezie, E., Duchateau, L., Goethals, K. and Tuyttens, F.A.M. (2017a) Animal well-being and behavior. Broiler chickens dead on arrival: associated risk factors and welfare indicators. *Poultry Science* 96, 259–265. doi: 10.3382/ps/pew353

Jacobs, L., Delezie, E., Duchateau, L., Goethals, K. and Tuyttens, F.A.M. (2017b) Impact of the separate pre-slaughter stages on broiler chicken welfare. *Poultry Science* 96, 266–273. doi: 10.3382/ps/pew361

Jäger, H.C., McKinley, T.J., Wood, J.L.N., Pearce, G.P., Williamson, S. *et al.* (2012) Factors associated with pleurisy in pigs: a case-control analysis of slaughter pig data for England and Wales. *PLoS ONE* 7. doi: 10.1371/journal.pone.0029655

Jarvis, A.M., Selkirk, L. and Cockram, M.S. (1995) The influence of source, sex class and pre-slaughter handling on the bruising of cattle at two slaughterhouses. *Livestock Production Science* 43, 215–224. doi: 10.1016/0301-6226(95)00055-P

Jarvis, A.M., Messer, C.D.A. and Cockram, M.S. (1996) Handling, bruising and dehydration of cattle at the time of slaughter. *Animal Welfare* 5, 259–270.

Jensen, T.B., Kristensen, H.H. and Toft, N. (2012) Quantifying the impact of lameness on welfare and profitability of finisher pigs using expert opinions. *Livestock Science* 149, 209–214. doi: 10.1016/j.livsci.2012.07.013

Johnson, D.C. (1972) Diagnosis, pathology, and etiology of tenosynovitis in broilers and broiler breeders. *Avian Diseases* 16, 1067–1072. doi: 10.2307/1588830

Jones, S.D.M., Schaefer, A.L., Robertson, W.M. and Vincent, B.C. (1990) The effects of withholding feed and water on carcass shrinkage and meat quality in beef cattle. *Meat Science* 28, 131–139.

Julian, R.J. (2005) Production and growth related disorders and other metabolic diseases of poultry - a review. *Veterinary Journal* 169, 350–369. doi: 10.1016/j.tvjl.2004.04.015 ER

Kenny, F.J. and Tarrant, P.V. (1987) The behaviour of young Friesian bulls during social re-grouping at an abattoir. Influence of an overhead electrified wire grid. *Applied Animal Behaviour Science* 18, 233–246. doi: 10.1016/0168-1591(87)90219-X

Kephart, K.B., Harper, M.T. and Raines, C.R. (2010) Observations of market pigs following transport to a packing plant. *Journal of Animal Science* 88, 2199–2203. doi: 10.2527/jas.2009-2440

Kester, E., Holzhauer, M. and Frankena, K. (2014) A descriptive review of the prevalence and risk factors of hock lesions in dairy cows. *The Veterinary Journal* 202, 222–228.

Kestin, S.C., Gordon, A., Su, G., and Sorensen, P. (2001) Relationships in broiler chickens – between

lameness, live weight, growth rate, and age. *Veterinary Record* 148, 195–197.

Kilbride, A.L., Gillman, C.E. and Green, L.E. (2009) A cross-sectional study of the prevalence of lameness in finishing pigs, gilts and pregnant sows and associations with limb lesions and floor types on commercial farms in England. *Animal Welfare* 18, 215–224.

Kittelsen, K.E., Granquist, E.G., Kolbjørnsen, O., Nafstad, O. and Moe, R.O. (2015a) A comparison of post-mortem findings in broilers dead-on-farm and broilers dead-on-arrival at the abattoir. *Poultry Science* 94, 2622–2629. doi: 10.3382/ps/pev294

Kittelsen, K.E., Granquist, E.G., Vasdal, G., Tolo, E. and Moe, R.O. (2015b) Effects of catching and transportation versus pre-slaughter handling at the abattoir on the prevalence of wing fractures in broilers. *Animal Welfare* 24, 387–389. doi: 10.7120/09627286.24.4.387

Kjaer, J.B., Su, G., Nielson, B.L. and Sorenson, P. (2016) Foot pad dermatis and hock burn in broiler chickens and degree of inheritance. *Poultry Science* 85, 1342–1348.

Knage-Rasmussen, K.M., Rousing, T., Sorensen, J.T. and Houe, H. (2015) Assessing animal welfare in sow herds using data on meat inspection, medication and mortality. *Animal* 9, 509–515. 10.1017/S1751731114002705

Knauer, M., Stalder, K.J., Karriker, L., Baas, T.J., Johnson, C. *et al.* (2007) A descriptive survey of lesions from cull sows harvested at two Midwestern US facilities. *Preventive Veterinary Medicine* 82, 198–212. doi: 10.1016/j.prevetmed.2007.05.017

Knezacek, T.D., Olkowski, A.A., Kettlewell, P.J., Mitchell, M.A. and Classen, H.L. (2010) Temperature gradients in trailers and changes in broiler rectal and core body temperature during winter transportation in Saskatchewan. *Canadian Journal of Animal Science* 90, 321–330.

Knowles, T.G. and Broom, D.M. (1990) The handling and transport of broilers and spent hens. *Applied Animal Behaviour Science* 28, 75–91.

Knowles, T.G., Maunder, D.H., Warriss, P.D. and Jones, T.W. (1994) Factors affecting the mortality of lambs in transit to or in lairage at a slaughterhouse, and reasons for carcase condemnations. *Veterinary Record* 135, 109–111. doi: 10.1136/vr.135.5.109

Knowles, T.G., Kestin, S.C., Haslam, S., Green, L.E., Butterworth, A. (2008) Leg disorders in broiler chickens prevalence risk factors and prevention. *PLoS ONE* 3(2), e1545. doi: 10.1371/journalpone.0001543

Ko, E.Y., Cho, J., Cho, J.H., Jo, K., Lee, S.M. *et al.* (2018) Reduction in neck lesion incidence in pork carcass using transdermal needle free foot and mouth vaccine. *Korean Journal of Food Science and Animal Resources* 38, 1155–1158.

Konold, T., Sivam, S.K., Ryan, J., Gubbins, S., Laven, R. and Howe, M.J.H. (2006) Analysis of clinical signs associated with bovine spongiform encephalopathy in casualty slaughter cattle. *The Veterinary Journal* 171, 438–444. doi: 10.1016/j.tvjl.2005.02.020

Kranen, R.W., Lambooij, E., Veerkamp, C.H., Van Kuppevelt, T.H. and Veerkamp, J.H. (2000) Haemorrhages in muscles of broiler chickens. *Worlds Poultry Science Journal* 56, 93–126.

Kristensen, H.H. and Wathes, C.M. (2000) Ammonia and poultry welfare: a review. *World's Poultry Science Journal* 56, 235–245.

Lassen, J., Sandøe, P. and Forkman, B. (2006) Happy pigs are dirty! – conflicting perspectives on animal welfare. *Livestock Science* 103, 221–230.

Laywel (2006) Welfare implications of changes in production in production systems for laying hens. Photographic scoring system. Available at: laywel.eu (accessed 25 July 2019).

Le, T.H., Norberg, E., Hielsen, B., Madsen, P., Nilssen, K. and Lundelheim, N. (2015) Genetic correlation between leg conformation in young pigs, sow reproduction, and longevity in Danish pig populations. *Acta Agriculturae Scandinavica, Section A Animal Science* 65, 132–138.

Leruste, H., Brscic, M., Heutinck, L.F.M., Visser, E.K., Wolthuis-Fillerup, M. *et al.* (2012) The relationship between clinical signs of respiratory system disorders and lung lesions at slaughter in veal calves. *Preventive Veterinary Medicine* 105, 93–100. doi: 10.1016/j.prevetmed.2012.01.015

Leslie, K.E. and Petersson-Wolfe, C.S. (2012) Assessment and management of pain in dairy cows with clinical mastitis. *The Veterinary Clinics of North America. Food Animal Practice* 28, 289–305. doi: 10.1016/j.cvfa.2012.04.002

Li, X., Xu, P., Zhang, C., Sun, C., Li, X. *et al.* (2019) Genome wide association study identifies variants in the CAPN9 gene association with umbilical hernias in pigs. *Animal Genetics* 50(4). doi: 10.1111/age.12760

Linden, A., Desmecht, D., Amory, H., Daube, G., Lecomte, S. and Lekeux, P. (1995) Pulmonary ventilation, mechanics, gas exchange and haemodynamics in calves following intratracheal inoculation of *Pasteurella haemolytica. Journal of Veterinary Medicine A* 42, 531–544.

Llonch, P., King, E.M., Clarke, K.A., Downes, J.M. and Green, L.E. (2015) A systematic review of animal based indicators of sheep welfare on farm, at market and during transport, and qualitative appraisal of their validity and feasibility for use in UK abattoirs. *Veterinary Journal* 206, 289–297. doi: 10.1016/j.tvjl.2015.10.019

Lorenz, I., Earley, B., Gilmore, J., Hogan, I., Kennedy, E. and More, S.J. (2011) Calf health from birth to weaning. III. Housing and management of calf pneumonia. *Irish Veterinary Journal* 64. doi: 10.1186/2046-0481-64-14

Lundeheim, N., Lundgre, H. and Rydhmer, L. (2014) Shoulder ulcers in sows are genetically correlated to

leanness of young pigs and to litter weight. *Acta Agriculturae Scandinavica Section A Animal Science* 64, 67–72.

Lundmark, F., Hultgron, J., Rockinsberg, I., Wahlberg, R. and Berg, C. (2018) Non-compliance and followup in Swedish official and private animal welfare control of dairy cows. *Animals* 8(5), 72.

Lupo, C., Chauvin, C., Balaine, L., Petetin, I., Péraste, J. *et al.* (2008) Postmortem condemnations of processed broiler chickens in western France. *Veterinary Record* 162, 709–713.

Lupo, C., Bougeard, S., Balaine, L., Michel, V., Petetin, I. *et al.* (2010) Risk factors for sanitary condemnation in broiler chickens and their relative impact: application of an original multiblock approach. *Epidemiology and Infection* 138, 364–375. doi: 10.1017/S0950268809990549

Mach, N., Bach, A., Velarde, A. and Devant, M. (2008) Association between animal, transportation, slaughterhouse practices, and meat pH in beef. *Meat Science* 78, 232–238. doi: 10.1016/j.meatsci.2007.06.021

Mader, T.L., Davis., M.S. and Brown-Brandl, T. (2005) Environmental factors influencing heat stress in feedlot cattle. *Journal of Animal Science* 84, 712–719.

March, S., Brinkman, J. and Winkler, C. (2007) Effect of training on the inter-observer reliability of lameness scoring in dairy cattle. *Animal Welfare* 16, 131–133.

Martínez, J., Segalés, J., Aduriz, G., Atxaerandio, R., Jaro, P. *et al.* (2006) Pathological and aetiological studies of multifocal interstitial nephritis in wasted pigs at slaughter. *Research in Veterinary Science* 81, 92–98. doi: 10.1016/j.rvsc.2005.10.005

Mathur, P.K., Vogelzang, R., Mulder, H.A. and Knol, E.F. (2018) Genetic selection to enhance animal welfare using meat inspection data from slaughter plants. *Animals* 8. doi: 10.3390/ani8020016

Mayne, R.K. (2005) A review of the aetiology and possible causative factors of foot pad dermatitis in growing turkeys and broilers. *World's Poultry Science Journal* 61, 156–267.

McCausland, I.P. and Millar, H.W.C. (1982) Time of occurrence of bruises in slaughtered cattle. *Australian Veterinary Journal* 58, 253–255.

McKeith, R.O., Gray, G.D., Hale, D.S., Karth, C.R., Griffin, D.B. and Savell, J.W. (2012) National Beef Quality Audit-2011: Harvest-floor assessments of targeted characteristics that affect quality and value of cattle, carcasses, and byproducts. *Journal of Animal Science* 90, 5135–5142.

McNally, P.W. and Warriss, P.D. (1996) Recent bruising in cattle at abattoirs. *Veterinary Record* 138, 126–128. doi: 10.1136/vr.138.6.126

Meat and Livestock Commercial Services (2013) An Evaluation of Food Chain Information (FCI) and Collection and Communication of Inspection Results

(CCIR). Final Report – Project FS145002. Available at: https://www.food.gov.uk/sites/default/files/media/document/796-1-1409_Evaluation_of_Food_Chain_Information_FS145002.pdf (accessed 15 April 2020)

Mendes, Â.J., Ribeiro, A.I., Severo, M. and Niza-Ribeiro, J. (2017) A multilevel study of the environmental determinants of swine ascariasis in England. *Preventive Veterinary Medicine* 148, 10-20. doi: 10.1016/j.prevetmed.2017.09.012

Meyns, T., Van Steelant, J., Rolly, E., Dewulf, J., Haesebrouck, F. and Maes, D. (2011) A cross-sectional study of risk factors associated with pulmonary lesions in pigs at slaughter. *Veterinary Journal* 187, 388–392. doi: 10.1016/j.tvjl.2009.12.027

Michel, V., Prampart, E., Mirabito, L., Allain, V., Arnould, C. *et al.* (2012) Histologically-validated footpad dermatitis scoring system for use in chicken processing plants. *British Poultry Science* 53, 275–281. doi: 10.1080/00071668.2012.695336

Miles, D.M., Miller, W.W., Branton, S.L., Maslin, W.R. and Lott, B.D. (2006) Ocular responses to ammonia of broiler chickens. *American Association of Avian Pathologists* 50, 45–49.

Morrissey, K.L.H., Brockhurst, S., Baker, L., Widowski, T.M. and Sandilands, V. (2016) Can non-beak treated hens be kept in commercial furnished cages? Exploring the effects of strain and extra environmental enrichment on behaviour, feather cover and mortality. *Animals* 6(3), 17. doi: 3390/ani6030017

Mouttotou, N., Hatchell, F.M., Lundervold, M. and Green, L.E. (1997) Prevalence and distribution of foot lesions in finishing pigs in south-west England. *Veterinary Record* 141, 115–120.

Mouttotou, N., Hatchell, F.M. and Green, L.E. (1999) Foot lesions in finishing pigs and their associations with the type of floor. *Veterinary Record* 144, 629–632.

Munoz, C., Campbell, A. and Hemsworth, P.H. (2018) Animal-based measures to assess the welfare of extensively managed ewes. *Animals* 8(1), 2. doi: 10.3390/ani80100002

Munoz, C.A., Campbell, A.J.D., Hemsworth, P.H. and Doyle, R.E. (2019) Evaluating the welfare of extensively raised sheep. *PLoS ONE* 14(6), e0218603. doi: 10.137-1/journal.pone.0218603

Murray, A.C. and Johnson, C.P. (1998) Importance of the halothane gene on muscle quality and preslaughter death in western Canadian pigs. *Canadian Journal of Animal Science* 78, 543–548.

Murray, R.D., Downham, D.Y., Merritt, J.R., Russell, W.B. and Manson, F.J. (1994) Observer variation in field data describing foot shape in dairy cattle. *Research in Veterinary Science* 56, 265–269. doi: 10.1016/0034-5288(94)90140-6

Nagaraja, T.G. and Chengappa, M.M. (1998) Liver abscesses in feedlot cattle: a review. *Journal of Animal Science* 76, 287–298. doi: 10.2527/1998.761287x

Nagaraja, T.G. and Lechtenberg, K.F. (2007) Liver abscesses in feedlot cattle. *Veterinary Clinics of North America: Food Animal Practice; Topics in Nutritional Management of Feedlot Cattle* 23, 351–369. doi: 10.1016/j.cvfa.2007.05.002

Nalon, E., Conte, S., Maes, D., Tuyttens, F.A.M. and Devillers, N. (2013) Assessment of lameness and claw lesions in sows. *Livestock Science* 156, 10–23. doi: 10.1016/j.livsci.2013.06.003

Neary, J.M., Gary, F.B., Holt, T.N., Thomas, M.G. and Enne, R.M. (2015) Mean pulmonary arterial pressure in Angus steers increase from cow-calf to feedlot finishing phases. *Journal of Animal Science* 93, 3854–3861.

Nery, L.C., Santos, L.R., Daroit, L., Marcolin, J. and Dickel, E.L. (2017) Microbiological, physicochemical, and histological analyses of broiler carcasses with cachexia. *Brazilian Journal of Poultry Science* 19, 595–600.

Neumann, E.J., Hall, W.F., Stevenson, M.A., Morris, R.S. and Ling, M.T. (2014) Descriptive and temporal analysis of post-mortem lesions recorded in slaughtered pigs in New Zealand from 2000 to 2010. *New Zealand Veterinary Journal* 62, 110–116. doi: 10.1080/00480169.2013.853278

Newberry, R.C., Webster, A.B., Lewis, N.J. and Van Arnam, C. (1999) Management of spent hens. *Journal of Applied Animal Welfare Science* 2, 13–29.

Newman, J.H., Holt, T.N., Cogan, J.D., Womack, B., Philliips, J.A. III *et al.* (2015) Increased prevalence of *EPAS1* variant in cattle with high altitude pulmonary hypertension. *Nature Communications* 6, article 6863. doi: 10-1038/ncomms7863

Nielsen, S.S. (2014) The apparent prevalence of skin lesions suspected to be human inflicted in Danish finishing pigs at slaughter. *Preventive Veterinary Medicine* 117, 200–206.

Nielsen, S.S., Michelsen, A.M., Jensen, H.E., Barington, K., Opstrup, K.V. and Agger, J.F. (2014) The apparent prevalence of skin lesions suspected to be human-inflicted in Danish finishing pigs at slaughter. *Preventive Veterinary Medicine* 117, 200–206. doi: 10.1016/j.prevetmed.2014.08.003

Nielsen, S.S., Nielsen, G.B., Denwood, M.J., Haugegaard, J. and Houe, H. (2015) Comparison of recording of pericarditis and lung disorders at routine meat inspection with findings at systematic health monitoring in Danish finisher pigs. *Acta Veterinaria Scandinavica* 57. doi: 10.1186/s13028-015-0109-z

Nielsen, S.S., Denwood, M.J., Forkman, B. and Houe, H. (2017) Selection of meat inspection data for an animal welfare index in cattle and pigs in Denmark. *Animals* 7. doi: 10.3390/ani7120094

Norton, R.A., Macklin, K.S. and McMurtrey, B.L. (1999) Evaluation of scratches as an essential element in the development of avian cellulitis in broiler chickens. *Avian Diseases* 43, 320–325. doi: 10.2307/1592624

Ochala, J., Ahlbeck, K., Radell, P.J., Eriksson, L.I. and Larsson, L. (2011) Factors underlying the early limb muscle weakness in acute quadriplegic myopathy using an experimental ICU porcine model. *PLoS ONE* 6, e20876.

OIE (2019) Transport of animals by land. Chapter 7.3. *Terrestrial Animal Health Code*. World Organisation for Animal Health, Paris.

Olsen, H.G., Kjelgaard-Hansen, M., Tveden-Nyborg, P., Birck, M.M., Hammelev, K.P. *et al.* (2016) Modelling severe Staphylococcus aureus sepsis in conscious pigs: are implications for animal welfare justified? *BMC Research Notes* 9, 1–10. doi: 10.1186/s13104-016-1888-7

Ontario Court of Justice (2014) R. v. Maple Lodge Farms. *Ontario Court of Justice* 212, 1–38. Available at: https://www.canlii.org/en/ (accessed 14 April 2020)

Ostanello, F., Dottori, M., Gusmara, C., Leotti, G. and Sala, V. (2007) Pneumonia disease assessment using a slaughterhouse lung-scoring method. *Journal of Veterinary Medicine Series A* 54, 70–75. doi: 10.1111/j.1439-0442.2007.00920.x

Pagot, E., Pommier, P. and Keïta, A. (2007) Relationship between growth during the fattening period and lung lesions at slaughter in swine. *Revue De Medecine Veterinaire* 158, 253–259.

Pearson, E.G. (1981) Differential diagnosis of icterus in large animals. *California Veterinarian* 35, 25–31.

Petersen, H.H., Enoe, C. and Nielsen, E.O. (2004) Observer agreement on pen level prevalence of clinical signs in finishing pigs. *Preventive Veterinary Medicine* 64, 147–156. doi: 10.1016/j.prevetmed.2004.05.002 ER

Petersen, H.H., Nielsen, E.O., Hassing, A., Ersbøll, A.K. and Nielsen, J.P. (2008) Prevalence of clinical signs of disease in Danish finisher pigs. *Veterinary Record* 162, 377. doi: 10.1136/vr.162.12.377

Pfeifer, M., Eggemann, L., Kransmann, J., and Scjhmitt, A.O. (2019) Inter- and intra-observer reliability of animal welfare indicators for on-farm self-assessment of fattening pigs. *Animal* 13, 1712–1720. doi: 10.1017/5175173118003701

Phythian, C.J., Michalopoulou, E. and Duncan, J.S. (2019) Assessing the validity of animal-based indicators of sheep health and welfare: do observers agree? *Agriculture* 9(5), 88. doi: 10.3390.agriculture 9050088

Pluym, L., Van Nuffel, A. and Maes, D. (2013) Treatment and prevention of lameness with special emphasis on claw disorders in group-housed sows. *Livestock Science* 156, 36–43. doi: 10.1016/j.livsci.2013.06.008

Pointon, A., Jackowiak, J., Slade, J. and Paton, M. (2008) Review of surveillance data capture systems in abattoirs. Meat & Livestock Australia Limited. Available at: https://www.mla.com.au/research-and-development/search-rd-reports/final-report-details/Product-Integrity/Review-of-surveillance-data-capture-systems-in-abattoirs/2835 (accessed 15 April 2020)

Raj, A.B.M., Gregory, N.G. and Austin, S.D. (1990) Prevalence of broken bones in broilers killed by different stunning methods. *Veterinary Record* 127, 285–287.

Rakestraw, P.C. (1996) Fractures of the humerus. *Veterinary Clinics: Food Animal Practice* 12, 153–168. doi: 10.1016/S0749-0720(15)30440-0

Reinhold, P., Rabeling, B., Günther, H. and Schimmel, D. (2002) Comparative evaluation of ultrasonography and lung function testing with the clinical signs and pathology of calves inoculated experimentally with *Pasteurella multocida*. *Veterinary Record* 150, 109–114.

Rezac, D.J., Thomson, D.U., Siemens, M.G., Prouty, F.L., Reinhardt, C.D. and Bartle, S.J. (2014) A survey of gross pathologic conditions in cull cows at slaughter in the Great Lakes region of the United States. *Journal of Dairy Science* 97, 4227–4235. doi: 10.3168/jds.2013-7636

Ritter, M.J., Ellis, M., Berry, N.L., Curtis, S.E., Anil, L. *et al.* (2009) Transport losses in market weight pigs: I. A review of definitions, incidence, and economic impact. *Professional Animal Scientist* 25, 404–414.

Roeber, D., Belk, K.E., Field, T.G., Scanga, J.L. and Smith, G.C. (2001) National market cow and bull beef quality audit, 1999. A survey of producer related defects in market cows and bulls. *Journal of Animal Science* 79, 658–665.

Romero, M.H., Uribe-Velasquez, L.F., Sanchez, J.A. and Miranda-de la Lama, G.C. (2013) Risk factors influencing bruising and high muscle pH in Colombian cattle carcasses due to transport and pre-slaughter operations. *Meat Science* 95, 256–263. doi: 10.1016/j.meatsci.2013.05.014

Sanchez-Vazquez, M. and Lewis, F.I. (2013) Investigating the impact of fasciolosis on cattle carcass performance. *Veterinary Parasitology* 193, 307–311. doi: 10.1016/j.vetpar.2012.11.030

Sanchez-Vazquez, M., Strachan, W.D., Armstrong, D., Nielen, M. and Gunn, G.J. (2011) The British pig health schemes: integrated systems for large-scale pig abattoir lesion monitoring. *Veterinary Record* 169, 413. doi: 10.1136/vr.d4814

Sandøe, P., Forkman, P., Hakansson, F. *et al.* (2017) Should the contribution of one additional lame cow depend on how many other cows are lame? *Animal* 7(12). doi: 10.3390/ani7120096

Saraiva, S., Saraiva, C. and Stillwell, G. (2016) Feather condition and clinical scores as indicators of broiler welfare at the slaughterhouse. *Research in Veterinary Science* 107, 75–79.

Schärrer, S., Schwermer, H., Presi, P., Lindberg, A., Zinsstag, J. and Reist, M. (2015) Cost and sensitivity of on-farm versus slaughterhouse surveys for prevalence estimation and substantiating freedom from disease. *Preventive Veterinary Medicine* 120, 51–61. doi: 10.1016/j.prevetmed.2015.01.020

Schemann, A.K., Hernández-Jover, M., Hall, W., Holyoake, P.K. and Toribio, J. (2010) Assessment of current disease surveillance activities for pigs post-farmgate in New South Wales. *Australian Veterinary Journal* 88, 75–83. doi: 10.1111/j.1751-0813.2009.00543.x

Schild, S.L.A., Rousing, T., Jensen, H.E., Barington, K. and Herskin, M.S. (2015) Do umbilical outpouchings affect the behaviour or clinical condition of pigs during 6h housing in a pre-transport pick-up facility? *Research in Veterinary Science* 101, 126–131. doi: 10.1016/j.rvsc.2015.06.005

Schlageter-Tlelo, A., Bokkers, E.A.M., Grootkoerkamp, P.W.G., Van Hertern, T., Viazzi, S. *et al.* (2014) Effect of merging levels of locomotion scores for dairy cows on intra- and inter-rates reliability and agreement. *Journal of Dairy Science* 97, 5533–5542.

Schleicher, C., Scheriau, S., Kopacka, I., Wanda, S., Hofrichter, J. and Köfer, J. (2013) Analysis of the variation in meat inspection of pigs using variance partitioning. *Preventive Veterinary Medicine* 111, 278–285. doi: 10.1016/j.prevetmed.2013.05.018

Schoning, P. and Hamlet, M.P. (1989a) Experimental frost-bite in Hanford miniature swine. I. Epithelial changes. *British Journal of Experimental Pathology* 70, 41–49.

Schoning, P. and Hamlet, M.P. (1989b) Experimental frost-bite in Hanford miniature swine. II. Vascular changes. *British Journal of Experimental Pathology* 70, 51–57.

Schulze, B., Wocken, C. and Spiller, A. (2006) Relationship quality in agri-food chains: supplier management in the German pork and dairy sector. *Journal on Chain and Network Science* 6, 55–68. doi: 10.3920/JCNS2006.x065

Schwägele, F. (2005) Traceability from a European perspective. *Meat Science* 71, 164–173. doi: 10.1016/j.meatsci.2005.03.002

Shadbolt, P.V., Mitchell, W.R., Blackburn, D.J., Meek, A.H. and Friendship, R.M. (1987) Perceived usefulness of the collection of subclinical and other disease entities detected at slaughter. *Canadian Veterinary Journal* 28, 439–445.

Shearer, J.K., Stock, M.L., Van Amstel, S.R. and Coetzee, J.F. (2013) Assessment and management of pain associated with lameness in cattle. *Veterinary Clinics of North America – Food Animal Practice* 29, 135–156. doi: 10.1016/j.cvfa.2012.11.012

Souza, A.P.O., Taconeli, C.A., Plugge, N.F. and Molento, C.F.M. (2018) Broiler chicken meat inspection data in Brazil: a first glimpse into an animal welfare approach. *Brazilian Journal of Poultry Science* 20, 547–554.

St.-Hilaire, S. and Sears, W. (2003) Trends in cellulitis condemnations in the Ontario chicken industry between April 1998 and April 2001. *Avian Diseases* 47, 537–548. doi: 10.1637/6067

Stafford, K.J., Mellor, D.J., Todd, S.E., Gregory, N.G., Bruce, R.A. and Ward, R.N. (2001) The physical state and plasma biochemical profile of young calves on arrival at a slaughter plant. *New Zealand Veterinary Journal* 49, 142–149. doi: 10.1080/00480169.2001.36222

Stafford, K.J. and Mellor, D.K. (2015) Painful husbandry procedures in livestock and poultry. In: Grandin, T. (ed.) *Improving Animal Welfare: A Practical Approach*. CAB International, Wallingford, UK, pp. 96–124.

Stärk, K.D.C. (2000) Epidemiological investigation of the influence of environmental risk factors on respiratory diseases in swine – a literature review. *The Veterinary Journal* 159, 37–56. doi: 10.1053/tvjl.1999.0421

Stärk, K.D.C., Alonso, S., Dadios, N., Dupuy, C., Ellerbroek, L. *et al.* (2014) Strengths and weaknesses of meat inspection as a contribution to animal health and welfare surveillance. *Food Control* 39, 154–162. doi: 10.1016/j.foodcont.2013.11.009

Strappini, A.C., Frankena, K., Metz, J.H.M. and Kemp, B. (2012) Intra- and inter-observer reliability of a protocol for post mortem evaluation of bruises in Chilean beef carcasses. *Livestock Science* 145, 271–274. doi: 10.1016/j.livsci.2011.12.014

Strappini, A.C., Metz, J.H.M., Gallo, C.B. and Kemp, B. (2009) Origin and assessment of bruises in beef cattle at slaughter. *Animal* 3, 728–736. doi: 10.1017/S1751731109004091

Strappini, A.C., Metz, J.H.M., Gallo, C., Frankena, K., Vargas, R., De Freslon, I. and Kemp, B. (2013) Bruises in culled cows: When, where and how are they inflicted? *Animal* 7, 485–491. doi: 10.1017/S1751731112001863

Straw, B., Bates, R. and May, G. (2009) Anatomical abnormalities in a group of finishing pigs: prevalence and pig performance. *Journal of Swine Health and Production* 17, 28–31.

Swaby, H. and Gregory, N.G. (2012) A note on the frequency of gastric ulcers detected during post mortem examination at a pig abattoir. *Meat Science* 90, 269–271.

Tarrant, P.V., Kenny, F.J., Harrington, D. and Murphy, M. (1992) Long distance transportation of steers to slaughter: effect of stocking density on physiology, behaviour and carcass quality. *Livestock Production Science* 30, 223–238.

Tauson, R., Kjaer, J., Maria, G., Cepero, R. and Holm, K-E. (2005) Applied scoring of integument and health in laying hens. *Animal Science Papers and Reports* 23, 153–159.

Thomson, D.L., Longeragan, G.H, Hennington, J., Ensley, S. and Bawa, B. (2015) Description of novel fatigue syndrome in feedlot cattle following transportation. *Journal of the American Veterinary Medical Association* 247, 66–72.

Tiong, C.K. and Bin, C.S. (1989) Abattoir condemnation of pigs and its economic implications in Singapore. *British Veterinary Journal* 145, 77–84. doi: 10.1016/0007-1935(89)90013-4 van Staaveren, N., Doyle, B., Manzanilla, E.G., Calderón Díaz, J.A., Hanlon, A. and Boyle, L.A. (2017) Validation of carcass lesions as indicators for on-farm health and welfare of pigs. *Journal of Animal Science* 95, 1528–1536. doi: 10.2527/jas2016.1180

Vogeler, C.S. (2019) Market based governors of farm animal welfare: a comparative analysis of public and private in Germany and France. *Animals* 9(5), 287. doi: 10.3390/ani9050267

Von Keyserlingk, M.A.G., Barrientos, A., Ito, K., Galo, E. and Weary, D.M. (2012) Benchmarking cow comfort on North American freestall dairies: lameness, leg injuries, lying time, facility design, and management for high-producing Holstein dairy cows. *Journal of Dairy Science* 95, 7399–7408.

Wall, R. and Lovatt, F. (2015) Blowfly strike: biology, epidemiology and control. *In Practice* 37, 181–188. doi: 10.1136/inp.h1434

Wallgren, T., Westin, R. and Gunnarsson, S. (2016) A survey of straw use and tail biting on Swedish pig farms rearing undocked pigs. *Acta Veterinaria Scandinavica* 58, 84. doi: 10.1186.13028-016-0266-84

Watson, E., Marier, E. and Weston, J. (2011) *MC1001: Review of historic ante mortem and post mortem inspection data – Final report*. Veterinary Laboratory Agency, London.

Welfare Quality® (2009a) Welfare Quality® assessment protocol for cattle. Welfare Quality® Consortium. Lelystad, Netherlands. Available at: http://www.welfarequality.net/media/1088/cattle_protocol_without_veal_calves.pdf (accessed 15 April 2020)

Welfare Quality® (2009b) Welfare Quality® assessment protocol for pigs (sows and piglets, growing and finishing pigs). Welfare Quality® Consortium. Lelystad, Netherlands. Available at: http://www.welfarequality.net/media/1018/pig_protocol.pdf (accessed 15 April 2020)

Welfare Quality® (2009c) Welfare Quality® assessment protocol for poultry (broilers, laying hens). Welfare Quality® Consortium. Lelystad, Netherlands. Available at: http://www.welfarequality.net/media/1019/poultry_protocol.pdf (accessed 15 April 2020)

Wellehan, J.F.X. (2003) Frostbite in birds: Pathophysiology and treatment. *Compendium on Continuing Education for the Practising Veterinarian* 25, 776–781.

Wester, T., Häggblad, E., Awan, Z.A., Barratt-Due, A., Kvernebo, M. *et al.* (2011) Assessments of skin and tongue microcirculation reveals major changes in porcine sepsis. *Clinical Physiology & Functional Imaging* 31, 151–158. doi: 10.1111/j.1475-097X.2010.00994.x

White, M. (1999) Skin lesions in pigs. *In Practice* 21, 20–29. doi: 10.1136/inpract.21.1.20

White, B.J. and Renter, D.G. (2009) Bayesian estimation of the performance of using clinical observations and harvest lung lesions for diagnosing bovine respiratory disease in post-weaned beef calves. *Journal of Veterinary Diagnostic Investigation* 21, 446–453. doi: 10.1177/104063870902100405

Wideman, R.F. (2001) Pathophysiology of heart/lung disorders: pulmonary hypertension syndrome in broiler chickens. *World's Poultry Science Journal* 57, 289–307.

Wildman, E.E., Jones, G.M., Wagner, P.E., Boman, R.L., Troutt, H.F. *et al.* (1982) A dairy cow body condition scoring system and its relationship to selected production characteristics. *Journal of Dairy Science* 65, 495–501.

Wilkins, L.J., McKinstry, J.L., Avery, N.C., Knowles, T.G., Brown, S.N. *et al.* (2011) Papers: Influence of housing system and design on bone strength and keel bone fractures in laying hens. *Veterinary Record* 169, 414. doi: 10.1136/vr.d4831

Winter, A.C. (2008) Lameness in sheep. *Small Ruminant Research* 76, 149–153. doi: 10.1016/j.smallrumres.2007.12.008 ER

Wyneken, C.W., Sinclair, A., Veldkamp, T., Vinco, L.J., and Hocking, P.M. (2015) Foot pad dermatitis and pain assessment in turkey poults using analgesia and objective gait analysis. *British Poultry Science* 56, 522–530.

Zinpro (2016) First step locomotion scoring videos. Available at: www.zinpro.com/video-library/dairy-locomotion-video#/videos/list(2016) (accessed 26 December 2016).

Zinpro (no date) Dairy Claw Lesion Identification. Available at: https://www.zinpro.com/lameness/dairy/lesion-identification (accessed 21 February 2020).

Zunderland, J.J., Schepers, F., Bracke, M.B.M., Hartog, L.A., denKemp, B. and Spoolder, H.A.M. (2011) Characteristics of biter and victim piglets apparent before a tail-biting outbreak. *Animal* 5, 767–775.

Zurbrigg, K., van Dreumel, T., Rothschild, M.F., Alves, D., Friendship, R.M. and O'Sullivan, T.L. (2019) Rapid communication: a comparison of cardiac lesions and heart weights from market pigs that did and did not die during transport to one Ontario abattoir. *Translational Animal Science* 3, 149–154. doi: 10.1093/tas/txy124

17 Approaches to Legislation and Enforcement to Minimize Welfare Issues Associated with Slaughter

MICHAEL COCKRAM*

Sir James Dunn Animal Welfare Centre, Atlantic Veterinary College, University of Prince Edward Island, Canada

Introduction

This chapter uses examples of legislation on slaughter mainly from North America and Europe to illustrate approaches to the drafting and enforcement of legislation, highlighting common themes, underlying principles and issues that have implications for animal welfare. In most countries, there is legislation designed to offer various levels of protection to farmed animals when they are slaughtered for human consumption in slaughterhouses (subsequently referred to simply as slaughter legislation). An appreciation of the risks of suffering during slaughter and the role of legislation in mitigating this risk is indicated by the priority that was given in many countries to the early introduction of slaughter legislation (Radford, 2001; Vapnek and Chapman, 2010) and by the presence of this legislation even when no equivalent national legislation has been introduced to protect farmed animals before they are sent to slaughter (Cowan, 2011). The development of global standards, such as recommendations on slaughter by Office International des Epizooties (OIE, now known as the World Organisation for Animal Health) (OIE, 2016), and the value of slaughter legislation in supporting international trade in meat products have provided governments with an incentive to introduce and update slaughter legislation. Most countries have some form of slaughter legislation that is to varying degrees consistent with OIE standards (Stafford and Mellor, 2009; Abyaneh et al., 2019). However, in countries with a federal system, e.g. USA and

Canada, there can be national legislation that regulates federal activities, but not all States and Provinces necessarily have legislation that provides protection to animals that are slaughtered within their local jurisdiction (Whiting, 2013; Animal Welfare Institute, 2017; Fraser et al., 2018). Some legislation is not comprehensive in the degree of protection that it provides. Some types of animals can be excluded and some slaughter procedures are exempt from some requirements.

Many different approaches are used in legislation to minimize the animal welfare issues that can occur during slaughter. In some parts of the world, e.g. the European Union (EU), there is detailed legislation that has widespread support, whereas in others, e.g. the USA, there is less support for legislation and more reliance on self-regulation and the use of voluntary schemes (Cowan, 2011).

Given that enforcement of food safety and animal welfare regulations occur at the same location, it is perhaps not surprising that there is considerable overlap between their approaches to legislation and enforcement. It is of interest to note the manner in which slaughter legislation has evolved to take account of developments in both regulatory policy and approaches to the regulation of food safety. The emphasis has moved away from prescriptive legislation that detailed how slaughter procedures should be conducted, with heavy reliance on direct inspection to identify non-compliance and the punishment of offenders. Regulatory policy is now often based on a cooperative model where

* Email: mcockram@upei.ca

the objective is to prevent identifiable animal welfare issues from occurring, and, when they do occur, to resolve these as rapidly as possible and attempt to update management procedures that will reduce the risk of their reoccurrence. Slaughterhouses are given responsibility for demonstrating their compliance with regulations and the enforcement agency is more focused on the oversight of these internal procedures rather than undertaking comprehensive and continuous direct inspection of each activity where animal welfare could be at risk. A broad range of enforcement tools is often available to facilitate a proportional approach to non-compliance that depends on factors such as the degree of suffering likely caused, the history of compliance and whether the slaughterhouse has a systematic procedure to reduce the risk of reoccurrence.

For legislation to be effective in achieving its objectives, it must be drafted well and adequately enforced. There is criticism of the manner of the enforcement of legislation both by industry, due to concern about its effects on economic performance, and by some pressure groups that are already concerned about the ethics of animal slaughter and then see graphic evidence of animal suffering during slaughter. Many companies and their industry associations have introduced policies, animal welfare standards and procedures to reduce the risk to their public and commercial reputation from non-compliance with animal welfare legislation.

Most legislation consists of primary legislation (e.g. Acts) that describe the underlying principles and secondary legislation (e.g. Regulations) that implement detailed provisions (e.g. methods of slaughter) and can be revised more easily and quickly than the primary legislation (Vapnek and Chapman, 2010). It is not the intention to describe the legislation present in each country in detail, as this can be readily obtained elsewhere and is subject to regular revision. It is important to note that where aspects of legislation and its enforcement are described, summary wording is often used rather than the original legal text. Therefore, to clarify legal aspects, it is important to refer to the original legal text.

Merits of Legislation

Due to different cultural attitudes to animals and the relative priority given to commercial activity, there are major differences in the perception of the need for legislation to protect the welfare of animals at slaughter and the relative merits of voluntary or self-regulation versus legal regulation (Matheny and Leahy, 2007; Harlow and Rawlings, 2009). The principle that a society should legislate to prevent cruelty and impose a common animal welfare standard is dependent on a society's view on factors such as individual freedom, whether there is a culture of legal compliance and enforcement, and the balance of political forces that operate to decide public policy (Radford, 2001; Broom, 2009). In Europe, 'The protection of animals at the time of slaughter or killing is a matter of public concern that affects consumer attitudes towards agricultural products' (Council Regulation (EC) No. 1099/2009). In the USA, the Humane Methods of Slaughter Act (HMSA) was introduced because 'It is the policy of the United States that the slaughtering of livestock and the handling of livestock in connection with slaughter shall be carried out only by humane methods, as provided by Public Law ...'.

The major reasons for legal regulation are:

- to control risks to animal welfare;
- to level the commercial 'playing field' of compliance for companies involved in slaughter;
- to provide public accountability and assurance, without a conflict of interest; and
- to deter practices found to be morally unacceptable to society (Swanson, 2008).

In some countries, it is seen as the government's responsibility to set and enforce animal welfare standards that reflect societal expectations and industry realities. In this context, government intervention can be justified to:

- reduce the impact of market negative 'externalities', such as animal suffering, and/or to encourage positive 'externalities', such as policies to improve animal welfare;
- provide 'public goods', i.e. things that are shared by and benefit many in society, but which are not directly linked to any payment, e.g. high levels of animal welfare; and
- achieve social goals, for example in pursuit of a 'caring society' (Farm Animal Welfare Council, 2008).

Compliance with legal regulation is not without direct costs to the industry that is regulated and indirectly to the national economy, in terms of competitiveness, international trade and economic output, and there are costs to governments that have to provide funding for the resources to introduce, inform and enforce the regulations (Bennett *et al.*, 2018). However, this has to be balanced against positive potential market benefits, for example from facilitating access to international markets by adopting internationally recognized high animal welfare standards for the production of meat and from avoiding the enormous adverse reputational costs to the whole sector (including the compliant majority) if publicity shows animal abuse by rogue operators (Bonafos *et al.*, 2010). Even companies that are regularly subject to enforcement activity for non-compliance use the fact that their procedures are subject to government oversight and regulation as a marketing tool in their publicity. There are also important indirect economic benefits from legally regulated standards to prevent animal suffering. For example, regulations on animal handling and effective stunning can result in safer and better working conditions for employees, improved meat quality and food safety and more efficient commercial practices (Hotis, 2006; Council Regulation (EC) No 1099/2009).

Industry has sometimes lobbied for minimal or no legal regulation with the following arguments.

- Voluntary regulation is more effective in achieving the desired outcome of minimizing risks to animal welfare.
- The market economy is the best way of determining what animal welfare standards the consumer desires.
- There is insufficient hard scientific evidence to justify many of the detailed animal welfare regulations that are sometimes proposed (Croney and Millman, 2007).
- Rigid prescriptive regulations restrict innovation and are slow to revise in line with commercial developments.
- The slaughter industry is already over-regulated and adopts high standards.
- Proposals for further regulation are mainly a mechanism for those opposed to animal slaughter to make the industry unsustainable.

It has also been suggested that it is not realistic for some slaughter procedures to always be performed with 100% efficiency, and that achievable performance targets that are included within voluntary standards have provided better improvements in animal welfare than legislation that in the USA requires, for example, mechanical stunning to be effective first time, otherwise the operator is not in compliance with the legislation (GAO, 2010).

Leaving consumers to decide which meat products to purchase on the basis of their ethical views is attractive for those who believe totally in an unregulated market economy (Sullivan, 2013). However, even if consumers were sufficiently informed about the relevant issues, most shoppers are influenced by factors such as price, appearance, advertising and habit, and their immediate priorities, rather than having to make a considered decision on all the relevant ethical issues connected with each purchase of a specific meat product. In addition, many consumers do not wish to think about the origin of meat products and do not like to dwell on the slaughter required to produce their meat. As discussed by Radford (2001), legal regulation can be seen as a reflection of a 'society's perceived collective values' and removes 'from the individual the responsibility of making a moral decision on every purchase'. Many of the benefits of improved animal welfare can be achieved by the adoption of voluntary standards as well as legal regulation (Broom, 2017). However, legal regulation provides an absolute minimal standard that applies to all slaughter plants specified in the legislation; it is relatively comprehensive in the coverage of risks to animal welfare; and the details and basis for the provisions in the regulations, and the criteria used for their enforcement, are transparent and publicly available (Lundmark *et al.*, 2018). Paolucci *et al.* (2015) audited a number of slaughter plants in Italy and found that, prior to the adoption of Council Regulation (EC) No 1099/2009, not all slaughter plants would have been in compliance with the legislation and they did not have the facilities, equipment and procedures necessary to reduce the risk of suffering.

Another option for the adoption of animal welfare standards is the use of Codes of Practice. These can provide practical advice on how to implement legal regulations, provide additional provisions to prevent welfare issues, and are often formulated using a consensus approach following input from industry and other stakeholders, leading to good industry 'buy-in'. They sometimes have legal status, for example by reference in legislation or by establishing industry norms of standard practice that are referenced during court proceedings. However, conflicts of interest can arise during the code development process if commercial interests inhibit the development of strict welfare standards or if there is a fear of subsequent assimilation of the code into law (Dale, 2009).

Types of Legislation

Cruelty provisions

The purpose of animal welfare legislation is to prevent suffering, not to punish people who are conducting socially accepted businesses (Whiting, 2013). For example, in the UK, an offence of cruelty cannot be committed if it is carried out during humane slaughter. However, in the absence of effective legislation and enforcement, cruel procedures can occur during slaughter. Examples of cruel procedures on conscious animals that are prohibited by legislation, but might otherwise occur, are:

- beating, throwing, kicking, dragging or dropping;
- poking out eyes, cutting tendons or the spinal cord to restrain or immobilize; and
- scalding, skinning, leg removal or other carcass dressing procedures (Stevenson *et al.*, 2014).

Although some slaughter legislation contains provisions that include the prosecution of cruelty as a criminal offence, this is often not an easy enforcement tool to use. It requires the prosecution to show that a person was motivated to commit a guilty act (mens rea) in that they intended the action and its consequences (Radford, 2001).

Developments in regulatory policy affect the design and objectives of slaughter legislation

Traditionally regulation was enacted by two separate parties: (i) the government as the regulator (mainly using prescriptive regulations, direct inspection and, if necessary, enforcement consisting of withdrawal of a licence to slaughter, a fine and occasionally criminal prosecution); and (ii) industry as the regulated entity (who, if found to be not in compliance with the legislation, would pay any penalty and/or follow the direct instructions of the inspectorate). This 'command and control' regulation was often written as standards that prescribed an approved procedure for a particular process (OECD, 2011; Gunningham and Sinclair, 2017).

In contrast, performance-based and management-based regulations are more flexible and less prescriptive. Performance-based regulations set objectives or standards for outcomes, such as what problems must be solved, or the goals to be achieved, and allow the regulated party some flexibility to determine how they will meet these objectives, rather than prescribing how to achieve these outcomes (OECD, 2011; Gunningham and Sinclair, 2017).

This allows them to identify processes that are cheaper and more efficient and allows innovation and faster adoption of new technology (OECD, 2002). Management-based regulation (or process-based regulation) requires businesses to demonstrate that they are meeting regulatory objectives through management processes that ensure a systematic approach to controlling and minimizing risks (OECD, 2002, 2011). The move away from command and control regulation has led to a focus more on management structures, incentives and self-regulation, with less reliance on conventional sanctions. In this 'enforced self-regulation' the regulator imposes a requirement for businesses to assess, control and monitor the risks to animal welfare at their establishment. The business determines and implements its own internal rules and procedures to fulfil the regulator's policy objectives (Fairman and Yapp, 2005). With enforced self-regulation, the role of enforcement changes from identifying contraventions of rules designed to reduce risk, to assessing the systems that the business has in place for risk management. The move towards enforced self-regulation has occurred with the increased adoption of Hazard Analysis and Critical Control Point (HACCP) schemes. In these types of schemes, food businesses have to identify the hazards present within their operations, implement and monitor controls, and document this process. The business has to devise systems and rules to control the risks it creates. It has to implement these systems, monitor the results and record the outcomes (Gunningham and Sinclair, 2017). A risk is a combination of the likelihood of an adverse event (hazard, harm) occurring and of the potential magnitude of the damage caused (e.g. the number of animals affected and the severity of the harm) (OECD, 2014).

In Canada, this regulatory approach has been adopted in the Safe Food for Canadians Act 2012 and Safe Food for Canadians Regulations (SOR/2018-108) (Government of Canada, 2019a,b) (Box 17.1). This legislation contains some specific prescriptive regulations on how animals must be handled and slaughtered. In addition, it contains performance-based and management-based regulations that require the slaughter plant to:

- make an assessment of welfare risks;
- monitor procedures;
- undertake corrective action to address any deviations from humane handling and slaughter; and

- develop written preventive measures that are effective at controlling the animal welfare risks in their establishment and provide evidence to demonstrate that they are effective at reducing and controlling animal welfare risks during all slaughter activities.

The required written preventive measures and evidence must include:

- a description of the performance criteria chosen to evaluate the expected outcome of each of the measures taken to control the risks;
- monitoring procedures for each slaughter activity associated with an animal welfare risk;
- corrective action procedures to be implemented for deviations from the expected outcomes of the measures in place;
- verification procedures used to check that the monitoring procedures are effectively implemented;
- procedures for conducting an animal welfare audit, on a regular basis, to evaluate the overall outcome of the measures; and
- documentation to prove implementation and show the supporting documents used to develop the plan.

The performance criteria can be written in a manner that recognizes that some procedures are

not always 100% efficient and that corrective action will only be required by the slaughter plant for equipment and processes if they fall below the agreed performance standard (critical control limits). However, corrective action is required if any animals experience suffering as a result of a less than perfect procedure (CFIA, 2019d). Provision of general information, advice and guidance from the regulator on the legislation and how it will be enforced (e.g. CFIA, 2019c) makes it easier for regulated entities to understand and meet their obligations (Harlow and Rawlings, 2009).

In the USA, the Humane Methods of Slaughter Act (HMSA) contains concisely worded performance-based regulations on handling and stunning in that they are required to be humane. However, the scope of the HMSA has attracted criticism (Mariucci, 2008). There is a prescriptive requirement for stunning by a single blow or gunshot, electrical or chemical methods, or other means that are rapid and effective, before restraint (shackling and hoisting) and exsanguination. The HMSA is a federal act that provides authority for the enforcement agency (United States Department of Agriculture, Food Safety and Inspection Service) (USDA FSIS) to introduce detailed regulations on facility design and operation, handling, stunning and enforcement (Code of Federal Regulations,

2017). There are no regulations that require slaughter plants to adopt written protocols. However, it is beneficial for an establishment to have a written document in place as it demonstrates to FSIS that procedures have been established to assure compliance with the HMSA, and it is taken into consideration if enforcement action is contemplated (FSIS, 2004, 2013). The following requirements are suggested for the development and maintenance of a systematic approach to humane handling and slaughter.

- Conduct an initial assessment of where and under what circumstances livestock may experience excitement, discomfort or accidental injury while being handled, and where and under what circumstances stunning problems may occur.
- Design facilities and implement practices that will minimize excitement, discomfort and accidental injury.
- Periodically evaluate handling methods to ensure that they minimize excitement, discomfort or accidental injury, and periodically evaluate stunning methods to ensure that all livestock are rendered insensible to pain by a single blow.
- Respond to the evaluations, as appropriate, by addressing problems immediately and by improving those practices and modifying facilities when necessary to minimize excitement, discomfort and accidental injury to livestock (FSIS, 2011).

Although poultry are not included in the HMSA, FSIS directives (FSIS, 2005) describe the use of a written systematic approach to humane handling similar to that described above for the HMSA, together with reference to industry guidelines on poultry welfare at slaughter (National Chicken Council, 2019). This is an example of co-regulation where the regulatory role is shared between government and industry by the enforcement agency endorsing an industry code of practice (OECD, 2002).

In the EU, Council Regulation (EC) No. 1099/2009 of 24 September 2009 on the protection of animals at the time of killing contains performance-based requirements to prevent avoidable pain, distress or suffering, including the provision of physical comfort, protection from injury and avoidance of prolonged withdrawal of feed and water. There are management-based regulations that require standard operating procedures (SOPs) to be developed and implemented for all the different operations, for example receiving animals, lairage,

restraint, stunning and exsanguination. The SOP has to detail the process so that it:

- explains the role of each individual in the activity it covers and all of their duties and responsibilities, and
- details who is responsible for: ensuring that the process is carried out correctly; carrying out assessments on critical stages, including monitoring for signs of unconsciousness; and taking any action necessary to ensure that the process is fully compliant with legislation.

Guides to good practice have been developed by industry (e.g. British Meat Processors Association, 2015; British Poultry Council, 2015) to assist with compliance with slaughter legislation.

Relationships Between Slaughter Legislation and Food Safety Legislation

There are many relationships between humane slaughter legislation and food safety legislation. In the EU, scientific advice on animal welfare issues is provided through the European Food Safety Authority (EFSA, 2019) as part of an integrated food chain approach to food safety (Horgan and Gavinelli, 2006). Many food safety regulations require a slaughter plant to adopt HACCP-based procedures (Hulebak and Schlosser, 2002). This change in the philosophy of food legislation, in which the emphasis moved from prescriptive legislation to legislation based on an assessment of risk, identification of Critical Control Points (CCPs) in the process where it is necessary to control these hazards, establishment of critical limits to monitor the effectiveness of control measures at CCPs and monitoring of CCPs (Green and Kane, 2014), has been mirrored in the way in which some humane slaughter regulations have been written.

Oversight of food safety at slaughterhouses is an important policy priority for governments (Henson and Caswell, 1999) and this has resulted in detailed legislation, establishment of an enforcement agency and the permanent presence of food safety inspectors at slaughterhouses. It was cost-efficient to add the regulation of humane slaughter to the food safety duties of the food safety agency. However, there are several consequences arising from adding the regulation of humane slaughter to existing food safety duties (Welty, 2007; Roy, 2015).

- Given the risk to human health, food safety is the overwhelming priority of the enforcement agency, rather than animal welfare (Leary *et al.*,

2016), as shown by examples of the names of various agencies, namely, the USDA Food Safety and Inspection Service (FSIS, 2019a), the UK's Food Standards Agency (FSA, 2019a) and the Canadian Food Inspection Agency (CFIA, 2019a).

- Most inspectors undertake their food safety work post-mortem by continual inspection of carcasses and processes, rather than ante-mortem or during slaughter, and therefore additional time and resources have to be provided to undertake inspections ante-mortem and during slaughter.
- Undertaking animal welfare duties requires specialist knowledge in addition to that required for food safety duties.
- Inspectors can be overburdened by having to undertake a range of duties.
- A greater range of enforcement tools, e.g. those related to meat inspection, can be available to enforce humane slaughter regulations.

As slaughter plants are a food business, non-compliance with legal regulations can be treated as a food safety violation. These administrative enforcement measures can include restrictions or prohibition of placing meat products on the market, suspension of meat inspection operations and closure of all or part of the business (Kettunen *et al.*, 2017), revoking or suspending a slaughter plant's licence and condemnation of carcasses as unfit for human consumption due to animal welfare issues. There are several examples from the USA on the use of food safety regulations to achieve animal welfare outcomes.

1. The federal meat inspection regulations require that all non-ambulatory cattle be condemned (FSIS, 2009). The incident that led to this regulation (abusive handling of non-ambulatory cattle) prompted FSIS to request that the company involved undertake a voluntary recall of all beef produced by that plant during the previous 2 years (USDA, 2009).
2. Poultry are not included in the HMSA. Some protection for poultry is provided by regulating food safety requirements (rather than by a specific animal protection regulation) contained in the Poultry Products Inspection Act in that it requires that poultry must die from slaughter. The associated regulations require that live poultry be handled in a manner that is consistent with good commercial practices (which is taken to mean that they should be treated humanely) and in a manner that results in thorough bleeding of the poultry carcass, and ensures that breathing has stopped before scalding, so that the birds do not drown (FSIS, 2005).

Carcasses of poultry showing evidence of having died from causes other than slaughter are condemned. Good commercial practice is assessed using the following criteria.

- Employees should be trained in handling birds with no fracturing of the legs of birds to hold them in shackles, or throwing live birds into a discard barrel.
- In cold weather, birds are not allowed to freeze inside cages or become frozen to cages.
- In warm weather, birds are not allowed to die from heat exhaustion.
- Employees should not drive over live birds with equipment or trucks.
- Employees should be trained in the proper use of stunning equipment and birds are not allowed to enter the scalder while still breathing (FSIS, 2015).

The effectiveness of the use of meat inspection legislation to regulate the humane slaughter of poultry in the USA has been heavily criticized (Animal Welfare Institute, 2016) and the exclusion of poultry from the HMSA is significant. The evidence that poultry can experience suffering is as strong as it is for mammals (Gentle, 2011) and they are just as (if not more) susceptible to welfare issues at slaughter as mammals. The total weight of poultry production in the USA is similar to that for red meat production; and in terms of numbers of animals, poultry slaughter is measured in billions of animals per year, whereas total red meat production is measured in millions of animals per year (USDA, 2016).
3. The Federal Meat Inspection Act provides authority for the appointment of inspectors at slaughter plants to prevent inhumane slaughtering of livestock by examining and inspecting the methods used for handling and slaughter.
4. If the handling and slaughter of livestock are not compliant with the HMSA, FSIS can refuse to provide or can temporarily suspend meat inspection at a slaughter plant, until the establishment furnishes satisfactory assurances on future handling and slaughter.
5. Inspectors can slow the slaughter line speed if there are deficiencies in carcass preparation or if carcass inspection requires more time.

Animal Welfare Expertise Present in Slaughterhouses Due to Legislation

Legislation can require the presence of specific types of trained people at slaughterhouses with a duty to oversee compliance with regulations on humane slaughter, namely an animal welfare officer and a veterinarian.

Animal welfare officer

In the EU, Council Regulation (EC) No. 1099/2009 requires slaughterhouse operators (other than small slaughterhouses) to appoint an animal welfare officer. The animal welfare officer is employed by the slaughterhouse to act as the contact point for the enforcement agency, provide guidance to the other employees, ensure that SOPs are developed and put into practice, and require completion of any remedial actions necessary to ensure compliance with regulations (European Commission, 2012). The animal welfare officer must have sufficient authority and technical competence to undertake their duties, including possession of a certificate of competence for all the operations taking place in the slaughterhouse for which they are responsible. The animal welfare officer must keep records of their actions and report to the slaughterhouse operator on animal welfare issues, especially if these require a managerial decision.

Veterinary inspector

A veterinarian is required to be present at most slaughterhouses to evaluate the health of animals before they are slaughtered (ante-mortem inspection and assessment of the food chain information provided on each consignment of animals). Their other duties include monitoring the welfare of live animals and slaughter operations. Veterinarians make professional decisions guided by: their knowledge, understanding and experience of the issues; their adherence to ethical behaviour, professional standards and guidelines; and the legal framework (Devitt et al., 2014). They give priority to animal welfare, while appreciating the need to balance animal welfare with other demands on the slaughterhouse operator (Whiting, 2013). However, in situations where there is only one veterinarian present in the same slaughterhouse for a prolonged period, there is a risk of not recognizing issues that require intervention and so job rotation has been suggested (Luukkanen and Lunden, 2016). Veterinarians are highly educated and have been considered to be the best-qualified generalists to oversee animal welfare matters (Farm Animal Welfare Council, 2003). Whether the existence of a veterinary qualification is

in itself sufficient to constitute the expertise required has been questioned (Radford, 2001). Veterinarians require specialist knowledge for the supervision of the welfare of animals at slaughter. Studies and audits have indicated that they would often benefit from an improved understanding of the principles of animal behaviour and welfare (Hötzel et al., 2018). A report by the European Commission's Food and Veterinary Office (FVO) concluded that insufficient training of veterinarians on animal welfare at slaughter contributed to an inadequate assessment of the effectiveness of stunning, resulting in unnecessary suffering where electrical methods were used (FVO, 2008).

Enforcement

Legislation on its own is not sufficient; to be effective in achieving its policy goal it has to be enforced (Radford, 2001; OECD, 2014). Ineffective enforcement can occur from under-inspection or insufficient or poorly implemented enforcement action (OECD, 2014).

Developments in regulatory policy affect the objectives, approach and type of tools available for the enforcement of slaughter legislation

Compliance strategy

The overall aim of most regulatory policies is to achieve the highest possible levels of compliance with the law at the least cost to the regulated businesses. The predominant enforcement approach used for slaughter legislation is a compliance strategy that recognizes that most businesses want to comply with the law, and therefore a cooperative and proportional response to non-compliance is adopted. With this approach, enforcement has become a process of negotiation rather than confrontation. The compliance strategy has the main objective of securing compliance and remedying a problem, rather than punishing the offender (Gunningham and Sinclair, 2017).

The regulations are written to reflect that the primary responsibility for compliance and animal welfare lies with the regulated business. Regulations often require self-monitoring, and inspections by the enforcement authority focus on verifying how effective the self-monitoring and risk-management systems implemented by the business operator are.

However, it is still important for the regulatory agency to assess whether these systems work in practice and not only on paper.

If primary control measures, which are advice and negotiation, fail to induce appropriate correction of non-compliance, an enforcement agency can force an establishment to comply with regulations by using administrative enforcement measures, also called coercive measures or formal enforcement actions (Kettunen *et al.*, 2015).

Administrative procedures versus criminal prosecution

Administrative tools such as improvement notices are used rather than criminal justice proceedings. Criminal sanctions are costly and time-consuming for both businesses and regulators (Harlow and Rawlings, 2009). Administrative processes can be used to intervene at an early stage and obtain a rapid improvement in the situation (Radford, 2001). For example, in the EU, a certificate of competence is required to undertake specified procedures (Council Regulation (EC) No 1099/2009). This certificate can be suspended or revoked if the holder:

- is no longer assessed to be a fit and proper person;
- is no longer competent to carry out the operations which the certificate authorizes;
- has failed to comply with any provision of the regulations; or
- has been convicted of an offence under any animal welfare legislation (FSA, 2019b).

Prosecutions are rare and are normally only taken when there is repeated non-compliance with administrative procedures. With slaughter legislation, the regulatory officials are permanently located within the business's premises, and therefore the use of administrative procedures is more conducive to maintaining a continuing relationship with the business (Kettunen *et al.*, 2017).

Factors affecting the type of enforcement action

The type of enforcement action taken is dependent on a number of factors, including:

- whether any animal suffering occurred (e.g. injury or distress);
- the severity of suffering;
- the compliance history of the establishment;

- whether the specific non-compliance occurs repeatedly;
- whether the establishment has protocols and management procedures in place to reduce the risk of suffering;
- the response of the operator to an inspection and the identification of violations; and
- whether the incident was:
  - the result of an error of judgement;
  - the result of an unjustifiable or deliberate act; or
  - accidental.

Compliance history

If there has been a history of repeated and systematic violations, the enforcement response is greater (e.g. immediate escalation of sanctions) than for an establishment that previously had good compliance, where they are given an opportunity to correct the situation (OECD, 2014).

Opportunity to remedy non-compliance before taking enforcement action

Informing a business of an intention to take action and offering them an opportunity to discuss the specific compliance issue and put it right before action is taken is considered good regulatory practice. In the USA, FSIS often issues a notice of intended enforcement action (NOIE) to enable an establishment to respond to a non-compliance with corrective action before any enforcement action is taken (FSIS, 2017). The NOIE requests that the establishment responds with a document that:

- identifies the specific reason(s) why the events described occurred;
- describes the specific action(s) that will be implemented to eliminate the cause of the incident and prevent future recurrences;
- describes the specific future monitoring activity or activities that the establishment will employ to ensure that the actions implemented are effective; and
- provides supporting documentation and records associated with the proposed corrective actions and preventive measures.

Severity of animal welfare issue

In the UK, the Food Standard Agency (FSA) uses a numerical score from 1 to 4 (1 = Welfare compliant;

2 = No immediate risk to welfare; 3 = Potential risk to welfare; 4 = Welfare critical) to indicate the severity of an animal welfare issue (FSA, 2019b). Inspectors are required to take enforcement action every time animal welfare is compromised and an animal is suffering. If the welfare of an animal is compromised, the inspector must take direct action, for example to ensure that an animal is killed as soon as possible (FSA, 2019b). Some acts are considered unacceptable and they are described as egregious inhumane treatment (FSIS, 2011) or deliberate acts of cruelty (CFIA, 2019d). In these cases, immediate action is required by the operator and/or by the inspector to address the issue.

Escalating enforcement action

Most enforcement strategies involve step-wise interventions characterized by an 'enforcement pyramid'. Informal advice and discussions may be followed by persuasion, formal warnings, administrative action and, rarely, by criminal proceedings (Gunningham and Sinclair, 2017) (Fig. 17.1).

Use of food safety procedures to enforce animal welfare regulations

In the USA, the HMSA is enforced using a range of potential enforcement tools related to food safety regulation (Federal Meat Inspection Act) (FSIS, 2004). If non-compliance is observed, one or more of the following enforcement actions might be undertaken.

- Non-compliance report: a document is issued to the slaughter plant that describes the violation and the actions needed to correct the deficiency.
- Regulatory control action: a reject tag (as used in meat inspection for the retention or rejection of a meat product as not fit for human consumption) is placed on a piece of equipment or an area of the plant that was involved in harming or inhumanely treating an animal. The tag

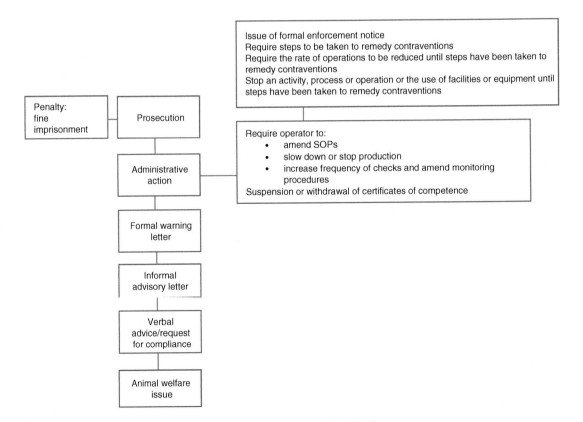

Fig. 17.1. A simplified example of escalating enforcement action (FSA, 2019b).

prohibits the use of a particular piece of equipment or area of the facility until the equipment is made acceptable.

- Suspension of plant operations: inspection services at the plant can be stopped immediately. The facts are documented and provided to plant management and senior management in the agency. They assess the facts supporting the suspension and take any final action. This acts as an economic deterrent, but it is common for a plant to be shut down for less than a day. As soon as the plant provides an acceptable plan for corrective actions and preventive measures, the suspension is removed. If this corrective action is approved, the enforcement action is deferred.
- Withdrawal of plant operations: if the plant fails to respond to concerns about repeated and/or serious violations, inspection services at the plant are withdrawn and products cannot enter interstate or foreign commerce. The plant must then reapply for and be awarded a grant of inspection before it may resume operations.

Publicizing enforcement action

Some enforcement agencies have adopted 'naming and shaming' strategies, including the publication of results of inspections, prosecutions and notices, or use of high-profile prosecutions. These deterrent measures are aimed at increasing the costs associated with reputational damage, increasing the perception of the probability of detection and as a means of satisfying public concerns over the level of enforcement of legal regulations (OECD, 2014; Gunningham and Sinclair, 2017). Enforcement actions from the past year that FSIS has taken against establishments that have been found in violation of the HMSA are published by FSIS (2019b).

Assessment of the effectiveness of enforcement

Assessing the effectiveness of inspection and enforcement by an agency is difficult. Improvements or deterioration in outcomes cannot be directly attributed to the activities of an enforcement agency, because of the large number of other factors that can influence these outcomes (OECD, 2014). The effectiveness of legislation cannot be reliably assessed by the number of enforcement actions taken. Enforcement action is a reflection of failure, as it is not required if there is compliance

with the regulations (Radford, 2001). Reporting a small number of records of enforcement activity does not necessarily mean that compliance is high: it may just be a reflection of a lack of inspection resources or lax enforcement. The numbers of reported cases of enforcement action are low in relation to the numbers of animals that are slaughtered (FSA, 2015c, 2019c; FSIS, 2019c). Performance measurement of effectiveness requires the use of a range of indicators from various sources and random statistically-representative surveys conducted periodically to determine industry compliance in critical areas (OECD, 2014). These can include the results of independent audits conducted for industry (Grandin, 2010) and those from enforcement agencies. In the EU, audits of compliance by member states with Council Regulation (EC) No 1099/2009 are published by the European Commission's Food and Veterinary Office (FVO, 2015, 2019). In the UK, the Food Standards Agency (FSA, 2015b) publishes the results of compliance audits.

Difficulties with enforcement

There have been claims that there has been significant under-enforcement of legislation on humane slaughter, especially in the USA (Jones 2008; Mariucci, 2008; Friedrich, 2015; Animal Welfare Institute, 2017). In the USA, the US General Accounting Office was concerned that the enforcement records kept by USDA FSIS were incomplete and that enforcement actions were inconsistent (GAO, 2004). In the next report, it considered that inconsistencies were due to incomplete guidance and inadequate training of inspectors and there was inadequate analysis of enforcement action across districts and plants (GAO, 2010). At that time, the GAO concluded that FSIS could not ensure that it was preventing the abuse of livestock at slaughter plants or meeting its responsibility to enforce the HMSA effectively (GAO, 2010). There are several factors that can potentially result in under-enforcement of legislation (Friedrich, 2015).

Commercial pressure

Regulatory or agency capture is a term used to identify situations where a regulator works very closely with the regulated party with the intention of assisting them in complying, but over time becomes subservient to the industry they are tasked to regulate, with an outcome contrary to the original policy objectives of the legislation. In this situation, the regulatory authority becomes identified with the regulated industry and facilitates the goals of the industry rather than the legislation. Industry groups can be well organized and devote considerable resources to lobbying government and the regulatory agency to restrict regulatory activity. Where agency personnel either come from the regulated industry or return to it after completing their public service, there is at the very least a perception that enforcement might not be as rigorous as it could be (OECD, 2011, 2014; Whiting, 2013; Friedrich, 2015).

Regulatory ossification can occur where industry lobbying is so unrelenting in its scale and effectiveness that it overwhelms the consultation stages prior to the introduction or revision of regulations that would restrict the industry's commercial activity (Friedrich, 2015). Opponents of legal regulation can also attempt to weaken enforcement agencies by restricting their authority, organizational capabilities and enforcement resources, leading to ineffective enforcement programs (Gray and Scholz, 1993).

Political pressure on a regulatory agency

The leadership of a regulatory agency can be influenced by the commercial pressure from industry that often lobbies government heavily to avoid regulatory enforcement (OECD, 2014). An independent regulatory agency, therefore, provides some protection from political and commercial interests (OECD, 2011). Many regulatory agencies have a management structure that directly influences the scope of the enforcement of regulations by individual inspectors at the plant level and any subsequent action that is taken over reported non-compliance. For an infringement of the regulations to proceed to enforcement action, it will often have to pass through multiple layers of management.

Insufficient funds to conduct enforcement activities

A regulatory agency requires funding for a range of activities, for example to employ sufficient staff, to provide guidance for industry, to train their staff and to undertake enforcement action. Where government does not provide sufficient funding for animal welfare duties and sufficient funds cannot be recovered from industry, there is an obvious danger of under-enforcement of animal welfare and a focus of scarce resources on food safety (Animal Welfare Institute, 2017; FSA, 2018).

Insufficient time allocated to inspection and enforcement

In the USA, as a consequence of concerns over the balance of resources allocated to animal welfare versus food safety issues, the regulatory agency now records the time that inspectors spend verifying compliance with regulations on handling and slaughter (Humane Activities Tracking System) and there are requirements on the frequency of inspection activities and their predictability in terms of how, where and when inspections are conducted (FSIS, 2011). In England, the Mandatory Use of Closed Circuit Television in Slaughterhouses (England) Regulations, 2018 were introduced to improve the effectiveness and efficiency of the monitoring and enforcement of animal welfare requirements in slaughterhouses. Undercover video evidence had demonstrated major welfare issues in some slaughterhouses. The previous voluntary use of closed-circuit television (CCTV) by the slaughter industry in England had not been comprehensive, in terms of the number of slaughterhouses covered, the areas where CCTV was present and the access to CCTV footage that was provided to the enforcement agency (Farm Animal Welfare Committee, 2015).

Intimidation by slaughter plant

Inspectors can, in some circumstances, be subject to intimidation, violence and harassment. Although most incidents have been reported as having been resolved informally, the enforcement agency may, in extreme circumstances, protect their employees by the withdrawal of inspection and veterinary services (FSA, 2015a).

Types of infringements

A review of non-compliance records issued by FSIS in 2016 (Animal Welfare Institute, 2017) found that the most frequent causes of incidents were:

- lack of worker training in humane handling techniques;
- use of inappropriate stunning devices;
- improper shot placement, often in connection with inadequate restraint;

　　　　　　　　　　　　　　　　　　　　　　　M. Cockram

- lack of routine testing and maintenance of stunning equipment; and
- lack of functional back-up stunning devices.

These findings were similar to the analysis of non-compliance records between January 2001 and March 2003 reported by GAO (2004), in which the most common type of violation was related to ineffective stunning, either as a result of multiple stunning attempts eventually resulting in unconsciousness of the animal, or the animal remaining conscious after stunning. Other non-compliances were caused by poor pen/ground conditions, inadequate access to water and feed, and handling issues related to 'disabled or sick' animals, use of excessive force and excessive use of electric prods.

An analysis of FSIS enforcement actions over the period July 2017 to June 2019 (FSIS, 2019b) showed that almost all enforcement leading to either a Notice of Intended Enforcement or a Notice of Suspension of Inspection was due to problems in undertaking effective stunning. The exceptions were handling incidents where, for example, animals were driven over a non-ambulatory animal; or an animal was kicked or hit with a shovel or rod, or died due to entrapment in handling equipment leading to the stunning area, or when an animal broke a leg when it fell from a shackle before ritual slaughter. Enforcement action due to ineffective mechanical stunning was taken when multiple attempts, i.e. more than two shots, were required to achieve unconsciousness. In many cases this appeared to be a consequence of failure to restrain the animal sufficiently, incorrect shot placement on the head, poor maintenance of stunning equipment and ammunition, use of firearms with insufficient power to cause effective stunning, and failure to have a working back-up stunner readily available. In many cases an animal was left too long, i.e. several minutes, in pain and distress between the application of the first shot that caused a penetrating hole in its head and the time that it was stunned successfully. The use of a variety of different firearms and ammunition in the descriptions of enforcement for ineffective stunning was indicative of a lack of knowledge on the suitability of equipment to cause effective stunning, especially of bulls and boars with thick skulls (Atkinson *et al.*, 2013; Whiting and Will, 2019). For pigs, the difficulty in locating the area of the skull over the brain when using captive bolt stunning equipment and firearms to stun pigs (Leary *et al.*, 2016) did not appear to be appreciated by some establishments. In several cases, pigs were observed to regain consciousness after electrical stunning and sometimes after exsanguination, and slaughter employees did not always recognize this. As identified by the Animal Welfare Institute (2017), the HMSA and associated regulations and directives do not contain the same types of requirements for training and assessment of competencies as those contained in, for example, Council Regulation (EC) No. 1099/2009. There is also no specific requirement for appropriate back-up stunning equipment to be immediately available and used if the original stunning equipment fails.

A review of audits conducted by the European Commission's Food and Veterinary Office (FVO, 2015) identified the following compliance issues with the EU regulation on slaughter (Council Regulation (EC) No 1099/2009):

- lairage capacities sometimes exceeded;
- lack of feeding or bedding for animals after more than 12 h in the lairage;
- some animals unfit for transport arriving for slaughter;
- inadequate documented procedures for assessing loss of consciousness after stunning; and
- inadequate electrical stunning of poultry.

Published data on enforcement action by the FSA in the UK following non-compliance with regulations (Table 17.1) provide examples of the types of issues recorded by inspectors and what action was taken. However, this data might not provide useful information on the prevalence of welfare issues. The high level of compliance might, of course, be due to the UK slaughter industry undertaking near-perfect operations. However, other evidence suggests that welfare issues still occur at slaughterhouses. The low number of recorded events might be due to a range of issues, such as problems with a central database, lack of standardized recording methods, inspectors not recording their observations, not undertaking inspections in areas of the slaughterhouse where non-compliance occurs, or not undertaking inspections at an appropriate time or for sufficient duration. The types of welfare issues recorded are affected by the specific legislation in the UK, the training and direction provided to the inspectors by the management of the enforcement agency, the species and local factors, such as the thermal environment, and methods of transport, handling and slaughter. In 2011, a 1-week assessment

Table 17.1. UK Food Standards Agency data on the number of records of non-compliance with slaughter regulations 2017–2018 (FSA, 2019a).

		Type of animal			
		Cattle	Pigs	Poultry	Sheep and goats
Area of slaughterhouse	Unloading	13	2	12	1
	Lairage	35	27	23	75
	Movement and restraint	22	12	97	28
	Stunning	59	19	37	34
	Bleeding	3	5	33	13
Management responsibilities for compliance such as up to date Standard Operating Procedures		44	10	49	54
No. of animals affected by non-compliance		822	358	20,439	6,009
Throughput during period of recording (no. of animals slaughtered)		3,560,142	17,435,960	1,997,819,000	26,272,949
Enforcement action	Verbal advice	115	47	104	121
	Written advice[a]	57	30	107	77
	Welfare enforcement notice	26	5	56	44
	Referred for further investigation and potential prosecution	11	5	63	14

[a]Letter outlining issues with compliance and requesting correction of issues

of 328 establishments in Great Britain reported that 99% were fully compliant, or only demonstrated minor deficiencies with the requirements of the slaughter legislation (FSA, 2012). The minor deficiencies included: no back-up stunner available; no water available for pigs; and overcrowding. Major deficiencies included: entrapment in a pen; no water available for pigs kept overnight; and inadequate bleeding of poultry. Further details were provided in a survey conducted in 2013 of inspectors' assessments on compliance with various aspects of the regulations (FSA, 2015b).

The UK Food Standards Agency (FSA) published detailed records of non-compliance with animal welfare regulations for the slaughter of animals between April 2011 and March 2014 (FSA, 2017). An analysis of these records showed that considerable attention was given to welfare issues associated with the handling and transport of broilers to slaughter. Many of these issues were related to injuries from poor handling, birds not in an upright posture, trapping of live birds, and overcrowding in crates and modules. Poor transport conditions resulting in heat stress and inadequate ventilation or cold stress from inadequate protection from rain and cold weather were associated with incidents where the prevalence of dead-on-arrivals exceeded normal thresholds. The inspectors recorded many incidents where the prevalence of breast blisters,

hock burn and foot pad dermatitis indicated poor on-farm conditions. Several incidents were caused by poor lairage management. These included loose birds, inadequate ventilation and live birds wetted from spray from pressure hoses or from passing through the crate wash. There were some incidents of poor shackling practices, with some birds left too long inverted in the shackles before stunning. There was a relatively small number of events recorded where the stunning equipment was not operated correctly, for example the level of water in the electric stunner bath was too low, or the current was too low. Some birds received pre-stun electrical shocks, some were not properly stunned, and one bird was drowned in the water-bath. There were many events where the neck-cutting equipment was not operated effectively and many birds were either not cut or were bled poorly. Inadequate performance or competency of slaughtermen was recorded as an issue. Almost half of the incidents were dealt with by offering verbal advice; written advice was provided in 3.5% of events; 14% were referred to management for further action; and 34% were referred to the regulatory authority responsible for the enforcement of transport and on-farm regulations. In the 102 events recorded where there was evidence of avoidable pain, distress or suffering during stunning or killing, 87% were dealt with by offering verbal advice, written advice was provided in 8% of events and 4% were referred to management for further investigation.

For cattle, most of the recorded events related to transport to slaughter and were associated with: transport in late pregnancy; injury; lameness; non-ambulatory, weak and blind animals; and overcrowding. Issues related to poor on-farm management included in-growing horns, overgrown hooves, emaciation, abscesses and tumours. For cattle, most of the recorded events for lairage management were due to failure to provide clean drinking water and feed, inadequate or no bedding, and overcrowding in pens. Handling issues recorded were delays in the race and stunning box, injuries and inappropriate use of goads and sticks. Some poor handling methods and the escape of cattle were recorded. Inadequate or no head restraint for stunning was recorded. In the 89 events recorded where there was evidence of non-compliance during stunning or killing, most of the events were related to inadequate stunning, too long a period between stunning and exsanguination, and too short a period between exsanguination and dressing. Other recorded events included an absence of back-up stunning equipment, no slaughter licence, and inadequate maintenance of captive bolt and electrical stunning equipment. In the 13 events recorded where there was evidence of avoidable pain, distress or suffering during stunning or killing, ten were dealt with by offering verbal advice and written advice was provided in the other three events.

For pigs, most of the recorded events related to transport to slaughter and were associated with injuries (including tail bites and slap marks), lameness, transport in late pregnancy and conditions affecting fitness for transport, including prolapses and hernias. Issues related to poor on-farm management were emaciation, overgrown hooves and abscesses. For pigs, most of the recorded events for lairage management were due to failure to provide clean drinking water, risk of injury from poor maintenance of equipment, overcrowding in pens and inadequate lighting. Many events were due to poor handling, including dragging by ears or tails and excessive slapping. For pigs, most of the issues of non-compliance during slaughter were due to inadequate display of the current applied during stunning, ineffective stunning, lack of back-up stunning equipment, lack of slaughter licence, delays in exsanguination after stunning and live pigs entering the scalding tank. None of the events where a live pig entered the scalding tank or when the ears were removed before bleeding was completed was considered by the inspectors to demonstrate evidence that the pigs suffered any avoidable pain, distress or suffering during killing, i.e. they were coded as a score 3 (potential risk to welfare), and only verbal or written advice was provided.

Conclusions

Slaughter legislation to protect the welfare of animals remains a controversial topic. There are divergent views on its necessity and effectiveness in enhancing animal welfare. This chapter has argued the merit of legislation to protect animals during slaughter in that slaughter is a process where animals are at risk of suffering, and they benefit from the external oversight that legislation provides. There are close relationships between the regulation of animal welfare and food safety within slaughterhouses. The evolution of regulatory policies has influenced the approach to slaughter legislation. Within legal regulations, responsibility is placed on the slaughterhouse operator to develop internal policies and procedures to mitigate animal welfare risks and monitor outcomes so that they can take corrective action as soon as a problem is identified. The role of the regulator has expanded from an enforcement role to one that facilitates and cooperates with the operator to achieve compliance with regulations and reduce risks to animal welfare. Emphasis is placed on the verification of procedures and corrective actions undertaken by the slaughterhouse. There are challenges in enforcing slaughter legislation and it is difficult to assess the effectiveness of enforcement. Reports provided by enforcement agencies indicate that compliance with legislation is high. Although there is independent evidence that standards in slaughterhouses have improved, critics suggest that improved inspection and enforcement would show that there are major issues that still need to be addressed. Reports on the types of infringements of regulations that occur indicate the continued need for legislation and in some cases revision of current regulations. Many of the welfare issues described could be addressed by more training and by dissemination of current knowledge and understanding of best practice.

References

Abyaneh, H.K., Dabaghian, A., Rezaeigolestani, M. and Amanollahi, D. (2019) Compliance with OIE animal welfare standards in slaughterhouses in Tehran province, Iran: an introductory survey. *Journal of Applied Animal Welfare Science* 1–8. doi: 10.1080/10888705.2019.1577735

Animal Welfare Institute (2016) The Welfare of Birds at Slaughter in the United States. The Need for Government Regulation. Available at: https://awionline.org/sites/default/files/products/FA-Poultry-Slaughter-Report-2016.pdf (accessed 15 April 2020).

Animal Welfare Institute (2017) Humane Slaughter Update. Federal and State Oversight of the Welfare of Farm Animals at Slaughter. Available at: https://awionline.org/sites/default/files/products/FA-HumaneSlaughterReport-2017.pdf (accessed 15 April 2020).

Atkinson, S., Velarde, A. and Algers, B. (2013) Assessment of stun quality at commercial slaughter in cattle shot with captive bolt. *Animal Welfare* 22, 473–481. doi: 10.7120/09627286.22.4.473

Bennett, R., Balcombe, K., Jones, P. and Butterworth, A. (2018) The benefits of farm animal welfare legislation: the case of the EU broiler directive and truthful reporting. *Journal of Agricultural Economics* 70, 135–152. doi: 10.1111/1477-9552.12278

Bonafos, L., Simonin, D. and Gavinelli, A. (2010) Animal welfare: European legislation and future perspectives. *Journal of Veterinary Medical Education* 37, 26–29. doi: 10.3138/jvme.37.1.26

British Meat Processors Association (2015) Animal health & welfare. BMPA Guide to Good Practice: Welfare at Slaughter. Available at: https://britishmeatindustry.org/resources/animal-health-and-welfare (accessed 15 April 2020).

British Poultry Council (2015) The Protection of Animals at the Time of Killing. Guidance for Poultry. Available at: http://www.britishpoultry.org.uk/identity-cms/wp-content/uploads/2017/11/2015_11_Poultry_GGP_final.pdf (accessed 15 April 2020).

Broom, D.M. (2009) Animal welfare and legislation. In: Smulders, F.J.M. and Algers, B. (eds) *Welfare of Production Animals: Assessment and Management of Risks*. Wageningen Academic Publishers, Wageningen, the Netherlands, pp. 339-352. doi: 10.3920/978-90-8686-690-8

Broom, D.M. (2017) Animal Welfare in the European Union. Directorate General for Internal Policies, European Union. https://www.europarl.europa.eu/RegData/etudes/STUD/2017/583114/IPOL_STU(2017)583114_EN.pdf (accessed 15 April 2020)

CFIA (2019a) Canadian Food Inspection Agency, Ottawa. http://www.inspection.gc.ca (accessed 15 April 2020).

CFIA (2019b) Guidelines for animal welfare Preventive Control Plans and self-audits for the slaughter of food animals. Canadian Food Inspection Agency, Ottawa. Available at: http://www.inspection.gc.ca/food/food-specific-requirements-and-guidance/meat-products-and-food-animals/guidelines-animal-welfare/eng/1523882301730/1523882392898 (accessed 15 April 2020).

CFIA (2019c) Food-specific requirements and guidance – Meat products and food animals. Canadian Food Inspection Agency, Ottawa. Available at: http://www.inspection.gc.ca/food/food-specific-requirements-and-guidance/meat-products-and-food-animals/eng/1523875902268/1523875902549 (accessed 15 April 2020).

CFIA (2019d) Operational guideline: Humane care and handling of food animals. Canadian Food Inspection Agency, Ottawa. Available at: http://www.inspection.gc.ca/food/compliance-continuum/guidance-for-inspectors/sip/humane-care-and-handling-of-food-animals/eng/1546041921629/1546042699855 (accessed 15 April 2020).

Code of Federal Regulations (2017) Part 313 Humane Slaughter of Livestock. Office of the Federal Register, Washington, DC. Available at: https://www.govinfo.gov/content/pkg/CFR-2017-title9-vol2/xml/CFR-2017-title9-vol2-part313.xml (accessed 15 April 2020).

Council Regulation (EC) No 1099/2009 of 24 September 2009 on the protection of animals at the time of killing. Available at: https://eur-lex.europa.eu/eli/reg/2009/1099/2018-05-18 (accessed 15 April 2020).

Cowan, T. (2011) Humane Treatment of Farm Animals: Overview and Issues. Congressional Research Service. Available at: https://crsreports.congress.gov/product/pdf/RS/RS21978 (accessed 15 April 2020).

Croney, C.C. and Millman, S.T. (2007) Board-invited review: The ethical and behavioral bases for farm animal welfare legislation. *Journal of Animal Science*, 85, 556-565. doi: 10.2527/jas.2006-422

Dale, A. (2009) Animal welfare codes and regulations – the devil in disguise? In: Sankoff, P. and White, S. (ed.) *Animal Law in Australasia*. Federation Press, Alexandria, NSW, Australia, pp. 174-212.

Devitt, C., Kelly, P., Blake, M., Hanlon, A. and More, S.J. (2014) Dilemmas experienced by government veterinarians when responding professionally to farm animal welfare incidents in Ireland. *Veterinary Record Open* 1. doi: 10.1136/vropen-2013-000003

EFSA (2019) Animal welfare at slaughter. European Food Safety Authority. Available at: http://www.efsa.europa.eu/en/topics/topic/animal-welfare-slaughter (accessed 15 April 2020).

European Commission (2012) The Animal Welfare officer in the European Union. https://ec.europa.eu/food/sites/food/files/animals/docs/aw_prac_slaughter_awo-brochure_24102012_en.pdf. (accessed 15 April 2020).

European Commission (2019) Health and Food Audits and Analysis. Available at: https://ec.europa.eu/food/audits_analysis_en (accessed 15 April 2020).

FVO (2008) Final Report of A Mission Carried Out In Italy from 10 to 14 March 2008 in Order to Evaluate the System of Control for Animal Welfare During Transport and at the Time of Slaughter and Killing. Food and Veterinary Office, European Commission, Brussels. Available at: http://ec.europa.eu/food/audits-analysis/

audit_reports/details.cfm?rep_id=2033 (accessed 15 April 2020).

FVO (2015) Overview Report. Animal welfare at slaughter in Member States. Food and Veterinary Office, European Commission, Brussels. Available at: http://ec.europa.eu/food/fvo/overview_reports/act_getPDF.cfm?PDF_ID=430 (accessed 15 April 2020)

FVO (2019) Audit Reports. Food and Veterinary Office, European Commission, Brussels. Available at: http://ec.europa.eu/food/audits-analysis/audit_reports/index.cfm (accessed 15 April 2020)

Fairman, R. and Yapp, C. (2005) Enforced self-regulation, prescription, and conceptions of compliance within small businesses: The impact of enforcement. *Law & Policy* 27, 491–519. doi: 10.1111/j.1467-9930.2005.00209.x

Farm Animal Welfare Council (2003) Report on the Welfare of Farmed Animals at Slaughter or Killing Part 1: Red Meat Animals. Farm Animal Welfare Council, London.

Farm Animal Welfare Council (2008) Opinion on Policy Instruments for Protecting and Improving Farm Animal Welfare. Farm Animal Welfare Council, London. Available at: https://assets.publishing.service.gov.uk/government/uploads/system/uploads/attachment_data/file/325046/FAWC_opinion_on_policy_instruments_for_improvement_of_farm_animal_welfare.pdf

Farm Animal Welfare Committee (2015) Opinion on CCTV in slaughterhouses. Farm Animal Welfare Committee, London. Available at: https://assets.publishing.service.gov.uk/government/uploads/system/uploads/attachment_data/file/400796/Opinion_on_CCTV_in_slaughter-houses.pdf

Federal Meat Inspection Act. US Code Title 21—Food and Drugs Chapter 12—Meat Inspection. US Department of Agriculture, Washington, DC. Available at: https://www.fsis.usda.gov/wps/portal/fsis/topics/rulemaking/federal-meat-inspection-act

FSA (2012) FSA 12/05/08 Open Board – 22 May 2012 Results of The 2011 FSA Animal Welfare Survey in Great Britain. Food Standards Agency, London. Available at: https://webarchive.nationalarchives.gov.uk/20171207164502/https://www.food.gov.uk/sites/default/files/multimedia/pdfs/board/fsa120508.pdf (accessed 15 April 2020)

FSA (2015a) Dealing with unacceptable behaviour by business operators – withdrawal of inspection and veterinary services. Food Standards Agency, London. Available at: https://www.food.gov.uk/sites/default/files/media/document/proposed-policy-unacceptable-fbo-behaviour.pdf (accessed 15 April 2020).

FSA (2015b) Results of the 2013 animal welfare survey in Great Britain. Food Standards Agency, London. Available at: https://webarchive.nationalarchives.gov.uk/20171207164502/https://www.food.gov.uk/enforcement/sectorrules/animal-welfare/animal-welfare-survey (accessed 15 April 2020)

FSA (2015c) FSA 15/06/05 Board Meeting – 3 June 2015. update on animal welfare. Food Standards

Agency, London. Available at: https://acss.food.gov.uk/sites/default/files/meeting/minutes/fsa1507013-june2015-mins.pdf (accessed 15 April 2020)

FSA (2017) Enforcement of animal welfare regulations at slaughter. Food Standards Agency, London. Available at: https://webarchive.nationalarchives.gov.uk/20171207180651/https://www.food.gov.uk/about-us/data-and-policies/foia/foirelease/foiaeir2014/regulations-at-slaughter (accessed 15 April 2020)

FSA (2018) Food Standards Agency FSA 18-09-05, Board Meeting – 19th September 2018, Animal Welfare Update, Funding for Delivery of Animal Welfare Official Controls. Food Standards Agency, London. Available at: https://www.food.gov.uk/sites/default/files/media/document/fsa-18-09-05-animal-welfare-update-amends.pdf (accessed 15 April 2020)

FSA (2019a) Food Standards Agency. https://www.food.gov.uk/ (accessed 15 April 2020)

FSA (2019b) Manual for Official Controls. Chapter 2.3 Animal Welfare. Food Standards Agency, London. Available at: https://www.food.gov.uk/sites/default/files/media/document/chapter-2.3-animal-welfare_4.pdf (accessed 15 April 2020)

FSA (2019c) Animal Welfare. Reports of our checks. Food Standards Agency, London. Available at: https://www.food.gov.uk/business-guidance/animal-welfare#reports-of-our-checks (accessed 15 April 2020)

FSIS (2004) Humane Handling and Slaughter Requirements and the Merits of a Systematic Approach to Meet Such Requirements. Federal Register 69 54625-5425. USDA Food Safety and Inspection Service, Washington, DC. Available at: https://www.federalregister.gov/documents/2004/09/09/04-20431/humane-handling-and-slaughter-requirements-and-the-merits-of-a-systematic-approach-to-meet-such-requirements (accessed 15 April 2020)

FSIS (2005) Treatment of Live Poultry Before Slaughter. Federal Register 70 no. 187. USDA Food Safety and Inspection Service, Washington, DC. Available at: https://www.federalregister.gov/documents/2005/09/28/05-19378/treatment-of-live-poultry-before-slaughter (accessed 15 April 2020)

FSIS (2009) Federal Meat Inspection Regulations. Requirements for the Disposition of Cattle that Become Non-Ambulatory Disabled Following Ante-Mortem Inspection. Federal Register 74 (51) 11463-11466. USDA Food Safety and Inspection Service, Washington, DC. Available at: https://www.federalregister.gov/documents/2009/03/18/E9-5987/requirements-for-the-disposition-of-cattle-that-become-non-ambulatory-disabled-following-ante-mortem (accessed 15 April 2020).

FSIS (2011) Directive: Humane Handling and Slaughter of Livestock. USDA Food Safety and Inspection Service, Washington, DC. Available at: https://www.fsis.usda.gov/wps/wcm/connect/2375f4d5-0e24-4213-902d-d94ee4ed9394/6900.2.pdf?MOD=AJPERES (accessed 15 April 2020)

FSIS (2013) FSIS Compliance Guide for a Systematic Approach to the Humane Handling of Livestock. USDA Food Safety and Inspection Service, Washington, DC. Available at: https://www.fsis.usda.gov/wps/wcm/connect/da6cb63d-5818-4999-84f1-72e6dabb9501/Comp-Guide-Systematic-Approach-Humane-Handling-Livestock.pdf?MOD=AJPERES (accessed 15 April 2020)

FSIS (2015) Humane Handling of Livestock and Poultry. Food Safety Inspection and Service. An Educational Guidebook Based on FSIS Policies. USDA Food Safety and Inspection Service, Washington, DC. Available at: https://www.fsis.usda.gov/wps/wcm/connect/96407439-2142-40c7-8e16-c24949f637ce/humane_handling_booklet.pdf?MOD=AJPERES (accessed 15 April 2020)

FSIS (2017) Administrative enforcement action decision-making and methodology. USDA Food Safety and Inspection Service, Washington, DC. Available at: https://www.fsis.usda.gov/wps/wcm/connect/45df5d0d-ab22-4f32-a32f-fddcbef73917/5100.3.pdf?MOD=AJPERES

FSIS (2019a) USDA Food Safety and Inspection Service. Available at: https://www.fsis.usda.gov (accessed 15 April 2020)

FSIS (2019b) Humane Handling Enforcement Actions. USDA Food Safety and Inspection Service, Washington, DC. Available at: www.fsis.usda.gov/wps/portal/fsis/topics/regulatory-compliance/regulatory-enforcement/humane-handling-enforcement-actions/humane-handling-enforcement-actions (accessed 15 April 2020)

FSIS (2019c) Quarterly Enforcement Reports. USDA Food Safety and Inspection Service, Washington, DC. Available at: https://www.fsis.usda.gov/wps/portal/fsis/topics/regulatory-compliance/regulatory-enforcement/quarterly-enforcement-reports/qer-index (accessed 15 April 2020)

Fraser, D., Koralesky, K.E. and Urton, G. (2018) Toward a harmonized approach to animal welfare law in Canada. Canadian Veterinary Journal 59, 293–302.

Friedrich, B. (2015) When the regulators refuse to regulate: Pervasive USDA underenforcement of the Humane Slaughter Act. Georgetown Law Journal, 104, 197-227.

GAO (2004) United States General Accounting Office Report to Congressional Requesters Humane Methods of Slaughter Act USDA has addressed some problems but still faces enforcement challenges January 2004 GAO-04-247. United States General Accounting Office, Washington, DC. Available at: https://www.gao.gov/new.items/d04247.pdf (accessed 15 April 2020)

GAO (2010) Humane Methods of Slaughter Act. Actions are needed to strengthen enforcement. GAO-10-203. United States General Accounting Office, Washington, DC. Available at: https://www.gao.gov/new.items/d10203.pdf (accessed 15 April 2020)

Gentle, M.J. (2011) Pain issues in poultry. Applied Animal Behaviour Science 135, 252–258. doi: 10.1016/j.applanim.2011.10.023

Government of Canada (2019a) Safe Food for Canadians Act 2012. Available at: https://laws-lois.justice.gc.ca/eng/acts/S-1.1/ (accessed 15 April 2020)

Government of Canada (2019b) Safe Food for Canadians Regulations (SOR/2018-108). Available at: https://laws-lois.justice.gc.ca/eng/regulations/SOR-2018-108/index.html (accessed 15 April 2020).

Grandin, T. (2010) Auditing animal welfare at slaughter plants. Meat Science 86, 56–65. doi: 10.1016/j.meatsci.2010.04.022

Gray, W.B. and Scholz, J.T. (1993) Does regulatory enforcement work? A panel analysis of OSHA enforcement. Law & Society Review 27, 177–213. doi: 10.2307/3053754

Green, R.M. and Kane, K. (2014) The effective enforcement of HACCP based food safety management systems in the UK. Food Control 37, 257–262. doi: 10.1016/j.foodcont.2013.09.016

Gunningham, N. and Sinclair D. (2017) Smart regulation. In: Drahos, P. (ed.) Regulatory Theory: Foundations and Applications. ANU Press, Canberra, Australia, pp. 133–148.

Harlow, C. and Rawlings R. (2009) Law and Administration. Cambridge University Press, Cambridge, UK.

Henson, S. and Caswell, J. (1999) Food safety regulation: an overview of contemporary issues. Food Policy 24, 589–603. doi: 10.1016/S0306-9192(99)00072-X

Horgan, R. and Gavinelli, A. (2006) The expanding role of animal welfare within EU legislation and beyond. Livestock Science 103, 303–307. doi: 10.1016/j.livsci.2006.05.019

Hotis, C. (2006) The anthropological machine at the abattoir: The Humane Methods of Slaughter Act. University of Chicago Legal Forum 1, 503–531.

Hötzel, M.J., Mota, S.M., Ludtke, C.B. and Poletto, R. (2018) Knowledge and attitudes of official inspectors at slaughterhouses in southern Brazil regarding animal welfare. Revista Brasileira De Zootecnia 47.

Hulebak, K.L. and Schlosser, W. (2002) Hazard analysis and critical control point (HACCP) history and conceptual overview. Risk Analysis 22, 547–552. doi: 10.1111/0272-4332.00038

Humane Methods of Slaughter Act (HMSA) U.S. Code, Title 7 Chapter 48. Available at: https://www.govinfo.gov/content/pkg/USCODE-2015-title7/pdf/USCODE-2015-title7-chap48.pdf (accessed 15 April 2020)

Jones, D. (2008) Crimes Without Consequences: The Enforcement of Humane Slaughter Laws in the United States. Animal Welfare Institute, Washington, DC. Available at: https://awionline.org/sites/default/files/publication/digital_download/SlaughterReport-1235136209-3588.pdf

Kettunen, K., Nevas, M. and Lundén, J. (2015) Effectiveness of enforcement measures in local food control in Finland. *Food Control* 56, 41–46. doi: 10.1016/j.foodcont.2015.03.005

Kettunen, K., Nevas, M. and Lundén, J. (2017) Challenges in using administrative enforcement measures in local food control. *Food Control* 76, 34–41. doi: 10.1016/j.foodcont.2017.01.002

Leary, S., Underwood, W., Anthony, R., Corey, D.G.T., Gwaltney-Brant, S. *et al.* (2016) *AVMA Guidelines for the Humane Slaughter of Animals*, 2016 edition. American Veterinary Medical Association, Schaumburg, Illinois. Available at: https://www.avma.org/KB/Policies/Pages/Guidelines-Humane-Slaughter-Animals.aspx

Lundmark, F., Berg, C. and Röcklinsberg, H. (2018) Private animal welfare standards – opportunities and risks. *Animals* 8. doi: 10.3390/ani8010004

Luukkanen, J. and Lundén, J. (2016) Compliance in slaughterhouses and control measures applied by official veterinarians. *Food Control* 68, 133–138. doi: 10.1016/j.foodcont.2016.03.033

Mariucci, J.L. (2008) The Humane Methods of Slaughter Act: deficiencies and proposed amendments. *Journal of Animal Law* IV, 149–181.

Matheny, G. and Leahy, C. (2007) Farm-animal welfare, legislation, and trade. *Law and Contemporary Problems* 70, 325–358. doi: 10.2307/27592172

National Chicken Council (2019) *Animal Welfare for Broiler Chickens. Animal Welfare Guidelines and Audit Checklist.* National Chicken Council, Washington, DC. Available at: https://www.nationalchickencouncil.org/industry-issues/animal-welfare-for-broiler-chickens/ (accessed 15 April 2020)

OECD (2002) Regulatory Policies in OECD Countries. From Interventionism to Regulatory Governance. OECD Reviews of Regulatory Reform. Organisation for Economic Co-operation and Development. OECD Publishing, Paris. Available at: https://doi.org/10.1787/9789264177437-en

OECD (2011) *Regulatory Policy and Governance. Supporting Economic Growth and Serving the Public Interest.* OECD Publishing, Paris. Available at: http://dx.doi.org/10.1787/9789264116573-en

OECD (2014) *Regulatory Enforcement and Inspections, OECD Best Practice Principles for Regulatory Policy.* OECD Publishing, Paris. Available at: https://doi.org/10.1787/9789264208117-en

OIE (2016) *Terrestrial Animal Health Code. Slaughter of Animals.* Office International des Epizooties, Paris. Available at: http://www.oie.int/index.php?id=169&L=0&htmfile=chapitre_aw_slaughter.htm (accessed 15 April 2020)

Paolucci, G., Cagnasso, D., Cassani, F. and Pattono, D. (2015) Council Regulation (EC) no. 1099/2009: State of the art and its application in a local health unit in Piedmont, Italy. *Italian Journal of Food Safety* 4, 10–12. doi: 10.4081/ijfs.2015.4520

Poultry Products Inspection Act (PPIA) United States Code Title 21 – Food and Drugs, Chapter 10. Available at: https://www.govinfo.gov/content/pkg/USCODE-2017-title21/html/USCODE-2017-title21-chap10-sec453.htm (accessed 15 April 2020)

Radford, M. (2001) *Animal Welfare Law in Britain: Regulation and Responsibility.* Oxford University Press, Oxford, UK.

Roy, E. (2015) Cruelty on your plate: the misadministration of the Humane Methods of Slaughter Act. *Mid-Atlantic Journal on Law and Public Policy* 3, 92–116.

Stafford, K.J. and Mellor, D.J. (2009) The implementation of animal welfare standards by member countries of the world organisation for animal health (OIE): analysis of an OIE questionnaire. *OIE Revue Scientifique et Technique* 28, 1143–1164.

Stevenson, P., Battaglia, D., Bullon, C. and Carita, A. (2014) Review of animal welfare legislation in the beef, pork, and poultry industries. Food and Agriculture Organization, Rome. Available at: http://www.fao.org/3/a-i4002e.pdf (accessed 15 April 2020)

Sullivan, S.P. (2013) Empowering market regulation of agricultural animal welfare through product labeling. *Animal Law* 19, 391–442.

Swanson, J.C. (2008) The ethical aspects of regulating production. *Poultry Science* 87, 373–379.

The Mandatory Use of Closed Circuit Television in Slaughterhouses (England) Regulations (2018). Available at: https://www.legislation.gov.uk/uksi/2018/556/contents/made (accessed 15 April 2020)

USDA (2009) Oversight of the Recall by Hallmark/Westland Meat Packaging Company. USDA Food Safety and Inspection Service, Washington, DC. Available at: https://www.fsis.usda.gov/wps/wcm/connect/9347d28e-59ba-471c-9099-5dc9a121aa0b/Audit_Report_Hallmark-Westland_Recall.pdf?MOD=AJPERES (accessed 15 April 2020)

USDA (2016) Overview of the United States Slaughter Industry. US Department of Agriculture, Washington, DC. Available at: https://downloads.usda.library.cornell.edu/usda-esmis/files/b5644r52v/jd473028z/7w62fc23r/SlauOverview-10-27-2016.pdf (accessed 15 April 2020)

Vapnek, J. and Chapman, M. (2010) *Legislative and regulatory options for animal welfare.* Food and Agriculture Organization of the United Nations, Rome. Available at: http://www.fao.org/3/i1907e/i1907e00.htm (accessed 15 April 2020)

Welty, J. (2007) Humane slaughter laws. *Law and Contemporary Problems* 70, 175–206.

Whiting, T.L. (2013) Policing farm animal welfare in federated nations: the problem of dual federalism in Canada and the USA. *Animals* 3, 1086–1122.

Whiting, T.L. and Will, D. (2019) Achieving humane outcomes in killing livestock by free bullet. I: Penetrating brain injury. *The Canadian Veterinary Journal [La Revue Veterinaire Canadienne]* 60, 524–531.

18 Ethical Issues: Introduction to Chapters 18a–e

TEMPLE GRANDIN

Department of Animal Science, Colorado State University, USA

It is important for people in the meat industry to understand different ways that people outside the industry view the use of animals for food. There are five short sub-chapters in Chapter 18. Two contributions discuss the ethical importance of good animal welfare and why it must be taken seriously.

Two other contributors discuss ethical reasons for not eating meat, from the viewpoint of animal rights and animal protection. Another chapter discusses the value of meat in the diet and methods such as improved grazing that can mitigate environmental problems.

18a Animal Rights Viewpoint: The Abuse of Animals Won't Stop Until We Stop Eating Meat

University Center for Human Values, Princeton University, USA

(Reprinted with permission from Peter Singer, *The Guardian*, 11 February 2015.)

Forty years after I wrote Animal Liberation, it's easy to think little has changed: but attitudes to the meat-eating industry, and our speciesism, are changing.

When *Animal Liberation* was published, I hoped that, 40 years on, there would be no more slaughterhouse – and therefore, no more newspaper stories about atrocities like the one at an abattoir in the north of England. The arguments against our oppression of animals seemed to me so clear and irrefutable that surely a powerful movement would arise, consigning these abuses to history, as the anti-slavery movement had put an end to the African slave trade.

At least, that is what I thought in my optimistic (or naïve) moments. In my more pessimistic (or realistic) moments, I understood the vastness of the task of changing habits as deeply ingrained as eating meat, and transforming philosophical outlooks as fundamental as speciesism.

More than 200 years after the abolition of the slave trade, racism is still with us, and even slavery, though everywhere illegal, still exists. How could I expect ending speciesism and animal slavery to be easier or more swift than ending racism and human slavery?

Against the background of those more realistic assumptions we can deplore the fact that animals are still being mistreated on a vast scale, but we should not despair. In many parts of the world, including Europe and the US, there has been tremendous progress in changing attitudes to animals.

A powerful animal advocacy movement has emerged, and it has made a difference for billions of animals.

In 1971, when a few other students and I set up a display in Oxford to show passers-by how their eggs and veal were produced, people asked if we really imagined that we could win against the political and financial might of the agribusiness industry. But the animal movement has challenged that industry with success, achieving reforms across the entire European Union that require farm animals to have more space and better living conditions, and similar changes have now become law in California as well. Admittedly, these changes are still far from giving factory-farmed animals decent lives, but they are a significant improvement on what was standard practice before the reforms came into effect.

Perhaps even more satisfying is the number of people who have abandoned eating animals entirely, and the others who have cut down their meat consumption for ethical reasons. In the 1970s, to be a vegetarian was to be a crank – a thought reflected in the self-mocking name of what was then London's best vegetarian restaurant, Cranks. If you used the term 'vegan' you invariably got a blank look and had to explain what it meant.

Despite all this, it is probably still true that there are more animals suffering at the hands of humans now than ever before. That is because there are more affluent people in the world than ever before, and satisfying their demand for meat has meant a vast expansion of factory farming, especially in China. But to see this as an indication that animal advocates have made no progress would be like saying that because there are more slaves in the world now than

©CAB International 2020. *The Slaughter of Farmed Animals* (eds T. Grandin and M. Cockram)   299

there were in the 1800s, the anti-slavery movement has made no progress. With the world's population now more than seven times what it was in 1800, numbers do not tell the whole story.

Progress is not steady. There will always be periods in which we seem to be treading water, or even going backwards. Periodically articles appear about the resurgence of fur, for example, but I doubt that fur will ever be as uncontroversially accepted as it was 40 years ago. The fact that newspapers give extensive coverage to stories about the abuse of animals being slaughtered for food (not only about abused dogs, cats or horses) is itself a sign of progress.

Meanwhile, there is a simple lesson to draw from the videos released by Animal Aid investigators: if you turn animals into things to use, and give workers complete control over them, it will never be possible to stop the occurrence of the kind of abuse allegedly shown in the videos. Sacking one or two workers merely makes a scapegoat out of them. (Think about what that word tells us about our traditional attitude to animals.) The problem is not one or two workers, nor the practice of halal slaughter, but the system, and the system will not change until people stop buying meat.

18b Ethical Defence of Eating Meat: The Place of Meat Eating in Ethical Diets

Frédéric Leroy[1]*, Miki Ben-Dor[2], Frank M. Mitloehner[3]

[1]Industrial Microbiology and Food Biotechnology (IMDO), Faculty of Sciences and Bioengineering Sciences, Vrije Universiteit, Brussels, Belgium; [2]Department of Archaeology and Ancient Near Eastern Cultures, Tel Aviv University, Israel; [3]Department of Animal Science, University of California, Davis, USA

Summary

Meat can be part of an ethical diet. The inclusion of animal produce in the diet offers nutritional robustness, especially in vulnerable populations. This is part of the ethical justification of meat eating. The ecological argument against meat eating needs to be put in perspective. Improved grazing methods can improve biodiversity and topsoil formation. A vegan society could lead to disastrous monocropping.

Learning Objectives

- Role of meat in a healthy diet.
- Meat is key part of early human diets.
- Learn how livestock can mitigate ecological damage.
- Learn about problems with a vegan world view.

Introduction

Despite its longstanding rank as a health food, meat is now often represented as intrinsically harmful to humans, animals and the planet (Leroy, 2019). This shift is due to three intertwined narratives that relate its consumption to disease, ecological dam-age and animal welfare issues. The evolution is partially driven by honest concern, scientific opinion and dietary guidelines, which are not free from bias and inconsistency (Ioannidis, 2018), and propagated by mass media, ideologists and vested interests in a post-truth setting (Leroy et al., 2018a). Whereas meat's expanding production is sometimes blamed on agri-food lobbying (GRAIN/IATP, 2018), an increasingly popular plant-based market is in its turn supported by various investors and food processors (Murphy, 2018). Coupled with a deceptive health discourse, the ultra-processing of low-priced materials (e.g. corn, soy, oil) into meat imitations generates profit margins that are not achievable with raw materials and fresh foods. Attributing symbolic value to products of inferior quality via (lifestyle) branding is how industry exploits a consumerist need to accumulate 'cultural' capital (Baudrillard, 1970; Ulijaszek et al., 2012). The public debate is therefore polarized and prone to manipulation by various agendas, including ideological ones (Banta et al., 2018). In this chapter, the three above-mentioned narratives (i.e. health, planet and animals) will be critically assessed. Moreover, it will be argued that there is (and should be) a prominent place for livestock and meat traditions within ethical worldviews.

---

* Email: Frederic.Leroy@vub.be

Meat Eating Brings Health and Nutrients, Not Disease

It is commonly stated by health institutions (e.g. IARC, 2015; WHO, 2015; NHS, 2018) and in academic literature that meat eating is related to increased mortality (Larsson and Orsini, 2014) and the development of cardiometabolic diseases (Pan et al., 2011; Abete et al., 2014; Yang et al., 2016; Kim and Je, 2018), cancers (Huang et al., 2013; Carr et al., 2016) and intestinal illness (Cao et al., 2018). Extrapolation of such data to causal interpretations and explicit dietary guidelines is nevertheless unsound (Alexander et al., 2015; Klurfeld, 2015; Feinman, 2018; Leroy et al., 2018b). Meat's relative risk (RR) levels obtained from epidemiological studies are generally much below two, far beneath what is reported for true risk factors. Compare, for instance, how excessive visceral fat generates an RR of 5.9 for colorectal cancer (Yamamoto et al., 2010), whereas for red meat this value is below 1.2. The latter RR levels would be unacceptable as proof in most epidemiological research outside nutrition (Shapiro, 2004; Klurfeld, 2015), especially considering the profusion of false-positive results and the large bias and uncertainty in the datasets (Bofetta et al., 2008; Young and Karr, 2011). Particularly problematic are the use of food frequency questionnaires (Archer et al., 2018; Feinman, 2018) and the poor disentanglement from other lifestyle factors associated with Western-style meat eating, such as low-quality diets, obesity, smoking and limited physical activity (Alexander et al., 2015; Fogelholm et al., 2015; Wang et al., 2016; Grosso et al., 2017; Turner and Lloyd, 2017; Hur et al., 2018). These problems are reflected in the fact that observational claims from nutritional epidemiology are commonly dismissed or even refuted in randomized controlled trials (RCTs) (Young and Karr, 2011), as shown for meat as well (Turner et al., 2015; O'Connor et al., 2017). Moreover, RCTs are not necessarily unproblematic either (Krauss, 2018). Transposition of results from intervention studies to actual risk level can be questionable, as RCTs looking into meat intake do not consider normal dietary context and rely on poor biomarkers (Turner and Lloyd, 2017; Kruger and Zhou, 2018). Also, evidence is usually cherry-picked, so that conflicting data is simply ignored. Inconvenient examples include the multiple studies where meat avoidance is not (or even positively) associated with mortality and disease (e.g. Key et al., 2009; Burkert et al., 2014; Iguacel et al., 2019; Okuyama et al., 2018; Yen et al., 2018).

Not only is the evidence to incriminate meat inadequate, but also the latter deserves reappraisal as a key element of our species-adapted diet (cf. Cordain et al., 2000; Stanford and Bunn, 2001; Leroy and Praet, 2015; Gupta, 2016). The appearance of Homo, 2.5 million years ago (Mya), parallels the emergence of stone tools and animal bones in archaeological sites (Pante et al., 2018), intensifying after the rise of Homo erectus some 1.9 Mya (Pickering and Domínguez-Rodrigo, 2010; Domínguez-Rodrigo and Pickering, 2017). Increased reliance on animal food, at the expense of fibrous plants, explains such adaptations as increased body and brain size and reduced mandible and teeth size (Aiello and Wheeler, 1995; Stanford and Bunn, 2001). Continuous signs of preference for the hunting of large animals (Broughton et al., 2011; Speth, 2012) and the punctuated extinction of large carnivores, but not of medium-size or small ones, around 1.5 Mya, suggests that Homo took a prominent position in the large carnivore guild (Lewis and Werdelin, 2007; Werdelin and Lewis, 2013). Whereas reliance on animal foods appears throughout the Pleistocene (Stiner, 2002; Richards amd Trinkaus, 2009; Balter et al., 2012), signs of increasing plant eating emerge gradually starting about 0.04 Mya at the Upper Palaeolithic (Kuhn and Stiner, 2001). The latter culminated in the transition to plant domestication at 0.01 Mya, which paralleled the domestication of livestock in most regions (Vigne, 2011). Physiological and life-history phenomena further indicate human reliance on animal foods throughout evolution. Unlike herbivores and omnivores, the human stomach is among the most acidic in the animal kingdom (Beasley et al., 2015), which protects humans from meat-borne pathogens and is typical of carnivores and scavengers. Also, human fat tissue has a cellular structure, which is typical of carnivores. 'These figures suggest that the energy metabolism of humans is adapted to a diet in which lipids and proteins rather than carbohydrates, make a major contribution to the energy supply' (Pond and Mattacks, 1985). A comparison of the age at weaning of herbivores, omnivores and carnivores highlights the 'emergence of carnivory as a process fundamentally determining human evolution' (Psouni et al., 2012). Earlier age at weaning is made possible by the replacement of maternal milk with the high nutrition density of meat and fat (Kennedy, 2005).

This brief review of the archaeological and physiological signatures of meat consumption underlines that it has been a key part of human nutrition during the past 2.5 million years. On an evolutionary basis, meat has thus been delivering valuable nutrients, of which some are not easily obtained from plants (Pereira and Vicente, 2013; Young et al., 2013; McNeill, 2014; Leroy et al., 2018b). This is in particular the case for essential amino acids (lysine, threonine and methionine being in short supply in plant-based diets), long-chain omega-3 fatty acids (EPA/DHA), B vitamins (of which vitamin B_{12} is limited to animal products only), vitamins A and K_2, and minerals such as selenium, zinc and iron. Other components that may be suboptimal without meat include taurine, creatine and carnosine. Including meat in the diet is particularly meaningful to prevent deficiencies in young females (Fayet et al., 2014), to improve the thriving and cognitive development of infants and children (Hulett et al., 2014; Tang and Krebs, 2014; Cofnas, 2019) and to prevent or treat malnutrition and sarcopenia in the elderly (Shibata, 2001; Phillips, 2012; Rondanelli et al., 2014). Avoidance of animal products can result in malnutrition (Ingenbleek and McCully, 2012) and deficiencies (Wongprachum et al., 2012, Foster et al., 2013; Pawlak et al., 2014; Woo et al., 2014; Brantsæter et al., 2018; Naik et al., 2018). Furthermore, it is associated with depression and eating disorders (Zhang et al., 2017; Barthels et al., 2018; Hibbeln et al., 2018) and may lead to neurological problems (Kapoor et al., 2017). Taken together, the fact that inclusion of animal products in the diet offers nutritional robustness, especially in vulnerable populations, is part of the ethical justification of meat eating.

Livestock Is Part of the Solution for the Mitigation of Ecological Damage

The ecological argument against meat eating equally needs to put in perspective (Fairlie, 2011). It is commonly assumed that the farming of livestock *as such* is too water- and land-intensive and therefore wasteful. First, 87% of the water used by livestock is green water originating from rainfall, which in the case of grazing beef equals 94% (Mekonnen and Hoekstra, 2010). With respect to land use, the debate needs to bear in mind that a quarter of the global agricultural area consists of non-convertible pastures and rangelands (1.3 billion ha) (Mottet et al., 2018) also referred to as 'marginal land'. Although the

option of rewilding should not be overlooked, exclusion of livestock from food production would leave marginal land that, in the context of food production, can only be dedicated to ruminant grazing, as unexploited. This is also primordial for rural development, as livestock in such areas contribute to the livelihoods and nutritional security of millions of farmers (430 million out of 729 million poor people in rural and marginal areas are livestock farmers; FAO, 2020), as well as the empowerment of women (Mottet et al., 2018). Livestock provide high-quality nutrition, asset savings, traction and manure nutrients for use as fertilizers in regions where cropping is problematic. The argument that animal feed competes with crops directly suitable for the human diet is partially true but also needs nuance. Contrary to overblown estimates of 6–20 kg grain per 1 kg meat, the actual number is close to 3 kg (Mottet et al., 2018). Additionally, 86% of livestock feed is not suitable for human consumption, consisting of forage as well as crop residues and by-products that otherwise would represent an environmental burden. For ruminants, only 5% of the feed directly competes with human food (mostly grain and some soybean meal) (Mottet et al., 2018). Cattle thus contribute to global food security, as they need only 0.6 kg of human-edible feed protein to produce 1 kg of animal protein, which has a higher biological value and makes them net contributors to global human-edible protein production (Mottet et al., 2017, 2018; FAO, 2018).

With respect to climate change, livestock are said to generate 14.5% (7.1 gigatons CO_2-eq per year) of the total greenhouse gas (GHG) emissions, largely because of feed production (45% of contribution; including deforestation) and enteric fermentation by ruminants (39%) (Gerber et al., 2013). This is worrying but needs contextualization. First, the metric viewing ruminant-derived methane as many times more harmful than CO_2 is unjustified, because atmospheric stabilization of the latter can only be obtained upon a massive reduction (80%) compared with a smaller drop of the former (30%) (Fairlie, 2017). Second, the 14.5% number reflects vast regional heterogeneity. In the USA, direct livestock GHG emissions from manure and enteric fermentation account for only 3% of the anthropogenic GHG emissions, far below the 26% of CO_2-eq by the transportation sector (Place and Mitloehner, 2012). Therefore, a global mitigation of 30% and more might be achieved if the practices of the 25% most efficient producers were to be adopted worldwide, especially with respect to ruminant systems with low productivity in Latin America, sub-Saharan Africa and South Asia (Gerber *et al.*, 2013). Additionally, better grazing land management has the potential to offset emissions via grassland carbon sequestration (Gerber *et al.*, 2013; Teague *et al.*, 2016; Stanley *et al.*, 2018). Grazing plays a role in ecosystem shaping, whereby ruminants take over the role of wild herbivores, manure-fertilize cropland and grassland, and improve biodiversity and topsoil formation. Yet, to be able to benefit from the potential assets of livestock management, interventions will be needed through further productivity improvements, adjustment of grazing pressure to improve carbon sequestration and build topsoil, and better integration in the circular bioeconomy (e.g. enhancing the use of by-products) (Mottet *et al.*, 2018). Larger shifting of ruminant grain feeding to grazing and improved channelling of waste streams to efficient conversion by pigs and poultry hold important potential (Fairlie, 2011).

To sum up, and as stated in the FAO report by Gerber *et al.* (2013), 'the livestock sector *should* be part of any solution to climate change' (our emphasis). Although there are reasons to consider a reduction of livestock numbers, its elimination would be unwise. A vegan society could easily lead to disastrous monocropping, driven by fossil fuel-derived fertilizers and resulting in topsoil depletion and biodiversity losses. Grass would need to be kept down with herbicides in the absence of grazing, and by-products of cropping would be left to waste (Fairlie, 2018). In the West, it would reinforce reliance on the import of crops (e.g. soy, bananas, coconuts, rice) and the formation of apocalyptic greenhouse landscapes (as currently found in Almeria) (MailOnline, 2013). A first priority in reducing climate change contributors should be in the drastic reduction of fossil fuel use and the associated rapid extraction of carbon deposits, which needed millions of years to accumulate (Fairlie, 2017).

Vegan Ideology Leads to Problematic Worldviews

Human–animal interactions, either through hunting or livestock keeping, have been fundamental to our biosocial development (Leroy and Praet, 2015). The heavily ritualized and culturally entrenched relationship with animals, although intimately linked to killing for food, has been driving the very evolution of our species. When not seen all too anthropocentrically, it can even be valued as a rich and symbiotic

association between humans and animals. In contrast to ferocious life in the wild, humanely kept livestock animals are (or should be) receiving a decent life, feed during winter and a fast death. According to Baggini (2014), it is not against livestock's *interests* or *nature* to be farmed, nor is there a good reason to deny that farming can provide a good life. Moreover, the number of sentient beings killed during crop harvesting or for pest control likely exceeds the death toll of animal husbandry per unit of food (Davis, 2003; Archer, 2011), although numbers are uncertain (Fischer and Lamey, 2018). Refusing to eat meat points toward an alienated relationship with nature and a failure to grasp the dynamics of life and death, which seems typical for the Western urban mindset (Fairlie, 2018). Whilst traditional societies, in particular hunter-gatherer groups, display a respectful attitude toward animal killing (Leroy and Praet, 2017), vegan belief often refers to a biocentric Garden-of-Eden concept (Sánchez Sábaté *et al.*, 2016), with death being a 'contaminant essence' (Testoni *et al.*, 2017). In such worldview, a strict nature/culture compartmentalization would be required, by fencing off crop production from wildlife to avoid the otherwise necessary killing of vermin. To eliminate animal killing altogether, vegan ideologists may even consider intervening in wildlife (i.e. *within* the nature side of the binary), for instance by pursuing genetic engineering of carnivores into herbivores or by phasing out wildlife populations via sterilization and confinement of the remaining animals to parks (Moen, 2016). It may even be preferable to some vegans to have no animals at all, rather than have them subjected to a nature that is red in tooth and claw (Moen, 2016). Considering that some theorists are in favour of legally imposing veganism on society at large (e.g. Deckers, 2013), such ideas are alarming indeed.

Conclusions

There are issues of concern related to current animal production systems that will need to be addressed on a global level. Yet, the historically unprecedented societal stigmatizing of meat eating as being severely detrimental to humans, animals and the planet is astonishing. Meat as such *does* hold a main place in ethical dietary behaviour, although there is margin for correction and improvement of its aspects of healthiness, sustainability and animal welfare. This may or may not mean that less meat should be consumed, produced by more suitable livestock management and with increased attention for animal welfare criteria, but certainly not that meat should be *avoided*. Meat has to be credited for being at the basis of our wider biosocial evolution, as it is a nutrient-dense key element of our species-adapted diet and has contributed to both our biological and behavioural idiosyncrasies, including its rich influence on cultural heritage and livelihoods. This is also valid for livestock since Neolithic times and, more broadly, for human–animal interactions going back to our earliest existence as hunter-gatherers. Properly organized and animal-friendly livestock management may not only reduce environmental impact but may even be part of the solution to mitigate climate change. A switch to a meat-free world would represent a reinforcement of the problematic nature/culture binary and a mass experiment of unknown proportions, of which the outcome is not only unpredictable but also leading to its own set of ethical concerns.

Acknowledgements

FL acknowledges financial support of the Research Council of the Vrije Universiteit Brussel, including the SRP7 and IOF342 projects, and in particular the Interdisciplinary Research Program 'Tradition and naturalness of animal products within a societal context of change' (IRP11).

References

Abete, I., Romaguera, D., Vieira, A.R., Lopez de Munain, A. and Norat, T. (2014) Association between total, processed, red and white meat consumption and all-cause, CVD and IHD mortality: a meta-analysis of cohort studies. *British Journal of Nutrition* 112, 762–775.

Aiello, L.C. and Wheeler, P. (1995) The expensive-tissue hypothesis: the brain and the digestive system in human and primate evolution. *Current Anthropology* 36, 199–221.

Alexander, D.D., Weed, D.L., Miller, P.E. and Mohamed, M.A. (2015) Red meat and colorectal cancer: a quantitative update on the state of the epidemiologic science. *Journal of the American College of Nutrition* 34, 521–543.

Archer, M. (2011) Ordering the vegetarian meal? There's more animal blood on your hands. *The Conversation*. Available at: http://theconversation.com/ordering-the-vegetarian-meal-theres-more-animal-blood-on-your-hands-4659 (accessed 15 April 2020).

Archer, E., Marlow, M.L. and Lavie, C.J. (2018) Controversy and debate: memory based methods paper 1: The fatal flaws of food frequency questionnaires and other memory-based dietary assessment methods. *Journal of Clinical Epidemiology* 104, 113–124.

Baggini, J. (2014). *The Virtues of the Table*. Granta Publications, London.

Balter, V., Braga, J., Télouk, P. and Thackeray, J.F. (2012) Evidence for dietary change but not landscape use in South African early hominins. *Nature* 489, 558–560.

Banta, J.E., Lee, J.W., Hodgkin, G., Yi, Z., Fanica, A. and Sabate, J. (2018). The global influence of the Seventh-Day Adventist church on diet. *Religions* 9, 251.

Barthels, F., Meyer, F. and Pietrowsky, R. (2018) Orthorexic and restrained eating behaviour in vegans, vegetarians, and individuals on a diet. *Eating and Weight Disorders* 23, 159–166.

Baudrillard, J. (1970) *The Consumer Society*. Myths and Structures. Gallimard, Paris.

Beasley, D.E., Koltz, A.M., Lambert, J.E., Fierer, N. and Dunn, R.R. (2015) The evolution of stomach acidity and its relevance to the human microbiome. *PLoS ONE* 10, e0134116.

Brantsæter, A.L., Knutsen, H.K., Johansen, N.C., Nyheim, K.A., Erlund, I. *et al*. (2018) Inadequate iodine intake in population groups defined by age, life stage and vegetarian dietary practice in a Norwegian convenience sample. *Nutrients* 10, E230.

Boffetta, P., McLaughlin, J.K., LaVecchia, C., Tarone, R.E., Lipworth, L. and Blot, W.J. (2008). False-positive results in cancer epidemiology: a plea for epistemological modesty. *Journal of the National Cancer Institute* 100, 988–995.

Broughton, J.M., Cannon, M.D., Bayham, F.E. and Byers, D.A. (2011). Prey body size and ranking in zooarchaeology: theory, empirical evidence, and applications from the northern Great Basin. *American Antiquity* 76, 403–428.

Burkert, N.T., Muckenhuber, J., Großschädl, F., Rásky, E. and Freidl, W. (2014). Nutrition and health – the association between eating behavior and various health parameters: a matched sample study. *PLoS One* 9, e88278.

Cao, Y., Strate, L.L., Keeley, B.R., Tam, I., Wu, K., Giovannucci, E.L. and Chan A.T. (2018) Meat intake and risk of diverticulitis among men. *Gut* 67, 466–472.

Carr, P.R., Walter, V., Brenner, H. and Hoffmeister, M. (2016) Meat subtypes and their association with colorectal cancer: systematic review and meta-analysis. *International Journal of Cancer* 138, 293–302.

Cofnas, N. (2019) Is vegetarianism healthy for children? *Critical Reviews in Food Science and Nutrition*, 59(13), 2052–2060. doi: 10.1080/10408398.2018. 1437024

Cordain, L., Brand Miller, J., Boyd Eaton, S., Mann, N., Holt, S.H.A. and Speth, J.D. (2000) Plant–animal subsistence ratios and macronutrient energy estimations in worldwide hunter-gatherer diets. *American Journal of Clinical Nutrition* 71, 682–692.

Davis, S.L. (2003) The least harm principle may require that humans consume a diet containing large herbivores. *Journal of Agricultural and Environmental Ethics* 16, 387–394.

Deckers, J. (2013) In defence of the vegan project. *Bioethical Inquiry* 10, 187–195.

Domínguez-Rodrigo, M. and Pickering, T.R. (2017) The meat of the matter: an evolutionary perspective on human carnivory. *Azania: Archaeological Research in Africa* 52, 4–32.

FAO (2018) More fuel for the food/feed debate. Available at: http://www.fao.org/ag/againfo/home/en/news_archive/2017_More_Fuel_for_the_Food_Feed.html (accessed 15 April 2020).

FAO (2020) Reducing enteric methane for improving food security and livelihoods. The role of ruminants in food security and livelihoods. Available at: http://www.fao.org/in-action/enteric-methane/background/thero-leofruminants/en/ (accessed 15 April 2020).

Fairlie, S. (2011) *Meat: a Benign Extravagance.* Permanent Publications, East Meon, UK.

Fairlie, S. (2017) Is grass-fed guilt-free? *The Land* 22, 6–9.

Fairlie, S. (2018) Is eating meat ethical or sustainable? Available at: https://www.lowimpact.org/is-eating-meat-ethical-simon-fairlie-interview (accessed 15 April 2020).

Fayet, F., Flood, V., Petocz, P. and Samman, S. (2014) Avoidance of meat and poultry decreases intakes of omega-3 fatty acids, vitamin B12, selenium and zinc in young women. *Journal of Human Nutrition and Dietetics* 27, 135–142.

Feinman, R. (2018) What's really wrong with medical research and how to fix it. *Journal of Evolution and Health* 2, article 10.

Fischer, B. and Lamey, A. (2018) Field deaths in plant agriculture. *Journal of Agricultural and Environmental Ethics* 31, 409–428.

Fogelholm, M., Kanerva, N. and Männistö, S. (2015) Association between red and processed meat consumption and chronic diseases: the confounding role of other dietary factors. *European Journal of Clinical Nutrition* 69, 1060–1065.

Foster, M., Chu, A., Petocz, P. and Samman, S. (2013) Effect of vegetarian diets on zinc status: a systematic review and meta-analysis of studies in humans. *Journal of Science of Food and Agriculture* 93, 2362–2371.

Gerber, P.J., Steinfeld, H., Henderson, B., Mottet, A., Opio, C. *et al.* (2013) Tackling climate change through livestock – a global assessment of emissions and mitigation opportunities. Food and Agriculture Organization of the United Nations (FAO), Rome. Available at: http://www.fao.org/3/a-i3437e.pdf (accessed 15 April 2020).

GRAIN/IATP (2018) Emissions Impossible. How big meat and dairy are heating up the planet. Available at:https://www.grain.org/article/entries/5976-emissions-impossible-how-big-meat-and-dairy-are-heating-up-the-planet (accessed 15 April 2020).

Grosso, G., Micek, A., Godos, J., Pajak, A., Sciacca, S. *et al.* (2017) Health risk factors associated with meat, fruit and vegetable consumption in cohort studies: a comprehensive meta-analysis. *PLoS One* 12, e0183787.

Gupta, S. (2016) Brain food: clever eating. *Nature* 531, S12–S13.

Hibbeln, J.R., Northstone, K., Evans, J. and Golding, J. (2018) Vegetarian diets and depressive symptoms among men. *Journal of Affective Disorders* 225, 13–17.

Huang, W., Han, Y., Xu, J., Zhu, W. and Li, Z. (2013) Red and processed meat intake and risk of esophageal adenocarcinoma: a meta-analysis of observational studies. *Cancer Causes and Control* 24, 193–201.

Hulett, J.L., Weiss, R.E., Bwibo, N.O., Galal, O.M., Drorbaugh, N. and Neumann, C.G. (2014) Animal source foods have a positive impact on the primary school test scores of Kenyan schoolchildren in a cluster-randomised, controlled feeding intervention trial. *British Journal of Nutrition* 111, 875–886.

Hur, S.J., Jo, C., Yoon, Y., Jeong, J.Y. and Lee, K.T. (2018) Controversy on the correlation of red and processed meat consumption with colorectal cancer risk: an Asian perspective. *Critical Reviews in Food Science and Nutrition* 59(21), 3526–3537.

IARC (2015) IARC Monographs evaluate consumption of red meat and processed meat. Press release n°240. Available at: https://www.iarc.fr/en/media-centre/pr/2015/pdfs/pr240_E.pdf (accessed 15 April 2020).

Iguacel, I., Miguel-Berges, M.L., Gómez-Bruton, A., Moreno, L.A. and Julián, C. (2019) Veganism, vegetarianism, bone mineral density, and fracture risk: a systematic review and meta-analysis. *Nutrition Reviews* 77(1), 1–18.

Ingenbleek, Y. and McCully, K.S. (2012) Vegetarianism produces subclinical malnutrition, hyperhomocysteinemia and atherogenesis. *Nutrition* 28, 148–153.

Ioannidis, J.P.A. (2018) The challenge of reforming nutritional epidemiologic research. *Journal of the American Medical Association* 320, 969–970.

Kapoor, A., Baig, M., Tunio, S.A., Memon, A.S. and Karmani, H. (2017) Neuropsychiatric and neurological problems among vitamin B12 deficient young vegetarians. *Neurosciences* 22, 228–232.

Kennedy, G.E. (2005) From the ape's dilemma to the weanling's dilemma: early weaning and its evolutionary context. *Journal of Human Evolution* 48, 123–145.

Key, T.J., Appleby, P.N., Spencer, E.A., Travis, R.C., Roddam, A.W. and Allen, N.E. (2009) Mortality in British vegetarians: results from the European Prospective Investigation into Cancer and Nutrition (EPIC-Oxford). *American Journal of Clinical Nutrition* 89, 1613S–1619S.

Kim, Y. and Je, Y. (2018) Meat consumption and risk of metabolic syndrome: results from the Korean population and a meta-analysis of observational studies. *Nutrients* 10, E390.

Klurfeld, D.M. (2015) Research gaps in evaluating the relationship of meat and health. *Meat Science* 109, 86–95.

Krauss, A. (2018) Why all randomised controlled trials produce biased results. *Annals of Medicine* 50, 312–322.

Kruger, C. and Zhou, Y. (2018) Red meat and colon cancer: a review of mechanistic evidence for heme in the context of risk assessment methodology. *Food Chemistry and Toxicology* 118, 131–153.

Kuhn, S.L. and Stiner, M.C. (2001) The antiquity of hunter-gatherers. In: Panter, Brick, C., Layton, R. and Rowley-Conwy, P. (eds) *Hunter–Gatherers: Interdisciplinary Perspectives*. Cambridge University Press, Cambridge, UK, pp. 99–142.

Larsson, S.C. and Orsini, N. (2014). Red meat and processed meat consumption and all-cause mortality: a meta-analysis. *American Journal of Epidemiology* 179, 282–289.

Leroy, F. (2019) Meat as a pharmakon: an exploration of the biosocial complexities of meat consumption. *Advances in Food and Nutrition Research* 87, 498–446.

Leroy, F. and Praet, I. (2015) Meat traditions: the co-evolution of humans and meat. *Appetite* 90, 200–211.

Leroy, F. and Praet, I. (2017) Animal killing and postdomestic meat production. *Journal of Agricultural and Environmental Ethics* 30, 67–86.

Leroy, F., Brengman, M., Ryckbosch, W. and Scholliers, P. (2018a) Meat in the post-truth era: mass media discourses on health and disease in the attention economy. *Appetite* 125, 345–355.

Leroy, F., Aymerich, T., Champomier-Vergès, M.-C., Cocolin, L., De Vuyst, L. *et al.* (2018b) Fermented meats (and the symptomatic case of the Flemish food pyramid): are we heading towards the vilification of a valuable food group? *International Journal of Food Microbiology* 274, 67–70.

Lewis, M.E. and Werdelin, L. (2007) Patterns of change in the Plio-Pleistocene carnivorans of eastern Africa. In: *HomininEnvironments in the East African Pliocene: an assessment of the faunal evidence*. Springer, pp 77–105.

MailOnline (2013) Britain's vegetable garden: The sea of Spanish greenhouses as large as the Isle of Wight where the food UK eats is grown. Available at: https://www.dailymail.co.uk/news/article-2303943/Britains-vegetable-garden-The-sea-Spanish-greenhouses-large-Isle-Wight-food-eat-grown.html (accessed 15 April 2020).

McNeill, S.H. (2014) Inclusion of red meat in healthful dietary patterns. *Meat Science* 98, 452–460.

Mekonnen, M.M. and Hoekstra, A.Y. (2010) *The green, blue and grey water footprint of farm animals and animal products*. Value of Water Research Report Series No. 48. UNESCO-IHE, Delft, the Netherlands.

Moen, O.M. (2016) The ethics of wild animal suffering. *Nordic Journal of Applied Ethics* 10, 91–104.

Mottet, A., de Haan, C., Falcuccia, A., Tempio, G., Opio, C. and Gerber, P. (2017) Livestock: on our plates or eating at our table? A new analysis of the feed/food debate. *Global Food Security* 14, 1–8.

Mottet, A., Teillard, F., Boettcher, P., De' Besi G. and Besbes, B. (2018) Domestic herbivores and food security: current contribution, trends and challenges for a sustainable development. *Animal* 12, s188–s198.

Murphy, N. (2018) Plant-based protein market booming. *Food Technology & Manufacturing*. Available at: https://www.foodprocessing.com.au/content/ingredients/news/plant-based-protein-market-booming-23276113 (accessed 15 April 2020)

Naik, S., Mahalle, N. and Bhide, V. (2018) Identification of vitamin B12 deficiency in vegetarian Indians. *British Journal of Nutrition* 119, 629–635.

NHS (2018) Red meat and the risk of bowel cancer. Available at: https://www.nhs.uk/live-well/eat-well/red-meat-and-the-risk-of-bowel-cancer (accessed 15 April 2020).

O'Connor, L.E., Kim, J.E. and Campbell, W.W. (2017) Total red meat intake of ≥0.5 servings/d does not negatively influence cardiovascular disease risk factors: a systemically searched meta-analysis of randomized controlled trials. *American Journal of Clinical Nutrition* 105, 57–69.

Okuyama, H., Hamazaki, T., Hama, R., Ogushi, Y., Kobayashi, T., Ohara, N. and Uchino, H. (2018) A critical review of the consensus statement from the European Atherosclerosis Society Consensus Panel 2017. *Pharmacology* 101, 184–218.

Pan, A., Sun, Q., Bernstein, A.M., Schulze, M.B., Manson, J.E. *et al.* (2011) Red meat consumption and risk of type 2 diabetes: 3 cohorts of US adults and an updated meta-analysis. *American Journal of Clinical Nutrition* 94, 1088–1096.

Pante, M.C., Njau, J.K., Hensley-Marschand, B., Keevil, T.L., Martin-Ramos, C. *et al.* (2018) The carnivorous feeding behavior of early *Homo* at HWK EE, Bed II, Olduvai Gorge, Tanzania. *Journal of Human Evolution* 120, 215–235.

Pawlak, R., Lester, S.E. and Babatunde, T. (2014) The prevalence of cobalamin deficiency among vegetarians assessed by serum vitamin B12: a review of literature. *European Journal of Clinical Nutrition* 68, 541–548.

Pereira, P.M. and Vicente, A.F. (2013) Meat nutritional composition and nutritive role in the human diet. *Meat Science* 93, 586–592.

Phillips, S.M. (2012) Nutrient-rich meat proteins in offsetting age-related muscle loss. *Meat Science* 92, 174–178.

Pickering, R.T. and Domínguez-Rodrigo, M. (2010) Chimpanzee referents and the emergence of human hunting. *Open Anthropology Journal*, 3.

Place, S.E. and Mitloehner, F.M. (2012) Beef production in balance: considerations for life cycle analyses. *Meat Science* 92, 179–181.

Pond, C.M. and Mattacks, C.A. (1985) Body mass and natural diet as determinants of the number and volume of adipocytes in eutherian mammals. *Journal of Morphology* 185, 183–193.

Psouni, E., Janke, A. and Garwicz, M. (2012) Impact of carnivory on human development and evolution revealed by a new unifying model of weaning in mammals. *PLoS ONE* 7, e32452.

Rondanelli, M., Perna, S., Faliva, M.A., Peroni, G., Infantino, V. and Pozzi, R. (2015) Novel insights on intake of meat and prevention of sarcopenia: all reasons for an adequate consumption. *Nutrición Hospitalaria* 32, 2136–2143.

Richards, M.P. and Trinkaus, E. (2009) Isotopic evidence for the diets of European Neanderthals and early modern humans. *Proceedings of the National Academy of Sciences* 106, 16034–16039.

Sánchez Sábaté, R., Gelabert, R., Badilla, Y. and Del Valle, C. (2016) Feeding holy bodies: a study on the social meanings of a vegetarian diet to Seventh-day Adventist church pioneers. *HTS Theological Studies* 72, UNSP a3080.

Shapiro, S. (2004) Looking to the 21st century: have we learned from our mistakes, or are we doomed to compound them? *Pharmacoepidemiology and Drug Safety* 13, 257–265.

Shibata, H. (2001) Nutritional factors on longevity and quality of life in Japan. *Journal of Nutrition, Health and Aging* 5, 97–102.

Speth, J.D. (2012) *Paleoanthropology and Archaeology of Big-game Hunting*. Springer-Verlag, New York.

Stanford, C.B. and Bunn, H. (2001). *Meat-eating and Human Evolution*. Oxford University Press, Oxford, UK.

Stanley, P.L., Rowntree, J.E., Beede, D.K., DeLonge, M.S. and Hamm, M.W. (2018) Impacts of soil carbon sequestration on life cycle greenhouse gas emissions in Midwestern USA beef finishing systems. *Agricultural Systems* 162, 249–258.

Stiner, M.C. (2002) Carnivory, coevolution, and the geographic spread of the genus *Homo*. *Journal of Archaeological Research* 10, 1–63.

Tang, M. and Krebs, N.F. (2014) High protein intake from meats as complementary food increases growth but not adiposity in breastfed infants: a randomized trial. *The American Journal of Clinical Nutrition* 100, 1322–1328.

Teague, W.R., Apfelbaum, S., Lal, R., Kreuter, U.P., Rowntree, J. *et al.* (2016) The role of ruminants in reducing agriculture's carbon footprint in North America. *Journal of Soil and Water Conservation* 71, 156–164.

Testoni, I., Ghellar, T., Rodelli, M., De Cataldo, L. and Zamperini, A. (2017) Representations of death among Italian vegetarians: an ethnographic research on environment, disgust and transcendence. *European Journal of Psychology* 13, 378–395.

Turner, N.D. and Lloyd, S.K. (2017) Association between red meat consumption and colon cancer: a systematic review of experimental results. *Experimental Biology and Medicine* 242, 813–839.

Turner, K.M., Keogh, J.B. and Clifton, P.M. (2015) Red meat, dairy, and insulin sensitivity: a randomized crossover intervention study. *American Journal of Clinical Nutrition* 101, 1170–1179.

Ulijaszek, S., Mann, N. and Elton, S. (2012) *Evolving Human Nutrition. Implications for Human Health*. Cambridge University Press, Cambridge, UK.

Vigne, J.-D. (2011) The origins of animal domestication and husbandry: a major change in the history of humanity and the biosphere. *Comptes Rendus Biologies* 334, 171–181.

Wang, X., Lin, X., Ouyang, Y.Y., Liu, J., Zhao, G. *et al.* (2016) Red and processed meat consumption and mortality: dose-response meta-analysis of prospective cohort studies. *Public Health Nutrition* 19, 893–905.

Werdelin, L. and Lewis, M.E. (2013) Temporal change in functional richness and evenness in the eastern African Plio-Pleistocene carnivoran guild. *PLoS ONE* 8, e57944.

WHO (2015) Q&A on the carcinogenicity of the consumption of red meat and processed meat. World Health Organization, Rome. Available at: http://www.who.int/features/qa/cancer-red-meat/en (accessed 15 April 2020)

Wongprachum, K., Sanchaisuriya, K., Sanchaisuriya, P., Siridamrongvattana, S., Manpeun, S. and Schlep, F.P. (2012) Proxy indicators for identifying iron deficiency among anemic vegetarians in an area prevalent for thalassemia and hemoglobinopathies. *Acta Haematologica* 127, 250–255.

Woo, K.S., Kwok, T.C. and Celermajer, D.S. (2014) Vegan diet, subnormal vitamin B-12 status and cardiovascular health. *Nutrients* 6, 3259–3273.

Yamamoto, S., Nakagawa, T., Matsushita, Y., Kusano, S., Hayashi, T. *et al.* (2010) Visceral fat area and markers of insulin resistance in relation to colorectal neoplasia. *Diabetes Care* 33, 184–189.

Yang, C., Pan, L., Sun, C., Xi, Y., Wang, L. and Li, D. (2016) Red meat consumption and the risk of stroke: a dose-response meta-analysis of prospective cohort studies. *Journal of Stroke and Cerebrovascular Diseases* 25, 1177–1186.

Yen, H., Li, W.Q., Dhana, A., Li, T., Qureshi, A. and Cho, E. (2018) Red meat and processed meat intake and risk for cutaneous melanoma in white women and men: two prospective cohort studies. *Journal of the American Academy of Dermatology* 79, 252–257.

Young, S.S. and Karr, A. (2011) Deming, data and observational studies. *Significance* 8, 116–120.

Young, J.F., Therkildsen, M., Ekstrand, B., Che, B.N., Larsen, M.K. *et al.* (2013) Novel aspects of health promoting compounds in meat. *Meat Science* 95, 904–911.

Zhang, Y., Yang, Y., Xie, M.S., Ding, X., Li, H. *et al.* (2017) Is meat consumption associated with depression? A meta-analysis of observational studies. *BMC Psychiatry* 17, 409.

18c Animal Welfare Viewpoint: Why Should Industry Worry About Food Animal Quality of Life?

BERNARD E. ROLLIN

Department of Philosophy, Colorado State University, USA

Summary

Animal agriculture often has resistance to public scrutiny. A CEO of a major European swine company said that the agricultural industry must listen to society because they can shut it down. Sound science is not sufficient to fully understand animal welfare. An animal can be productive and have poor welfare because its *Telos* or natural behaviours cannot be performed. The industry has a choice. It can either self-regulate or face an uncertain future. Societal changes such as the rise of artificial meat and the demise of animal exhibitions and circuses may be a harbinger of where society is heading. If the animal industry fails to acquiesce to the demands of society, it may be forced to do so.

Learning Objectives

- Make the reader see a perspective that is outside the meat industry.
- Sound science is not a substitute for ethics.
- The animal industry must not ignore societal demands.

Introduction

I am often asked by my cattle-producer friends why they should have to listen to members of the general public regarding animal welfare when the public knows virtually nothing about animal production; what the public 'knows' is often grossly wrong or misinformed; and producers themselves are the true experts concerning animal welfare. The best response to this query I have encountered came from a commentary by the CEO of a European swine company. What he said in essence was the following: 'Why listen to society in general? Because they can close you down tomorrow!'

His response contains two elements. First, in a democracy, the general public can dictate policy through the political process even regarding things they do not understand. Second, and equally devastating, the public can refrain from buying your product.

Regarding the first element, in my work on animal research I have seen this happen repeatedly. In the early 1980s, I was invited to Australia to help facilitate a political dialogue on the regulation of animal research. Historically, all over the world, the research community has been extremely resistant to public accountability. Among the options being considered by the Australian Senate was a complete ban on any animal research in Australia, a point stressed by the chairman of the relevant Senate committee. The fact that that did not occur was largely due to the presence of a robust approach to regulation of animal research suggested by me that was in fact adopted, what one sociologist referred to as 'enforced self-regulation'.

A very similar pattern occurred in the USA. When I was pressing for oversight of animal research by institutional animal care and use committees in the early 1980s, there was also well-supported legislation advanced that would have cut the multibillion-dollar federal research budget by up to 60% and directed the money towards creating alternatives to animal use. (When I asked the woman responsible for the bill what she meant by 'alternative', she replied, 'Oh you know, a plastic dog that howls when you cut it and bleeds ketchup!') Public support for animal research has been steadily declining and the research community is seriously discussing increasing transparency (Foundation for Biomedical Research, 2018).

Similar moves have also occurred with US agriculture. Many consumers have put their dollars into purchasing organic animal products, under the mistaken belief that organic entails good animal welfare. This is demonstrably false, as I have shown in writing. For example, when organic rules forbid the use of antibiotics for treating painful afflictions like foot rot, the animals suffer considerably more than if antibiotics had been deployed.

To understand the claim that the US public will support animal production if they are convinced that the animals live under conditions assuring a good quality of life, one must first understand some basic features of ethics. Ethics may be divided into three categories: personal ethics; societal ethics; and professional ethics. Personal ethics are the individualized rules by which a person determines what they believe is right and wrong. A moment's reflection reveals that diverse personal ethics fail to assure the possibility of a functional and robust society. The reason, as Thomas Hobbes pointed out, is that one ends up with variegated individual ethics, virtually assuring 'a war of each against all', a state of chaos and anarchy.

Societies Have a Consensus Ethic

The only way to avoid this is to create a relatively strong societal consensus ethic that everyone is obliged to obey. Even in US democratic society, driven in principle by a major commitment to individual freedom, there exist strict ethically based laws against robbery, murder, sexual assault, child abuse and other actions that compromise the ability of individuals to live a decent life. In fact, one way to assure the loss of freedom is to flagrantly violate societal ethical principles and concerns.

Professions are subgroups of society that are given the job of performing tasks of great importance and requiring specialized training, education and skill. Medicine, veterinary medicine, accounting and law are paradigm cases of professions. Professions are allowed to regulate themselves as long as their rules of self-regulation are consonant with societal ethics. Society in essence says to professions, 'You regulate yourselves the way we would regulate you if we genuinely understood what you do and what it takes to do it.' If a profession violates societal expectations, it risks being regulated by people who do not understand how it operates.

The draconian rules governing accounting in the wake of numerous scandals is an excellent example of how this occurs.

There is ample evidence of great societal concern about animal welfare across the world regarding all animal use. Understanding this is absolutely essential to anyone in animal agriculture. One can see this all across the Western world. For example, the demise of killer whale shows at Sea World and the end of the 125-year reign of Ringling Brothers circus, in spite of the love the public has previously had for animal shows, eloquently bespeaks what is happening in society, as does the regulation of animal research over the past three decades, despite the research community's threats to society that any regulation will impair human health. Also attesting to this is the tight legislative control on animal agriculture in Europe.

Ethics and Animal Welfare

Unfortunately, people in animal-using areas, particularly agriculture, lack full understanding of the concept of animal welfare. It is generally seen as strictly a matter of 'sound science' in both agriculture and veterinary medicine. There is no doubt that there is a scientific component to animal welfare. One certainly needs to know a fair amount about the animals' needs and natures in order to address them. But one can never forget that, in the context of human use of animals, the concept of animal welfare entails an ethical decision on what we owe animals and to what extent. In the early 1980s, the agricultural community produced a document known as the *CAST Report*, addressing animal welfare. In that report, it was argued that all we owe animals is what it takes to get them to be maximally productive (CAST, 1981). Clearly, any ethical component therein was totally self-serving.

In contradistinction, the Farm Animal Welfare Council (FAWC), a British committee that grew out of the Brambell commission, chartered by the British government to investigate farm animal welfare, defined animal welfare in terms of the famous *Five Freedoms* (www.fawc.org.uk).

1. Freedom from Hunger and Thirst – by ready access to fresh water and a diet to maintain full health and vigour.
2. Freedom from Discomfort – by providing an appropriate environment, including shelter and a comfortable resting area.

3. Freedom from Pain, Injury or Disease – by prevention or rapid diagnosis and treatment.

4. Freedom to Express Normal Behaviour – by providing sufficient space, proper facilities and company of the animal's own kind.

5. Freedom from Fear and Distress – by ensuring conditions and treatment which avoid mental suffering.

The ethic implicit in the FAWC definition could not be more different than what is in the Cast Report.

Lessons from Ancient Philosophies

Since there is a wide variety of ethical positions on human moral obligations to animals, there is also as wide a variety of definitions of animal welfare. The obvious question that arises is this: whose definition of animal welfare will and should prevail? Will it be the industry definition, that of advocates for animal welfare, or something else?

In order to answer this question, we can borrow an account of general human obligations from the ancient philosophers known as the Stoics (Inwood, 2003). This account is as applicable today as when it was formulated in ancient times. For those among us who are not moved by moral arguments, there exists an undeniable argument from self-interest. In their account of the nature of human life, the ancient Stoic philosophers articulated a powerful metaphor that admirably fits the requirement that we all act in accord with societal ethics. Paraphrasing them, social ethics can be schematized as an oxcart on its way to a nearby town. You are chained to the oxcart. You have two choices: you could dig in your heels and resist, in which case you will arrive at the town broken and bleeding. Or you could walk when the oxcart walks, rest when it rests, in which case you will be unscathed.

Dealing with ethical issues raised by your activities is very much analogous to the Stoic point. It is far easier to self-regulate and do the right thing than to wait for society to impose it upon you. You understand your own activities far better than society does. You are far more concerned with preserving your freedom of action than the rest of society is. And most important, you understand what can practically be done without imposing great harm on the regulated area. In most cases, society wants to see a problem solved and will impose a putative solution with a heavy hand. Self-regulation, if permitted, will accomplish far more in a far less onerous manner. The emergence of an industry devoted to creating 'artificial

meat', in which even meat companies are investing, is a harbinger of where society may turn if the animal industry fails to acquiesce to the demands of society.

Agriculture Must Not Ignore Societal Demands

I can provide a vivid personal example of what can happen if the agricultural industry disregards these demands. Last year, I was visited by a very well-known animal activist seeking my support for a new campaign. Although she was better informed than most about the beef industry, what she wanted to accomplish was thoroughly impractical. She was concerned about unusually snowy winters where animals out on range had no access to shelter. She wanted ranchers to set up shelters at regular intervals wherein animals could escape from the snow. If ranchers failed to do this, on her plan they would lose federal reimbursement for cattle that died under snowy conditions.

Using North Dakota as an example, I asked her if she had any idea of the size of a large North Dakota ranch. She did not. I explained to her that ranches in North Dakota can easily exceed 100,000 acres. I also explained to her that one could not know in advance where such shelters were needed. Snow accumulation varies with the wind and a place requiring shelter one year might not need it the next. I also conveyed to her that of all contemporary agriculturalists, ranchers undoubtedly had the greatest concern for their animals.

To evidence my point, I told her about the statue that stands in front of the agriculture building at Colorado State University. Entitled '20% chance of flurries', it depicts an elderly rancher on horseback carrying a lost calf across the saddle in the middle of a snowstorm. Realistically rendered, even showing his windblown duster and white snowdrifts, it eloquently bespeaks the rancher ethic, with the cattleman risking his life to bring home the baby animal. Clearly, his motivation is not financial. I advised her to drive to ranch country to see how impracticable her suggestion was. To her credit, she was willing to learn. I also pointed out to her that it was precisely her kind of concern about leaving animals under natural conditions that led to the kind of high-confinement agriculture she despised. This is an excellent example of societal ignorance underlying good intentions.

Returning to our main point: if the concept of animal welfare irreducibly involves animal ethics, whose ethics will determine the relevant concept of animal welfare? And the answer is: those of society in general and those of the consumer. We have already seen changes in such practices as raising veal in crates mandated by consumer concern.

Here is a personal example of how this works. In 2008, I was approached by Smithfield Farms, the largest pork producer in America, for advice on managing societal animal welfare concerns. I told them that they should abolish gestation crates immediately, because the public abhors them. I told them that 80% of the public would display such an attitude. I then challenged them to poll consumers. They did and told me that I was wrong. Their polling indicated not 80%, but 78%! They went on to tell me that they would abolish gestation crates in their facilities by 2018 and have scrupulously kept their word. Gratifyingly, they also asked me to speak to the *Wall Street Journal* to explain the change in policy.

Western society has always had a societal ethic for animal treatment, both in terms of what is prohibited and in terms of what is encouraged. The prohibitive ethic forbade deliberate, sadistic, purposeless infliction of pain and suffering on animals and outrageous neglect such as not feeding and watering. That ethic is encoded in the anti-cruelty laws of every civilized country, both for the sake of animals and because of the empirically confirmed insight that numerous psychopaths begin with abusing animals and 'graduate' to people (Ascione *et al.*, 1999). The ethic of encouragement was *good husbandry*, which formed the basis for animal agriculture historically. Producers did everything they could to place animals in the optimal environment for which they had evolved, and then provide food during famine, water during drought, protection from predation, whatever medical attention was available. This ethic was based in the strongest of all human motivations – self-interest. If one failed to provide good husbandry, the animals did not produce. This ethic underlies the 23rd Psalm.

End of Husbandry

By the mid-20th century, these venerable ethical principles for animal treatment were no longer sufficient. Whereas traditional animal agriculture involved, as it were, putting square pegs in square holes, round pegs in round holes and creating as little friction as possible, ever-increasing industrialization allowed for putting animals into environments not congenial to them, by using what I call 'technological sanders', that allowed us to force square pegs into round holes. Productivity was unaffected, but animal welfare was severely compromised (Rollin, 2008).

This was not a result of cruelty, but rather an attempt to improve productivity and efficiency, with erosion of animal welfare an unfortunate side effect. Similarly, the mid-20th century rise of large amounts of research and safety and efficacy testing on animals caused a great deal of suffering, although no rational person would call it deliberate sadistic cruelty. Thus, a new animal ethic was demanded by society to cover the infliction of pain, suffering, deprivation and frustration of animal nature that resulted from these new uses.

New ethics do not come from nowhere, nor are they created *ex nihilo*. As Plato pointed out, new ethical ideas have to be rooted in established ethics. In Plato's language, if one is attempting to change the ethics of an individual or a population, one cannot *teach*, one must *remind*. In other words, one must show the person or society that the ethic you are pressing is not new, but rather, implicitly or explicitly, contained in or a consequence of ethical principles they already hold and believe.

To put the point another way: changing a person's ethical beliefs is very much like physical combat. You can pit your force against that of your opponent, as occurs with football linesman or in sumo competition. Alternatively, you can use your opponent's force against them, as occurs in judo. In American history, Prohibition represented an attempt on the part of a minority to move the majority away from drinking. Inevitably, it failed and had many pernicious consequences, including actually increasing the amount of drinking in society.

Contrast this with Martin Luther King's approach to civil rights and Lyndon Johnson's civil rights legislation. As himself a Southerner, Johnson realized that even Southerners would acquiesce to the following two propositions, fundamental to American ethics: all humans should be treated equally; and black people were human – they just had never bothered to draw the relevant conclusion.

If Johnson had been wrong about this point, if 'writing this large' in the law had not 'reminded' people, civil rights would have been as ineffective as Prohibition. (For some readers with teenagers at home, they realize that while moral judo may sometimes work, force never does.)

At the same time, recall that Western society has gone through almost 50 years of extending its moral categories for humans to people who were morally ignored or invisible – women, minorities, the handicapped, children, citizens of the third world. (As late as the mid-1970s, the National Institutes of Health (NIH) had different and weaker moral standards for the use of Third World research subjects in federally funded research.) So a plausible and obvious move is for society to continue in its tendency and attempt to extend the moral machinery it has developed for dealing with people, appropriately modified, to animals.

In the US Constitution, specifically in the Bill of Rights, fundamental features of human nature are protected against infringement for the sake of the general welfare. These of course include freedom of speech, freedom of movement, holding on to one's property, not being tortured, freedom of expression, freedom of religion. Animals also possess fundamental natures determined by their biology – what Aristotle called their *Telos*. Being allowed to express and satisfy the interests dictated by their nature is as important to animals as avoiding pain. This is evidenced eloquently by certain animals chewing their legs off to escape from steel-jawed traps, showing that freedom is more important to them than pain.

Under traditional, husbandry-based agriculture, animal nature was respected, with such respect sanctioned by producer self-interest. Under industrial agriculture, this is no longer the case. It is clear that society and the social ethic see the actualization of animal *Telos* as fundamental to animals enjoying a positive quality of life. If respect for their natures is no longer presuppositional to animal use, society wishes to see it embodied in legislation – hence the articulation of the 2100 pieces of legislation pertaining to animal welfare promulgated across the USA in 2004. Hence too the evidence from Gallup polls. A Gallup poll conducted in 2003 showed that 75% of the public wanted legislated guarantees of farm animal welfare. By 2012, it had risen to 90% (Gallup 2003, 2012). Hence the

relentless consumer thrust to eliminate gestation crates, battery cages, veal crates and all other high-confinement systems violative of animal nature. The same ethic prevails across all animal use. When I was a young man, zoos were in essence impoverished prisons for animals. Today those zoos would no longer survive.

The lesson for animal agriculture is plain. Society is very unlikely to abandon animal products. But it is clear that respect for the animals' needs and natures as determined by their *Telos* is presuppositional to societal comfort with animal production, as such respect determines animal quality of life. I would thus strongly advise the agricultural community to clean up its own house with respect to how animals are produced. Cows on pasture, chickens pecking freely, pigs allowed to roam on pasture with other pigs are ancient and iconic images with which all of us have been brought up. The issue is one of fairness and common decency, as well as self-protection. There is no reason to believe that animals have a concept of death or loss of life. But there is ample evidence that they worry how they live.

References

Ascione, F. and Arkow, P. (1999) *Child Abuse, Domestic Violence, and Animal Abuse*. Purdue University Press, West Lafayette, Indiana.

CAST (1981) *Scientific Aspects of the Welfare of Food Animals*. Report #91, November 1981. Council for Agricultural Science and Technology, Ames, Iowa.

Foundation for Biomedical Research (2018) Animal researchers debate transparency. 27 June 2018. Available at: *http://www.sciencemag.org/news/2018/06/cataclysmic-wake-call-can-more-candor-win-back-support-animal-research*

Gallup (2003, 2012) Polls available at: http://www.gallup.com (accessed 15 April 2020).

Inwood, B. (2003) *The Cambridge Companion to the Stoics*. Cambridge University Press, Cambridge, UK.

Rollin, B. (2008) The ethics of agriculture: the true end of husbandry. In: Dawkins, M.S. and Bonney, R. (eds) *The Future of Farming: Renewing the Ancient Contract*. Blackwell, Oxford, UK, pp. 7–19.

18d Animal Protectionist Viewpoint: Inhumane Slaughter Should be a Crime

ANDY LAMEY

Department of Philosophy, University of California, San Diego, USA

Recent decades have seen a shift in how society views the moral status of farmed animals. Up until the 1950s, American law permitted slaughterhouse workers to stun cows and pigs with multiple blows of a sledgehammer and to shackle and hoist them while still conscious. Today approximately half of the slaughter facilities in the USA use Temple Grandin's system of humane slaughter. Grandin's audit-based approach seeks to catalogue and minimize the frequency with which workers use cattle prods, require more than one shot of a stun gun to render animals insensitive, and other practices that were once considered perfectly acceptable (Lamey, 2019a). The increased use of Grandin's system has at key points been due to animal protection advocates applying pressure to the fast food industry (Singer, 1999: 166–176), but its popularity is not due to such advocacy alone. National opinion surveys indicate widespread support for regulations designed to reduce the suffering of farmed animals (ASPCA, 2019).

Rather than a passing fad, heightened concern with the well-being of farm animals is here to stay. Yet the institutionalization of this concern has not gone far enough. Use of systems such as Grandin's is currently voluntary when it should be mandatory. If we are serious about the welfare of farmed animals, we will make it a crime to kill them without making their death as merciful as possible.

Animals on American farms currently have few legal protections. In principle, federal law requires that they be quickly rendered unconscious before being killed, and that when they are transported across state lines for slaughter they be unloaded every 28 h to receive food and rest. In practice, both regulations have only the faintest impact. The slaughter law excludes chickens, which constitute over 98% of land animals killed for food, as well as kosher and halal slaughter. The transportation regulations are punishable by a maximum fine of $500 and in any event are rarely enforced, a fact that also holds true for the few state-level laws concerned with the welfare of farmed animals. Most states expressly exclude farmed animals from their anti-cruelty statutes.

Advocates for the welfare of farmed animals should support legislation requiring every slaughter facility to use Grandin's system. The fact that humane slaughter is already employed at many facilities, including those that kill chickens, shows that the industry can accommodate itself to humane slaughter in a systematic way. A wide range of businesses, from bars to contractors to dentists, have to meet licensing requirements as a condition of doing business. When it comes to the business of slaughtering, a basic cost of doing business should be a binding commitment to making the process as painless as possible.

The main reason for doing so is ethical. We take it for granted that our moral concern with our fellow human beings should be backed up with the force of law. We make it a crime to needlessly abuse members of our own species, including some with cognitive abilities less advanced than those of pigs and other 'livestock'. Although increased concern with the well-being of farmed animals is now widely affirmed, the rhetoric is not adequately joined with legal force. Taking the interests of animals seriously requires closing the gap between what we say they deserve and the painful outcomes that are all too likely to occur in slaughter facilities that do not allow welfare auditing.

I have argued elsewhere that animals have an interest not only in avoiding suffering but also in not being killed (Lamey, 2019b). Given this, it may seem incoherent to propose banning the inhumane elements of slaughter but not slaughter itself. As far as sheer morality is concerned, this criticism is sound. Killing animals for food when plant-based alternatives are widely available is morally indefensible. The law, however, must take into account factors beyond morality, including whether a legal command is likely to be obeyed. The widespread popularity of meat eating suggests that the public is unlikely to accept a ban on killing animals for food any time soon. A measure enforcing the new consensus on animal suffering, but which stops short of banning killing, is a compromise justified by crude political considerations regarding what the meat-eating majority, rightly or wrongly, is willing to abide by. Precisely because it would stop short of full justice for animals, such a law would have a greater chance of being enforced. At the same time it would do nothing to prevent continued advocacy regarding the moral wrong of killing animals for food.

A second possible objection is that such a reform is unlikely to happen, because lawmakers have historically shown little interest in the well-being of farmed animals (often, it is said, because agricultural agencies have been 'captured' by the industry they purportedly regulate). But introducing a bill in a legislature is not the only way to bring the law to bear on slaughterhouses. In recent years California, Florida, Colorado and other states have introduced animal welfare reforms through ballot initiatives. Where lawmakers have been reluctant to act, the public has repeatedly endorsed measures to limit the cruelty of industrial agriculture. Initiatives obliging slaughter facilities to commit to humane slaughter are no more likely to fail than previous initiatives that outlawed sow gestation crates or required layer hens to live cage-free.

As with any legal change, banning inhumane slaughter would require answering many questions of detail, such as whether kosher and halal slaughter facilities should continue to be allowed to kill without stunning. As it stands, however, the discussion around farmed animal welfare is often framed as a matter of voluntary ethical concern. If we are serious about the needs of animals, we will recognize that their interest in avoiding suffering can no longer be viewed as an optional matter that slaughter facilities can accept or reject at their discretion. We will instead recognize that their well-being is so important that inadequate commitment to protecting it should be a crime.

References

ASPCA (2019) Farm Animals Need our Help. American Society for the Prevention of Cruelty to Animals. Available at: https://www.aspca.org/animal-cruelty/farm-animal-welfare (accessed 4 August 2019).

Lamey, A. (2019a) The animal ethics of Temple Grandin: a protectionist analysis. *Journal of Agricultural and Environmental Ethics* 32(1), 143–164.

Lamey, A. (2019b) *Duty and the Beast: Should We Eat Meat in the Name of Animal Rights?* Cambridge University Press, Cambridge, UK.

Singer, P. (1999) *Ethics into Action: Henry Spira and the Animal Rights Movement.* Melbourne University Press, Melbourne, Australia.

18e Animal Welfare Viewpoint: My Thoughts on Use of Animals for Food

Department of Animal Science, Colorado State University, USA

Animal Welfare Perspective

I get asked all the time. How can you care about animals and be involved in slaughtering them? When my career started in the early 1970s, the cattle in the feedlots had a good life. In the dry Arizona climate, feedlot pens remained dry and the cattle had plenty of water and shade. Cattle handling was terrible, but I viewed it as a solvable problem. There were a few feedlot managers and ranchers who handled cattle quietly. I remember one ranch in particular. It was Singing Valley Ranch run by Bill and Penny Porter. Their beautiful cattle had a wonderful life. It became obvious that improving cattle handling was possible. The local Swift plant in Tolleson, Arizona was brand new when I started visiting it early in my career. Stunning was done well and the stunner was carefully maintained.

Management of large US slaughter plants in the 1970s was often better compared with the 1980s and 1990s. When the US industry suddenly expanded, they went through a sloppy phase where stunners were seldom repaired and handling was often brutal. If I had entered the industry in the 1980s or had been exposed to muddy disgusting feedlots early in my career, my career might have gone down a different path. The problems observed early in my career were viewed as fixable.

Welfare Auditing by Major Customers

In 1999, I was hired by McDonalds and Wendy's International to implement animal welfare auditing of the large abattoirs where they bought beef and pork. The scoring system I developed is described in Grandin (1998, 2005) and in Chapter 12.

The effectiveness of this programme is clearly illustrated in Bob Langert's book *The Battle to Do Good* (Langert, 2019). Bob Langert was the corporate manager at McDonalds who hired me. In my work with several large meat buyers, I saw animal welfare change from an abstract issue to something real. I took top managers on their first tours of farms and slaughterhouses. When they saw something bad, it motivated them to implement changes. It was like the TV show 'Undercover Boss'. They were sometimes shocked at what they saw.

During that year, I saw more positive change than I had seen in my previous 25 years. The good news was that animal welfare could be greatly improved without expensive remodeling and purchase of major equipment. Simple improvements such as stunner maintenance, non-slip flooring, changing lighting and better employee supervision brought all but three abattoirs out of 75 up to a decent welfare standard. More tips on how to improve animal handling are in Chapter 6. At three plants, a new general manager greatly improved animal welfare.

Lamey (2019) criticized the scoring system described in this book because it allows 5% of the cattle to have a missed stun. This is where the practical world collides with ideals. For any process, it is impossible to be perfect. The conditions were much worse before the audits started. A numerical cut-off provides clear guidelines to assist a buyer when they have to remove a poor slaughter plant from their approved supplier list. Industry guidelines are clear on acts of abuse that have a zero tolerance. Breaking tails or dragging fully conscious animals is *never* acceptable. Employees need to be trained and given a list of acts of abuse.

An employee who commits an act of abuse should be fired from their job.

The Animals Must Have a Life Worth Living

The cattle that I worked with in the 1970s had a life worth living. Unfortunately, a relatively new problem started occurring with lameness, heat stress and feedlot cattle that die when they are almost at slaughter weight. The problem crept up slowly. It was caused by a combination of factors such as: (i) heavier at a younger age; (ii) genetic selection for heavier carcasses; (iii) excessive grain in the ration; and (iv) feeding beta agonists. This is discussed in Grandin and Whiting (2018) and in this book. Some of these animals are stiff and sore and their lives are miserable. This problem does not occur in all feedlot cattle. There are 10–20% of feeders who push the animal's biology too hard and compromise welfare. It happens when animal weight gain is maximized. Young managers starting a career in the feedlot industry are often not aware that feedlot cattle 20 years ago were seldom lame. This is why I call this 'bad becoming normal'. The industry did not like it when I spoke out on this issue. This resulted in a backlash against me by some people in the beef industry. This was a very difficult time for me.

Improving Slaughter was Easy

Compared with problems on the farm, improving slaughterhouses was easy. Today the biggest welfare issues I have observed in modern slaughter plants are problems caused by poor conditions on the farm. This is why this book has extensive information on monitoring on-farm welfare issues at the abattoir (see Chapters 4 and 16). When I stand at the truck unloading ramp, I am often not happy with what I see. Fortunately, a few good things have started happening. Recently one really progressive large slaughter plant stopped buying cattle that were lame or had high levels of liver abscesses.

Ethical Issues

The contribution by Andy Lamey discusses my views on the ethics of eating meat. There are more extensive essays on my views in Grandin (1995) and Grandin and Johnson (2010). In many of my writings, I have stated that an animal being killed by a predator has a worse death than a cow or pig in a modern slaughterhouse. Lamey stated that animal death in the wild is required to sustain ecosystems (Lamey, 2019). People killing animals for food may harm ecosystems if it is done in an irresponsible way. This brings up a fundamental issue about moral values concerning the natural world. One viewpoint is: if it is natural, then it is acceptable. This is not an abstract issue for me. I have been on a ranch and seen a calf that was partially skinned alive by coyotes. The rancher shot it to put it out of its misery. These are complicated issues. The purpose of these short sub-chapters in Chapter 18 are to enable the reader to see different perspectives. This can encourage people to have constructive dialogue instead of getting into hyper-polarized arguments.

References

Grandin, T. (1995) *Thinking in Pictures*. Vintage Books, Random House, New York.

Grandin, T. (1998) Objective scoring of animal handling and stunning practices at slaughter plants. *Journal of the American Veterinary Medical Association* 212, 6–9.

Grandin, T. (2005) Maintenance of good animal welfare standards in beef slaughter plants by use of auditing programs. *Journal of the American Veterinary Medical Association* 226, 370–373.

Grandin, T. and Johnson, C. (2010) *Animals Make us Human*. Houghton Mifflin Harcourt, New York.

Grandin, T. and Whiting, M. (2018) *Are We Pushing Animals to Their Biological Limits? Welfare and Ethical Implications*. CAB International, Wallingford, UK.

Lamey, A. (2019) The animal ethics of Temple Grandin: a protectionist analysis. *Journal of Agricultural and Environmental Ethics* 32, 143–164.

Langert, B. (2019) *The Battle to Do Good*. Emerald Group, Bingley, UK.

Index

behaviour
    abnormal 252, 254, 255
    escape 41, 44, 126, 129, 130, 138
    following 95
    lying 65–66
    responses 9
    sexual 64
    signs of pain 12, *12*
    social 20
behavioural principles
    stockmanship and abattoir facility design
        90–111
bellowing, cattle 36
benchmarking
    meat inspection 265
    mortality rate 52
    quality defects 80
best-practice guidelines 5, 57
beta agonists 40, 43, 97, 188, 235–236, 317
bilirubin 83
biliverdin 81
biosecurity 8, 56, 265
biphasic carbon dioxide and oxygen system
        128–129, **128**
bison 180
bleed rails 183
bleed-out 111, 112, 169
bleeding *see* exsanguination
blinding 104, 150
blindness 54
blinking 193, 196, **197**, 198, 199, 218
blood
    aspiration of 165, 166
    flow 14, 208
    odours 181
bobby veal calves 50, 51
body
    condition 3, 56, 262
        score 251, **252**, 254, 255
    temperature 59, 63, 230
bone fractures 7, 8, 52, 231, 232, 261
bovine bruising 85, **85**, 86
    see also cattle bruising
bovine respiratory disease 265
brain
    avian 203, 204
    blood flow 208
    Charolais cow **207**
    death 169, 195, 197
    eye movements 216, **217**
    haemorrhage 205, *206*, 207, 214
    Holstein cow 207, **207**
    lesions 215
    physiology 202–229
    righting reflex 211, **215**
    sheep **203**
    structures 204–205

stunning 214
    electrical 112, 207–209
    gas 209–210
    mechanical 205–207
    penetrating captive bolt 205–207, **206**, *207*, **207**
brainstem 206, 207, 210, 214, 215, 221
breast blisters 3
breathing
    absence 220
    rhythmic 193, 197, 198, 219–220, **220**, 221
breeding
    genetic selection 97
    livestock 39–40, 56
    practices 56, 234
brisket disease 263
broilers
    CAS 123
    cold stress 62–63
    flip over disease 234
    foot pad lesions 247, **249**, 250
    LAPS 12, 119, 129, **129**
    leg fractures 53
    lesions 258
    mortality 58
    on-farm stocking density 258
    pneumatic captive bolt guns 154
    poor health 51
    skin scratches 260
    stunning
        captive bolt 116
        water-bath 114, 170
    welfare assessments 20, 257
    wing fractures 53, 56
bruising 3, 81–83, 256
    age 83–84, 236
    assessment 78, 79, 81, 82, 87, 88
    auction markets 84
    carcass 79, 80
    cattle (bovine) 17, 78–89, **85**, **86**
    causes 83–84, 85, 236, 237
    colour 81–83, **83**, 85
    definition 81
    driving instruments 261
    economic impacts 44, 78, 80
    exsanguination 84–85
    fresh 83
    gates **167**
    handling 79–80, 84, 85, 87
    impacting factors *see* risk factors
    livestock 261
    meat 80
    metal equipment 238
    monitoring
        programmes 78
        and scoring 86–87, **86**
    occurrence location 86, 87
    old 83, 237

movements 211, 215–216
  reflex 169, 193, **196**, 198, 214, 215, 216, 221
    brain 211, **215**
rights
  animal 299–300
  civil 312
ritual slaughter 159, 160
  without pre-stunning 168–169
  see also religious slaughter
rotating box 161, **163**, 164, **164**

safety
  employees 36, 156
  threats 16
  see also food safety
sanctions, criminal 287
scalding 222, 256
scoring
  aggregate 249
  numerical 182, 184, 188, 249
  tools 246, 250
    categories 247, 249
    differences in numbering 249
    gait 53, 56
    lameness 251
    welfare outcome indicators 2–3
    yes/no scoring 247
  vocalization 177, 179
secondary legislation 280
security, food 303
self-regulation 279, 280, 282, 310, 311
sensibility, definition 193
sensory information 202–203
separation distress 163
septicaemia 263–264
serpentine race systems 101
sexual behaviour 64
shackling 44, 111, 113, 160, 165
  and hoisting system 35–36
  poultry 41, 112–113, **113**, 114, 123
shechita slaughter 202
  see also religious slaughter and kosher slaughter
sheep 8, 96, 255
  blood vessels 168
  body condition score 255
  brain **203**
  cortisol 180–181
  following behaviour 95
  foot rot 255
  hair coat condition 255
  heat stress 235
  joint problems 255
  lambs 61, 151, 229
  lameness 254–255
  lesions 255
  lighting 10, 12
  LOP 168

muscle pH 61
poor on-farm conditions, indicators
    254–255
restrainers **163**
stress 7, 16, 180–181
stunning
  captive bolt 7, 151–152, **152**
  electrical 7, 132–136
unconsciousness 168–169
V restrainers 160
vocalization scoring 162–164
sheep dogs 96
shipping, long-distance 42–43
short-term stress 230
shot placement, improper 290
sick animals 53
single file races 41–42, 95, 98, 101
skin
  conditions 260–261
  erythema 261
  injuries 17
  lesions 254, 260–261
  pliability 18
skull, penetrating captive bolt stunning 207
slaughter without stunning 159, 160, 171
slaughterhouses 6–7, 317
  welfare expertise 285–286
slaughtermen, competency 292
slippery floors 237
slips 180, 183
slopes 101–102
social behaviour 20, 64
social ethics 311
social goals 280
societal ethics 310, 311
society, caring 280
solar radiation 61
species-specific vocalization 193, 197
speciesism 299
spinal cord 150, 209
squealing 177, 230, 231
stair steps 102, **102**
Standard Operating Procedures (SOPs) 175, 182, 183,
    184, 185, 186, 284, 286
stocking density 64, 261
stockmanship, behavioural principles 90–111
stockyards 44, 97
stomach ulcers 246
stress 9, 12, 14, 15, 204–205
  causes 12, *13*, 14
  cold 36, 61, 62–63, 292
  distress 12, 14
  factors 14–15
  genetics 14–15
  goats 180–181
  handling 2, 35, 41–42
  hormones 90
  pheromones 181

CABI – who we are and what we do

This book is published by **CABI**, an international not-for-profit organisation that improves people's lives worldwide by providing information and applying scientific expertise to solve problems in agriculture and the environment.

CABI is also a global publisher producing key scientific publications, including world renowned databases, as well as compendia, books, ebooks and full text electronic resources. We publish content in a wide range of subject areas including: agriculture and crop science / animal and veterinary sciences / ecology and conservation / environmental science / horticulture and plant sciences / human health, food science and nutrition / international development / leisure and tourism.

The profits from CABI's publishing activities enable us to work with farming communities around the world, supporting them as they battle with poor soil, invasive species and pests and diseases, to improve their livelihoods and help provide food for an ever growing population.

CABI is an international intergovernmental organisation, and we gratefully acknowledge the core financial support from our member countries (and lead agencies) including:

Discover more

To read more about CABI's work, please visit: **www.cabi.org**

Browse our books at: **www.cabi.org/bookshop**,
or explore our online products at: **www.cabi.org/publishing-products**

Interested in writing for CABI? Find our author guidelines here:
www.cabi.org/publishing-products/information-for-authors/